my dearest Hogg my baby is dead – will
you come to me as soon as you can –
I wish to see you – It was perfectly
well when I went to bed – I awoke in
the night to give it suck it appeared
to be *sleeping* so quietly that I would
not awake it – it was dead then but we
did not find that out till morning – from
its appearance it evidently died of
convulsions –

Will you come – you are so
calm a creature & Shelley is afraid
of a fever from the milk – for I am
no longer a mother now

Mary

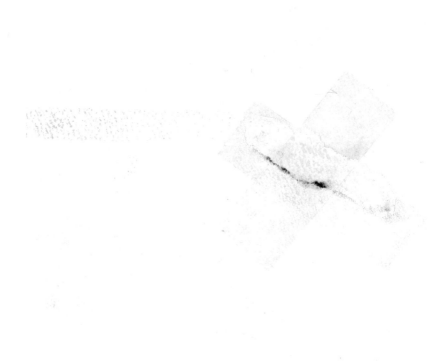

The Letters of Mary Wollstonecraft Shelley

THE LETTERS
of
MARY WOLLSTONECRAFT SHELLEY

VOLUME I

"A part of the Elect"

Edited by Betty T. Bennett

THE JOHNS HOPKINS UNIVERSITY PRESS
BALTIMORE AND LONDON

The publication of this volume has been aided by grants
from The Carl and Lily Pforzheimer Foundation, Inc.,
and the Andrew W. Mellon Foundation.

 Manufactured in the United States of America

The Johns Hopkins University Press, Baltimore, Maryland 21218
The Johns Hopkins Press Ltd., London

Library of Congress Catalog Card Number 79–24190
ISBN 0–8018–2275–0
Library of Congress Cataloging in Publication data will be found
on the last printed page of this book.

Frontispiece: Mary Wollstonecraft Shelley, a miniature
by Reginald Easton, courtesy of the Bodleian Library.

End papers: (front) letter from Mary Godwin to Thomas Jefferson Hogg, 6 March 1815, courtesy of The Carl H. Pforzheimer Library; (back) letter from Mary Wollstonecraft Shelley to Jane Williams Hogg, 31 August 1827, courtesy of Lord Abinger and the Bodleian Library.

To Jennie and Mayer Edelman,
Gary Thomas, and Matthew and Peter Bennett

Contents

Acknowledgments

IN UNDERTAKING this edition, I had little idea of the time and travel it would call for; of the scores of collectors, libraries, museums, and book dealers to be located, corresponded with, visited; or, most unexpected, of the encouragement, assistance, and many kindnesses I would receive from an international community dedicated to literary studies, whose members have shared and shored my enthusiasm for assembling the letters of Mary Shelley. I wish particularly to thank Professors Alice G. Fredman, Donald H. Reiman, and Charles E. Robinson, who unstintingly gave their judgments and suggestions, read and reacted to the first draft of this manuscript, and buoyed my spirits through some of the more difficult phases of this project.

For use of their manuscripts, as well as other assistance in preparing this edition, I am indebted to Lord Abinger, The Carl and Lily Pforzheimer Foundation, John Murray, and Professor Jean de Palacio.

For answering innumerable questions and providing other assistance in preparing this edition, I am indebted to Dr. Bruce Barker-Benfield, of the Bodleian Library; Dr. Alan S. Bell, of the National Library of Scotland; and Doucet D. Fischer, Ricki B. Herzfeld, Mihai H. Handrea, and Robert Yampolsky, of The Carl H. Pforzheimer Library. To Professors Kenneth Neill Cameron and Leslie A. Marchand I am grateful for general and specific guidance in the world of Romantic studies.

Among those who have helped in the search for letters, illustrations, or supplemental material or have otherwise assisted in the preparation of this edition are: Joanne Allen, Martin J. Bromley, Linette F. Brugmans, Arlene Canner, Lydia Chabza, David R. Cheney, Sir Joseph L. W. Cheyne, Florence Consentino, Michael Denci, Daniel J. Donno, Wilfred S. Dowden, Clement Dunbar, Herb and Merrilyn Edelman, Richard P. Feinberg, Paula Feldman, Irwin F. Fredman, James D. Galbraith, C. M. Gee, Stephen Gill, Aaron W. Godfrey, Norman Goodman, Rosemary Graham, Theodore Grieder, Carolyn J. Guthrie, Richmond Y. Hathorn, David Holmes, Ian Hustwick, Mary Jacobus, Nicholas A. Joukovsky, Norman O. Jung, Hilton Kelliher, Charles Kim, V. J. Kite, Clara E. Lida, Jacob Lipkind, John Manners, Edwin W. Marrs, Jr., Marylebone Library, Prince Alexander Mavrocordato, Winifred A. Meyers, Mario Mignone, E. B. Murray, Virginia Murray, E. G. Protopsaltis, M. Byron Raizis, Elias Rivers, Mary Robertson, Timothy D. Robson, Thomas Rogers, The Royal Commission on Historical Manuscripts, John R. Russell, William St. Clair, Helen Sherman, Marion Stocking, Emily W. Sunstein, Lola L. Szladits, Robert H. Taylor, Roslyn S. Teicher, James Thorpe, Joseph A. Tursi, Eugene Weinstein, Herbert Weisinger, Alice S. Wilson, Iris Zavala, Paul M. Zall.

Permissions to publish manuscript letters, as well as other courtesies regarding them, were given by: Avon County Library (Bath Reference Library); Bodleian Library; Boston Public Library; The British Library; Columbia University Library; Fales Library, New York University; The Houghton Library, Harvard University; The Huntington Library, San Marino, California; India Office Library and Records; Lilly Library, Indiana University, Bloomington, Indiana; University of Iowa Libraries; London Borough of Camden, from the collections at Keats House, Hampstead; Keats-Shelley Memorial House, Rome; The Brotherton Collection, University of Leeds; George S. MacManus Co.; Maggs Bros.; John Murray; Newstead Abbey, Nottingham Museums; Henry W. and Albert A. Berg Collection, The New York Public Library, Astor, Lenox and Tilden Foundations; Harkness Collection (#12), Manuscripts and Archives Division, The New York Public Library, Astor, Lenox and Tilden Foundations; The Historical Society of Pennsylvania; The Carl and Lily Pforzheimer Foundation; The Pierpont Morgan Library; Princeton University Library; Gordon N. Ray; The Rosenbach Museum and Library; The Trustees of the National Library of Scotland; Scottish Record Office; The Robert H. Taylor Collection, Princeton; William Luther Lewis Collection, Texas Christian University; Humanities Research Center, The University of Texas at Austin; William K. Bixby Papers, Washington University Libraries, St. Louis, Missouri; Wellesley College Library; Chapin Library, Williams College.

Permissions to publish the illustrations, as well as other courtesies regarding them, were given by: Lord Abinger; Bodleian Library; The Huntington Library, San Marino, California; Professor Leslie A. Marchand; The National Portrait Gallery, London; Newstead Abbey, Nottingham Museums; The Carl and Lily Pforzheimer Foundation.

Fellowships from the National Endowment for the Humanities, the American Council of Learned Societies, and The Huntington Library, San Marino, California; a grant from The Carl and Lily Pforzheimer Foundation; and a faculty grant-in-aid from the State University of New York at Stony Brook have provided me with exceptional time for research and the ability to travel in this country and abroad to work first-hand with manuscripts of the letters and other pertinent material.

I am deeply grateful to Gary Thomas, who has encouraged this project by helping in the search for letters, reading first drafts, and participating in countless discussions about Mary Shelley; and to my parents, Jennie and Mayer Edelman, and my sons, Matthew and Peter Bennett, for allowing Mary Shelley to become a part of our family circle.

Introduction

In a letter of 3 October 1824, Mary Wollstonecraft (Godwin) Shelley (1797–1851) eulogized the members of the Shelley-Byron circle as "a part of the Elect." Prominent among those who participated in that extraordinary literary world was Mary Shelley herself—author, editor, and woman of learning. The recognition her works achieved during her lifetime, however, has since been generally overshadowed by the fame of her husband, Percy Bysshe Shelley (1792–1822), and her parents, William Godwin (1756–1836) and Mary Wollstonecraft (1759–1797). Studies of the Shelley circle, even those concerned principally with Mary Shelley, have focused primarily on her family relationships, treating her life and works as literary footnotes. Frederick L. Jones, editor of the most complete collection of her letters before this edition (*MWS Letters* [1944]), followed in that tradition when he wrote in his introduction: "It is as the wife of Shelley that she excites our interest and arouses our desire to know as much about her as we can" (p. xxix). For Jones, Mary Shelley's life after Shelley's death was important for her decisive contribution to the establishment of the poet's posthumous reputation and because "she reared and educated Shelley's only surviving son" and "continued her association with Shelley's old friends." Almost as an aside, Jones commented: ". . . and she is a remarkable woman in her own right." This and other such selective approaches have produced biographical studies that fail to probe deeply into the details and complexities of Mary Shelley's personality and behavior and, aside from commentary on *Frankenstein* (1818), have largely deflected critical inquiry away from Mary Shelley as a creator and creation of the romantic period.

In fact, her literary activity included five novels after *Frankenstein*: *Valperga* (1823), *The Last Man* (1826), *Perkin Warbeck* (1830), *Lodore* (1835), and *Falkner* (1837). Except *Valperga*, all of her novels went into at least a second printing during her lifetime. She wrote one novella, *Matilda* (1819, pub. 1959); two travel books, *Six Weeks' Tour* (1817) and *Rambles in Germany and Italy* (1844); two mythological dramas, *Proserpine* (1820, pub. 1832) and *Midas* (1820, pub. 1922); five volumes of *Lives* (1835–39) of Italian, Spanish, Portuguese, and French writers for Lardner's *Cabinet Cyclopedia* (*Lives*); more than two dozen short stories; essays; translations; reviews; and poems. As Shelley's editor, she brought out Shelley's *Posthumous Poems* (1824), *Poetical Works* (1839), and *Essays, Letters* (1839, dated 1840), the latter two containing her biographical notes, which have been an invaluable resource for Shelley scholarship. These achievements and her family relationships, interacting with the socio-political movements of the first half of the nineteenth century, place Mary

Shelley in the mainstream of the period and give her letters special biographical and historical significance. They are the expressions of a highly gifted, well-educated, and perceptive woman, and they reflect all aspects of her dramatic personal and professional life, portraying her development from almost the beginning of her youthful commitment to become an author through the fulfillment of that ambition.

Consciousness of herself as an author is one of the pervading themes of Mary Shelley's letters. She frequently writes of projects finished and unfinished, aspirations, feelings of failure and satisfaction, efforts to publish, reactions to reviews and friends' opinions, exhaustion from overwork, deadlines, lost manuscripts, revisions, self-reappraisal. When Shelley's death (8 July 1822) left her with no income, she expressed self-confidence in her ability to earn a living through her writing: "I think that I can maintain myself, and there is something inspiriting in the idea" (7 March 1823). She found solace in continuing her habits of writing and study: "I study—I write—I think even to madness & torture of the past—I look forward to the grave with hope—but in exerting my intellect—in forcing myself to real study—I find an opiate which at least adds nothing to the pain of regret that must necessarily be mine for ever" (28 February 1823). Protracted negotiations with Shelley's father, Sir Timothy Shelley, wrung from him, towards the close of 1823, only a modest allowance against Shelley's estate (see 9–11 September 1823, nn. 11 and 12), which she had to supplement. Dependent on her writing for additional income, Mary Shelley, as are many professional authors, was aware that some works were motivated primarily by financial gain. Her letters show, however, that she maintained her determination to develop and fulfill her aesthetic ideals. When she advised Leigh Hunt to write for magazines to earn the money he needed, she characterized her own situation: "I write bad articles which help to make me miserable—but I am going to plunge into a novel, and hope that its clear waters will wash off the ⟨dirt⟩ mud of the magazines" (9 February 1824).

More than thirteen hundred letters will be included in this edition. The 395 letters in this first volume, dated 25 October 1814 through 31 August 1827, trace her growth from novice author (Shelley arranged the anonymous publication of *Frankenstein* with Lackington) through her reliance, when a widow, on introductions and recommendations to publishers by established writers, such as Charles Lamb, Horace Smith, and Godwin, to eventual self-reliance that enabled her to negotiate directly and persistently for herself and others with some of the leading publishers and editors of the day, including Henry Colburn, John Murray, Alaric A. Watts, and John Bowring.

Her works, varied in style and quality, are too extensive and complex for brief summation. Two recent studies, William Walling's *Mary Shelley* and Jean de Palacio's *Mary Shelley dans son oeuvre*, offer lengthy and provocative analyses of her novels, resolving some important issues while raising others. There remains, however, a great deal more to be considered about this author who, sensitive to a host of personal and historical influences, developed a literary voice quite her own, which was nurtured rather than subsumed by the achievements of Godwin, Wollstonecraft, and Shelley.

Godwin's influence on Mary Shelley is substantial. She read and reread his political works, deriving much of her vision of an egalitarian social order from his theories of political and social justice. His fiction provided a model for her own; the most obvious instance is in the similarities in her *Frankenstein* and his *Caleb Williams.* From Godwin she learned the value in studying history (a lesson Godwin also taught Shelley) and the habit of intensive research, demonstrated in many of her works, including her two historical novels (*Valperga* and *Perkin Warbeck*) and the biographical essays in Lardner's *Cabinet Cyclopedia* (*Lives*).

Before her relationship with Shelley began, Mary Shelley had an "excessive & romantic attachment" to her father (30 October 1834). She had regarded him as a "God" [5 December 1822], and throughout her life she valued his opinion of her work, which he usually, but not always, admired and encouraged. One work he disapproved of was her 1819 novella *Matilda*, the story of a father's incestuous passion for his daughter. Her letters show that Godwin neither arranged for its publication nor responded to her many requests to have the fair-copy manuscript returned to her. When she sent him the manuscript of *Valperga* to publish for his own financial benefit (see 28 May 1821, n. 5), he took it on himself to delete passages that he thought detracted from the novel, which he otherwise praised. His opinion in 1824 that Mary Shelley lacked the talent for dramaturgy (see 9 February 1824, n. 5) persuaded her to give up her attempt to write for the theater, a decision she later regretted.

The 1814–27 letters, which underscore Mary Shelley's almost unfaltering devotion to her father, describe her unhappiness when Godwin refused to accept her elopement with the married Shelley, her later reconciliation with her father, her distress to the point of illness in 1820–22 because of Godwin's incessant demands on the Shelleys for money (see for example 30 June 1820 for the Shelleys' previously unpublished letters on Godwin's finances). When she returned to England after Shelley's death, she came again into Godwin's circle, customarily seeing him several times a week. Through him she renewed the literary friendships of her youth, and she gladly accepted from Godwin's associates recommendations of her work to publishers and editors. Mary Shelley had returned to England, and remained there, in order to gain an allowance from Sir Timothy Shelley (see 7 January 1823, n. 1; c. 5 April 1823). These letters show that another restraint on her deeply desired return to Italy was Godwin's financial reliance on the young widow combined with his insistence that she stay in England.

It was also from Godwin that Mary Shelley learned to idolize her mother, who died ten days after Mary Shelley's birth. Although many contemporaries deplored the unconventional life and radical ideas of Mary Wollstonecraft, the Godwin circle encouraged her daughter to worship this pioneer of equal rights for men and women and to measure herself and others against the heritage of her mother's ideals. On 3 November 1814 Mary Shelley praised her friend Isabella Booth by writing that "she adores the shade of my mother." On 18 August 1823 she wrote: "Mrs K [*Kenney*] says that I am grown very like my Mother, especially in Manners . . . the most flattering thing anyone c[d] say to me. . . ." She avidly read her mother's works, which, along with Godwin's (and later Shelley's), fostered her own political views. Through their special relationship to Mary Shelley and their influence on many of their contemporaries and hers, William Godwin and Mary Wollstonecraft in a double sense helped shape her into a child of the romantic period who developed and maintained a commitment to literature and to political reform.

The letters of 1814–27 demonstrate her early and consistent concern with political events; they display a vehement antimonarchism and an abiding belief in the freedom of the individual. The many letters she wrote expressing enthusiastic support of uprisings against tyrannical acts of government in Spain, Italy, Greece, and England substantiate her self-depiction in her letter of 24 March 1820: "You see what a John or rather Joan Bull I am so full of politics—." She formed a close friendship with Prince Alexander Mavrocordato, a leader of the Greek war of independence against Turkey, and was his confidant before he left Italy for Greece in June 1821. Her political concerns did not end—as some critics contend—with Shelley's death: She continued to keep in contact with Mavrocordato; her letters to and about Trelawny testify to her continued attention to the Greek battle for freedom; her 1826 novel, *The Last Man*, has politics as a central theme; she reacted to the death of Canning in 1827 as a blow to the cause of European liberty.

At the same time that the young Mary Godwin was introduced to the new political ideas of the age through Godwin, she was introduced to the new literary ideas as well. She was present during many literary conversations between Godwin and his associates and was encouraged to make use of Godwin's extensive library. In 1811–12 Godwin took her, along with the other children in the household, to attend his friend Samuel Taylor Coleridge's lectures on literature at the Royal Institution (Godwin, Journal). William Wordsworth was also Godwin's friend, and throughout her life Mary Shelley alluded to or quoted from the works of both Wordsworth and Coleridge. The romantic period revered nature and the individual, and Mary Shelley's letters resonate with her responses to plains, mountains, lakes, trees, the sea and sky, storms and calms. She sometimes used copies of these letters as sources for details for her fiction and travel books, just as Wordsworth sometimes used his sister Dorothy Wordsworth's journal observations for his poetry. Some of the letters, particularly those written after Shelley's death, resemble the topographical-meditative poetry so popular in the period—characterized by a description of a specific place followed by associations and reflections that it inspired. Her confessional tendency, not only in her letters to Jane Williams but also to others, including Leigh Hunt, John Howard Payne, and Maria Gisborne, is another indication of the influence of an age that celebrated the self-revelations of Jean-Jacques Rousseau, Wordsworth, and Lord Byron. The 1814–27 letters, as well as most of Mary Shelley's professional writing of this period, place her in the Romantic tradition in their expression of an aesthetic dependent on the curative role of nature, the dignity of the individual, and the conviction that love, not force, is the only valid means of restructuring the life of the individual and the society.

The variety of Mary Shelley's correspondents illustrates how cosmopolitan a daughter of her age she was. A friend or acquaintance of many prominent people, she wrote letters containing anecdotes about, or allusions to, Shelley, Godwin, Lord Byron, Coleridge, Charles and Mary Lamb, John Keats, William Hazlitt, Sir Walter Scott, Lady Sydney Morgan, Leigh Hunt (see 8 April 1827 for Hunt's previously unpublished addition to Mary Shelley's letter), Edward John Trelawny, Thomas Medwin, John Howard Payne, Prosper Mérimée, Caroline Norton, Thomas Love Peacock, Thomas Moore, Washington Irving. The letters provide an invaluable source of information about these and others who constituted literary and nonliterary society in Britain and elsewhere. Her many observations on living conditions, politics, royalty, manners, customs, housing, diet, dress, recreation, travel, schooling, finance, and transportation are often couched in comparative terms—past with present, one country played against another—adding considerable perspective to the insights she offers on contemporary society. Because of her particular interests, a large number of letters deal in depth with literature, opera, theater, musical entertainments, ballet, recitals, museums, and exhibitions. And it is not surprising that letters frequently allude to what her contemporaries wrote and read or that she gives considerable information about publishing practices and their effects on the world of letters. Her detailed accounts of so many aspects of the period, narrated in terms of her individual experiences and expectations, make nineteenth-century history direct and alive.

Tutored in intellectual thought and literary aspiration, Mary Godwin met an ideal mate in Shelley—poet, political radical, and admirer of Godwin and Wollstonecraft. The rapid development of their love, which culminated in their 28 July 1814 elopement, and Shelley's influence on his partner-protégée, have been described numerous times. Critics have seldom considered, however, the complexities of a relationship in which both parties are young and committed to literary careers. Mary Shelley, at the time of their elopement, was one month short of her seventeenth birthday, but among the possessions she took with her were her writings, to which she added on the tour a story called "Hate." Clearly, she represented for Shelley the ideal companion that he felt his first wife had failed to become. Their passion for each other and for literature found early expression: Their first child was born on 22 February 1815; the notebook of their elopement journey, kept mostly by Mary Shelley with occasional entries by Shelley, became the source of *Six Weeks' Tour*, published anonymously in 1817 and then included by Mary Shelley in Shelley's *Essays, Letters* in 1839. She later acknowledged what other evidence reveals, namely, that she, not Shelley, was its primary author. While *Six Weeks' Tour* was being printed, Shelley, in addition to attending to the publication of several of his own works, helped Mary Shelley see through the press the novel that is probably more familiar to people worldwide than any other romantic work: *Frankenstein.* Some critics, beginning with Sir Walter Scott (see 14 June 1818) and continuing to the present (see E. B. Murray, *Keats-Shelley Memorial Bulletin* 29 [1978]: 50–68), have believed that Shelley was entirely or largely the author of *Frankenstein.* Both Shelleys denied this attribution. Rather, Shelley is to be credited for contributing to *Frankenstein* the judgment and suggestions of an astute and committed editor, a favor Mary Shelley returned when she became his editor.

That Shelley influenced Mary Shelley is easily demonstrated and documented by her letters. Godwin had provided his daughter with a far richer intellectual experience than women of that period ordinarily enjoyed, and Shelley continued the educational process, sharing with her the benefits of his own wide knowledge, acquired at school and through independent, avid reading. Five years her senior, he had devoted himself to literature from his early adolescence, supported and indulged by his wealthy father. With few obstacles in his path, Shelley supplemented, shaped, and refined his school lessons. His dismissal from Oxford for refusing to answer questions about the authorship of the *Necessity of Atheism* (1811) ended only his formal education, as the lists of his prodigious reading in Mary Shelley's *Journal* attest. The *Journal* and the letters also record that Mary Shelley read a large number of the same books. Their dedication to the development of two literary careers is also demonstrated by daily schedules that included time for each to read and write and living quarters that generally provided each with a separate study.

Critics have stressed that Mary Shelley's relationship with Shelley introduced into her life personal and Shelleyan philosophic love. They have ignored, however, other experiences that contributed significantly to the growth of a gifted and intelligent but dependent girl into an accomplished author and independent woman, both anomalies in her era. Surely one of the central experiences in Mary Shelley's life was motherhood. During the eight years the Shelleys were together she was pregnant five times, the last pregnancy ending in a nearly fatal miscarriage. Of the four children born, the first, a girl, lived from 22 February to 6 March 1815; the second, William, lived from 24 January 1816 to 7 June 1819; the third, Clara Everina, from 2 September 1817 to 24 September 1818. Only Percy Florence, born 10 November 1819, survived both his parents. Following the death of William, Mary Shelley, then childless, wrote: "I feel that I am no[t] fit for any thing & therefore not fit to live but how must that heart be moulded which would not be broken by what I have suffered—" (29 June 1819). At that time she seemed almost to wish that she had forgone her union with Shelley rather than have endured the deaths of her children (see *Journal*, 4 August 1819). After Shelley's death all that survived of their shared life was Percy Florence Shelley and their manuscripts. Her newly published letters to Jane Williams, which indicate her almost superstitious fear that Percy Florence would die young, also show how completely she erased all blemish from her memory of Shelley and began her devoted task of gathering and publishing his writings shortly after his death. She had been accustomed to worshipping her dead mother and communing with her through her mother's works; in the same way, she would now relate to Shelley through his poetry and prose.

The letters not only record the depth and duration of her mourning after each death but also constitute a primary source of information about Mary Shelley's response to Shelley's philosophy of expansive rather than exclusive love. Her letters to Thomas Jefferson Hogg make clear that she participated in a three-sided love experiment with Shelley and Hogg in 1815. The degree of her involvement remains a matter of speculation, though these letters strongly suggest the affair between Mary Shelley and Hogg was not consummated (see 1 January 1815). Other letters refer to her awareness that throughout her union with Shelley other women, including Claire Clairmont (Mary Shelley's stepsister), Sophia Stacey, Teresa Emilia Viviani, and Jane Williams, became Shelley's major though temporary love objects and inspirations, although she remained his "best Mary." Moreover, each of these women was, to a greater or lesser degree, a member of the Shelley circle with whom Mary Shelley had her own special friendship.

The woman against whom Mary Shelley reacted most strongly during Shelley's life and after was her stepsister, and aspects of Shelley's relationship with Claire Clairmont remain unresolved to this day. Many Shelley biographers have thought it quite possible that he and Claire Clairmont had a liaison in 1814–15, the period during which Mary Shelley was pregnant and Shelley encouraged her and Hogg in their relationship. Aside from the amount of time Shelley and Claire Clairmont spent together and Mary Shelley's open annoyance at the attention her stepsister demanded and received, there is no clear evidence to document such a liaison (see 1 January 1815, n. 1). Nor is there any clear evidence that Shelley and Claire Clairmont were the parents of Shelley's "Neapolitan child" (see 18 June 1820, n. 1).

Biographers have maintained that towards the end of his life Shelley fell in love with Jane Williams and have questioned whether Shelley would have long remained with Mary Shelley. Mary Shelley was aware of Shelley's interest in Jane Williams, but—perhaps because she had seen such attractions grow and wane before or because the Williamses were evidently devoted to each other—it seems that she expressed no personal animosity towards Jane Williams. On the contrary, after Shelley and Edward Williams drowned, she regarded Jane Williams as her dearest friend and mourned the loss of Edward Williams as one whom she had truly loved.

The lives of the two young widows provide interesting parallels and telling differences: Both were left with almost no financial means; both tenaciously refused to give up the guardianship of their children to affluent relatives; both returned to England; both sought and gained financial support from the families of their spouses. But whereas Mary Shelley regarded herself as a writer capable of selling her work, Jane Williams had neither expectation of nor ambition for independence or career. In 1827, quite in keeping with the conventions of the day, she again took the role most readily accepted for women by becoming Mrs. Thomas Jefferson Hogg.

Mary Shelley was profoundly shaped and influenced by Shelley's artistry, intellect, and political philosophy; but their relationship, which provided her with such requisite conditions for writing as support, encouragement, intellectual dialogue and guidance, also brought pregnancies, child care, domestic responsibilities and tragedies, financial worries, and a transient existence in Italy. These demands on her time and energy might well be seen as impediments or challenges to the development of a young writer; but as her letters demonstrate, despite turmoil and tragedy, her literary objectives and enthusiasm persisted.

Her decision after Shelley's death to devote her life both to their son and to the publication of her own and Shelley's works was not a simple one. Alternative ways of life were offered, forcing her to reconsider her course. Some options she unequivocally dismissed, particularly her father-in-law's offer that she give up Percy Florence to a guardian of his choice in return for Sir Timothy Shelley's supporting him. Other possibilities were treated with more ambivalence, including the courtships of John Howard Payne and Prosper Mérimée and her friendships with other men. Although the deep loneliness she endured after Shelley's death figures prominently in her correspondence and her *Journal*, many of her letters of the same period, as well as Godwin's Journal, record her participation in a busy social schedule, including tea visits, dinner parties, theater, and opera. Her loneliness was obviously rooted not in the absence of friends and family but in the loss of the intimacy she and Shelley had shared, in retrospect hallowed by her imagination.

In the years 1823–27, Mary Shelley did not lead a life devoid of adult love; rather, her love was in great measure transferred to a number of women. Her strong feelings for female friends (a tendency of her mother's as well) began before she met Shelley. These letters unfold the story of her disappointment at losing the friendship of Isabella Booth, whose husband disapproved of Shelley, and the restoration of that friendship after Mary Shelley returned to England. But the letters make clear that the primary object of Mary Shelley's adoration and confidence was Jane Williams, whose lack of loyalty shocked and depressed Mary Shelley (see 22

August 1827 to John Howard Payne, n. 1). The newly published letters of July and August 1827 display Mary Shelley's efforts to disguise her anguish at the insincerity of her friend, whom she loved for herself and as a living bond with their days in Italy with Shelley and Edward Williams (see 18 October [1823]). New letters also provide the biographical data that led to previously unknown information about Mary Shelley and her circle of friends. For example, Jane Williams was pregnant when she and Hogg began to live together as man and wife in spring 1827. In November she gave birth to a girl, baptized Mary Prudentia Hogg, whose first name quite likely honored Mary Shelley (see 28 July 1827, n. 2). Furthermore, the letters give details of Mary Shelley's friendship with Isabel Robinson Douglas and with the eccentric Mary Diana Dods, who pseudonymously published books and short stories as David Lyndsay, a fact unknown until this edition (see 30 October 1826 to Alaric A. Watts, n. 2).

Mary Shelley wrote of herself: "A pen in hand my thoughts flow fast" (6 January 1825), which partially explains the air of spontaneity as well as the many minor errors in her letters. But her haste was not motivated by indifference to letter writing. On the contrary, Mary Shelley frequently commented in her letters on the high value she placed on letters as literature, as literary and biographical source, and as personal communication. During Shelley's lifetime she asked Thomas Love Peacock to save Shelley's letters because she intended to copy them when they returned to England (10 November 1818). After Shelley's death she gathered his letters, originals and copies, and published a selection of them in *Essays, Letters*. She and Shelley included two letters each in *Six Weeks' Tour*, and she revised passages from letters for her fiction and for *Rambles in Germany and Italy*. In 1827 she was instrumental in convincing Teresa Guiccioli to allow Thomas Moore to glean information from Byron's letters for his biography (see 3 July 1827 and 20 August 1827 for previously unpublished letters on the subject). Discreet in deciding whether a letter addressed to one person ought to be read by others, she often recognized the efficiency of sharing letters and sometimes directed correspondents to give her letters to others to read. She realized that friends showed her letters to others, and she, too, asked to read letters not addressed to her. In her letter to Leigh and Marianne Hunt explaining why she wished that they had opened and read Trelawny's letter to her before forwarding it, she wrote that she knew Trelawny showed her letters to others, which made her "less scrupulous" (not "unscrupulous," as in Jones, *MWS Letters*) about allowing them to read Trelawny's letters (13–14 August 1823). Her occasional complaints as she grew older about making personal letters public were almost certainly the result of publications she regarded as indiscreet, since, throughout her life, she shared her letters and Shelley's by publishing them, by borrowing and lending letters, and by giving letters as remembrances to special friends or acquaintances.

She was relatively open not only in sharing letters but also in her letter-writing style, which is frank about her own feelings and diverse in tone and topic. The melancholia and depression of many of her letters have long been a subject for critics, who have cited them to argue that Mary Shelley had little or no sense of humor. A number of the newly published 1814–27 letters, however, together with some of the previously published letters of this period, are marked by humor and playfulness and call for a reevaluation of Mary Shelley's personality. Examples of her humor are her use of a variety of nicknames, including "Pecksie," "Pecksey Dor," "Dormouse," and "Maie"; the high-spirited and sometimes flirtatious nature of some of her letters to Hunt, before and after Shelley's death; her ebullient letter to her friend Maria Gisborne in which she announces Percy Florence's birth (see c. 13 November 1819); her merry description of her unconventional behavior at the theater (see 11 June 1826). The new letters, together with the old, also call into question another canard of Mary Shelley criticism: that she was a cold, unexpressive woman. These letters exhibit a wide range of responses: joy of her love of Shelley and of their children; optimism about her writing; pride in Shelley's writing; love of friends; amusement over human foibles; excitement over books, theater, opera, art; exhilaration over landscape. These contrast and sometimes comingle with grief over the deaths of Shelley and their children; dismay and anger at accusations of incest against Shelley (see 10 August 1821 to Shelley; 10 August 1821 to Isabella Hoppner); wryness at the outcome of Shelley's friendship with Emilia Viviani (see 7 March 1822); hostility towards Claire Clairmont; disappointment over lost friendships; frustration at financial pressures. Her commentaries on these experiences may be faulted for their occasional repetitiveness, but not for their want of emotion.

This edition, with several hundred previously unpublished letters supplementing old material, will contain twice the number of Mary Shelley's letters as any earlier publication. Though letters remain unlocated, indicated by gaps during some periods and references to unfound correspondence, the collection here develops a far more complete narrative and presents a newly realized Mary Shelley for critical scrutiny. Transcribing the letters from manuscripts, many not before available, has allowed for the correction of thousands of errors in past editions (including misreadings, misdatings, and standardized punctuation and capitalization) that served to emphasize her shortcomings and underestimate her strengths. Focusing the annotations primarily on Mary Shelley has yielded significant insights from scores of her statements unannotated in the past. For example, her own writing and politics become recognizable as dominant themes in the life of Mary Shelley. And she emerges from her explicit and implicit self-revelations as a woman of great strength and energy; this is nowhere more movingly demonstrated than in her 1822–23 mourning letters, which are interfaced with her persistent requests, through intermediaries and directly, that Sir Timothy Shelley grant her an allowance. Old letters are given fresh perspective by new letters and by replies of correspondents to unfound letters, revealing that conclusions about Mary Shelley have often been based on inadequate information. One instance is the notion that she sought only conventional society after Shelley's death, here dispelled by the facts of her friendship with Mary Diana Dods and her role in the lives of Dods and Isabel Robinson Douglas. Another instance is the correspondence of her friends indicating that after the birth of Percy Florence, the Shelleys remained in Florence to permit Mary Shelley to do research about that city, which is a principal setting of *Valperga* (see c. 13 December 1819, n. 4).

These early letters place Mary Shelley in the tradition of romantic letter writing not because they are creative and reflective in the same way as are Lamb's or Byron's, Shelley's or Keats's, but because their own creativity and reflectiveness add a different, equally important, perspective to our understanding of the romantic period. Her elopement and life with Shelley, her writing career, her self-dependence in widowhood, and her publications of Shelley's works are rooted in romantic defiance of conventions and in belief in the ability of the individual to change those conventions. Because of her own varied interests and her sensitivity to the concerns of her correspondents, Mary Shelley's letters (except when brief or about business) are generally not confined to any one topic. A passage about literature may follow one about housekeeping; a discussion of the Tuscan landscape may precede an urgent request for baby clothes or combs or pencils. Though she occasionally played in her letters, she never posed. At times her self-awareness becomes maudlin, her candor chiding, her observations sentimental; but the voice that pervades is analytical, forthright, contemplative, and caring.

And perhaps the most important characteristic of Mary Shelley, confirmed by her letters, was her enduring will not merely to survive but to create and to contribute to the world in which she lived. Readers interested exclusively in literary or historical detail or in the status of women will value parts of her letters and perhaps wish that she had not strayed from those subjects. But the diversity of her concerns develops a counterpoint, the minor themes giving depth and nuance to the major themes of her life and letters: the Godwin, Shelley, and Byron circles; her career; her responses to and reflections on nineteenth-century European society.

Editorial Notes

MARY SHELLEY'S known extant letters date from October 1814, two months after her seventeenth birthday, through September 1850, one month after her fifty-third birthday and five months before her death, on 1 February 1851. The earliest collection of her letters is *Shelley Memorials* (1859); the most complete collection is *MWS Letters* (1944), edited by Frederick L. Jones, which numbers 705 letters. Many of these letters, however, are brief summaries, simple citations of dates and recipients, or material taken from imperfect copies. A major difficulty—then and now—was locating the letters, which are widely scattered throughout the world. To find them, I wrote hundreds of letters of inquiry to libraries, collectors, dealers, and colleagues in Africa, Australia, Europe, New Zealand, and North America. I also placed advertisements in journals and newspapers and searched through old auction records and dealers' catalogues. This process yielded more than thirteen hundred letters, several hundred of which were previously unpublished. The total is an approximation because new letters keep turning up (even as this first volume was going to press, two previously unpublished letters were located).

The Carl H. Pforzheimer Library, the Bodleian Library, The Huntington Library, Lord Abinger, John Murray, the British Library, and Professor Jean de Palacio hold the largest collections of Mary Shelley's letters; the rest are in the hands of diverse collectors and libraries. Since Jones's pioneer work, much of the correspondence that he had to take from copies has been made accessible, including the 118 letters formerly owned by Sir John Shelley-Rolls, now at the Bodleian Library. And most important, significant collections of previously unpublished letters have been made available for this edition, including the letters of Lord Abinger, John Murray, and The Carl H. Pforzheimer Library. In the interest of presenting the letters as faithfully as possible, I have newly transcribed almost all of the unpublished and previously published letters from manuscript (exceptions are noted).

Mary Shelley's letters are consistent primarily in their inconsistency. Spelling and punctuation are irregular and variable; dates are often omitted, partial, or incorrect. Errors in words, phrases, and sentences are largely uncorrected. The variety of subject matter together with the irregularities of writing style, creates an impression of haste, unselfconsciousness, and spontaneity, which reveals as much about the author as the words themselves. Rather than follow the tradition of past editors who silently corrected these irregularities, with some minor exceptions explained herein, I have reproduced the letters as Mary Shelley wrote them, adding bracketed material for clarification when the original might cause unnecessary distraction.

The letters are arranged in chronological order; letters to the same person on the same day are distinguished by letters after the date. Almost all letters in this edition are from manuscript, indicated by MS. in the textual notes. If, however, a letter is from a copy, it is taken from the earliest copy or printed form of the letter. If a later publication of a printed text is substantially superior, it will be cited along with the first publication.

Following is a description of editorial principles, including minor exceptions to the original manuscript:

1. The name of the addressee is given at top left. The names of addressees identified but not given appear in square brackets: [ ]. A name in square brackets that is preceded by a question mark indicates editorial conjecture. Unidentified addressees are represented by a square bracket containing only a question mark: [?].

2. Previously unpublished letters have an asterisk preceding the addressee's name. Partially published letters that omit a significant portion of the original manuscript are treated as unpublished; however, they are cited.

3. The place of writing is given at top right, although Mary Shelley sometimes gave this information at the close of letters. If a letter was written from several places, the first and last place are given at top right (the latter appears in the body of the letter as well). Place of writing is supplied in square brackets when no place is given in the manuscript. A place in brackets preceded by a question mark indicates editorial conjecture.

4. The date of writing also is given at top right, although Mary Shelley sometimes dated letters at their close. Dates in square brackets are taken from postmarks, context, or information other than the original manuscript. Questionable dates are explained in footnotes. Conjectural dates are bracketed and preceded by a question mark. Letters written over a number of days are placed under their earliest date, but the last possible date of writing is also cited. Letters that I have been unable to date I place at their earliest possible date, the conjectured date (or dates) preceded by a question mark and in brackets. Editorial references to dates give the day, the month, and then the year.

5. The complimentary close is separated from the letter except when followed by additional text or when so informal as to be considered part of the text.

6. Postscripts appear in Mary Shelley's letters on envelopes and address sheets; in margins; and at times are cross-written (see below). In this edition, all postscripts follow the signature. Postscripts written anywhere except after the letter are preceded by an editorial note (in square brackets) indicating their place in the manuscript.

7. The following information appears after each letter:
   a. Address of recipient
   b. Postmarks
   c. Endorsement
   d. Indication that the letter is unpublished or a citation to previous publication. Letters published in *MWS Letters* and elsewhere are cited to Jones's edition. Otherwise, earliest publication is cited.
   e. Source of text. Letters from original manuscripts are indicated by MS. preceding name of present holder.
   f. Translator, if other than editor.

8. Footnotes are numbered for each letter.

9. I have made countless corrections of previously published letters; however, only corrections of particular significance are called to the reader's attention.

10. Although Mary Shelley's irregularities have been retained, *sic* is avoided. Easily understood irregularities, such as a word or even a name spelled differently in the same letter or the substitution of *you* for *your*, are left as given, unless context requires clarification. Questionable spellings caused by uncrossed *t*'s, undotted *i*'s, and partial letters are silently corrected. Words that might cause the reader difficulty are followed by a square bracket containing the intended word in italics, and when necessary, omitted letters of words are inserted in the text in curly brackets: {   }. Where omission of entire words proves distracting, a curly bracket is inserted. Occasionally, based on context, I venture an editorial conjecture within those brackets.

The following is a list of Mary Shelley's common misspellings: aboutt, abroard, ach, agreably, ajustment, ammeliorated, ancle, appartments, arrisen, asortment, assylum, atatch, atmospher, bankrupcy, batchelors, befal, carrige, cathederal, centinels, chamberi, comming, concious, consolotary, contemtible, corteous, cotons, craked, credibilty, crost, dayly, dicision, delettanti, demonination, descicion, desart, develope, devision, dipt, disagreable, disipated, dispair, dissappoint, docter, Dutchess, embarassing, enclined, evedently, exageration, exersize, exhiliarating, exiliarating, exitement, hacnied, headach, herse, hypoccrisy, immagination, immagine, impassable, improvisaing, independant, indicision, indure, insuferably, intirely, invelloped, irrisistibly, jiwellers, labratory, lodgeings, Medames, medecines, meer, negociations, occurences, orriginal, parr, patrole, peice, phisical, precipieces, prest, privarications, publickly, quarelled, reatreat, reccommended, releive, sciszars, scolars, seige, seing, seperated, shiped, sincerly, skrewing, somthing, staid, stile, stopt, synonimous, synomimies, takeing, teusday, threatning, toothach, tost, untill, upolsterer, Venise, verry, violance, walzing, witnissed.

11. Abbreviations remain, followed, when necessary, by the complete word italicized in brackets. For example, *w*^{d} is not spelled out, but *T—y*

[*Trelawny*] is. Abbreviated names are followed by the full name italicized in brackets only the first time they are used in a letter unless context requires additional clarification. *S.* for Shelley and *LB* or Lord B for Byron appear frequently and are spelled out only if confusion might arise in a particular context.

12. False starts or obvious slips have been silently omitted. Deleted words that have significance are enclosed in angled brackets: 〈 〉 A variety of means, including ultraviolet and infrared light, have been used to rescue these words. Even partial readings of such passages are given, in the hope that future readers may be able to fill in or correct material.

13. Words missing due to holes, torn seals, or deterioration of the manuscript are treated as follows: If enough of a partial word remains to suggest the full word, the remainder will be supplied in square brackets. Wholly conjectural words will be given in square brackets, italicized and followed by a question mark. Uncertain readings will be given in square brackets, italicized and preceded by a question mark. Missing words that offer no sound basis for conjecture will be represented by empty square brackets. Words torn from manuscripts that can be read on fragments adhering to the seals, unless they are of particular significance, have been silently inserted.

14. Mary Shelley's punctuation conforms to no system. She generally uses a dash instead of a period or comma (though at times she uses a dash in addition to other punctuation), and she usually omits end punctuation. A double space has been left after an apparent sentence ending without punctuation that is followed by a sentence beginning with a capital letter. Unpunctuated sentences run on unless clarity requires emendation; in which case punctuation will be supplied in curly brackets. Paragraphing has been added to avoid unclear, run-on postscripts. The length of dashes has been standardized.

15. Like many of her contemporaries, Mary Shelley was inconsistent in her use of capitalization. These inconsistencies have been retained.

16. Words or phrases written between lines, unless unusual in content or placement, have been silently inserted into the line. An asterisk is substituted for Mary Shelley's footnote indication *x* when confusion may arise.

17. Portions of letters that contain cross-writing—that is, horizontal writing crossed by vertical writing, giving a gridlike effect—are preceded by the indication [*cross-written*].

18. Superior letters like those in *M^rs^* and *30th* are retained, but the dash or dot below is omitted; *&* and *&c* are also retained.

19. Not represented are underscorings in addresses, dates, and signatures or punctuation following addresses and dates.

20. Letters in French and Italian are followed by translations. Errors or variants in Mary Shelley's French and Italian are not corrected. Foreign words and phrases are translated in footnotes unless they are cognates or are clear by their context.

21. Persons included in the list entitled "Biographical Names" in *Webster's Seventh New Collegiate Dictionary* are not identified unless context requires additional information.

The first two volumes of this edition will contain indexes of proper names. A complete index will be given in volume three. Volume three will also contain a list of letters located too late for inclusion in their appropriate chronological order and a list of letters unlocated but noted from auction records and other sources.

Editorial Symbols

[?]	Unidentified addressee
[London]	Non-given but certain addressee, place, date
[?London]	Editorial conjecture of addressee, place, date
[ ]	Word torn from text or otherwise obliterated
mo[on]	Editorial conjecture of word torn from text or otherwise obliterated
[*moon?*]	Uncertain editorial conjecture of word torn from text or otherwise obliterated
[?*moon*]	Uncertain reading
[*P. 1, top*]	Editorial information
M^{rs} G [*Godwin*]	Abbreviated name supplied
and [*an*]	Clarification of word
{ }	Word or letter omitted
{moon}	Editorial conjecture of omitted word or letter
⟨ ⟩	Deletion restored

Abbreviations

Abinger MS.	The manuscripts and letters of William Godwin, Mary Wollstonecraft Shelley, Percy Bysshe Shelley, and others in the possession of Lord Abinger (many of which are now on deposit at the Bodleian Library).
Altick, *The Cowden Clarkes*	Richard D. Altick. *The Cowden Clarkes.* London: Oxford University Press, 1948.
Alumni Cantabrigienses	*Alumni Cantabrigienses.* Edited by John Venn and J. A. Venn. 10 vols. Cambridge: At the University Press, 1922–47.
Alumni Oxonienses	*Alumni Oxonienses.* Edited by Joseph Foster. 4 vols. Oxford: Parker & Co., 1888–91.
Angeli, *Shelley and His Friends in Italy*	Helen Rossetti Angeli. *Shelley and His Friends in Italy.* London: Methuen & Co., 1911.
Annual Register	*The Annual Register, or a View of the History, Politics, and Literature.* London: Baldwin, Cradock, and Joy [various dates].
Beavan, *James and Horace Smith*	Arthur H. Beavan. *James and Horace Smith.* London: Hurst and Blackett, 1899.
Beddoes, *Letters*	*The Letters of Thomas Lovell Beddoes.* Edited by Edmund Gosse. London: Elkin Mathew & John Lane, 1894.
Blunden, *"Examiner" Examined*	Edmund Blunden. *Leigh Hunt's "Examiner" Examined.* London: Cobden-Sanderson, 1928.
Blunden, *Leigh Hunt*	Edmund Blunden. *Leigh Hunt, A Biography.* London: Cobden-Sanderson, 1930.
Brewer, *The Holograph Letters*	*My Leigh Hunt Library, the Holograph Letters.* Edited by Luther A. Brewer. Iowa City: University of Iowa Press, 1938.
Brown, *Godwin*	Ford K. Brown. *The Life of William Godwin.* London: J. M. Dent & Sons, 1926.
Brown, *Letters*	*The Letters of Charles Armitage Brown.* Edited by Jack Stillinger. Cambridge, Mass.: Harvard University Press, 1966.
Burke's Landed Gentry	John Burke *et al.*, eds. *Genealogical and Heraldic History of the Landed Gentry.* London [various dates].
Burke's Peerage	John Burke *et al.*, eds. *Genealogical and Heraldic History of the Peerage, Baronetage and Knightage.* London [various dates].
Byron, *Correspondence*	*Lord Byron's Correspondence.* Edited by John Murray. 2 vols. London: John Murray, 1922.

Byron, *Letters and Journals*	*Byron's Letters and Journals.* Edited by Leslie A. Marchand. Cambridge, Mass.: The Belknap Press of Harvard University Press, 1973–.
Byron, *Poetry*	*The Works of Lord Byron: Poetry.* Edited by Ernest Hartley Coleridge. 7 vols. London: John Murray, 1898–1903.
Byron, *Works*	*The Works of Lord Byron: Letters and Journals.* Edited by Rowland E. Prothero. 6 vols. London: John Murray, 1898–1901.
Cameron, *The Golden Years*	Kenneth Neill Cameron. *Shelley: The Golden Years.* Cambridge, Mass.: Harvard University Press, 1974.
Cameron, *The Young Shelley*	Kenneth Neill Cameron. *The Young Shelley: Genesis of a Radical.* New York: Macmillan Co., 1950.
CC Journals	*The Journals of Claire Clairmont, 1814–1827.* Edited by Marion Kingston Stocking with the assistance of David Mackenzie Stocking. Cambridge, Mass.: Harvard University Press, 1968.
Charnwood, *Call Back Yesterday*	Dorothea Charnwood. *Call Back Yesterday.* London: Eyre and Spottiswoode, 1937.
Clarke, *Recollections of Writers*	Charles Cowden Clarke and Mary Cowden Clarke. *Recollections of Writers.* London: Low, 1878.
Cline, *Pisan Circle*	C. L. Cline. *Byron, Shelley and their Pisan Circle.* London: John Murray, 1952.
Donner, *The Browning Box*	H. W. Donner, ed. *The Browning Box; or, The Life and Works of Thomas Lovell Beddoes.* London: Oxford University Press, 1935.
Dowden, *Shelley*	Edward Dowden. *The Life of Percy Bysshe Shelley.* London: Kegan Paul, Trench & Co., 1886.
Ebers, *The King's Theatre*	John Ebers. *Seven Years of the King's Theatre.* London: William Harrison Ainsworth, 1828.
Fenner, *Leigh Hunt and Opera Criticism*	Theodore Fenner. *Leigh Hunt and Opera Criticism: The "Examiner" Years, 1808–1821.* Lawrence: University Press of Kansas, 1972.
Genest, *English Stage*	John Genest, ed. *Some Account of the English Stage from the Restoration in 1660 to 1830.* 10 vols. Bath: n.p., 1832.
Gisborne, *Journals and Letters*	*Maria Gisborne & Edward E. Williams, Shelley's Friends, Their Journals and Letters.* Edited by Frederick L. Jones. Norman: University of Oklahoma Press, 1951.
Godwin, Journal	Manuscript journal of William Godwin, 1788–1836 (Abinger MS.).
Grylls, *Clairmont*	R. Glynn Grylls. *Claire Clairmont: Mother of Byron's Allegra.* London: John Murray, 1939.
Grylls, *Mary Shelley*	R. Glynn Grylls. *Mary Shelley: A Biography.* London: Oxford University Press, 1938.
Haydon, *Diary*	*The Diary of Benjamin Robert Haydon.* Edited by Willard Bissell Pope. 5 vols. Cambridge, Mass.: Harvard University Press, 1960–63.

Hogg, *Shelley*	Thomas Jefferson Hogg. *The Life of Percy Bysshe Shelley*. In *The Life of Percy Bysshe Shelley . . .* , edited by Humbert Wolfe. 2 vols. London: J. M. Dent & Sons, 1933.
Hunt, *Autobiography*	*The Autobiography of Leigh Hunt.* Edited by Roger Ingpen. 2 vols. New York: E. P. Dutton & Co., 1903.
Hunt, *Correspondence*	*The Correspondence of Leigh Hunt.* Edited by Thornton Hunt. 2 vols. London: Smith, Elder and Co., 1862.
Hunt, *Lord Byron and Some of His Contemporaries*	Leigh Hunt. *Lord Byron and Some of His Contemporaries.* London: Henry Colburn, 1828.
Ingpen, *Shelley in England*	Roger Ingpen. *Shelley in England: New Facts and Letters from the Shelley-Whitton Papers.* London: Kegan Paul, Trench, Trubner & Co., 1917.
Irving, *Journals and Notebooks*	Washington Irving. *Journals and Notebooks.* Edited by Henry A. Pochmann. Madison: University of Wisconsin Press, 1969–70. Vol. I, *1803–1806*, edited by Nathalia Wright; vol. III, *1819–1827*, edited by Walter A. Reichart.
Johnstone's Guide	Johnstone's *London Commercial Guide*, August 1817.
Jones, "New Letters"	Frederick L. Jones, ed., "Mary Shelley to Maria Gisborne: New Letters, 1818–1822." *Studies in Philology* 52 (January 1955): 39–74.
Lamb, *Letters* (Lucas)	*The Letters of Charles Lamb to Which Are Added Those of His Sister Mary Lamb.* Edited by E. V. Lucas. 3 vols. London: J. M. Dent & Sons, 1935.
Lamb, *Letters* (Marrs)	*The Letters of Charles and Mary Anne Lamb.* Edited by Edwin W. Marrs, Jr. 3 vols. to date. Ithaca: Cornell University Press, 1975–.
Lovell, *Medwin*	Ernest J. Lovell, Jr. *Captain Medwin: Friend of Byron and Shelley.* Austin: University of Texas Press, 1962.
Lucas, *Charles Lamb*	E. V. Lucas. *The Life of Charles Lamb.* London: Methuen & Co., 1905.
Lyles, *MWS Bibliography*	W. H. Lyles. *Mary Shelley: An Annotated Bibliography.* New York: Garland, 1975.
McAleer, *The Sensitive Plant*	Edward C. McAleer. *The Sensitive Plant: A Life of Lady Mount Cashell.* Chapel Hill: University of North Carolina Press, 1958.
Marchand, *Byron*	Leslie A. Marchand. *Byron: A Biography.* 3 vols. New York: Alfred A. Knopf, 1957.
Marshall, *Mary Shelley*	Mrs. Julian [Florence A.] Marshall. *The Life and Letters of Mary Wollstonecraft Shelley.* 2 vols. London: Richard Bentley & Son, 1889.
Marshall, *The Liberal*	William H. Marshall. *Byron, Shelley, Hunt and the Liberal.* Philadelphia: University of Pennsylvania Press, 1960.
Medwin, *Conversations*	*Medwin's Conversations of Lord Byron.* Edited by Ernest J. Lovell, Jr. Princeton: Princeton University Press, 1966.

Medwin, *Shelley*	Thomas Medwin. *The Life of Percy Bysshe Shelley.* Edited by H. Buxton Forman. London: Oxford University Press, 1913.
Moore, *Accounts Rendered*	Doris Langley Moore. *Lord Byron: Accounts Rendered.* London: John Murray, 1974.
Moore, *The Late Lord Byron*	Doris Langley Moore. *The Late Lord Byron.* New York: Harper & Row, 1961.
Moore, *Letters*	*The Letters of Thomas Moore.* Edited by Wilfred S. Dowden. 2 vols. Oxford: Clarendon Press, 1964.
Moore, *Memoirs*	Thomas Moore. *Memoirs, Journal and Correspondence.* Edited by Lord John Russell. 8 vols. Boston: Little, Brown and Co., 1853.
MWS, *Collected Tales*	Mary Wollstonecraft Shelley. *Collected Tales and Stories.* Edited by Charles E. Robinson. Baltimore: Johns Hopkins University Press, 1976.
MWS, *Falkner*	Mary Wollstonecraft Shelley. *Falkner: A Novel.* 3 vols. London: Saunders and Otley, 1837.
MWS, *Frankenstein*	Mary Wollstonecraft Shelley. *Frankenstein; or, The Modern Prometheus.* 3 vols. London: Lackington, Hughes, Harding, Mayor, & Jones, 1818.
MWS Journal	Manuscript journal of Mary Shelley (Abinger MS.).
MWS *Journal*	*Mary Shelley's Journal.* Edited by Frederick L. Jones. Norman: University of Oklahoma Press, 1947.
MWS, *The Last Man*	Mary Wollstonecraft Shelley. *The Last Man.* 3 vols. London: Henry Colburn, 1826.
MWS Letters	*The Letters of Mary W. Shelley.* Edited by Frederick L. Jones. 2 vols. Norman: University of Oklahoma Press, 1944.
MWS, *Lives* (1835–37)	Mary Wollstonecraft Shelley (with others). *Lives of the most Eminent Literary and Scientific Men of Italy, Spain, and Portugal.* The Cabinet of Biography, edited by the Rev. Dionysius Lardner, vols. 86–88. London: Longman, Orme, Brown, Green, & Longman; and John Taylor, 1835–37.
MWS, *Lives* (1838–39)	Mary Wollstonecraft Shelley. *Lives of the most Eminent Literary and Scientific Men of France.* The Cabinet of Biography, edited by the Rev. Dionysius Lardner, vols. 102 and 103. London: Longman, Orme, Brown, Green, & Longman; and John Taylor, 1838–39.
MWS, *Lodore*	Mary Wollstonecraft Shelley. *Lodore.* 3 vols. London: Richard Bentley, 1835.
MWS, *Matilda*	Mary Wollstonecraft Shelley. *Mathilda.* Edited by Elizabeth Nitchie. Chapel Hill: University of North Carolina Press, 1959.
MWS, *Midas*	Mary Wollstonecraft Shelley. *Midas.* In *Proserpine & Midas. Two Unpublished Mythological Dramas by Mary Shelley*, edited by A[ndré] [Henri] Koszul. London: Humphrey Milford, 1922.

MWS, *Perkin Warbeck*	Mary Wollstonecraft Shelley. *The Fortunes of Perkin Warbeck, A Romance.* 3 vols. London: Henry Colburn and Richard Bentley, 1830.
MWS, *Proserpine*	Mary Wollstonecraft Shelley. *Proserpine, a Mythological Drama in Two Acts.* In *The Winter's Wreath.* London: G. and W. B. Whittaker, 1832 [1831].
MWS, *Rambles in Germany and Italy*	Mary Wollstonecraft Shelley. *Rambles in Germany and Italy, in 1840, 1842, and 1843.* 2 vols. London: Edward Moxon, 1844.
MWS, *Six Weeks' Tour*	Mary Wollstonecraft Shelley with Percy Bysshe Shelley. *History of a Six Weeks' Tour through a Part of France, Switzerland, Germany, and Holland: with Letters Descriptive of a Sail round the Lake of Geneva, and of the Glaciers of Chamouni.* London: T. Hookham, Jun. and C. and J. Ollier, 1817.
MWS, *Valperga*	Mary Wollstonecraft Shelley. *Valperga: or, the Life and Adventures of Castruccio, Prince of Lucca.* 3 vols. London: G. and W. B. Whittaker, 1823.
Nicoll, *English Drama*	Allardyce Nicoll. *A History of English Drama, 1660–1900.* Vol. IV, *Early Nineteenth Century Drama, 1800–1850.* London: Cambridge University Press, 1960.
Nitchie, *Mary Shelley*	Elizabeth Nitchie. *Mary Shelley.* New Brunswick: Rutgers University Press, 1953.
Norman, *After Shelley*	*After Shelley: The Letters of Thomas Jefferson Hogg to Jane Williams.* Edited by Sylva Norman. London: Oxford University Press, 1934.
Norman, *Flight of the Skylark*	Sylva Norman. *Flight of the Skylark: The Development of Shelley's Reputation.* London: Max Reinhardt, 1954.
Origo, *The Last Attachment*	Iris Origo. *The Last Attachment.* London: Jonathan Cape & John Murray, 1949.
Overmyer, *America's First Hamlet*	Grace Overmyer. *America's First Hamlet.* New York: New York University Press, 1957.
Palacio, *Mary Shelley*	Jean de Palacio. *Mary Shelley dans son oeuvre: Contributions aux études shelleyennes.* Paris: Editions Klincksieck, 1969.
Paul, *Godwin*	C. Kegan Paul. *William Godwin: His Friends and Contemporaries.* 2 vols. London: Henry S. King & Co., 1876.
Payne, *Letterbook*	Manuscript letterbooks of John Howard Payne. Columbia University Library [various dates].
PBS Letters	*The Letters of Percy Bysshe Shelley.* Edited by Frederick L. Jones. 2 vols. Oxford: Oxford University Press, 1964.
Peacock, *Memoirs*	"Memoirs of Percy Bysshe Shelley." In *The Works of Thomas Love Peacock*, vol. VIII, edited by H. F. B. Brett-Smith and C. E. Jones (*Halliford Edition*). London: Constable & Co., 1934.

Peacock, *Works*	*The Works of Thomas Love Peacock.* Edited by H. F. B. Brett-Smith and C. E. Jones (*Halliford Edition*). 10 vols. London: Constable & Co., 1924–34.
Reiman, *The Romantics Reviewed*	Donald H. Reiman, ed. *The Romantics Reviewed: Contemporary Reviews of British Romantic Writers.* 9 vols. New York: Garland Publishing, 1972.
Rennie, *Traits of Character*	Eliza Rennie. *Traits of Character; Being Twenty-Five Years' Literary and Personal Recollections By A Contemporary.* 2 vols. London: Hurst and Blackett, 1860.
Robinson, *Diary*	*Diary, Reminiscenses, and Correspondence of Henry Crabb Robinson.* Edited by Thomas Sadler. 3 vols. London: Macmillan, 1869.
Robinson, *On Books*	Henry Crabb Robinson. *On Books and Their Writers.* Edited by Edith J. Morley. 3 vols. London: J. M. Dent & Sons, 1938.
The Romance	*The Romance of Mary W. Shelley, John Howard Payne and Washington Irving.* With remarks by F. B. Sanborn. Boston: Boston Bibliophile Society, 1907.
St. Clair, *Trelawny*	William St. Clair. *Trelawny: The Incurable Romancer.* London: John Murray, 1977.
S & M	*Shelley and Mary.* 4 vols. London: privately printed, 1882.
SC	Kenneth Neill Cameron and Donald H. Reiman, eds. *Shelley and his Circle, 1773–1822.* 6 vols. Cambridge, Mass.: Harvard University Press, 1961–73.
Scott, *New Shelley Letters*	*New Shelley Letters.* Edited by W. S. Scott. New Haven: Yale University Press, 1949.
Shelley, *Complete Works*	*The Complete Works of Percy Bysshe Shelley.* Edited by Roger Ingpen and Walter E. Peck (Julian Edition). 10 vols. London and New York: E. Benn, 1926–30.
Shelley, *Essays, Letters*	*Essays, Letters from Abroad, Translations and Fragments by Percy Bysshe Shelley.* Edited by Mary W. Shelley. 2 vols. London: Edward Moxon, 1840 [1839].
Shelley Memorials	*Shelley Memorials: From Authentic Sources. Edited by Lady Shelley. To Which is Added An Essay on Christianity, By Percy Bysshe Shelley: Now First Printed.* Edited by Lady [Jane] Shelley. London: Smith, Elder and Co., 1859.
Shelley, *Poetical Works* (1839)	*The Poetical Works of Percy Bysshe Shelley.* Edited by Mary W. Shelley. 4 vols. London: Edward Moxon, 1839.
Shelley, *Poetical Works* (Forman)	*The Poetical Works of Percy Bysshe Shelley.* Edited by Harry Buxton Forman. 4 vols. London: Reeves & Turner, 1876–77.
Shelley, *Poetical Works* (OSA)	*The Complete Poetical Works of Percy Bysshe Shelley.* Edited by Thomas Hutchinson. Oxford University Press, 1960.
Shelley, *Poetry and Prose*	*Shelley's Poetry and Prose.* Edited by Donald H. Reiman and Sharon B. Powers. New York: Norton & Co., 1977.

Shelley, *Posthumous Poems*	*Posthumous Poems of Percy Bysshe Shelley.* Edited by Mary W. Shelley. London: John and Henry L. Hunt, 1824.
Shelley's Prose Works	*The Prose Works of Percy Bysshe Shelley.* Edited by Harry Buxton Forman. 4 vols. London: Reeves & Turner, 1880.
Smiles, *John Murray*	Samuel Smiles. *A Publisher and His Friends: Memoir and Correspondence of the Late John Murray.* 2 vols. London: John Murray, 1891.
Smith, *A Sentimental Library*	Harry B. Smith. *A Sentimental Library.* Privately printed, 1914.
Steffan, *Byron's Don Juan*	Truman Guy Steffan. *Byron's Don Juan.* 2d ed. 4 vols. Austin: University of Texas Press, 1971.
Tatchell, *Leigh Hunt*	Molly Tatchell. *Leigh Hunt and His Family in Hammersmith.* London: Hammersmith Local History Group, 1969.
Taylor, *Early Collected Editions*	Charles H. Taylor, Jr. *The Early Collected Editions of Shelley's Poems.* New Haven: Yale University Press, 1958.
Trelawny, *Adventures*	Edward John Trelawny. *Adventures of a Younger Son.* Edited by William St. Clair. London: Oxford University Press, 1974.
Trelawny, *Letters*	*Letters of Edward John Trelawny.* Edited by H. Buxton Forman. London: Oxford University Press, 1910.
Trelawny, *Recollections*	*Trelawny's Recollections of the Last Days of Shelley and Byron.* With an Introduction by Edward Dowden. London: Humphrey Milford, 1931.
Trelawny, *Records*	Edward John Trelawny. *Records of Shelley, Byron, and the Author.* 2 vols. London: Basil Montagu Pickering, 1878.
Van Doren, *Peacock*	Carl Van Doren. *The Life of Thomas Love Peacock.* London: J. M. Dent & Sons, 1911.
Walling, *Mary Shelley*	William A. Walling. *Mary Shelley.* New York: Twayne Publishers, 1972.
Wardle, *Hazlitt*	Ralph M. Wardle. *Hazlitt.* Lincoln: University of Nebraska Press, 1971.
Wheatley, *London*	Henry B. Wheatley. *London Past and Present: Its History, Associations, and Traditions.* 3 vols. London and New York: John Murray and Scribner & Welford, 1891.
White, *Shelley*	Newman Ivey White. *Shelley.* 2 vols. London: Secker & Warburg, 1947.
White, *Unextinguished Hearth*	Newman Ivey White. *The Unextinguished Hearth: Shelley and His Contemporary Critics.* Durham: Duke University Press, 1938.
Williams, *Journals and Letters*	*Maria Gisborne & Edward E. Williams, Shelley's Friends, Their Journals and Letters.* Edited by Frederick L. Jones. Norman: University of Oklahoma Press, 1951.

Wise, *Shelley Library*	Thomas James Wise. *A Shelley Library: A Catalogue of Printed Books, Manuscripts and Autograph Letters by Percy Bysshe Shelley, Harriet Shelley and Mary Wollstonecraft Shelley*. London: privately printed, 1924.
Wollstonecraft, *A Short Residence*	Mary Wollstonecraft. *Letters Written during a Short Residence in Sweden, Norway, and Denmark*. London: Joseph Johnson, 1796.
Wollstonecraft, *Posthumous Works*	Mary Wollstonecraft. *The Posthumous Works of the Author of a Vindication of the Rights of Woman*. Edited by William Godwin. 4 vols. London: Joseph Johnson, 1798.

List of Letters

Previously unpublished letters are marked by an asterisk.

The Letters of Mary Wollstonecraft Shelley

To Shelley[1] [5 Church Terrace, Pancras 25 October 1814][2]

For what a minute did I see you yesterday—is this the way my beloved that we are to live till the sixth[3] in the morning I look for you and when I awake I turn to look on you—dearest Shelley you are solitary and uncomfortable why cannot I be with you to cheer you and to press you to my heart oh my love you have no friends why then should you be torn from the only one who has affection for you—But I shall see you tonight and that is the hope that I shall live on through the day—be happy dear Shelley and think of me—why do I say this dearest & only one I know how tenderly you love me and how you repine at this absence from me—when shall we be free from fear of treachery?—

I send you the letter I told you of from Harriet and a letter we received yesterday from fanny[4] the history of this interview I will tell you when I come—but perhaps as it is so rainy a day Fanny will not be allowed to come at all—

My love my own one be happy—

I was so dreadfully tired yesterday that I was obliged to take a coach home forgive this extravagance but I am so very weak at present[5] & I had been so agitated through the day that I was not able to stand a morning rest however will set me quite right again and I shall be quite well when I meet you this evening—will you be at the door of the coffee house at five oclock as it is disagreeable to go into those places and I shall be there exactly at that time & we will go into St. Pauls where we can sit down

I send you Diogenes as you have no books—Hookham[6] was so ill tempered as not to send the books I asked for

PUBLISHED: Jones, #1. TEXT: MS., Bodleian Library (MS., Shelley, c. 1, ff. 129–30).

1. On 28 July 1814 William Godwin wrote in his journal, "Five in the morning," thereby noting the elopement of his daughter Mary Wollstonecraft Godwin with Percy Bysshe Shelley. Accompanied by Jane (also called Mary Jane) Clairmont (1798–1879), Mary Godwin's stepsister, the couple toured Europe for six weeks and kept an account of their travels, published as *History of a Six Week's Tour through a Part of France, Switzerland, Germany, and Holland: with Letters Descriptive of a Sail round the Lake of Geneva, and of the Glaciers of Chamouni* (London: T. Hookham, Jr., and C. and J. Ollier, 1817), hereinafter cited as *Six Weeks' Tour.* On 13 September they returned to London without funds to find that almost all of their former friends disapproved of their elopement and of Shelley's treatment of his wife, Harriet Westbrook Shelley (1795–1816), and daughter, Ianthe (1813–76). Shelley and Mary Godwin's residence in London was marked by constant financial embarrassment until May 1815 (see 26 April 1815). Shelley had to pay past debts and immediate living expenses not only for his current house-

hold, which included Jane Clairmont, but also for his wife and daughter and for Godwin, who refused to see the elopers but used go-betweens to continue to draw on Shelley's resources. Shelley and Mary Godwin often changed their lodgings while Shelley tried to negotiate for funds. From the night of 23 October until 9 November 1814, aided by his friend Thomas Love Peacock, Shelley lived apart from Mary Godwin in order to avoid arrest for debt. To elude detection by bailiffs, Shelley and Mary Godwin met daily at different hours and locations, including St. Pancras, Holborn Street, Southampton Buildings, and a number of coffeehouses. The first five letters printed here were written during this period of forced separation. In *Lodore* (1835) Mary Shelley wrote a fictionalized account of the tribulations and restorative love of these days. (The dates and details of the events reflected in these letters are found in *MWS Journal, CC Journals*, and *PBS Letters*. For an account of the six-week tour, see *SC*, III, 342–75.)

2. Date established through *MWS Journal*, 25 October 1814. Mary Godwin's letters were written from 5 Church Terrace, Pancras, the lodgings she, Shelley, and Jane Clairmont had taken on 27 September.

3. Bailiffs were not permitted to make arrests from midnight Saturday until midnight Sunday, allowing debtors to come from hiding for a twenty-four-hour period each week. If Mary Godwin had been referring to their Sunday meeting, she would have named 30 October, the first Sunday after their separation and the writing of this letter. The text suggests rather that Mary Godwin expected to be permanently reunited with Shelley on 6 November, an expectation he shared (see *PBS Letters*, #269, #270).

4. Fanny Imlay (1794–1816), Mary Godwin's half sister through Mary Wollstonecraft's liaison with Gilbert Imlay (1754–?1828). The letter was to Jane Clairmont asking her to meet Fanny the next day. Jane Clairmont complied and found that Fanny had been sent as an emissary bearing Godwin's proposal that she leave Mary Godwin and Shelley and "go into a family" (*CC Journals*, 24 October 1814; *MWS Journal*, 25 October 1814).

5. Mary Godwin was often indisposed during this period due to pregnancy.

6. Thomas Hookham, Jr. (1787–1867), publisher and friend of Shelley and Peacock. Hookham and his brother, Edward T. Hookham, were Peacock's publishers, and they introduced Shelley to Peacock (Carl Dawson, *His Fine Wit: A Study of Thomas Love Peacock* [Berkeley: University of California Press, 1970], pp. xiii, 37). Hookham and Shelley were briefly estranged because Hookham disapproved of the elopement.

TO SHELLEY [5 Church Terrace, Pancras 27 October 1814][1]

My own love

I do not know by what compulsion I am to answer you but your porter says I must so I do—

By a miracle I saved your £5[2] & I will bring it—I hope indeed; oh my loved Shelley we shall indeed be happy

I meet you at three and bring heaps of Skinner street news[3]—Heaven bless my love & take care of him

his own Mary

PUBLISHED: Jones, #2. TEXT: MS. (photcopy), Lilly Library, Indiana University.

1. Date established through *MWS Journal* and *CC Journals*, 27 October 1814.

2. Shelley had pawned his microscope at Davidson's for £5 on 24 October (*CC*

Journals). Writing to his wife of his dire financial straits, Shelley alludes to this sale of their "last valuable" and implores her to "send quick supplies" (*PBS Letters*, #269). According to *MWS Journal, CC Journals*, and Mary Godwin's Letter of [25 October 1814], Mary Godwin and Jane Clairmont had taken a coach on 24 October. Since prior to pawning the microscope they had no money, perhaps Peacock supplied them with their fare or they spent some small part of the £5.

3. Early in the day, Fanny Imlay left a letter from herself and Charles Gaulis Clairmont (1795–1850), Jane Clairmont's brother and Mary Godwin's stepbrother, which Mary Godwin carried to Shelley that afternoon (*MWS Journal; CC Journals*).

To Shelley [5 Church Terrace, Pancras 28 October 1814][1]

So this is the end of my letter—dearest love what do they mean—I detest Mrs G. [*Godwin*][2] she plagues my father out of his life & then—well no matter—why will not Godwin follow the obvious bent of his affections & be reconciled to us—no his prejudices the world & she—do you not hate her my love—all these forbid it—what am I to do trust to time of course—for what else can I do

Goodnight my love—tomorrow I will seal this blessing on your lips dear good creature press me to you and hug your own Mary to your heart perhaps she will one day have a father till then be every thing to me love—& indeed I will be a good girl and never vex you any more I will learn Greek[3] and—but when shall we meet when I may tell you all this & you will so sweetly reward me—oh we must meet soon for this is a dreary life I am weary of it—a poor widowed deserted thing no one cares for her—but—ah love is not that enough—indeed I have a very sincere affection for my own Shelley—

But Good night I am woefully tired & so sleepy—I shall dream of you ten to one when naughty one—you have quite forgotten me—

Take me—one kiss—well that is enough—tomorrow

Published: Jones, #3. Text: MS., Bodleian Library (MS., Shelley, c. 1, f. 131).

1. Date established through *MWS Journal*, 28 October 1814.

2. Very little is known about Mary Jane Vial (?Devereux) Clairmont Godwin (1768–1841) before her marriage to Godwin on 21 December 1801 in two separate ceremonies, first under the (probably assumed) name Clairmont and then under the name Vial. The paternity of her children, Charles Gaulis Clairmont and Jane Clairmont, remains obscure, although evidence suggests that both may have been illegitimate. Mrs. Godwin was credited with being an industrious woman who established and ran the M. J. Godwin Company, a publishing firm that specialized in children's books. Henry Crabb Robinson's description of her as a "meritorious wife" but of doubtful sincerity and integrity in her dealings with others seems generally accurate (Robinson, *On Books*, I, 235; *CC Journals*, pp. 13–16; White, *Shelley*, I, 667–68, 671, 673, 674, 683; Dowden, *Shelley*, II, 541–49). The relationship between Mary Godwin and her stepmother was never amicable. In this instance, Mary Godwin's ire concerned a letter she had received from Mrs. Godwin this same evening at six (*MWS Journal*).

3. Mary Godwin was a most willing and apt student to Shelley, who in turn was a most committed mentor (see the lists in *MWS Journal* indicating their combined readings).

To Shelley [5 Church Terrace, Pancras ?2 November 1814][1]

I enclose you a letter [ ][2] I would not advise you [ ] all your estate or to [ ] Post obits from too many people—Sir John Shelley[3] I think the best to treat with—Yet till you have some money from some of them do not break with any—

But you know all about this better than I do—So goodnight—may you sleep as well as though it wer[e] in my arms—but I know you wont—dearest love Goodnight

[ ] to send the enclosed [ ] scribbled it all over so [ ] as it is—but I have for [ ] a time for meeting [a]t three o'clock exactly just at Holborn bars—I know you will be punctual for you know how I dislike walking up an down in a public place

ADDRESS: Percy Bysshe Shelley Esq. PUBLISHED: Jones, #5. TEXT: MS., Bodleian Library (MS., Shelley, c. 1, f. 128).

1. From 30 October through 1 November Mary Godwin and Shelley were reunited. On 2 November she wrote to Shelley twice—a long letter in the afternoon and, at the end of the day, "a goodnight to my love" (*MWS Journal*).

2. The manuscript is badly torn.

3. Sir John Shelley (1772–1852), head of the Michelgrove Shelleys and M.P. for Lewes, was a kinsman of Shelley's (White, *Shelley*, I, 7). He refused the loan (*MWS Journal*).

To Shelley [5 Church Terrace, Pancras 3 November 1814][1]

Dearest Love—I am so out of spirits I feel so lonely but we shall meet tomorrow so I will try to be happy—Grays inn Gardens is I fear a dangerous place yet can you think of any other.

I received your letter tonight I wanted one for I had {not} received one for almost two day but do not think I mean any thing by this my love—I know you took a long long walk yesterday so you could not write but I who am at home who do not walk out I could write to you all day love—

Another circumstance has made me feel more solitary that letter I received today[2]—dear Shelley you will say I was deceived I know I am not—I know her unexampled frankness and sweetness of character but what must that character be who resists opinions preach——

Oh dear what am I writing I am indeed disappointed—I did think Isabel perfectly unprejudiced—she adores the shade of my mother—but then a married man it is impossible to knock into some peoples heads that Harriet is selfish & unfeeling and that my father might be happy if he chose—by that cant concerning <u>selling</u> <u>his</u> <u>daughter</u> I should half suspect that there has been some communication between ⟨my⟩ the Skinner St. folks and them

Higho love such is the world

How you reason & philosophize about love—do you know if I had been asked I could not have given one reason in its favour—yet I have as great an opinion as you concerning its exaltedness and love very tenderly to prove my theory—adieu for the present it has struck eight & in an hour or two I will wish you goodnight.

Well so now I am to write a goodnight with the old story of I wish I could say it to you—yes my love it has indeed become an old story but I hope the last chapter is come—I shall meet you tomorrow love & if you do but get money love which indeed you must we will defy our enemies & our friends (for aught I see they are all as bad as one another) and we will not part again—Is not that a delightful word it shall cheer my dreams

No answer from Hooper[3]—I wish he would write oh how I long {to} be at our dear home where nothing can trouble us neither friends or enemies—dont be angry at this you know my love they are all a bad set—But Nantgwilt do you not wish to be settled there at a home you know love—with your own Mary nothing to disturb you studying walking & other such like amusements—oh its much better {I} believe not to be able to see the the light of the sun for mountains than for houses

You dont say a word in your letter—you naughty love to ease one of my anxietie not a word of Lambert of Harriet of Mrs Stuart[4] of money or anythink [*anything*]—but all the reasonings you used to persuade Mr Peacock love was a good thing Now you know I did not want converting—but my love do not be displeased at my chattering in this way for you know the expectation of a letter from you when absent always makes my heart jump so do you think it says nothing when one actually arrives.

Your own Mary who loves you so tenderly

PUBLISHED: Jones, #4. TEXT: MS., Bodleian Library (MS., Shelley, c. 1, ff. 126–27).

1. Date established through *MWS Journal*, 3 November 1814.

2. From David Booth (1766–1846), lexicographer. In 1812 and 1813, for reasons of health, Mary Godwin had been sent by Godwin to live with the family of William Thomas Baxter, a manufacturer of canvas, in Dundee, Scotland. There she formed a deep friendship for Isabella Baxter, who in 1814 married Booth, widower of Isabella's sister Margaret and some twenty years her senior. According to contemporary law, it was illegal for Booth to marry his deceased wife's sister. On 4 and 23 October Mary Godwin had written to Isabella Booth (the letters are unlocated), but Booth, disapproving of the elopement and probably concerned about his own questionable matrimonial status, refused to allow the continuation of the friendship. In 1817 and 1818 attempts were made to change Booth's mind, but the friendship of Isabella Booth and Mary Shelley was not renewed until after Shelley's death (see *SC*, II, 558–59; [24 September 1817](*a*); 30 December 1817; [3 March] 1818; [5 March 1818]; 9–11 September [1823]).

3. Shelley had lived in Mr. Hooper's house at Nantgwillt, Wales, in 1812. Before or on 28 October 1814 Shelley had written to Mr. Hooper to learn whether the house was available (*PBS Letters*, #274).

4. John Lambert, Godwin's creditor, was threatening Godwin with arrest (*PBS Letters,* #277). Mrs. Stewart was one of the most pressing of Shelley's creditors (*PBS Letters,* #278).

To Thomas Jefferson Hogg[1] [2 Nelson Square, Blackfriars Road]

January 1 1815[2]

Dearest Hogg

As they have ⟨all⟩ both[3] left me and I am here all alone I have nothing better to do than take up my pen and say a few words to you—as I do not expect you this morning.

You love me you say—I wish I could return it with the passion you deserve—but you are very good to me and tell me that you are quite happy with the affection which from the bottom of my heart I feel for you—you are so generous so disinterested that no one can help loving you But you know Hogg that we have known each other for so short a time and I did not think about love—so that I think that <u>that</u> also will come in time & then we shall be happier I do think than the angels who sing for ever or even the lovers of Janes[4] world of perfection. There is a bright prospect before us my dear friend—lovely—and—which renders it certain—wholly dependant on our selves—for Shelley & myself I need promise nothing—nor to you either for I know that you are persuaded that I will use every effort to promote your happiness & such is my affection for you that it will be no hard task—

But this is prattle—I tell you what you know so well already—besides you will be here this evening—The sun shines it would be a fine day to visit the divine Theoclea[5] but I am not well enough—I was in great pain all night & this morning & am but just getting better

Affectionately yours

Mary

You need not answer this scrall

ADDRESS: Thomas Jefferson Hogg Esq. / Arundel Street / 34 Strand. POSTMARKS: (1) Two Py Post / Unpaid / West Lambth; (2) 7 o'clock / 1 Ja / 1815 NT. PUBLISHED: Scott, *New Shelley Letters*, p. 80; *SC*, III, #270. TEXT: MS., Pforzheimer Library.

1. Thomas Jefferson Hogg (1792–1862) and Shelley became close friends while at Oxford, from which both were expelled on 11 March 1811 for refusing to answer questions about Shelley's pamphlet *The Necessity of Atheism.* In October 1811 Hogg attempted to seduce Harriet Shelley, which caused a temporary rift in the friendship. Shelley's unconventional views of marriage, however, allowed him to forgive Hogg, whom Shelley held culpable mainly because he tried to force a relationship on an unwilling Harriet Shelley (White, *Shelley*, I, 170–74).

On 14 November 1814 Hogg paid his first call on the elopers. Uncertain about Hogg's ability to sympathize with his radical views, Shelley decided that a renewal of their friendship would depend on Hogg's response to Mary Godwin. Hogg, "pleased with Mary" (Shelley entry, *MWS Journal*), became a frequent caller. In the spirit of Shelley's philosophy of disinterested love and with Shelley's knowledge and encouragement, on 1 January 1815 Hogg sent Mary Godwin a gift accompanied by a declaration of love. Mary Godwin reciprocated, in this letter, indicating her willingness to "think about love" and the "bright prospect" before them. Evidently she came to enjoy Hogg's attentions. Her strongest motivation in this experimental relationship, however, seems to have been to please Shelley by embodying his doctrine of love unrestrained by social convention, and typically her expressions of affection for Hogg are overshadowed by her love for Shelley (see *SC*, III, 423–57, 461–73; and White, *Shelley*, I, 388–93, 400–402).

Some scholars have speculated that during this period Shelley and Claire Clairmont (see below, n. 4) had a love affair. Reviewing the various analyses of the Mary Godwin-Hogg and the Claire Clairmont-Shelley relationships, Kenneth N. Cameron argues that the journals and letters of 1815 offer evidence that "love affairs were planned" in accord with "Shelley's sex ethic . . . that although sensuality without love as a basis for sexual relations was abhorrent, people genuinely in love should have relations regardless of marriage ties; sexual relations must be viewed only as one segment of a complex emotional relationship." Cameron also suggests that if the affairs "materialized," they were of brief duration ("A New Shelley Legend," in *An Examination of the Shelley Legend*, ed. Newman I. White [Philadelphia: University of Pennsylvania Press, 1951], pp. 107–10). The question of a sexual relationship between Claire Clairmont and Shelley arose again in the scandal of the Neapolitan child (see 18 June 1820, n. 1).

2. Mary Godwin, Shelley, and Claire Clairmont lived at 2 Nelson Square, Blackfriars Road, from 9 November 1814 to 10 January 1815.

3. Shelley had invited Hogg to call on Mary Godwin before evening, indicating that he and Claire Clairmont would be gone for the day, since Mary Godwin wished to speak with Hogg alone (*PBS Letters*, #283).

4. In November 1814 Jane Clairmont changed her name to Clara; she later changed it to Clary, then to Clare, and finally to Claire. The elder Godwins always referred to her as Jane, but Mary Godwin and Shelley complied with her wishes, although in the transitional period, they sometimes reverted to Jane. From this point, I will refer to her as Claire Clairmont, the name by which she was generally known.

5. Apparently one of the statues John Bacon (1777–1859) exhibited at his studio/home at 17 Newman Street. Bacon, who exhibited at the Royal Academy from 1792 to 1824, was famous in his day primarily for sculpting monuments, which he produced in prolific numbers (see *The European Magazine* 67 [January–June 1815]: 3–4; and Rupert Gunnis, *Dictionary of British Sculptors, 1660–1851* [London, Abbey Library, 1968]).

To Thomas Jefferson Hogg [4] January—1815[1] Nelson Square

My dearest Hogg

I have been trifling away my time thinking it early when to my infinite astonishment I learn that it is past two—It is useless to think of going to Theoclea today—but tomorrow will do as well—

Shelley & Jane are both gone out & from the number & distance of the places that they are going to I do not expect them till very late—perhaps you can come and console a solitary lady in the mean time—but I do not wish to make you a truant so do not come against your consience.

You are so good & disinterested a creature that I love you more & more—

By the bye when Shelley is in the country we shall never be alone so perhaps this is the last opportunity for a lone time but still I do not wish to persuade you to do that which you ought not.

With one kiss Goodbye

Affectionately yours—Mary

If you cannot come now perhaps you can come earlier this evening than usual

ADDRESS: T. J. Hogg Esq. / Holroyd Esq— / Gray's Inn. PUBLISHED: Scott, *New Shelley Letters*, p. 81; *SC*, III, #271. TEXT: MS., Pforzheimer Library.

1. On 4 January Shelley and Claire Clairmont were away during the day, and Hogg visited in the evening, when plans were made for the next day. On 5 January Mary Godwin, Claire Clairmont, and Shelley went to Hogg's for breakfast, after which they all went to see the statue *Theoclea* at Newman Street (*MWS Journal*).

To Thomas Jefferson Hogg

43 Southampton Buildings
[6 January 1815][1]

Dear Alexy

Will you come with me to Theoclea—I wait here at Mrs Peacocks[2] for your answer. By an advertisement in the paper we learn that this & tomorrow are the last days[3]—will you not see that lovely creature again?

Yours very truly Mary.

I only ask you for the pleasure of your company, not because I want some-one to go with me, so you refuse if you are busy.

ADDRESS: Mr. Hogg Mr. Holroid Grays Inn. PUBLISHED: Scott, *New Shelley Letters*, pp. 81–82. TEXT: Scott, *New Shelley Letters*.

1. On 6 January *MWS Journal* records: "Walk to Mrs. Peacock's with Clara. Walk with Hogg to Theoclea."

2. Sarah Love Peacock (1754–1833), Peacock's mother.

3. "National Works in Sculpture, 17, Newman-street.—We are requested to state that Mr. Bacon will be under the necessity of finally closing his Exhibition on Saturday next, after which, as his men will be removing the several works, it will be impossible to admit visitors. He will, however, be flattered in the visits of amateurs of art during the present week—N.B. Visitors are merely required to give in their own cards" (*Morning Chronicle*, 6 January 1815).

To Thomas Jefferson Hogg

[2 Nelson Square, Blackfriars Road
7 January 1815]

Dearest Hogg

I send you what you asked me for[1]—I sincerely believe that we shall all be so happy. My affection for you a{l}though it is not now exactly as you would wish will I think dayly become more so—then what can you have to add to your happiness—I ask but for time—time which for other causes beside this—phisical causes[2]—that must be given—Shelley will be subject to these also—& this dear Hogg will give time for that love to spring up which you deserve and will one day have

All this—you know is sweet hope but we need not be prudent now—for I will try to make you happy & you say it is in my power

Most affectionately yours
Mary

ADDRESS: T. Jefferson Hogg Esq. / Arundel Street / 34 Strand. POSTMARKS: (1) Two Py Post / Unpaid / Gt [?George] St; (2) 7 [o']clock / JA. 7 / 1815 NT. PUBLISHED: Scott, *New Shelley Letters*, p. 82; *SC*, III, #272. TEXT: MS., Pforzheimer Library.

1. Mary Godwin enclosed, wrapped in two sheets of paper, a three-ringlet lock of her lovely, golden-brown hair. On the outer wrapper she wrote, "To alexy from his affectionate Mary." Alexy was a pet name for Hogg, taken from his pseudonymous novel, *Memoirs of Prince Alexy Haimatoff. Translated from the Original Latin MSS. Under the Immediate Inspection of the Prince, by John Brown, Esq.* (London: T. Hookham, Jun. and E. T. Hookham, 1813).

2. This reference to Mary Godwin's pregnancy as a reason for delaying any sexual relationship with Hogg indicates that such a relationship was at least discussed. There seems to be no evidence that a sexual consummation ever took place.

TO THOMAS JEFFERSON HOGG

[41 Hans Place][1] Monday morning
[error for Tuesday morning
24 January 1815][2]

When you return to your lodgings this evening dearest Alexy I hope it will cheer your solitude to find this letter from me that you may read & kiss before you go to sleep—.

My own Alexy I know how much & how tenderly you love me and I rejoice to think that I am capable of constituting you happiness—we look forward to joy & delight—in the summer when the trees are green when the suns { } brightly & joyfully when dearest Hogg I have my little baby with what exquisite pleasure shall we pass the time—you are to teach me Italian you know & how many books we will read together but our still greater happiness will be in Shelley—I who love him so tenderly & entirely whose life hangs on the beam of his eye and whose whole soul is entirely wrapt up in him—you who have so sincere a friendship for him to make him happy—no we need not try to do that for every thing we do will make him that without exertion but to see him so—to see his love his tenderness dear dearest Alexy these are joys that fill your heart almost to bursting & draw tears more delicious than the smiles of love from your eyes.

When I think of all that we three in ea————

Here have been called away for a couple of hours from finishing your letter so I can not finish the sentence I began or say much more—for when the course of ones feelings is interrupted they will not run rightl[y] again besides now Shelley & Clar[e] are talking beside me which is not a very good accompaniment when one is writing a letter to one, one loves

Goodnight then—Good dreams to my Alexy— Mary

ADDRESS: Thomas Jefferson Hogg Esq / 34 Arundel Street / Strand. POSTMARK: 7 o'Clock / 24. JA / 1815 NT. PUBLISHED: Scott, *New Shelley Letters*, p. 83; *SC*, III, #275. TEXT: MS., Pforzheimer Library.

1. From 10 January to 8 February Mary Godwin, Shelley, and Claire Clairmont lived at 41 Hans Place.

2. This letter is dated "Monday morning," although the postmark indicates that

it was delivered the night of 24 January, which was a Tuesday. The interruption of "a couple of hours" referred to by Mary Godwin would not have delayed the letter twenty-four hours, since the two-penny post made deliveries six times a day within London, from 8 A.M. to 7 P.M. (see *SC*, II, 923–24). It is likely that in this instance, as in many others, Mary Godwin misdated her letter.

TO THOMAS JEFFERSON HOGG [1 Hans Place 2 March 1815][1]

My own dear Hogg—you must come to us today in our new lodgeings—for it is such a fine day that we have determined {to} remove—for this is a very horrid place and we are in great danger of arriving without any money for the old woman is determined to fleece us—

What a horrid man that Peacock is talking of nothing but greek letters and type[2]—

I write in hurry for the sun is hastening away and I ought to journey by its light

We shall see you tonight and soon always—which is a very happy thing
Your most affectionately

the Maië[3]

Mal il soit qui mal il pense
bring my garters[4]

ADDRESS: T. J. Hogg Esq / Holroyd Esq / Holborn Court / 4 / Grays Inn. PUBLISHED: Scott, *New Shelley Letters*, p. 84; *SC*, III, #278. TEXT: MS., Pforzheimer Library.

1. From 8 February to 2 March, Mary Godwin, Shelley, and Claire Clairmont lived at 1 Hans Place. On 2 March they moved to 13 Arabella Road, Pimlico.

2. In her *Journal* for 1 March, Mary Godwin wrote: "In the evening Peacock comes. Talk about types, editions, and Greek letters all the evening. Hogg comes."

3. Shelley and Hogg had three pet names for Mary Godwin during this period: the Maië, Pecksie, and Dormouse.

4. A misquotation of "Honi soit qui mal y pense" ("Evil to him who evil thinks"), the motto of the Order of the Garter, founded by Edward III (1312–77) in the mid-fourteenth century. According to an unauthenticated legend, Edward III made this comment to rebuke those who laughed suggestively when he put on his leg a garter dropped by a countess who was dancing with him.

Mary Godwin's letter of 7 January made clear that no intimacy between her and Hogg might take place prior to the birth of her child. On 22 February Mary Godwin gave birth to a seven-month's girl, and from that day through 2 March she remained at home (MWS Journal). The garters were probably a purchase Hogg was to make for Mary Godwin.

TO THOMAS JEFFERSON HOGG [13 Arabella Road, Pimlico 6 March 1815]

My dearest Hogg my baby is dead[1]—will you come to me as soon as you can—I wish to see you—It was perfectly well when I went to bed—I awoke in the night to give it suck it appeared to be sleeping so quietly that

I would not awake it—it was dead then but we did not find that out till morning—from its appearance it evedently died of convulsions—

Will you come—you are so calm a creature[2] & Shelley is afraid of a fever from the milk—for I am no longer a mother now

Mary

ADDRESS: T. J. Hogg Esq. / Holroyd Esq. / Holborn Cou[r]t / 4 Grays Inn. PUBLISHED: Scott, *New Shelley Letters*, p. 84; *SC*, III, #279. TEXT: MS., Pforzheimer Library.

1. On 22 February 1815 Shelley recorded in the MWS Journal: "Maie perfectly well & at ease. The child is not quite 7 months. The child not expected to live." On 6 March Mary Godwin wrote in her Journal: "find my baby dead—Send for Hogg—talk—a miserable day—in the evening read fall of the Jesuits. H. sleeps here—" Hogg remained through the next day while Shelley and Claire Clairmont went into town, most likely to make burial arrangements. The infant's name, the cause of her death, and her burial place are unknown.

2. This quality of Hogg's made him especially welcome to the Shelley household, distressed not only by the death of the child but also by a recent medical opinion that Shelley was dying of consumption. Hogg spent his holidays, from 9 March until his return to courts on 17 April, with Mary Godwin and Shelley (White, *Shelley*, I, 393; *MWS Journal*).

To THOMAS JEFFERSON HOGG

[13 Arabella Road, Pimlico
24 April 1815]

Dear Jefferson

I am not hardhearted but Clary will explain to you how we are obliged to go away—you will perceive that it was indispensable[1]

we shall return tomorrow night or the next morning so dear Jefferson do not think very hard of the p[oor] Pecksey who would not for all the world make you uncomfortable for a moment if she could help it.—

Clary says that she will not get lodgeings so will you—but she will of course alter her mind—dear Jefferson love me all the time as I do you

affectionately yours

The Pecksey Dor to answer for

we shall be very very glad to see you tomorrow evening if you can spare time at Salt Hill[2]—

I will write however & you must go to A. Row[3] for the letter as I shall send it by coach you must not tell Clare of the invitation[4]

write directly as C. shall direct

ADDRESS: Jefferson———. PUBLISHED: Scott, *New Shelley Letters*, p. 85; *SC*, III, #286. TEXT: MS., Pforzheimer Library.

1. Their sudden flight to Salt Hill (later called Slough), about twenty-five miles west of London, was occasioned by fear that bailiffs had discovered their whereabouts.

2. The third page of Mary Godwin's letter contains an incomplete note by Shelley that reads: "My dear friend / We shall be absent from London one day & one." Mary Godwin wrote her letter around and between these lines.

3. Probably a reference to Hogg's lodgings at 34 Arundel Street (*SC*, III, 465).

4. One of the many instances throughout her life that demonstrated Mary Godwin's desire to be free of Claire Clairmont's presence, which often irritated her.

TO THOMAS JEFFERSON HOGG Windmill Inn—Salt Hill
April 25—1815[1] (*a*)

Dear Jefferson

It would have required more than mortal fortitude (and such the Pecksie does not boast of) to have resisted the sight of Green fields and yew trees & have jogged up to London again—when your letters arrived Shelley's distich was truly applicable

On her hind paws the Dormouse stood
In a wild & mingled mood
Of Maiëishness & Pecksietude

Would it be treating you ill & would it be too much expence Shelley said that it would not be too much expence I said that you would not be angry with a dormouse who had escaped from her London Cage to green fields & acorns—dear Jefferson I am sure that you are not so selfish (pardon the word) as to be <u>very</u> <u>very</u> sorry.

Well here am I sitting in a parlour of the Windmill Inn seeing the little white pales of the garden before where the yew & Cypress flourishes in great abundance after I have written to you & Clary I mean to construe some Ovid & to be very industrious.

What a shocking place London is how truly I hate it Would that I were never to enter it again—dear Jefferson do give up the Law and come down & pass your days here—ay at the Windmill Inn if you please I am sure that it's a better place than the Inns of Court.

Now nothwithstanding your ill humour which would not allow you to write to me yesterday night—I expect a very long letter tomorrow & a very kind forgiving one too or I never will speak to you again.

Well Jefferson take care of yourself and be good—the Pecksie will soon be back all the better for her Dormouseish jaunt & remember nothing take away from my Maiëishness

For Maië girls are Maië girls
Wherever they're found
In Air or in Water
or In the ground

Now think of me very kindly while I am away & receive me kindly when I come back or I will be no more

Your affectionate Dormouse———

I will write again in the evening or early tomorrow & tell you all the sights that I have seen

ADDRESS: Jefferson Hogg Esq. / 34 arrundel Street / Strand. PUBLISHED: Scott, *New Shelley Letters*, pp. 86–87; *SC*, III, #287. TEXT: MS., Pforzheimer Library.

1. Mary Godwin wrote two letters to Hogg on 25 April—one in the morning and one in the evening—which were sent to Hogg, along with a letter from Shelley, the morning of 26 April. These three letters made clear that although Mary Godwin would have been pleased if Hogg came to Salt Hill, she was unwilling to shorten her stay in the country to return to London to see him. Shelley's letter also indicates his willingness to continue to share their "common treasure" (*PBS Letters*, #287).

TO THOMAS JEFFERSON HOGG [Windmill Inn, Salt Hill 25 April 1815] (*b*)

My dear Jefferson

I am no doubt a very naughty Dormouse but indeed you must forgive me—Shelley is now returned—he went to Longdills[1]—did his business & returned he heard from Harriets attorney that she meant (if he did not make a handsome settlement on her) to prosecute him for atheism.—

How are you amusing yourself with the Pecksie away very doleful no doubt but my poor Jefferson I shall soon be up again & you may remember that even if we had staid you would not have seen much of me as you must have been with me—

Do you mean to come down to us—I suppose not Prince Prudent well as you please but remember I should be very happy to see you. If you had not been a lawyer you might have come with us—

Rain has come after a mild beautiful day but Shelley & I are going to walk as it is only showery

How delightful it is to read Poetry among green shades Tintern Abbey thrilled me with delight—

But Shelley calls me to come for
The sun it is set
And Night is coming

I will write perhaps by a night coach or at least early tomorrow—

I shall return soon & remain till then an affectionate but

Runaway Dormouse

ADDRESS: ⟨Mr⟩ Jefferson Hogg Esq / Arrundel Street / 34 / Strand. POSTMARKS: (1) COLNBROOK / Penn[y Post]; (2) B / 26 AP 26 / 1815. PUBLISHED: Scott, *New Shelley Letters*, pp. 87–88; *SC*, III, #288. TEXT: MS., Pforzheimer Library.

1. Pynson Wilmot Longdill, Shelley's solicitor, was negotiating with William Whitton, Shelley's father's solicitor, for an agreement by which Shelley would sell to Sir Timothy Shelley his reversionary interest in part of his grandfather's estate valued at £18,000 in return for an annual income of £1,000 and a lump sum of £7,400. These negotiations resulted from the death of Shelley's grandfather, Sir Bysshe Shelley (b. 1752), on 6 January 1815. Sir Bysshe left an estate of £220,000 and a will that tried to force Sir Timothy Shelley, Shelley, and their heirs to keep

the family fortune intact. Shelley, however, concerned with his present circumstances rather than with his future income, refused to comply with the terms of the will. In order to retain full control of an eventual inheritance valued at £80,000, he disclaimed his rights to that part of the estate valued at £140,000, believing, correctly, that his father, fearing that Shelley would deplete the estate through post-obit bonds, would negotiate a settlement with him (see Ingpen, *Shelley in England*, pp. 449–54, 644–45; and *SC*, IV, 605–7).

To Thomas Jefferson Hogg

Windmill Inn Salt Hill
April 26th 1815.

Dear Jefferson

You must not go to courts very early tomorrow as it is most likely we shall be with you about nine—We shall try to get a place in the mail which comes into London about seven so you must rise early to receive the Dormouse all fresh from grubbing under the oaks.

But you must know that I think it very dangerous for Shelley to remain in London—the Bailiffs know Longdill to be his attorney and of course will place spies there and indeed what part of London can he walk about free in—none I fear—Have you not thought of this & what do you think of it now—but more of this when we meet.

The Dormouse is going to take a long ramble to day among green fields & solitary lanes as happy as any little Animal could be in finding herself in her native nests again—I shudder to think of breathing the air of London again—Jefferson Jefferson it is your duty {to} not keep any creature away from its home so come—I shall expect you tonight and if you do not come I am off—not for London I promise you—

But dear Jefferson all things considered the danger of Shelley remaining in London and my hatred of it do you not think that you ought to come to Salt Hill incontinently—Remember I shall believe that your love is all a farce if you do not—so I expect you Adieu—though he is but a bad sort of a personage yet he is good enough for you A Dieu[1] therefore

Yours—as we shall see when we know how you behave

A Runaway Dormouse

you have not chosen to write to me very well I know by this what you are good for

I wish if there is time that you would send us some money as I do not think we shall have quite enough[2]

ADDRESS: Jefferson Hogg Esq. / Arrundel Street / 34 Strand. PUBLISHED: Scott, *New Shelley Letters*, pp. 88–89; *SC*, III, #290. TEXT: MS., Pforzheimer Library.

1. An irreverant pun on *A Dieu* as "a God."

2. The frank manner of this request suggests that Hogg had been called on to provide assistance before. This period of financial distress ended on 13 May, when Shelley and Sir Timothy Shelley signed an agreement that brought Shelley £4,500.5.6 in cash, payment of Shelley's debts in the amount of £2,899.14.6, and an annual income of £1,000, in quarterly payments. From his annuity, Shelley arranged for

his estranged wife to receive an annual payment of £200. Shelley received his first quarter's payment on 24 June 1815 (White, *Shelley*, I, 397–98). A year later the Court of Chancery ruled that Sir Timothy could not purchase the reversion, whereupon Shelley and Sir Timothy came to a new agreement. Shelley's allowance was to continue and, on a post-obit bond, Shelley would receive funds sufficient to cover debts incurred during the year of negotiations (White, *Shelley*, I, 429–30).

To Shelley

July 27—1815—Clifton[1]

My beloved Shelley, what I am now going to say is not a freak from a fit of low spirits—but it is what {I} earnestly entreat you to attend to and to comply with—

We ought not to be absent any longer indeed we ought not—I am not happy at it—when I retire to my room no sweet Love—after dinner no Shelley—though I have heaps of things very particular to say—in fine either you must come back, or I must come to you directly—You will say shall we neglect taking a house—a dear home?—No my love I would not for worlds give up that—but I know what seeking for a house is and trust me it is a very very long job too long for one love to undertake in the absence of the other—Dearest, I know how it will be—we shall both of us be put off day after day with the hopes of the success of the next days search for I am frightened to think how long—do you not see it in this light my own love—We have been now a long time seperated and a house is not yet in sight and if even if ⟨I⟩ you should fix on one which I do not hope for ⟨above⟩ in less than a week then the settling &c indeed, my love, I cannot bear to remain so long without ⟨me⟩ you—so if you will not give me leave —expect me without it some day—and indeed it is very likely that you may for I am quite sick of passing day after day in this hopeless way—

Pray is Clary with you?[2] for I have enquired* several times & no letters—but seriously it would not in the least surprise me if you have written to her from London & let her know that you are there without me that she should have taken some such freak—

The Dormouse has hid the broach—& pray why am I for ever & ever to be denied the sight of my case?—have you got it in your own possession? or where is it—it would give me very great pleasure if you would send it me—I hope you have not already appropriated it for if you have I shall think it un-Pecksie of you—as Maië was to give it you with her own hands on your birthday[3]—but it is of little consequence for I have no hope of seing you on that day—but I am mistaken—for I have hope & certainty for if you are not here on or before the 3rd of August I set off on the 4th in early coach so as to be with you in the evening of that dear day at least—

Tomorrow is the 28th of July[4]—dearest ought we not to have been together on that day—indeed we ought my love & I shall shed some tears to think we are not—do not be angry dear love—Your Pecksie is a good girl & is quite well now again—except a headach when she waits so a{n}xiously for her loves letters—dearest best Shelley pray come to me—pray pray do not stay away from me—this is delightful weather and you better we might have a delightful excursion to Tintern Abbey—my dear dear Love—I most earnestly & with tearful eyes beg that I may come to you if you do not like to leave the searches after a house

It is a long time to wait even for an answer—tomorrow may bring good news but I have no hope for you only set off to look after 4 in the afternoon —& what can be done at that hour of the day—You cannot . . .

* at Lynmouth

PUBLISHED: Jones, #17. TEXT: MS., Bodleian Library (MS., Shelley, c. 1, ff. 144–45).

1. After they toured the southern coast of Devonshire for part of the summer, Mary Godwin, again pregnant, remained at Clifton, a suburb just to the west of Bristol, while Shelley went to London to search for a house.

2. On 13 May—to the satisfaction of Mary Godwin—Claire Clairmont had gone to live with a Mrs. Bicknell at Lynmouth, about sixty miles northeast of Bristol (*MWS Journal*).

3. On or just before 4 August, Shelley's birthday, the couple took up residence at Bishopsgate, the eastern entrance of Windsor Park, where they remained for the next nine months (Dowden, *Shelley*, I, 525n).

4. The anniversary of their elopement.

To [?Fanny Imlay][1] Hôtel de Sécheron, Geneva. 17 May 1816[2]

We arrived at Paris on the 8th of this month, and were detained two days for the purpose of obtaining the various signatures necessary to our passports, the French government having become much more circumspect since the escape of Lavalette.[3] We had no letters of introduction, or any friend in that city, and were therefore confined to our hotel, where we were obliged to hire apartments for the week, although when we first arrived we expected to be detained one night only; for in Paris there are no houses where you can be accommodated with apartments by the day.

The manners of the French are interesting, although less attractive, at least to Englishmen, than before the last invasion of the Allies: the discontent and sullenness of their minds perpetually betrays itself. Nor is it wonderful that they should regard the subjects of a government which fills their country with hostile garrisons, and sustains a detested dynasty on the throne, with an acrimony and indignation of which that government alone is the proper object. This feeling is honourable to the French, and encouraging to all those of every nation in Europe who have a fellow feeling with the oppressed, and who cherish an unconquerable hope that the cause of liberty must at length prevail.

Our route after Paris, as far as Troyes, lay through the same uninteresting tract of country which we had traversed on foot nearly two years before, but on quitting Troyes we left the road leading to Neufchâtel, to follow that which was to conduct us to Geneva. We entered Dijon on the third evening after our departure from Paris, and passing through Dôle, arrived at Poligny. This town is built at the foot of Jura, which rises abruptly from a plain of vast extent. The rocks of the mountain overhang the houses. Some difficulty in procuring horses detained us here until the evening closed in, when we proceeded, by the light of a stormy moon, to Champagnolles, a little village situated in the depth of the mountains. The road was serpentine and exceedingly steep, and was overhung on one side by half distinguished precipices, whilst the other was a gulph, filled by the darkness of the driving clouds. The dashing of the invisible mountain streams announced to us that we had quitted the plains of France, as we slowly ascended, amidst a violent storm of wind and rain, to Champagnolles, where we arrived at twelve o'clock, the fourth night after our departure from Paris.

The next morning we proceeded, still ascending among the ravines and vallies of the mountain. The scenery perpetually grows more wonderful and sublime: pine forests of impenetrable thickness, and untrodden, nay, inaccessible expanse spread on every side. Sometimes the dark woods descending, follow the route into the vallies, the distorted trees struggling with knotted roots between the most barren clefts; sometimes the road winds high into the regions of frost, and then the forests become scattered, and the branches of the trees are loaded with snow, and half of the enormous pines themselves buried in the wavy drifts. The spring, as the inhabitants informed us, was unusually late, and indeed the cold was excessive; as we ascended the mountains, the same clouds which rained on us in the vallies poured forth large flakes of snow thick and fast. The sun occasionally shone through these showers, and illuminated the magnificent ravines of the mountains, whose gigantic pines were some laden with snow, some wreathed round by the lines of scattered and lingering vapour; others darting their dark spires into the sunny sky, brilliantly clear and azure.

As the evening advanced, and we ascended higher, the snow, which we had beheld whitening the overhanging rocks, now encroached upon our road, and it snowed fast as we entered the village of Les Rousses, where we were threatened by the apparent necessity of passing the night in a bad inn and dirty beds. For from that place there are two roads to Geneva; one by Nion, in the Swiss territory, where the mountain route is shorter, and comparatively easy at that time of the year, when the road is for several leagues covered with snow of an enormous depth; the other road lay through Gex, and was too circuitous and dangerous to be attempted at so late an hour in the day. Our passport, however, was for Gex, and we were told that we could not change its destination; but all these police laws, so severe in themselves, are to be softened by bribery, and this difficulty was at length overcome. We hired four horses, and ten men to support the carriage, and departed from Les Rousses at six in the evening, when the sun had already far descended, and the snow pelting against the windows of our carriage, assisted the coming darkness to deprive us of the view of the lake of Geneva and the far-distant Alps.

The prospect around, however, was sufficiently sublime to command our attention—never was scene more awfully desolate. The trees in these regions are incredibly large, and stand in scattered clumps over the white wilderness; the vast expanse of snow was chequered only by these gigantic pines, and the poles that marked our road: no river or rock-encircled lawn relieved the eye, by adding the picturesque to the sublime. The natural silence of that uninhabited desert contrasted strangely with the voices of the men who conducted us, who, with animated tones and gestures, called to one another in a patois composed of French and Italian, creating disturbance where, but for them, there was none.

To what a different scene are we now arrived! To the warm sunshine and to the humming of sun-loving insects. From the windows of our hotel we see the lovely lake, blue as the heavens which it reflects, and sparkling with golden beams. The opposite shore is sloping and covered with vines, which however do not so early in the season add to the beauty of the prospect. Gentlemen's seats are scattered over these banks, behind which rise the various ridges of black mountains, and towering far above, in the midst of its snowy Alps, the majestic Mont Blanc, highest and queen of all. Such is the view reflected by the lake; it is a bright summer scene without any of that sacred solitude and deep seclusion that delighted us at Lucerne.

We have not yet found out any very agreeable walks, but you know our attachment to water excursions. We have hired a boat, and every evening at about six o'clock we sail on the lake, which is delightful, whether we glide over a glassy surface or are speeded along by a strong wind. The waves of this lake never afflict me with that sickness that deprives me of all enjoyment in a sea voyage; on the contrary, the tossing of our boat raises my spirits and inspires me with unusual hilarity. Twilight here is of short duration, but we at present enjoy the benefit of an increasing moon, and seldom return until ten o'clock, when, as we approach the shore, we are saluted by the delightful scent of flowers and new mown grass, and the chirp of the grasshoppers, and the song of the evening birds.

We do not enter into society here, yet our time passes swiftly and delightfully. We read Latin and Italian during the heats of noon, and when the sun declines we walk in the garden of the hotel, looking at the rabbits, relieving fallen cockchaffers, and watching the motions of a myriad of lizards, who inhabit a southern wall of the garden. You know that we have just escaped from the gloom of winter and of London; and coming to this delightful spot during this divine weather, I feel as happy as a new-fledged bird, and hardly care what twig I fly to, so that I may try my new-found wings. A more experienced bird may be more difficult in its choice of a bower; but, in my present temper of mind, the budding flowers, the fresh grass of spring, and the happy creatures about me that live and enjoy these pleasures, are quite enough to afford me exquisite delight, even though clouds should shut out Mont Blanc from my sight. Adieu!

M.[4]

PUBLISHED: Jones, #18. TEXT: *Six Weeks' Tour*, pp. 85–97.

1. This letter, as well as that of 1 June (following) and two letters by Shelley, was published in *Six Weeks' Tour.* Shelley's letters, dated 12 July and 22 July–2 August, identify the addressee as T.P., Thomas Love Peacock. Shelley's second letter (*S&M*, I, 104–13) and the first, which will appear in *SC*, VII, both show that the contents as published in *Six Weeks' Tour* are largely those of the actual letters, but with considerable literary emendations and the omission of personal matters (finances, housing, and so on). Because Mary Godwin's letters contain no addressee, it has been assumed that hers were not actual letters but a travel narrative in the epistolary form then popular. Two letters written by Fanny Imlay to Mary Godwin strongly suggest that they are answers to Mary Godwin's letters in *Six Weeks' Tour.* On 29 May Fanny Imlay wrote: "Papa has given to me this space of paper to fill & seal. I received Mary's letter on Monday morning I can assure you, it was very precious to me—France is in so strange a state that I could not feel easy for your safety till I heard that you had actually arrived—" Mary Godwin's 17 May letter begins by announcing their arrival and giving details of France that could well mesh with Fanny Imlay's remarks about the strange state of France at that time. In closing her letter of 29 May, Fanny Imlay expressed her hope that there was a letter already en route to her in response to one she had written about a fortnight earlier (Abinger MS.; *S&M*, I, 93–94). Fanny Imlay's letter of 29 July indicates she had just received a letter from Mary Godwin describing the weather in Switzerland, a subject treated in Mary Godwin's letter of 1 June in *Six Weeks' Tour.* These letters clearly establish that a steady correspondence was carried on by the sisters, and it is quite likely that Mary Godwin's letters to Fanny Imlay formed the basis of her letters in *Six Weeks' Tour*, as Shelley's letters to Peacock were the basis of his. Mary Godwin may have omitted any identification of her correspondent because of the notoriety attached to Fanny Imlay's birth or in fear of stimulating fresh notoriety in connection with her suicide on 9 October 1816, an event Godwin wished to keep secret. In 1844 Mary Shelley again combined notes from her travels with lengthy passages from actual correspondence to publish them as *Rambles in Germany and Italy in 1840, 1842, and 1843*, 2 vols. (London: Edward Moxon, 1844).

2. On 3 May, with their son William (born 24 January 1816) and again accompanied by Claire Clairmont, Shelley and Mary Godwin sailed from Dover en route to Geneva. In the spring of 1816 Claire Clairmont had formed a secret liaison with Byron. When Byron left England for Geneva on 25 April, Claire Clairmont determined to follow him. She revealed the affair to Shelley, who for her sake and because of his own interest in meeting Byron, agreed to go to Geneva instead of Italy (*SC*, IV, 677–79, 720–21).

3. Antoine-Marie Chamans, comte de La Valette (1769–1830), French politician, held political and military posts under Napoleon. When Louis XVIII came to power, La Valette was arrested and condemned to death, but with the aid of his wife and three Englishmen (Sir Robert Wilson; Michael Bruce; and Captain John Hely-Hutchinson, afterwards third Earl of Donoughmore), he escaped from prison in December 1815 and was safely conveyed out of France.

4. In later editions of *Six Weeks' Tour* Mary Shelley altered this signature to "M.S."

To [?Fanny Imlay][1] Campagne C[hapuis], near Coligny. 1 June 1816[2]

START

You will perceive from my date that we have changed our residence since my last letter. We now inhabit a little cottage on the opposite shore of the lake, and have exchanged the view of Mont Blanc and her snowy aiguilles for the dark frowning Jura, behind whose range we every evening see the sun sink, and darkness approaches our valley from behind the Alps, which are then tinged by that glowing rose-like hue which is observed in England to attend on the clouds of an autumnal sky when day-light is almost gone. The lake is at our feet, and a little harbour contains our boat, in which we still enjoy our evening excursions on the water. Unfortunately we do not now enjoy those brilliant skies that hailed us on our first arrival to this country. An almost perpetual rain confines us principally to the house; but when the sun bursts forth it is with a splendour and heat unknown in England. The thunder storms that visit us are grander and more terrific than I have even seen before. We watch them as they approach from the opposite side of the lake, observing the lightning play among the clouds in various parts of the heavens, and dart in jagged figures upon the piny heights of Jura, dark with the shadow of the overhanging cloud, while perhaps the sun is shining cheerily upon us. One night we enjoyed a finer storm than I had ever before beheld. The lake was lit up—the pines on Jura made visible, and all the scene illuminated for an instant, when a pitchy blackness succeeded, and the thunder came in frightful bursts over our heads amid the darkness.[3]

But while I still dwell on the country around Geneva, you will expect me to say something of the town itself: there is nothing, however, in it that can repay you for the trouble of walking over its rough stones. The houses are high, the streets narrow, many of them on the ascent, and no public building of any beauty to attract your eye, or any architecture to gratify your taste. The town is surrounded by a wall, the three gates of which are shut exactly at ten o'clock, when no bribery (as in France) can open them. To the south of the town is the promenade of the Genevese, a grassy plain planted with a few trees, and called Plainpalais. Here a small obelisk is erected to the glory of Rousseau, and here (such is the mutability of human life) the magistrates, the successors of those who exiled him from his native country, were shot by the populace during that revolution, which his writings mainly contributed to mature, and which, notwithstanding the temporary bloodshed and injustice with which it was polluted, has produced enduring benefits to mankind, which all the chicanery of statesmen, nor even the great conspiracy of kings, can entirely render vain. From respect to the memory of their predecessors, none of the present magistrates ever walk in Plainpalais. Another Sunday recreation for the citizens is an excursion to the top of Mont Salêve. This hill is within a league of the town, and rises perpendicularly from the cultivated plain. It is ascended on the other side, and I should judge from its situation that your toil is rewarded by a delightful view of the course of the Rhone and Arve, and of the shores of the lake. We have not yet visited it.

There is more equality of classes here than in England. This occasions a greater freedom and refinement of manners among the lower orders than we meet with in our own country. I fancy the haughty English ladies are greatly disgusted with this consequence of republican institutions, for the Genevese servants complain very much of their scolding, an exercise of the tongue, I believe, perfectly unknown here. The peasants of Switzerland may not however emulate the vivacity and grace of the French. They are more cleanly, but they are slow and inapt. I know a girl of twenty, who although she had lived all her life among vineyards, could not inform me during what month the vintage took place, and I discovered she was utterly ignorant of the order in which the months succeed one another. She would not have been surprised if I had talked of the burning sun and delicious fruits of December, or of the frosts of July. Yet she is by no means deficient in understanding.[4]

The Genevese are also much inclined to puritanism. It is true that from habit they dance on a Sunday, but as soon as the French government was abolished in the town, the magistrates ordered the theatre to be closed, and measures were taken to pull down the building.

We have latterly enjoyed fine weather, and nothing is more pleasant than to listen to the evening song of the vine-dressers. They are all women, and most of them have harmonious although masculine voices. The theme of their ballads consists of shepherds, love, flocks, and the sons of kings who fall in love with beautiful shepherdesses. Their tunes are monotonous, but it is sweet to hear them in the stillness of evening, while we are enjoying the sight of the setting sun, either from the hill behind our house or from the lake.

Such are our pleasures here, which would be greatly increased if the season had been more favourable, for they chiefly consist in such enjoyments as sunshine and gentle breezes bestow. We have not yet made any excursion in the environs of the town, but we have planned several, when you shall again hear of us; and we will endeavour, by the magic of words, to transport the ethereal part of you to the neighbourhood of the Alps, and mountain streams, and forests, which, while they clothe the former, darken the latter with their vast shadows.—Adieu!

M.

PUBLISHED: Jones, #19. TEXT: *Six Weeks' Tour*, pp. 98–106.

1. See 17 May 1816.

2. By the end of May Shelley and his party had moved to a cottage variously called Montalègre, Maison Chapuis, or Campagne Chapuis. On 10 June Byron rented the Villa Diodati, a short walk away (H. W. Häusermann, *The Genevese Background* (London: Routledge and Kegan Paul, 1952). The two poets and their companions spent the summer in each other's company. The Shelley party remained at Lake Geneva until 29 August.

3. Byron described such a storm in *Childe Harold* 3. 92. Mary Godwin included her impressions of Alpine storms and scenery in *Frankenstein*, which she began that June in fulfillment of a pact made by herself, Claire Clairmont, Shelley, Byron, and Byron's physician, John William Polidori (1795–1821), to each write a ghost story. Only Mary Godwin and John Polidori (who incorporated Byron's idea for a ghost story into *The Vampyre: A Tale* [London, 1819]) completed the agreement. The fragment Byron wrote was published at the end of *Mazeppa, A Poem* (London: John Murray, 1819; see Marchand, *Byron*, II, 628–29, 787).

4. Perhaps Mary Godwin's first impressions of Elise (Louise) Duvillard, the Swiss servant who returned with them to England as William's nurse (see 29 May 1817, n. 9).

To Shelley[1] December 5th 1816 Bath New Bond Street[2]

Sweet Elf

I got up very late this morning so that I could not attend Mr West.[3] I dont know any more Good night.

December 5th 1816 Bath

Sweet Elf

I was awakened this morning by my pretty babe and was dressed time enough to take my lesson from Mr West and (Thank God) finished that tedious ugly picture I have been so long about—I have also finished the 4 Chap. of Frankenstein which is a very long one & I think you would like it.

And where are you? and what are you doing my blessed love; I hope and trust that for my sake you did not go outside this wretched day, while the wind howls and the clouds seem to threaten rain. And what did my love think of as he rode along—Did he think about our home, our babe and his poor Pecksie? But I am sure you did and thought of them all with joy and hope.—But in the choice of residence—dear Shelley—pray be not too quick or a⟨t⟩tatch yourself too much to one spot—Ah—were you indeed a winged Elf and could soar over mountains & seas and could pounce on the little spot—A house with a lawn a river or lake—noble trees & divine mountains that should be our little mousehole to retire to—But never mind this—give me a garden & absentia Clariæ and I will thank my love for many favours.

If you, my love, go to London you will perhaps try to procure a good Livy, for I wish very much to read it—I must be more industrious especially in learning latin which I neglected shamefully last summer at intervals, and those periods of not reading at all put me back very far.

The morning Chronicle as you will see does not make much of the riots which they say are entirely quieted and you would almost be enclined to say out of the mountain comes forth a mouse[4] although I dare say poor Mrs Platt[5] does not think so

The blue eyes of your sweet boy are staring at me while I write this he is a dear child and you love him tenderly, although I fancy your affection will encrease when he has a nursery to himself and only comes to you just dressed and in good humour—Besides when that comes to pass he will be a wise little man for he improves in mind rapidly—Tell me shall you be happy to have another little squaller? You will look grave on this, but I do not mean anything.

Leigh Hunt[6] has not written;—I would advis[e] letter addressed to him at the Examiner offic[e] if there is no answer tomorrow—he may not be at the vale of Health for it is odd that he does not acknowledge the receipt of so large a sum. There have been no letters of any kind today.

Now, my dear, when shall I see you? Do not be very long away! take care of yourself; & take a house. I have a great fear that bad weather will set in. My airy Elf, how unlucky you are! I shall write to Mrs G. [*Godwin*] but let me know what you hear from Hayward and Papa as I am greatly interrested in those affairs.[7] Adieu, sweetest, Love me tenderly and think of me with affection whenever any thing pleases you greatly

Your affectionate girl
Mary W. G.

[*P. 4, sideways*] I have not asked Clare but I dare say she would send her love although I dare say she would scold you well if you were here My compts & remembrances to Dame Peacock & son[8]—but {do} not let them see this—sweet, adieu

ADDRESS: Percy B. Shelley Esq / Great Marlow / Bucks. POSTMARK: [B]ATH / [DEC.] 5 / [18]16. PUBLISHED: Jones, #20. TEXT: MS., Bodleian Library (MS., Shelley, c. 1, ff. 146–47).

1. On their return to England on 8 September, Shelley first went to London on business and then to Marlow to find a house; Mary Godwin and Claire Clairmont went to Bath. This plan was devised to keep from the Godwins the fact that Claire Clairmont was expecting Byron's child.

2. The date of this letter appears in the manuscript prior to the second greeting, which suggests that the brief opening note was written on 4 December. However, both the MWS Journal and *PBS Letters* (#372) attest that Shelley was still at Bath on 4 December. The postmark date of 5 December confirms Mary Godwin's assigned date (thereby precluding the possibility that the letter was written on 5 and 6 December). Having found no evidence in the manuscript of the letter, the Journal, or elsewhere to substantiate any of my own speculations about the opening of this letter, I assign the authorial date to the letter and acknowledge the mystery of the first brief note.

3. Possibly John West (1772–1836), miniature painter and drawing master, who lived in Bath from at least 1795 to 1833. John West was the father of Joseph West (b. 1797). This information was kindly furnished by V. J. Kite, Area Librarian, Bath Reference Library.

4. Horace *Epistles* 3. #139.

5. The *Morning Chronicle* of 4 December reported that it was the intention of rioters, on 2 December, to collect arms, return to their meeting in Spa-field, and then proceed to Carlton House, the residence of the Prince Regent. Mr. Platt, a neighbor of Godwin's on Skinner Street, was wounded by rioters demanding firearms.

6. James Henry Leigh Hunt (1784–1859), poet, essayist, editor, and co-owner

of the *Examiner*, a weekly newspaper. Shelley admired Hunt for his liberal views and had written to him on a number of occasions, at one time offering him money (which Hunt declined) when he was jailed for libeling the Prince Regent. A deep friendship developed between the two men after Hunt's article "Young Poets" (on Keats, Shelley, and Reynolds) appeared in the *Examiner* on 1 December, the same day on which Shelley received a letter from Hunt. Mary Godwin's letter suggests that Shelley sent funds to Hunt at that time (see *PBS Letters*, #373; *SC*, V, 401–3). On 12 December Shelley visited the Hunts at their home in the Vale of Health, Hampstead.

7. Fanny Imlay, in her letter of 3 October, had reminded Mary Godwin that Shelley had promised Godwin £300 (*S&M*, I, 143–46). On 6 December Mrs. Godwin sent Mary Godwin £100. Dowden infers that Godwin negotiated on Shelley's behalf with Richard William Hayward (Godwin's, and sometimes Shelley's, solicitor) and obtained £100 more than the sum promised him, which he sent to Shelley for his own use (Dowden, *Shelley*, II, 63).

8. At Marlow, Shelley stayed with Peacock and his mother.

To Shelley[1]

Bath. Dec. 17th 1816

My beloved friend

I waited with the greatest anxiety for your letter—You are well & that assurance has restored some peace to me.

How very happy shall I be to possess those darling treasures that are yours—I do not exactly understand what Chancery has to do in this and wait with impatience for tomorrow when I shall hear whether they are with you—and then what will you do with them? My heart says bring them instantly here—but I submit to your prudence

You do not mention Godwin—When I receive your letter tomorrow I shall write to Mrs G. [*Godwin*] I hope yet I fear that he will show on this occasion some disinterrestedness—Poor dear Fanny if she had lived until this moment she would have been saved for my house would then have been a proper assylum for her[2]—Ah! my best love to you do I owe every joy every perfection that I may enjoy or boast of—Love me, sweet, for ever—But I {do} not mean———I hardly know what I I mean I am so much agitated

Clare has a very bad cough but I think she is better today Mr Cam[3] talks of bleeding if she does not recover quickly—but {she} is positively resolved not to submit to that—She sends her love

My sweet love deliver some message from me to your kind friends at Hamstead—Tell Mrs Hunt that I am extremely obliged to her for the little profile she was so kind as to send me[4] and thank Mr H. [*Hunt*] for his friendly message which I did no{ } hear

These Westbrooks—But they have nothing to do with your sweet babes they are yours and I do not see the pretence for a suit but tomorrow I shall know all

Your box arrived today I shall send soon to the upolsterer—for now I long more than ever that our house should be quickly ready for the reception of those dear children whom I love so tenderly then there will be a sweet brother and sister for my William who will lose his pre-eminence as eldest and be helped third at table—as his Aunt Clare is continually reminding him—

Come down to me sweetest as soon as you can for I long to see you and embrace—As to the event you allude {to} be governed by your friends & prudence as to when it ought to take place—but it must be in London[5]

Clare has just looked in—she begs you not to stay away long—to be more explicit in your letters and sends her love

You tell me to write a long letter and [I] would but that my ideas wander and my hand trembles come back to reassure me my Shelley & bring with you Your darling Ianthe & Charles—Thank your kind friends I long to hear about Godwin

Your Affectionate Companion
Mary—W.G.—

Have you called on Hogg I would hardly advise you—Remember me sweet in your sorrows as well as your pleasures they will I trust soften the one and heighten the other feeling Adieu

Be resolute for Desse[6] plainly wishes to procrastinate and make out a bill for his worthy ⟨children⟩ patron—How it would please me if old Westbrook were to repent in his last moments and leave all his fortune away from that miserable and odious Eliza[7]

ADDRESS: Percy Bysshe Shelley Esq / Messrs Longdill & Butterfield / 5 Gray's Inn Square / London. POSTMARKS: (1) BATH / 17 DE 17 / [1816]; (2) E / 18 DE 18 / 1816. PUBLISHED: Jones, #21. TEXT: MS., Bodleian Library (MS., Shelley, c. 1, ff. 148–49).

1. On 10 December Harriet Westbrook Shelley's body had been found in the Serpentine, Hyde Park, an apparent suicide. On 15 December a letter from Thomas Hookham, Jr., informing Shelley of her death took Shelley to London to obtain custody of his two children from this marriage, Ianthe and Charles (b. 30 November 1814). The Westbrook family refused to give the children to Shelley and took the matter to the Court of Chancery to prevent Shelley from ever having custody of his children. This letter is in response to Shelley's letter of 16 December, which describes his anguish at these events (*PBS Letters*, #374).

2. Fanny Imlay had committed suicide on 9 October 1816 at the Mackworth Arms Inn, Swansea, Wales, by taking an overdose of laudanum.

3. A surgeon who resided at 7 Alfred Street, Bath.

4. Marianne Kent Hunt (1788–1857) had married Leigh Hunt in 1809. One of her artistic hobbies was cutting profile silhouettes out of paper (see 27 November [1823]; 11 December [1823]; 9 February [1824]; 29 July [1824]; 10 October [1824]; [?14 October–November 1826]).

5. Shelley had written: "I have seen Longdill . . . I told him that I was under contract of marriage to you; & he said that in such an event all pretences to detain the children would cease" (*PBS Letters*, #374). On 30 December Mary Godwin and Shelley were married at St. Mildred's Church, London, with the Godwins as witnesses. Longdill's opinion about custody of the children, however, proved incorrect.

6. Attorney to John Westbrook, Harriet Shelley's father.

7. Shelley had grown to dislike Eliza Westbrook, Harriet Shelley's older sister,

prior to the dissolution of his relationship with his first wife. Now he wrote to Mary Godwin that "the beastly viper her sister" drove Harriet Shelley to suicide in order to be their father's sole heir, an accusation he repeated to Byron (*PBS Letters*, #374, #381). That Harriet Shelley did not share Shelley's feelings towards her sister is demonstrated by her suicide letter to Eliza Westbrook, in which she requested that Ianthe remain permanently with her "dear sister" (*PBS Letters*, #374, n. 1).

To Lord Byron   Bath—Jan. 13th 1817[1]

Dear Lord Byron

Shelley being in London upon business I take upon myself the task & pleasure of informing you that Clare was safely delivered of a little girl yesterday morning (Sunday · January 12) at four.[2] She sends her affectionate love to you and begs me to say that she is in excellent spirits and as good health as can be expected. That is to say that she has had a very favourable time and has now no other illness than the weakness incidental to her case.

A letter ought not to be sent so far with out a little more news. The people at present are very quiet waiting anxiously for the meeting of parliament—when in the Month of March, as Cobbett boldly prophesies a reform will certainly take place.

For private news if you feel interest in it, Shelley has become intimate with Leigh Hunt and his family. I have seen them & like Hunt extremely. We have also taken a house in Marlow to which we intend to remove in about two months—And where we dare hope to have the pleasure of your society on your return to England. The town of Marlow is about thirty miles from London.

My little boy is very well and is a very lively child.

It is a long time since Shelley has heard from you and I am sure nothing would give him greater pleasure than to receive news of your motions & enjoyments.

Another incident has also occurred which will surprise you, perhaps; It is a little piece of egotism in me to mention it—but it allows me to sign myself—in assuring you of my esteem & sincere friendship

Mary W. Shelley[3]

ADDRESS: To the Right Honourable / Lord Byron / M. Hentsch-Banquier / Genêve / Switzerland. POSTMARKS: (1) E / PAID / 18 JA 18 / 1817; (2) F17 / 191. PUBLISHED: Jones, #23. TEXT: MS., John Murray.

1. Because the letter is postdated 18 January and its postmark is from London rather than from Bath, it has been conjectured that it may have been forwarded in Mary Shelley's letter of 17 January to Shelley, along with her letter of 13 January to Marianne Hunt, and that Shelley, on receipt of these letters, also wrote to Byron (*PBS Letters*, #381) and sent his letter under cover of Mary Shelley's letter to Byron (*SC*, V, 83–84). While the conjecture that Shelley mailed both letters may be valid, the postal fee on Mary Shelley's letter of 17 January (9 pence, the fee of a single-sheet letter between Bath and London) establishes that her two letters of

13 January were not enclosed in her 17 January letter, but were perhaps sent under cover of another (unlocated) letter.

2. The baby was first called Alba, a name similar to Albè, Claire Clairmont and the Shelleys' nickname for Byron. At Marlow she was referred to as "Miss Auburn" (Dowden, *Shelley*, II, 124; *SC*, V, 391–92), perhaps an allusion to her hair (see *PBS Letters*, #401). Byron wanted the child to be christened Allegra, but on 9 March 1818 Claire Clairmont had her christened as Clara Allegra Byron. Donald H. Reiman suggests that this name was chosen because Allegra was not on the approved lists of saints' names with which Catholics and Anglicans of the period could be christened (*SC*, V, 365). Although this may have been the reason, it is obvious that the Christian name selected would be a reminder of the child's mother.

3. See 17 December 1816, n. 5.

To Marianne Hunt — Bath Jany 13th 1817

My dear Mrs Hunt

I am going to trouble you with a very impertinent commission—but Mr Shelley's thoughtlessness must be my excuse. Will you be so very kind as to ask him for his dirty linen and send it to the wash for him

If you trouble yourself to answer t[his] impertinent billet will you let me know how your health is and if you take the exercise that you ought. How is Mr Hunt & the dear little children? In a month or six weeks I hope to see you and soon after to be favoured with your promised visit.

Will you also tell me how Mr Shelley continues under the vexation of this hateful business.[1]

Kiss the children for me. & every kind remembrance to M^r H.

Yours very sincerely
Mary W. Shelley

ADDRESS: Mrs. Hunt. PUBLISHED: Jones, #22. TEXT: MS. (photocopy), Humanities Research Center, University of Texas at Austin.

1. The Chancery suit for custody of Shelley's children.

*To Shelley — Bath. Jan 17—1817

My sweet Love

You were born to be a don Quixote and if that celebrated personage had ever existed except in the brain of Cervantes I should certainly form a theory of transmigration to prove that you lived in Spain some hundred years before & fought with Windmills.[1] You were very good in this except in one thing—which was sitting up all night—which indeed you ought not to do especially when you are so fagged all day.

I wait for the Chancellor's decision with anxiety and yet with great hope —Take care of your own health, sweet, love & all will go well—You wish to be accurate and to give me the very words of Basil M.[2] but unfortunately that was the only part of your letter of which I did not understand a single word—part of it was covered with the seal & the rest nearly illegible

If you have not sent the nipple shield for Clare pray send it without fail by to nights mail as she is in great want of it—send also a pretty book for me. Hunt has some old romances—of King Arthur & the Seven Champions I would take great care of them if he would lend them to me—& pray ask Papa for a nice history that I can get here for I am in sad want of books to read in the sick chamber—But pray send the thing for Clare if you have not sent it already which I trust you have. The baby is well.

Blue eyes—gets dearer and sweeter every day—he jumps about like a little squirrel—and stares at the baby with his great eyes—

We have bad weather—& I am when I think at all—in wretched spirits come back with good news my best absent love & we shall be happy—Never before have you been so long away—it is very melancholy. Is Saturday the day certainly—oh that it were past and it were post time Sunday—But I am afraid you will not have time to write much that day—if so pray send a parcel by the mail sunday Enclosing news—& a lb of Green & 2 lb of black tea—for if I have to wait untill teusday I shall be quite sick with expectation

adieu best & dearest—Clare writes to day & directs to Longdills—Have you sent Mrs Hoopers[3] money pray send me word—and if you have not pray do or we shall have another very dangerous visit from Mary H.

send me news of your protegèe[4] Clare writes I entreat you most earnestly & anxiously to take care how you answer it—Be kind but make no promises & above all do not say a word that may imply any responsibility on your part for her future actions—I shall most likely not see your letter but I shall be very anxious for its [ ] contents for you are warmhearted [ ] & indeed sweetest very indiscreet—[ ] pardon this but [*p. 1, top*] pray attend to it—Have you given Mrs G. [*Godwin*] money for your night shirt do not love [*lose?*] any clothes—dearest adieu be well & happy but remember a white mouses advise—

Yours tenderly
M.W.S.

ADDRESS: P. B. Shelley Esq. / Leigh Hunt Esq. / Vale of Health—Hampstead / Near London. POSTMARKS: (1) F. / 17 JA 17 / 1817; (2) 10 oClock / JA. 17 / 1817 F. Nn. UNPUBLISHED: partially, in Smith, *A Sentimental Library*, p. 176. TEXT: MS., The Robert H. Taylor Collection, Princeton.

1. From 7 October through 7 November 1816 Shelley read *Don Quixote* aloud to Mary Godwin and Claire Clairmont (*MWS Journal*).

2. Basil Montagu (1770–1851), a prominent attorney and an old friend of Godwin's, was one of Shelley's representatives in the pending Chancery suit (*SC*, II, 563).

3. Shelley owed £30 to Mrs. Hooper, his landlady at Lynmouth in 1812 (White, *Shelley*, I, 252).

4. Perhaps a reference to Thornton Leigh Hunt (1810–73), the Hunts' precocious eldest child, who spent much time in the poet's company during this period (Dowden, *Shelley*, II, 104–5).

TO LEIGH HUNT Marlow[1]—March 2—1817

Dear Hunt

Shelley & Peacock have started a question which I do not esteem myself wise enough to decide upon—and yet as they seem determined to act on it I wish them to have the best advise. As a prelude to this you must be reminded that Hamden[2] was of Bucks and our two worthies want to be his successors for which reason they intend to refuse to pay the taxes as illegally imposed—What effect will this have & ought they to do it is the question? Pray let me know your opinion.

Our house is very political as well as poetical and I hope you will acquire a fresh spirit for both when you come here[3] You will have plenty of room to indulge your self in and a garden which will deserve your praise when you see it—flowers—trees & shady banks—ought we not to be happy and so indeed me [*we*] are in spite of the Lord Chancellor and the suspension act.[4] But I can assure you we hope for a great addition to it when you are so kind as to come to us. By the bye could you not come down with Shelley and stay only a day or two—just to view your future abode—It would give me great delight to see you—and I think the tout ensemble would give you some pleasure But for all this I know you will not come—but if one or two would—Mrs Hunt for instance would lose her headach I am quite certain in three minutes—

I have not yet seen the Examiner but when I do I shall judge if you have been disturbed since we left you—The present state of affairs[5] is sufficient to rouse any one I should suppose except (as I wish to be contemptuous) a weekly politician—This however as I have not seen your paper is rather cat's play—if you have been good it will pass off very well but if you have not I shall be very sorry but I send it depending that you have pleased yourself this week.

We will hasten every thing to have you down and you shall be indulged in sopha's hair brushes & hair brushers to you hearts content but then in return you & Mrs Hunt must leave off calling me Mrs S. for I do not half like the name[6]

Remember us all with kindness & believe me your very sincere friend

Mary W. S.

Let me know if you have been at peace since our departure—And if you all have taken advantage of these fine days to improve your health & spirits by exercise. S. has been very well. In one of the parcels will you send down the hair[7] that you have got for me—

Do you know if you could get in town a small ivory casket in which I could put those memorials—

ADDRESS: Leigh Hunt Esq / Vale of Health / Hampstead. PUBLISHED: Jones, #24. TEXT: MS., Huntington Library (HM 2734).

1. From 2 to 18 March, while arranging their new house at Marlow, the Shelleys resided with Peacock and his mother.

2. John Hampden (1594–1643) was an English Parliamentary leader famous

for his opposition to Charles I, particularly in matters of taxation. Marlow is in Buckinghamshire, the county where Hampden lived and which he represented in Parliament in the last years of his life.

3. As an economy measure, the Hunts gave up their Vale of Health home and accepted the Shelleys' invitation to stay with them at Marlow for an extended visit. They remained at Marlow from 6 April through 25 June (*MWS Journal*; *SC*, V, 227–28).

4. John Scott, Baron Eldon (1751–1838), as Lord Chancellor of England, had heard the case between Shelley and the Westbrooks for the custody of Ianthe and Charles on 24 January. Eldon's decision, handed down on 27 March, deprived Shelley of the custody of his children (Dowden, *Shelley*, II, 76–95). Shelley wrote to Mary Shelley: "The only manner in which I could get at the children in the common course of law, is by Habeas Corpus, & that supposes a delay of some weeks" (*PBS Letters*, #380). On 24 February an act to suspend habeas corpus was presented to Parliament. On 25 March the act was passed, and it was in effect until 29 January 1818.

5. The great agitation for reform in 1817 was reflected in Hunt's weekly *Examiner* and in Shelley's pamphlet *A Proposal for Putting Reform to the Vote throughout the Kingdom* (London: C. and J. Ollier, 1817).

6. Mary Shelley preferred to have less formality between herself and the Hunts. Subsequently the Hunts addressed her as Mary or by the pet name Marina.

7. Perhaps locks of hair from Leigh and Marianne Hunt, for whch Mary Shelley requests the "small ivory casket."

To Marianne Hunt

Marlow. March—2nd 1817

My dear Mrs Hunt

It is said that our days for letter writing fade as we grow older (and I, you know, am an old woman) and for some time I felt it so myself—but I know not how it is but ever since I have left you I think I could write all day long and wish to hear as often from you all—I wish at one time to describe our house to you but that is useless as you will soon see it—It is indeed a delightful place very fit for the luxurious literati who enjoy a good library—a beautiful garden and a delightful country surrounding it—

But I meant this to be a letter of business as there are two or three things that I am impertinent enough to imagine your kindness warrants my asking you to do for me.

First—If you have not sent my clothes do not wait for Shelleys departure but let me have them without delay.

Secondly—Will you take the trouble to furnish me with a little stock of haberdashery as I cannot well get it here—This includes—a quantity of White Chapel needles—balls of cotton of all sizes tapes—some black sewing silk and silk of other colours—pins—a pair of large and one of smaller sciszars and any other article of the same nature that you may deem necessary Will you also get from Clare[1] all the clothes she has got of Wills

And now tell me how your headachs are and if any thing has disturbed you since our departure—If nothing new has happened—pray remember—sufficient for the day is the evil thereof—and do not disturb yourself by prognostics—This may be a difficult but I believe it to {be} an attainable art and surely it is very desirable—Believe me, my poor Mary Anne, All your fears and sorrows shall fly when you behold the blue skies & bright sun of Marlow—and feel its gentle breezes (not winds) on your cheeks—We enjoy in this town a most delightful climate—and rivers—woods and flowering fields make no contemptible appendage to a bright sky.

How does Clare go on—is she content and happy—And is her babe thriving. My Willy is cutting some more teeth which occasions a little fretting but upon the whole he goes on very well.

Give my love to Miss K.[2] & the Children

Affectionately yours
Mary W. S.

Will you be so kind as to enclose in your next letter a paper of accounts that I gave you to take care of for me. We do not mean to take Marlow servants—Can you contrive that S. should see some while in London

ADDRESS: Mrs Hunt / Vale of Health / Hampstead. PUBLISHED: Jones, #25. TEXT: MS., Huntington Library (HM 2735).

1. Claire Clairmont arrived in London from Bath on 18 February, bringing with her William Shelley (MWS Journal). By 22 February, the MWS Journal indicates, Elise Duvillard was also in London; presumably she had brought Alba with her. Apparently Alba stayed with the Hunts while Albion House, which Shelley had leased in Marlow, was being prepared. Claire Clairmont, however, probably did not stay at the Hunts' but, according to MWS Journal, 20 and 21 February, was at quarters within walking distance. These precautions were no doubt taken to avoid any suspicion that might arise about Alba's identity. The Shelleys moved into Albion House on 18 March, Claire Clairmont arrived a few days after, and the Hunts brought Alba on 6 April (MWS Journal).

2. Elizabeth (Bessy) Kent (?1790–1861), Marianne Hunt's sister and the author of *Flora Domestica, or the Portable Flower Garden* (London, 1823); *Sylvan Sketches; or a Companion to the Park and Shrubbery: with illustrations from the works of the Poets* (London, 1825), for which Hunt supplied poetic quotations; and *New Tales for Children* (London, 1831). Bessy Kent was Hunt's particular friend and confidante. It has been speculated that she was in love with Hunt, and Thornton Hunt commented that she "might have seemed a better companion" for Hunt (Blunden, *Leigh Hunt*, pp. 39, 359). Rumors of an illicit liaison between Bessy Kent and Hunt were brought to public attention in reviews of Hunt's *Story of Rimini* in 1816 (Reiman, *The Romantics Reviewed*, Part C, I, 86–89). Richard Benjamin Haydon (1786–1846), English artist and friend of Keats, in an angry assault on Hunt's character wrote in his diary entry of 20 January 1817: "His poor wife has led the life of a slave, by his smuggering fondness for her Sister, without the resolution or the desire to go to the full extent of a manly passion, however wicked. He likes & is satisfied to corrupt the girl's mind without seducing her person . . ." (*Haydon, Diary*, I, 83; for Haydon and Shelley, see 13 May 1818). Mary Shelley's sympathetic understanding of Marianne Hunt's antagonism towards her sister (see, for example, 19–20 February [1823]) may have resulted from Mary Shelley's antipathetic feelings towards the role Claire Clairmont played in her own household.

To Leigh Hunt March 5th 1817. Marlow. 1 o'clock

My dear Hunt

Although you mistook me in thinking that I wished you to write about politics in your letters to me—as such a thought was in fact far from me; yet I cannot help mentioning your last weeks Examiner, as its boldness gave me extreme pleasure. I am very glad to find that you wrote the leading article which I had doubted as there was no significant hand.[1] But though I speak of this do not fear that you will be teazed by me on these subjects when we enjoy your company at Marlow. When there, you shall never be serious when you wish to be merry; and have as many nuts to crack as there are words in the petitions to parliament for reform. A tremendous promise.

Have you never felt in your succession of nervous feelings one single disagreable truism gain a painful possession of your mind and keep it for some months. A year ago, I remember my private hours were all made bitter by reflections on the certainty of death[2]—and now the flight of time has the same power over me. Every thing passes and one is hardly concious of enjoying the present before it becomes the past. I was reading the other day the letters of Gibbon. He entreats Lord Sheffield to come with all his family to visit him at Lausanne & dwells on the pleasure such a visit will occasion. There is a little gap in the date of his letters and then he complains that his solitude is made more irksome by their having been there and departed. So will it be with us in a few months when you will all have left Marlow. But I will not indulge this gloomy feeling. The sun shines brightly —and we shall be very happy in our garden this summer.

Do you know that I am wicked enough to wish to run away from this place and to come to Hamstead untill Saturday—as our furniture does not arrive untill then & Mrs Peacock is not so bright or agreable a companion as my poor dear Mary Anne and to tell you a little truth I do not like Peacock a millionth part so well as I do you.[3] But this freak must not extend further than my fancy—the conversations I should promise myself must dwindle into letters and the music will be disipated long before it reaches me (this being an Irishcism—)—And as it is I will put bye my writing untill I am in a merrier mood more according with yours. For I had a dream tonight of the dead being alive which has affected my spirits.[4]

8 oclock P.M.

I send this letter in a parcel to Clare containing her music—among which there are two or three songs that I should like you to learn—the Rantz des Vaches[5]—and the Macellois hymn[6] with the french words which Clare will teach you to pronou[nce] if necessary. Now do not think this im[pertinent] in me—for it is taken from your own report as I never heard you speak two words of french in my life. But when I see you for convenience sake you must either learn that or I italian that we may not always shock one another with our vernacular tongue. A thing Moliere's philosopher[7] could not endure.

I suppose you have not been to the opera—Peacock will be disappointed by the alteration this week as he wished very much to see Figaro.[8] When a child I used to like going to the play exceedingly. and more from association than any thing else I liked it afterwards: but I went seldom principally from feeling the delight I once felt wearing out—but this last winter it has been renewed—and I again look forward to going to the theatre as a great treat quite exquisite enough, as of old, to take away my appetite for dinner. A play, in fact, is nothing unless you have people you like with you, & then it is an exquisite pleasure.

Take care of yourself—Give my love to Miss K. [*Kent*] & tell her to be good & I will love her.

Adieu—Be not very angry with us for being such new friends—for I like you too well to wish you forget me—or to be other than as I am

Affectionately Yours
Marina

ADDRESS: Leigh Hunt Esq. PUBLISHED: Jones, #26. TEXT: MS., Huntington Library (HM 2737).

1. "Friends of Revolution—Taxation" appeared in the 23 February *Examiner.* The "significant hand" ☞ was used by Hunt to sign most of his contributions to the *Examiner.*

2. The year before had been the first anniversary of the death of her baby girl on 6 March 1815.

3. While in Marlow readying Albion House, the Shelleys lived with Peacock and his mother.

4. The anniversary of the death of her baby girl may have caused dreams of Harriet Shelley, since Mary Shelley had felt resentment toward Harriet Shelley when she gave birth to Charles Shelley, Shelley's legal son—the child Mary Shelley carried would be illegitimate (*MWS Journal*, 6 December 1814). The anniversary might also have provoked dreams of Fanny Imlay, who, like the baby, was an illegitimate child, or of Mary Wollstonecraft Godwin, about whose death Mary Shelley expressed feelings of responsibility (see, for example, "Mathilda by Mary Wollstonecraft Shelley," ed. Elizabeth Nitchie, in *Studies in Philology*, extra ser., 3 [October 1959]; see also [?–] 18 January 1822, n. 18. Although Nitchie spells the title of the novella *Mathilda*, Mary Shelley consistently spelled her heroine's name *Matilda*).

5. *Ranz des Vaches*, or *Kuhreigen*, the song form of the cattlebreeding populace of Switzerland. More than fifty of these songs exist, and many composers, including Rossini, in *William Tell*, have made arrangements of these songs for voice and instrument. Perhaps Mary Shelley was referring to "Appenzell" or "Gruyére," the most popular of these songs.

6. The *Marseillaise*, which Shelley had translated in 1810.

7. The "maître de philosophie" in *Le Bourgeois Gentilhomme* (1670).

8. Mozart's *Marriage of Figaro*, at the King's Theatre.

To Marianne Hunt

March 5—1817 Marlow

My dear Mrs Hunt

I have received the parcel & your very kind letter this evening—and I thank {you} for the latter a thousand times. All my clothes however—are not come; no gowns being in the parcel which I want very much. But I suppose they will come by Shelley.

A spencer that fits Mary[1] would I think just do for Will. I wish it to button behind. I would rather also that it should be crimson as that soils less than scarlett.

I have written a long letter to Hunt & as you and he are one and as my affection for you both is I believe pretty nearly equal (if you will not be jealous) perhaps you will excuse a long letter as I am rather prest for time—Not but that I have plenty to say.

But I must not forget to praise my good girl for her resolutions & exhort her to fortify them by every forcible argument I know of. And indeed to see or know of the content & pleasure Hunt feels when you & Bessy agree must be enough to make you appear so at least especially as with Hunt every symptom of generosity touches him deeply when any thing that looks (in his opinion) towards the other side of the question makes him angry—cultivate his affection & cherish & enjoy his society & I am sure my dear Mary Anne will find her prospects clear very sensibly.

Our furniture will arrive saturday morning and if Hunt will let me use a selfish argument you would be very useful to me. But upon second thoughts do not let him see this ugly sentence as your greatest use must be towards him—& besides he does not like being teazed—

William is very well—How is your little one after being weaned[2]—Give my love to all the children.

Do not fear Hunt's boldness—I do not think that that does any harm if he steers clear of societies & libels and what he says is not libelous certainly.

I am glad to hear of the health of Clare's babe—poor girl she must be lonely—

Shelley mentions M^rs^ G's [*Godwin's*] favour is she not an odious woman

I hope we shall see you very soon and this air will certainly drive away all headachs

Your affectionate friend
Mary W. ⟨G.⟩ S.

I wrote to Shelley today if he had departed before the letter arrived burn it

ADDRESS: Mrs Hunt. PUBLISHED: Jones, #27. TEXT: MS., Huntington Library (HM 2736).

1. Mary Florimel Hunt (1814–c. 1845), the Hunts' eldest daughter.
2. Swinburne Hunt (1816–27), the Hunts' fourth child.

To Leigh Hunt

Marlow. March 18—1817

My dear Friend

We have not received any letter from you but have heard from Clare that your friend, Mr Horace Smith[1] is ill I hope however than [*that*] when you receive this you will find him so far restored as to free you from anxiety. The Examiner of this week, also says a great deal for you—I am glad to see you write much and well as it shews that your mind is at peace. I am now writing in the Library of our house in which we are to sleep tonight for the first time—It is very comfortable & expectant of its promised guests —The statues are arrived[2] and every thing is getting on—Come then, dear, good creatures, and let us enjoy with you the beauty of the Marlow sun and the pleasant walks that will give you all health spirits & industry.

Hogg is at present a visitor of Peacock—I do not like him and I think he is more disagreable than ever[ ] I would not have him come every week to disturb our peace by his ill humour and noise for all the w[orld] Both of ⟨these wise ones⟩ the menagerie were very much scandalized by the praise & sonnet of Keats[3] and mean I believe to petition against the publication of any more. It was tra{n}sferred to the Chronicle—Is that an honour?

I have a word or two to say to Mrs Hunt & not having any more paper in the house to night & it being too late to get more I must with this country excuse cut short my letter to you—Write & if you wish it you shall have a long answer—

Your Affectionate Friend
Marina

It is very impertinent to give the lady the last place but I did not know how little paper I had when I began

My dear Mary anne—

My little red box is not yet arrived & I am in agony—I hope it is sent if not pray send it with the rest of the things mentioned in the list. What about a servant—If you get one let her be a good cook for I think we must have two and I can easily get a housemaid do not entirely agree with one untill you let me know.

Have you given Clare Lord B's letters yet—she mentions that you had not in a letter we had from her today they will give her so much pleasure

William is very well & can now walk alone, but I am afraid his teeth will put him back again—how is Swynburne and the rest of your babies—kiss them for me and give my love to Miss Kent.

I hope Hunt will criticise Melincourt[4] next week Have you been to see Cymbeline[5] or the opera—

Take care of yourself, my dear girl, I long to see you all down here & hope, for Hunts sake, that we shall by that time have received the long withheld hairbrush

Most Affectionately Y^s
Mary W. S.

Shelley sends his love to you all

ADDRESS: [*in Shelley's hand*] Leigh Hunt Esq / Vale of Health / Hampstead. POSTMARK: 4 o'Clock / MR. 19 / 1817 EV. PUBLISHED: Jones, #28. TEXT: MS., Huntington Library (HM 2738).

1. Horace Smith (1779–1849), stockbroker and author, became an ardent supporter of Shelley after Hunt introduced the two in late 1816 or January 1817 (*SC*, V, 404). His interest in Shelley and Mary Shelley continued after Shelley's death.

2. Shelley put full-size casts of Apollo and Venus in their study (White, *Shelley*, I, 505).

3. Keats's poem "Written on a Blank Space at the End of Chaucer's Tale of 'The Floure and the Lefe' " was printed in the *Examiner* of 16 March, preceded by Hunt's laudatory comments, and reprinted in the *Morning Chronicle* (*SC*, V, 408–9).

4. Peacock's novel, published in February or March 1817.

5. At the Theatre Royal, Covent Garden.

To Shelley Skinner St.[1] May 29th 1817

My best Love

I have not heard from you today nor indeed since you left me—nor did I write last night for in some way I entirely forgot all about writing untill it was too late.

We have bad weather now but it was fine during your voyage with south east winds; you are now arrived & I hope safe under covert with your pretty Will man whom kiss a million of times for me Saturday I shall kiss him myself.

Papa is not in very good spirits the money affairs are at a stand—I wish I could see him happy; he is full of care and I fear that there is no way to relieve this. I suppose you have nothing more of the proposal made to Longdill[2]

I have been once to the play to see Kean in Barbarossa[3] teusday night but otherwise I have been at home. Yesterday evening Papa supped with Hazlitt at Dr. Walcots[4] and I amused myself with reading the 3rd Canto of Childe Harold.[5] It made me dreadfully melancholy—The lake—the mountains and the faces associated with these scenes passed before me—Why is not life a continued moment where hours and days are not counted—but as it is a succession of events happen—the moment of enjoyment lives only in memory and when we die where are we?

Manfred[6] is advertized—I long to see it{.} if the weather is tolerable I shall call in Albermarle St. before I return and if possible see Murray and ask a question or two about our faithless Albe but do not say a word of this as I may learn nothing or worse.[7]

Of course Gifford did not allow this courtly bookseller to purchase F.[8] I have no hope on that score but then I have nothing to fear.

I am very well here but so intolerably restless that it {is} painful to sit still for five minutes—

Pray write—I hear so little from Marlow [tha]t I can hardly believe that you and Will man live there

Give my love to such of my guests as care about it—to Clare and Miss Alba Tell Elise I shall buy clothes for Aimèe[9] and that I hope she has been a good girl.

Adieu dearest—Welcome me with smiles and health

Your affectionate
Pecksie

Send Charles's[10] letter—I will not close this letter just yet that if I feel in better spirits after dinner I may say so.

Good bye pretty one—I smile now and shall again when I see you saturday

ADDRESS: Percy B Shelley Esq. / Grt Marlow / Bucks. POSTMARK: [ ] MY / 29 / 1817. PUBLISHED: Jones, #29. TEXT: MS., Bodleian Library (MS., Shelley, c. 1, ff. 215–16).

1. From 22 to 31 May, while trying to arrange for the publication of *Frankenstein*, Mary Shelley stayed with her father. (Mrs. Godwin was in France at the time [see *SC*, V, 204]). Shelley, who had come to London with her, had returned to Marlow on 26 May (*MWS Journal*).

2. Shelley first introduced himself to Godwin, whose works he greatly admired, in a letter of 3 January 1812. In his second letter he informed Godwin that he was "heir by entail to an estate of 6000£ per an" (*PBS Letters*, #157, #159). Godwin, always in debt, readily accepted the young heir's financial assistance, calling on Shelley for money even when Shelley was himself hard-pressed. In March and April 1817 Godwin again tried to secure money from Shelley (Dowden, *Shelley*, I, 395. *SC*, I, 14; IV, 600–602; V, 203–5). The proposal to Pynson Wilmot Longdill, Shelley's lawyer, to which Mary Shelley refers, is probably in connection with Godwin's latest plan for Shelley to raise money in order to aid him.

3. Mary Shelley had seen Edmund Kean (1787–1833) in *Barbarossa*, by John Brown (1715–66), at the Theatre Royal, Covent Garden, on 27 May (MWS Journal).

4. John Wolcot (1738–1819), physician and author, who since the 1780s had written poetry on the Whig side under the name Peter Pindar.

5. Shelley had brought the manuscript to John Murray, Byron's publisher, in September 1816 (*PBS Letters*, #361, #362). Byron's friend Scrope Davies was also entrusted to bring a copy to Murray (Byron, *Letters and Journals*, V, 113). The copy Davies carried was discovered in a trunk in the vaults of Barclays Bank Ltd. in December 1976 (Elma Dangerfield, "The Literary Find of the Century," *The Byron Journal*, 1977, pp. 5–9). It has been argued that Davies delivered his copy after Shelley delivered his and that John Murray returned it because Byron had given it to Davies as a gift (John Clubbe, "Scrope Davies Reconsidered," *The Byron Journal*, 1978, pp. 4–6).

6. Published by John Murray on 16 June 1817.

7. The Shelley's had had no response from Byron about the birth of Alba. Mary Shelley means that Shelley should not mention her intended inquiry about the "faithless Albe" to Claire Clairmont, who was with Shelley at Marlow.

8. William Gifford (1756–1826), author of *The Baviad* (1794) and *The Maeviad* (1795) and editor of the *Quarterly Review*, was chief literary advisor to John Murray. Mary Shelley believed that Gifford would advise John Murray against publishing *Frankenstein*. John Murray rejected it on 18 June.

9. Emily W. Sunstein, in "Louise Duvillard of Geneva, the Shelleys' Nursemaid" (to be published in the 1980 *Keats-Shelley Journal*), identifies the Shelleys' nursemaid Elise as Louise Duvillard, born 28 April 1795 at Geneva; Aimée Romieux as Elise Duvillard's half sister, born 20 January 1816; and other family members.

10. Charles Clairmont.

Mary Shelley and Shelley to Leigh and Marianne Hunt[1]

Great Marlow June 29th [error for 30 June] 1817

[*Added by Mary Shelley*] You may see by this letter that Shelley is very unwell—he always writes in this manner when ill—He was well yesterday untill the evening but today he is worse than I have known him for some time—Perhaps the decrease of heat in the weather has to do with it.

The babes are all well[2]—John has been a very good boy and Mary better within this last day or two. Swynburne is quite well

What about the Alpha Cottage[3] it is dear and I should think too far from the theatres is there no other choice.

Please Mary Anne send flannel for petticoats & flannels and a pattern of the latter—and lawn (not too expensive with a pattern shirt & cap.

The statues are not of a snowy but a milky whiteness but I think begin to l[ook] more creamy today.[4]

Miss Kent is very attentive to the children—she bids me tell you that they are well and that she does not write today—

How do you like Canova[5]—One of you write & tell us a little news of yourselves

You know the news we have had concerning the little Faithless[6]—Clare is of course unhappy and consequently cross or so—I do not wonder that she should be unhappy—I suppose he is over head & ears in love with some Venetian—

Give our love to Thornton

Adieu little babes—take care not to loose one another in the streets for fear one of you should be kidnapped but take hold of one another's hands & walk pretty

Affectionately Ys
M.W.S.

Address: Leigh Hunt Esq. / J. Hunt Esq / Maida Vale / Paddington / London. Postmarks: (1) MARLOW / 33; (2) 10 o'Clock / JY. 1 / 1817 F Nn. Published: Jones, #30; *SC*, V, #404. Text: MS., Pforzheimer Library.

1. For the part of this letter written by Shelley, see *SC*, V, #404. Shelley's portion of this letter and the postmark indicate that the Shelleys wrote it on 30 June (see *SC*, V, 225–31).

2. On 25 June the Hunts and Thornton (accompanied by Shelley) had gone to London to arrange for a new home, leaving the three younger Hunt children—John (1812–46), Mary, and Swinburne—behind in the care of Bessy Kent until 12 July.

3. A possible new home for the Hunts. They decided to move to 13 Lisson Grove.

4. Casts of Apollo and Venus that Marianne Hunt, an amateur artist, had scraped on 23 and 24 June (see 18 March 1817; *MWS Journal*). These statues were quite possibly made by Robert Shout, who, along with his father Benjamin and then his son Charles, from 1778 to 1823 was a well-known maker of plaster copies of great statues such as the *Venus* and the *Apollo* (Gunnis, *Dictionary of British Sculptors*).

5. Antonio Canova (1757–1822), one of the most celebrated sculptors of the period, exhibited at the Royal Academy from 1817 to 1823. Mary Shelley had seen Canova's sculptures while she was in London (MWS Journal, 24 May 1817).

6. Byron had not responded to the Shelleys' three previous letters when Shelley heard news of him and wrote again on 9 July. Byron's silence is explained by the fact that he did not receive his first information of Alba's birth until May (*SC*, V, 243–44).

SHELLEY TO LORD BYRON Marlow, July 9. 1817.

[*Postscript by Mary Shelley*][1] Alba has blue eyes and had dark hair which has fallen off and there is now a dispute about the colour Clare says that it is auburn.—

William and she are very good friends

ADDRESS: To the Right Hon. / Lord Byron / to the care of / Messieurs Siri and Wilhelin / Venice. POSTMARKS: (1) F 17 / 92; (2) VENEZIA / [ ]. PUBLISHED: *PBS Letters*, #401; *SC*, V, #408. TEXT: MS., Pforzheimer Library.

1. Mary Shelley's postscript was added to Shelley's letter to Byron proposing various plans for the care of Alba. Shelley wrote: "She continues to reside with us under a feigned name. But we are somewhat embarrassed about her. We are exposed to what remarks her existence is calculated to excite" (*SC*, V, 241). David Booth, among others, thought Alba was Claire Clairmont's daughter by Shelley (*SC*, V, 391–92).

TO MARIANNE HUNT Marlow August 6—1817

My dear Marianne

In writing your congratulations to Shelley on his birthday did not your naughty heart smite you with remorse—did you not promise to look at some broaches and send me the descriptions and prices—but the 4th of August arrived and I had no present—

I am exceedingly obliged to you for the loan of the caps—but a nurse—I have a great aversion to the having a Marlow woman—but I must be provided by the 20th What am I to do—I dare say Mrs Lucas is out at present but she may be disengaged by that time.[1]

I am sorry to observe by your letter that you are in low spirits—cheer up my dear little girl—and resolve to be happy—let me know how it is with you and how your health is as your time advances[2]—If it were of any use I would say a word or two against your continueing to wear stays—such confinement cannot be either good for you or the child—and as to shape I am sure they are very far from becoming

We are all well here—our dog who is a malicious beast whom we intend to send away has again bitten poor little Will-man without any provocation for I was with him and he went up to him to stroke his face when the dog snapped at his fingers. Miss Alba is perfectly well & thriving—she crows like a little cock although (as Shelley bids me say—) she is a hen—

Our sensations of indignation have been a little excited this morning by the descicion of the Master of Chancery—He says the children are to go to this old clergyman in Warwickshire who is to stand instead of a parent—and [*an*] old fellow who no one knows and never saw the children this is somewhat beyond credibilty did we not see it in black & white—Longdill is very angry that his proposition is rejected and means to appeal from the master to the Lord Chancellor[3]

I cannot find the sheet of M[rs] J.H.[4] I send you two or three things of yours—the stone crop and the soap dish must wait untill some one goes up to town

I am afraid Hunt takes no exercise or he would not be so ill—I see however that you go to the play tolerably often—How are you amused—

The gown must not be dear—but you are as good a judge as I of what to give Milly[5] as a kind of payment from Miss Clifford's Mamma for the trouble she has had—

Longdill thought £100 per ann. sufficient for both Shelleys' children to provide them with clothes and every thing—Why then should we pay £70 for A.[6]

The country is very pleasant just now—but I see nothing of it beyond the garden—I am ennuied as you may easily imagine from want of Exercise which I cannot take—The cold bath is of great benefit to me—By the bye what are we to do with it—have you a place for its reception—It is of such use for H's health that you ought not to be without it—We can easily get another—If you should chance to hear of any very amusing book send it in the parcel if you can borrow it from Ollier[7]

Adieu—take care of yourself and do not be dispirited—All will be well one day I do not doubt—

I send you £3—

Shelley sends his love to you all and thanks for your [g]ood wishes and promised present—pray when is this [in]tended parcel to come—Affectionately Y[s]

MW.S.

[*Postscript by Shelley*] I will write to Hunt tomorrow or the day after—meanwhile kindest remembrances to all, & thanks for your dreams in my favour.—Your incantations have not been <u>quite</u> powerful enough to expel evil from all revolutions of time. Poor Mary's book came back with a refusal, which has put me rather in ill spirits.[8] Does any kind friend of yours Marianne know any bookseller or has any influence with one? Any of those good tempered Robinsons? All these things are affairs of interest & preconception.—

You have seen Clarke[9] about this loan. Well, is there any proposal, anything in bodily shape? My signature makes any security in fact infallible tho not in law.—even if they would not take Hunts.—I shall have more to say on this—the while—Your faithful friend

PBS.

ADDRESS: Mrs. Hunt. PUBLISHED: Jones, #31. TEXT: MS., Luther A. Brewer Collection, University of Iowa.

1. The caps and nurse were in preparation for the birth of Clara Everina Shelley, born 2 September 1817.

2. Marianne Hunt was expecting her fifth child, born 4 December and named Percy Bysshe Shelley Leigh Hunt.

3. On 1 August the court had decided that Shelley's children should be placed with the Reverend John Kendall and his wife, the Westbrooks' nominees, rather than with Longdill, Shelley's nominee. Shelley appealed the decision, and his second choices, Dr. and Mrs. Thomas Hume, were appointed on 28 April 1818 (*SC*, VI, 649–52).

4. Mrs. John Hunt, wife of Leigh Hunt's brother.

5. Amelia "Milly" Shields, who lived near Marlow and served the Shelleys until December 1819 (see 28 December 1819).

6. Because of the increasing awkwardness involved in hiding Alba's identity, the Shelleys contemplated placing Alba in the care of "two very respectable young ladies in this town" if Byron consented (*PBS Letters*, #401).

7. Charles Ollier (1788–1859), author and editor, and his brother James conducted a publishing and bookselling company from 1817 to 1823. During this period they published all but one of Shelley's individually issued works. Later, as literary advisor to Henry Colburn and Richard Bentley, Ollier was instrumental in the publication of Mary Shelley's novels, including *The Last Man* (Colburn, 1826); *The Fortunes of Perkin Warbeck, A Romance* (Colburn and Bentley, 1830); *Lodore* (Bentley, 1835); and the 1831 reprint of *Frankenstein* in Colburn and Bentley's Standard Novels series. He was also associated with the publication of works by Keats, Hunt, Hazlitt, Peacock, Godwin, Trelawny, and Medwin (*SC*, V, 124–29).

8. *Frankenstein* was turned down by Ollier (*PBS Letters*, #404).

9. Possibly Charles Cowden Clarke (see 9–11 September [1823], n. 13.)

To Shelley [Marlow 24 September 1817] (*a*)[1]

You told me, dearest, to write you long letters but I do not know whether I can today as I am rather tired—my spirits however are much better than they were—and perhaps your absence is the cause—ah! my love you cannot guess how wretched it was to see your languour and encreasing illness. I now say to myself perhaps he is better—but then I watched you every moment & every moment was full of pain both to you and to me—write my love, a long account of what Lawrence says[2]—I shall be very anxious untill I hear

I do not see a great deal of our guests—they rise late and walk all the morning—This is something like a contrary fit of Hunt's, for I meant to walk today & said so but they left me and I hardly wish to take my first walk by myself[3]—however I must tomorrow if he shews the same want of tact. Peacock dines here every day uninvited to drink his bottle I have not seen him—he morally disgusts m[e] and Marianne says that he is very ill tempered

I was much pained last night to hear from Mr B. [*Baxter*] that Mr Booth is illtempered and jealous towards Isabell—& Mr B. thinks that she half repents her marriage—so she is to {be} another victim of that ceremony—Mr B is not at all pleased with his son in law but we can talk of that when we meet[4]—

Pray, dearest, come back in better health looking cheerful & pleased with me & your two pretty babes—Alba—is quite well

Did you take the Examiner away with you—if you did send it back—tell me also what money you took and if you took £1 from my table—

A letter came from Godwin today—very short—You will see him tell me how he is—You are loaded with business—the event of most of which I am very anxious to learn and none so much as whether you can do any thing for my father—

If you have not time—or what I fear are too languid to write let Clare[5] & tell her what news you have—I sent a parcel yesterday—if you have not received it you had better send to the White H. Cel. for it.[6]

I will write before dinner tomorrow and a longer letter

Adieu my own one—come back as quickly as you may—with bright eyes and stout limbs

Had I not better in future direct my letters to Longdills of [*or*] Skinner St. as they arrive so late at Paddington.

Your own P[?] M

ADDRESS: P. B. Shelley Esq / L. Hunt Esq / 13 Lisson Grove North / Paddington—London. POSTMARKS: (1) MARLO[W]; (2) 10 o'Clock / SP. 25 / 1817 F N[n]; (3) C / 25 SE 25 / 1817. PUBLISHED: Jones, #32. TEXT: MS., Bodleian Library (MS., Shelley, c. 1, f. 214).

1. The postmarks indicate that this letter was mailed in Marlow on 24 September and received in London on the twenty-fifth. Shelley had gone to London on 23 September, immediately upon completing *Laon and Cythna,* to arrange for its publication.

2. Shelley was to consult Dr. William Lawrence (1783–1867) about his extremely deteriorated health (*PBS Letters,* #411; for an account of Lawrence and the Shelleys, see Hugh L. Luke, Jr., "Sir William Lawrence: Physician to Shelley and Mary," *Papers on English Language and Literature* 1 [Spring 1965]: 141–52, and corrections in *SC,* V, 144).

3. Her first walk after the birth of Clara Everina on 2 September.

4. William Baxter, Isabella Booth's father, was a guest of the Shelleys from 25 to 29 September. Favorably impressed with Shelley, Baxter encouraged his daughter to reestablish her friendship with Mary Shelley (see 26 September 1817), but Isabella Booth's husband strongly objected to Shelley and refused to permit the friendship (for a full account of the Baxter-Booth-Shelley relationship in the fall of 1817, see *SC,* V, 371–92).

5. Claire Clairmont had accompanied Shelley to London.

6. White Horse Cellar, Piccadilly, starting place of mail coaches and stages to Oxford, Bristol, and western towns generally.

To Shelley [Marlow 24 September 1817] (*b*)

Dont let Clare come down on my account as Mr B. [*Baxter*] is here

I send you my dearest another proof[1]—which arrived tonight in looking it over there appeared to me some abruptnesses which I have endeavoured to supply—but I am tired and not very clear headed so I give you carte blanche to make what alterations you please

I wrote today by the post—my love to Clare the babes are all very well
The Hunts go up tomorrow[2] they say—Will C [*Clare*] come down or not
Goodnight dearest & best—be well & I am happy

PUBLISHED: Jones, #33. TEXT: MS., Bodleian Library (MS., Shelley, c. 1, ff. 217–18).

1. *Frankenstein* was accepted for publication by Lackington, Allen & Co. before 22 August 1817. Its author's identity was kept secret, and Shelley handled all the negotiations with the publisher and made stylistic revisions in the proofs (*PBS Letters,* #408, #410, #412, #418, #419, #438, #444).

2. The Hunts left Marlow the next day, as expected (*MWS Journal*).

TO SHELLEY Marlow. Sept. 26. 1817

You tell me to decide between Italy and the sea[1]—I think—dearest—if, what you do not seem to doubt but which I do a little, our finances are in sufficiently good a state to bear the expence of the journey—our inclination ought to decide—I feel some reluctance at quitting our present settled state but as we <u>must</u> leave Marlow I do not know that stopping short on this side {of} the channel would be pleasanter to me than crossing it. At any rate, my love, do not let us encumber ourselves with a lease again. However consult in your own mind and say frankly in your next, if your feelings are decided enough on the subject—if Italy would not give you far more pleasure than a settlement on the coast of Kent—If it would say so & so be it—Perhaps A. [*Alba*] renders the thought of expence pretty nearly equal whichever way you decide.[2] Do you glow with the thoughts of a clear sky—pure air & burning sun—You would then enjoy life. For my own part I shall have tolerable health anywhere and for pleasure Italy certainly holds forth a charming prospect—But are we rich enough to enjoy ourselves when there.

I do not get strength so quickly as I could wish. I have finished the bottle of aperient medecine[3] and as I cannot get on at all without it I wish you would write to Furnival for more—I have not been out yet this day was too windy & rainy and indeed the season advances very fast which renders A.'s affairs pressing we must decide to go ourselves or send her within a month.

It is well that your poem was finished before this edict was issued against the imagination but my pretty eclogue will suffer from it[4]—By the bye talking of authorship do get a sketch of Godwin's plan from him—I do not think that I ought to get out of the habit of writing and I think that the thing he talked of would just suit me. I am glad to hear that G. [*Godwin*] is well I told you that after what had passed he would be particularly gracious. As to Mrs G. [*Godwin*] somthing very analogous to disgust arises whenever I mention her that last accusation of Godwins adds bitterness to every feeling I ever felt against her.

Send William[5] a present of fruit and a little money.—Pray also dearest do get the state of you accounts from your banker—and also (for I might as well pack all my commissions into one paragraph send my broach down as soon as you can and as your hair is to be in it have a lock ready cut when you go to the jewellers—Get your hair cut in London—For any other commission be sure to consult your tablets.

You{r} babes are quite well but I have had some pain in perceiving or imagining that Willy has almost forgotten me—and seems to like Elise better—but this may be fancy & will certainly disappear when I can get out and aboutt again—Clara is well and gets very pretty. How happy I shall be when my own dear love comes again to kiss me and my babes—As it seems that your health principally depends upon care pray dearest take every possible precaution—I have often observed that rain has a very bad effect upon {you}—if therefore you have rain in London do not go out in it.

Clare told me to send Harry[6] today to Maidenhead to wait for her which I did but she has not come but I suppose I shall receive an explanation by tomorrow's post

Adieu—dearest—Come back as soon as you may and in the mean time write me long long letters—

Your own Mary

Mr B. [*Baxter*] thinks that Mr Booth keeps Isabel from writing to me he has written to her today warmly in praise of us both and telling her by all means not to let the acquaintance cool & that in such a case her loss would be much greater than mine. He has taken a prodigious fancy to us and is continually talking of & praising Queen Mab which he vows is the best poem of modern days.[7]

ADDRESS: P. B. Shelley Esq. PUBLISHED: Jones, #34. TEXT: MS., Bodleian Library (MS., Shelley, c. 1, ff. 212–13).

1. Dr. Lawrence had told Shelley that his best hope for recovery from his pulmonary illness was to cease writing and remove to a warmer climate (White, *Shelley*, I, 538).

2. If they decided on Italy, the Shelleys could take Alba to Byron themselves (*PBS Letters*, #411).

3. A laxative, which she requests Shelley to get from Dr. Furnivall, a surgeon of Egham who attended her at the birth of Clara. (Dr. Furnivall was the father of Frederick J. Furnivall, the Victorian literary scholar who founded the first Shelley Society.)

4. *Laon and Cythna* was complete, but *Rosalind and Helen*, an eclogue suggested to Shelley by Mary Shelley's friendship with Isabella Booth, remained unfinished when Dr. Lawrence ordered Shelley to discontinue writing. Shelley completed *Rosalind and Helen* at the Bagni di Lucca (Baths of Lucca) during August 1818 (*PBS Letters*, #475).

5. William Godwin, Jr. (1803–32), the son of William Godwin and Mary Jane Clairmont Godwin and half brother to Mary Shelley.

6. The Shelleys' manservant at Marlow. He had a variety of household duties, including the care of the garden (Dowden, *Shelley*, II, 111, 123).

7. Shelley's *Queen Mab; A Philosophical Poem: with Notes* (London, 1813).

To Shelley Marlow—Sept—28th 1817

Dearest Love

Clare arrived yesterday night and whether it might be that she was in a croaking humour (in ill spirits she certainly was) or whether she represented things as they really were I know not but certainly affairs did not seem to wear a very good face—She talks of Harriet's debts to a large amount & something about Longdills having undertaken for them so that they must be paid—She mentioned also that you were entering into a post-obit transaction—Now this requires our serious consideration—on one account. These things (post-obits) as you well know, are affairs of wonderful length—and if you must complete one before you settle on going to Italy Alba's departure ought certainly not to {be} delayed. You do not seem enough to feel the absolute necessity there is that she should join her father with every possible speed. Write me a long letter concerning all these things and put the letter into the post yourself—be particular in this for Hunt's servant is so neglectful that I did not receive your last letter untill today consequently no one went to Maidenhead to meet Clare and she waited some hours uncomfortably at the Inn by herself untill the Marlow coach came.—

You are teazed to death by all kinds of annoying affairs—dearest—how much do I wish that I were with you but that is impossible—but pray in your letters do be explicit and tell me all your plans. You have advertized the house but have you given Maddocks[1] any orders about how to answer the applicants. And have you yet settled for Italy or the Sea—and do you know how to get money to convey us there and to buy the things that will be absolutely necessary before our departure? And can you do any thing for my father before we go? Or after all would it not be as well to inhabit a small house by the sea shore where our expences would be much less than they are at present—You have not mentioned yet to G. [*Godwin*] your thoughts of Italy but if you determine soon I would have you do it as those things are always better to be talked of some days before they take place.

I took my first walk today. What a dreadfully cold place this house is—I was shivering over a fire and the garden looked cold and dismal but as soon as I got into the road I found to my infinite surprise that the sun was shining and the air warm and delightful—I wish Willy to be my companion in my future walks—to further which plan will you send down if possible by Mondays coach (and if you go to Longdills it will be very possible—for you can buy it at the corner of Southampton buildings and send it to the coach at the old Bailey) a seal skin fur hat for him it must be a fashionable round shape for a boy mention particularly and have a narrow gold riband round it—that it may be taken in if too large—it must measure round & let it be rather too large than too small—but exactly the thing would be best—He cannot walk with me untill it comes which makes me in a greater hurry for it—besides if you send it Monday you can enclose a word of news and as there is no post on that day it would be a great comfort to me—Do you call on Longdills every day—if you do had I not better direct my letters there

Tell Marianne to be so kind as to lose no time about my pelisse as I shall want it soon—She had better send it to Thompson's in the Strand[2] where Clare has sent the other. Give my love to these good folks I hope Marianne has now recovered from her imprudent walk of so many hours—for with her hours are of more consequence than miles in her walks.

William is peevish in the house—but happy in the air he is just cutting a double tooth. Clara is very well—but my milk will not come in any quantity to satisfy her—We have sent the ass away for she was far gone with foal and would not give any milk—the little lady takes cows milk—

I will now tell you something that will make you laugh if you are not too teazed and ill to laugh at any thing—Ah! dearest—is it so?—You know not how melancholy it makes me sometimes to think how ill & comfortless you may be and I so far away from you—But to my story—In Elise's last letter to her chere amie Clare put in that Mad^me^ Clairmont was very ill so that her life was in danger and added in Elise's person that she (Elise) was somewhat shocked to pe{r}ceive that Mademoiselle Clairmont's gaiety was not abated by the douloureuse situation of her amiable sister—Jenny replies—"Mon amie, avec quel chagrin j'apprends la maladie de cette jolie et amiable Mad^me^ Clairmont; pauvre, chere dame comme je la plains—Sans doute elle aime tendrement son mari et en etre separèe pour toujours—en avoir la certitude et le sentir—quelle cruelle chose—qu'il doit entre un mechant homme pour quitter sa femme je ne sais ce qu'il y-a mais cette jolie et jeune femme me tient singulierment au cœur; je l'avoue que je n'aime point Mam^lle^ sa sœur—Comment!! avoir a craindre pour les jours d'une si charmante sœur et n'en pas perdre un grain de gaite—elle me met in colere.[3]

Here is noble resentment thrown away—really I think this mystification of Clare's a little wicked although laughable.

I am just now surrounded by babes Alba is scratching and crowing—William amusing himself with wrapping a shawl round him and Miss Clara staring at the fire. It is now only four o'clock so I shall put bye my letter for the present to finish it after dinner—Adieu—dear love—I cannot express to you how anxious I am to hear from {you}—your health—affairs & plans.
½ past Seven.

I have waited untill the last minute that I might learn from Maddocks some news of the next house but he is out and I cannot—However I will tomorrow.

I do not think that the cows milk agrees well with Clara as she has been disordered ever since she took it—Furnival mentioned that he could get an ass think about this & write about it to him if you think it right—

Clare wants her box sent down by the first conveyance. She sends her love to you and in proper gradations to the rest of the folks at 13 Lisson Grove Has virtue deserted them?

Perhaps you had better not get William's hat as it may not fit him or please me

Now pray, dearest—dearest love write me a long letter tell me that this absence does not make you wretched but that you keep up your spirits—tell me what you have decided on and what your difficulties are

I think you took up my journal of our first travels with you if you did tell me if you have done any thing with it or if you have any prospect—if you have I will go on instantly with the letters[4]

Adieu dearest love I want to say again that you may fully answer me how very <u>very</u> anxious I am to know the whole extent of your present difficulties & pursuits and remember also that if the this post-obit is to be a long business Alba must go before it is finished

Willy is just going to bed—When I ask him where you are he makes me a long speech that I do not understand—but I know my own one that you are away and I wish that you were with me—come soon my own—only love

Your affectionate girl,
MW.S.

What of Frankenstein? and your own poem have you fixed on a name[5]

Give my love to Godwin—when M^rs^ G [*Godwin*] is not by or you must give it to her too and I do not <u>love</u> her. Did Marianne get a parcel sent Saturday to Maiden Lane

ADDRESS: Percy B. Shelley Esq / Leigh Hunt Esq / 13 Lisson Grove North / Paddington / London. POSTMARKS: (1) MARLOW; (2) [   ] Clock / SP. 29 / 1817 Nn; (3) C / 29 SE 29 / 1817. PUBLISHED: Jones, #35. TEXT: MS., Bodleian Library (MS., Shelley, c. 1, ff. 206–7, 210–11).

1. Robert Madocks, a Marlow cabinetmaker, was probably the local agent for Mr. Tylecote, the owner of Albion House (*SC*, V, 516 n. 6) and Shelley's "petty banker" at Marlow (White, *Shelley*, I, 517–18). Shelley gave him the responsibilities of selling the Shelleys' twenty-two-year lease on Albion House, of looking after property at Marlow when the Shelleys went to Italy, and of discharging some of Shelley's debts (*PBS Letters*, #415, #457). Shelley remained in debt to Madocks as late as July 1821 (White, *Shelley*, II, 299), and years later Madocks sold to C. S. Middleton, a biographer of Shelley's, fragments of manuscripts Shelley left at Marlow (Dowden, *Shelley*, II, 137).

2. John Thompson, 425 Strand, linen draper (*Johnstone's Guide*, August 1817).

3. "My friend, with what sadness I learn of the sickness of this pretty and amiable Mad^me^ Clairmont; poor, dear lady how I pity her—Without doubt she loves her husband tenderly and to be separated forever from him—to be certain of it and to feel it—how cruel—how mean a man he must be for leaving his wife—I don't know what it is but this pretty, young woman is singularly dear to my heart. I admit I don't like Mademoiselle her sister—Really!! to have to fear for the life of such a charming sister and not to lose a grain of gaiety over it—she makes me angry."

The joke is based on Claire Clairmont's two identities: At Geneva she was "Madame" (George Paston and Peter Quennell, *To Lord Byron* [London: John Murray, 1939], pp. 211–12), as she was at Bath. This suggests that Claire Clairmont was expecting to drop her pose if Alba were placed in someone else's care.

4. "Letters from Geneva," of 1816, appended to *Six Weeks' Tour*, published in

December 1817. From 9 August through 10 October Mary Shelley was preparing *Six Weeks' Tour* (*MWS Journal*).

5. *Laon and Cythna* was first printed in November 1817. Fearing prosecution because of the antireligious sentiments in the poem and the incestuous relationship between the title characters, Shelley's printer, Buchanan McMillan, and publisher, Ollier, insisted that the poem be altered. Shelley changed the language of a few religious passages and changed the lovers from siblings, and Ollier republished it as *The Revolt of Islam* in January 1818 (*MWS Journal*, 14–16 December 1817; *SC*, V, 141–67, 350–53).

TO SHELLEY Marlow Sept 30th 1817

You will have received, my dearest—an answer to most of your questions in the two letters you have seen of mine since the one that has arrived today from you. We must make our decision instantly. Let us, past all doubt quit this house You have no conception of how cold it is—As the winter advances none of the back rooms receive any sun at any time—The garden looks bleak shaded as it is by the house now that the sun does not rise high in the horizon while the road in front is warm and cheerful—let us flit therefore (as the Scotch people call it) as soon as possible—I hope by tomorrows post Maddocks will receive directions from you how to answer the people that apply.

But Italy or the Sea. Clare has hinted post-obits[1] &c to me which makes it appear doubtful to me whether we can go this winter—Perhaps I incline to a quiet home on the Kent coast—there it must be for warmth—but all must be decided by your own feelings concerning your health—Make your determination and I will abide by it—but Alba—indeed my love her departure must not be delayed—I have given my opinion concerning that in my former letters.

After all—dear Shelley—indicision will be our bane talk with Godwin and Hunt or if you will consult only with your own mind—but determine in one way instantly or I foresee that we shall get into a scrape—You must see plainly that we cannot wait thus undecided long—so make the effort and resolve

Tell Hunt I like everything in his political article of this week except the title.[2] How are they all—and the piping fawns & the piping babes with fa praparar

Alba makes me hestitate chiefly about going abroad—I do not well see how she is to get there unless we take her. Clare talks of the imprudence of sending her through the means of the Hunts—and then you know she has talked to you about promises of writing and sending accounts[3]—now this is all very well if there were any practicability in the thing—but promises with Albe! the first object that engaged his attention would put them all out of his head—and negotiated by letter also—why it is the labour of several months to get any kind of answer from him and then if he makes objections and you have to answer the child can never depart—in fact Clare although she in a blind kind of manner sees the necessity of it, does not wish her to go and will instinctively place all kind of difficulties in the way of our as it is very difficult task—Our going would obviate all this and the actual expence of the journey would not be greater. Let these weigh with you in a ponderous weight for if by imprudent delay we find (which is indeed far from being improbable) that the fair prospect of Alba's being brought up by her father is taken away how shall we reproach ourselves—Clare also will then see the extreme evil & distress of her situation & not easily forgive us for having destroyed her childs fortune by want of firmness —I almost dread the answer you may receive from the capricious Albe to your capitulations[4]

Have you seen Cobbett's 23 No. to the Borough mongers—Why he appears to be making out a list for a proscription—I actually shudd[er] to read it—a revolution in this country would [not?] be bloodless if that man has any power in it He is I fear somewhat of a Marius perhaps of a Marat[5]—I like him not—I fear he is a bad man—He encourages in the multitude the worst possible human passion revenge or as he would probably give it that abominable Christian name retribution.[6]

Now dearest I believe I have said all I can say on the subject—humbly offering my reasons and leaving it to you as the manly part to decide

I am pretty well—and my milk comes in greater quantities Clara and William are well

Affectionately Yours
Mary

[*P. 4, with address*] I sent to Hookhams for some books a day or two ago and they have not come.

ADDRESS: Percy B. Shelley Esq / Leigh Hunt Esq / 13 Lisson Grove North / Paddington / London. POSTMARKS: (1) MARLOW / 33; (2) 10 o'Clock / OC. 1 / 1817; (3) C / 1 OC 1 / 1817. PUBLISHED: Jones, #36. TEXT: MS., Bodleian Library (MS., Shelley, c. 1, ff. 208–9).

1. Again with insufficient funds to meet his own debts, as well as those of Hunt and Godwin, Shelley signed a post-obit bond with William Willats, an accountant, on 31 January 1818. In exchange for £2,000, Shelley agreed to pay Willats £4,500 within three months of the death of Sir Timothy Shelley (*SC*, V, 478–83).

2. "Porcupine Renewing His Old Quills, Or Remarks on Mr. Cobbett's Strange and Sudden Bristling Up Against Sir Frances Burdett," *Examiner*, 28 September 1817.

3. Claire Clairmont wanted assurances that Byron would regularly inform her about Alba after he became her guardian.

4. See Shelley's letter to Byron of 24 September 1817, in which he wrote: "Clare is well, but anxious. I have said nothing to her which you do not authorize" (*PBS Letters*, #411).

5. Gaius Marius (157–86 B.C.), Roman general and consul who derived his political power from army veterans rather than from the aristocracy; Jean Paul Marat (1743–93), journalist of the French Revolution who wrote on behalf of the working classes and the poor and was a leader of the faction that advocated the massacre of those formerly in power.

6. See 7 October 1817.

To Shelley [Marlow] Thursday [?2 October 1817]

My dear Love

Your letter received per parcel tonight was very unsatisfactory. You decide nothing and tell me nothing—You say—"the Chancery expences must be paid but you do not say whether our going to ⟨England⟩ Italy would o[b]viate this necessity—You say Longdill has not undertaken for all the debts but you do not mention for how much he has and { } far those would help us or send us away

Now dearest Pray come down by friday (the day you receive this) if possible but at least I earnestly entreat you come by saturday's coach—I assure you that it is of the utmost consequence that we should see one another—I cannot come to London—If you presence is indispensable in London you could return Monday but I think from the account you give of folks dilitoriness you might be spared for a few days

However it may be my love I most earnestly entreat you to come—I do not understand what you are doing or how things are going on pray come—I shall expect you indeed on Saturday for if you reflect I think you will perceive with me the necessity of our meeting indeed my love nothing can be done without it

How happy shall I be to see my dearest Shelley

I would use more arguments but I think it is plain—May I not expect you Saturday?

Your own

Come in the inside of the coach or do not come—High Wycombe coach was overturned last friday and a person killed

[*On a separate leaf*] I almost think of writing my letter over again as the enclosed is so wild I fear you will not attend to it—but I am so firmly convinced of the necessity of our seeing each other but I have not time (as it is near 12) for argument and I have used persuasion but I hope you will see it as I do—and come without delay—if you do not such is my view of the necessity I almost think I shall wean Clara & come up by the monday's coach—yet surely you will not put me to so cruel an alternative yet our meeting is necessary for our desicion and our immediate desicion is necessary

I shall wait for your coming or answer to this with the utmost anxiety

On no account send down the girl you mention I will tell you my reasons when I see you

[*On a third leaf*] I have written long letters explanatory of all I feel—Yours are still undecided—Little Alba's affairs weigh heavily on my mind I am not at peace untill she is on her way to Italy—Yet you say nothing of all this—in fact your letter tells me nothing

I wish to hear extremely the account of your money at the bankers

I earnestly hope that you have written to C.C.[1]

I shall be truly miserable if you do not come saturday—I think then I must come up myself yet cows milk does not agree with the child & to bring her & lodgeings in town is an expence & discomfort I cannot think of

Oh my love pray pray do come every thing will go wrong if you do not—

How wretched this unsettled state of our affairs Makes me—how I wish we had not come to Marlow—I dare say after all you will not come if so God knows what I shall do but you will surely you will if it is only to hinder my being unhappy

ADDRESS: Jones, #37. TEXT: MS., Bodleian Library (MS., Shelley, c. 1, ff. 194–96).

1. In January 1817 Charles Clairmont had written Shelley from France asking for money so that he might marry a Frenchwoman. Receiving no reply from Shelley, he wrote to Mary Shelley on 9 August, imploring her to have Shelley respond (*S&M*, I, 211–17). Shelley, who had supplied Charles Clairmont with funds in the past, refused him on this occasion.

TO SHELLEY

Marlow October 5—1817

I am rather tired, my best beloved—with a letter I have written to the Hunts—but this you will hold no excuse for not writing to you—and in fact I have many things to say—but the hope that you will be enabled to keep your promise & return teusday[1] makes me keep back many questions & thoughts that will be better answered then.

Your babes are very well—But Willy suffers from the cold—I want sadly some flannell for petticoats both for him and myself—indeed the poor little fellow is very susceptible of cold and suffers a good deal—But Marianne would give so high a price—and I do not like to ask M[rs] G. [*Godwin*] and you are no judge—I do not want Welch flannell but it ought to be thick and good—if you do venture to buy it get 8 yrd[s] M[r] Baxter is a good judge of those things but I should not like to ask him. Put the enclosed to him in the post.

Clara is rather disordered—cows milk evidently does not agree with her—If you have not written to Furnival do by the next post and ask his opinion of milk and bread. I get on very well without medecine[2]—Now do write & tell him to direct his answer to Marlow.

In Geneva women who suckle a{re} forbidden to drink beer but are ordered wine—I think a little Madeira would do me good—not pure but mixed with water for I feel the want of some supporting drink—If you think the same as I do bring a bottle with you. I can get no chocolate here.

Remember dearest to bring me a good thick book to write extracts in—ruled—I send you a list of some books that I selected from the Manuel du Libraire[3] which I think might be useful to me especially those I have marked under would you try to get them or some of them—Bring down also your proofs.[4]

How happy shall I be—my own dear love to see You again—Your last was so <u>very</u> very short a visit and after you were gone I thought of so many things I had to say to you and had no time to say—Come teusday dearest and let us enjoy some of each others company come and see your sweet babes and the little commodore who is lively and an uncommonly interesting child—I never see her without thinking of the expressions in my Mother's letters concerning Fanny—If a mother's eyes were not partial she seemed like this Alba—she mentions her intelligent eyes & great vivacity. But this is a melancholy subject

I have written to Hunt but tell him over & above that our piano is in tune and that I wish he would come down by monday's coach to play me a few tunes[5]—He will think I jest but it would really give me the greatest pleasure—I would make love to him pour passer le temps that he might not regret the company of Marianne & Thornton—I do not tell you to tell him the latter part of this message but you may if you please—

I shall not hear from you tomorrow unless indeed you write by the coach nor shall I write for you will not receive the letter if you com[e] teusday Hunt might come with you. I feel un[commonly?] kindly towards him for his kindness to you

Good night my own best Shelley—tell me have you suffered from you journey—tell me also dearest if I may expect you—But you will answer this in person if I may

A thousand kisses for you my own one

Your affectionate Pecksie

I had occasion to send to Peacocks for a book & in my billet I asked why they had not sent for the paper—the answer returned was—Mrs Peacocks compts and she did not think that it was convenient to us to lend the paper and therefore Mr Peacock had told her not to send.

ADDRESS: Percy B. Shelley. PUBLISHED: Jones, #38. TEXT: MS., Bodleian Library (MS., Shelley, c. 1, ff. 204–5).

1. Shelley had joined Mary Shelley at Marlow on Friday evening, 3 October, and had returned to London Saturday morning, 4 October (*MWS Journal*).

2. See 26 September 1817, n. 3.

3. The *Manuel du Libraire*, first published at the end of 1809 in Paris, is a compendium, by author, of rare, valuable, and unusual books in all languages, from the beginning of typography.

4. Though Shelley was also receiving proofs of *Frankenstein* and *Six Weeks' Tour* at this time, "your proofs" probably refers to *Laon and Cythna*, part of which was printed and sent to a publisher for consideration by 13 October.

5. Leigh Hunt was a highly gifted singer, accomplished pianist, and music critic (see Fenner, *Leigh Hunt and Opera Criticism*).

To Shelley

Marlow Oct 7th—1817

You complain of this weather—Dear Love but I have seldom known any more pleasant—out in the air that is to say—for in the house we are glad to creep over {to} the fire as if it where [*were*] Christmas.

Your account of our Expences is by very much too favourable You say that you have only borrowed 250[1] our debts at Marlow are greater than you are aware of besides living in the mean time and articles of dress that I must buy—Now we cannot hope to sell the house for £1200—And to think of going abroard with only about £200 would be madness for that would not much more than carry us there and then we have to live untill the end of december—In fact I do not think we can go if we cannot find some means of raising money

I know not how it is my love but in the middle of the day I feel my spirits sink—the children every thing annoys me and I am not well again untill after dinner—I know I ought to take some nourishment at that time—but bread is the only thing I can take and that has no effect in sustaining or raising me—sometimes when the child comes to suck at that time I feel hardly able to support myself.

I shall expect you wednesday my own love—and Willy who has become much better tempered will I have no doubt be very glad to see you. The behaviour of this child to the two little girls would be an argument in favour of those who advocate instinctive natural affection He will not go near Alba and if she approaches him he utters a fretful cry untill she is removed—but he kisses Clara—strokes her arms & feet and laughs to find them so soft and pretty and the other day when he got a twig of mignionet after he had smelt it and handed it all round he put it to her nose to scent. As for the little lady herself she is quite a little doll—so diminutive yet well made and upright—already holding her little head steadily on her shoulders.

I must say that the paragraph from my letter which Hunt has done me the honour to quote—cuts a very foolish figure—it is so femeninely expressed that all men of letters will on reading it acquit me of having a masculine understanding. If Hunt had told me he meant to put any thing of mine in I think I could have worded it with more print-worthy dignity.[2] Give my love to him and a kiss to poor little Polly who I hope is getting on better with the model of Hunt than she did with mine[3]—How are the children. Have you sent—dear, the parcel to Thompsons[4] & did the porter ask for the pelisse?

Remember my book—for transcribing

I want to practise drawing a little before I go to Italy—I have accordingly purchased pencils but find that it is too cold to draw from nature—could you get me a drawing or two to copy—I do not like prints Ask Marianne they may be either pencil drawings or water coloured

By the bye I do think that we have a whole packet of Hunts prints down here—if so you can take them up with you when you return to London. I suppose that the little gentleman[5] will not come down to play me Donne l'Amore and Auld Robin Gray.

I sent for some books to Hookhams but I fancy that I did not mention Goldsmith's Animated Nature[6] Will you write a 2[d] post[7] letter about it—

Bring down your proofs—& if you can my broach you could order one at any of the jewellers or I think if you went into any one in the Strand of

[*or*] Picadilly you might get a pretty one—it ought not to exceed £3 the price of the other—

Clare sends her love—The little bright eyed Commodore is as bluff as ever & as gay—Have you written to Furnival? And (what I dread to ask) C.C. [*Charles Clairmont*]?[8]

Adieu my own love—Get rid of that nasty side ach—You will tell me that the Italian sun will be the best physician—be it so—but money money

Come wednesday[9]—I long to see you

Most affectionately your Pecksie

ADDRESS: Percy Bysshe Shelley Esq / Messrs Longdill & Butterfield / 5 Gray's Inn Square / London. POSTMARKS: (1) MARLOW / [ ]; (2) C / 8 OC 8 / 1817. PUBLISHED: Jones, #39. TEXT: MS., Bodleian Library (MS., Shelley, c. 1, ff. 202–3).

1. Shelley had borrowed £250 from Horace Smith (*PBS Letters*, #415).

2. The lead article in the *Examiner* of 5 October, entitled "Porcupine Renewing His Old Quils, Or Remarks on Mr. Cobbett's Strange and Sudden Bristling Up Against Sir Francis Burdett [Concluded from Last Week.]," contained a footnote by Hunt: "A lady of what is called a masculine understanding, that is to say, of great natural abilities not obstructed by a bad education, writes thus in a letter to her husband: "Have you seen Cobbett's No. 23 . . . Retribution [see 30 September 1817]. This attack, by the bye, of our fair friend's on the Christian vocabulary, seems no longer warrantable. . . ."

3. Polly Rose was a girl whom the Shelleys partially adopted while they were at Marlow in order to "educate her" (Dowden, *Shelley*, II, 123). Polly must have accompanied the Hunts to Lisson Grove, perhaps to help temporarily with one of the Hunt children, that is, "the model of Hunt."

4. See 28 September 1817.

5. Hunt (see 5 October 1817).

6. *An History of the Earth and Animated Nature* (1774).

7. Two-penny post.

8. See [?2 October 1817].

9. In his letter of 8 October Shelley wrote that he would return to Marlow on 9 October unless prevented. Shelley returned on 10 October and left the evening of 12 October (*MWS Journal*).

TO SHELLEY [Marlow 14 October 1817][1]

I intended—my best love—to have sent the letters[2] by tomorrow mornings coach I shall not be able but depend on them by the next day

I do not at all expect you by tomorrow evening but perhaps the day after—And do the Godwins come? I shall write to them by this post

Your babes are quite well—Clara's eyes begin to emulate the pretty commodore's and Willy is fonder of her than ever—he is a sweet little fellow I wonder how he will like Italy.

Hunt was hardly strong enough in his paper today—The horror of a man's dying in the street was represented as terrible but was it enough impressed on his reader the superabundant capacity of ⟨his readers⟩ the spectators to have relieved him[3]

I cannot write a long letter today but I will a very long one by tomorrow —by the parcel I shall send which will be sent to Hookhams

Your own Pecksie

Bring down with you when you come a piece of cambric muslin which you can get at Maltby's in Holborn a{t} 12/^{o}p^{r} piece. Also three y^{ds} of cambric muslin or thick jaconet—1½ y^{d} wide fit for frocks for William—enough of the smallest and plainest pattern plaid to make him a frock—and also of maroon coloured cloth to make a frock & spencer. ask Marianne the quantity but tell her to allow for their being wider than hers.—send also to the dyers for his pelisse [*p. 1, upside-down*] and whatever else may be ready— You had better send all these things by the coach the first thing.

ADDRESS: Percy B. Shelley Esq / Leigh Hunt Esq / Lisson Grove North / Paddington / London. POSTMARKS: (1) MARLOW; (2) 10 o'Clock / OC. 15 / 1817 F Nn; (3) C / 15 OC 15 / 1817. PUBLISHED: Jones, #40. TEXT: MS., Bodleian Library (MS., Shelley, c. 1, f. 199).

1. The contents of this letter and the morning postmark indicate that Mary Shelley wrote this letter on 14 October.

2. Mary Shelley was transcribing Shelley's and her letters for *Six Weeks' Tour.*

3. Hunt's leading article in the *Examiner* of 12 October, "Fellow-Creatures Suffered to Die in Streets," was an account of a discharged seaman who died from exposure after sleeping three nights in the streets of Covent Garden Market.

TO SHELLEY Marlow Oct 16—1817

So you do not come this night—Love—Nor any night—you are always away and this absence is long and becomes each day more dreary—.

Poor Curran![1] So he is dead and a sod is on his breast as four years ago I heard him prophecy would be the case within that year.

Nothing is done you say in your Letter and indeed I do not expect anything to be done this many months—This—if you continued well—would not give me so much pain except on Alba's account—If she were with her father I could wait patiently but the thought of what may come between the cup and the lip—between now and her arrival at Venice is a heavy burthen on my soul He may change his mind—or go to Greece—or to the devil and then what happens—My dearest Shelley be not I entreat you too self negligent—Yet what can you do? If you were here you might retort that question upon me but when I write to you I indulge false hopes of some miraculous answer springing up in the interval. Does not Longdill treat you ill—he makes out long bills and does Nothing. You say nothing of the late arrest[2] what may be the consequences and may not they detain you for lex longa est[3] and may you not be detained many months for Godwin must not be left unprovided—All these things make me run over the months and know not where to put my finger & say—during this your Italian journey shall commence—

Yet when I say that it is on Alba's account that I am anxious—this is only when you are away and with too much faith I believe you to be well—When I see you—drooping and languid—in pain and unable to enjoy life then on your account I ardently wish for bright skies & an Italian sun—

You will have received I hope the manuscript that I sent yesterday in a parcel to Hookhams[4]—I am glad to hear that the printing goes on so well—bring down all that you can with you.

If he were free and I had no anxiety what delight would Godwins visit give me—as it is I fear that it will ma[ke] me dreadfully melancholy—cannot you come with him—by the way you write I hardly expect you this week but is it really so!

I think Alba's remaining here exceedingly dangerous. Yet I do not see what is to be done.

Your babes are well—Clara already replies to her nurse's caresses by smiles—and Willy kisses her with great tenderness

Yours very affectionately

Send instantly also several lb of tea—and I wish you would purchase a gown for Milly with a little note with it from Marianne that it may appear to come from her[5]—You can get one I should think for 12/ or 14/ but it must be stout—such a kind of one as we gave to the servant at Bath

Have you seen any thing of Mr Baxter?

Will you send the things I mentioned without delay

When do you think of coming

Be sure to send to the dyers for Williams pelisse and what else may be ready. [*P. 1 top, upside-down*] Willy has just said Good night to me he kisses the letter and says Good night to you   Clara is asleep

ADDRESS: Percy B. Shelley Esq / Leigh Hunt Esq / 13 Lisson Grove North / Paddington / London. POSTMARKS: (1) MARLOW; (2) 10 o'Clock / OC. 17 / 1817 F Nn; (3) C / 17 OC [17] / 1817. PUBLISHED: Jones, #41. TEXT: MS., Bodleian Library (MS., Shelley, c. 1, ff. 200–201).

1. John Philpot Curran (1750–1817), Irish judge, patriot, and old friend of Godwin's, had died on 14 October. When Godwin finished writing his novel *Mandeville*, interrupted by his grief over Curran's death, he dedicated it "to the memory of the sincerest friend I ever had, the late John Philpot Curran" (*SC*, V, 498).

2. Shelley was arrested and held for two days because of a debt owed to a maternal uncle, Captain John Pilford. Shelley's total debts at the time are estimated at more than £1,500. The dates and details of this arrest are unknown (see Ingpen, *Shelley in England*, pp. 522–26).

3. "The law takes much time."

4. The transcription of the letters for *Six Weeks' Tour.*

5. The Hunts, guests of the Shelleys at the end of September, had failed to tip the nursemaid Milly Shields (White, *Shelley*, I, 543).

TO SHELLEY

Marlow—Oct. 18—1817 Saturday

Mr Wright has called here today,[1] my dearest Shelley and wished to see you. I can hardly have any doubt that his business is of the same nature as that which made him call last week—You will judge but it appears to me that an arrest on Monday will follow your arrival sunday. My love—you ought not to come down—a long—long week has past and when at length I am allowed to expect you I am obliged to tell you not to come—This is very cruel.[2]

You may easily judge that I am not happy—My spirits sink during this continued absence—Godwin too will come down he will talk as if we meant to stay here and I must—must I? tell fifty privarications or direct lies—when I thought that you would be here also I ⟨contented⟩ knew that your presence would lead to general conversation but Clare will absent herself we shall be alone and he will talk of our private affairs—I am sure that I shall never be able to support it.

And when is this {to} end?—do not answer this question by saying come up to town directly—Remember we lost all the little property we had at Bishopgate by going up to town—here we have much more to loose & I must not leave this house untill such things as we do not dispose of are put in a place of safety

But Italy appears farther off than ever and the idea of it never enters my mind but Godwin enters also & makes it lie heavy at my heart—Had you not better speak—you might relieve me from a heavy burthen—Surely he cannot be blind to the many heavy reasons that urge us—your health the indispensable one if every other were away—I assure you that if my Father said—Yes you must go—do what you can for me—I know that you will do all you can—I should far from writing so melancholy a letter prepare every thing with a light heart—arrange our affairs here and come up to town to wait patiently the effect of your efforts—I know not whether it is early habit or affection but the idea of his silent quiet disapprobation makes me weep as it did in the days of my childhood.

I am called away by the cries of Clara I must go to feed her and there will be no time to resume this letter.

I shall not see you tomorrow God knows when I shall see you—Clare is forever wearying with her idle & childish complaints—can you not send me some consolation

Ever your affectionate
Mary

What about Pilfords arrest?[3] You never mention business. [*P. 4, with address*] Give the bearer a shilling.[4]

ADDRESS: P. B. Shelley. PUBLISHED: Jones, #42. TEXT: MS., Bodleian Library (MS., Shelley, c. 1, ff. 197–98).

1. Probably J. S. Wright, a Great Marlow attorney. In January and February 1818 Shelley wrote three checks to Wright totaling £66.4.9, possibly because Wright was dunning Shelley (*SC*, V, 316, n. 4).

2. Shelley was still threatened with arrest for debt. He nevertheless returned to Marlow on Sunday, 19 October, accompanied by Godwin, and remained there until 22 October without incident.

3. See 16 October 1817, n. 2.

4. This indicates that Mary Shelley's letter was sent by private messenger (perhaps a wagon or coach driver) rather than by post. Since the cost of postage for a letter was less than a shilling, perhaps the letter was accompanied by proofs.

TO CHRISTINA BAXTER[1] Marlow Nov. 4—1817

[De]ar Christy

After so long a silence I hardly know how to begin my letter to you. On my part it has not been the silence of coldness.[2] But we can talk of this when we see one another so I will hasten to the object of my letter.

In a letter that I have received from your father today he says that he shall try to get a house that you may join him but that the rest of the family cannot come untill Newburgh brewery is sold. I know that it is a long job to get a house to ones mind and as your father longs for your society and as I am sure you wish to be with him Can not you come to England and make our house your home for some time where you will be nearer to him[3] and as he comes down here [ ] then for a week or so the addition of [his daugh]ter to our society will be very delightf[ul to] him.

We have no acquaintances here belonging to the town as country town friends are not very agreable but Jane (or as you must now call her Clare) lives with us who is nearly the same creature as she was when you visited Skinner Street. I hope you will be good friends with her and we now and then have a visitor or two from London. These are all the allurments I can hold out to you besides Shelleys and my society and a library of books. Will you come?

Tell me a little of Isabells health which I fear is bad. perhaps this place would do her good as it is warmer that [*than*] bleak Newburgh [but h]er father says that she cannot quit [her f]amily.

Remember me to Betsy & Robert very [ ] and tell Cowley[4] that I have not forgotten him & shall be very glad to see him kiss my old friend Izy[5] for me & Catherine[6] too although I do not know her. I long to see the little things and introduce them to my babes although the language of each will I am afraid at first be unintelligi[ble] to the other—Although I speak by anticipation for neither of mine can speak yet

Affectionately yours
Mary W. Shelley

ADDRESS: Miss / Miss Christy Baxter / Woodside / Newburgh / Fife N.B. PUBLISHED: *SC*, V, 341–42. TEXT: MS., National Library of Scotland.

1. Christina Baxter, Isabella Booth's sister, was also a childhood friend of Mary Shelley's. At age ninety-one she gave an interviewer her recollections of Shelley, Mary Shelley, and Harriet Shelley, which were published in the *Dundee Courier* on 8 July 1922 (*SC*, II, 558).

2. In September 1815 Christina Baxter had sent Fanny Imlay "a very impertinent letter," which Fanny Imlay had forwarded to Mary Godwin on 16 April 1816. Mary Godwin commented that the letter "professes friendship but such friendship we see

how much worth it is" (MWS Journal; see also *SC*, V, 334–35). Apparently no answer was sent to Christina Baxter's letter.

3. David Booth believed that the Shelleys' invitation to Christina Baxter was actually the first step of a plot through which Isabella Booth would accompany the Shelleys to Italy (*SC*, V, 390).

4. Isabella Booth had five sisters and two brothers, among them Elizabeth, Robert, and John Cowley (*SC*, II, 558–59).

5. Pet name for Isabella Booth.

6. Isabella Booth's daughter.

To William T. Baxter — Marlow ⟨Nov⟩ Dec. 3rd 1817

My dear sir   You receive the cheque enclosed for the money[1]

Isabell promised to write to me some time ago and not having performed this promise I am afraid that she is ill will you let me know about this.

Shelley is not well—he has a cough this house is so very damp—all the books in the library are mildewed we must quit it. Italy is yet uncertain.

Have you yet received a copy of Shelley's poem[2] he has ordered one to be sent—and above all have you read Mandeville[3] & what do you think of it.

When you write to Izy tell her that I shall send her a parcel in a few days.

William & Clara are both well—Clara is very much grown & William grows Daily I think—He suffers however when the weather is the least cold for his complexion is so delicate

Remember me to Mrs Booth. when may we expect you both or one of you at Marlow

Will you oblige Peacock by sending down all the Cobbetts that have been published since No. 25.

Clare & Shelley desire their best remembrances to you and your son in la[w]

Most sincerely y[ours]
MWShelley

ADDRESS: Mr W. T. Baxter / 117 Dorset Street / Salisbury Square / Fleet Street. POSTMARKS: (1) [   ] paid; (2) 4 o'Clock / DE. 4 / 1817 EV. PUBLISHED: Jones, #44; *SC*, V, #432. TEXT: MS., Pforzheimer Library.

1. Shelley's check for £7 to Baxter was probably reimbursement for cash Baxter advanced or purchases he made for the Shelleys (*SC*, V, 346–47, 367–68).

2. Shelley's *Laon and Cythna.*

3. Godwin's novel, published 1 December 1817.

Shelley to William Godwin[1] — Marlow 7 December 1817

[*Postscript by Mary Shelley*] Will you ask Mamma to be so kind as to get next door to 41[2] half a yard and a nail of gold band for Willy's hat and send it by [?the] next coach.

All our loves—

ADDRESS: William Godwin, Esq. / 41 Skinner St. Holborn / London. POSTMARKS: (1) MARLOW / [ ]; (2) C / 8 DE 8 / 1817. PUBLISHED: Jones, #45. TEXT: MS., Bodleian Library (MS., Shelley, c. 1, ff. 184–86).

1. *PBS Letters*, #429.

2. The Godwins' residence and book-publishing firm were at 41 Skinner Street. According to *Johnstone's Guide*, the building next door, at 26 Skinner Street, was the firm of W. & J. Welch, straw hat manufacturers, and next to that, at 25 Skinner Street, was Griffen & Sons, ribbon manufacturers.

MARY SHELLEY AND SHELLEY TO WILLIAM T. BAXTER[1]

Marlow, Dec. 30 1817

[*P. 1, top, upside-down*]

My dear Sir—

You see I prophesied well three months ago when you were here—I then said that I was sure that Mr B. [*Booth*] was averse to our intercourse and would find some means to break it off[2]—I wish I had you by the fire here in my little study and it might be double double, toil & trouble but I would quickly convince you that your girls are not below me in station[3] & that in fact I am the fittest companion for them in the world but I postpone the argument untill I see you for I know (pardon me) that viva voce is all in all with you

ADDRESS: Mr Will. Thos Baxter / 20 / Little St Thos the Apostles / London. POSTMARKS: (1) MARLOW / [33]; (2) D / 31 DE 31 / 1817. PUBLISHED: Jones, #46; *SC*, V, #441. TEXT: MS., Pforzheimer Library.

1. *PBS Letters*, #431; *SC*, V, #441.

2. Baxter's letter to Shelley of 29 December indicated that he had changed his feelings about Shelley and wished the friendship of the families to gradually fade. The Shelley's attributed this change in attitude to the influence of his son-in-law David Booth.

3. Baxter contended that Shelley's higher "rank and fortune" and the unconventional behavior they allowed him would adversely affect Baxter's family.

TO WILLIAM T. BAXTER

[119 Great Russell Street Bloomsbury Square][1] Feb. 3. [error for 3 March] 1818[2]

My dear Sir

Be so kind as to deliver the enclosed to your daughter[3]

In a few days we quit England for a long journey at such a time I could wish that all who have been our friends would be still so—but this is useless

With the most heart felt wishes for your happiness & welfare

Yours very sincerely
MaryWShelley

ADDRESS: Mr Willm Thos Baxter / Mr Thos Baxter / 3 Colledge Green / City. POSTMARKS: (1) [ ]ory [ ] / Unpaid / GIR[ ]EISIBY; (2) [ ] / 3. MR. / [1]818 Nn; (3) Postal fee: 2. PUBLISHED: The *Star* (London), 22 March 1894; *SC*, V, 507. TEXT: MS., National Library of Scotland.

1. The Shelleys had moved to 119 Russell Street (London) on 10 February.

2. In all previous printings, this letter has been dated 3 February 1818, in accordance with Mary Shelley's dating. Mary Shelley was then at Marlow, but the postmarks indicate that it was sent by two-penny post within London, which has lead to the assumption that Mary Shelley sent the letter to Shelley to post (*SC*, V, 507). The MWS Journal gives no indication of a letter written to Isabella Booth on 3 February, but it does indicate one for 3 March written from 119 Great Russell Street, Bloomsbury Square, just eight days before the Shelleys' departure for Italy. (The printed *Journal* omitted reference to the 3 March letter.) Looking at Mary Shelley's letter of "3 February," we find that the postmark date on this letter is unmistakably "3. MR"; this explains the method of mailing, the context, and the MWS Journal entry. (Claire Clairmont, who was with the Shelleys in London, also confused the months and days in her *Journal* entry of 1 March [*CC Journals*].)

3. Shelley and Claire Clairmont visited William Baxter on 2 March (*CC Journals*). Mary Shelley's Journal recounts: "Isabel is arrived but neither comes or sends." On 3 March: "No news of Isabell I write to her."

To Isabella Booth [119 Great Russell Street Bloomsbury Square 5 March 1818]

My dear Izy

As you directed to {me} at Marlow and I was {in} London a day was lost and I am afraid you did not receive mine which contained my address

How I long to see you—if you can send me a note when I may expect you[1] that I may contrive that we may not be interrupted—⟨send⟩ bring little Izy with you

your own MaryW.S.

Mrs Shelley
119 Great Russell St.
Bloomsbury square

ADDRESS: Mrs Booth. ENDORSED: Mrs. Shelley. PUBLISHED: *SC*, V, #463. TEXT: MS., Pforzheimer Library.

1. We may infer that Isabella Booth planned to visit her childhood friend. Mary Shelley's Journal, however, gives no indication as to whether the meeting took place.

Shelley to Leigh Hunt[1] Calais. March 13—1818[2]

[*Postscript by Mary Shelley*] Shelley is full of business & desires me to finish this hasty notice of our safety—The children are in high spirits & very well. Our passage was stormy but very short both Alba and William were sick but they were very good and slept all the time—We now depart for Italy with fine weather & good hopes.

Farewell my dear Friends
May you be happy.—

Your affectionate friend
MaryWS

ADDRESS: Mr. Leigh Hunt / 13 Lisson Grove North / Paddington / London / Angleterre. POSTMARKS: (1) P.611 / CALAIS; (2) FPO / MR. 16 / 1818; (3) 12 o'Clock / MR. 16 / 1818 Nn; (4) 4 o'Clock / 16. MR / 1818 EV. PUBLISHED: Jones, #48. TEXT: MS. (photocopy), W. L. Lewis Collection, Texas Christian University.

1. *PBS Letters*, #458.

2. On 11 March the Shelleys, their children, Claire Clairmont, Allegra, and their servants, Elise and Milly Shields, traveled to Dover, and on 12 March they crossed to Calais, where they remained overnight (*MWS Journal*).

MARY SHELLEY AND SHELLEY TO LEIGH AND MARIANNE HUNT

Lyons, March 22 1818[1]

[*Cross-written by Mary Shelley, pp. 1–3 of Shelley's letter*] Now, my dear Hunt & my dear Marianne, we see Jura & Mont Blanc again from the windows of our hotel and the Rhone rushes by our window—The sun shines bright and it is a kind of Paradise which we have arrived at through the valley of the shadow of death—for certainly the greater part of our journey here was not the most pleasant thing in the world—I think if Peacock had been with us he would have taken fright and returned. The first night after quitting Calais we slept at St. Omers—we arrived after the shutting the gates—The postillions craked their whips to give signs of our approach and a female voice was heard from the battlements demanding the name and number of the invaders she was told that it was some English ladies with their children and she departed to carry the intelligence to the Governor who lived half a mile off—In about half an hour the gates were thrown open and about a dozen soldiers came out headed by this female who demanded our passport—she received it and began to read it when recollecting herself she said—Mais, Medames you will remember the guard. We told her that we certainly would Ah then—said she—you may enter directly—So we passed through the various windings of the fortifications and through three immense gates which were successively closed after us with a clanking sound. But these are the frontier towns and when we came to the middle of France we found nothing of this. The largest towns here are not fortified—but these kind of things appear to spring up in the north of France—that is that part of it that borders Flanders like mushrooms or toadstools great large round things with a ditch & wall round them swarming with people—There is Douai—with I do not know how many thousand inhabitants—who ever heard of Douai?[2] Why to be born in such a town is like living out of the circle of human things—an ambitious individual of Douai would almost like Erostratus[3] wish to burn down a fine building or two to let his fellow men know that there was such a place in the world. Now Lyons is a pleasant city and very republican—The people have suffered dreadfully—you know the horrors they went th{r}ough in the revolution and about six months ago they were not much better off.[4] If it had not been for Napoleon said one man to us, my head would not have been where it is he brought peace to us—and I say nothing but there are people who wish him back—When the Angouleme party had the lead dreadful atrocities were committed here mais ce Monsieur q'on appelle Louis XVIII is a better man and restrained them.[5]

This same man told us some horrible facts which could never have been committed if there was liberty of the press and such things could have been published. I do not relate them for you do not like to hear of inhumanities

Such is our little history at present—Is yours a pleasant one—You have promised to write often—and I am sure that here your kindness would stand instead of promise or any thing else—it would bind you to us exiles who love you very sincerely and wish to hear every good news concerning you. Shelley's health is infinitely improved and I hope the fine climate we now enjoy and are proceeding to will quite restore him—The children bear the journey exceedingly well and thus far we are fortunate and in good spirits. La prima donna[6] desires her love to you and Bessy

Adieu—We will write again soon and hope to find a letter waiting for us from you at Milan

Most affectionately yours, my dear friends—MWS

ADDRESS: Mr Leigh Hunt / 13 Lisson Grove North / Paddington / London / Angleterre. POSTMARKS: (1) P 58 P / LYON; (2) FPO / MR. 30 / 1818; (3) 12 o'Clock / MR. 30 / 1818 Nn; (4) 4 o'Clock / 30. MR / 1818 EV. PUBLISHED: *SC*, VI, #469. TEXT: MS., Pforzheimer Library.

1. On 13 March the Shelley party left Calais. They traveled through Saint Omer, Douai, La Fère, Rheims, Saint Dizier, Langres, Dijon, and [?Thounu(s) *or* Thomirey] and arrived at Lyons on 21 March. They remained at Lyons for four days, staying at the Hôtel de l'Europe (*MWS Journal*).

2. Douai was well-known as a center of English Catholic scholarship from 1562 through 1793.

3. Erostratus (or Herostratus) burned down the temple of Artemis at Ephesus in order to gain a place in history.

4. The "horrors" six months past may have resulted from the revelation in June 1817 of a seditious conspiracy in Lyons (*SC*, VI, 529).

5. In 1816 Louis XVIII had suppressed the Angoulême party, an ultraroyalist group (*SC*, VI, 529).

6. A playful allusion to Claire Clairmont's singing artistry.

To Leigh and Marianne Hunt

Milan—[6] April 1818[1]

My dear Friends

We have at length arrived in Italy. After winding for several days through vallies & crossing mountains and passing Cenis we have arrived in this land of blue skies & pleasant fields. The fruit trees all in blossom and the fields green with the growing corn—Hunt already says—I should like this. Indeed as we passed along the mountainous districts of Savoy we often said—Hunt would not like this—but the first evening that we arrived in Italy every thing appeared changed. We arrived at Susa the first Italian town at the foot of Cenis about six in the evening and Shelley and I went to look at a triumphal arch that had been erected to the honour of Augustus—It was nearly in perfect preservation and most beautifully situated surrounded by mountains—The path under it was preserved in beautiful order a green lane covered with flowers a pretty Italian woman went with us and plucked us a nosegay of violets.

Italy appears a far more civilized place than France—you see more signs of cultivation and work and you meet multitudes of peasants on the road—driving carts drawn by the most beautiful oxen I ever saw—They are of a delicate dove colour with eyes that remind you of, and justify the Homeric epithet ox-eyed Juno. In France you might travel many miles and not meet a single creature. The inns are infinitely better and the bread which is uneatable in France is here the finest and whitest in the world. There is a disconsolate air of discomfort in France that is quite wretched In Italy we breathe a different air and every thing is pleasant around us.—At Turin we went to the opera—it was a little shabby one and except the lights on the stage the house was in perfect darkness—there were two good singers and these the people heard but during the rest of the time you were deafened by the perpetual talking of the audience.—We have been also at the opera of Milan.[2] The house is nearly as large as that of London and the boxes more elegantly fitted up. The scenery and decorations much more magnificent Madame Camporesi[3] is the Prima Donna but she was ill and we did not hear her—indeed we heard nothing For the people did not like the opera which had been repeated for every night for these three weeks so not one air was heard. But the ballet was infinitely magnificent—It was (strange to say) the story of Othello—but it was rather a tragic pantomime than a ballet—There was no dancer like Mam^lle^ Milanie[4] but the whole was in a finer stile—The corps de ballet is excellent and they throw themselves into groups fit for a scluptor [*sculptor*] to contemplate. The music of the ballet was very fine and the gestures striking. The dances of many performers which are so ill executed with us are here graceful to the extreme. The theatre is not lighted and the ladies dress with bonnets and pelisses which I think a great pity—The boxes are dear—but the pit—in which none but but respectable people are admitted is only eighteen pence so that our amusement is very cheap.

I like this town—The ladies dress very simply and the only fault of their costume is the length of their petticoats so that Marianne's pretty feet would be quite hid. We think however of spending the summer on the banks of the lake of Como which is only twenty miles from here. Shelley's health is infinitely improved and the rest of the chicks are quite well—How are you all—And how do you like Don Garcia and il barbiere di Seviglia.[5] We half expected a letter to have arrived before us—but the posts travel very slowly here. Let us have long letters.—Do you see Peacock and is he in despair[6] Remember me to all friends and kiss your babes for me.

I almost forgot to mention that we spent one day at 30 miles from

Geneva Elise's Mother and father-in-law and little girl came to see her [ ][7] Aimee is very beautiful with eyes something lik[e] but sweeter than William's—a perfect shaped nose and a more beautiful mouth than her Mothers expressive of the greatest sensibility

Adieu—My dear Hunt & Marianne La Prima Donna sends her Affectionate remembrances and Shelley his love

Most affectionately yours
MaryWShelley

Direct to us
Mess. Marietti-Banquiers
Milano
Italie

Tell Ollier that S. has not received his parcel but that he can send the proofs[8] to Peacock for revision.

We left several things at our lodgings in Great Russel St. to be sent you—among the rest have you received William's service—if not have {the} kindness to enquire for it. for I should be very sorry that it should be lost.

Shelley wishes you to call at the first jewellers on the left hand side of the way in New Bond St—as you enter it from Oxford St. where we bough[t] Marianne's broach—Shelley left a ring to be mended and forgot to call for it

Tell Peacock to send Beppo[9] & some pins with the first parcel—& sealing wax these things are so bad here

ADDRESS: Mr Leigh Hunt / 13 Lisson Grove North / Paddington / London / Angleterre / Inghilterra. POSTMARKS: (1) FPO / AP. 23 / 1818; (2) 12 o'Clock / AP. 23 / 1818 Nn; (3) 4 o'Clock / 23. AP / 1818 EV. PUBLISHED: Jones, #49. TEXT: MS., Huntington Library (HM 2739).

1. Shelley wrote to Peacock telling him about the opera and ballet that he, Mary Shelley, and Claire Clairmont had seen the previous night (*MWS Journal*), which dates Shelley's letter as 6 April. In the same letter, Shelley asked for news of Hunt "to whom Mary is now writing" (*PBS Letters*, #460). Both Shelley's and Mary Shelley's letters were received in England on 23 April. On 25 March the Shelley party had left Lyons. Traveling through Tour-du-Pin, Chambery, Saint Jean-de-Maurienne, Mt. Cenis, Susa, and Turin, they had arrived at Milan on 4 April.

2. La Scala.

3. Violante Camporese (1785–1839), a soprano who excelled in works by Mozart.

4. The Shelleys had been greatly impressed by the dancing of Mlle Milanie, whom they had seen during their last month in England (*PBS Letters*, #460, #462; Peacock, *Works*, VIII, 81–82, 107; *SC*, V, 504).

5. Leigh Hunt wrote a review of Manuel Garcia's performance in *Il Barbiere de Siviglia* for the *Examiner* of 12 April 1818 (Fenner, *Leigh Hunt and Opera Criticism*, pp. 216, 260).

6. Possibly an allusion to Claire Clairmont's rejection of Peacock's proposal of marriage, made in 1818 (*CC Journals*, p. 143, n. 41).

7. On 27 March at Chambéry they visited with Jeanne Elizabeth Duvillard Romieux, Louis Romieux, and Aimèe Romieux (identified by Emily W. Sunstein

[see 29 May 1817, n. 9]). In accordance with the common usage of the day, "father-in-law" could refer to either a stepfather, as in this case, or to the parent of one's spouse (see 9–11 September [1823], n. 14).

8. Of the incomplete *Rosalind and Helen.*

9. Shelley had undertaken to bring Byron's poem *Beppo*, published by John Murray in January 1818, to Byron. Having left it behind, Shelley arranged for Peacock to send it on (*PBS Letters*, #464).

SHELLEY TO THOMAS LOVE PEACOCK[1] Milan April 30. 1818

[*By Mary Shelley*] P.S. If you see Hunt Give my love—to him & his Marianne—tell him I am going to buy some airs for him from an opera we saw here

Be so kind as to remember the things I mentioned in S's last for our midsummer parcel and add Beppo—(if possible) Le proces de Fualdes[2]—

ADDRESS: T. L. Peacock, Esqr. / Great Marlow / Bucks / Angleterre. POSTMARKS: (1) FPO / MY. 14 / 1818; (2) G / MY / 14 / 1818. PUBLISHED: Jones, #50. TEXT: MS., Bodleian Library (MS., Shelley, c. 1, ff. 231–32).

1. *PBS Letters*, #466.

2. Antoine Bernardin Fualdes, *Cause célèbre: Procès des prévenus de l'assassinat de M. Fualdès, ex-magistrat à Rhodez* . . . (Paris: Pillet, 1817). On 5 July Peacock indicated that he had sent this along with other publications and items requested by the Shelleys (Peacock, *Works*, VIII, 196).

TO LEIGH AND MARIANNE HUNT Leghorn—May 13. 1818[1]

My dear Friends

We have been many weeks absent from England and we have had no letter from you—I hope however that there is a letter on the road and that this letter will only make you say—Have they not yet had our letter and not—Indeed I must write soon—We have as you may perceive by the date of my letter travelled farther south since I last wrote—we have passed through a country which we { } would be the delight of Hunt—Beautiful hedges blooming with hawthorn in flower and roses—beautiful lanes are bounded by these and the corn fields are planted with rows of trees round which the vines twist themselves and are festooned from tree to tree so as to form the most pleasant leafy Alleys in the world—After travelling several days through a country like this blooming and fertile like a perpetual garden we came to the Appenines which we crossed in a most violent wind so that Clare was very much afraid that the carriage would blow over—Here we quitted the scene which would be so pleasant to Hunt but we found it again in the vale of the Arno along the banks of the river where nothing was wanting to the beauty of the scene but that the river should be capable of reflecting its banks but unfortunately it is too muddy—Pisa is a dull town situated on the banks of the Arno—it has a fine cathederal but not to be compared to that of Milan—and a tower which has been so shaken by an earthquake that it leans many feet on one side—Its gallery of pictures or whatever it contains we did not see putting that off untill our return to the town—One thing however which disgusted me so much that I could never walk in the streets except in misery was that criminals condemned to labour work publickly in the streets heavily ironed in pairs with a man with a gun to each pair to guard against their escape—These poor wretches look sallow and dreadfully wretched and you could get into no street but you heard the clanking of their chains.

I think this circumstance made us quit Pisa sooner than we otherwise should—and we came here to Leghorn to present a letter to a friend[2]—we shall stay here however but a short time for we intend to pass the summer at Florence. The people that we know here have been many years in Italy and have seen a great deal of the society in the principal towns here—There seems to be a very pleasant way of going on here if the members that compose the company are as agreable as is their manner of visiting—One lady keeps open house in the evening and the rest resort to her—there are no refreshments and the English complain that they do not know what to do when they come in for there is no appearance of receiving visits—for the company instead of assembling altogether are dispersed in parties about the room. They told us that whenever you call at an Italian house the servant always puts her head out of window and demands chi è whatever time of day or night it may be—The proper answer to this question is amici but those people {who} do no[t] know the proper reply are terribly puzzled to know what to answer to this chi è which meets them at every corner—one of their friends visiting a house after having been kept a long time in the street while they were screaming chi è to him from the window and he was exhausting all answers to them but the right one—at length he made his way to the stairs which as they always are in Italy, were dark and as he was groping along the mistress of the house called out chi è and the poor man quite confounded not recognizing the voice—called out Bruta bestia, andate al diavolo—and rushed out of the house.

This town is a noisy mercantile one and we intend soon to quit it—It cannot be compared to Milan—which was a very pleasant city large and populous yet quiet. There is no opera and there was an excellent one at Milan—particularly one singer who is famous in all Italy of the name of David[3]— he has a tenor voice and sing in a softer & sweeter way than you ever hear in England—In Italy except the first night or two you can never hear any thing of the opera except some favourite airs—for the people make it a visiting place & play cards and sup in the boxes so you may guess that the murmur of their voices rises far above the efforts of the singers—but they became silent to hear some of David's songs which hardly at all accompanied—stole upon the ear like a murmur of waters while Mad. Camporesi ran up the octaves beside him in a far different manner

You will be pleased to hear that Shelley is much better than he was—I suppose you all in England go on as you did when we left you but I should like to know how all you{r} little babes are—Do you see much of Peacock—and tell me if you go often to the opera and if any changes have taken place in that singing Paradise. We are the same as we were except that before we left Milan Alba was sent to Venise where they dress her in little trousers trimmed with lace & treat her like a little princess.

There lives here in Leghorn and we are going to see her an Aunt of Marianne's favourite Mr Haydon—that Hero de se who has lately send her over his bust in marble and promises to come and see her when his picture is finished but you {know} when that will be or rather you do not know as it goes on in the same manner as Penelope's web. He writes long letters to his relations here and I fancy they think him a little God[4]

What weather have you in England—here it is very pleasant although not so hot as I expected but we have peas and strawberries for dinner and I fancy you will not have them for another month.—but this place is cooler than more inland towns on account of its vicinity to the sea which is here like a lake without tides blue and tranquil

Shelley and Clare send their love. Adieu my dear Hunt and Marianne—May Æsculapius keep you in health which prayer I have no doubt he will hear if you do not remain at home so much as you used—

Most affectionately yours
MaryWShelley

ADDRESS: Leigh Hunt Esq. / 13 Lisson Grove North / Paddington / London / Angleterre / Inghilterra. POSTMARKS: (1) LIVORNO; (2) FPO / MY. 28 / 1818; (3) 12 o'Clock / MY. 28 / 1818 Nn; (4) A [ ]lock / 28. MY / 1818 EV. PUBLISHED: Jones, #51. TEXT: MS., Huntington Library (HM 2740).

1. From 9 through 12 April the Shelleys looked for a house at Lake Como. Deciding to rent the Villa Pliniana for the summer, they remained at Milan. From Milan Shelley wrote Byron three letters about the care of Allegra, the third on 28 April, when Allegra was sent to Byron at Venice, in the care of Elise and Byron's messenger (*SC*, VI, 542–47, 576–77). Unable to rent the Villa Pliniana, the Shelleys left Milan on 1 May. Traveling through Piacenza, Parma, Modena, Bologna, Barberino, and La Scala, they arrived at Pisa on 7 May and stayed at the Tre Donzelle until 9 May. On 8 May they had word from Elise that she and Allegra were at Venice (*MWS Journal*). On 9 May the Shelleys and Claire Clairmont went to Leghorn (Livorno), where they stayed for a few days at the Acquila Nera and then at La Croce di Malta until their departure for the Bagni di Lucca on 11 June (White, *Shelley*, II, 14, n. 27).

2. Maria James Reveley Gisborne (1770–1836). On 9 May Mary Shelley delivered a letter of introduction to Maria Gisborne from Godwin, which read in part: "You perhaps recollect an unfortunate female infant, of which I was the father, that you took into your house, & were kind enough to protect for a week, a very few days after its birth" (*SC*, V, #465). When she cared for the infant Mary Godwin, Maria Gisborne was married to Henry Reveley. A member of Godwin's liberal circle of friends, she was a particular friend of Godwin's. When she was widowed two years after Mary Wollstonecraft's death, Godwin asked her to marry him, but she preferred John Gisborne, a merchant. She married Gisborne in 1800, and accompanied by her thirteen-year-old son, Henry Reveley, they went to Italy in 1801. The Shelleys quickly developed the greatest admiration for Maria Gisborne, and although they thought John Gisborne a bore, they became, with the exception

of an estrangement in 1820–21 (see 25 September 1820), lifelong friends of the Gisbornes, as demonstrated in the Shelleys' letters, *MWS Journal*, and Gisborne, *Journals and Letters* (Dowden, *Shelley*, II, 205–9).

3. Giovanni Davide (1789–c. 1851), tenor.

4. Benjamin Robert Haydon's aunt was Mrs. Partridge, whom Shelley, Mary Shelley, and Claire Clairmont visited on 5 June (*MWS Journal*). The marble bust is acknowledged by Mrs. Partridge in her letter to Haydon of 7 April 1818 (*Benjamin Robert Haydon: Correspondence and Table Talk*, ed. F. W. Haydon, 2 vols. [London: Chatto and Windus, 1876], I, 332). The Shelleys and the Hunts did not get along with Haydon (see 2 March, 1817), who was introduced to Shelley by Hunt in 1817 at a dinner party at which Shelley and Hunt argued with Haydon about Christianity (Haydon, *Diary*, II, 80–87, 372–73). Mary Shelley's antipathy to Haydon may have been in response to Haydon's dislike of Shelley.

TO MARIA GISBORNE Hotel di Malta. Leghorn. Monday morng. [?18] May 1818

Dear Madam

The weather appears favourable enough for the sea and we wait your decision—But pray allow me to ask you to name an early hour. We ought rather to think of returning than of setting off at five, as you know with the chances of the wind and water we may be detained longer than we intend—

If you are not for the sea, are you for a long walk this evening?[1]

Your's truly obliged M.W.S.

PUBLISHED: Jones, "New Letters," pp. 41–42. TEXT: John Gisborne Notebook No. 2, Abinger MS., Bodleian Library.

1. The Shelleys and the Gisbornes walked together almost every evening during the Shelleys' stay at Leghorn (*MWS Journal*).

TO MARIA GISBORNE H. di Malta. [28] May 1818[1]

Dear Madam

Mr Shelley has returned, and I send you some of the fruits of his arrival—We intend to wait on you at six this Evening, if the slight rain does not intimidate you from a walk to the Steam Engine

most truly your's
MWS.

PUBLISHED: Jones, "New Letters," p. 42. TEXT: John Gisborne Notebook No. 2, Abinger MS., Bodleian Library.

1. On 28 May Shelley returned to Leghorn from a two-day trip to the Bagni di Lucca, where he had been looking for a house. In the evening the Shelleys, the Gisbornes, and Henry Reveley went to see the steam engine that Henry Reveley was constructing for a steamer projected to run between Leghorn, Genoa, and Marseilles. The young engineer's enterprise greatly interested Shelley, who eventually invested between £250 and £350 in it before it finally was abandoned (*SC*, VI,

943. For details of Shelley's involvement with the construction of the steam engine, see Dowden, *Shelley*, II, 208–9, 303–6; White, *Shelley*, II, 16–17, 206–7; *PBS Letters*; and Mary Shelley's letters of 5 October 1819 and [27–30 November 1819]).

To Maria Gisborne H. di Malta. 1. June 1818

Dear Madam

May I take the liberty to ask you to lend me your Ariosto? We had only one Volume of our's, and I have finished it.

I hope you feel no ill effects from last night's walk. It is the first of June, and we are longing for a fire here in Italy!

Your's truly obliged. MWS.

PUBLISHED: Jones, "New Letters," p. 42. TEXT: John Gisborne Notebook No. 2, Abinger MS., Bodleian Library.

To Maria Gisborne H. di Malta. [2] June 1818[1]

My Dearest Madam

The pattern appears to me to do very well—I have but one linen sheet, I find—I think I ought to have four pair in all—You do not ask the size, but let them be like your's—But I am quite ashamed to give you so much trouble—Mr Gisborne seems to think the weather too unfavourable for our walk to Mrs Patridge's[2]—if therefore I do not hear from you to the contrary, we shall see you about six. Remembrance to M^{r} R [*Reveley*]—

PUBLISHED: Jones, "New Letters," p. 43. TEXT: John Gisborne Notebook No. 2, Abinger MS., Bodleian Library.

1. Mary Shelley's journal for 2 June records, "Cold dismal weather—Walk in the evening with S. Claire—& Mr & Mrs G." The Journal for 3 June notes "rain all day" and has no mention of the Gisbornes.

2. See 13 May 1818, n. 4.

To Maria Gisborne Croce di Malta. [?4] June 1818[1]

Dear Madam

Not knowing whether you would wish me to send the money by your servant, we shall bring it with us this Eveng. I am exceedingly obliged to you for the trouble you have taken for me.

MWS.

PUBLISHED: Jones, "New Letters," p. 43. TEXT: John Gisborne Notebook No. 2, Abinger MS., Bodleian Library.

1. The place of this letter in John Gisborne's Notebook and the MWS Journal entries for 2 and 3 June suggest that this letter was written on 4 June.

To Maria Gisborne Livorno Friday morning. [5 June 1818][1]

Dear Madam

The physician will be with us at 7 this evening[2]—Shall we come this evening earlier for our walk and then you can return with us at the right hour?—

I send you somthing that will amuse you

Most truly yours
Mary W. Shelley

Compts to Mr G. [*Gisborne*] and Il Re della Macchina[3]

ADDRESS: Mrs. Gisborne. PUBLISHED: Jones, "New Letters," pp. 43–44; *SC*, VI, #482. TEXT: MS., Pforzheimer Library.

1. At the top of this letter John Gisborne wrote: "C. di Malta / June 1818." The only Friday in June that the Shelleys were at Leghorn was 5 June. On Thursday, 11 June, they departed for the Bagni di Lucca.

2. On 5 June the Shelleys walked to Mrs. Partridge's with the Gisbornes, Claire Clairmont, and Henry Reveley; a Mr. Bilby called (MWS Journal; see also 13 May 1818; and 17 August 1818).

3. A playful allusion to Henry Reveley as "The King of the Machine."

To [Sir Walter Scott][1] Bagni di Lucca[2] 14 June—1818

Sir

Having received from the publisher of Frankenstein the notice taken of that work in Blackwood's magasine, and intelligence at the same time that it was to your kindness that I owed this favourable notice I hasten to return my acknowledgements and thanks, and at the same time to express the pleasure I receive from approbation of so high a value as yours.

Mr Shelley soon after its publication took the liberty of sending you a copy[3] but as both he and I thought in a manner which would prevent you from supposing that he was the author we were surprised therefore to see him mentioned in the notice as the probable author,[4]—I am anxious to prevent your continuing in the mistake of supposing Mr Shelley guilty of a juvenile attempt of mine; to which—from its being written at an early age, I abstained from putting my name—and from respect to those persons from whom I bear it. I have therefore kept it concealed except from a few friends.

I beg you will pardon the intrusion of this explanation—

Your obliged &c &c
Mary Wollst^ft^ Shelley.

PUBLISHED: Irving Massey, "Mary Shelley, Walter Scott, and 'Maga,'" *Notes and Queries*, 207 (November 1962): 420–21. TEXT: MS., National Library of Scotland.

1. *Frankenstein* was very favorably reviewed by Sir Walter Scott in *Blackwood's Edinburgh Magazine* 2 (March 1818): 613–20. For a discussion of the contemporary reviews of *Frankenstein*, most of which were favorable, see Grylls, *Mary*

Shelley, pp. 315–19. For a listing of contemporary reviews, see Lyles, *MWS Bibliography*.

2. On 11 June the Shelley party had removed to Casa Bertini at the Bagni di Lucca.

3. *PBS Letters*, #443.

4. See *SC*, V, 471–73.

To Maria Gisborne Casa Bertini Bagni di Lucca June 15—1818

My dear Madam

It is strange after having been in the habit of visiting you daily, now for so many days to have no communication with you; and after having been accustomed for a month to the tumult of Via Grande to come to this quiet scene, where we hear no sound except the rushing of the river in the valley below—While at Livorno I hardly heard the noise, but when I came here I felt the silence as a return to something very delightful from which I had been long absent. We live here in the midst of a beautiful scene and I wish that I had the imagination and expressions of {a} poet to describe it as it deserves and to fill you all with an ardent desire to visit it—We are surrounded by mountains covered with thick chestnut woods—they are peaked and picturesque and sometimes you see peeping above them the bare summit of a distant Appenine{.} vines a{re} cultivated on the foot of the mountains—The walks in the woods are delightful; for I like nothing so much as to be surrounded by the foliage of trees only peeping now and then through the leafy screen on the scene about me—You can either walk by the side of the river on [*or*] on commodious paths cut in the mountains, & for ramblers the woods are intersected with narrow paths in every direction—our house is small but commodious and exceedingly clean for it has just been painted and the furniture is quite new—we have a small garden and at the end of it is an arbour of laurel trees so thick that the sun does not penetrate it—Nor has my prediction followed us that we should every where find it cold—although not hot the weather has been very pleasant—we see the fire flies in an evening—somewhat dimmed by the brightness of the moon—

And now I will say a few words of our domestic economy—<u>albeit</u> I am afraid the subject has tired you out of your wits more than once—Signor Chiappa[1] we found perfectly useless—he would talk of nothing but himself and recommended a person to cook our dinner for us at 3 pauls a day—So, as it is, Paolo[2] (whom we found exceedingly useful) cooks and manages for us, and a woman comes at 1 paul a day to do the dirty work—we live very comfortably and if Paolo did not cheat us he would be a servant worth a treasure for he does everything cleanlily & exactly without teizing us in any way—So we lead here a very quiet pleasant life—reading our Canto of Ariosto[3]—and walking in the evening am[ong] these delightful woods—we have but one wish—you know what that is but you take no pity on us, and exile us from your presence so long—that I quite long to see you again—Now we see no one—the Signor Chi{a}ppa is a stupid fellow and the Casino is not open that I know of—at least it is not at all frequented, when it is every kind of amusement goes on there particularly dancing which is divided into four parts—English & french country dances; quadrilles; walzes; & Italian dances, these take place twice a week on which evenings the ladies dress but on others they go merely in a walking dress.

We have found among our books a volume of poems of Lord Byrons which you have not seen—some of them I think you will like—but this will be a novelty to recommend us on our return—I begin to be very much delighted with ariosto the beginning of the nineteenth canto is particularly beautiful—It is the wounding [*p. 1, cross-written*] of Medoro and his being relieved by Angelica who for a wonder shews herself in the light of {a} sympathizing and amiable person

Mr Shelley is tolerably well he desires to be most kindly rememembered to you & Mr Gisborne not forgetting the Macchinista[4] who although he has seen very little of him is {a} favourite of his from certain phisiognomonical reasons—you will also have the kindness to present my best remembrances both to him and M^r G— [*Gisborne*] Clare desires to be remembered—But we all of us repine that we must send such messages and that you are not all here when I could express to {you} by words how much I am

My dear Mrs Gisborne
Most obliged & Affectionately yours
Mary Wollstonecraft Shelley

Has Mr Reveley made a Calleidoscope? and do you find as much pleasure as the Londone{r}s in looking through it?[5]

ADDRESS: Alla Signora / Signora Gisborne / 1091 Via Genesi / Fuore della porta di Capucini / Livorno. POSTMARKS: (1) LUCCA; (2) 19 GIUGNO. ENDORSED: Baths of Lucca / 15 June / Recd 19 Do / Ans 21st Do. PUBLISHED: Jones, #52. TEXT: MS., Bodleian Library (MS., Shelley, c. 1, ff. 264–65).

1. G. B. del Chiappa, owner of Casa Bertini (Dowden, *Shelley*, II, 211).

2. Paolo Foggi, the Shelleys' Italian servant, who later formed an illicit relationship with Elise, the Swiss nursemaid. In Naples, towards the end of 1818, the Shelleys discovered that Elise was pregnant and arranged for the marriage of Foggi and Elise prior to dismissing them sometime between the end of December 1818 and 22 January 1819 (22 January 1819; *PBS Letters*, #491; White, *Shelley*, II, 67). Foggi subsequently spread scandalous rumors concerning Shelley and Claire Clairmont and tried to blackmail Shelley (18 June 1820; [10 August 1821] to Shelley; 10 August 1821 to Isabella Hoppner).

3. Mary Shelley read *Orlando Furioso* from 30 May through 19 July. On 15 June she read Canto 19 (*MWS Journal*).

4. "Engineer," that is, Henry Reveley.

5. On 21 June Maria Gisborne responded: "Kaleidoscopism is at this moment with us in a most triumphant state . . . but as we are not eagle eyed our initiation into this delightful science has occasioned us many a headache" (Abinger MS.; *S&M*, I, 289). Henry Reveley had built a kaleidoscope from a description sent to the Shelleys by Hogg (*SC*, VI, 764, 766–67).

TO MARIA GISBORNE Bagni di Lucca 2 July—1818

My dear Madam

An Earthquake for the Steam Engine and thus to swallow up Mr Reeveley's whole territory is somewhat a harsh remedy yet I would wish for one that could transport it (if you will not come without it) to these Bagni where I am sure you would be enchanted with every thing except the English that are crowded here to the almost entire exclusion {of} Italians; so that I think it would be easier to have a conversazione of Italians in England than here in their native country—We see none but English, we hear nothing but English spoken—The walks are filled with English Nurserymaids, a kind of aninal [*animal*] I by no means like, & dashing staring Englishwomen, who surprise the Italians who always are carried about in Sedan Chairs, by riding on horseback—For us we generally walk Except last Teusday, When Shelley and I took a long ride to il prato fiorito; a flowery meadow on the top of one of the neighbouring Appenines—We rode among chestnut woods hearing the noisy cicala, and there was nothing disagreable in it except the steepness of the ascent—The woods about here are in every way delightful especially when they are plain with grassy walks through them—they are filled with sweet singing birds and not long ago we heard a Cukcoo—Mr Shelley wishes to go with me to Monte Pelerino[1]—the highest of the Appenines at the top of which there is a shrine—It is distant about 22 miles—Can it be there that the Italian palates were deceived by unwholesome food (to talk of that hideous transaction in their own cool way)—? and would you think it advisable for us to make this pilgrimage?—we must go on horseback and sleep in one of the houses on the mountain.

I have had a letter from my father—he does not appear very well in health but I hope the summer will restore him—He says in his letter—"I was extremely gratified by your account of Mrs Gisborne. I have not seen her, I believe, these twenty years; not, I think, since she was Mrs Gisborne. And yet by your description she is still a delightful woman. How inexpressibly pleasing it is to call be back the recollection of years long past, and especially when the recollection belongs to a person in whom one deeply interrested oneself, as I did in Mrs Reveley! I can hardly hope for so great a pleasure, as it would be to me to see her again."

We are now in the 36th Canto of Ariosto How very entertaining it is, and how exceedingly beautiful are many of the stories—Yet I cannot think him so great {a} poet as Spenser although as I said before a much better story teller [ ] I wonder if I shall like Tasso better!

Shelley intends to write in a day or two and in the mean time both Clare and he desire to be kindly remembered to you all

My dear Mrs Gisborne
Yours Affectionately & obliged
Mary W. Shelley

A friend in England[2] asks us if a family of 3 persons can live at Pisa with 4 servants—an excellent storehouse furnished, a horse & chaise—a garden of 2 acres—denying themselves no comforts required by a respectable family—for less than £500 per annumm—I say no—What do you say?

You know letters may come directed to Miss Clairmont[3]

ADDRESS: Alla Signora / Signora Gisborne / 1091 Via Genesi / Fuore della porta di Capucini / Livorno. POSTMARKS: (1) LUCCA; (2) 8 LUGLIO. ENDORSED: 2nd July 1818. PUBLISHED: Jones, #53. TEXT: MS., Bodleian Library (MS., Shelley, c. 1, ff. 266–67).

1. On 12 and 13 August 1820 Shelley walked to a shrine on the top of Monte San Pellegrino, which inspired him to write *The Witch of Atlas* (*MWS Journal*; Shelley, *Poetry and Prose*, p. 347).

2. Almost certainly Horace Smith (*SC*, VI, 562).

3. A request that the Gisbornes ask at the post office for Claire Clairmont's mail, as well as for theirs, and forward it on.

To Maria Gisborne — Bagni di Lucca 26 July 1818

My Dear Madam

We are exceedingly obliged to you for the trouble you have taken in sending our letters,[1] which have been very welcome to us; containing among other things, public news, which at least borders on good. All English heads in England are filled with the general Election, which appears to be turning out more favourably for the free party than was expected. Of all the eight members for the Metropolis, not one is ministerial—But you have forgotten these things, although you will, I daresay, feel indignant at what we hear about that class, of which Coleridge is, if not actively engaged, yet more than openly appears, since he writes for the most detestable of all papers—the Courier—One of our friends says—Brougham is standing for Westmoreland against the Lowthers—Wordsworth has published an address to the freeholders, in which he says, "they ought not to choose so poor a man as Brougham—riches being the only guarantee of political integrity—he goes further than this, and actually asserts, that the Commons ought to be chosen by the Peers—"[2]

We have had a letter from my father, who appears much better in health than when he wrote last—he is, he says, over head and ears in an answer to Malthus,[3] a work which will be the more interesting, since Malthus is the work from which all the rich have, ever since it has been written, borrowed excuses and palliations for their luxury and hard-heartedness—

The weather here is hot, so hot, that it has induced us to engage our house for another month, as we suppose that Florence will be intolerable in August—We live here seeing no one reading for ever almost—I do not much like the Casino, since there are no persons that we know there; it would otherwise be pleasant enough. Our only amusement is a ride, which Shelley and I often take, in the cool of the evening. I ought to tell you that no English go to the Casino; partly because the festa di ballo is is always on a Sunday—There are several rich English here—Lord Kensington—Admiral Fremantle &c—the latter are very gay, and have Lord and Lady Berghersh on a visit at their house, and give balls &c. The princess Paolina is here—she is handsome, but I do not like in her that she associates with the high ministerial English—the people, who especially dethroned her brother[4] She goes to their balls, and either has, or is to have a conversazione principally for them—

We have finished Ariosto, and are now reading the Aminta of Tasso—a sweet pastoral! I think I shall like Tasso better than Ariosto, for although I bestow little value on correctness by itself, I like it united to the genius and spirit of poetry—and how Ariosto runs on sometimes for stanza with—nothing!

How do you like Schlegel?[5] I suppose you have finished it—how much finer a view does he take of the tragic poets than that Frenchman Barthelemy,[6] who, if he could without an anachronism in his work, would, I doubt not, have preferred Racine to Sophocles—

Mr Shelley is tolerably well—Clare has been very unwell, but is now better—They both desire to be remembered to you, all with kindness—My Dear Mrs Gisborne

Your's obliged and truly
M.WS.

PUBLISHED: Jones, "New Letters," pp. 44–46. TEXT: John Gisborne Notebook No. 2, Abinger MS., Bodleian Library.

1. Shelley wrote to Godwin, Horace Smith, and Peacock on 26 July, perhaps in response to letters received (*MWS Journal*).

2. Wordsworth's pamphlet *Two Addresses to the Freeholders of Westmoreland* (1818) was part of his active support of the candidacy of Lord William Lowther, who defeated Henry Brougham. Lord Lowther was the eldest son of Wordsworth's patron, the Earl of Lonsdale (Mary Moorman, *William Wordsworth: A Biography*, 2 vols. [Oxford: Clarendon Press, 1957–65], vol. II, *The Later Years, 1803–1850*, pp. 344–56).

3. Godwin's letter of 7 July 1818 begins: "You will I dare say be glad to hear that I am now over head and ears in my Answer to Malthus" (*S&M*, I, 296). Godwin's essay, *Of Population. An Enquiry Concerning the Power of Increase in the Numbers of Mankind, Being an Answer to Mr. Malthus's Essay on that Subject*, was published in 1820 by Longman, Hurst, Rees, Orme, and Brown.

4. Pauline Bonaparte Leclerc Borghese (1780–1825), the sister of Napoleon, had married the Italian Prince Camillo Borghese in 1803.

5. In May Shelley had loaned the Gisbornes his copy of A. W. Schlegel's *Lectures on Dramatic Art and Literature* (*PBS Letters*, #467), which he had read in March (MWS Journal, 16–21 March 1818).

6. On 26 July the Shelleys completed their readings of Abbé J. J. Barthélemy's *Voyage du Jeune Anacharsis en Grèce vers le milieu du quatrième siècle avant l'ère vulgaire* (Paris, 1817) (*MWS Journal*).

To Maria Gisborne Bagni di Lucca Agust 17—1818

My dear Madam

It gave me great pleasure to receive your letter after so long a silence, when I had begun to conjecture a thousand reasons for it and among others illness;—in which I was half right.—Indeed I am much concerned to hear of Mr Reveley's attack, and sincerely hope that nothing will retard his speedy recovery. His illness gives me a slight hope that you might now be induced to come to the baths if it were even to try the effect of the hot baths. You would find the weather cool for we already feel in this part of the world that the year is declining by the cold mornings and evenings—I have another selfish reason to wish that you would come which I have a great mind not to mention, yet I will not omit it as it might induce you—Shelley and Clare are gone (they went today) to Venise on important business[1] and I am left to take care of the house—now if all of you or any of you would come and cheer my solitude it would be exceedingly kind—I dare say you would find many of your friends here—Among the rest there is the Signora Felichi whom I believe you knew at Pisa.

Shelley & I have ridden almost every evening Clare did the same at first but she has been unlucky and once fell from her horse and hurt her knee so as to knock her up for some time. It is the fashion here among all the English to ride on horseback; and it is very pleasant on these fine evenings; when we set out at sunset and are lighted home by Venus, Jupiter and Diana—three of the greatest deities—who kindly lend us their light after the sleepy Apollo is gone to bed—The road which we frequent is raised somewhat above and overlooks the river affording some very fine points of view among these woody mountains.

Still we know no one; we speak to one or two people at the Casino and that is all—We live in our studious way going on with Tasso whom I like—but who, now I have read more than half his poem I do not know that I like so well as Ariosto.—Shelley translated the Symposium in ten days[2] (an anecdote for Mr Bilby)[3] It is a most beautiful piece of writing,—I think you will be delighted with it—It is true that in many particulars it shocks our present manners, but no one can be a reader of the works of antiquity unless they can transport themselves from these to other times and judge not by our but by their morality

Shelley is tolerably well in in health—the hot weather has done him good—Clare too I think is better—I must just mention that one of our friends[4] has sent us a parcel directed to you—by ship I believe—but he does not expressly mention how.

We have been in high debate nor have we come to any conclusion—concerning the land or sea journey to Naples—We have been thinking that when we want to go that although the equinox will be past yet the ecquinoctial winds will hardly have spent themselves—and I cannot express to you how I fear a storm at sea with two such young children as William and Clara—Do you know the periods when the Mediterranean is troubled and when the Wintry Halcyon days come—However it may be we shall certainly see you before we proceed southward

We have been reading Eustace's tour through Italy[5]—I do not wonder the Italians reprinted it—among other select specimens of his way of thin[king] he says that the Romans did not derive their arts and learning from the Greeks—That the Italian ladies are chaste and the Lazzeeroni[6] honest and industrious—And that as to assassination and highway robbery in Italy it is all a calumny—no such things were ever heard of—Italy was the garden of Eden and all the Italians Adams and Eves untill the Blasts of Hell (i.e. the French for by that polite name he designates them) came. By the bye an Italian servant stabbed an English one here—it was thought dangerously at first but the man is doing better.

I have scribbled a long letter and I dare say you have long wished to be at the end of it—Well now you are—So my dear Mrs Gisborne with best remembrances to Mess. G. [*Gisborne*] and R [*Reveley*]

Yours obliged and affectionately
MaryWShelley

If your heart should be moved to come and visit me be so kind as to encrease Mr Dunn's[7] debt and bring a few pounds of tea with you

ADDRESS: Alla Signora / La Signora Gisborne / 1091 Via Genesi / Fuore della porta di Capucini / Livorno. POSTMARKS: (1) LUCCA; (2) 21 AGO[STO]. ENDORSED: Recd. 22 Aug / Ans. PUBLISHED: Jones, #54. TEXT: MS., Bodleian Library (MS., Shelley, c. 1, ff. 268–69).

1. Claire Clairmont had received letters from Elise on 14 and 16 August informing her that Allegra was no longer at Byron's house. Alarmed and anxious to see Allegra, Claire Clairmont set out for Venice on 17 August, accompanied by Shelley, who intended to convince Byron to allow Claire Clairmont to spend some time with her daughter (Dowden, *Shelley*, II, 221).

2. From 9 to 17 July. He corrected it on 20 July, at which time Mary Shelley began transcribing it (*MWS Journal*; *PBS Letters*, #475).

3. One of the difficulties in identifying Mr. Bilby, who was a friend of the Gisbornes and may have been "the physician" (see [5 June 1818]), has been the variant spelling of his name as *Beilby* in *S&M*, *MWS Journal*, and *MWS Letters*. It should be pointed out that in the manuscript of the Journal (see *SC*, VI, 599–600) and the manuscripts of Mary Shelley's letters the name is consistently spelled *Bilby*.

4. Thomas Love Peacock (*PBS Letters*, #472, n. 1).

5. John Chetwode Eustace, *A Tour through Italy, Exhibiting a View of Its Scenery, Etc.*, 3 vols. (London, 1813).

6. Lazzaroni, a name given by the Spaniards to the lower classes in Naples.

7. Henry Dunn (1776–1867), an Englishman, operated a British general store at Leghorn (*MWS Letters*, I, 57, no. 6).

TO MARIA GISBORNE — Este [c. 13] September—1818[1]

My dear Mrs Gisborne

I hasten to write to you to say that we have arrived safe and yet I can hardly call it safe since the fatigue has given my poor <u>Ca</u> an attack of dysentery and although she is now some what recovered from that disorder she is still in a frightful state of weakness and fever as [*and*] is reduced to be so thin in this short time that you would hardly know her again[2]—the physician of Este is a stupid fellow but there is one come from Padua & who appears clever—so I hope under his care she will soon get well, although we are still in great anxiety concerning her

I found Mr Shelley very anxious for our non arrival for besides other delays we were detained a whole day at Florence for a signature to our passport—The house at Este is exceedingly pleasant with a large garden and quantities of excellent fruit—I have not yet been to Venise and know not when I shall since it depends upon the state of Clara's health—I hope Mr Reveley is quite recovered from his illness—and I am sure the Baths did him a great deal of good—so now I suppose all your talk is how you will get to England—Shelley agrees with me that you could live very well for your £200 per an. in Marlow or some such town, and I am sure you would be much happier than in Italy—how all the English dislike it—The Hoppners[3] speak with the greatest acrimony of the Italians & Mr Hoppner says that he was actually driven from Italian society by the young men continually asking him for money—everything is saleable in Venise—even the wives of the gentry if you will pay well—It appears indeed a most frightful system of society

Well—when shall we see you again soon I dare say—I am so much hurried that you will be kind enought to excuse the abruptness of this letter—I will write soon again and in the mean time write to me—Shelley & Clare desire the kindest rememembrances—

My dear Mrs Gisborne

Affectionately yours,
MaryWS.

Casa Capucini
Este
September—1818—
send our letters—to this direction

ADDRESS: Alla Signora / La Signora Gisborne / Via Genesi / Fuore della Porta di Capucini / Livorno. POSTMARKS: (1) ESTE; (2) 18 SETTEMBRE. ENDORSED: Recd. 19th. Sept / Ansd. 20 Nov. PUBLISHED: Jones, #55. TEXT: MS., Bodleian Library (MS., Shelley, c. 1, ff. 270–71).

1. On 23 August Shelley had written Mary Shelley a lengthy letter explaining that Byron was willing to allow Claire Clairmont to have an extended visit with Allegra and would lend I Capuccini, his villa at Este, to the Shelleys and Claire Clairmont for that purpose. In response to Shelley's hasty summons, Mary Shelley packed their belongings and, together with the two children, Paolo Foggi, and Milly Shields, left on 31 August for Este, arriving there on 5 September (*MWS Journal*).

Mary Shelley's description in this letter of her daughter Clara's illness agrees with Shelley's letter dated 13 September, which suggests that they wrote on or about the same day.

2. On 24 September the Shelleys grew greatly alarmed at Clara's condition and

carried her to Venice for medical attention. Mary Shelley's Journal entry of 24 September reads: "We go to Venise with my poor Clara who dies the moment we get there—"

3. Richard Belgrave Hoppner (1786–1872) and his Swiss-born wife Isabella Hoppner (née May). Hoppner had been the English Consul General at Venice since 1814. Shelley had met the Hoppners when he and Claire Clairmont went to see Allegra, who, either at the Hoppners' suggestion or at Byron's request, was staying with them (*PBS Letters*, #479; Marchand, *Byron*, II, 747).

To Lord Byron

Este—Oct. 3—1818

I take advantage of an opportunity of a person going to Venise to send you Mazeppa and your ode with I hope not many errors and those partly from my not being able to decypher your M.S.[1]

It will give me great pleasure (if the Fornaretta will permit)[2] if you will send me your Don Juan[3] by the bearer—you may trust him as we often employ him—At any rate write a line to say that you have received this safe as I do not like to send your M.S. untill I know that my copy is in your hands—You will see by my copying Mazeppa so quickly that there is more of pleasure than labour in my task. MWS Allegra is perfectly well[4]

PUBLISHED: Jones, #56. TEXT: MS., John Murray.

1. Mary Shelley transcribed Byron's *Mazeppa* and *Ode on Venice* from 1 through 4 October (*MWS Journal*; Marchand, *Byron*, II, 754).

2. Margarita Cogni, one of Byron's mistresses at Venice, called La Fornarina because she was a baker's wife. Mary Shelley may be alluding to the fact that La Fornarina read and sometimes kept letters to Byron from other women (Byron, *Letters and Journals*, VI, 195).

3. Mary Shelley is perhaps offering to transcribe the first canto of *Don Juan*, which Byron had recently completed. Byron may have expressed to her what he wrote on 19 September to Thomas Moore about transcribing the canto: "But the bore of copying it out is intolerable; and if I had an amanuensis he would be of no use, as my handwriting is so difficult to decipher" (Byron, *Letters and Journals*, VI, 68). After Shelley's death, Byron paid Mary Shelley to copy some of his new cantos (Marchand, *Byron*, III, 1042).

4. The Shelleys returned Allegra to Byron on 29 October.

To Maria Gisborne

Este. Nov. 2nd 1818

My Dear Mrs Gisborne

I have not heard from you since we parted[1]—but I hope that nothing has occasioned this, except your dislike of letter writing—Several events have occurred to us since then, and the principal one, the death of my little Clara—I wrote to tell you of her illness, and the dreadful state of weakness that succeeded to it—In this state she began to cut all her teeth at once—pined a few weeks, and died—

Soon after this, William grew rather ill, and as we were now soon frightened, and there is no good doctor at Este, Shelley and I took him to Venice, where we staid about a fortnight.[2] It is a pleasant town to visit—it's appearance is so new and strange: but the want of walks and variety must render it disagreeable for a continuous residence—The Hoppners[3] find it so—they have lived between four and five years here, and are heartily sick of it. We liked almost every thing,—however I must here except three things, as the disagreements of the city—1st its inhabitants—2nd its streets to walk in—3rd its canals at low water. These are tolerable deductions, and yet there is enough to like without liking these. The inhabitants I dislike, because they are some of the worst specimens of Italians, and to you, who have lived so long in the country, and know their characteristics, this is saying every thing. The streets I dislike because they are narrow and dirty, and above all because they carry zucche[4] about to sell, the sight of which always makes me sick. and I dislike the canals at low water, because they are never cleaned, and the horrid smell makes my head ache, and so now, I daresay, you will think me reasonable enough in all my dislikes—

Well; tomorrow, god permitting, we set out for Naples[5]—but having been forced to delay our journey so long, we must give up the hope of seeing you until next June, when we think of coming north again. We go to Naples by Rimini and Ancona—Will you therefore be so kind as to direct our letters to (Ferma in Posta)[6] Napoli. Write to us also, and tell me if you have any further projects for returning to England. I have been speaking to Shelley, and he says that there is a very heavy tax upon books entering England—he thinks as much as 9d per bk.

I will write to you again from Naples—I need not say, if you could send us any introductions for that place, you would infinitely oblige us. Shelley and Clare desire to be kindly remembered.

I hope Mr Reveley is entirely recovered, and that you and Mr G. [*Gisborne*] are in good health. What news of the Steam Engine? Mr Webb has received 200 Cr. on Shelley's account,[7] I enclose an order for you to receive it. You will be so kind as to pay yourselves and Mr Dunn, and to keep the rest for more letters and parcels. Have you received our's sent so long ago? The name of the ship it is sent by is—We have actually lost the letter in which it is mentioned. We think it was either the Sisters, or the Northumberland; and the Captain's name Nainor—Adieu—

Your's affectionately and
Sincerely
M.WS.

PUBLISHED: Jones, "New Letters," pp. 46–47. TEXT: John Gisborne Notebook No. 2, Abinger MS., Bodleian Library.

1. When Mary Shelley went to join Shelley and Claire Clairmont at Este on 31 August, she was accompanied as far as Lucca by Maria Gisborne, who had been visiting her at the Bagni di Lucca (*MWS Journal*).

2. From 12 to 31 October. Shelley returned to Este from 24 to 29 October to take Allegra back to Venice (*MWS Journal*).

3. When Clara died, the Hoppners showed great kindness to the Shelleys (*PBS*

Letters, #482). During the Shelleys' stay in Venice they were almost daily in the Hoppners' company (*MWS Journal*).

4. Gourds.

5. They left Este on 5 November, stopping at Bologna from 8 to 10 November and at Rome from 20 through 27 November. Shelley left Rome on 27 November; the others followed the next day. On 1 December Mary Shelley recorded: "A long and fatiguing journey. We arrived at Naples about 6 o'clock" (*MWS Journal*).

6. Meaning "Hold at Post Office."

7. Webb & Co. was a banking firm at Leghorn (*SC*, VI, 942–43).

SHELLEY TO THOMAS LOVE PEACOCK[1]

Bologna.
[10 November 1818]

[*Shelley's letter is in Mary Shelley's hand. She added this explanatory note at the top of page 1*] I write out Shelley's letter because he has written so wide that it takes up too much room—Take care of these letters because I have no copies & I wish to transcribe them when I return to England. [*Postscript by Mary Shelley, p. 4*] send a pair of pointed scissars in your next parcel & a penknife

ADDRESS: Thomas L. Peacock Esq / Great Marlow / Bucks / Inghilterra Angleterre. POSTMARKS: (1) FPO / DE. 8 / 1818; (2) C / DE / 8 / [1]818. PUBLISHED: Jones, #57. TEXT: MS., Bodleian Library (MS., Shelley, c. 1, ff. 259–60).

1. For Shelley's letter, see *PBS Letters*, #486. Shelley's four-page letter, cross-written on all four sheets, was copied by Mary Shelley in a small hand in order to avoid cross-writing. Shelley then decided to add to the letter and found it necessary to again cross-write. Mary Shelley's transcription varies in some details from Shelley's original (Bodleian Library [MS., Shelley, c. 1, ff. 253–54]).

SHELLEY TO THOMAS LOVE PEACOCK[1]

Rome. [20] Nov. 1818[2]

[*Postscript by Mary Shelley, p. 4*] be so kind as to send 12—Brookman & Langdon pencils 3BB—3B—3F—3HF—so marked{.} untill the end of February—you had better direct your letters ferma in posta Napoli—after that time we return to Rome

ADDRESS: T. L. Peacock Esq / Great Marlow / Bucks / Inghilterra / Angleterre. POSTMARKS: (1) FPO / DE. 12 / 1818; (2) DE / 12 / 1818. PUBLISHED: Jones, #58. TEXT: MS., Bodleian Library (MS., Shelley, c. 1, ff. 255–56).

1. *PBS Letters*, #487.

2. The Shelleys reached Rome on 20 November. On 27 November Shelley left to look for lodgings in Naples. Mary Shelley, Claire Clairmont, William, and their servants departed for Naples on 28 November (*MWS Journal*).

TO MARIA GISBORNE

Naples. [c. 3] Dec 1818[1]

My dear Mrs. Gisborne

I hasten to answer your kind letter as soon as we are a little recovered from the fatigue of our long journey although I still feel wearied and overcome by it—so you must expect a very stupid letter. We set out from Este the day after I wrote to you—we remained one day at Ferrara & two at Bologna looking at the memorials preserved of Tasso and Ariosto in the former town and at the most exquisite pictures in the latter—Afterwards we proceeded along the coast Road by Rimini Fano Fossombrone &c—We saw the divine ⟨acquaduct⟩ waterfall of Terni—And arrived safely at Rome. We performed this journey with our own horses with Paolo to drive us which we found a very œconomical & a very disagreable way so we shall not attempt it again—To you who have seen Rome I need not say how enchanted we were with the first view of Rome and its antiquities—one draw back they have at present which I hope will be fully compensated for in the future—The ruins are filled with galley slaves at work—They are propping the Coliseum & making very deep excavations in the forum. We remained a week at Rome and our fears for the journey to Naples were entirely removed they said there that there had not been a robbery on the road for 8 months—This we found afterwards to be an exageration but it tranquillized us so much that Shelley went on first to secure us lodgings and we followed a day or two after—We found the road guarded and the only part of the road where there was any talk of fear was between Terracina and Fondi where it was not thought advisable that we should set out from the former place before daylight—Shelley travelled with a Lombard merchant & a Neapolitan priest—he remained only two nights {on} the road—and he went veterino,[2] so you may guess he had to travel early & late—The priest—a great strong muscular fellow was almost in convulsions with fear—to travel before daylight along the Pomptine Marshes—There was talk of two bishops murdered & that touched him nearly—The Robbers spare foreigners but never Neapolitan men if they are young & strong so he was the worst off of the party—the Merchant did not feel very comfortable & they were both surprised at Shelley's quietness—That quiet was disturbed however between Capua & Naples by an assassination committed in broad daylight before their eyes—{a} young man ran out of a shop on the road followed by a woman armed with a great stick & a man with a great knife—the man overtook him & stabbed him in the nape of the neck so that he fell down instantly stone dead—The fearful priest laughed heartily at Shelley's horror on the occasion—

Well we are now settled in comfortable lodgings which S. took for 3 louis a week opposite the Royal gardens[3]—you no doubt remember the situation—we have a full view of the bay from our windows—so I think we are well off—As yet we have seen nothing but we shall soon make some excu{r}sions in the environs—

I will write soon again but the journey has quite knocked me up—Be so kind as to send our parcel as soon as you can directed to the care of M. Falconet Bankers—Naples

Use our little purse in paying for our letters & parcels—William is very well—S. & Clare send their kindest remembrances—Excuse this stupid scrawl

Ever yours affectionately
Mary W. Shelley

Shelley left his card at the door of Sig. Castellani but he has not returned his call.

ADDRESS: Alla Signora / La Signora Gisborne / Via Genesi / Fuore della Porta dei Capucini / Livorno. POSTMARKS: (1) NAP 1818 / [ ] DIC; (2) 18 DICEMBRE. ENDORSED: Naples Dec. 1818 / recd 26 Dec / Ans 15th Jany. PUBLISHED: Jones, #59. TEXT: MS., Bodleian Library (MS., Shelley, c. 1, ff. 272–73).

1. They arrived at Naples at about 6:00 P.M. on 1 December. Mary Shelley's statements in this letter that she writes as soon as they "are a little recovered" from travel fatigue but while they have yet "seen nothing" suggests that the letter was written before 5 December, when they began their sightseeing excursions with a visit to a museum and the theater (MWS Journal).

2. A *vetturino* was the owner of a coach who contracted to take passengers a certain distance and provide them with food and shelter, all for a fixed price (see letters dated 23 July [1823] through 3–5 August [1823] for Mary Shelley's description of travel by *vetturino*).

3. Their lodgings were at 250 Riviera di Chiaia.

SHELLEY TO THOMAS LOVE PEACOCK[1]

Naples.
[17–19] December 1818[2]

[*Postscript by Mary Shelley*] You had better direct all your letters to Livorno & not here—and when you send another parcel I wish you would contrive to get 2 hairbrushes & a small tooth comb from Florriste hairdresser—Germain St. behind St. James Church—

ADDRESS: T. Peacock Esqr / Great Marlow / Bucks, Inghilterra / Angleterre. POSTMARKS: (1) NAP. 1818 / 22 DIC; (2) FPO / JA. 9 / 1819; (3) C / JA / 9 / [1]819. PUBLISHED: Jones, #61. TEXT: MS., Bodleian Library (MS., Shelley, c. 1, ff. 257–59).

1. *PBS Letters*, #488.

2. The last excursions Shelley described in his lengthy letter took place between 16 and 19 December. On 19 December Mary Shelley recorded in her journal that Shelley had written letters that day.

SHELLEY TO LEIGH HUNT[1]

Naples. [?20] Dec. 1818

[*By Mary Shelley, p. 1, top*] Ollier has orders to pay Marianne £5—I owe her part of it & with the other I wish her to pay £1—to the taylor who made my habit if he calls for it—his charge will be more but do not pay it him

ADDRESS: Leigh Hunt Esq / 8 York Buildings—New Road / London / Angleterre / Inghilterra. POSTMARKS: NAP 1818 / 22 DIC; (2) FPO / JA. 9 / 1819. PUBLISHED: Jones, #60. TEXT: MS., Berg Collection, New York Public Library.

1. *PBS Letters*, #489.

To Maria Gisborne Naples. 22nd Jany 1819

My Dear Mrs Gisborne

We received your Bill of Lading last night, and we hope soon to have the box—It will be a great amusement to us, although I read almost all the books that it contains, at Venice. Another parcel is on its way, but we have not yet heard by what ship it sails.

Naples is, I can easily conceive, to most people, a delightful residence—We live on the Chiaiia, just opposite the royal gardens, so that we have a full view of the lovely bay, and can hear the dashing of the waves of the sea. We have been to Vesuvius, Herculaneum, Pompeii, the Studii,[1] so that you may guess, we have enjoyed ourselves somewhat here; especially since Shelley, partly through the prescriptions of our English surgeon,[2] and partly by riding on horseback, enjoys better health than he ever did before during the winter season; and has some hopes of an entire cure. Yet we have been dreadfully teized, and that has, in some degree, taken away from our gusto for this place, and besides, I long to return to Rome, which city I like better than any I was ever in.

We are very studious here, and we are all reading "Sismondi's Histoire des Republiques Italiennes du moyen âge,"[3] which since we have visited many of the towns, the history of which he treats of, is exceedingly interesting. I have been reading also Virgil's Georgics, which is, in many respects, the most beautiful poem I ever read—He wrote it at Baiæ; and sitting at the window, looking almost at the same scene that he did—reading about manners little changed since his days, has made me enjoy his poem, more, I think, than I ever did any other.

I should think that you must find Livorno very dull—I, although continually seeing novelties, begin to get home-sick. The Italians are so very disagreeable, and you live in the same kind of solitude that we do—There is no life here—They seem to act as if they had all died fifty years ago, and now went about their work like the ghostly sailors of Coleridge's enchanted ship[4]—except indeed when they cheat. Yet no doubt, there would be many things to teize one in England, and I remember when I set my foot on the shore at Calais, I seemed to break the thread of my annoyances. but I find care to be the thing that Horace describes it to be[5]—and yet mine came from outward circumstances in a great part, and not from my self. The reports, you mention, have nothing to do with these—I seldom suffer them to torment me.[6] When we see you again, we can talk them over, if you have any curiosity on the subject—but it was a kind of treat when we came to Italy to be acquainted with friends who knew nothing of us, as it were, in a public light—and that kept me silent.

You see I am not in very good spirits today—how can one be, when the scirocco blows, especially as I am made stiff by riding a very pretty, but very hard gallopping horse yesterday. We have got rid of our Italian Paolo,[7] after he has made, I fancy, £100—by us. lately he has cheated us through thick and thin.

You ask me news of my father. We have not had a letter from him for above a month. When he wrote last, he said, that he was over head and ears in his answer to Malthus. M^rs^ G—'s [*Godwin's*] health seems to be getting worse daily—

I have several anecdotes to tell you about Lord Byron's particular friend, who is no Colonel.[8] He must bore you dreadfully, I should think—

Have you heard the news from Spain?[9] A plot was discovered at Madrid by the Inquisition, and seven hundred people killed—but the insurgents, to the number of 18,000, have surrounded Madrid—The Queen, who was far advanced in pregnancy, died of fright. The King attempted to escape, and, it is universally believed here, is killed—besides the old King of Spain, who lived here, has died of the gout, and they are very busy in trying to find out how to bury him[10]—Some of their ceremonies are ghastly and laughable at the same time—On account of these misfortunes happening to their relations, the Royal Family have forbidden Carnival to be celebrated.

Shelley and Miss Clairmont desire their kindest remembrances—We shall see you, the good spirit willing, next June—but the devil is getting more and more power in the world every day—I hope however his antagonist will allow you to return to England when we do, so that we shall not lose the Fine Arts, and our friends at the same time—

Ever affectionately your's
M. WS

PUBLISHED: Jones, "New Letters," pp. 48–50. TEXT: John Gisborne Notebook No. 2, Abinger MS., Bodleian Library.

1. These visits were made on 16, 5, 22, and 19 December, respectively (*MWS Journal*).

2. Almost certainly identified as Dr. Roskilly in *SC*, VI, 768.

3. Simonde de Sismondi, *Histoire des republiques italiennes du moyen âge* (Paris, 1808–18).

4. *The Rime of the Ancient Mariner* 5. 329–44.

5. *Odes* 3. 1. 40: "*Post equitem sedent atra Cura*," or "behind the horseman sits black Care," which means that no matter what the speed or distance, one cannot escape from care.

6. Perhaps rumors about the Shelleys' elopement.

7. Elise, recently married to Paolo Foggi and about to give birth, was also dismissed at Naples (see 15 June 1818, n. 2).

8. Robert Finch (1783–1830) was a self-conferred colonel. The Shelleys referred to him as Colonel Calicot, after a fraudulent character in Thomas Moore's *The Fudge Family in Paris, Edited by Thomas Brown, the Younger* (London: Longman, 1818). For an account of Finch as Colonel Calicot, see Elizabeth Nitchie, *The Reverend Colonel Finch* (New York: Columbia University Press, 1940); see also 26 April 1819.

9. A Carbonari conspiracy in Valencia, not Madrid, against the local authorities, headed by General Grancisco Elío, at the beginning of January 1819. The conspiracy was discovered, and Elío ordered thirteen executed and some twenty-two imprisoned. The Inquisition aided in the prosecution and trials (Iris M. Zavala,

Masones, cumuneros y carbonarios [Madrid: Siglo XXI Editores, 1971], p. 27) Queen Isabel of Portugal, second wife of Ferdinand VII of Spain, died at the end of December 1818 from a miscarriage or from illness resulting from a previous miscarriage. The miscarriage has been attributed to poor health rather than to political fears (Miguel Morayta, *Historia general de España*, 9 vols. [Madrid, 1896]; VI, 490). Rumors of Ferdinand's death proved false.

10. Charles IV, King of Spain from 1788 to 1808, died on 19 January 1819, while visiting the court of his brother Ferdinand I, King of the Two Sicilies, at Naples.

SHELLEY TO THOMAS LOVE PEACOCK[1] [Naples 23–24 January 1819]

[*Postscript by Mary Shelley, p. 5, top*] Direct your next letters to Rome—You have not yet sent us the name of the ship which brings the 2nd parcel—Be so kind as to enclose in the next a set {of} letters (counters) for William—and some dozens of mother of pearl buttons—

ADDRESS: Impostata Gen 24 / Thos. L. Peacock Esq. / New Hummums / London / Inghilterra Angleterre. POSTMARKS: (1) NAP. 18[19] / 26 GE; (2) FPO / FE. 16 / 1819. PUBLISHED: Jones, #62. TEXT: MS., Bodleian Library (MS., Shelley, c. 1, ff. 281–83).

1. *PBS Letters*, #491.

TO MARIA GISBORNE

Naples—Friday Feb. 19th
[error for 26 February] 1819[1]

My dear Mrs. Gisborne

We leave Naples sunday next with the regret every one must feel at leaving so lovely a place—We are however going to Rome for 3 months and that idea is the only one that can compensate for quitting this beautiful country—Unfortunately it has happened that illness has confined Mr Shelley a great deal to the house & it is only lately also that we have bought carriage horses so that we leave Naples just as we begin to feel its real value.

We have one consolation that we have visited most of the places to be <u>seen</u> — Pæstum — Pompeii — Herculaneum — Vesuvius — Baiae — Lago d'Agnano—Caccia d'Astroni—Caserta[2] &c—We have had generally favourable weather for our excursions except that to Pæstum & then it was not so bad as it might have been.

And what are you doing all this time—Still at Livorno—It must be a truly dismal place in the Winter—any town in all Italy would be better but it is always the way when from the abstract fear of moving one puts off leaving a place for years (long years) one becomes entangled & can not get out when one would—but for ever Livorno I hope not—we shall be at Florence in the summer—try to come there.

We have received our books & am obliged to you for the trouble you have taken. I fancy anothere box may have arrived by this time although we have not received the name of ship or captain but if Mr G. [*Gisborne*] would some day give a peep in at the custom house I should be infinitely obliged to him.

A sirocco has broken half the glass out {of} our windows so I am very cold—our landlord (un vero birbante)[3] wants to make us pay—is that fair? Adieu I hope you will write to me at Rome

Affectionately yours
Mary W Shelley

Kind Compts to Mr G. and Mr R. [*Reveley*] If you want to read a true picture of Italians read the two last Chapters of Sismondi's history of the republics of the middle ages—they are very well written.

ADDRESS: Alla Signora / La Signora Gisborne / Via Genesi / Fuore della Porta dei Capucini / Livorno. POSTMARKS: (1) NAP. 1819 / 2 MAR; (2) 7 MARZO. PUBLISHED: Jones, #63. TEXT: MS., Bodleian Library (MS., Shelley, c. 1, ff. 331–32).

1. Although Mary Shelley dated this letter 19 February, the correct date must be 26 February, since the Shelleys visited Paestum on 24 February. They left Naples on 28 February ("Sunday next"), and the letter bears a postmark of 2 March.

2. The dates of these visits are provided in *MWS Journal*: 5 December 1818, Herculaneum; 8 December, Baiae; 16 December, Vesuvius; 22 December 1818 and 25 February 1819, Pompeii; 10 February, Caserta; 11 February, Lago d'Agnono; 11 and 14 February, Caccia d'Astroni.

3. "A real rascal."

TO MARIANNE HUNT

Corso—Rome—March 12th 1819[1]

My dear Marianne

You must have thought my silence long between our letters from Lucca & those from Naples—I wrote you a long one from Venice but the laudable love of gain (buscare as they call it—i.e. gaining their livelihood) which burns with zealous heat in the breast of every Italian caused the hotel keeper to charge the postage & to throw the letter in the fire together with several others—I wrote to you soon after the death of my little girl which event I dare say Peacock has mentioned

We quitted Naples about a fortnight ago with great regret the country is the divinest in the world and as spring was just commencing it appeared that we left it when we just began to value it—but Rome repays for every thing—How you would like to be here! We pass our days in viewing the divinest statues in the world—you have seen the casts of most of them but the originals are infinitely superior & besides you continually see some new one—of heavenly beauty that one never saw before—There is an Apollo—it is Shelleys favourite—in the museum of the Capitol he is standing leaning back with his feet crossed—one arm supports a lyre the other hand holds the instrument to play on it and his head is thrown back as he is in the act of being inspired and the expression of his countenance especially the lower part is more beautiful than you can immagine—There are a quantity of female figures in the attitude of the Venus di Medicis generally taller and slimmer than that little plump woman but I dare not say so graceful although I do not see how they can be surpassed—There is a Diana hunting—her dress girded about her—she has just let fly an arrow and watches its success with eagerness & joy. Nothing can be more venerable than the aspects of the statues of the river Gods that abound here—indeed it is a scene of perpetual enchantment to live in this thrice holy city—for add to these statues beautiful pictures and the fragments of magnificent architecture that meet your eye at every turn as you walk from one Street to Another—The other evening we visited the Pantheon by moon light and saw the lovely sight of the moon appearing through the round aperture above & lighting the columns of the Rotunda with its rays—But my letter would never be at an end if I were to try {to} tell a millionth part of the delights of Rome—it has such an effect on me that my past life before I saw it appears a blank & now I begin to live—In the churches you hear the music of heaven & the singing of Angels—

But how are you all this time—my dear girl—And how are all your children? We were very much amused by some Examiners that we received in Peacocks parcel although they were very old—We had Hunts' letter at Naples e[x]pressing all his doubts & difficulties about the proposed j[our]-ney[2]—I am afraid indeed that you will decl[are it] impracticable although you both {would} be infinitely delighted At Naples there is a delightful opera although I do not know how you would like the Italian mode of managing it—They play the same opera for a year together and nothing is listened to of it except the favourite airs—Nothing is heard in Italy now but Rosini & he is no favourite of mine—he has some pretty airs—but they say that when he writes a good thing he goes on copying it in all his succeeding operas for ever and ever—he composes so much that he cannot always be called on for something pretty & new—

Shelley is suffering his cure—he is teazed very much by the means but it certainly does him a great deal of good William speaks more Italian than English—when he sees any thing he likes he cries O Dio che bella—

He has quite forgotten french for Elise has left us—She married a rogue of an Italian servant that we had and turned Catholic—Venise quite spoiled her and she appears in the high road to be as Italian as any of them she has settled at Florence—Milly stays with us & goes on [*p. 1, cross-written*] very well except that during her exile her tender affection for every thing English makes her in love with every Englishman that she meets—

Adieu My dear Marianne—What modelling are you about? In stone or in what materials?—I dare say you wont understand this[3]—Adieu keep yourself as well as you can & do not forget us—

Ever yours affectionately MaryWShelley

Shelley & Clare desire with me a thousand kind loves to Hunt & Bessy—Do you ever see Hogg—how he would scream & beat his sides at all the fine things in Rome—it is well that he is not or he would have broken many a rib in his delights or at least bruised them sorely—

ADDRESS: Mrs Leigh Hunt / 8 York Buildings—New Road / London / Inghilterra / Angleterre. POSTMARKS: (1) FPO / AP. 3 / 1819; (2) 2 o'Clock / AP. 3 / 1819 A.Nn. PUBLISHED: Jones, #64. TEXT: MS., Huntington Library (HM 2741).

1. They arrived at Rome on 5 March and took lodgings for two days at the Villa di Parigi. On 7 March they moved to the Palazzo Verospi on the Corso (White, *Shelley*, II, 84).

2. See *PBS Letters*, #488 and #489, for Shelley's invitations to the Hunts to join them in Italy.

3. A playful query about whether Marianne Hunt was pregnant again. At this time the Hunts had five children—Thornton, John, Mary, Swinburne, and Percy (1817–99)—and were expecting another, born 28 September 1819 (d. post 1863) and named [James] Henry Sylvan Leigh Hunt.

To Leigh Hunt

Rome Teusday—April 6th 1819

My dear Hunt

Your long kind letter was very welcome to us for it told us a little about you after a long ignorance[1]—You seem in good spirits and I hope this is not meer appearance and that every thing is well with you—and that at least you see the end of your difficulties—To tell you the truth both Shelley and I thought that we left you free—and had easy minds upon that score—So you still remember us & wish us back to England—and for your sake I wish that we were there but I fear on our return to be envelloped not only in a bodily but a mental cloudy atmosphere whose simoonic wind sometimes contrives to reach us even in this country of sunshine—so we have determined & very soon we shall not be able to change our determination to stay here another year—In a couple of months we shall return to Naples where circumstances will keep us a long time[2] And we shall be in Rome again at this time next year—You cannot come you say—indeed I always feared that you could not but you would like Italy very much—so if you feel enclined some cold day next autumn take ship and come & find us on the shores of the bay of Naples enjoying a brighter sun than ever peers through the mists of your England

I suppose that Peacock shews you Shelley's letters so I need not describe those objects which delight us so much here—We live surrounded by antiquity ruined and perfect besides seeing the lovely pictures of your favourite Raphael who is the Prince or rather God of painting (I mean a heathen God not a bungling modern divinity) and there are delightful painters besides him Guido would be a great favourite of yours—you would not like Domenichino so well, he is so fond of painting that scapegoat of all that is shrivelled & miserable in human nature Saint Jerolymo but there are some very beautiful pictures of his—And then you know Rome is stuffed with the loveliest statues in the world—a much greater number than one has any idea of untill one sees them and most of them in the most perfect state:—besides our eternal visits to these divine objects—Clare is learning singing—I painting & S is writing a poem[3] so that the belle arte take up all our time—Swiny[4] ought to be here to see the statues—We took our Will-man to the Vatican & he was delighted with the Goats & the Cavalli and dolefully lamented over the man rotto[5] which is his kind of language

Your account of your nephew Henry interested us very much it shews a very generous nature to undertake the cause of the absent especially one so little known as Shelley is to him[6]—Pray convey Shelleys thanks to him and let us know if his health is improved—We must thank you also for your delicasy about meeting the Turnurs[7]—These people are very strange; but I always understood that their distaste to us originated with Alfred Boinville and he it seems is not of the present party—but Turnur is a bad envious man & a slanderer so if we saw them we should at least keep a kind of barrier in the way of intimacy Mrs Boinville is a very delightful woman but has the unhappy knack of either forgetting or appearing to forget her friends as soon as they turn their backs—

You seem certain that Southy did not write the number in the quarterly[8] but if he spares us in print he does not in conversation as we have good authority to know and that he speaks in the grossest manner—but this is all nothing—

So you would put in a word with me about Hogg (& Polypheme also—I do not know if you think they are alike but I believe that the gentleman does himself—but I have written a book in ⟨favor⟩ defence of Polypheme—have I not?)[9]—You say that you think that he has a good heart—and so do I—but ⟨you⟩ who can be sure of it—he wraps himself up in a triple veil—and places or appears to place a high wall between himself & his fellows—This want of confidence & frankness must in its natural course be repaid by a kind of mistrust—& that—with his manners which when unrelieved by the presence of half a dozen people, always disgust me make him as a constant daily-hourly visitor, which he insists upon being with us, absolutely intolerable—I hope when we return we shall be out of the reach of any but his sunday visits.

Shelley's doctor (not an Italian, they never do any good) has been of service to him & I hope that he will be of more but the bright sun of this blue sky is of more use than a myriad of medecines & a cold day (we have none of them now) casts him back—The rest of us are well—If it is not that I suffer from ill spirits—God knows why but I have suffered more from them ten times over than I ever did before I came to Italy evil thoughts will hang about me—but this is only now and then—

Give our loves to the darling of Aix la Chapelle—she never writes & never will I dare say although I have written to her several tim[es] but of course she has more to do than ever[10]—y[et] of an evening she might—as she has before now gossip a little with me—Our best remembrances to Bessy and our friends that you may chance to see—God knows when we shall see them if some chances came about it might be in 3 months but it will not be so I promise you;[11] so wait another year and stay till I date again Rome April 1820 and then we may see some glimmering—

It is a long time since we have heard from Venise—but all goes on as badly there with the noble poet[12] as ever I fear—he is a lost man if he does not escape soon—Allegra is there with a friend of his and ours[13] & if fortune will so favour us things shall remain as they are concerning her another year but I fear we shall be obliged to move—it is a long story and as usual people have behaved ill but do not mention these things in your letters—Adio—The Romans speak better Italian & have softer voices than their country men—Keep yourself well & walk out every day—we do—

Affectionately yours MaryWS.

ADDRESS: Leigh Hunt Esq / York Buildings—New Road / London / Inghilterra / Angleterre. POSTMARKS: (1) FPO / AP. 24 / 1819; (2) 12 o'Clock / AP. 24 / 1819 Nn. PUBLISHED: Jones, #65. TEXT: MS., Huntington Library (HM 2742).

1. Hunt's letter of 9 March was the first they had received since Hunt's (unlocated) letter of January 1819 (*SC*, VI, 794; the text of Hunt's letter is on pp. 790–93).

2. Mary Shelley was again pregnant. The Shelleys planned to return to Naples because Dr. John Bell (1763–1820), the English doctor they had met in Rome, expected to be in Naples, and they wished him to attend the birth of their child (see 9 April 1819; 30 May 1819; *MWS Journal*, 22, 29, 31 March 1819). Later in this letter Mary Shelley credits Dr. Bell with helping to improve Shelley's health.

3. The drafts of acts 2 and 3 of *Prometheus Unbound*, completed on 6 April (*PBS Letters*, #498).

4. Swinburne, the Hunts' third son.

5. "Broken" man, perhaps meaning broken statues.

6. Hunt's letter of 9 March contained a lively account of "a zealous defense of Shelley" by Hunt's nephew.

7. Cornelia Boinville Turner, wife of Thomas Turner (a lawyer and friend of Godwin's), and Alfred Boinville were the daughter and son of Mrs. Harriet Collins Boinville. In 1813 Shelley and Harriet Shelley had become intimates of the Boinville circle, and Shelley became an ardent admirer of Mrs. Boinville and her daughter. Thomas Turner believed Shelley was in love with his wife and was particularly hostile toward Shelley (*PBS Letters*, #92; *SC*, IV, 605–16). Even after the Boinville circle broke with Shelley following his elopement with Mary Godwin, his admiration for them continued. Mary Shelley's gratitude is for Hunt's refusal to meet the Turners until he learned that they were interested in restoring their friendship with Shelley (Dowden, *Shelley*, I, 377–88. *SC*, II, 275–78; IV, 609–20).

8. Shelley at the time believed that Southey had attacked him and Hunt in the *Quarterly Review* 18 (January 1818): 324–33, published in June 1818. However, John Taylor Coleridge had written the *Quarterly* article (*SC*, VI, 617, 708, 742–43).

9. That is, *Frankenstein*.

10. A reference to Marianne Hunt and the care of her increasing family (see 12 March 1819, n. 3).

11. Perhaps a reference to Shelley's expectation of being summoned to England at his father's death.

12. Byron (see *PBS Letters*, #488).

13. The Hoppners.

SHELLEY TO THOMAS LOVE PEACOCK[1] Rome. 6 April 1819

[*Postscript by Mary Shelley, p. 1*] The date of your last letter received by us is Jan. 31st it is the 16th[2] You have been a long time without writing— Pray tell me how Marianne St. Croix is?[3]

ADDRESS: Thos. Peacock Esq / 5 York St. Covent Garden / London / Angleterre / Inghilterra. POSTMARK: FPO / AP. 27 / 1819. PUBLISHED: Jones, #66. TEXT: MS., Bodleian Library (MS., Shelley, c. 1, f. 287).

1. *PBS Letters*, #498.
2. Peacock's sixteenth letter to the Shelleys.
3. Peacock and Marianne St. Croix had had a romance from 1814 through 1819 (see 24–25 November 1819, n. 4. For details of their relationship, see H. F. B. Brett-Smith's "Biographical Introduction" to Peacock, *Works*; *SC*, I, 100–102; *MWS Journal*, pp. 17, 20, 27, 28, 34, 44, 213).

TO MARIA GISBORNE Rome April 9th 1819

My Dear Mrs Gisborne,

You will have received Shelley's letter inviting you to Naples[1]—but you will not come—I wish you would; but how many things do I wish as uselessly as I do this. We shall stay all the summer and perhaps the autumn somewhere on the shores of the Bay—I am with child—and an eminent English surgeon will be there[2]—that is one reason for going, for we have no faith in the Italians.

We are delighted with Rome, and nothing but the Malaria would drive us from it for many months—It is very busy now with the funzioni of the holy week, and the arrival of the Emperor of Austria,[3] who goes about to see these things preceded by an officer, who rudely pushes the people back with a drawn sword, a curious thing that a fellow, whose power only subsists through the supposed conveniences of the state of the complaisance of his subjects, should be thus insolent—Of course, we keep out of his track; for our English blood, would, I am afraid boil over at such insolence.

The place is full of English, rich, noble—important and foolish. I am sick of it—I am sick of seeing the world in dumb show, and but that I am in Rome, in the city where stocks and stones defeat a million of times over my father's quoted maxim, "that a man is better than a stock or a stone,"[4] who could see the Apollo, and a Dandy spying at it, and not be of my opinion—Our little Will is delighted with the goats and the horses and the men rotti,[5] and the ladie's white marbel feet.

We saw the illuminated cross in St Peter's last night, which is very beautiful; but how much more beautiful is the Pantheon by Moonlight![6] As superior, in my opinion, as is the ancient temple to the modern church! I don't think much of S. Peter's after all—I cannot—it is so cut up—it is large—and not simple.

I am very much grieved to hear that Mr Webb[7] is become your enemy! I am afraid he will check all your endeavours, and, be as steady as you will, the life of a contender with the wealthy must be, at least, an anxious one. I hate Livorno, and it always makes me melancholy to think that you are cooped up there, where you are confined from all that can interest you in life, or where there can be any field for Mr Reveley's industry, but I know you will not change it—perhaps you are right!

My father is now engaged in a lawsuit[8]—the event of which will be to him the loss or not of £1500—You may conceive how anxious I am, as well as he; for my part, I am so devoured by ill spirits, that I hardly know what or where I am.

Adieu my Dear Mrs Gisborne—Mr Shelley desires his kindest remembrances, and believe me,

Affectionately your's
MWS

PUBLISHED: Jones, "New Letters," pp. 50–51. TEXT: John Gisborne Notebook No. 2, Abinger MS., Bodleian Library.

1. *PBS Letters*, #497.

2. John Bell.

3. Francis II (1768–1835), Holy Roman Emperor from 1792 to 1806, as Francis I, Emperor of Austria from 1804 to 1835 and former Grand Duke of Tuscany.

4. Used here in the sense of graven images (see *Jeremiah* 2: 27).

5. See April 6 1819 to Leigh Hunt, n. 5.

6. The Shelleys had seen the Pantheon first in the daytime and then by moonlight on 9 March (*MWS Journal*).

7. A banker at Leghorn (see 2 November 1818).

8. Godwin had lived rent-free for many years in his Skinner Street house. The demand for the accumulated rent resulted in a lawsuit that Godwin finally lost on 1 May 1822 (Brown, *Godwin*, pp. 339–46, 349).

To Maria Gisborne [Rome] Monday—April 26th 1819

My dear Mrs Gisborne

We already begin to feel or think that we begin to feel the effects of the Roman air—producing colds—depression & even fever to the feeblest of our party, so we emigrate a month earlier than we intended—& on the seventh of May leave this delightful city for the Bay of Naples intending if possible to settle for some months at Castel del Mare[1]—The physicians prognosticate good effects to Shelley from a Neapolitan summer—he has been very unwell lately & is very far from well now—but I hope that he is getting up again

Yesterday evening I met at a Conversatizione the true model of Biddy Fudge's lover—an Englishman with "the dear Corsair expression half savage half soft"—with the beautiful mixture of "Abelard & old Blucher"—& his forehead "rather bald but so warlike" and his mustachios on which the lamp shone with as fine an effect as the sun did upon Biddy's Hero—that when I heard his [*him*] called Signore Colonello I could not retain a smile which nearly degenerated into laughter when I thought that we had Colonel Calicot in Rome—Presently he began in very good Italian which although Englishly pronounced yet is better spoken than any other Englishman that I have heard—to give an account of his warlike feats and how at Lisbon he had put to flight thirty well armed & well mounted robbers (he on foot) with two pistols that never missed their aim—There can be but one such man in the world as you will be convinced when I tell you that while I was admiring his extraordinary prowess Clare whispered to me It is Colonel Finch —you asked me to tell you what I had heard of him at Venise—only one or two shabby tricks two [*too*] long for a letter & that an officer who served in Spain of the same regiment to which he pretends to belong vows that there was no Col^nel^ Finch there—report says that he is a parson & Lord B's nick name for his particular friend—is the Reverend Colonel Finch[2]—

We have been very gay in Rome as I dare {say} you have heard with the visit of the Emperor of Austria who they whisper wishes to take the Roman states into the keeping of the holy Roman Empire—this would be a fall to say the least of it from ⟨Hell to⟩ nothingness to Hell—There was a feast given at the Capitol—the three palaces were joined by a gallery and the whole hung with silk and illuminated in the most magnificent manner & the dying Gladiator surrounded by his Apollo's & Venuses shone forth very beautifully—There were very fine fire works—& a supper not at all in the Italian taste for there was an abundance which did honour to the old Cardinal who superintended the fête—every one was pleased & the Romans in extacies—I have not room to tell you how gracefully the old venerable Pope fulfilled the Church ceremonies—or how surprised & delighted we were with the lighting up of St. Peters—all that must serve for gossip when we meet—when will that be?—

We saw nobody at Naples—but we see a few people here[3]—The Italian character does not improve upon us—By the bye we have given an introduction for you (which I do not think will be presented) to a Roman lady, a painter and authoress, very old—very miserly & very mean—a Sig^ra^ Dionigi[4] perhaps you knew her—She says that she [*p. 1, top*] thinks that she remembers your name—

I am in better health & spirits than when I last wrote & make no ceremony of writing without receiving answers—S. & Clare desire best remembrances—

Affectionately Y^s^ MWS.

[*P. 4, partially cross-written*] We expect with little hope but many wishes your answer concerning your visit to Naples—Pray come if it is not impossible & give very little latitude to that word—

I can hardly tell you what to do about directing our letters—for a week or ten days have the kindness to direct them to Naples & after that perhaps you had better keep them till we write

Did you not say that you knew a herb for the destruction of fleas—be so kind as to send us its name

PUBLISHED: Jones, #67. TEXT: MS., Bodleian Library (MS., Shelley, c. 1, ff. 333–34).

1. Castellammare di Stabia, a few miles south of Pompeii on the Gulf of Naples.

2. Robert Finch, Byron's acquaintance (22 January 1819, n. 8; Byron, *Letters and Journals*, V, 136). Mary Shelley had seen Finch on 25 April (*MWS Journal*).

3. Details of the social activities of the Shelleys and Claire Clairmont during this period are provided in *MWS Journal* and *CC Journals*.

4. Marianna Candida Dionigi (1756–1826), painter, antiquary, author, "a centre of intellectual culture in Rome, and able to gather many strangers to her conversazioni" (Dowden, *Shelley*, II, 255). From 12 March through 27 April the Shelleys and Claire Clairmont were frequently in the company of Signora Dionigi. (For a biographical sketch of Marianna Dionigi, see *CC Journals*, pp. 462–64.)

To Maria Gisborne — [Rome] April 27— [1819]

We have just received Mr Gisborne's letter with the dreaded but expected refusal—If you must waste away 2 or 4 years Cannot you spare a few months out of that time—You will say no—& yet I think that you might say yes—Will you?

The Tale you mention of Lord Byron's[1] is on the same subject as one that he commenced in Switzerland and I little doubt therefore but that the information is t[r]ue—I shall be very curious to see it—I know the [s]tory of it already which is very dramatic & striking—And I dare say that we shall like it better than the poetry in which he is engaged at present which is in the Beppo style[2]—What a miserable thing it is that he should be lost as he is among the worst inhabitants of Venise—

Well I am afraid that we shall not see you this year which is a very great disappointment to us—especially as at Castel a Mare we shall most likely live a solitary life & not see a single creature—so take pity on us if you can—

Most affectionately Ys. MWShelley

ADDRESS: A Madame / Madame Gisborne / Poste Restante / Livorno. POSTMARK: 2 MAGGIO. ENDORSED: Recd.—Ansd. 17 May. PUBLISHED: Jones, #68. TEXT: MS., Bodleian Library (MS., Shelley, c. 1, f. 335).

1. The *New Monthly Magazine* (11 [1 April 1819]: 193–206) and Sherwood, Neely, and Jones simultaneously published *The Vampyre*, a story they attributed to Lord Byron. It was actually Byron's former physician, John William Polidori, who wrote the story, elaborating on an idea of Byron's for a ghost story he intended to write as part of the ghost-story-writing pact made at Geneva in 1816 (see 1 June 1816, n. 3). Printed with *The Vampyre* was an "Extract of a Letter from Geneva," which in its denial of Lord Byron's "having two sisters as the partakers of his revels," goes on to name Shelley ("a gentleman well known for extravagance of doctrine and for his daring") and "Miss M.W. Godwin and Miss Clermont, (the daughters of the celebrated Mr. Godwin)." Godwin saw *The Vampyre* and after some brief negotiations, had the offending passages removed (*SC*, VI, 777–81). For Polidori and *The Vampyre*, see *The Diary of Dr. John W. Polidori, 1816*, ed. W. M. Rossetti (London: E. Matthews, 1911), pp. 11–24.

From Mary Shelley's response, we may surmise that the Gisbornes had seen or heard of a revised version of the publication.

2. *Don Juan.*

To Maria Gisborne Rome May 11th 1819

My Dear Mrs Gisborne

You will think us strange people that we stay on another month in Rome. But when we determined to go, we did not know a creature in Rome, and we began to long for the country—but since that we have met with an old friend (Miss Curran),[1] and that has induced us to stay longer. Will you then be so kind to send me as soon as possible, word, how many letters you have forwarded to Naples, as I am anxious for some that may have been sent—

We have changed our lodgings for the last month, as Shelley did not find the air of the Corso agree with him, and we now live at the Trinita dei Monti,[2] which, of course, you well remember. It is the best air in Rome. We wish very much to hear how you are going on, and if you still look forward to a long addition to your long stay at Livorno. And if by chance you should hit upon our long lost box—I wish you were to be with us this summer, but you will not, I am sure, although I think it would give you pleasure.

Adieu! I will write again before we leave Rome.

Most affectionately your's
M.WS.

PUBLISHED: Jones, "New Letters," p. 52. TEXT: John Gisborne Notebook No. 2, Abinger MS., Bodleian Library.

1. Amelia Curran (1775–1847), artist, was the daughter of John Philpot Curran, one of Godwin's dearest friends (see 16 October 1817). Claire Clairmont's *Journal* entry for 23 April reads, "Drive in the Borghese—We think we see Miss Curran," and that for 24 April, "Leave a card at Miss Curran's." From 27 April, when Amelia Curran called on them, until their departure from Rome, the Shelleys and Claire Clairmont were almost daily in the company of Amelia Curran, who painted portraits of the Shelleys, Claire Clairmont, and William. (Claire Clairmont sat for her portrait on 5 and 6 May; Shelley, on 7 and 8 May; William, on 14 May; and Mary Shelley, on 28 May [*MWS Journal*; *CC Journals*].) On 7 May, the day the Shelleys had planned to leave Rome, Amelia Curran was working on the portraits of Claire Clairmont and Shelley, and they therefore decided to put off their departure for Naples (Dowden, *Shelley*, II, 265–66). It is possible that Maria Gisborne was also acquainted with Amelia Curran, since Godwin had written a letter on 14 July 1814 introducing his friend's daughter to Maria Gisborne, who then resided in Rome (MS. of Godwin's letter, Huntington Library [HM 7414]; *SC*, V, 498).

2. On 7 May they had moved to 65 Via Sistina, next-door to Amelia Curran, who lived at 64 Via Sistina (*CC Journals*).

To Maria Gisborne Rome Sunday—May 30th 1819

My Dear Mrs Gisborne—

Another letter—another plan—You will think us strange people—We leave Rome ⟨next⟩ tomorrow week We take a veterino—to where?—To Lucca—We shall see you this summer—I hope you will be glad of this—

Several reasons have joined to force us to this—The Surgeon who is to attend on me follows the Princess Paulina Borghese[1] to the Baths of Lucca & will be either at Pisa or Florence at the time we want him[2]—Besides this what weighs more with us is that the heat of this southern climate disagrees with William—He has had a dangerous attack of worms and it is only yesterday & today that he is convalescent—We are advised above all things to pass the summer is [*in*] as cool a place as possible—We have turned our eyes therefore to the Baths of Lucca & if we cannot get a house there we shall about the town of Lucca or the Baths of Pisa—Pray is the latter a cool place or not?—

We shall therefore I trust see you all this summer—Indeed you must come to console us for quitting Rome which we do with the greatest regret—However we must & shall return there—We shall most likely spend the winter a{t} Pisa a place reccommended particularly for Shelley's health.

Now we have one favour to ask you in this which is to procure us a servant—I think it had better be a woman since we must necessarily remain for some time about the same place—Perhaps the same Caterina you thought of before—She or He must cook tolerably since a chance might allow us to see people—They must market as honestly as an Italian can—If she could iron it would be a very great & almost a necessary convenience to us—I should not want her to wash—The wages you will judge yourself—as they would not quit Tuscany except to go to Lucca I should think 2 seq. a month enough but you will see—The servant must eat in the house—I have a very great objection to board wages—

I cannot tell you how glad we shall be to see you again—We should like of all things to have a house near you by the seaside at Livorno but the heat would frighten me for William who is so very delicate—and we must take the greatest possible care of him this summer—We shall at least be within reach of a good English Physician & we have the most rooted contempt & in any case of illness the greatest dread of Italian Medicos

Of course you will send us no more letters—If William's illness causes us to retard our journey we will write but I think we may pronounce[3] that {we} shall set out Sunday 7th of June. We shall[4] be six days on our journey so on Saturday the 13th Let us find at the Croce di Malta at Lucca our servant waiting for us—I hope you will not have much trouble in this and I ought to make you many apologies for teazing you so much—but your kindness makes us bold as we trust your goodness as we should to friends of many years standing.

You will exceedingly oblige us if you will write to us by this servant to say if you think the baths of Pisa very hot or if you know of any place about Lucca that would do for us—and if you could favour us with any kind of introduction at Lucca—

Adieu—My dear Mrs Gisborne—Give our kindest remembrance to Mess. G. [*Gisborne*] & R. [*Reveley*] & believe me Most affectionately yours

Mary W Shelley

ADDRESS: A Madame / Madame Gisborne / Post Restante / Livourne. POSTMARK: 6 GIUGNO. ENDORSED: Recd. 11 June. Ansd. PUBLISHED: Jones, #69. TEXT: MS., Bodleian Library (MS., Shelley, c. 1, ff. 336–37).

1. See 26 July 1818.

2. Dr. John Bell, who did not attend the birth of Percy Florence Shelley at Florence because of his own serious illness, from which he died at Rome on 15 April 1820 (*SC*, VI, 784). Bell wrote to Shelley explaining the severity of his illness (*S&M*, II, 463–64).

3. The original letter is torn after *pr*; the word is completed from the John Gisborne Notebook copy.

4. The original letter is torn after *sha*; the word is completed from the John Gisborne Notebook copy.

MARY SHELLEY AND CLAIRE CLAIRMONT TO MARIA GISBORNE[1]

Rome Thursday June 3rd June 5th 1819

Dear Mrs Gisborne

Mary tells me to write for her for she is very unwell and also afflicted. Our poor little William is at present very ill[2] and it will be impossible to quit Rome so soon as we intended—She begs you therefore to forward the letters here and still to look for a Servant for her as she certainly intends coming to Pisa—She will write to you a day or two before we set out. William has a complaint of the Stomach but fortunately he is attended by Mr Bell who is reckoned even in London one of the first English Surgeons. I know you will be glad to hear that both Mary & Mr Shelley would be well in health were it not for the dreadful anxiety they now suffer.

June 5th

[*Added by Mary Shelley*] William is in the greatest danger—We do not quite despair yet we have the least possible reason to hope—Yesterday he was in the convulsions of death and he was saved from them—Yet we dare not must not hope—

I will write as soon as any change takes place—The misery of these hours is beyond calculation—The hopes of my life are bound up in him—

Evers your affectionately

MWS.

I am well and so is S. although he is more exhausted by watching than I am.—William is in a high fever.

ADDRESS: A Madame / Madame Gisborne / Poste Restante / Livourne. POSTMARK: 16 GIUGNO. ENDORSED: Recd. 16 June. Ans. CC. & M.W.S. PUBLISHED: Jones, #70. TEXT: MS., Bodleian Library (MS., Shelley, c. 1, ff. 292–93).

1. Jones noted that the endorsement and contents of the unsigned portion of this letter indicated that the writer was Claire Clairmont and not, as assumed in *S&M* (II, 381) and Marshall, *Mary Shelley* (I, 242), Amelia Curran. The John Gisborne Notebook verifies that Claire Clairmont was the writer, for his copy of the unsigned portion is headed "From Clare," and the portion dated 5 June, "From Mary."

2. William first became ill on 25 May, but by the evening of 28 May he seemed

convalescent (*MWS Journal*; and letter of 30 May 1819). On 2 June he again fell ill, and Claire Clairmont recorded on that day: "William very ill—Mr. Bell calls three times . . . I sit up with Willy." On 3 June, Mary Shelley recorded: "William is very ill but gets better towards the evening—" William died at noon on 7 June, a victim of the malaria epidemic that swept Rome in 1819, 1820, and 1821 (*SC*, VI, 838) and was buried at the Protestant Cemetery in Rome. The Shelleys left Rome on 10 June but arranged with Amelia Curran to erect a tombstone. When William's grave was unearthed in 1822 in order to bury him near his father, the grave was found to contain the remains of an adult (Dowden, *Shelley*, II, 268). The precise place of William Shelley's grave remains unknown.

TO AMELIA CURRAN — Leghorn—June 27 1819

My dear Miss Curran

I wrote to you twice on our journey and again from this place but I found the other day that Shelley had forgotten to send the letter—and I have been so unwell with a cold these last two or three days that I have not been able to write

We have taken an airy house here[1] in the vicinity of Leghorn for three months and we have not found it yet too hot—the country around us is pretty so that I dare say that we shall do very well—

I am going to write another stupid letter to you—yet what can I do—I no sooner take up my pen than my thoughts run away with me—& I cannot guide it except about <u>one</u> subject & that I must avoid—So I entreat you to join this to your many other kindnesses & to excuse me—I have received the two letter forwarded from Rome—My father's lawsuit[2] is put off untill July—It will never be terminated—

I hope that you have quitted the pestilential air of Rome[3] & have gained a little health in the country—Pray let us hear from you for both Shelley & I are very anixous—more than I can express—to know how you are. Let us hear also if you please—anything you may have done about the tomb[4]—near which I shall lie one day & care not—for my own sake—how soon—I never shall recover that blow—I feel it more now than at Rome—the thought never leaves me for a single moment—Everything on earth has lost its interest to me

You see I told you than [*that*] I could only write to you on one subject how can I since do all I can (& I endeavour very sincerely) I can think of no other—so I will leave off—

Shelley is tolerably well & desires his kindest remembrances—

Most affectionately yours
Mary WShelley

Direct were [*here*]—Ferma in Posta, Livorno—& Pray write soon—& tell us of your painting & your occupations—

ADDRESS: Alla Signora Curran / 64 Via Sistina / Roma. POSTMARK: LIVORNO. PUBLISHED: Jones, #71. TEXT: MS., Bodleian Library (MS., Shelley, c. 1, ff. 338–39).

1. The Shelleys and Claire Clairmont left Rome on 10 June and arrived on 17 June at Leghorn, where they remained for one week. They then moved to the Villa Valsovano, a short distance from Leghorn.

2. For back rent (see 9 April 1819).

3. The malaria epidemic that claimed the life of William also struck Amelia Curran (*SC*, VI, 838).

4. For William Shelley (see 3–5 June 1819).

To Marianne Hunt — Leghorn—June 29th 1819

My dear Marianne

Although we have not heard from you or of you for some time I hope you are going on well—that you enjoy our [*your*] health and see your children lively about you—

You see by our hap how blind we mortals are when we go seeking after what we think our good—We came to Italy thinking to do Shelley's health good—but the Climate is not any means warm enough to be of benefit to him & yet it is that that has destroyed my two children—We went from England comparatively prosperous & happy—I should return broken hearted & miserable—I never know one moments ease from the wretchedness & despair that possesses me—May you my dear Marianne never know what it is to loose two only & lovely children in one year—to watch their dying moments—& then at last to be left childless & for ever miserable

It is useless complaining & I shall therefore only write a short letter for as all my thoughts are nothing but misery it is not kind to transmit them to you—Since Shelley wrote to Hunt we have taken a house in the neighbourhood of Leghorn be so kind as to inform Peacock of this—and that he must direct to us Ferma in Posta, Livorno & to let us know whether he has sent any letter to Florence—I am very anxious to know whether or not I am to receive the clothes I wrote to you about[1]—for if we do not I must provide others and although that will be a great expense & trouble yet it would be better for me to know as soon as possible if any one can or will send them—Peacock seems too much taken up in his new occupations[2] to think about us & he unfortunately is the only person whom I can have the slightest hope would do such a thing—If you would write to let me know whether you have them or indeed what you know about them it would exceedingly oblige me—but I know that your domestic concerns leave you no time therefore I do not expect that you can do me this favour I wish I had brought them with me—but one can only learn by experience how slowly & badly every thing is done for the absent—do not think that I reproach you by these words—I know that you can do nothing and who else is there that would care for my convenience or inconveniences

I am sorry to write to you all about thes[e] petty affairs [y]et if I would write any thi[ng] else about [my]self it would only be a list of hours spent [in] tears & grief—Hunt used to call me serious wh[a]t would he say to me now—I feel that I am no[t] fit for any thing & therefore not fit to live but how must that heart be moulded which would not be broken by what I have suffered—William was so good so beautiful so entirely attached to me—To the last moment almost he was in such abounding health & spirits—and his malady appeared of so slight a nature—and as arising simply from worms inspired no fear of danger that the blow was as sudden as it was terrible—Did you ever know a child with a fine colour—wonderful spirits—breedings worms (and those of the most innocent kind) that would kill him in a fortnight—we had a most excellent English surgeon to attend him and he allowed that these were the fruits of this hateful Italy—

But all this is all nothing to any one but myself & I wish that I were incapable of feeling that or any other sorrow—Give my love to Hunt keep yourselves well and happy

Yours—MWShelley

If the child's things are not sent at least as soon as this letter arrives they will come too late but if I had hopes that any one would take the trouble to send them at least—I would only make up the things perfectly necessary in expectation of the others

ADDRESS: Mrs. Hunt / 8 York Buildings / New Road / London / Angleterre. POSTMARKS: (1) LIVORNO; (2) FPO / JY. 17 / 1819; (3) 12 o'Clock / JY. 17 / 1819 Nn. PUBLISHED: Jones, #72. TEXT: MS., Huntington Library (HM 2745).

1. Clothes for the baby the Shelleys expected in November.

2. In May 1819, after a training period, Peacock was appointed Assistant to the Examiner in the East India Company. He remained with the company—as Senior Assistant to the Examiner from 1830 and Examiner from 1836—until his retirement in March 1856 (*SC*, VI, 710, 721).

To Marianne Hunt

Leghorn—August 28—1819

My dear Marianne

We are very dull at Leghorn and I can therefore write nothing to amuse you—We live in a little country house at the end of a green lane surrounded by a podère these podère are just the things Hunt would like—they are like our kitchen gardens with the difference only that the beautiful fertility of this country gives them—a large bed of cabages is very unpicturesque in England—but here the furrows are alternated with rows of grapes festooned on their supporters—it is filled with olive, fig and peach-trees and the hedges are of myrtle which have just ceased to flower—their flower has the sweetest faint smell in the world like some delicious spice—green grassy walks lead you through the vines—the people are always busy—and it {is} pleasant to see three or four of them transform in one day a bed of indian corn to one of celery—they work this hot weather in their shirts or smock frocks (but their breasts are bare) their brown legs nearly the colour only with a rich tinge of red in it with the earth they turn up—They sing not very melodiously but very loud—Rossini's music—

Mi revedrai ti revedro[1] and they are accompanied by the cicala a kind of little beetle that makes a noise with its tail as loud as Johnny[2] can sing—they live on trees and three or four together are enough to deafen you—it is to the cicala that Anacreon has addressed an ode which they call to a grasshopper in the English translations

Well here we live—I never am in good spirits—often in very bad—and Hunt's portrait[3] has already seen me shed so many tears that if it had his heart as well as his eyes he would weep too to in pity—but no more of this or a tear will come now—and there is no use for that—

By the bye a Hint Hunt gave about portraits[4]—the Italian painter's are very bad—they might make a nose like Shelleys & perhaps a mouth—but I doubt it; but there would be no expression {in} it—They have no notion of any thing except copying again and again their old masters—and somehow mere copying however divine the original does a great deal more harm than good—

Shelley has written a good deal and I have done very little since I have been in Italy[5]—I have had so much to see—and no [*so*] many vexations—independant of those which God has kindly sent to wean me from the world if I were too fond of it—S. has not had good health by any means—and when getting better fate has ever contrived something to pull him back—he never was better than the last month of his stay in Rome except the last week—then he watched 60 miserable—deathlyke hours without closing his eyes & you may think what good that did him—

We see the examiners regularly now four together just two months after the publication of the last—these are very delightful to us—I have a word to say to Hunt of what he says concerning Italian dancing—the Italians dance very badly—they dress for their dances in the ugliest manner—the men in little doublets with a hat and feather—they are very stiff—nothing but their legs move—& they twirl and jump with as ill grace as may be—it is not for their dancing but their pantomime that the Italians are famous—you remember what we told you of the ballêt of Othello—they tell a story by action so that words appear perfectly superfluous things for them—In that they are graceful—agile impressive & very affecting so that I delight in nothing so much as a deep tragic ballêt—but the dancing—unless as they sometimes do—they dance as common people—for instance the dance of joy of the Venetian citizens on the return of Othello—is very bad indeed—

I am much obliged to you for all your kind offers and wishes—Hunt would do Shelley a great deal of good—but that we may not think of—His spirits are tolerably good—But you do not tell me how you get on—How Bessy is & where she is—Remember me to her—Clare is learning thorough base[6]—& singing—We pay 4 crowns a month for her master—lessons 3 times a week cheap work this—is it not—at Rome we pay 3 shillings a lesson & the master stayed two hours—The one we have now is the best in Leghorn—I write in the morning—read latin till two when we dine—then I read some English book & two cantos of Dante with Shelley—In the evening our friends the Gisbornes come so we are not perfectly alone—I like M[rs] Gisborne very much indeed but her husband is most dreadfully dull and as he is always with her we have not so much pleasure in her company as we otherwise should—Her son is the pattern of good boys—Thornton & Johnny should take pattern by him—he is only thirty years of age and always does as he is bid—this is no exageration although that age he is under as complete a subordination as few boys of twelve are—this however is all to his praise for hes [*he*] is very clever—and he ought to . . .[7]

[ ]ve sent the things I wrote for or will without delay[8]—for indeed I need them—if you have not slip in a pair of baby's stays for a pattern—but pray send them immediately and what is of as much consequence send me the bill of lading the moment you get it—you know that I shall be in the most wretched state ever poor woman was if you do not let me have them.

I am obliged to Hunt for his page of excuses—give my love to him and tell him that I vote that for the future he should follow Boccaccio's example who always makes his people begin prestamente their tales without any excuses at all—Tell him that I read that most delightful author at Rome—and that his letter joined to my recommendations has persuaded Shelley to begin him—he is now reading him regularly through and is quite enchanted by his mixture of hilarity and Pathos—

I call this a long letter—Will Hunt call it a gigantic paragraph[9] and pray what does he mean.

POSTMARK: FPO / SE. 11 / 1819. PUBLISHED: Jones, #73. TEXT: Humanities Research Center, University of Texas at Austin (a partial copy by Mary Shelley); Charnwood, *Call Back Yesterday*, p. 201.

1. From Rossini's *Tancredi.*

2. John Hunt, the Hunts' second child.

3. The portrait of Hunt, a copy by the artist of the "portrait taken in chalk as large a life half length by Mr. Wildman, Thornton's drawing Master," was received by the Shelleys sometime between 16 and 20 August 1819 (*SC*, VI, 606, 877; *MWS Journal*).

4. Hunt's letter accompanying his portrait asked for "a head or heads" in return, a request he repeats in his letter of 6 September 1819 (*SC*, VI, 609, 886).

5. Shelley had completed *Rosalind and Helen* and had written *Julian and Maddalo, Lines written among the Euganean Hills*, the first three acts of *Prometheus Unbound*, and *The Cenci.* From 4 August through 12 September 1819 Mary Shelley wrote *Matilda*, which remained unpublished until 1959 (MWS, *Matilda*). Mary Shelley was also working on her novel *Valperga*, conceived at Marlow and researched from the time of her arrival in Italy, but not completed until 1 December 1821 (see 30 June 1821; *MWS Journal*).

6. A method of indicating an accompanying part by the bass notes only together with figures designating the chief intervals and chords to be played above the bass notes (*Harvard Dictionary of Music*).

7. The remainder of this letter is taken from Charnwood, *Call Back Yesterday.*

8. Clothes for the expected baby, of which Mary Shelley reminded the Hunts in

her letter of 29 June and Shelley reminded them in his letter of 15 August (*PBS Letters*, #508).

9. In his letter to Shelley of 8 July Hunt had promised to write often to the Shelleys "& shall dispatch another letter next week, addressed to Mary, which I hope will induce her to oblige me with one of those gigantic paragraphs which she entitles a letter also" (*SC*, VI, 841). Hunt's letter to Shelley of 12 September defines "gigantic paragraphs" as "short letters written in large characters" (*SC*, VI, 905).

SHELLEY TO CHARLES OLLIER[1] Leghorn, Sep. 6. 1819

[*Postscript by Mary Shelley, p. 4*] The parcel must be taken to the wharf —the vessel that sails soonest for Leghorn be particularly enquired for: the parcel delivered to the Captain—a bill of lading taken & dispatched to us by the next post—

ADDRESS: Messrs. Ollier / Booksellers / Vere Street / Bond Street / London / Inghilterra / Angleterre. POSTMARKS: (1) LIVORNO; (2) FPO / SI. 21 / 1819. PUBLISHED: *PBS Letters*, #513. TEXT: *PBS Letters*, #513.

1. *PBS Letters*, #513.

TO AMELIA CURRAN Leghorn—Sept. 18—1819

My dear Miss Curran

We certainly lost your first letter concerning the engraving of La Cenci so perhaps some good person is at work for us here as well as at Rome—I am sorry that you have had so much trouble especially, as it is in vain—of course if the two years were not inadmissible a 1,000 sequins[1] would be—What Shelley thought of was an engraving of a fit size to place as a frontispiece to his tragedy[2] but he has now given up the thought of its being done in Italy, as we trust to your copy—which you know you are to do very beautifully for us—it will be doing us both a very great favour—

We shall quit Leghorn in about a fortnight but as yet we do not know where we go—The autumn here is very delightful & not at all too hot—we are so much more north than you—I regret this for I regret Rome & God knows when we shall see it again—not this winter for we cannot stir before it will be too cold for travelling—not in the summer for then we shall not seek so hot a residence—the next winter is a possible thing—but then I fear you will be thinking of returning to England

Nothing more has been said about the tomb—we still encline to a pyramid as the most durable of simple monumental forms—when you return to Rome do not be angry with me for requesting you to inform yourself of the following particulars—What would be the size of a pyramid built of the most solid materials & covered with white marble at the price of £25 sterl—and also what would be the size of an obelisk built in the same manner & at the same price? When we know these things I think we can decide—You are so kind that you see I trouble you without ceremony & hope that you will accept our thanks & gratitude without being angry with us for the trouble we give you—I wish all the people that we depend upon were as good as you are—the most pressing entreaties on my part as well as Clares cannot draw a single line from Venise[3]—It is now 6 months since we have heard even in an indirect manner from there—God knows what has happened or what has not—I suppose S. must go to see what has become of the little thing—yet how or when I know not, for he has never recovered from his fatigue at Rome and continually frightens me by the approaches of a dysentery—besides we must remove—my lying in & winter are coming on so we are wound up in an inextricable dilemma—this is very hard upon us—& I have no consolation in any quarter for my misfortune has not altered the tone of my father's letters[4]—so I gain care every day & can you wonder that my spirits suffer terribly—that time is a weight to me—& I see no end to this—

Well to talk of something more interesting—Shelley has finished his tragedy & it is sent to London to be presented to the managers—it is still a deep secret & only one person, Peacock who presents it, knows anything about it in England—with S.'s public & private enemies it would certainly fall if known to be his—his sister in law[5] alone would hire enough people to damn it—It is written with great care & we have hopes that its story is sufficiently polished not to shock the audience—we shall see

Continue to direct to us at Leghorn for if we should be gone they will be faithfully forwarded to us—And when you return to Rome just have the kindness to enquire if there should be any stray letter for us at the post office

I hope the country air will do you real good—You must take care of yourself—remember that one day you will return to England & that you may be happier there—Affectionately Yours

MWS.

[*P. 1, top*] Shelley desires his kindest remembrances & thanks—he will write soon—Clare &ce—Have you paid Bandeloni, her music master?—if not pray do—

ADDRESS: Miss Curran / Alla Casa della / Signora Rosalinda Rotonda / Roma / per Gensano. POSTMARKS: (1) LIVORNO; (2) 25 SETTEMBRE. PUBLISHED: Jones, #74. TEXT: MS., Bodleian Library (MS., Shelley, c. 1, ff. 340–41).

1. A sequin, the French form of the Italian *zecchino*, was worth at that time about nine shillings. The amount quoted, then, is approximately £450.

2. On 5 August Shelley had asked Amelia Curran to inquire about the cost of a good engraving of the portrait of Beatrice Cenci, then in the Colonna Palace in Rome (*PBS Letters*, #507). On 8 August Shelley finished *The Cenci* and arranged for 250 copies to be printed at Leghorn. On 9 September, having asked Peacock to offer it to Covent Garden for production with its authorship a secret, Shelley sent either a printed copy or proof sheets to Peacock (*SC*, VI, 895, 899). The play was rejected by Covent Garden. In March 1820 Charles Ollier published the printed copies that Shelley had sent to him (*PBS Letters*, #513; *SC*, VI, 926). Mary Shelley's "Note on *The Cenci*," in Shelley, *Poetical Works* (1839), II, 273–80,

gives a detailed account of Shelley's intentions regarding the writing, proposed production, and printing of *The Cenci.*

3. From the Hoppners or Byron about Allegra. Shelley's letter of 18 October 1819 indicated that he had heard from Hoppner by that time (*PBS Letters*, #520).

4. Ever in debt and at this time particularly worried about the lawsuit for back rent, Godwin wrote pressing and unpleasant letters in his attempt to draw further upon Shelley's financial resources (*SC*, II, 852).

5. Eliza Westbrook.

TO LEIGH HUNT Leghorn—Sept. 24th 1819

My dear Hunt

How very thankful we are to you for your Monday letters[1]—this is truly kind of you—and yet we have both been very ungrateful, and not answered them as we ought—For me I hardly need make any excuse—for I am so seldom in a humour when any letter of mine could be in any degree amusing or acceptable—& Shelley has for these last days been so occupied with our friends here ⟨in trying to persuade them to do so⟩ from various causes—that with that, and his poem[2] which you will have received—and his spanish—for Clare's brother has been here[3]—he has passed 15 months in Spain—and Shelley having made some progress in spanish before he came he wished to take advantage of his short stay here to improve himself more—with all these things his time has been fully taken up—Yesterday he went to Florence to take lodgeings for us I shall be confined there some time next month—& we shall probably spend the whole of the winter there—some what dully to be sure, since we shall not know a soul there—and there is little to amuse us in looking at one another and ⟨seei⟩ reading there what we already too well know—yet I am the worst at this, for latterly Shelley's spirits have been tolerably good—& his health much improved although the variableness of this climate is not very good for him—The transitions from heat to cold are worse here than in England—for instance 3. days ago we had the finest weather in the world—so hot that you could not stir out in the middle of the day—& now it has become as cold as sometimes I have felt it at Christmas in England—This will not last for when the wind changes it will become warm again—in the mean time we freeze in an Italian built house that lets in the wind on every side—no fire places & stone floors—The Italians although having so much hotter weather than we & feeling the heat more than we—yet are not nearly so sensible to the cold as us—and take very few precautions against the cold season except holding a little earthen ware pot with charcoal in it in their hands—

In my last letter I answered your kind words about pictures—Italian artists cannot make portraits—we may chance to find an ⟨Italian⟩ English or German it [*at*] Florence & if so I will persuade Shelley to sit—as for me it would have been very well 6 months ago but now I could not persuade myself to sit to be painted—I can assure you I am much changed—the world will never be to me again as it was—there was a life & freshness in it that is lost to me—on my last birthday when I was 21—I repined that time should fly so quickly and that I should grow older so quickly—this birthday—now I am 22—although the time since the last seems to have flown with speed of lightning yet I rejoiced at that & only repined that I was not older—in fact I ought to have died on the 7th of June last[4]—

I am very much obliged to Marianne for the trouble she has taken about my commissions of course the parcel has been sent long ago—in your next letter I hope to have the bill of lading or at least the name of the Captain & vessel—& then it will entirely depend on whether the vessel quits London directly—I am very anxious for some of the things—

It gives me great pleasure to hear that you have such good hopes of Thornton Pray how does Jhonny get on & have you now another?[5] How very happy you must feel amidst all their noise & bother ⟨if⟩ when you think of our desolate situation—Marianne might well laugh if it were a laughing matter at the recollection of my preachments about having so large a familly when I now say that I wish I had a dozen—any thing but none—or one—a fearful risk on whom all one's hopes and joy is placed—

Why do I write about this—why because I can write of nothing else & that is why I write so seldom

My best & most affectionate wishes are with you—take care of yourselves & pray write still every week—Clare sends her love—to Bessy also—is she still with her brother[6]—pray tell us—

Your's ever
MaryWShelley

I must say a word of Mr Gisborne[7] whom you will see—you will find him a very dull man—but if you take any trouble about him you will be well repaid when Mrs G. joins him for she is an excellent ⟨friend⟩ woman—& what you will think praise—very much attached to Shelley—to me too perhaps but I am nothing now & it is impossible any one can much like so dull a person

As you talked of moving at Michaelmas I direct this letter to the E. [*Examiner*] office—a letter was sent yesterday with a poem[8] in it directed to York Buildings

ADDRESS: Leigh Hunt Esq / Examiner Office / 19 Catherine St—Strand / London / Angleterre. POSTMARKS: (1) LIVORNO; (2) FPO / OC. 9 / 1819. PUBLISHED: Jones, #75. TEXT: MS., Huntington Library (HM 2744).

1. In his letter of 23 August 1819 Hunt had promised to write to the Shelleys every Monday morning and had requested that they do the same (*SC*, VI, 880). Mary Shelley's letter indicates that the Shelleys did not comply with the suggestion, and her letter of 24–25 November 1819 shows that Hunt had discontinued his Monday letters.

2. Shelley wrote *The Mask of Anarchy* in early September and sent it to Hunt on 23 September for publication in the *Examiner*. The poem was Shelley's response to the 16 August 1819 "Peterloo Massacre," in which mounted, armed militiamen

and hussars charged into a peaceful assembly of several thousand men, women, and children gathered to hear a speech on political reform in St. Peter's Field, outside Manchester. Various authorities have cited the number of persons killed as between 6 and 9 and the persons wounded as between 80 and 418 (White, *Shelley*, II, 105; *SC*, VI, 893).

3. Charles Clairmont remained with the Shelleys from 4 September until 10 November 1819.

4. The day William died.

5. See 12 March 1819, n. 3. Several times in her letters, Mary Shelley wrote the Hunts' second child's name as "Jhonny."

6. Marianne Hunt's letter of 14 July–4 August 1818 informed the Shelleys that Bessy Kent had gone to live with her brother Thomas Kent (*SC*, VI, 606).

7. John Gisborne had left Leghorn for England on 12 September (*MWS Journal*), but Mary Shelley's letter of 18 June 1820 indicates that he never reached his destination.

8. See above, n. 2.

SHELLEY TO LEIGH HUNT[1] — Livorno, Sept. 27, 1819

[*Postscript by Mary Shelley*] Direct your letters 'ferma in Posta Firenze.'

ADDRESS: Leigh Hunt, Esq., Examiner Office, 19, Catherine Street, Strand, London. POSTMARK: FPO / OC. 12 / 1819. PUBLISHED: Hunt, *Lord Byron and Some of His Contemporaries*, I, 393–95 (incomplete); Charnwood, *Call Back Yesterday*, 201–4. TEXT: Charnwood, *Call Back Yesterday*.

1. *PBS Letters*, #517.

TO MARIA GISBORNE — Florence[1] Oct. 5—1819

My dearest Mrs Gisborne

I should have written to you before but we were detained one day longer on our journey than we counted and did not arrive time enough on Saturday to write—Except the last miles I was not at all fatigued but the roads near Florence are so exceedingly bad that it would have been bad for me were not our carriage so easy[2]—

Well we are now tolerably settled in our lodgings which are convenient in their way but one always feels uncomfortable at removing from a house to oneself to one occupied in common with others—We talk a great deal about you & long to know some news of the steam engine[3] of course we shall have a letter in the course of the week—

I only write you this line to say we have arrived safe & well for as to letter writing that must be transferred to Shelley for {I} find my hand trembles even with these few words—you will not judge of my affection by a short letter—and you will repay me I am sure by a long one—reflecting how solitary & dull we must be here—& you can write a long letter if you please as Mrs G. will prove when she sits beside a fine coal fire her spectacles on—&—but you can fill up the rest of the picture—

I have a favour to ask of you which I know you will not delay in doing—

this is that you will make up a parcel of—Our Tales of my Landlord—Frankenstein—Birbecks—journal & letters—Cobbetts year's residence—The reviews that we have—⟨Revolt of Islam⟩—The two last Cantos of Childe Harold[4]—& ½ lb. of the very best green tea that you can possibly get—at whatever price—& send these by the very first quick & sure conveyance to Pisa directed to Madame Mason[5]—Casa Silva—Via Mala gonella—Pisa—

I send you the list of books that you have of ours—

Clare & Shelley send their best love to you & I would say to Henry[6] but that would not do from the young lady so take out her name & only remember her kindly to him as well as my self—Shelley longs for a letter from him Adieu

Most Affectionately Yours
M WS.

I am very anxious about our Neapolitan box

Townley tea was tried & found wanting perhaps there is better at Dunns

You will of course open the box from Naples—be so kind as to inclose in it for me the very finest small tooth comb you can get and a brush for it—

I can get a comb here but it is not fine enough

ADDRESS: A Madame / Madame Gisborne / Ferma in Posta / Livorno. POSTMARKS: (1) FIRENZE; (2) 8 OTTOBRE. ENDORSED: Received 7th October 1819 / Ansd 11th Do. PUBLISHED: Jones, #76. TEXT: MS., Bodleian Library (MS., Shelley, c. 1, ff. 342–43).

1. The Shelleys and Claire and Charles Clairmont had left Leghorn on 30 September and arrived at Florence on 2 October, taking lodgings at Palazzo Marini, 4395 Via Valfonda.

2. For a discussion of the carriage, see *SC*, III, 153–80.

3. See [28] May 1818.

4. Walter Scott, *Tales of My Landlord*, 3d series, 4 vols. (Edinburgh: Archibald Constable, 1819); Morris Birkbeck, *Notes On a Journey through France, from Dieppe through Paris and Lyons, to the Pyrennees, and back through Toulouse . . .*, 2d ed. (London: William Phillips, 1815); William Cobbett, *A Year's Residence in the United States of America* (New York: Privately printed, 1818). Each item requested has a line through it, indicating that the Gisbornes used Mary Shelley's letter as a checklist. There is a line drawn through "The two last Cantos of Childe Harold," and "the 4th only" is written above it.

5. The Shelleys had brought with them to Italy a letter of introduction from Godwin to Mrs. Mason, whose real name was Margaret King Moore, Lady Mount Cashell (1773–1835), and who had been Mary Wollstonecraft's pupil some thirty years earlier. In 1791 Margaret King had married Stephen Moore, the second Earl of Mount Cashell, by whom she had eight children, but had separated from him in 1805; she and George William Tighe had lived together in Italy for many years—as Mr. and Mrs. Mason—with their daughters Laura and Nerina. (For a full account of Mrs. Mason's life, see McAleer, *The Sensitive Plant.* Although the Shelleys' letters to Mrs. Mason have not been found, forty-two letters written by Mrs. Mason (thirty-seven to Mary Shelley, five to Shelley) are extant, and they give ample evidence of the friendship and kind counsel Mrs. Mason gave the Shelleys and particularly Claire Clairmont (Abinger MS.; Dowden, *Shelley*, II, 315–18).

6. It appears that Henry Reveley proposed marriage to Claire Clairmont in 1820 (*CC Journals*, p. 469).

SHELLEY TO LEIGH HUNT[1] Florence, Nov. 2 1819

[*Postscript by Mary Shelley to Marianne Hunt*] At the end of August Hunt wrote to say that my parcel[2] was to be sent the next day—Sept. 12th he said his letter had been put off that he might give us news of it yet not a word of news did he give—nor has since—Ah Marianna mia—I hope you and your babe[3] are well—Kiss him for me—Clare begs her love to you all—

[*On address page*] make Ollier pay the postage of this

ADDRESS: Leigh Hunt Esq. / Examiner Office / 19 Catherine St. Strand / London / Inghilterra. POSTMARKS: (1) FIRENZE; (2) FPO / NO. 16 / 1819. PUBLISHED: Jones, #77. TEXT: MS., Bodleian Library (MS., Shelley, c. 1, ff. 303–4).

1. *PBS Letters*, #526.
2. One of many reminders about clothes for her expected baby.
3. The Hunts' sixth child, [James] Henry Sylvan Leigh, born 28 September 1819.

TO MARIA GISBORNE Florence November 4th 1819

My Dear Mrs Gisborne

I am not yet confined—this is very provoking, for my time is past, and I have no enjoyment of life in my present state—I expect it tonight—tomorrow—very soon.

Shelley desires a thousand apologies to Mr G [*Gisborne*]—for not writing—for these last three days he has been deeply engaged in writing a letter in Carlisle's affair[1]—but next post you will certainly have a letter from him—

The parcel you last sent me was nearly three weeks coming. As I am in great need of the things contained in the Box you have heard of, you will infinitely oblige me if you will send it by as speedy a conveyance as you can—sans delai[2]

Our best loves most affectionately to all

Your's M.WS.

Thanks for your trouble about the Cenci[3]—We have heard no news of it.

Papa's affair is not come on yet. his letter contained that information simply—We have heard from Venice from Mr H. [*Hoppner*] A [*Allegra*] is with her papa, and, he says, will go to England with him in the spring—Shelley called at Madme Tonelli[4]—he heard that she was gone to England. He will call again tomorrow.

My head is so heavy that I am almost asleep as I write this—

PUBLISHED: Jones, "New Letters," pp. 52–53. TEXT: John Gisborne Notebook No. 2, Abinger MS., Bodleian Library.

1. Shelley wrote a five-sheet letter in defense of Richard Carlile (1790–1843), a bookseller convicted of blasphemous libel for publishing passages of Paine's *Age of Reason* and of republishing Palmer's *Principles of Nature*. Shelley sent his defense, addressed to the editor of the *Examiner*, on 6 November, but Hunt did not publish it (*PBS Letters*, #527; *SC*, VI, 1084).

2. The box from the Hunts reached the Shelleys about 13 December (see [?13 December 1819]).

3. On 13 or 14 October 1819 Shelley had requested that the Gisbornes "send the Cenci's which are at the printers to England by the next ship.—I forgot it in the hurry of departure" (*PBS Letters*, #518).

4. Jones has noted the following reference in a letter Shelley wrote from Florence to Claire Clairmont in Leghorn on 25 September: "Give my compts. to the Siga. Tolonei [*sic*], and pay her at the interval you think fit eleven crowns, and say that I have given a receipt for it. Say that I am going to see her house, etc., etc." (Shelley, *Complete Works*, X, 85). Shelley and Charles Clairmont were in Florence from 23 to 25 September looking for lodgings (*MWS Journal*).

To Maria Gisborne — Florence. [9 November 1819][1]

My Dear M^rs^ G—

As there was no number put to the direction of Sg^re^ Büyel—Via di Fossi, Shelley was unable to find him out—Will you let us know the exact direction? Our's is 4395 Via Valfonda, Piazza Vecchia di S. Maria Novella—

My father's letter, received today, contains the worst possible news. The affair of his house is given against him, and in a month from the date of his letter, he will be come upon for £1,500—They talk of compromise &c, but he has nothing, so, I suppose, S—must go to England—We shall wait for one more return of post—for my part, I see nothing but despair—His journey, to say the least, is next door to death for him—but while I have life, I expect nothing but misery. I am not yet confined—

Ever Your's—M.WS.

PUBLISHED: Jones, "New Letters," pp. 53–54. TEXT: John Gisborne Notebook No. 2, Abinger MS., Bodleian Library.

1. Gisborne notes that this letter was written "Tuesday on or just before 10 November." Since Mary Shelley's *Journal* indicates that they received bad news from London on Tuesday, 9 November, and she informs Maria Gisborne of her "father's letter, received today," we may date this letter 9 November.

*To Maria Gisborne — [Florence c. 13 November 1819][1]

The little boy takes after me, and has a nose that promises to be as large as his grandfather's—I have not yet seen his form, but I enput it to be the quintessence of beauty, entracted from all the Apollos, Bacchus's, Loves and dawns of the Study and the Vatican.

His health is good, and he is very lively, and even knowing for his age—although like a little dog I fancy his chief perfection lies in his nose, and that he smells me out, when he becomes quiet the moment I take him.

We have had for the last fifteen days a tempo patetico,[2] as Maria calls it—true enough, it is always crying. perhaps some little misfortune has happened la su, and that il figlio is infreddato,[3] or the padre got a stroke of the palsy, and all the pretty angels and cherubs are weeping.

Maria must depart—She does nothing, and is in every way disagreeable—Addio, Cara mia amica!

UNPUBLISHED: TEXT: John Gisborne Notebook No. 2, Abinger MS., Bodleian Library.

1. In the John Gisborne Notebook, Mary Shelley's 4 November letter is run into her letter that begins, "I have promised a lady," to which a date of [27–30 November] may be assigned. Gisborne's copy of the [27–30 November] letter is accurate through the line in the third paragraph of the postscript that concludes, "ought hardly to have united yourself to our eccentric star." At this point, rather than completing the text of the letter, he transcribes the present four paragraphs, which I conjecture to be part of a letter written shortly after the birth of Percy Florence on 12 November. It is likely that these paragraphs (perhaps accompanying a note by Shelley) first announced the birth of Percy Florence. In his letter to the Gisbornes of 16 November, Shelley comments, "Mary & the babe continue well" (*PBS Letters*, #532).

2. "Melancholy weather."

3. "The son is suffering from a cold."

TO MARIANNE HUNT Florence—Nov 24th (November 25th) 1819

My dear Marianne

At length I am afraid Hunt has got tired of his monday remembrances[1] —I cannot tell you how this vexes me; perhaps he thinks that my little Percy will serve instead—but why not have two pleasant things instead of one? Ask him to be very good, and to continue his practise, which was the pleasantest in the world—tell him we have few friends in any part of Italy —none in Florence—& none whom we we love as well as we love him: make him always consider it a black monday when he does not write a little to us.

A few days before we left Leghorn which is now 2 months ago Shelley sent ⟨an ode to Hunt⟩ a poem called the mask of anarchy[2] Hunt does not mention the reception of it—it was directed to York buildings—and he is anxious to know whether it has been received—you will have received several other large packets from him—you will ask Ollier for money to pay for these extra extraordinary letters—but just let us hear of their safe arrival—We have to thank Bessy for her kindness in transcribing Hunt's kindness[3]—but it so happened that the practical Peacock had thought it worth while to send those three Examiners themselves to us by post—pray how is the said gentleman going on—he is not yet married & says he does not think about it—I am afraid his Marianne[4] does & somewhat bitterly—she had rather perhaps that he were still faithfully rusticating at Marlow; for this shepherd-King has I am afraid forgotten his crook & his mistress—do not shew him this gossip of mine concerning him on any account—

After writing this long page I need not tell you that I am very well—& the little boy also—he was born a small child but has grown so during this first fortnight that if his little face were not always the same one might almost think him a changed child he takes after me—You see I say more about him than Hunt did of his little Harry but he is my only one and although he is so healthy and promising that for the life of me I cannot fear yet it is a bitter thought that all should be risked on one yet how much sweeter than to be childless as I was for 5 hateful months—Do not lett us talk of those five months: when I look back on all I suffered at Leghorn I shudder with horror yet even now a sickening feeling steps in the way of every enjoyment when I think—of what I will not write about

I hope all your children are well—they must all be grown quite out of our knowledge—years can hardly give steadiness to Thornton—& Johnny & Mary are yet in the jumping age give them a kiss they & the three younger ones—including the little stranger—

You have no notion how many admirers Hunt has got here by means of his picture especially among our lady acquaintances (English) I had corked up in my memory a number of soft & tender exclamations concerning his eyes & his hair & his forehead &c—I have forgotten them unfortunately—but really from the effect his phisiognomy produces on all who see him & the warmth with which people defend him after seeing it who were cool before—and their vows that indeed he cannot be the Bristol Hunt[5] I should think that his friends ought to club to have his picture painted by Owen or Lawrence[6] & exhibited & then no one would think ill of him more—

Shelley in his last letter mentioned something about his return to England[7] —but this is very vague—I hope—how ardently you may guess that it will not be—but in any case keep it quite a secret as if he came hardly a creature must know it.—We have been pursued by so much ill luck that I cannot hope & dare not that things will turn out well—but his return would be in so many ways so dreadful a thing that I can not dwell long enough upon the idea as to conceive it possible—We do not think of all returning—Since we have returned to Tuscany we have lived for the first time in an œconomical manner & it would be madness to break this up besides that arrests & a thousand other things render it impossible that we should be known to be in England—

(November 25th) Another post day & no letter from any of you who I must tell you are the only people from whom we receive any letters except concerning business—Peacock's corespondence having degenerated since the time he had nought to do but to tune his pipe in Bisham wood—I could ask a thousand questions about you & yours but I am afraid that they would not be answered & so instead I will talk to you of ourselves. You may judge by what Shelley has sent to England[8] that he has been very busily employed—and besides this he often spends many hours of the day at the gallery admiring & studying the statues & pictures—There are many divine ones—he says—for my part I have not seen any thing except one peep I took at the Venus di Medici which is not a striking statue—both from its size & the meaningless expression of the countenance the form requires study to understand its full merit.

Claire[9] has got now a very good singing master & is getting on exceedingly well—Tell Hunt that there is a beautiful song—Non temete, O Madre Amata—of Azziolis'[10]—only a few copies of which were printed—I wish he could get it to sing to me when I return. When will that be? I must answer with the nursery rhyme—When I grow rich.

After having heard that the box you so kindly sent was shipped from Genoa we have heard no more of it—fortunately a box from Peacock contained the things I so indispensably needed—but I am now in great want of the flannel for the child—

I long to hear from you—I wish you could squeeze a hour for a letter—Love from all to all—Have you received Peter Bell 3rd[11] &c—Yours affectionately & entirely

MaryWShelley.

ADDRESS: Mrs. Hunt / Examiner Office / 19. Catharine Street / Strand / London. POSTMARKS: (1) FIRENZE; (2) FPO / DE. 15 / 1819. PUBLISHED: Jones, #78. TEXT: MS., Huntington Library (HM 2744).

1. See 24 September 1819.

2. See 24 September 1819.

3. The *Examiners* of 26 September, 3 October, and 10 October contained Hunt's attack on the *Quarterly Review* for its vitriolic review of Shelley's *Laon and Cythna* in April 1819.

4. Marianne St. Croix (see 6 April 1819 to Peacock). Whether Peacock ever proposed to Marianne St. Croix remains uncertain. However, on 20 November 1819 Peacock proposed marriage to Jane Gryffydh (Peacock, *Works*, VIII, 217–18); she accepted, and they were married in Wales in March 1820 (*SC*, I, 102).

5. Henry "Orator" Hunt (1773–1835), a leading radical spokesman imprisoned for two and a half years (1820–1822) because of his participation in Manchester's "Peterloo" in August 1819.

6. William Owen (1769–1825) and Sir Thomas Lawrence (1769–1830).

7. Shelley had written to Hunt: ". . . some circumstances have occurred, not necessary to explain by letter, which make my pecuniary condition a very difficult one . . . it is probable that I shall pay you a visit in the spring" (*PBS Letters*, #529). On 18 November Shelley had written Amelia Curran that he might have to return to England to arrange the large sum of money Godwin required because the lawsuit for back rent had been decided against him (*PBS Letters*, #534).

8. Between 14 August and 17 November 1819 Shelley had sent *Julian and Maddalo, The Cenci, The Mask of Anarchy*, "Letter to the Editor of the *Examiner*" (concerning Richard Carlile), *Prometheus Unbound, Peter Bell the Third*, and several shorter poems. Shelley had requested that the Gisbornes send *The Cenci* and *Prometheus Unbound* in mid-October, but they were not sent to Ollier until mid-December (*PBS Letters*, #551).

9. This marks the end of the evolution, begun in late 1814, of Mary Jane Clairmont's name to Claire Clairmont. (Marion Kingston Stocking points out that in old age she added the name Constantia in acknowledgment of Shelley's poem to her [*CC Journals*, p. 13].) Mary Shelley generally uses the spelling *Claire* from this time forward.

10. Possibly Bonifacio Asioli (1769–1832), the most famous of a family of composers and a prolific composer of songs, cantatas, operas, and duets.

11. Shelley had written the poem in Florence during the latter part of October and on 2 November had sent it to Hunt to give to Ollier for immediate publication

(*PBS Letters*, #526). It was not published until 1840, when Mary Shelley included it in the second edition of Shelley, *Poetical Works* (1839).

To Maria Gisborne [Florence 27–30 November 1819][1]

My dear M[rs] G.

I have promised a lady here to write to you on a subject on which I think your trinity can be of service to her by giving her some necessary information—This lady has a son of 14 years of age who in a year will take up his commission—in the East Indian service—he is she says quite wild from India—but she wishes to make use of this year in giving him some mathematical instruction either here or at Pisa—The difficulty in this is that he does not understand the least Italian & she does not wish him to lose his time while he acquires this language—Nor does he understand french—so that her object is to get an introduction to some person sufficiently qualified who could teach him in English—This lady w[d] prefer Florence to Pisa as she is settled here—but I am afraid your counsels would be confined to Pisa—do you think Foggi[2] would be of any use on such an occasion—He wishes to begin from the beginning Henry perhaps might suggest something with regard to Florence.

I have still no news of my box which is very provoking since it gave out so much better hopes at the beginning.

What on earth can have come to the Sig[ra] Tonelli[3]—S. called there—the servant said—la famiglia sta in Inghilterra—you must help us out of this dilemma as we do not know what to do—if the Sig[ra] T. would send any one to our house to receive the money before noon on any day some one of us would be at home—to pay it—

I hope all is going on well with you & that this dreadful weather either does not exist at Livorno or that your health does not suffer by it—

When are we to see you?

Affectionately Yours
MWS.

[*Postscript written in pencil*] This letter was to have been sent last post—I have now received your letter—I hope to get the box today—

Shelley Calderonized on the late weather—he called it an epic of rain with an episode of frost & a few similes—concerning fine weather—

We have heard from England although not from the bankers but Peacocks letter renders the affair darker than ever[4]—Ah my dear friend you in your slow & sure way of proceeding ought hardly to have united yourself to our eccentric star I am afraid that you will repent & it grieves us both more than you can immagine that all sh[d] have gone so ill—but I think we may rest assured that this is delay & not loss—It can be nothing else

I write in haste—a carriage at the door to take me out & Percy asleep on my knee

Adieu.

Charles is at Vienna by this time he did not go by the steam boat to Trieste[5]—

be so kind as to let us know how we ought to direct to C.C. ferma in Posta Vienna[6]

[*In Shelley's hand*] Next Post or the Post after my bankers are to write & explain—Of course I shall soon send the good news—

[*In Mary Shelley's hand*] Our box is not yet come

ADDRESS: A Madame / Madame Gisborne / Livorno. POSTMARKS: (1) FIRENZE; (2) 1 DECEMBRE. ENDORSED: Recd. 1st Dec Ansd Do. PUBLISHED: Jones, #79. TEXT: MS., Bodleian Library (MS., Shelley, c. 1, ff. 344–46).

1. This letter was postmarked 1 December at Leghorn. The courier carried mail from Florence to Livorno on Tuesdays, Thursdays, and Saturdays. Mail was delivered in one day (*L'Indispensabile almanacco . . . per L'anno 1819* [Florence, 1818], p. 249). Since Mary Shelley said in her postscript that this letter was to be sent by the last post, we may assume that she began the letter on Saturday, 27 November, and completed it on Tuesday, 30 November.

2. Ferdinando Foggi, professor of law at the University of Pisa. The Shelleys had become acquainted with him through the Gisbornes and the Masons, who knew him to carry parcels for friends on trips between Florence and Pisa and also to give language lessons (*CC Journals*, p. 189, n. 68).

3. Maria Gisborne replied on 20 December: "she never stirs from home; yet I wish Mr. Shelley had seen her. She thinks the imbroglio of his not seeing her inexplicable" (Gisborne, *Journals and Letters*, p. 61).

4. In order to finance Henry Reveley's steamboat, Shelley had written to his bankers, Brooks, Son & Dixon, to draw a bill on them to the order of Webb & Co. at Leghorn. Shelley had miscalculated his balance on deposit, and Brooks had informed Peacock of an insufficiency of funds to meet the £200 bill. Upon receipt of Peacock's information (28 October), Shelley wrote to Brooks (30 October [*PBS Letters*, #525]). At the same time, he drew upon Horace Smith for £100, which he sent to the Gisbornes on 7 December. On 23 December Shelley received another £100, which he had had with the banker Torlonia at Rome. He sent this £100 also to the Gisbornes. (For a detailed explanation of Shelley's complicated accounts from October through December 1819, see *SC*, VI, 939–44.) Shelley's letter of 23 December indicated that the Gisbornes had led him to believe that the steamboat would be completed in three months (*PBS Letters*, #542).

5. Charles Clairmont had left Florence for Vienna on 10 November. Shelley had written to Henry Reveley that Charles Clairmont would write him (Shelley) an account of the Trieste steamboat and that he in turn would transmit it to Reveley (*PBS Letters*, #533).

6. That is, the proper phrase in German.

TO MARIA GISBORNE [Florence] Thursday. [?2 December 1819][1]

My dear M[rs] G.

I am become uneasy about this felucca which seems to be above a month coming from Genoa—I am afraid that it is cast away & all the little boy's flannel petticoats are gone to the bottom—

Now my confinement is well over & I am getting well & strong I hope you are beginning to consider your promised visit which was to take place about this time—It would give me so much pleasure & would be so very agreable to see you here—do think seriously about coming soon

The little boy is nearly 3 times as big as when he was born—he thrives well & cries little & is now taking a right down earnest sleep with all his heart in his shut eyes

There {are} some ladies come to this house who know Shelley's family[2] —the younger one was entousiasmée to see him—the elder said that he was a very shocking man—but finding that we became the mode she melted and paid us a visit she is a little old welshwoman without the slightest education—she has got an Italian master & has entered into the difficult part of the language—the singulars & plurals—the il's & the lo's & is to turn masculines into feminines & feminines into masculines—but she says she does not think she shall ever learn for she cannot help mixing welsh with her italian & besides it spoils her french—she speaks the sweetest french as you may judge by her telling her master Je ne peus lire aucune plus[3]—

The younger lady was a ward of one of Shelley's uncle's—she is lively & unaffected—she sings well for an english delettanti & if she would learn the scales would sing exceedingly well for she has a sweet voice So there is a great deal of good company for Clare who is as busy as a bee among them all serving as an interpreter to their masters—She has a most excellent singing master & he now teaches several other young ladies who are here—one who had had a very cross master in England when told to sing Sol burst into tears—the poor man was aghast—non capisco questo effetto[4]

I do not know why I write all this gossip to you—pray lett us hear of you & the steam boat & the felucca—

Affectionately Y[rs] MWS.

[*P. 1, top*] The rains confined Shelley to the house so much that he could not go to la Sig[ra] Tonelli[5]—today he has been—they say that she is still in England

PUBLISHED: Jones, #80. TEXT: MS., Bodleian Library (MS., Shelley, c. 1, ff. 347–48).

1. Mary Shelley dated this letter simply "Thursday." Between the salutation and the first line, "1st December 1819" was written in by John Gisborne, who also dated this letter "1 December 1819" in his Notebook copy. It is likely, therefore, that Mary Shelley wrote this letter on Thursday, 2 December, and that John Gisborne, in transcribing the letter into his Notebook, mistakenly thought Thursday was 1 December.

2. Sophia Stacey (the ward of Shelley's uncle Robert Parker) and her traveling companion, Corbet Parry-Jones. On 11 November the two women moved into the house where the Shelleys were living. Extracts from Sophia Stacey's journal indicate that she very much admired Shelley, who in turn grew quite fond of her. Her singing particularly pleased him, inspiring him to write a number of lyrics, including: "To Sophia," and "On a Faded Violet." When the women left the Palazza Marini for Rome on 29 December, they carried with them a letter of introduction from Shelley to Signora Dionigi (*PBS Letters*, #544). For information about Sophia Stacey, as well as extracts from her journal, see Angeli, *Shelley and His Friends in*

Italy. Sophia Stacey's journal was never printed in full, and White comments that it seems to have disappeared (*Shelley*, II, 172–75).

3. Very poor French for "I can no longer read."
4. "I do not understand this effect."
5. See [27–30 November 1819].

To Maria Gisborne [Florence ?13 December 1819][1]

You see—my dear Friend—by the receipt of your crowns[2] that we have recovered £100 of our money—there is still £100 in jeopardy—but we must hope & pray, & perhaps by dint of giving it up as lost we may find it again—I have intended for some time to write to you, but you cannot tell how my time is taken up in provoking trifles, which leave no trace behind—except indeed I may call the encreasing size of the little boy a trace—for the cause of that encrease is the great cause of my idleness—first breakfast late on his account—then after as soon as I have dressed him & put him to sleep I must seize the little leisure for a walk which is now so perfectly necessary to me—on my return—dinner—for young & old—dressing—then it is evening—& for these last evenings—a lady here & a very amiable one having been far too ill to go to the fire in the common sitting room of Mad^me^ DuP.[3] she has been with us—thus cutting up the few short remaining hours—but yesterday having taken a walk long enough to make my feet blister I have been obliged to cut it short today & this occasions this long letter of excuses. After all for several reasons I am very sorry that we have come to pass the winter at Florence especially this early season—attendance for me I could have got quite as good & far cheaper at Pisa—we should have been within a more possible distance of you—& I am too much confined to the house to see Florence well—and as we do not know an Italian soul here I can do nothing towards any plan of study that I may have meditated[4]—besides the weather at Pisa I hear is far milder—but there is now no remedy—for it w^d^ not accord with our œconomical plan to move again so soon—besides Claire has got so good a singing master & is getting on so prosperously in her sol fa's that I sh^d^ be sorry to break in upon her studies untill she had made a progress that would not fear a falling off when she left him. Shelley talks of coming to you—but the weather I am afraid will not permit it—his general health is much improved but he has a pain settled in his side which is taking so rhumatic an appearance that we fear cold & damp more than ever—We think of a course of warm baths for him in May—pray how far is Casciano[5] from Pisa? And now let me talk about you & ask you about your spirits—mine were very bad some days ago—they are better now—but always irregular We do not live here in the extreme solitude that you do—for we mix a little with the people down stairs because some of them are tolerably agreable people & others assert a claim to our acquaintance on the score of being acquainted with S.'s family. but you never see any one except those whom you shut out when you can—This is a melancholy thing—one does not wish you to go into the society that surrounds you but one grieves that you do not know any worth your friendship—I wish the steam boat were stocked & manned & bound for England—if you were not overcome by money cares there & think you would be happier among your country people [ ]

Can you not indeed take your money[6] from [the?] stocks without the consent of Henry's Uncle?—& his [obst]inacy—for obstinate no doubt he will be, may be cruel to you—Yet God knows what you would do with your money—although I am afraid that English funds are become more uncertain than foreign ones—

We have received our box[7]—it contained no books—it was a silly, expensive affair—but that was not my fault—I did the best I c^d^ & that you know is a consolation—Mad^me^ T. [*Tonelli*] is paid[8]—I have no other news for you—except that poor little Zoide[9] writes to say that she is unhappy so she is to come home—of course—the W's [*Webbs*] will storm but from what I have heard of Zoide's character I am sure that if she complains her mother is justified in taking her away.[10]

If you hear of any one coming to Florence would you send 4 brach.[11] to match the enclosed?

Affectionately Y^s^ MWS

Would you buy for me also a gown of a close pink stripe—not like the enclosed but of good material—if it is no wider than that buy 9 brach. if wider 8. send it by the first good conveyance—I have no room for apologies for troubling you but I am not the less obliged and in return I send you somthing [*cross-written*] to amuse you—the bane & antidote[12]—the bane from the quarterly the antidote from Blackwoods Edinburgh Magazine, a publication as furious as the quarterly but which takes up the arms singularly enough in Shelley's defence—we half think that unless it is Mitching Mallecho (See Hamlet Act III—Sc. II) that it must be by Walter Scot who is the only liberal man of that faction

If Henry goes to Pisa ask him to remember my request concerning the list of books from his astronomer—is the Genoese steam boat bad or good for you? We are anxious to hear concerning it—I have begun reading with Shelley the Conquista de Mexico by Solis—We have read very little as yet—have the kindness to send us the meaning of tamaño & alcabalas[13]

ADDRESS: A Madame / Madame Gisborne / Livorno. POSTMARKS: (1) FIRENZE; (2) [?15] DECEMBRE. ENDORSED: Recd 15th Dec. Ansd. 1819. PUBLISHED: Jones, #81. TEXT: MS., Bodleian Library (MS., Shelley, c. 1, ff. 349–50).

1. The copy of this letter in the John Gisborne Notebook is dated 13 December.
2. See [27–30 November 1819].
3. The Shelleys resided at Madame Merveilleux du Plantis's lodging house.
4. Mary Shelley's "study" was very likely related to her novel *Valperga*. The Shelleys must have written to Mrs. Mason expressing Mary Shelley's wish to meet an Italian who might make historical books and records available to her, for she responded: "I am sorry to perceive that your visit to Pisa will be so much retarded,

but I admire Mary's courage & industry—I sincerely regret that it is not in my power to be of service to her in this undertaking—I have not been in Florence except once en passant these fifteen years & the few people I knew there have probably no recollection of me, nor if they had would it (for many & weighty reasons) be prudent to recall my name [i.e., *Lady Mount Cashell*] to their remembrance—All I can say is, that when you have got all you can there (where I suppose the manuscript documents are chiefly to be found) & that you come to this place, I have scarcely any doubt of being able to obtain for you many books on the subject which interests you—probably everything in print which relates to it is as easy to be had here as at Florence" (Abinger MS., [?November–December] 1819).

Maria Gisborne's lengthy response indicates that she, too, was unable to provide Mary Shelley with an introduction to an Italian who might aid her in her research (Gisborne, *Journals and Letters*, pp. 57–62).

5. Cascina is about ten miles east of Pisa.

6. Shelley had advised the Gisbornes to withdraw their money from British Government Funds, for he believed a revolution was near that would diminish or cancel their holdings, which were their main financial support (*PBS Letters*, #524, #528, #532).

7. The box sent by the Hunts in response to the Shelleys' many reminders.

8. See [27–30 November 1819].

9. Daughter of Madame Merveilleux du Plantis.

10. Maria Gisborne responded with surprise at Zoide's likely return to Florence, since she understood that Madame du Plantis was arranging for Zoide to serve as a governess in Mr. Webb's household, where Zoide's sister Louisa was already employed (Gisborne, *Journals and Letters*, p. 62).

11. *Bracciatura* (Italian), "yards."

12. The "bane" was the *Quarterly Review*'s extraordinarily harsh treatment of Shelley's *Laon and Cythna* (see 24–25 November 1819). The "antidote" was the highly laudatory review of Shelley's *Alastor; or, The Spirit of Solitude* (London: Baldwin, Cradock, and Joy; and Carpenter and Son, 1816) by John Gibson Lockhart in *Blackwood's Edinburgh Magazine* 6 (November 1819): 148–54. The latter review refuted the *Quarterly*'s attack and depicted Shelley as a poet of genius who would attain true splendor if he altered his perverted philosophical views (see Reiman, *The Romantics Reviewed*, Part C, I, 118–24).

13. Antonio de Solis y Ribadeneira, *Historia de la conquista de Méjico* (1684), translated by Charles Townsend (1724) as *History of the Conquest of Mexico.* Maria Gisborne responded: "Tamaño. So great. Alcabala a tax or duty on goods" (Abinger MS.; Gisborne, *Journals and Letters*, p. 61).

To Maria Gisborne — Florence Dec 28—1819

My dear Mrs Gisborne

I am glad that you are pleased with the Prometheus[1]—the last act though very beautiful is certainly the most mystic of the four—I am glad also that Spencer pleases you for he is a favourite author of mine—in his days I fancy translations & plagiarisms were not considered so disgraceful as they are now—You have not all of him & perhaps you have not read therefore the parts that I particularly admire—the snowy Florimel—Belphœbe and her squire lover who is half meant for Q. Elizabeth & Lord Essex—Britomart is only an imitation—she is cold & dull but these others

& the lovely Una are his own creations & I own I like them better than Angelica although indeed the thought of her night scene with Medoro[2] came across me & made me pause as I wrote the opinion—but perhaps it is not in pathos but in the simple description of beauty that Spencer excels—His description of the island of of bliss is an exact translation of Tasso's garden of Armida[3] yet how is it that I find a greater simplicity & spirit in the translation than in the original—yet so it is.

You cannot guess how busy & I may almost say now it is over uselessly busy I have been these last days—Milly has left us & for 3 days we were without a servant for the child (chi è bello e grasso) now we have a German-Swiss who speaks Italian perfectly who as much as I see of her I prefer to Milly[4] infinitely so we are fortunate so far & now I think of beginning to read again Study I cannot for I have no books & I may not call simple reading study for Papa is continually saying & writing that to read one book without others beside you to which you may refer is mere childs work—but still I hope now to get on with latin & Spanish—Do you know that if you could borrow for us Rousseaus Emile & Voltaires essai sur l'eprit des nations[5] either or both you would oblige us very much & send them with the stripped cotons which I wish you to send if the duty is not intolerable but I dare say your <u>sage</u> (I mean Giuseppe)[6] can manage that.

Shelley has given up the idea of visiting Leghorn before the finishing of the steam boat—he is rather better these last 2 or 3 days but he has suffered dreadfully lately from his side—he seems a changed man his numerous weaknesses & ailments have left him & settled all in his side alone for he never any other winter suffered such constant pain there—It puts me in mind of the mountain of ills in the Spectator—where mankind exchange ills one with the other—there they all take up their old evils again as the most bearable[7] I do not know whether this is Shelley's case.

Well—I hope the steam engine is getting on prosperously—give our best loves to it and our compts (as more respectful to the higher being) to its maker—I have a headach & will not scribble any more except to say that Papa's riddle[8] is not yet divined Your way of cutting the knot we all think the best but it were easier to set Pelion upon Ossa than to make him think so

Adieu my dear <u>good</u> friend (& wise too & <u>upright</u>) I cannot answer what you say about Zoide that must remain for gossip—Mad[me] M. [*Merveilleux du Plantis*] might go on exceedingly well & gain if she had the brains of a goose but her head is a sive & her temper worse than wildfire it is gunpowder & blows up every thing—We see a great deal of Louise she is a good girl clever too but lazy—what say you to her jilting poor Charles[9] & marrying the steam boat (or its maker) tell it or him (if you are not afraid) that she has lovely hair pretty eyes—nice neck & shoulders for the rest non c'è male—

You see I chatter on & nonsense [to]o that is the worst of it—adieu

Affectionately yours
MWS.

Our best remembrances to Mr. G. [*Gisborne*] & Mr. R. [*Reveley*] If by any chance you have not sent the Prometheus add the word bowers after from their obscurest[10] & in the other change it to it's mother fears awhile[11]

ADDRESS: A Madame / Madame Gisborne / Livorno. POSTMARKS: (1) FIRENZE; (2) 31 DECEMBRE. ENDORSED: Recd. 31st Dec., 1819. Ansd. PUBLISHED: Jones, #82. TEXT: MS., Bodleian Library (MS., Shelley, c. 1, ff. 351–52).

1. Shelley wrote the fourth act of *Prometheus Unbound* in the autumn of 1819 and sent it to the Gisbornes on 23 December to read and then mail to Charles Ollier (*PBS Letters*, #542).

2. Florimel, Belphoebe, Britomart, and Una are figures in Spenser's *The Faerie Queene* (1589–96); Angelica and Medoro are figures in Ariosto's *Orlando Furioso* (1532).

3. In *Gerusalemme liberata* (1575).

4. Amelia Shields, the Shelleys' servant from Marlow. Mrs. Mason helped them find their new servant, Carolina (McAleer, *The Sensitive Plant*, p. 132).

5. *Émile* (1762); *Essai sur les Mœurs et l'esprit des nations* (1753–56).

6. The Gisbornes' servant.

7. Joseph Addison, *The Spectator*, 23 June 1714 and 25 June 1714.

8. Godwin's legal entanglement about his back rent.

9. Zoide and Louise, the daughters of Madame Merveilleux du Plantis (see [?13 December 1819]). Charles Clairmont, who had visited the Shelleys until 10 November, had fallen in love with Louise, but she had rejected him (White, *Shelley*, II, 154).

10. *Prometheus Unbound* 4. 375.

11. *Prometheus Unbound* 4. 392.

TO MARIA GISBORNE

Florence Jany. 6th 1820

Dearest Mrs Gisborne,

If the pattern of buff is sufficiently like to make the front breadth and sleeves of a gown, the rest of which is made, be so kind as to send it.

The pink is not at all the thing I mean, being both cold and ugly, and not fit for washing. Excuse the trouble I have given you, and my present haste.

Affectionately Your's
MWS

I have, I imagine, a Box at Mr Webb's—Can one enquire? If yes, then send it me—I have the Bill of Lading—

PUBLISHED: Jones, "New Letters," p. 54. TEXT: John Gisborne Notebook No. 2, Abinger MS., Bodleian Library.

TO MARIA GISBORNE

Florence Jany. 12th 1820

Here is a fine Tuscan winter! Are you not in a passion, my Dear Mrs Gisborne? I am sure I am, and have every reason; for besides all pains in the side, of which Shelley has plenty, he had an attack last Friday of fever, just like, only more severe, the one he had on returning to Leghorn from Florence[1]—Wind! Frost! Snow! How can England be worse?

Are you yet reconciled to the idea that England is become a despotism? The freedom with which the newspapers talk of our most detestable governors is as mocking death on a death bed. The work of dissolution goes on, not a whit the slower—And cannot England be saved? I do hope it will—I enclose to you a letter we have received from a stock broker[2] on the subject—You see what he says, The rich alone support the government—The poor, and middling classes are, I believe, to a man, against them—But we have fallen, I fear, on evil days. There are great spirits in England. So there were in the time of Cesar and Rome. Athens flourished but just before the despotism of Alexander—Will not England fall? I am full of these thoughts;[3] but to talk of something else, what do you think of an idea that has crost our brains of taking a house, and settling, during our Exile, at Florence—We are tired of roving—We want our books—We dare not settle in a very warm climate on account of our child—It is true, it is cold at Florence, but seldom, they say, so cold as this. Do you think we could manage with two or three months in the summer at the baths of Lucca? We should then have some comforts about us, and when we felt ourselves en fonds, the steam boat would be our wings to carry us quickly there, and quickly back to see what curiosities we desired to visit.

I hope you have not been teazed any more by those rascally Italians—When you calculate a bargain with them, you ought always to put so much for law expences in your calculation—

I have not yet received the buff gown—you would much oblige me by letting me have it as soon as is convenient.

How does this cold weather agree with you, and your two Catastas[4] of wood? We are already in our fourth, but then we have two fires, and in our two first, to say nothing of the two last, were cheated above half by Maria, who sold it. She has left us long ago—She cheated us horribly—so does the one with us now—but she is a very good servant.

Adieu, dear Mrs G—! The day will be benvenuto when I see you again, and this new year, if I see much of you within it. In any case may it be a fortunate one for you.—for us—I am tired of wishing or hoping. All goes on de pire en pire[5]—so let us shut our eyes—though the lightening of misfortune will pierce through our tight-closed lids.

So with this fine poetical image once more Adieu. I hope Mr G— [*Gisborne*] does not suffer from the cold—Lord B— is at Ravenna—reforming—i.e. making love and becoming a methodist.—but tare! so again I recommend you to Jehovah. Your's affectionately.

M.WS.

Henry and his child[6] are not forgotten. A happy year to them both. May the boat have sailed 10,000 leagues, and he be married to an heiress of £10,000 within it. Return the letter that I send—By the bye, I send you none—for I have been looking it over and find it not worth sending. He is in a rage with Lord C—[7] and says that the finance must explode one day—Do sent the cotton for my gown—

PUBLISHED: Jones, "New Letters," pp. 54–56. TEXT: John Gisborne Notebook No. 2, Abinger MS., Bodleian Library.

1. On 23 September 1819 Shelley had gone to Florence to find lodgings, and on 25 September he had returned to Leghorn "very unwell" (*MWS Journal*).

2. Horace Smith. (For a discussion of Smith's liberal politics expressed in his correspondence, see Stuart Curran, "The View from Versailles: Horace Smith on the Literary Scene of 1822," *Huntington Library Quarterly* 40 [1977]: 357–71.) Mary Shelley may have been reacting to news of the repressive "six acts" passed by Parliament in December 1819. Her letter of [24 March] 1820 to Marianne Hunt contains a lengthy satirical attack against the "enslaved state" of England.

3. That Mary Shelley expressed the same political concerns in an unlocated letter of 11 January 1820 to Mrs. Mason is evident from Mrs. Mason's response of 14 January (Abinger MS.).

4. "Piles."

5. "Worse and worse."

6. That is, his steam engine.

7. Robert Stewart (1769–1822), Viscount Castlereagh by courtesy—he succeeded his father as Second Marquess of Londonderry in 1821—was blamed by liberals for atrocities in Ireland following the rebellion of 1798 and, as Secretary of War (1805–9) and Foreign Secretary (1812–22), for the Tory government's generally reactionary policies at home and abroad, including the "six acts."

To Maria Gisborne

Florence—Teusday morning
[18 January 1820]

I cannot tell you my dear Friend how much we are grieved a terrified at Henry's misfortune[1]—One misfortune seems to succeed another for you & to let you have no rest. What advise do you have for him? Indeed you ought to have Vacca[2]—I hope indeed that you will write directly to let us know how he is for I shall be very anxious, & so shall we all—untill we know that he begins to recover more rapidly—

And what a miserable winter you are passing—indeed—indeed it makes me truly unhappy to think of your sufferings—I should think that list to the doors & windows and a fire would have been better & upon my word you must still do somthing—think that the steam engine will soon relieve you & do spare a few pauls to buy a large folding skreen I have seen them here which spread at your backs as you sit by the fire would keep out the drafts

Your letter has made me so uncomfortable that I cannot talk of other things except to tell you that Percy is well & that Shelley although better still feels the effects of the cold in an extreme nervous irritability

Pray let me hear <u>particularly</u> how Henry gets on and what effects are likely to ensue from this contusion—And let me earnestly entreat you not to continue your system—you may do yourselves serious injury—I am sure that it is necessary for Henry to be kept warm & comfortable—It almost seems like a treason to my affection for you to have been living so miserably while we at least have been indulging ourselves in plenty of firing—You must not do this—Indeed you must not—but I feel alas that my words are fruitless though I would give the world that they were not

Pray write by return of post

Affectionately & Anxiously Yours,
MWS.

Now I do insist that you make Giuseppe look for a skreen.

Henry ought {not} to have been so complaisant to Foggi[3]—You lost yourselves by good nature to others & cruelty to yourselves—I sent yesterday for the parcel & it has not come—I shall send today

[*Postscript by Shelley*] My first impulse after the first shock of your melancholy letter was to come to you—Could I not be of use—think of this, & if in any manner I should be capable of being turned to the minutest profit I intreat you to send for me—Send us the minutest intelligence of poor Henry—present to him my most affectionate remembrances, & accept the same for all—

ADDRESS: A Madame / Madme Gisborne / Livorno. POSTMARKS: (1) FIRENZE; (2) 19 GENNAIO. ENDORSED: 18 Jany. 1820 / Recd. Dy ans Do. PUBLISHED: Jones, #83. TEXT: MS., Bodleian Library (MS., Shelley, c. 1, ff. 390–91).

1. A contusion (see [c. 19 February] 1820).

2. Andreà Vaccà Berlinghieri (1772–1826), of Pisa, internationally distinguished physician, humanitarian, and political liberal. Mrs. Mason's letters to the Shelleys during their stay at Florence continually suggest that Shelley's poor health might be remedied by consulting Vaccà (Abinger MSS.). There is also evidence that the Shelleys' thought of spending the winter of 1817–18 at Pisa was prompted by Vaccà's reputation (*SC*, V, 290–93). The Shelleys and Claire Clairmont met Vaccà in 1820 after their move to Pisa, and Vaccà became their friend and physician. (For a detailed biographical sketch of Vaccà, see *CC Journals*, pp. 464–66.)

3. Ferdinando Foggi (see [27–30 November 1819], n. 2).

To Amelia Curran

Florence Jan 19—1820

My dear Miss Curran

If you suffer from the cold in the same proportion that we do I hope that at least it has had the good effect of entirely curing your malaria fever I know that you are a bad correspondant or I should be somewhat alarmed at not hearing from you again. Rome, I fancy, is tolerably full of English—perhaps you have some friends whom you like there—How does your painting go on?—And when do you think of returning to England? I am afraid that you will answer all these questions in low spirits & with bad news—and at such a distance and with no arguments except those which your own sense and feelings can suggest—what can I say but I really think that you would be happier in Dublin or London where you would be forced to exertions which would allay the dark feeling of unhappiness—for by my own case I find that employment is the only cure to low spirits.

This letter will be presented to you with a copy of the Cenci which I hope you will like—It was refused by Covent Garden—& now that Miss O'Neil[1] is married I do not think could be brought out with effect anywhere I hope however that it will be liked in print.

Would you have the kindness to tell me what opportunities a lady & gentleman with no family or servants could have of boarding in Rome in a genteel Italian family or if there is any thing of {a} respectable boarding house which the English frequent—an Italian family or english if perfectly comfortable would be preferred—do not give yourself much trouble about these questions but just answer as you happen to know

I own that during all this time my heart is still at Rome—It is a place I cannot think of without a sigh and yet I long to be there yet God knows when we shall—the winter past we shall not move south during the summer—the weather has been & is still dreadfully cold—& Shelley has suffered very much—I am well and so is the little boy who thrives surprisingly

Pray let us hear from you soon as I am anxious concerning your health & mention the subject of Shelley's last letter[2]—I am afraid we trouble you very much but for that object I know you will find my excuse in your own heart—

A good new year to you. Kind remembrances from my companions & believe me, my dear Miss Curran Yours ever grateful

MaryWShelley

could a lady get good harp strings sent from Rome here?

As we think of leaving Florence to consult Vaccà[3] at Pisa be so kind as to direct to me when you have the kindness to write to Leghorn[4]

ADDRESS: Miss Curran / Al 'Ario della Regina / 64 Via Sistina / Ultimo Piano Roma. PUBLISHED: Jones, #84. TEXT: MS., Bodleian Library (MS., Shelley, c. 1, ff. 392–93).

1. Eliza O'Neill (1791–1872), whom Shelley had wanted to play the role of Beatrice in *The Cenci* (*PBS Letters*, #504), had married William Wrixon Becher (M.P., created a baronet in 1831) on 18 December 1819 and retired from the theater.

2. Shelley had written to Amelia Curran on 18 November 1819 about various matters, including the tombstone for William (*PBS Letters*, #534).

3. See [18 January 1820], n. 2.

4. The Shelleys informed their friends to write to them at Leghorn, with the understanding that the Gisbornes would always know their whereabouts and send their mail on to them. On 26 January the Shelleys and Claire Clairmont moved to Pisa, where they lodged at the Tre Donzelle.

Shelley to John and Maria Gisborne[1] [Pisa 9 February 1820]

[*Postscript by Mary Shelley*] Besides which you will catch perhaps a cold which will fall on your chest—which—&c &c[2]

ENDORSED: Pisa 9th Feb / 1820. PUBLISHED: *PBS Letters*, #549. TEXT: MS., Bodleian Library (MS., Shelley, c. 1, f. 357).

1. *PBS Letters*, #549.

2. Trying to convince the Gisbornes to visit them for more than one day, Mary Shelley playfully warns against the dangers of night travel.

TO MARIA GISBORNE Pisa. [c. 19 February] 1820[1]

When the weather clears up, my Dear M^rs G— the carnival being ended, I shall expect to see you, for really I want to talk over your plans terribly with you, but one can say little or nothing in a letter—Nor can I receive your answer and then return mine without so many days interval, that I shall not mention them till I see you.

I have a favour to ask of you, "That by advertisement or any other way, you would let it be known throughout Leghorn that some one wants a Bible, to buy a good Quarto Bible, with the Apocrypha, (senza[2] no) and then make the bargain for me, and send it.

I send you the comb S. bought for me—it is so awkwardly made, that it tears my hair to pieces—Could you contrive to exchange it for 2 or 3 small ones, three or four fingers wide and four or five or six long, you would very much oblige me—

I have borrowed from a lady here the enclosed book to send you. I hope it will please you. Bring, or send it, when you have done with it—I am very uneasy about your Dante—I have a story that will make you laugh about that mad woman (anche disagreeable) Mrs Merveilleux du Plantis—

We have a parcel coming by the Symmetry, Capt. Moore. Addio. Cara Mia—never mind the moon,[3] but bring your Nightcap instead—Do you not know that a lady's frilled Nightcap has the same effect upon night, as the fair moon herself, even though she be not envelopped in her silvery clouds.

I hope Henry does not feel his blow[4] now, or any effects from it. Love from all to all. Do not blush or be angry.

Affectionately your's M.WS

Will you send me also some Arrow root, or in default of that Tapioca. It is of the greatest consequence, my Dearest M^rs G— that we should have the Chiroplast[5] by the bearer—I will explain the pressure of the affair when I see you, but pray send it.

Would you have the kindness to order at your Stationers a dozen plain books like that the Prometheus was copied in. I think the price was three pauls or more, but perhaps you or Beppe[6] will remember—Write a line by the bearer to tell us how you all are, and pray send the Chiroplast

Affectionately Your's
M.WS

PUBLISHED: Jones, "New Letters," pp. 56–57. TEXT: John Gisborne Notebook No. 2, Abinger MS., Bodleian Library.

1. On the basis of Mary Shelley's opening comments concerning the end of carnival and the bad weather, we may conjecture a date of 19 February for this letter. Carnival ended on 15 February, and the weather at Pisa was clear enough to allow walks until 19 February, when it rained (*CC Journals*). John Gisborne's Notebook indicates that this letter and the next were written in "Feb. or March 1820" at Pisa "Near about the same date."

2. "Without."

3. A reference to the Gisbornes' intention to visit the Shelleys at Pisa for one day and return to Leghorn the same night.

4. See [18 January 1820].

5. A mechanical device to assist young pianists in correctly positioning their hands. The Chiroplast belonged to Madame du Plantis, who was angry because Claire Clairmont had taken it to Pisa (*CC Journals*, pp. 122–23). Shelley had sent the Chiroplast to Henry Reveley on 11 February so that he could make a drawing of it and a copy could be made. The instrument was misdirected to the British Consul's house, which led to delay and confusion (*PBS Letters*, #550).

6. Giuseppe, the Gisbornes' servant. Beppo and Beppe are nicknames for the name Giuseppe.

TO MARIA GISBORNE Pisa [?24 February] 1820[1]

My Dear M^rs^ G—

I suppose we must not expect you until the weather is more settled—God knows when that will be!

I wish you would inquire if the servant you named (Caterina) is out of place, for we want one sadly to do every thing but cook We wish her to be rather an upper servant that could iron &c. Milly you know left us. Our present nursery maid is ill, and though the servant I want is not exactly for the child, yet it would be better if she were accustomed to and fond of children. I think Caterina would suit us very well, if her last place has not spoiled her.

Would you have the kindness to send us our tea directly—Dogana[2] paid, if necessary. Shelley is not well, and we are all uncomfortable as usual, with a servant ill and cross. You know our fate of old. We have received the Bible—it appears to me that you were sadly cheated—Adieu—pray let us see you soon in this most ugly town.

Affectionately Your's
M. WS

PUBLISHED: Jones, "New Letters," pp. 57–58. TEXT: John Gisborne Notebook No. 2, Abinger MS., Bodleian Library.

1. John Gisborne's Notebook tells us that this letter was written at about the same time as Mary Shelley's letter of [c. 19 February] 1820. Mary Shelley's statement that they must not expect the Gisbornes "until the weather is more settled" suggests that she may have written this letter on 24 February, the first rainy day after the nineteenth (*CC Journals*). On 28 February the Gisbornes visited the Shelleys for one day, bringing with them the maid Caterina, whom Mary Shelley asks about in this letter (*MWS Journal*).

2. "Duty."

To Sophia Stacey [Pisa c. 5 March 1820][1]

Before we received your letter, my dear Miss Stacey, which had fancied us still at Florence, we had flown to Pisa, living very quietly while you are honoured by the hands of princes and the eyes of princesses. I told you that you would find Naples more gay than any town in all Italy—than in all the world, I do believe. Rome will come like a sombre matron clothed in black after the sparkling, dancing Naples—Penseroso after Allegro—but during Holy Week a majestic Penseroso that strikes the eye, and more than Naples, if we omit the Prince of Batavia,[2] interests the heart. I hope that you will be able to get into the Sistine Chapel. Mr. Shelley and I have a plan of going there next year when all the English will have hastened to the coronation and we shall have Rome *all to ourselves*. It was so extremely crowded when we were there that we could gain admittance to few of the fêtes. . . .

I have just received your letter of February 28th and hasten to acknowledge the kind communication. Both Mr. Shelley and I are much concerned to hear of your ill-health. I should have thought that the divine air of Naples would have thawed the cold you got in Via Valfonda and have revived you. I never found my spirits so good since I entered upon *care* as at Naples, looking out on its delightful Bay. The sky, the shore, all its forms and the sensations it inspires, appear formed and modulated by the Spirit of Good alone unalloyed by any evil. Its temperature and fertility would, if men were free from evil, render it a faery habitation of delight—but as a Neapolitan said of it, *'E' un Paradiso abitato dai diavoli.'*[3] But Rome is formed by men—a city in the midst of a desert, its associations and being are entirely human. Its hills are mole-hills even when compared with the low Apennines of Naples, but they are giants to us which once bestrode the world. Many of them are formed alone by the ruins of materials brought there by man. And the Coliseum is his masterpiece. But a truce to Rome. It is my *hobby-horse*, and as it is only a stupid wooden fellow that cannot carry me thither, he must needs stay in his stable if he will not alter his course. I hope you will go to Paestum, and in doing that you will have done more than many of our English Butterflies do—and it is ten to one if you get there without some fearful adventure. The inhabitants are so savage—clothed in rough sheep-skins with wolfish hearts, and no sweet outsides—a bridge also that has been building these twenty years and is not finished! We walked from that broken bridge to Paestum and returned in a cart drawn by oxen. . . .

We are much flattered by your affectionate remembrances and desires to see us—a desire entirely sympathized with by us. We shall remain here stationary until the end of May, when Mr. S. is ordered to the Baths of Lucca, where we shall accordingly pass the summer—I am afraid that it does not accord with your plans, *bella Sofia*, to pass it there likewise: will not you also be one of the swallows to return to see his new most excellent and most gracious majesty crowned?[4] Alas, but a few days ago he was but a good-for-nothing prince—bankrupt in character—but the crown that encircles the mortal temples of a king has regenerated him.

Let the friend of the Courier forgive my radicalism in favour of my being hers very affectionately,

Mary Shelley

[*In a postscript, followed by the well-known lines, "On a Dead Violet," Shelley adds:*] I promised you what I cannot perform; a song on singing: —there are only two subjects remaining. I have a few old stanzas on one which though simple and rude, look as if they were dictated by the heart. And so—if you tell no one *whose* they are, you are welcome to them.

[*The verses follow, after which he adds:*] Pardon these dull verses from one who is dull—but who is not the less ever yours, P.B.S.

When you come to Pisa continue to see us—Casa Frassi, Lung' Arno.

PUBLISHED: Jones, #86. TEXT: Angeli, *Shelley and His Friends in Italy*, pp. 102–5.

1. Claire Clairmont indicates in her *Journal* that they received Sophia Stacey's letter on 5 March, and Mary Shelley states that she answers it at once.

2. Louis Bonaparte (1778–1846), brother of Napoleon I and, from 1806 to 1810, King of Holland (the Batavian Republic from 1795 to 1806). He spent most of his later life involved in literary pursuits in Rome and Florence.

3. "It is a paradise inhabited by devils."

4. George III had died on 29 January 1820.

TO MARIA GISBORNE

[Pisa c. 10 March 1820][1]

Shelley has returned safe,[2] my dear Friend, a little cold or so, & very glad to see the fire again, but still more glad to have seen you, being one who pleases him more than a fire so that we have a plan of keeping you with us.

Seriously I have a very serious plan to propose to you so I will mend my very bad pen and you must collect strength & thought I will tell you all about it.

You say that you reflect with horror on the idea of going to England—and as you will stay too short a time to make it any pleasure to you—& as one of you must return—need you all go? My proposal is that you give your power of attorney to Mr G. [*Gisborne*] Send him & Henry off when you decide upon going & come & visit us. I need not tell you what a pleasure this will be to us—after our various misfortunes we want a little recreation & what can be more so than the presence of such a friend as you are, my dear Mrs Gisborne? It will fill up so many hours with pleasant conversation that are now spent in unhappy reflection and be one of greatest almost the only pleasure we have had {for} a long, long time.

Then consider the advantage that it may be of to you. It will save you the trouble of a long & fatiguing journey—The expence to Mr G. & Henry will be very trifling—I assure you that you with all your fears hardly foresee half the expences of living in London. but Henry may be with his uncle &

in various ways they may be accommodated—If they are obliged to remain in England you will be here to sell the furniture & by means of the Swiss vetturinos[3] may join them safely & well—again if they return, still there will be the expence of one returning saved—Your health is delicate—but perhaps they can go by Marseilles perhaps & in France for 2 if they travel hard posting will be fully as cheap as a vetturino & then the journey will be very quickly done to Paris & from Paris there are excellent diligences[4]—as you pay a horse a person one more person makes a considerable difference in the expence. You will suffer great discomfort if you go—You may stay here quite comfortably—

What say you, my dear Sir? Will you come over to our side of the question? Henry will take {care} of you on the journey & you will take care of him when you arrive at the jour{ne}y's end & poor dear Mrs Gisborne will be saved much care & pain.

If you accept our invitation return the answer soon that we may ascertain whether our good star has yet risen—but if you hesitate pray take a week to decide because I assure you that the more you reflect the better it will appear to you

The other day[5] as Clare & Shelley were walking out they beheld a little dirty blacksmith's boy running away from a tall long-legged man running with an umbrella under his arm after him crying <u>fermatelo</u> <u>fermatelo</u>—the boy got into a house & cried—son nella mia botega! non tocami! son nella mia botega—Shelley approached & asked cosa c'è for the tall umbrella gentleman had seized the boy by the collar—He (the tall man) cried "Cercate il governatore—subito cercate il governatore"—Ma perche? che cosa è?" "Signor n[on] fa niente che cosa sia—cercate il g[over]natore—subito cercatelo!"[6] & this with the greatest vehemence—a crowd collected—Clare twitched S. & remonstrated—Don Quixote did not like to leave the boy in thrawl but deafened by the tall strider's vociferations & overcome by Clare's importunities he departed—& the [*then*] Clare out of breath with terror as you may well suppose said 'for mercy's sake have nothing to do with those people it's the reverend Colonel Calicot Finch[7] so they escaped the attack.

Can you not get me darning needles 6·7·8 & 9 2 papers of the 3 first numbers one of 9. also a little case to put them in I have seen one here but they ask 10 pauls. And before 4 day are out 1 lb of arrowroot—

We received the tea & biscuits but as we owed most of the former to Mrs Mason pray send another lb when you send again.

If you visited us—the bright Giuseppe should come with you—take my word for it. it is an excellent plan for us all.

Affectionately yours MWS.

[*P. 1, upside-down*] The measles are all about us & Vaccà thinks that our Percy has it—but so slightly that if it get not worse it will be rather a benefit getting it over so easily than to be regretted his having caught it—he has the eruption but no fever.

ADDRESS: Alla Ornatissima Signora / Signora Maria Gisborne / Livorno. POSTMARKS: (1) PISA; (2) 12 MARZO. ENDORSED: recd. 12th March / Ans. PUBLISHED: Jones, #87. TEXT: MS., Bodleian Library (MS., Shelley, c. 1, ff. 394–95).

1. Mary Shelley's letters from Pisa generally took two days to reach the Gisbornes at Leghorn.

2. Shelley had visited the Gisbornes at Leghorn from 3 through 6 March.

3. See [c. 3] December 1818, n. 2.

4. Scheduled public-mail and passenger coaches.

5. On 8 March (*CC Journals*).

6. "*Stop him stop him.* . . . I am in my shop! don't touch me! I am in my shop! . . . 'Go get the governor—immediately go get the governor'—But why? what is it?' 'Signor it is not important what it is—go get the governor—immediately go get him!' "

7. See 22 January 1819.

TO MARIA GISBORNE — Pisa. [c. 11 March 1820][1]

We only send you the two last papers because we cannot find the others. In future, we shall be more regular. There is enough in these two to keep you talking till next week—There was nothing in the others.

Percy has got the measles very lightly—We go to other lodgings up stairs on Tuesday, and hope you will soon come to see us. I assure you Oscar[2] will play the Damma very well, even if you should be a night absent. My pen sputters. You cannot get from a library for me Voltaire's Essai sur l'ésprit, or Rousseau's Emile to send me.[3] Adieu! God keep you, and bless you, and send you to know the right way

Your's s——

PUBLISHED: Jones, "New Letters," p. 58. TEXT: John Gisborne Notebook No. 2, Abinger MS., Bodleian Library.

1. Although John Gisborne dates this letter "between 18th & 24 March," Jones assigns the date of c. 9 March, since the *MWS Journal* records Percy's measles on that day and the Shelleys removed to more spacious quarters at Casa Frasi on Tuesday, 14 March. Since Mary Shelley's [c. 10 March] letter indicates that Vaccà "thinks" Percy has measles, while this letter confirms that he has measles, it seems appropriate to assign a date of [c. 11 March].

2. The Gisbornes' dog.

3. Mary Shelley first requested these books in her letter of 28 December 1819.

TO MARIA GISBORNE — Pisa Teusday. [14 March 1820][1]

Dearest M[rs] G.

Do you think you could get a good woman cook for us—do pray look about—& write to me if you hear of one but <u>see</u> her before you write—the wages we w[d] give a{re} four crowns or 4 & ½ & she find bread & wine.—And in the mean time have the kindness to send me Celeste's address for Clare could not find the house.

I daily expect a parcel from you as I am in great want of the arrow root—I do not like not hearing from you since it makes me fear that you hesitate concerning my most reasonable proposition—you cannot conceive how very much you will dissapoint us if you refuse & how very much you will bore yourself by going to the desolate & enslaved England.

Today we move to pleasant roomy appartments—do come & see us & sleep at our house & do not be obstinate—do you not know that S. E.[2] is the bride and therefore there is no fear

That letter from My father that you last sent me had laid more than a month at the Leghorn Post Office—the delay has been a great evil to us—

Adieu be good & docile—& do not force me to write a long letter of reasoning—if you are not reasonable obey & if Mr Gisborne does not like to lose the dolce sua società[3] which is very natural let him think of the ornatissima[4] Sra Maria in the dust of travelling—in the vexations of saving in a country where you will find a pound will not go so far as a crown here let him trust the cara donna to us we will teach her no treason—One thing I insist upon which is if you hesitate that you come here to argue the point.

Adieu affectionately ys MWS.

ADDRESS: Signora Maria Gisborne / per ricapito al forno d'Isidoro / vicino al Ponte di S. Marco / Livorno. ENDORSED: Recd. 15 March / Ans. PUBLISHED: Jones, #88. TEXT: MS., Bodleian Library (MS., Shelley, c. 1, ff. 396–97).

1. Mary Shelley says that on the day of this letter they will move, and they moved on 14 March (*MWS Journal*).

2. That is, the steam engine is Henry Reveley's bride. Mary Shelley is apparently teasing Maria Gisborne for her unwillingness to leave the thirty-year-old engineer alone at Leghorn for more than one day.

3. "Sweetness of your company."

4. "Well-attired."

To William Godwin[1] [Pisa 14 March 1820]

What I fear is the business: how happy should we all be, if you had given it up, & were living without that load of evils!

PUBLISHED: *S&M*, II, 488A–488B; it is cited as a fragment of a Mary Shelley letter in Palacio, *Mary Shelley*, pp. 601–2. TEXT: MS. (photocopy), Abinger MS., Bodleian Library.

1. William Godwin's letter of 30 March 1820 to Mary Shelley begins: "In your letter of the 14th instant just received, you give me a subject to write upon, & I write accordingly." He goes on to quote part of Mary Shelley's letter, and then to express to both Shelleys his interest in remaining in the book-publishing business because of its intellectual stimulation.

To Maria Gisborne Pisa. Wednesday. [22 March 1820]

Cara Signora—

You are wrong, believe me, in saying that you ought to go to England—the duty consists in visiting us upon my word it does—But as I said before come & argue the point—We can now offer you a comfortable bed & indeed you must not be so particular—Percy has the measles still on him—it has made a very light but a very long course—he has not, by Vaccà's commands been outside the door this fort'night nor will he untill the weather becomes decidedly warm as yet we have had cold winds—My comming is out of the question—to be jolted with a child for 3½ hours is no joke—So pray do come to see us—As to your staying with us when Mr G. [*Gisborne*] & R. [*Reveley*] go to England the more I think of it the more excellent the plan seems argue the point with you I must.

Shelley is a good deal better these last ⟨two⟩ days & we are very busy translating Spinosa[1] I write from his dictation & we get on—by the bye I wish you w^d send me the vol of the Encyclopedia, if Henry can spare it, that gives a system of short hand for I want to learn one without delay.

I wish I could be certain that you could come to see us. Suppose you & Mr G. came seperately & in succession—now indeed there can be no objection to this it w^d planer all difficulties you might stay 3 days each & it w^d be no such mighty affair—after all you ought not to refuse all accommodation

Claires shoes suit extremely well be so kind as to pay for them—I want a pair of black ones for the house but will not pay more than 8 pauls—will he make a slim pair of stuff kid or morocco for this they must be made on the same last as my green stuff ones. If he does not remember, I will send him one. Two papers by a sbaglio[2] were omitted in your last packet—they shall come in the next.

Have you heard whether the Symetry[3] has left London

Affectionately Ys
MWS.

ADDRESS: A Madame / Madame Gisborne / Livorno. POSTMARKS: (1) PISA; (2) 24 MARZO. ENDORSED: Recd. 24th March / Ansd. 26th Do. PUBLISHED: Jones, #89. TEXT: MS., Bodleian Library (MS., Shelley, c. 1, ff. 398–99).

1. Shelley's interest in Spinoza began at least as early as 2 January 1813, when he wrote Thomas Hookham requesting a copy of the *Tractatus Theologico-Politicus*. Shelley's translation of this book spanned the years 1817–21 (*MWS Journal*, 17–20 September 1822). The copy of Spinoza's *Tractatus* that Shelley and Mary Shelley used is on deposit at The Carl H. Pforzheimer Library, and the annotations in it will be discussed in a forthcoming volume of *Shelley and His Circle* (*SC*).

2. "Mistake."

3. A ship by which the Shelleys expected a parcel (see [c. 19 February] 1820).

To Marianne Hunt Pisa. Feb 24th [error for 24 March] 1820[1]

We have at last received Bessy's letter my dear Marianne, when the long protracted silence of our poor dear friend made us fear that he must be engaged in some plot or other with T—d[2] or others so to engross his time that for three months (& during cold weather too) he could not send one look to Italy. But it appears that he is only engaged in the same plot that exercises all the world—viz. care. & I would write a great deal to say how melancholy it makes me to see all my friends oppressed by the same load—but I wish letters from Italy to be a recreation & to draw you out of your cares as much as vain words, & kind remem{bran}ces can. Although before I leave the subject of your cares my dear, let me advert to your health—Bessy says in her letter that Percy from a sickly infant is grown a fine stout boy—he appears to have been in the same case as Swinburne & I am afraid from the same cause—I could say a great many things to prove to you that a woman is not a field to be continually employed either in bringing forth or enlarging grain—but I say only, take care of yourself. And so I pass on to something else.

We are now comfortably settled in Pisa for 3 months more than we have already staid & then we go again to the Baths of Lucca. Shelley's health is so very delicate that little as he can bear cold—heat is almost more injurious to him & he is ordered to seek the coolest climate Tuscany affords i.e. the Baths of Lucca: besides the Baths themselves are recommended for him The most famous surgeon in all Italy lives at Pisa, Vaccà—he is a very pleasant man—a great republican & no Xtian—He tells Shelley to take care of himself & strengthen himself but to take no medecine. At Pisa we have an appartment on the Lung' Arno—a street that runs the length of the town on each side of the Arno, and the side which receives the southern sun is the warmest & freshest climate in the world—We have two bed rooms 2 sitting rooms kitchen servants rooms nicely furnished—& very clean & new (a great thing in this country for 4 guineas & a ½ a month—the rooms are light and airy—so you see we begin to profit by Italian prices—One learns this very slowly but I assure you a crown here goes as far in the conveniences & necessaries of life as £1 in England & if it were not for claims on us & expences that are as it were external or perhaps rather internal for they belong to ourselves & not to the Country we live in we sh[d] be very rich indeed. As it is for the first time in our lives we get on easily—our minds undisturbed by weekly bills & daily expences & with a little care we expect to get the things into better order than they are.

Only one thing teazes us—Elise has married & Milly has quitted us & we have only Italian servants who teaze us out of our lives—I am trying to get a Swiss & hope that I shall succeed. We see no society it is true except one or two English who are friends & not acquaintances—we might if we pleased but it is so much trouble to begin & I am so much confined & my time is so much taken up with my child that I sh[d] grudge the time—however in the summer or next winter we shall I think mix a little with the Italians Pisa is a pretty town but its inhabitants w[d] exercise all Hoggs vocabulary of scamps, raffs &c &c to fully describe their ragged-haired, shirtless condition. Many of them are students of the university & they are none of the genteelest of the crew. Then there are Bargees, beggars without number; galley slaves in their yellow & red dress with chains—the women in dirty cotton gowns trailing in the dirt—pink silk hats starting up in the air to run away from their ugly faces in this manner  (for they always tie the bows at the points {of} their chins—& white satiny shoes—& fellows with bushy hair—large whiskers, canes in their hands, & a bit of dirty party coloured riband (a symbol of nobility) sticking in their button holes) that mean to look like the lords of the rabble but who only look like their drivers—The Pisans I dislike more than any of the Italians & none of them are as yet favourites with me. Not that I much wish to be in England if I could but import a cargo of friends & books from that island here. I am too much depressed by its enslaved state, my inutility; the little chance there is for freedom; & the great chance there is for tyranny to wish to be witness of its degradation step by step, & to feel all the sensations of indignation & horror which I know I shd experience were I to hear daily the talk of the subjects or rather the slaves of King Cant whose dominion I fear is of wider extent in England than any where else. At present I have it double distilled through Galignani[3] & even thus frittered way it makes one almost sick. No—since I have seen Rome, that City is my Country, & I do not wish to own any other untill England is free & true that is untill the throne Cant the God or if you will the abominable idol before whom at present the english are offering up a sacrifize of blood & liberty, be over thrown. Cant has more power in parliament, & over the Kingdom than fear or any other motive—a man now in England wd as soon think of refusing a duel as of not listening to & talking the language of Cant & from the same motive—he wd be afraid of being turned out of society.

Besides these reasons you know many others, my dear Marianne, of an individual nature that keep us from returning. If we had no debts yet they wd instantly accumulate if we went back to England—& then Shelley's health—the more we see & hear the more we are convinced that this climate is absolutely necessary to him. Not that this is a Paradise of cloudless skies & windless air just now the libechio is blowing hurricanes—but they are equinoctial gales—but it {is} so much better than your northern island. But do not think that I am unenglishifying myself—but that nook of ci devant free land, so sweetly surrounded by the sea is no longer England but Castlereagh[4] land or New Land Castlereagh,—heaven defend me from being a Castlereaghish woman. What say you to Hunt's gravely putting a letter in his Examiner as from a Correspondant saying that on the approaching elections, & during the present state of the country it is dangerous to repeat the name of England which has become the watchword of rebellion & irreligion—& that while the land continues in its present demoralized & disturbed state that all loyal persons should distinguish themselves by assuming for their country the demonination [*denomination*] I before mentioned The more loyal one, which wd be Georgia is objectionable on account of the immorality of the women of the region that goes by that name,[5] which by association might have a bad effect on the imaginations of our chaste country women of unblemished reputation!!!!!—Is not this the talk of God Cant? & of his prime council the Exxxxxh Parliament? & of his prime organ the Courier newspaper?—But I really think an excellent plan might be made of it—All those who wish to become subjects of the new kingdom ought to be obliged to take an oath of citizenship not as Irish English or Scotch but as Castlereaghish—all that refused sh^d be put on the alien list—besides the Government should have the right to refuse subjects—what a picnic kingdom it w^d become! One of the first things w^d be to import a cargo of subjects from all various oppressed countries on the earth—not to free them but as good examples for the rest—A man w^d only have to enter himself a slave—a fool—a bigot—& a tyrant where he can; to become a Castlereaghishman. The form of their oath sh^d be—The king shall have my wealth—Castlereagh my obedience—his parliament my love—the Courier my trust—the Quarter[l]y my belief—Murray my custom—down with the Whigs & Radicals—So God help me. Their belief may be asily [*easily*] exprest—I believe in Cant—the creator of ⟨God⟩ this kingdom the Supporter of Castlereagh & maker &c of all good fortunes; The sole rule of life & the life of all morality—created by fear, falsehood & hate; brought into fashion by Castlereagh, for the use of Castlereagish-men & women—detested by the Whigs yet used by them—detested by the Radicals whom it detests—[ ] born long ago, but grew much since the French Revolution, & more since the establishment of the most holy kingdom New Land Castlereagh—May it never die—As it has changed all truth to a lie, so does it live in & by lies & may its food never fail; nor can it while we exist. I believe in all that Cant teaches, as it is revealed to me by the Courier, & the Quarterly, & sold to me by Murray—whom Cant bless. I believe in all plots Cant feigns & creates & will use none but the language of Cant unto my last day—amen!"—I really think I will write to Castlereagh on the subject it w^d be a God send to him such a kingdom, & save him a world of trouble in grinding & pounding, & hanging & taxing, the English that remain into Castlereaghish for all that w^d not accede to the terms of his agreement w^d be aliens & so an end to them.—You see what a John or rather Joan Bull[6] I am so full of politics—But I entreat you to adopt my vocabulary & call all that can support so vile a wretch as that detested Irishman by their proper name—do not degrade—the name of British they are & ever must be Castlereaghish—which pronounced in a short way Castleraish wont be very uncouth & will be very apt.

I hope that we shall soon hear of your health & well-being, my dear Marianne. Little Percy has got the measles very lightly—it is a much milder malady in this climate than with you—& he has it mildly for this climate—Do pray you or Hunt write—Bessy's letter is dated the 6th Jan^ry so God knows what may have happened since then—nothing ill I trust—

But we now begin to feel that we are not travellers but exiles—since our English friends neglect & forget us—What say you to this reproach? or will you consider it as one?—

Adieu—dear Marianne
Affectionately y^s ever
Marina W.S.

Pisa. (direct to us here.)

We have just re^d Hunt's letter—it is dreadful to see how much he is teazed—I hope, how sincerely that you are now going on better. do you write—Does he think I c^d write for his Indicator & what kind of thing w^d he like. Shelley will answer his letter next week—adieu

ADDRESS: Mrs. Leigh Hunt / Examiner Office / 19 Catherine St. Strand / London / Inghilterra / Angleterre. POSTMARKS: (1) Pisa; (2) FPO / AP. 8 / 1820. PUBLISHED: Jones, #85. TEXT: MS., Huntington Library (HM 2746).

1. Mary Shelley's date of 24 February 1820 is an error for 24 March 1820, for in this letter Mary Shelley refers to Percy's measles, which he contracted on 9 March, and to their comfortable apartments, to which they moved on 14 March (*MWS Journal*; *CC Journals*). Moreover, the letter from Bessy Kent to which this letter is a response was received on 19 March (*CC Journals*). Shelley answered Bessy Kent's and Hunt's letters mentioned in Mary Shelley's postscript on 5 April (*PBS Letters*, #557). These facts and the 8 April 1820 postmark all support 24 March as the probable date.

2. Arthur Thistlewood (1770–1820) was the leader of the Cato Street conspiracy, a radical plot to murder all the members of the British Cabinet on 23 February 1820. The conspirators were betrayed and arrested before they could execute their plan; Thistlewood and four others were condemned to death and were hanged on 1 May 1820. Shelley's letter to Ollier of 13 March 1820 also refers to the plot and Hunt's possible involvement in it (*PBS Letters*, #555).

3. *Galignani's Messenger*, a weekly Parisian English-language newspaper.

4. See 12 January 1820.

5. That is, the area of the Caucasus, now part of the Soviet Union.

6. In Shelley's *Oedipus Tyrannus; or Swellfoot the Tyrant*, written in August 1820, Queen Caroline is represented by Iona Taurina ("Joan Bull"), her enemy Castlereagh by Purganax (Greek transliteration for Castlereagh) (Carlos Baker, *Shelley's Major Poetry: The Fabric of a Vision* [Princeton: Princeton University Press, 1948], p. 179). Mary Shelley's attack in this letter and others and Shelley's *Oedipus Tyrannus* employ figures of speech, characters, and ideas common to a flood of satires, tracts, and cartoons of the period on the Queen Caroline controversy (see 19 July 1820).

TO MARIA GISBORNE — Pisa Sunday [26 March 1820][1]

Dear M^rs G—

Since you do not write surely you come—

What does the Spanish Consul say to the distress of his Monarch[2] Give him my compts & tell him that it m'ir cresce [*mi rincresce*] molto[3]—. Vaccà is delighted about it—The Rev. Colonel[4] has been impudent to Mad^me Tantini[5] & is dismissed—

The more I think of my plan the more it delights me—but I dare not think of it for you are so very unreasonable & cross.

Can you get us a good English Corkscrew—

Affectionately Y^s MWS

Last night I received your letter—Your arguments Do not appear to me conclusive—put [*but*] you know best—I sh^d think that unless Henry lets out the secret himself which he sh^d be cautioned against that his Uncle will not guess that he has just entered his eleventh year but will imagine him to be 30 & in that case will not {at} all be alarmed as [*at*] Gisbornes being with him—If your presnce in England is absolutely necessary for receiving the property into your own hands it is one thing but if you can get it without renouncing it it does not appear to me to be worth a journey to England—But in all this you must judge—but it vexes me that you do not talk of comming to see us—

Do you hear anything of the Symetry—?[6] Addio Carino—The month of march is nearly gone & bad weather with it I hope—

[*P. 1, upside-down*] Remember you can have a bed with us without the slightest inconvenience to us.

ADDRESS: Mrs. Gisborne. PUBLISHED: Jones, #90. TEXT: MS., Bodleian Library (MS., Shelley, c. 1, ff. 400–401).

1. There are two notes on this letter in another hand: "Pisa between 26 March and Good friday 1820" and "We have got a cook." The copy in John Gisborne's Notebook is dated 28 March, possibly due to a misreading of *Sunday* as *Tuesday*. Mary Shelley's comment that "March is nearly gone" suggests that she wrote on 26 March, the last Sunday of the month.

2. In January 1820 a meeting at Cadiz grew into a full-scale revolution in Spain against the tyrannical abuses of Ferdinand VII (who reigned 1814–33). The Spanish monarch was held captive by the revolutionaries from 1820 through 1823, during which time the constitution of 1812 was reinstated. On 15 March Claire Clairmont recorded in her *Journal*: "Report that the insurgent of Spain have twice defeated the troops under General Freyre. and are now called ⟨nat⟩ armèe nationale." Shelley contemplated going to Spain "on account of these glorious events" (*PBS Letters*, #557). He expressed his hopes for a republic in "Ode to Liberty," written between March and 12 July 1820 (see 22 January 1819).

3. "Is very regrettable to me."

4. See 22 January 1819.

5. Cecilia Liebrecht Tantini (b. 1772) and her husband, Francesco Tantini (1779–1831), a distinguished physician, were introduced to the Shelleys by Mrs. Mason (*CC Journals*, p. 130).

6. See [c. 19 February] 1820.

TO MARIA GISBORNE

Pisa. Good Friday [31 March] 1820

My dear Mrs Gisborne

I will send your box soon & perhaps a vol of Political Justice which I hear you have defended to the loss of <u>ancient</u> <u>friendship</u>. Shelley c^d not be persuaded to continue his subscription to Gaglignani untill he found the paper stopt so we shall not have it for some days—I suppose however that you have heard the news—that the Beloved Ferdinand has proclaimed the Constitution of 1812 & called the Cortes—The Inquisition is abolished —The dungeons opened & the Patriots pouring out—This is good. I sh^d^ like to be in Madrid now.[1]

Do you think that you c^d^ get me some little stockings or shoes that w^d^ wash for Percy—If not could not the Miss Riccis[2] manufacture some out of old ones—they new footed some very nicely for me so perhaps they could—his foot is the length of your middle finger—if it can be done w^d^ you set them to work—I want 4 p^rs^ Claires shoes I suppose are to cost 8 pauls—I sh^d^ not think he w^d^ not charge more.

You do not write but pray come I think you c^d^ manage it in the way I mentioned—

How does Mr G. [*Gisborne*] get on with Homer has he nearly finished the Iliad? You ought to have read it with him.

Adieu dear Mrs G. The sun shines & it is divine weather Shelley is not very well if I c^d^ get a pretty boat & come down in 2 hours I w^d^ come but a carriage & a child are discords—But you will come surely.

Very since{re}ly & for ever yours
MaryWS.

After all, like a goose I closed my letter having forgot the most particular thing I had to say—A gentleman of our acquaintance is going to Casciano[3] in May he will want a sitting room a bed room for himself & another for his servant—a man of the name of Passetti has asked 15 seq. per month for these accommodations—w^d^ you have the kindness to tell me what he ought to pay and the names of some reasonable lodging people there to apply to—& another facility you can thing [*think*] of—& the nearest to the baths—in short if you w^d^ kindly send me the information you judge necessary on the subject.

Addio Cara Mia

ADDRESS: Alla Ornatissima Signora / La Signora Maria Gisborne / Livorno. POSTMARKS: (1) Pisa; (2) 2 APRILE. ENDORSED: Pisa Good Friday / 1820 / Between the 26th March and the 9th April. PUBLISHED: Jones, #91. TEXT: MS., Bodleian Library (MS., Shelley, c. 1, ff. 402–3).

1. See [26 March 1820].

2. Carlotta and Apollonia Ricci, daughters of the Gisbornes' landlord at Leghorn (White, *Shelley*, II, 207).

3. Mrs. Mason had requested this information for Mr. Mason in her letter to Mary Shelley of 14 January (Abinger MS.).

To John Gisborne   Pisa—Teusday Evening. [4 April 1820]

My dear Sir

I am very much obliged to you for the trouble you take about my little commissions—it is very kind of you & I hope does not teaze you too much

—I hope M[rs] Gisborne is better. Shelley saw the noble scion of the Fudges[1] who said that Henry was ill—that & your letter has frightened us but as you do not mention it in your note I hope that he is better—

I return the stocking—it will do very well—but since the weather is so warm I will only have two pair—I have short coated the young Gentleman —& I feared that he w[d] feel cold but he is always hot & indeed it is most delightful weather—

Both we & our friend are very much obliged to you for your information concerning Casciano—It is the husband of M[rs] Mason I think I told you that he had been confined the whole winter with an attack of rhumatism—he has been ordered the baths this May—He is not in a state to take a trip there first but he thinks of sending his servant to look at the houses & then to decide—so perhaps we shall trouble you again.

After some days of weakness Shelley had a very bad nervous attack yesterday he is better today but not well

I wish you c[d] come to us for a few days as I mentioned one after the other—I c[d] not if I came sleep out on very many accounts—but thus we sh[d] really see somthing of you—

Tell M[rs] Gisborne to persuade you

Ever sincerly Yours
MaryWS.

I sent the box & a note—Be so kind as to send the 2 lb. of tea & 1 lb of arrow root.

ENDORSED: Ansd. 9 April. PUBLISHED: Jones, #92. TEXT: MS., Bodleian Library (MS., Shelley, c. 1, f. 404).

1. Robert Finch (see 22 January 1819, n. 8).

To Maria Gisborne Pisa Thursday Morning [?13 April 1820][1]

Dear M[rs] G.

Shelley has lost the paper[2] and as he never read it I am as much in the dark as ever—If it be possible & useful I sh[d] very much like to have the bath

I wish for love or money to get a chip hat before you go or I much fear I shall not get it {at} all—What of raw silk—perhaps your milliner or your Seraph cd tell you whether the silk I desire is used for netting if it is send a quantity—common netting silk is not the thing I want—if they do not know send me a pattern that I may get more if it is right.

If Henry w[d] lend us the whole of the Encyclopedia[3] in his absence he w[d] oblige us—When you come I have somthing to say about a piano—so remind me

You must expect me to shed tears when you go—I consider this as a mere trip which will bring you closer to us in future

Is your day fixed—By the arrangements made—S. cannot set off till Thursday week[4]

When we were at Leghorn we took our passport to the Police there who kept it & gave us a Carte de Suretè which was lost long ago—Shelley will want a passport for Bologna certainty [*certainly*] but whether afterwards for Ravenna or Venice non si sa—but I fancy for Ravenna can you aid us—perhaps a passport from the English Consul which we can get signed by other authorities here

Adieu The bobbin is not English Addio.

You{r}s for aye
MWS

ADDRESS: La Signora Maria. ENDORSED: [?] written a Short time before the 2 May / 1820 / The day of our departur[e]. PUBLISHED: Jones, #93. TEXT: MS., Bodleian Library (MS., Shelley, c. 1, ff. 405–6).

1. On Thursday, 20 April, the Gisbornes were at Pisa. On 28 April the Shelleys went to Leghorn; it seems improbable that Mary Shelley wrote the day before she was to see the Gisbornes. The only remaining Thursdays were 6 April, which was too far ahead of the date Shelley was to go to Ravenna, and 13 April, which I tentatively assign to this letter.

2. The paper most likely contained a list of items the Gisbornes offered to lend to the Shelleys while the Gisbornes were in England.

3. Henry Reveley complied, for on 28 April Claire Clairmont recorded in her *Journal* that she read the Encyclopedia, and on 5 May she recorded that Shelley "walks about ⟨w⟩ reading a great quarto Encyclopedia with another volume under his arm." Mary Shelley had previously asked to borrow the volume "that gives a system of shorthand" (see [22 March 1820]).

4. The purpose of Shelley's projected journey was to bring Allegra to Pisa for a visit. The impetus for this trip was Claire Clairmont's strong desire to see her child. When by 23 April Byron had not yet responded to her 16 March request that he send Allegra to Pisa, Claire Clairmont proposed to go (accompanied by Shelley) to Bologna and, if necessary, to Ravenna to fetch Allegra (Paston and Quennell, *To Lord Byron*, pp. 244–48; Dowden, *Shelley*, II, 229–30). Because Byron did not agree to this plan, the trip did not take place (see 8 May 1820).

SHELLEY TO JOHN AND MARIA GISBORNE[1] Pisa, April 13. 1820

[*Postscript by Mary Shelley, p. 1, top*] I want to hear concerning the hunting of Buffaloes. When you come have your lesson ready

We want a Schrevelius[2]—can you get us one reasonably? & we shall be much obliged to you—Also when you come bring 2 lb. of tea but do not send it the duty is so high

ADDRESS: Signor Giovanni Gisborne / Per ricapito al Forno / d'Isidoro / vicino al Ponte de S. Marco / Livorno. ENDORSED: Recd. Sunday 14 / April [Sunday was 16 April]. PUBLISHED: Jones, #94. TEXT: MS., Bodleian Library (MS., Shelley, c. 1, ff. 365–66).

1. *PBS Letters*, #558.

2. Cornelius Schrevelius, *Lexicon Manuale Græco-Latium et Latino-Græcum* (1663).

TO MARIA GISBORNE

Pisa May 2nd
[error for ?24 or 25 April] 1820[1]

Will you deign to look on this foglio in the midst of your most immediate bustle? and the tears of the lovely Carlotta and fairer Apollonia,[2] and having read, will you attend? That is far too much to ask, but however you will think I use my friends well, that I actually dare mention commissions at such a time.

In primis—Claire's shoes.—for she now walks barefoot.

In secundas. Your bath—If you have the kindness to lend it, do not forget to send it per Navicello before you go—

In tertio. My bonnet. If we do not hear from Ravenna in the meantime, Claire and Shelley set out on Wednesday week, but you will be beforehand, or you might have gone together. Pray write, so that we may know the day and hour of our last farewell. I will not scribble any more, for it would be a sin and a shame

Don't you hear Mr Gisborne? "Maria! Where are these stockings to go?" Now Henry—"Mamma! don't forget my razors—" Mamma! Maria! run for god's sake, or the house will be out of the windows.—

M.WS

PUBLISHED: Jones, "New Letters," pp. 59–60. TEXT: John Gisborne Notebook No. 2, Abinger MS., Bodleian Library.

1. Although John Gisborne dates this letter 2 May (the day the Gisbornes left for England), the contents strongly suggest a date of 24 or 25 April. In the third paragraph, Mary Shelley says Claire Clairmont and Shelley will set out for Ravenna on Wednesday week unless they hear from Ravenna. This agrees with Claire Clairmont's letter of 23 April to Byron, in which she says that she and Shelley will leave on 3 May, a Wednesday. On 30 April Claire Clairmont received Byron's objections to her plan (sent via Mrs. Hoppner), and she wrote on 1 and 2 May trying to reverse his decision (*CC Journals*). A date of 24 or 25 April seems appropriate because Mary Shelley asks the Gisbornes to pick the day of their last farewell, which took place on 28 April. The letter could not have been written prior to 24 April because the Gisbornes visited the Shelleys at Pisa on 20 and 21 April, and Shelley accompanied the Gisbornes back to Leghorn, returning to Pisa on 23 April (*CC Journals*). In light of the frequent communications of the friends, Jones's suggestion that this letter illustrates that Mary Shelley was not fully informed of her friends' plans seems less likely than the probability that John Gisborne misdated this letter, as he did a number of others in his Notebooks.

2. See [31 March] 1820, n. 2.

SHELLEY TO LEIGH HUNT[1]

Pisa. May 1. 1820

[*Postscript by Mary Shelley*] Do you know that you might write much longer letters if {you} wrote closer—besides at the top of each page you leave a full inch as you are so much accustomed to this way of writing that you cd not easily break yourself of it suppose when you came to the end of your paper you turned it topsy turvy and interlined it all the way—

I wish Marianne c[d] write but how can she? Bessy might her last letter was 6th of January

Everyours MWS.

The Gisbornes will bring a little remembrance for Marianne—I wish it had been more valuable or useful—but as it {   } not like letting you see friends from us without any thing from us

ADDRESS: Leigh Hunt Esq / 13 Mortimer Terrace / Kentish Town / London / Inghilterra. POSTMARKS: (1) FPO / MY. 16 / 1820; (2) 4 o'Clock / MY. 16 / 1820 EV. PUBLISHED: Jones, #95. TEXT: MS., Huntington Library (HM 20100).

1. *PBS Letters*, #563.

TO MARIA GISBORNE

Pisa May 8th 1820

My Dear M[rs] G—

I am glad to hear you staid so few hours (comparatively) under your awning;[1] and now welcome to Paris! What think you of the Alps, and how did you cross Cenis? You who are travelling must write long letters, and we that stay at home must ask questions, having nothing better to do—

The Ravenna journey does not take place.[2] He has written to say that the child shall not quit him. The Hoppners have behaved shamefully, but it is useless to detail in a letter.

I long for your English letters, and all the queer, and, I fear, the many disagreeable things that will strike you at first sight: in that unhappy land. But you will have little time there except for your own business, and perhaps will know more of the state of your Country from reading Galignani at Leghorn, than in England itself—

You have safe, no doubt, the list of Commissions, and you will remember that you had to scratch out the stockings for Shelley—Be so kind as to put in their place, a handsome square black net-veil—This, I fancy, can be got infinitely cheaper in France than in England—If so, you had better get it there—

The little boy is quite well, and so we are all as well as can be expected —only very hungry waiting for dinner, and very stupid, I don't know why, just now—so excuse this letter and write a great deal more entertainingly yourself, which, doubtless, you will do, being, though you don't know it, I believe, a very good letter writer.

I hope you have, during this dangerous transit, taken good and due care of your gentleman—that M[r] G—[*Gisborne*] has not suffered by the rheumatism on Mount Cenis, nor you by bad spirits or any other ill. I hope you are as happy as the day long, and with that I remain, Your affectionate friend

Mary Wollstonecraft Shelley[3]

[   ] Send your English address in your next letter.

[*Postscript by Shelley*] I wonder what makes Mary think her letter worth the trouble of opening—except indeed she conceives it to be a delight to decypher a difficult scrawl. She might as well have put as I will.—

My dear [*a scrawl*]

? ? ? ! !—? ? ? ; ; . ? !

yours a————

Take care of yourselves—& do you not forget your nightly journal. The silent dews renew the grass without effort in the night.—I mean to write to you, but not today.

All happiness attend you my dear friends.

As an excuse for mine & Mary's incurable stupidity I send a little thing about Poets;[4] which is itself a kind of an excuse for Wordsworth & ⟨?   ⟩. You may shew it Hunt if you like.

ADDRESS: Madame / Madame Gisborne / aux soins / de M. Louis Guibhard / Paris / La Francia. [*Further directed to*] Marche des Jacobins / hotel du Prince Regent. POSTMARKS: (1) Pisa; (2) Mai / 19 / 1820. ENDORSED: Pisa 8 May / 1820. PUBLISHED: Jones, "New Letters," pp. 60–61 (in part); *PBS Letters*, #565. TEXT: John Gisborne Notebook No. 2, Abinger MS., Bodleian Library; MS. of postscripts and address, Bodleian Library (MS., Shelley, c. 1, f. 367).

1. Maria Gisborne's *Journal*, 2 May–26 September, recounts portions of the Gisbornes' journey to London. The *Journal*, kept at the behest of the Shelleys, gives a detailed account of the Gisbornes' short voyage to Genoa on 2 May and describes the awning used for shelter on deck. Maria Gisborne must have sent this same information in a letter from Genoa, where the Gisbornes and Henry Reveley remained until setting off for Voltaggio on 5 May.

2. See [?24 or 25 April] 1820. Claire Clairmont recorded that she received a letter from Byron on 3 May and wrote to him on 4 May (*CC Journals*).

3. From this point, the letter is transcribed from the Bodleian MS.

4. Probably "An Exhortation" ("Chameleons feed on light and air"), which was published with *Prometheus Unbound* in 1820 (*PBS Letters*, #565, n. 6); it is dated "Pisa, April 1820" in the Harvard manuscript (MS., Harvard University Library).

SHELLEY TO LEIGH HUNT[1] [Pisa] May 26. 1820

[*Postscript by Mary Shelley*] select one of the later Indicators & send it by the Post

ADDRESS: Leigh Hunt Esq / 13 Mortimer Terrace / Kentish Town / London / Londra / Angleterre. POSTMARKS: (1) Pisa; (2) FPO / JU. 10 / 1820; (3) 4 o'Clock / JU. 10 / 1820 EV. PUBLISHED: *PBS Letters*, #568. TEXT: MS., Bodleian Library (MS., Shelley, c. 1, f. 374).

1. *PBS Letters*, #568.

TO MARIA GISBORNE Casa Ricci All' Origine. June 18—1820[1]

My dearest Mrs Gisborne

Where am I? Guess! In a little room before a deal table looking out on a poderè—Whose voice is that? Henry, does not your heart beat? By heaven, 'tis Miss Appolonia Ricci—Nay here we are we have taken possession—What do you say?—

The truth is, my dear friend, a variety of circumstances have occurred not of the most pleasant nature, since you left us and {we} have been obliged to reform our plans—We could not go to the baths of Lucca and finding it necessary to consult an attorney we thought of Del Rosso & came here—Are you pleased or vexed? Our old friend Paolo was partly the cause of this—by entering into an infamous conspiracy against us—there were other circumstances that I shall not explain till we meet—That same Paolo is a most superlative rascal—I hope we have done with him but I know not—since as yet we are obliged to guess as to his accomplices.

I wish your journal[2] would come—I long to know how you get on in England and in fact a myriad of circumstances. that your journal will explain—Tell my father I have not heard from him a long long time & am dreadfully anxious—the path of our life is a very thorny one as you well know—nor is my anxiety concerning him[3] is not the least of my troubles—You will imagine how teazed we were when I tell you that the fright I had gave our poor Percy a violent diarrhœa he is now well but we were much alarmed as the poor little thing suffered but he had no fever so he has lost none of his strength & is now blither than ever—he is the merriest babe in the world—Shelley of course is not well his troubles have given him a bilious attack

The day before we came here Annunziata[4] was brought to bed of a little girl—Giuseppe begged Shelley to acquaint you both that it is the image of M[r] Gisborne and that Carlotta & Appolonia both say that the resemblance is striking except the nose—I tell you this as he entreated with laughable gravity that we w[d] I do not know what he means for the child is as like the man in the moon in fact it is like Giuseppe—Anunziata got up the second day & is quite well yesterday There was a grand christening & a regalo—Isidoro the baker was Compare[5] & he sent ices—cakes—Rosoliglio & with the exception of the last—(though indeed they sent up a bottle of that) we had our share & of course gave a christening present the babe was dressed out in the most ridiculous manner it is very ugly and as black as a walnut table—She has a very large nose like her fathers so I wonder why that was excepted in the account of its resemblance—The Miss Riccis lament much the absent Caro Giovane—quanto è carino[6]—they say—

You seem to have suffered a great deal in your journey through France—& you will suffer the same I fear when you return—I long for your next letter pray be particular & journalize as you promised—I should write you a long letter if I were to relate all that has passed since we separated—but such things do not hurt by being kept—on the contrary they improve as we may then add the denouement to a strange commencement—

We purpose keeping possession of your premises for 1 or 2 months as it may happen—That is if you will not be angry—

And now let me ask you when we may expect you I assure you, deare{s}t friend, I long to see you very much You must arrange to be with us this winter for God knows where we shall be in the summer since the climate frightens us with regard to the babe—Thank Mr Gisborne for his kind letters—Shelley & Claire send their love to All of you—there you are

Il bravo giovane—Arrigo—

La Ornam Sig Maria △ Il erudito Sig. Giovanni

—Col. Calicot[7] is at Pisa—As to our books—why before I finish this letter I will consult with Shelley about them—so adieu for the present—Giuseppe is very ill I must consult about him too—As to the books you had better do nothing about them we are too unsettled—so do not send them—but have the kindness to ask Peacock four [*for*] Schrevelius's lexicon Jones's Greek grammar—& the Greek exercises Hogg used to do—& bring them with you—with regard to Giuseppe—he has a high fever & we are afraid to go near him so we have sent for the doctor—A present that I had intended for you is come since you left us—there is Caleb Williams for Henry—a Fleetwood & Essay on Sepulchres[8] for you so do not buy any of these.—It seems Giuseppe is not dying as Anunziata wd make us believe—it is not yet decided whether it is a worm or an intermittent fever—

There is one thing I want you to do which is to buy a cornelion seal neither too plain or too fine—& to get Shelleys coat of arms engraved on it [*p. 1, cross-written*] you can find the coat of arms in some book of baronatage that has been published since this thirty years under the name of Sir Bysshe or S Timothy—not Sir John—be so kind as to get this done as I wish for it very much—and get with it a gold ring for hanging seals & key &c—

Adieu dear Mrs G. if Henry is married present my congratulations to the bride—salted by a few tears from Appolonia Let him remember Le Morte Lancee & tremble—

I hope Mr Gisborne is well—we looked out for his fate in the Sortes Virgilia[9]—We found that with a feather in his cap he would be walking restlessly before the doors ruminating the fate of the old Fawn—We looked for it thinking of your evil prognostication and we find an evident coincidence—He will engage either on the Radical or Government side and walk an officer on watch before the tent of the general—no doubt on the eve of an engagement since he will {be} thinking of the last prophecy—that his mother's eyes should be wet by the grief of his funeral.—Now as he disappointed fate last time by not going to England[10] so he may this by not enlisting under the banners of either party

For us—so darkling is our destiny—neither Virgil or Homer wd unfold the recesses of time but spoke mysteriously of woes—so you see every thing combines—

Give our loves to Papa & Hunt & family—present our kind Compts. to Peacock & his bride[11] & tell us how Horace Smith likes his vases[12]—Again Adieu

Ever & for ever yours,
Mary WShelley

Shelley has taken possession of Henry's study

ADDRESS: Mrs. Gisborne / 26 Newman St. Oxford Road / London / Inghilterra / Angleterre. POSTMARKS: (1) LIVORNO; (2) FPO / JY. 5 / 1820. PUBLISHED: Jones, #96. TEXT: MS., Bodleian Library (MS., Shelley, c. 1, ff. 407–8).

1. On 15 June the Shelleys and Claire Clairmont took up temporary residence in the Gisbornes' home so that Shelley could consult with Leghorn lawyer Frederico Del Rosso about Paolo Foggi's scandalous gossip and attempted blackmail. The gossip dealt with the parentage of the infant girl Shelley called his "Neapolitan charge," Elena Adelaide Shelley, born 27 December 1819 at Naples and registered by Shelley as his and Mary Shelley's child. The fact that Mary Shelley was not the mother of this child resulted in a great deal of speculation as to her parentage. Paolo Foggi circulated the story that Claire Clairmont was the mother and Shelley the father (see 1 January 1815, n. 1; 7 July 1820; [10 August 1821] to Shelley; and 10 August 1821 to Isabella Hoppner). Marcel Kessel has argued that Claire Clairmont's illness on 27 December 1818 was due to her menstrual cycle, not childbirth ("The Mark of X in Claire Clairmont's Journals," *Publication of the Modern Language Association* 66 [December 1951]: 1180–83). Furthermore, when Claire Clairmont was five months pregnant with Allegra, she went to Bath rather than London for fear that her appearance would reveal her condition (see 5 December 1816, n. 1). It seems highly doubtful that Claire Clairmont, nine months pregnant, would have risked public discovery of another pregnancy by openly accompanying the Shelleys on sightseeing tours on which they were likely to be recognized (see *PBS Letters*, #488). White has argued that the child was not Shelley's at all and that it was given Shelley's name so that the legal entanglements involved in adopting a child at that time would be avoided. Others have suggested Elise Foggi as the mother and Shelley as the father (see Ursula Orange, "Elise: Nursemaid to the Shelleys," *Keats-Shelley Memorial Bulletin* 6 [1955]: 24–34). The mystery concerning the Neapolitan child, who died on 9 June 1820, remains unsolved to date. For discussions of the child and Foggi's attempted blackmail, see *PBS Letters*, #553, #556, #571, #575, #650, #651, #656; White, *Shelley*, II, 71–83, 201–3, 546–50; and Cameron, *The Golden Years*, pp. 66–73.

2. See 8 May 1820.

3. Mary Shelley was concerned about the lawsuit against Godwin for back rent. Her acute anxiety about the outcome of this case caused Shelley to tell the Gisbornes to address him at the Masons' should they have "any communications unfit for Mary's agitated mind" (*PBS Letters*, #571).

4. Annunziata was the wife of Giuseppe, the Gisbornes' servant.

5. "Godfather."

6. "How dear he is."

7. Robert Finch (see 22 January 1819, n. 8).

8. *Things as they are: or the Adventures of Caleb Williams*, 3 vols. (London, 1794); *Fleetwood: or the new man of feeling*, 3 vols. (London, 1805); *Essay on Sepulchres* (London, 1809)—all by Godwin.

9. *Sortes Vergilianæ*, a method of divination according to which the answer to a question posed is found by closing the eyes, opening a text of Virgil, and placing a finger on the page (see 7 March 1822).

10. See 24 September 1819, n. 7.

11. Peacock had married Jane Gryffydh on 22 March 1820.

12. Shelley had sent a gift of alabaster vases to Horace Smith (*PBS Letters*, #569), who acknowledged the gift on 4 September (*S&M*, II, 535).

To Amelia Curran Leghorn June 20th 1820

My dear Miss Curran

It is a very long time since I heard from you so that if I did not know your dislike to writing I should be afraid that somthing had happened—and that you were very ill—My heart—during all this time is at Rome—But I cannot conjecture when I shall be really there—still a letter with a Roman postmark would be a pleasant thing how much more welcome if from you!

I am afraid that you find great difficulties in executing our unhappy commission Shelley & I are therefore induced to entreat you to have the kindness to order a plain stone to be erected to mark the spot with merely his name & dates—(William Shelley born January 24, 1816—June 7—1819)—You would oblige us more than I can express if you w^d^ take care that this should be done.

Our little Percy is a thriving forward child but after what has happened I own it appears to me—a faded cloud—all these hopes that we so earnestly dwell upon.

How do you like the Cenci—It sells—you must know of which I am verry glad—If I could hear of any one going to Rome I w^d^ send you some other books to amuse you—for we had a parcel from England the other day—but we are entirely out of the world—

It will give me great pleasure to hear from you—to know when you leave Rome—and how your pictures encrease—Be sure I do not forget your nice study & your kind hospitality You{r} study how can I forget when we have so valuable a specimen of it that is dearer to me than I can well say[1]

Shelley desires his kindest remembrances what have become of our pictures—Claire is not yet reconciled to hers—How is St. George & all your friends—I would give a very great deal to look upon the divine city from the Trinità dei Monti—Is not my heart there?—

From Papa I have not heard a very long time—affairs seem gowing [*going*] on there badly but slower than a tortoise I hope not so surely towards their apparent end—

Farewell—I entreat you to write

Yours with affection
MaryWS.

I have heard your brothers life of your father much praised[2]—

Address: Miss Curran / 64 Via Sistina / Trinita de' Monti / Roma. Postmarks: (1) LIVORNO; (2) GIUG[NO]. Published: Jones, #97. Text: MS., Bodleian Library (MS., Shelley, c. 1, ff. 409–10).

1. The portrait of William. Mary Shelley then inquires about the portraits of Shelley, Claire Clairmont, and herself (see 11 May 1819, n. 1).

2. William Henry Curran, *The Life of the Right Honourable John Philpot Curran, Late Master of the Rolls in Ireland*, 2 vols. (London: Archibald Constable & Co., 1819).

*To Maria Gisborne Leghorn 30 June 1820[1]

My Dear Mrs Gisborne,

You may remember that when I saw you last at Pisa, I mentioned to you my anxiety at not being able to get £500, for my father in this distressing affair of the house—This affair still pends—now I have a proposal to make to you which I entreat you to consider, and at any rate to take in good part—

Having already got the sum of £100,—£400 remains to be raised—Shelley by this day's post sends a note enclosed to Horace Smith, by which he pledges himself to pay to any one who will lend this money £50—pr quarter from his income, and the interest of the money also quarterly—Now would you take up this note?[2] Would you advance £400, and receive £50—and interest quarterly which will liquidate the whole in two years

If you will—you know how it is with my father—I should be afraid to give the money into his hands, lest some pressing necessity should lessen it—You therefore would have the kindness to let him know that you have the money ready to be paid into his hands when the compromise should be agreed to between the parties—

As this is a compromise of £500 for above £1500, you see the benefit your compliance will confer on him—It will be a kindness I shall never forget; as it will, to say the least, put an end to a state of great anxiety and unhappiness—If however Prudence whispers, "No!" frankly declare so, and there is an end of the matter—You know me too well, I hope, to imagine that I shall love you the less.

If any other settlement of the payment would suit you better, mention it—Perhaps you will think our security as good as the Bank's—I think it is—for Heaven and Earth should not defer the payment—

We are in daily expectation of a letter from you—We have received none since M^rs G—'s put in at Rouen—But as we have lost one of my father's, I am afraid that this may be the case with the first sheet of your journal—

Giuseppe is recovered from his intermittent fever—Percy is tolerably well—Shelley is far from well, being nervous to an extraordinary degree—

Adieu—Ever most sincerely your's

M.W.S.

Unpublished. Text: John Gisborne Notebook No. 7, Abinger MS., Bodleian Library.

1. On 30 June Mary Shelley received a letter from Godwin. Donald H. Reiman has called to my attention that Mary Shelley's Journal entry for 1 July reads: "Write & send letters—To Hogg—Mrs. G. Papa—Mr Hamilton," and not "Write & read letters . . . ," as in the printed *Journal* (see *PBS Letters*, #572 [to Samuel Hamilton] and #574 [to Hogg], both dated 1 July 1820). John Gisborne's Notebook reveals that on 30 June Shelley addressed two letters to the Gisbornes—the first a letter accompanying his promissory note (see 30 June 1820, following), the second begun

on 30 June but not completed until 2 July (see *PBS Letters*, #571). The originals of Shelley's letters have not been located, and the John Gisborne Notebook is at present the only source of Shelley's 30 June letter and of a fuller version of Shelley's 30 June–2 July letter than the published text.

The Notebook also resolves the question of whether the poem Shelley enclosed in his 30 June–2 July letter was his *Letter to Maria Gisborne.* In his copy, John Gisborne placed an *X* over Shelley's phrase mentioning the poem and noted with another *X* at the end of the page that Shelley referred to "the letter in verse which precedes" in the Notebook. Copied out, just before Shelley's letter, is his *Letter to Mrs. Gisborne.*

2. The Gisbornes did not lend the money.

*SHELLEY TO JOHN GISBORNE[1] — Leghorn 30th June 1820

My Dear Sir—

On reconsideration I enclose the promissory note to you, and make it payable to you instead of H.S. [*Horace Smith*] I can add nothing to what Mary has said; but I write to urge you who can estimate the temptation of necessity, not to pay any money to Godwin before you perceive that the purpose for which the advance is made is on the point of accomplishment—I leave to your discretion the necessary delicacies to be observed—If you accede to the proposal, lose no time in acquainting Godwin with it—always however with the restriction of the conditions annexed by me to the application of the £500—I cannot express to you the relief that we should experience if it were possible to annul this detested business of the house, and the torturing correspondence it gives rise to, or our gratitude to those who may be our saviours from this evil.—a gratitude, which if any thing should interpose between your power and your will, is due no less to the intention than the act.

I need not say the money will be regularly paid—Hunt and I daresay H. Smith would sign any security collateral with mine—but that I daresay you think superfluous—Always affectionatly your's and your's

Percy B. Shelley

I have sent a letter for you to Ollier.

[*Postscript by Mary Shelley*] I need not say how anxious we shall be for your reply—direct always Pisa, and pray write often—write, I entreat you by return of post—

UNPUBLISHED. TEXT: John Gisborne Notebook No. 7, Abinger MS., Bodleian Library.

1. This heretofore unpublished letter by Shelley accompanied his note pledging to return £400 plus interest to the Gisbornes for a loan to clear Godwin's debt (see 30 June 1820 to Maria Gisborne; *PBS Letters*, #571).

TO MARIA GISBORNE — [Leghorn] July 7—1820

No letter! no letter! I do not believe that you are so wickedly faithless as not to write & therefore expect 2 sheets so very full that fuller were never seen—I send you a letter from Shelley[1] which as it is not addressed to any of the trinity in particular he as a courteous knight begs you as the lady fair to accept laying it humbly before the happy footstool which receives the envied weight of your most ladylike foot hoping that from thence not by its own worth[2] but by your most gracious favour it may rise to your[3] hands & thence be distilled into the precious fishponds of Heshbon[4] namely your mild, bright eyes.

Pray do not forget the commission I gave you concerning a piano as my friend is anxious concerning it it must be like yours; long with 6 oxtaves [*octaves*]. please to strike out of your list the fine silk stockings you were to buy & put in the stead 6 p^{r} of worsted stockings for a babe of a year & ½ & 12 of cotton

Our Babe is well & merry—We are still worshipping your Penates. Jeppe & his wife manque'd to scratch out each other's eyes the other night[5]—your pigeons lay eggs a l'envie l'un de l'autre—& the Miss Riccis are corteous & kind & greatly lament the Caro Giovane—

You have of course received our proposal[6] in which we trespassed so greatly on your kindness—I am most excessively anxious for y^{r} answer.

We have since writting the above received M^{r} G's [*Gisborne's*] extremely welcome letter—not but I am both vexed & angry with your faithless & unkind breaking of your promise—I built on a rock & I find sand—I hope you are ashamed—now this minute begin & continue your journal—The letter with our proposal was addressed 26 Newman St.—Continue to address us at Pisa Now pray—pray—write your journal

Ollier is a ninny or worse—Tell Hunt we never hear from him—He (Ollier) is ordered to give you a Melincourt & Headlong Hall[7] pray bring them with you as your friend here wants to see them. & remember to bring all the Indicators from Peacock from No. 16—We are delighted with them —Adieu Carina—Cattiva—Tell Henry that Appolonia pines & gets thin— Addio or si piace piu a lei a diavolio[8]—Ever & for ever Yours

M W S

The sun shines all day long—the north breezes blow—& the weather is actually paradisiacall—I give you joy of London smoke—Your friends seem very kind—there must be a fierce battle I think between bella Italia & smoky London. Could you not present Peter[9] to some bookseller not letting out Shelley's name & get it published so

[*P. 1, upside-down*] The enclosed[10] must on no account be published.— I hope you will bring Prometheus with you. Poor Mrs. Godwin! I knew it w^{d} be thus—

Dalla bellissima e superbissima villa del Grand Capitano Gaetano Ricci —Uffiziale dell' magnfico Ferdinando di Toscana[11]

ADDRESS: Mrs. Gisborne / To the care of Mess. Ollier / Booksellers / Vere Street. Bond Street / London Angleterre / Inghilterra. [*Redirected to*] 3 Carmarthen St. / Tottenham Cot Road. POSTMARKS: (1) LIVORNO; (2) FPO / JY. 22 / 1820;

(3) 4 o'Clock / JY. 22 / 1820 EV. PUBLISHED: Jones, #98. TEXT: MS., Bodleian Library (MS., Shelley, c. 1, f. 411).

1. *PBS Letters*, #575. After briefly mentioning the financial proposal put to the Gisbornes by the Shelleys to aid Godwin, Shelley goes on to advocate, in some detail, that the Gisbornes and Henry Reveley remain in England in order for Henry Reveley to make a career. In the second paragraph of his letter Shelley informs his friends that his "Neapolitan charge" (see 18 June 1820, n. 1) has died and that "the rascal Paolo has been taking advantage of my situation at Naples in December 1818 to attempt to extort money by threat[en]ing to charge me with the most horrible crimes." That Mary Shelley knew of the accusations made by Foggi is clear from her letter of 18 June. Although it remains unclear whether Mary Shelley knew of the existence of Elena Adelaide prior to 18 June, it seems likely that she knew of her by that time, since only the child's existence would have given Paolo Foggi's accusations sufficient substance to cause Shelley to be fearful and take legal action against him. Further, it seems unlikely that Shelley would have planned to have the child—who bore his family name and was legally registered as his and Mary Shelley's—join them or even be brought to the same locale as theirs (*PBS Letters*, #571) unless Mary Shelley knew of the child.

2. The original letter is torn; the word is supplied from the John Gisborne Notebook copy.

3. See above, n. 2.

4. *Song of Solomon* 7: 4.

5. An account of the lively quarrel between Giuseppe and Annunziata, the Gisbornes' servants, is given in Dowden, *Shelley*, II, 332–33.

6. 30 June 1820 to Maria Gisborne.

7. Peacock's satirical novels.

8. Another irreverent pun (see 26 April 1815, n. 1): "to God or if it pleases you more to the devil."

9. *Peter Bell the Third*, sent to Leigh Hunt on 2 November 1819 for him to give to Ollier for publication (*PBS Letters*, #526). It remained unpublished until Mary Shelley included it in the one-volume second edition of Shelley, *Poetical Works* (1839).

10. Unidentified.

11. "From the very beautiful and magnificent villa of the Grand Captain Gaetano Ricci—Official of the munificent Ferdinand of Tuscany."

TO MARIA GISBORNE — Leghorn July 19th 1820

My Dear Friend!

Seeing what a large sheet of paper I have before me, I think I should do more than my duty if I were to fill it, which I do not promise—You have done so much less than your duty, and your promise, that I am seriously vexed—I could not have believed when we parted at Leghorn, that for three months nearly I should not have seen a single line indited by the fairest faithless Maria. Do you wish the word at the top of the letter to dwindle into a mere name? or do you think, as Hogg does, that there is an instinctive intercourse between congenial souls that needs not the slow and troublesome formality of letter-writing? I do not, for I am sure, if put to the rack, I could not have guessed at your employments and thoughts during this long interval—Mr G—'s [*Gisborne's*] letter was very welcome, but it was not a journal[1]—I daresay you had the barbarity not to put down even any part of your talk with Papa—to leave it till your return is such a procrastination that you ought not even to have thought of, however, I expect a letter from you in a few days, and if one does not come, the fault will surely lie very heavy at your door—

I have now very seriously begun Greek—I pass five lines or more every day—reading them over again and again, so that now I may boast that I know perfectly sixty lines of Homer's Odyssey. I am much teazed from the want of a good grammar—S. wanted to persuade me to have Jones's sent out in sheets: but finding that a whole box would cost less than that, he has written to Peacock to beg him to send, without delay, a box.[2] If you have anything to send, pray consign it, as you will have several things to bring for us, perhaps you would like to send some of your books this way. But I should advise that nothing but books were sent. Pray do not forget to ask M[rs] Hunt for the remains of the flannel &c. that she bought for the last winter, but did not send. I wish you to bring that with you—as I shall want flannel next winter, and that will serve.

We are still at Casa Ricci, nor have we yet settled the date of our imigration—Necessity brought us here—You know Leghorn is no favourite with me—The rascal, whom I mentioned in my first letter from here, came and laid an accusation, but, through the means of Del Rosso,[3] he was ordered to quit Leghorn in four hours. The idea of going to Del Rosso was most fortunate, as otherwise we certainly should have been frightened again, if not excessively teazed. We now wait here until we receive our quarter, and afterwards perhaps for other arrangements; but we shall be guided by time. I wish very much to spend a month among mountains before the end of the summer—I think we shall go in a fortnight[4]—

I do not wonder you dislike the smoke and confinement of London. They say you are visited by some very hot weather. You can tell us how this weather is in comparison with Italy—

We have had some very hot hours, but the weather is so changeable that a very hot day we have not yet had—The country wants rain and the Cicalas sing in the trees, I suppose, entreating for dew, and telling the Gods that the dry leaves hurt the sweetness of their merry song. With this exception, the season is promising—the Vines are weighed down by their clusters, and the trees loaded with figs. Come and eat! Will you?

I am sorry to see an Advertisement in Galignani to say that on the first of the month a steam boat was to sail from Bourdeux to Leghorn and ply between here and Genoa—Will they have the start of us?

To ask something that has to do with business for us as you will guess—Will you tell me why the King of Naples set up a Confectioner's shop?[5] That rascal Galignani gave you a pretty account of the sale of the Cenci[6]—We know that Copies were sent for, and he sent word that none were to be had—It was only advertised once, so the matter is clear. It has been suppressed, doubtless, through the representations of our moral Country-men, who, as we have reason to know, hate Shelley (I hope they will include me in the Compliment) with ardour, and this is why only four Copies were sold—

The Queen! The Queen! The Queen![7] Does it not rain Queens in England, or at least orations sent post from Heaven with pleadings in favour of our heroic—magnanimous—innocent—injured—virtuous—illustrious and lion-hearted British one—full of painful feelings, delicate subject (not any scandal of the V.M.[8] I hope). Tantini said he saw her at the Campo Santo—She had on a black pelisse, tucked up to her knees, and exhibiting a pair of men's boots. A fur tippet that seemed as if it would cover ten such—a white cap, and a man's hat set on sideways.—to be sure, she is injured, but it is too great a stretch of imagination to make a God of a Beef-eater, or a heroine of Queen Caroline.—but I wish with all my heart downfall to her enemies, and that is no great stretch of compassion. Besides her, you have the coronation to carry joy to the hearts of H.M.'s subjects. Oh! they are a pretty set! Castlereagh's impudence and Brougham[9] speechifying—I believe the latter to be a good man at bottom, but he is naturally cautious, canny, as they say in his Country.—Apropos of Scotland, Ask Papa if it were not well to introduce Henry to Mr Booth—and ask him also how those good folks are going on—If he sees Isabel &c—

Are you not, or will you not be delighted to hear of the Revolution at Naples.[10] The Duke of Campochiaro was at the head of it—They assembled before the gates of the palace, and the old pastry Cook ordered the Soldiers to fire on them—they refused, and he was obliged to compromise by turning out his old ministry and filling their places by popular nobles and entreating the people's patience until a constitution should be formed. Thirty years ago was the era for Republics, and they all fell—This is the era for constitutions, I only hope that these latter may in the end remove the [?mothes] of the former. What a glorious thing it will be if Lombardy regains its freedom—and Tuscany—all is so mild there that it will be the last, and yet in the end I hope the people here will raise their fallen souls and bodies, and become something better than they are.

The friend of Mrs Mason asking where she ought to apply to receive and pay for the Piano, I gave them the direction of Clementi's shop, 26 Cheapside.[11] You will therefore have the kindness to acquaint Clementi of this. She desires me to convey her thanks to you for your kindness—

Annunziata departed with her new-born last Monday, to take her to the mountains. While she was here, Fortunata screamed all day—Now, we do not know that the child is in the house. That woman is a real Devil—I could no more endure her than the perpetual sight of a dozen crawling toads. I will not conclude without mentioning Percy—he is well—lively, and thriving—Shelley gets on pretty well, he has just concluded the translation of Homer's Hymn to Mercury I do not hear from you, and I am vexed—that is my last word, except indeed I add that I am ever your's

Mary WShelley

If your hearts did not very much encline you to Italy, I should say, accept C—'s offer.[12] Your instructions assuredly would be worth £100 p ann. and with the addition of one or two pupils, which you would easily get, you might be well and comfortably settled. But this is for your decision—I will just mention that our Parisian plan[13] has failed. It seems that the French are become surly having lost their politeness, and hating the English in an incredible manner—

PUBLISHED: Jones, "New Letters," pp. 62–66. TEXT: John Gisborne Notebook No. 2, Abinger MS., Bodleian Library.

1. Mary Shelley evidently expected Maria Gisborne to send the *Journal* to her in installments.

2. See *PBS Letters*, #576. On 18 June Mary Shelley asked Maria Gisborne to have Peacock send a number of books, including Jones's Greek grammar.

3. Lawyer (see 18 June 1820, n. 1).

4. On 4 August the Shelleys and Claire Clairmont left Leghorn, spent the night of 4 August with the Masons, and then went to the Bagni di Pisa (also called Bagni di San Giuliano), which was a short distance from Pisa, Lucca, and Leghorn.

5. Ferdinand I (1751–1825). Maria Gisborne responded: "The old confectioner whom you inquire about had one principal and one secondary object in setting up business—gain and amusement" (Gisborne, *Journals and Letters*, p. 65).

6. Shelley believed (erroneously) that *The Cenci* had ben piratically published by Galignani in Paris (*PBS Letters*, #561).

7. Caroline of Brunswick (1768–1821), separated from her husband the Prince of Wales (and from 1811 to 1820 Prince Regent) since 1796—they were married in 1795—returned to England in June 1820 to claim her rights as Queen (George III had died on 29 January). The Prince Regent objected to her claims and instigated a bill in the House of Lords to dissolve the marriage on the basis of accusations of adultery; this resulted in a great public debate in which Caroline's partisans characterized the charges as victimization of Caroline by a debauched monarch. The bill of divorce was abandoned on 10 November 1820. The Shelleys regarded Caroline as a woman of poor character, but they were far more antipathetic toward George IV and his cabinet. The dispute came to an end with the death of Caroline on 7 August 1821, shortly after George IV's coronation on 19 July 1821. Shelley satirized the scandal in *Oedipus Tyrannus, or Swellfoot the Tyrant*, written in August 1820 (see [24 March] 1820, n. 6).

8. For Virgin Mary, perhaps.

9. Henry Peter Brougham, Baron Brougham and Vaux (1778–1868), attorney, liberal politician, legal reformer, and one of the founders of the *Edinburgh Review* (to which he was a prolific contributor). He was Leigh and John Hunt's friend and defended them in their 1811 libel trials, but he was Byron's enemy (*SC*, III, 106–7; IV, 645–53. Marchand, *Byron*, II, 614).

10. Inspired by the success of the revolution in Spain in 1820, which forced Ferdinand VII to restore the constitution, a revolution began on 1 July in Naples under the leadership of General Guglielmo Pepe. The rebels demanded a democratic constitution, which Ferdinand I granted on 7 July and swore to on 13 July. On 23 March 1821, Austria, with the consent of Ferdinand I, crushed the revolution. The restoration of Ferdinand I as absolute monarch was followed by reprisals against the liberals under a police state.

11. Muzio Clementi (1752–1832), distinguished pianist, composer, and conductor. On 3 July 1811 he married Emma Gisborne, John Gisborne's sister. Clementi founded the firm of Clementi & Co., piano manufacturers and publishers of music.

12. In her *Journal* for 2 July, Maria Gisborne wrote: "Clementi has offerred to

instruct me, which would be an incalculable advantage to me should I determine to teach music. . . ."

13. A plan by which Claire Clairmont was to go to Paris. Following the text of Mary Shelley's letter is a cross-written addition by Shelley that refers to the poor relations between Mary Shelley and Claire Clairmont, the failure of the Paris plan, and the exertions of Mrs. Mason to find a substitute place for Claire Clairmont. (In her *Journal* for 4 July Claire Clairmont wrote: "'Heigh-ho the Clare, & the Ma / Find something to fight about every day—'") In concluding, Shelley cautioned the Gisbornes: "Of course you will not suppose that Mary has seen the enclosed, or this transverse writing—so take no notice of it in any letter intended for her inspection." The enclosure is unidentified, but Jones speculates that it may have been one of the "sad" poems, "Time Long Past" (*PBS Letters*, #577).

To Amelia Curran San Giuliano[1] August 17—[1820]

My dear Miss Curran

It gives me great pain to hear of your ill health Will this hot summer conduce to a better state or not—? I hope anxiously when I hear from you again to learn that you are better having recovered from your weakness—& that you have no return of your disorder

I should have answered your letter before but we have been in the confusion of moving we are now settled in an agreable house at the Baths of San Giuliano about four miles from Pisa—under the shadow of Mountains & with delightful scenery within a walk—We go on in our old manner with no change—I have had many changes for the worse—one might be for the better but that is nearly impossible—Our child is well & thriving which is a great comfort—& the Italian sky give Shelley health which is to him a rare & substantial enjoyment

I did not receive the letter you mention to have written in March and you also have missed one of our letters in which Shelley acknowledged the receipt of the drawings you mention & requested that the largest pyramid might be erected if they would case it with white marble for £25—However the whole had better stand as I mentioned in my last[2] for without the most rigorous inspection great cheating would take place & no female could detect them—when we visit Rome we can do that which we wish. Many thank for your kindness which has been very great.

I w^{d} send you the books I mentioned but we live out of the world & I know of no conveyance Mr. [*?Purriance*] says that he sent the life of your father by sea to Rome directed to you so doubtless it is in the custom house there—

How enraged all our mighty rulers are at the quiet revolutions which have taken place it is said that some one said to the Grand duke here ma si chi edono una constituzione qui?—Ebene la daro subito[3]—was the reply but he is not his own Master & Austria w^{d} take care that that sh^{d} not be the case—they say Austrian troops are coming here & the Tuscan ones will be sent to Germany. We take in Galignani & w^{d} send them to you if you liked —I do not know what the expense w^{d} be but I sh^{d} think slight.

If you recommence painting do not forget Beatrice [*Cenci*] I wish very much for a copy of that—you w[d] oblige us greatly by making one—Pray let me hear of your health—God know when we shall be in Rome—circumstances must direct—& they dance about like will o' the wisps—enticing & then deserting us—we must take care not to be left in a bog.

Adieu take care of yourself—Believe in Sh[elley]'s sincere wishes for your health & kind remembrances & in my being ever sincere[ly yrs]

MWShelley

Claire desires (not remembrances—if they are not pleasant) however she sends a proper message & says she w[d] be obliged to you if you let her have her picture[4] if you c[d] find a mode of conveying it.

Who was he with the long memory who remembered seeing me—somehow people always remember my features—even there { } have detected my identity who have not seen me since I was a month old—so I have hopes that when I go to Heaven I shall easily be recognized by my old friends

Do you know we lose many letters—having spies (not Government ones) about us in plenty—they made a desperate push to do us a desperate mischief lately—but succeeded no further than to blacken us among the English—so If you receive a fresh batch (or green bag)[5] of scandal against us—I assure you it is all a lie poor souls we live innocently as you well know—if we did not ten to one God w[d] take pity on us & we sh[d] not be so unfortunate.

ADDRESS: Miss Curran / 64 Via Sistina / Roma. POSTMARKS: (1) Pisa; (2) 24 AG[OSTO]. PUBLISHED: Jones, #99. TEXT: MS., Bodleian Library (MS., Shelley, c. 1, ff. 476–77).

1. The Shelleys had moved to Casa Prini, San Guiliano (also known as Bagni di Pisa, or Baths of Pisa) on 5 August.

2. See 20 June 1820.

3. "But do they demand a constitution here?—Very well I will give them one immediately" (see 19 July 1820).

4. The portrait of Claire Clairmont painted by Amelia Curran at Rome in 1819 (see 20 June 1820).

5. The notorious "green bag" (lawyer's briefcase), in which the government carried its accusations against Queen Caroline in 1820.

TO MARIA GISBORNE — Casa Prini—Bagni di San Giuliano

Sept. 25 1820

My dear M[rs] Gisborne

Having a thousand things to say & hear & the situation of things being now, on your account, convenient—C. [*Claire*] being for her health at Leghorn—I wish you w[d] come & repose, all three, from your fatigues here[1]—We have a pleasant house plenty of beds—& would be very glad to see you—as you must well know Do not answer this I entreat you with your accustomed refusal & intercede with M[r] G. [*Gisborne*] that he will not either—But come with him & Henry for a few days at least—Do you not owe this answer to my unanswered letters?—

Affectionately yours
MaryW.S.

ADDRESS: Mrs. Gisborne. ENDORSED: Sept. 25. / Oct. 5 Ansd. PUBLISHED: Jones, #100. TEXT: MS., Bodleian Library (MS., Shelley, c. 1, f. 412).

1. The Gisbornes had began their return journey to Leghorn on 3 September. On 3 October they were at Genoa, expecting to depart for Leghorn the next day, which would date their arrival as 5 October (Gisborne, *Journals and Letters*) (this is confirmed by the endorsement date on this letter). On the same day, Mary Shelley wrote again (a "P.S." to this letter) to renew her invitation. The Gisbornes declined the invitation, which disappointed and offended the Shelleys (see [?17 October] 1820). The serious rift that ensued between the friends, fueled by accusations against the Shelleys by Mrs. Godwin, was further intensified by Henry Reveley's abandonment of the steamboat project (*PBS Letters*, #591). The quarrel was somewhat patched after a few months, but not until the period of the Gisbornes' return to England in August 1821 were the friends fully reconciled.

To Maria Gisborne

Baths of San Giuliano Friday
Oct 5 1820

My Dear M^rs^ G—

This letter will be a P.S. to another of mine you will find at your house[1] —Your return has been so long delayed that you will have found the bird flown from your nest—Yet not for that need I revoke my invitation, or you refuse it, for Claire is on a visit, and therefore your H. [*Henry*] would meet with no temptations.

I long to bid you welcome back to Italy, and we are full of conjectures as to the cause of the length of {your} journey.—conjectures not untinged by anxiety: but I trust all is well.

Your's very sincerely
MaryWS

We shall not be in Pisa until the 1st of November—how could we { } in Italy? Is not this rainy weather the clear delightful season of Villeggiatura?[2]

PUBLISHED: Jones, "New Letters," p. 67. TEXT: John Gisborne Notebook No. 2, Abinger MS., Bodleian Library.

1. See 25 September 1820.
2. "Country holiday."

To Maria Gisborne

Baths of San Giuliano
Oct 16 [error for ?17 October] 1820[1]

My Dear Mrs Gisborne,

It is said that it is well that we do not foresee, on rising in the morning, the good night we shall have on going to bed—Whether it is well or not,

I do not pretend to say—at least affairs would then take a different turn, and I should not have bored you with my inopportune visit yesterday—

When I saw you yesterday, you said you had written me a foolish letter,[2] (foolish was your word, I think) but since you did not explain away any part of it, of course you meant that it should remain in full force.—a good dose on my return;—indeed I was tolerably astounded, and found Shelley in a state of considerable agitation—but this is not the purport of this letter—

A Veil is now taken off from what was mysterious yesterday, and I now understand your refusal to visit us, and Henry's curious and, at last, almost rude reply to my invitation—I see that the ban of the Empire is gone out against us, and they who put it on must take it off. Of course it is quite impossible that we should visit you until we have first received you at our house—It will give me the greatest pleasure to seal a mutual forgiveness with you here—But you must chose this—Our friendship rests on your sentence—and do not, I pray you, so write as we shall say, what does she mean? Either say, It is all over—or come. There can be no real cordiality until I have seen you here.

The very first fine day I shall ride over to Pisa, and send Henry his books,[3] as he desired. He has chosen to join himself to your accusations—He is young to do this—But what terms need be made with Pariahs—And such, thank God a thousand and a million times, we are, long—very long, may we so continue.—When you said that that filthy woman[4] said she would not visit Hunt how I glorified in our infamy. Now is the time! join them, or us—the gulph is deep, the plank is going to be removed—set your foot on it if you will, and you will not lose the sincere affection of one who loved you tenderly

Adieu—

Success crown all your plans

Your's

Mary W. Shelley

Shelley had written, but upon second thought he resolves to deliver this letter himself—By him I shall know the end of the affair. I make it rest upon that one point—after the manner of the refusal yesterday. Do you come, or not?

PUBLISHED: Jones, "New Letters," pp. 67–69. TEXT: John Gisborne Notebook No. 2, Abinger MS., Bodleian Library.

1. Mary Shelley went to Leghorn to see the Gisbornes on 16 October. The next day Shelley carried this letter to them (MWS Journal), which suggests that this letter was written on 17 October.

2. Maria Gisborne's letter may have contained some of the accusations made against Shelley by Godwin and against Mary Shelley by Mrs. Godwin that Maria Gisborne recorded in her *Journal*, pp. 38–39, 42, 43, 47–48.

3. Probably the encyclopedia the Shelleys borrowed in April 1820.

4. Almost certainly Mrs. Godwin.

*To [?   ]   Pisa   Monday Morning   [?29 October 1820—
December 1821][1]

My dear Friend

I am exceedingly obliged to you for your kindness, & send the saddle. It has never been used once:

I hope that you are getting better, all very hot weather is now over, so you may consider yourself convalescent; although at all times in Italy you ought to beware of exposing yourself to the sun.

Very sincerly your's
MaryW. Shelley

UNPUBLISHED. TEXT: MS., Pforzheimer Library.

1. The contents of this letter indicate that it was written after "all very hot weather was over," that is, in the fall. The Shelleys were at Pisa in 1820, from 29 October, at the Casa Galetti, Lung' Arno, and again in 1821, from 25 October. The only other references to saddles I have found in the Shelleys' correspondence are in regard to a saddle Henry Reveley "regenerated" for Mary Shelley in spring 1821, which Shelley asked Reveley to sell in summer 1821 (5 April [1821]; 19 April [1821]; *PBS Letters*, #640.) Perhaps the saddle mentioned in this letter is the "regenerated" one.

TO LEIGH HUNT   Pisa.   Il 3 Dec[re] [December]—1820.

Credete voi, amico mio caro, che ci è molto piacevole di scrivere mille, e poi mille lettere, e di recevere punto risposto? Crudel, perche? Davero non posso contare i giorni, le lunghe settimane, e le mese piu lunghe ancora che son passate, e nessun ci porta le di vostre lettere. Marianna e voi son egualmente infedele. Chi sa che mai sia divenuto di voi altri. Forse una stregua Laplandese vi abia trasportati non all'aria dolce, e ai paesi deliziosi del mezzogiorno; ma a qualche terra orrida, gelato e ruvidosa che abbia infredato tutto il vostro amore per noi. Pero credo per certo che voi in Inghilterra son piu duri ed aspri che noi, quando vedo che cosi pochi di tutti i nobili defendevano la disgraziata Regina, chi davero credo sia innocentissima. Mi fa gran' pietà questa donna; e quando si riflette della gran' differenza che esiste fra il scelerato re, e questa regina pietosa e buona, che visita un servo ammalato dal peste, s'arrabia; lui, il di cui carrattere voi stesso avete depinto tanto bene, come pessimo; e lei il di cui piu grande fallo e di divertirse colla sua servitù, invece di stare sola soletta quando i grandi servili d' Inghilterra l'hanno abandonata intieramente. Si sa bene che era i espioni che feciono il sentimento contra di lei, che esiste in Italia. Ma non ostante questo sentimento forte tutti i Italiani dicono che per certo la evidenza no era assai per condannarla—e davero mi pare che hanno un oppinione molto piu favorevole per lei dopo codesto processo che avante. Tutti son inorridito dalla indecenza del processo infame per sempre.

Recevemo intanto una lettera dalla cara Marianna, chi ci dice che voi ci avesse scritto una lettera, ma fin' ora questo foglio tanto sospirato non è arrivato.

Bisogna che vi parlerei, amico mio, d'una conoscenza che abiamo fatto con un Professore a Pisa.[1] Lui è davero il solo Italiano che ha cuore ed anima. Ha un spirito altissimo, un ingegno profondo, e un' elequequenza che trasporta. I poveri Pisani lo credano matto; e racontano tante storiette di lui che ci fa credere che davero è un poco stravagante, o per parlare in Inglese—eccentric. Ma lui dice—Mi credano matto e mi fa piacere chi si sbagliarebbero cosi; ma forse il tempo verrà quando vedrano che sia la pazzia di Bruto. Ogni sera viene ala nostra casa e sempre fa le nostre delizie colle di sue idee originale. Parla una bellissima lingua Italiana, tutto differente della idioma di oggi, che ci fa credere d' udire il Boccacio o il Macchiavelli parlando come scrissono.

Poi abiamo fatto conoscenza con un'Improvisatore[2]—un'uomo di gran' talento—e molto forte nel Greco, e con un genio poetico incomparabile. Improvise con un fuoco e justezza ammirabile. Il suo sujetto era il destino futuro d'Italia. Rammentò che Petrarca disse che ni le alpe altissime ni il mare bastava a difendere questo paese vaccillante e vecchio dai Padroni forestieri—Ma disse lui—vedo crescere le alpe—e alzare e turbare il mare stesso per impedire i di suoi nemici. Sfortunatamente lui, come qualchi poeti della nostra patria, trove piu piacere nei applausi momentarii d'un teatro e le feste che lo fanno le donne che di studiare per la posterità.

Vedete che intanto conoscemo ogni giorno un poco piu dei Italiani, e sentiamo un grandissimo interesso nella guerra minacciata a Napoli. che faranno? I nobili di Napoli sono independente e bravi; ma il popolo è schiavo. Chi sa si la milizia resistarano le arme degli Austrani.[3] Quanti e tanti Italiani sospirono per la libertà, ma come in ogni paese i poveri non hanno potere, e i ricchi mai vogliono rischiare i di loro denari—I Italiani amano i denari quasi dalle Inglese—I ricchi d'Inghilterra amano l'oro, ma i nobili d'Italia son inamorati di rame ed il spiccio i quattrini (half farthings) ricevono da loro tanto rispetto quanto i shillings con noi altri.

V'è un' altra conoscenza[4] nostra romanesca e patetica e una fanciulla di diece novi anni—figlia d'un nobile Fiorentino, bellissima—d'un gran' genio—chi scrive Italiana con un eleganza e delicatezza chi eguala i migliore autori della migliore età d'Italia—Ma è infelicissima—La sua madre è una pessima donna: e essendo gelosa dai talenti e la belezza della di sua figlia, la rinchiude in convento dove non vede mai che le cameriere e le idiote.[5] Ne esce mai ma chiusa in due piccole stanze che guardono—sulla kitchen gar[den] poco pittoresco del convento, lamenta sempre la sua pietosa condizione—La sola sua speranza è di maritarsi Ma la sua essistenza stessa e quasi un secreto—e che sposaliza rara! Vi diro, amico mio come si maritono in questo paese. E posso assicuravi della verita perche al momento che scrivo, ho davante i di miei occhi una proposizione per una ragazza Pisana—Il avvocato chi è impiegato per fare questa proposta manda una foglia che commincia cosi—"Il Giovane, col quale si desidera congiungersi in matrimonio con la Giovane proposta, è nel anno diece settimo: è statura grande, complesso, senza imperfezione, di ottima salute, robusto e avvenute. Egli è di candidi costumi, ed una saviezza incomparabile; è studioso, e bastantemente inoltrato nello studio delle belle lettere, a cui indefessamente si applica." Segue allora una descrizione della sua famiglia e la di sua fortuna e espetazione; e del dote che aspetta—e fenisce questo capo d'opera cosi. "Il matrimonio dovra effetuarsi due anni dopo la stipulazione del detto contratto. Allorche i Genitori della Giovane proposta verrano approvate le soprascritte condizione sara data immediate congnizione del Giovane di cui si tratta. È necessario in fine di sapersi l'eta della Giovane proposta." Ecco una sposalizia Italiana! Di piu hanno un grandissimo orrore dei Matrimonii che si fanno senza il consentimento dei Genitori. Sicuramente la tirannia domestica ha piu di forza qui nei oppinioni—e anzi nelle legge; tutt'ora che con pochi essetzione i genitori sono suavi ed indulgenti nei affari commune di giorno in giorno.—

Abiamo avuto punto inverno fin'ora—godiano d'un'aria dolce e un bel sole di decembre—le piove del' Autumno son passati—e il paese quantunque è spogliato e ignudo ride sotto i raggi d'un cielo chiarissimo—Lasciate—o mio amico i vostri guai—e per qualche minute godiate voi anche della mia bella Italia—Spero che questo foglio avra questo effetto—Dio vi guarda—voi e tutti che vi appartienono—Shelley e Chiarina mandono mille e poi mille salute affetuosi—addio—

la vostra amico costanto—Marina.

[*Translation*]

Do you think, my dear friend, that it is pleasurable to write a thousand, and then another thousand letters, and receive nothing in return? You are cruel, why? I really cannot count the days, the long weeks, and the even longer months that have passed without bringing any of your letters. Marianne and you are equally unfaithful. Who knows what may have become of you. Perhaps a Lapland witch has taken you not to the mild climate and the delightful lands of the south, but to some horrible land, frozen and coarse, which may have chilled all of your love for us. However, I believe for sure that you in England are harder and more severe than we, when I see that so few of all the noblemen have defended the disgraced Queen, who I really believe to be most innocent. I feel great pity for this woman; and when one reflects upon the great difference that exists between the wicked king, and this compassionate and good queen, who visits a servant sick with the plague, one becomes angry; he, whose character you yourself have painted so well, as horrible; and she whose greatest fault is to amuse herself with a servant, instead of staying all alone when the great servile ones of England had abandoned her completely. It is well known that it was the spies who created the feelings against her, who exist in Italy. But in spite of this strong feeling, all the Italians say the evidence was certainly not enough to condemn her—and really it seems to me that they have a much more favorable opinion of her since the trial than before. All are horrified by the indecency of this forever infamous proceeding.

We have in the meantime received a letter from dear Marianne, who tells us that you wrote to us, but up until now this much desired letter has not arrived.

I must tell you, my friend, of an acquaintance that we have made with a Professor in Pisa.[1] He is really the only Italian that has a heart and a soul. He has the highest mind, a profound genius, and an eloquence that transports. The poor Pisans believe him to be mad; and recount many tales about him that make one believe that he is a little odd, or to say it in English—eccentric. But he says—They believe me to be mad and it pleases me that they make this mistake; but perhaps the time will come when they will see that it is the madness of Brutus. He comes to our house every evening and always delights us with his original ideas. He speaks the most beautiful Italian tongue, completely different from today's idiom, which makes one believe that he might be hearing Boccaccio or Machiavelli speaking as he wrote.

We have also made the acquaintance of an Improvisatore[2]—a man of great talent—and very strong in Greek, with an incomparable poetic genius. He improvises with an admirable fire and precision. His subject is the future destiny of Italy. He recalled that Petrarch said that neither the very high Alps nor the sea was enough to defend this unsteady and aged country from the foreign masters—But he says—I see the Alps grow—and the sea rise and become agitated in order to impede the enemies. Unfortunately he, like some of the poets of our own country, finds more pleasure in the momentary applause of a theater and the fuss that the women make, rather than in studying for posterity.

You see that in the meantime we get to know a few more Italians every day, and we take a great interest in the threatened war at Naples. What will they do? The Noblemen of Naples are independent and brave; but the populace is enslaved. Who knows if the army will resist the Austrian troops.[3] How many Italians long for liberty, but as in every country, the poor do not have the power, and the rich never want to risk their money. The Italians love money almost more than the English do. The rich in England love gold, but the noblemen of Italy are in love with copper, and small coins—(half farthings) receive from them as much respect as we give to shillings.

We have another acquaintance, from Rome, and pathetic.[4] She is a young girl, nineteen years old—the daughter of a Florentine nobleman, beautiful —of great genius—who writes Italian with an elegance and delicacy to equal the best authors of the best Italian age. But she is miserably unhappy. Her mother is a terrible woman: and being jealous of the talents and the beauty of her daughter, she keeps her locked in a convent where she sees no one but the maids and the idiots.[5] She never goes out but stays closed up in two small rooms that look out upon a not very picturesque kitchen garden of the convent, always lamenting her pitiful situation. Her only hope is to marry but her very existence is almost a secret—what an exceptional wedding! I will tell you, my friend, how they marry in this country. And I can assure you it is true, because at the moment I am writing, I have in front of my eyes a proposal for a Pisan girl. The lawyer who is employed to handle this proposal sends a letter that begins thus—"The Youth, with whom it is desired to unite in matrimony the proposed Young Woman, is seventeen: he is tall, whole, without imperfections, in the best of health, robust and attractive. He is of innocent morals, and an incomparable wisdom; he is studious, and sufficiently advanced in the study of belles lettres, to which he applies himself indefatigably." There then follows a description of his family and his fortune and expectations; and of the dowry that he expects—and this masterpiece concludes thus. "The marriage must take place two years after the stipulation of the said contract. When the Parents of the proposed Young Woman have approved the above-mentioned conditions, the identity of the Young Man with whom they are dealing will immediately be made known to them. It is necessary finally, to know the age of the proposed Young Woman." Here is an Italian wedding! Furthermore, they have a tremendous horror of marriages made without parental consent. Surely domestic tyranny has more force here in the opinions—and even in the laws; still, but with few exceptions, the parents are gentle and indulgent in the common day-to-day affairs.

We have had no winter up until now—we enjoy mild weather and beautiful December sunshine. The autumn rains have passed—and the country everywhere is stripped and bare laughing beneath the rays of a very clear sky. Abandon your woes, my friend—and for a few moments may you also enjoy my beautiful Italy—I hope that this letter will have this effect. May God watch over you—you and all those that belong to you. Shelley and Claire send a thousand and a thousand affectionate regards—farewell

your constant friend—Mary.

ADDRESS: To be forwarded immediately / Leigh Hunt Esq / To the care of / Mess. Olliers—Booksellers / Vere St. / Bond St. / Londra / Angleterre. POSTMARKS: (1) Pisa; (2) FPO / DE. 19 / 1820. PUBLISHED: Jones, #101. TEXT: MS., Huntington Library (HM 2747). TRANSLATION: Ricki B. Herzfeld.

1. Francesco Pacchiani (b. 1771), a professor of logic and metaphysics and then of physical chemistry at the University of Pisa and a canon. He first fascinated the Shelleys with his brilliance and learning, and he introduced them to a number of people they came to value. Soon, however, they regarded him as coarse, hypocritical, and irresponsible and referred to him by his common nickname, "Il Diavolo." Mary Shelley based her character Benedetto Pepi in *Valperga* on Pacchiani (White, *Shelley*, II, 241–43; *CC Journals*, pp. 187–88).

2. Tommaso Sgricci (1789–1836), introduced to the Shelleys by Pacchiani on 1 December 1820. When he met the Shelleys, Sgricci had been an improvisor for seven years and had appeared in many major Italian cities. His ability to improvise poems, tragic scenes, and whole tragedies excited both Shelleys, particularly Mary

Shelley (White, *Shelley*, II, 243–45; Angeli, *Shelley and His Friends in Italy*, pp. 174–77; *CC Journals*, pp. 470–73).

3. See 19 July 1820, n. 10.

4. Teresa Emilia Viviani (1801–36), the inspiration of Shelley's *Epipsychidion*, introduced into the Shelley circle by Pacchiani at the end of November 1820. The daughter of the Governor of Pisa, Niccolo Viviani (to whose family Pacchiani was confessor), Teresa Emilia Viviani was kept in virtual isolation in the Convent of St. Anna school, apparently because of her mother's jealousy. The Shelleys and Claire Clairmont felt immediate sympathy for this beautiful, talented, and seemingly imprisoned young woman. After a short time she addressed Shelley as her "brother" and Mary Shelley and Claire Clairmont as her "sisters." By May 1821, however, Mary Shelley and Claire Clairmont were disillusioned with her; eventually Shelley came to share that disillusionment (White, *Shelley*, II, 247–70; for transcriptions of Teresa Emilia Viviani's letters to the Shelleys, see White, *Shelley*, II, 466–85).

5. Mary Shelley incorporated similar descriptions of the convent and the marriage customs in her 1824 story, "The Bride of Modern Italy" (MWS, *Collected Tales*, pp. 32–42), in which she satirized Teresa Emilia Viviani (see 7 March 1822; 2–5 October [1823], n. 17).

To [Marianne Hunt] [Pisa] Dec 3. 1820[1]

You must know that all intercourse between the G's [*Gisbornes*] & us is broken off—it were long & tedious in a letter to explain but they have behaved so as to pain & disappoint us extremely—that is to say on M^rs^ G's account for I do not count the others. And their folly (as is usual in such cases) equals their—what word shall I put—<u>baseness</u>—I hardly think the word too strong—however do not mistake it is an affair of pelf—but acting ill on that score that [*they*] had no write [*right*] to pretend to uprightness—enough of them.

I long exceedingly to hear from you again, my best girl—in about a week you could fill a sheet & send it to satisfy my anxiety

When shall we see you again—God only knows I foresee one only event which can bring us to England[2] Are we not wanderers on the face of the earth—take pity on us & by loving us still let us have some point in life—

How is your health

Yours affectionately for ever
Mary W Shelley

PUBLISHED: Jones, #102. TEXT: MS., British Library (Add. MSS. 38, 523, f. 56).

1. This note was most likely enclosed in Mary Shelley's letter of the same date to Leigh Hunt.

2. Probably a reference to the anticipated death of Shelley's father.

To Maria Gisborne 13. Dec [1820] Casa Galetti Pisa

My dear Mrs Gisborne

If you w^d^ have the kindness to send us a list of the things you have of ours I could more easily tell what should be sent to us—The articles of clothing if you will get them marked & rubbed a little on a red brick floor will pass the dogana[1] My parasol since I am not like an Italian afraid of the sun of December may remain safely in your custody.

We are very sorry to hear of M^r^ G's [*Gisborne's*] prolonged ill health—this weather is not I am afraid very favourable to him Shelley is by no means well—Vaccà says that his disease is entirely nervous and nephretic.

I had put the papers apart for you & by an accident many of them were destroyed I send all I can collect—The present crisis in England is wonderfully awful It appears like a huge crag tottering on the edge of a precipiece. We are also highly interested in the result of the Austrian counsels against Naples.[2]

I envy your Decameron evening—I am at present very busy with Greek & Calderon

I hope to hear that M^r^ G— gets better—has he seen Vaccà

I write in haste you will therefore excuse this scrawl—you will be so kind as to send the flannels—child's stockings* .&c without delay & you will much oblige youevr

M W S.

* new books, Lord Bacon, & the Greek Tragedians[3]

Endorsed: Casa Galetti / Pisa / 15 Dec 1820. Published: Jones, #104. Text: MS., Bodleian Library (MS., Shelley, c. 1, ff. 415–16).

1. "Customs inspection."
2. See 19 July 1820, n. 7, 10.
3. This note is quite likely in Shelley's hand.

To John Gisborne [Casa Galetti Pisa 14–24 December 1820][1]

We send the papers[2] but as we want them again be so kind as to return them by the first opportunity—directed Casa Galetti Lung'Arno—

I cant write a word more for I have a cold in my eyes

Yours
MWS.

Address: Signore Giovanni Gisborne / per ricapito al forno / d'Isidoro / via dei Cavalieri / Livorno. Endorsed: Pisa, Dec. 1820, Casa Galetti. Published: Jones, #103. Text: MS., Bodleian Library (MS., Shelley, c. 1, ff. 413–14).

1. The copy in John Gisborne's Notebook No. 2 is placed between 14 and 24 December 1820.
2. *Galignani's Messenger.*

To Maria Gisborne Pisa [?15 December 1820—January 1821][1]

My Dear Mrs Gisborne

Have the kindness to give Pepi the parcel of new books, combs, brushes, tape &c, leaving the rest for a future day.

I send you some fresh papers, but I believe that there is a vacuum—I cannot make it up however—The papers are exceedingly uninteresting—Pacchiani is no great favourite of our's—He disgusted S— by telling a dirty story—So much for him Adieu

Your's MWS

I hope M^r^ G— [*Gisborne*] is better—

PUBLISHED: Jones, #105. TEXT: John Gisborne Notebook No. 2, Abinger MS., Bodleian Library.

1. On 14 December Mary Shelley recorded in her *Journal*: "Pacchiani in the evening"; and Claire Clairmont recorded in hers for the same day: "Pacchiani in the Evening. He is indecent." John Gisborne's Notebook places the letter in January 1821.

To Maria Gisborne [Pisa ?25 December 1820][1]

My dear Mrs Gisborne

Have the kindness to consign to Pèpi all the articles contained in your list I send you the money as you wish be so good as to write a line to say that all is right.

I hope this mild weather agrees with you & Mr Gisborne. Winter has not begun yet—What a delicious climate this Italy is!

Pèpi is waiting therefore I have not time for another word

30 crowns

ENDORSED: December 1820 or January 1821. PUBLISHED: Jones, #106. TEXT: MS., Bodleian Library (MS., Shelley, c. 1, f. 464).

1. The original of this letter is undated, but John Gisborne's Notebook dates it 25 December 1820.

To Maria Gisborne [Pisa] Saturday—Dec 29th [?30 1820][1]

My dear Mrs Gisborne

Will you be so kind as to give Pepi the rest of the child's stockings—a flan. shirt—and Æschylus. I think Olliers Miscellany[2] was in your list—will you send it us.

Shelley has had a cold in his eyes which has prevented his writing and reading for above a fortnight—How does this cold weather agree with Mr Gisborne I hope he keeps close to the fire and lets the winds howl vainly

I am sorry that I cannot send the papers but Claire is gone to Florence[3] for a few weeks and I have promised to send them to her—she shall forward them to you thence or return them to me in numbers and then you shall have them if you do not think them too stale.

Ever truly yours. MWS.

ADDRESS: La Signora Maria Gisborne / Casa Ricci / Al'Origine / Livorno. PUBLISHED: Jones, #108. TEXT: MS., Bodleian Library (MS., Shelley, c. 1, f. 417).

1. Saturday was 30 December. Mary Shelley's Journal indicates that she wrote letters on 29 December; however, she often made entries for several days at one time, leading to confusion about days and dates.

2. *Ollier's Literary Miscellany in Prose and Verse*, no. 1 (London: C. and J. Ollier, 1820). *The Miscellany* published Peacock's "The Four Ages of Poetry," to which Shelley responded with *A Defence of Poetry*, sent to Ollier on 20 March 1821. The *Miscellany*, however, ceased with its initial issue. Mary Shelley tried to publish *A Defence of Poetry* in the *Liberal*, but it, too, ceased publication before the essay was included (see 6 November 1822). Shelley's essay was first published in 1840 in *Essays, Letters from Abroad, Translations and Fragments by Percy Bysshe Shelley*, brought out by Mary Shelley.

3. On 20 October Claire Clairmont went to Florence, where she was to spend a trial month as a paying guest at the home of Dr. Antonio Botji (1778–1827), physician (*CC Journals*, p. 179, n. 42). If arrangements proved satisfactory, Claire Clairmont was then to remain with the Botji family for at least three months longer. Her initial unhappiness prompted Shelley to call her to Pisa, where she joined the Shelleys on 21 November. On 23 December, however, she returned to Florence and, with the exception of visits to the Shelleys and other holidays, made her home with the Botji family until 7 June 1822, when she joined the Shelleys at Lerici. Mrs. Mason, believing it necessary that Claire Clairmont establish a life independent of the Shelleys, was instrumental in settling Claire Clairmont at Florence (see 19 July 1820; *PBS Letters*, #591, #595).

TO LEIGH HUNT [Pisa] December 29th—1820 (Jan. 1. 1821)

My dear Friend

We have been very anxious to hear from you since we saw that your paper had been honoured with the peculiar attention of the A.G.[1] Yet no letters comes. I am convinced that you will escape when it comes to trial—but an Acquittal must be bought not only with anxiety—fear & labour but also with the money you can so ill spare. Before this comes to hand you will of course have written—one of your letters which are as rare as Fountains in the Stony Arabia will have given us a brief pleasure Why do you not write oftener?—Ah! why are you not rich, peaceful and Enjoying? We have just been delighted with a parcel of your Indicators[2] but they also afford full proof that you are not as happy as you ought to be—Yet how beautiful they are. That one upon the deaths of young children was a piece of as fine writing & of as exquisite feeling as I ever read—To us you know it must have been particularly affecting—Yet there is one thing well apparent—You, my dear Hunt, never lost a child or the ideal immortality w[d] not suffice to your immagination as it naturally does thinking only of those whom you loved more from the overflowing of affection, than from their being the hope, the rest, the purpose, the support, and the ⟨reward⟩ recompense of life.

I hardly know whether I do not teaze you with too many letters, yet you have made no complaint of that, and besides you always like to hear about Italy[3] and it is almost impossible not to write somthing pleasing to you from this divine country, if praises of its many beauties and its delights be interesting to you. I have now an account to give you of a wonderful and beautiful exhibition of talent which we have been witnesses of.[4] An exhibition peculiar to the Italians and like their climate—their vegetation and their country fervent fertile and mixing in wondrous proportions the picturesque the cultivated & the wild until they become not as in other countries one the foil of the other but they mingle and form a spectacle new and beautiful We were the other night at the theatre where the Improvisatore whom I mentioned in my last letter delivered an extempore tragedy. Conceive of a poem as long as a Greek Tragedy, interspersed with choruses, the whole plan conceived in an instant—The ideas and verses & scenes flowing in rich succession like the perpetual gush of a fast falling cataract. The ideas poetic and just; the words the most beautiful, scelte[5] and grand that his exquisite Italian afforded—He is handsome—his person small but elegant—and his motions graceful beyond description: his action was perfect; and the freedom of his motions outdo the constraint which is ever visible in an English actor—The changes of countenance were of course not so fine as those I have witnissed on the English stage, for he had not conned his part and set his features but it was one impulse that filled him; an unchanged deity who spoke within him, and his voice su{r}passed in its modulations the melody of music. The subject was Iphigenia in Tauris. It was composed on the Greek plan (indeed he followed Euripides in his arrangement and in many of his ideas)—without the devision of acts and with chorus's. Of course if we saw it written there would have been many slight defects of management, defects—amended when seen—but many of the scenes were perfect—and the recognition of Orestes and Iphigenia was worked up beautifully.

I do not know how this talent may be appreciated in the other cities of Italy, but the Pisans are noted for their want of love and of course entire ignorance of the fine arts—Their opera is miserable, their theatre the worst in Italy. The theatre was nearly empty on this occasion—The students of the University half filled the pit and the few people in the boxes were foreigners except two Pisan families who went away before it was half over. God knows what this man w[d] be if he laboured and become a poet for posterity instead of an Improvisatore for the present—I am enclined to think that in the perfection in which he possesses this art it is by no means an inferior power to that of a printed poet—There have been few Improvisatores who have like him joined a cultivated education and acquirements in languages rare among foreigners—If however his auditors were refined—and as the oak or the rock to the lightning—feeling in their inmost souls the penetrative fire of his poetry—I sh^d^ not find fault with his making perfection in this art the aim of his exertions—But to Improvise to a Pisan audience is to scatter otto of roses among the overweighing stench of a charnel house:—pearls to swine were œconomy in comparison. As Shelley told him the other night He appeared in Pisa as Dante among the ghosts—Pisa is a city of the dead and they shrunk from his living presence. The name of this Improvisatore is Sgricci, and I see that his name is mentioned in your literary pocket book.[6] This has made me think that it were an interesting plan for this same pretty pocket book if you were to give some small interesting account—not exactly a biographical sketch, but anecdotical and somewhat critical of the various authors of the list. Sgricci has been accused of ca{r}bonarism whether truly or not I cannot judge—I should think not or he w^d^ be trying to harvest at Naples instead of extemporizing here. From what we have heard of him I believe him to be good and his manners are gentle and amiable—while the rich flow of his beautifully pronounced language is as pleasant to the ear as a sonata of Mozart. I must tell you that some wiseacre Professors of Pisa wanted to put Sgricci down at the theatre and their vile envy might have frightened the God from his temple if an Irishman who chanced to be in the same box with him had not compelled him to silence. The ringleader of this gang is called Rosini[7] a man, a speaker of folly in a city of fools—bad envious talkative presumptuous;—one—"chi mai parla bene di chichesisia—o di quei che vivono o dei morti."[8] He has written a long poem which no one has ever read and like the illustrious Sotherby[9] gives the law to a few distinguished Blues of Pisa Well good night; tomorrow I will finish my letter and talk to you about our unf[ortu]nate young friend, Emilia Viviani.

It is grievous to see this beautiful girl wearing out the best years of her life in a[n] odious convent where both mind and body are sick from want of the appropriate exercize for each—I think she has great talent if not genius—or if not an internal fountain how could she have acquired the mastery she has of her own language which she writes so beautifully, or those ideas which lift her so far above the rest of the Italians. She has not studied much and now hopeless from a five years confinement every thing disgusts her and she looks with hatred & distaste even on the alleviations of her situation. Her only hope is in a marriage which her parents tell her is concluded although she has never seen the person intended for her—Nor do I think the change of situation will be much for the better for he is a younger brother and will live in the house with his mother whom they say is molta secante[10]—Yet she may then have the free use of her limbs—she may then be able to walk out among the fields—vineyards & woods of her country and see the mountains and the sky and not be as now a dozen steps to the right and then back to the left another dozen which is the longest walk her convent garden affords—and that you may be sure she is very seldom tempted to take.

Winter began with us on Xmas day—not that we have yet had frost but a cold wind sweeps over us and the sky is covered with dark clouds and the cold sleet mizzles down—I understand that you have had as yet a mild winter—This and the plentiful harvest will keep the poor somewhat happier this year.—Yet I dare say you now see the white snow before your doors. Even warm as we are here Shelley suffers a great deal of pain in every way—perhaps more even than last winter.

(Jan 1. 1821) Although I almost think it of bad augury to wish you a good new year yet as I finish my letter on this day I cannot help adding the Compliments of the Season and wishing all happiness peace & enjoyment for this comming year to you my dear dear Marianne and all who belong to you—I thank you for all the good wishes I know you have made for us—We are quiet now—last year there were many turbulencies—perhaps during this there will be fewer—

We have made acquaintance with a Greek, a Prince Mauro Codarti[11]—a very pleasant man profound in his own language and who although he has applied to English little more than a month begins to relish its beauties & to understand the genius of its expressions in a wonderful manner—He was done up [*cross-written, p. 1*] by some alliance I believe with Ali Pacha[12] and has taken refuge in Italy from the Constantinopolitan bowstring. He has related to us some very infamous conduct of the English powers in Greece of which I sh^d exceedingly like to get the documents & to place them in Grey Bennett's of [*or*] Sir F. B.'s [*Francis Burdett*][13] hands—they might serve to give another knock to this wretched system of things.

We are very anxious to hear the event of the meeting of parliament as I suppose you all are in England—but perhaps we exiles are ultra-political—but certainly I have some hopes that something fortunate will soon happen for the state of things in England.

And Italy! The King of Naples has gone to Trophau[14] with the consent of his parliament and that is the latest news—we begin, we hope to see the ⟨golden⟩ crimson clouds of rising peace—And if all be quiet southward we have some thoughts of emigrating there next summer—

Adieu my dear Hunt

Most affectionately yours
Marina

[*Half-line deleted*] ⟨will⟩ be a better girl than last time—let her make up a small parcel—a dozen papers of middle sized pins—an asortment of good needles—a small pointed pair of Scissars—an excellent penknife of several blades—a few sticks of sealing wax—let the needles be in a very small morocco case such as they make on purpose for papers of needles—a steel topped thimble and some ounces of stocking cotton— [*half-line deleted*]—and send this to Horace Smith—asking him if he has sent our parcel if he has let it be sent to Peacock written on the outside to be sent to me by the next parcel—

Ollier will answer her demand for the amount of these things
Adieu

add also a few hundreds of Brama's pens.

ADDRESS: Leigh Hunt Esq. / Mess. Olliers. Booksellers / Vere St. Bond St. / London / Inghilterra / Angleterre. POSTMARKS: (1) PISA; (2) FPO / JA. 18 / 1821. PUBLISHED: Jones, #107. TEXT: MS., Huntington Library (HM 2748).

1. The Attorney General, who had prosecuted the *Examiner* for its comments concerning the trial of Caroline of Brunswick. On 25 February 1821 John Hunt (1775–1848), Leigh Hunt's brother and proprietor of the *Examiner*, was sent to prison for one year, and the sum of £1,000 was required as guarantee of proper future conduct (Blunden, *"Examiner" Examined*, pp. 106–8).

2. The *Indicator* was a weekly literary periodical edited and published by Hunt from 13 October 1819 to 21 March 1821 and continued by someone else under the name Onewhyn from 28 March 1821 to 30 August 1821 (*SC*, VI, 912–13, 915–16).

3. *Italy* is written over *Italians*.

4. On 21 December Mary Shelley, Shelley, and Claire Clairmont went to the theater to see Sgricci's improvisations of "a Canzone upon Pyramus & Thisbe" and a tragedy, "Iphegenia in Tauris" (*CC Journals*).

5. "Select."

6. The *Literary Pocket-Book; or, Companion for the Lover of Nature and Art*, an annual pocket calendar that contained a variety of useful data (currency rates; coach schedules; shop addresses; lists of persons in the arts, science, and government), as well as original prose and poetry. Begun by Leigh Hunt and printed for him by Charles and James Ollier, it appeared for five years beginning in 1819.

7. A professor at the University of Pisa, Rossini was a man of wide learning and a poet. He regarded Sgricci as mediocre and tried to stem his popularity (Dowden, *Shelley*, II, 368–69).

8. "Who never speaks well of anybody whatsoever—living or dead."

9. William Sotheby (1757–1833), an author prominent in London literary society. Mary Shelley's allusion here is to Byron's satire of Sotheby as "Botherby" in *Beppo*, stanzas 72–76. For Byron's reason for satirizing Sotheby, who was once his friend, see Byron, *Letters and Journals*, VI, 34–36.

10. "Very tiresome."

11. Prince Alexander Mavrocordato (1791–1865), Greek patriot and statesman and a major figure in the cause of Greek liberty. Introduced to the Shelleys by Pacchiani on 2 December 1820, Mavrocordato became a friend and frequent visitor. Although Shelley admired him as a political hero and dedicated *Hellas* to him, he did not develop any true rapport with Mavrocordato (*PBS Letters*, #626). Mary Shelley, however, became his close friend. He aided her in her studies of Greek, and she gave him English lessons. Mary Shelley's letters to Mavrocordato remain unlocated, but seventeen of his letters to her are extant (Abinger MSS.) and reveal the deep and active interest she had in political events in Greece, as well as her role as confidant to Mavrocordato until his departure for Greece on 26 June 1821 (Herbert Huscher, "Alexander Mavrocordato: Friend of the Shelleys," *Keats-Shelley Memorial Bulletin* 16 [1965]: 29–38).

12. Ali Pasha (1741–1822), "The Lion of Janina," was a Turkish brigand who became pasha of Janina in 1788 and through ruthless, capricious rule eventually established independent authority over Albania, Macedonia, Epirus, Thessaly, and the Morea, all technically answerable to the sultan. In 1820 Ali Pasha, in an attempt to gain further power, openly revolted against Sultan Mahmud II, which preoccupied the Turks and gave the Greeks the opportunity to rebel against Turkish rule (see 2 April 1821; 6–10 April 1822).

13. Henry Grey Bennet (1777–1836), later Earl of Tankerville, a leading liberal politician who represented Shrewsbury in 1806 and 1807 and from 1811 to 1826; and Sir Francis Burdett (1770–1844), radical political leader and advocate for reform whose strong criticism of the actions of the authorities at "Peterloo" brought him a fine of £2,000 and three months in prison.

14. The Congress of Troppau (in Silesia) of the Holy Alliance, attended by the emperors Alexander I of Russia and Francis I of Austria and representatives of Prussia and Great Britain, began on 20 October 1820. On 19 November Austria, Russia, and Prussia agreed to crush any changes of government due to revolution. At the subsequent Congress of Laibach (in Slovenia), from 26 January to 12 May 1821, the Holy Alliance authorized Austria to suppress the Neapolitan revolution, which it did by 7 March 1821.

To Claire Clairmont Pisa. Sunday night. Jan. [14–15] 1821

My dear Claire

I must now give you some account of my adventures since I last wrote—The Vicar of Wakefield for many years recorded no other migration than from the blue bed to the brown—mine is one of far greater importance since it purposes to narrate a migration from Pisa to Lucca. Yet do not be terrified at my formal beginning, & fancy robbers, and broken roads, & overturned coaches—no, I have no events to record except a journey hence to Lucca—a day spent there, and my return.

I mentioned that on thursday Sgricci was to give an Accademia which I had little hope of attending[1]—teusday and wednesday came, and I had still less—for Shelleys boils got worse—his face swelled dreadfully, and though not very ill he was in no travelling condition—However at his persuasian I cooked up a party with Pacchiani & thursday evening at 6 o'clock I, Babe, Pacchiani & Maria set out for Lucca. It has rained the whole day & the day before besides—but it held up as we went and we had a pleasant ride—It was eight when we arrived, and we hastened to the theatre—We entered the box of a friend of P.—there was no Sgricci—but a bad Orchestra—a screaming Prima donna & a worse Basso pouring forth melifluous notes on an inattentive audience. The Accademia was put off until the following night—& Pacchiani who had already missed one lesson in that week was obliged to return the next morning to Lucca—And how could I stay & go alone?

Pacchiani introduced me at the theatre to a friend of his called Georgine—a Mathematician & a man of talent—& very very gentlemanly in his way—It would seem that this gentleman took compassion on me, and he came early the next morning with a message from one of the first ladies of Lucca a friend of his to offer me her box & company if I would stay. So I staid and Pacchiani, to my infinite relief, returned to Pisa.

The Marchesa Eleonora Bernardini who was thus polite to me is thus described by Pacchiani—È richissima, ma questa nulla—è la prima donna di Lucca; buona come un angelo—ha piu genio che alcuna altra donna d'Italia—quando parla è come un bel libro—e scrive lettere venissime—come la Viviani; la stessa a cosa—ma ha l'uso del mondo—e poi è richissima, ma questa nulla—[2]

She is thus described by Sgricci è ricca assai—ma sicuro questa è nulla per lei perche spende quasi niente—le di lei erudizione e quella che nasce delle giornale—Lei è la piu gran' politica in Italia—ogni sera alla ma conversazione legge con voce alta le gazette—una dopo l'altra dal capo fin al ultimo—è dogmatica assai.[3]

I have seen so little of her that I can hardly decide between the two opinions, yet I will tell you what I think. I think that she is most exceedingly polite, easy mannered & pleasing—A Blue she certainly is—from her remarks on Sgricci's improvisaing and her evident struggles to bring all things into her square & height I should instantly decide that she had no genius—Her love of journals is probably true since she sent me a couple to amuse me—Well—she sent to ask me when I wd have her carrige & sent her secretary to conduct {me} to see some pictures in the town—and in the evening came for me to go with her to the theatre.

We went late and Sgricci had nearly finished his canzone—When it was over some one came to the box to call out—our male attendant—un certo cavaliere (who had known L.B. at Rome who had made him a Regalo[4] of his works) who presently returned to say that the duchess of Lucca who was present had ordered S. [*Sgricci*] to treat the subject of Ignez di Castro and that he did not know the story—Ignez is not as you said the daughter of Count Julian—I knew nothing of the story—the Sig^{ra} B. [*Bernardini*] little—so we made out a story among us which by the bye is little like the Ignezs of Camoens as I have since found though it may bear some affinity to the French tragedies on that subject. However while S. delivered the argument I heard someone in the pit say—Ha fallito nel 'istorica.[5] However unhistorical the argument of his tragedy might be Sgricci acquitted himself to admiration in the conduct and passion & poetry of his piece. As he went on he altered the argument as it had been delivered to him and wound up the tragedy with a scene both affecting and sublime. Peter of Arragon wished to marry his son Sancho to a Princess of France but Sancho obstinately refused and neither his mother's tears His fathers menaces curses or entreaties could induce him to comply. In truth he was already married to Inez and had two children. Pietro irritated by his sons opposition casts him into prison, and then Ignez to save her husband comes forward & confesses that she is the obstacle which causes his disobedience The Sig^{ra} B. had said that the story was that this came to late for that Sancho had already been put to death by his father who now put Ignez to death also. But Sgricci—as one inspired became possessed of the truth as he continued to improvise, and leaving this false route came upon that which was the real one without knowing it—Was he not inspired?—While Ignez is trying to move the compassion of the king, Sancho who had been freed by his mother comes in wild and aghast—The king pretended to {be} moved by their prayers—said that he would sanctify their marriage, & takes Ignez & the two children under his care giving orders for the ceremonial—the moment comes Sancho arrives in confidence and his bride is produced by his inexorable father—dead.—It seems impossible that a tragedy represented by one man should in any way create illusion—others complained of the want of it—yet when Pietro unveiled the dead Ignez, when Sancho died in despair on her body, it seemed to me as if it were all there; so truly & passionately did his words depict the scene he wished to represent. The Sig^ra^ B. said that it was una cosa mediocra to me it appeared a miracle. Of course this lady was not quite silent during the whole time & I lost much of the poetry though nothing of the scenic effect of this exhibition.

The next morning I returned early to Pisa and found S. a great deal better; though not well & still tormented with boils.

I like Pacchiani less & less. there is no truth in him—but a love of wealth and a boasting infinitely disgusting. It would require volumes to tell you all the ⟨violance⟩ proofs that dayly occur of this disposition. What think you of his relating how when David,[6] the divine David, first came out, how he seeing that he failed in some points of melody went to him & put him right, & how the applause of the Florentine audience crowned his instructions, & how the old David came to thank him. Emilia will perhaps relate to you the coin in which he intends to make her pay for his friendship so through her he is to gain favour & dinners from the English When he talks of any one the first words are—è ricco, ma questo e nullo—ma poi è richissimo. And then his innumerable host of great acquaintances!—he would make one believe that he attracts the great as a milk pail does flies on a summer morning.

Of Emilia I have seen little since I last wrote, but she was in much better spirits when I did see her than I had found her for a long time before. Sgricci is returned from Lucca and will I fancy soon proceed to Florence—We want very much to cook up an Accademia for him here—but we have no power—P. says that he can—perhaps he will—we shall see. To me, I own it is no slight delight to be a spectator (to use such a term) of the rich & continuous flow of his poetic extasies—I do believe them to be something divine—In a room he is amusing—I believe him to be good—time will shew if that be frankness which now looks like it—for as I read the other day in Sophocles—You may know whether a man be bad in a day but length of time alone discovers virtue. But on the theatre he is as a god—

Well good night—I will finish my letter tomorrow. I will keep back the papers a few days & then send them you with a parcel of such books as we have—and thus I think it will not be dearer than the postage of the papers.

(Monday Morning) you see that you need not complain of want of letters from me since I write quite enough in all conscience. I write generally of an evening after tea. You have no idea how earnestly we desire the transfer of Mxxxxn[7] to Florence—in plain Italian he is a Seccatura— He sits with us & be one reading or writing he insists upon interrupting one every moment to read all the fine things he either writes or reads— Besides writing poetry he translates—He intends he says to translate all the fine passages of Dante—& has already the canto concerning Ugolino. Now not to say that he fills his verses with all possible commonplaces he understands his author very imperfectly—and when he cannot make sense of the words that are he puts in words of his own and calls it a misprint—so sometimes falsifying the historical fact always the sense he produces something as like Dante as a rotten crab apple is like a fine nonpareil. For instance those lines of Dante—but I have not time or paper for examples. We have had a droll letter from Hogg which I will send in the promised parcel. We have heard from no one else—I think the Williams[8] may stay a month here since Mxxxxn has taken lodgeings for them & then proceed to Florence —I hope he will go before—or at least when they come he will be much with them for otherwise S does nothing but conjugate the verb seccare & twist & turn Seccatura in all possible ways. He is Common Place personified.—

Yesterday it rained all the afternoon—after a cloudy morning today is fine with I fancy a little tramontana. I wish you could stringere amicizia with Eliza[9]—but I fear the attempt is vain at least you can do nothing more than you have done until she answers your letter.

S. is now somewhat better—little Babe is well & merry—Do not send this long retarded stove for I fancy it would only be ready to be lighted the day of our departure from these disagreable lodgings

I envy you the Gallery—I do not know what you can envy in us since now we are dryed beyond our usual dustiness I do not think we shall come to Florence if we do it will be only in the progress of a tour which I do not think we shall make—

There is no news in the papers of any kind so be patient during the fine days I hope we are to have & before the next rainy weather comes, I hope you will receive them. Pray write to Emilia—Pacchiani asked me for your name yesterday since he is going, he says to write to you—if he does pray preserve the letter—for as I believe no one ever ever saw even his handwriting it w^d be a curiosity for a museum—

Ever Yours
Mary W.S.

ADDRESS: A Mademoiselle / Madlle de Clairmont / Chez M. le Professeur Bojti / vis-a-vis au Palazzo Pitti / Firenca. PUBLISHED: Jones, #109. TEXT: MS., British Library (Ashley 4020, ff. 1–4).

1. Mary Shelley's Journal records: for 11 January 1821, trip to Lucca; for 12 January, attendance of Sgricci's "Ignez di Castro"; 13 January, return to Pisa; 14 January, letter to Claire Clairmont.

2. "She is extremely rich but this is not important—she is the first lady of Lucca; as good as an angel—she has more talent than any other woman in Italy—when she speaks it is like a beautiful book—and she writes the finest letters—like la

Viviani; the same—but she has a knowledge of the world—and then she is very rich, but this is not important."

3. "She is very rich—but surely this means nothing to her, since she spends almost nothing—her erudition is that which comes from the papers—She is the biggest politician in all of Italy—every evening at the conversazione she reads the journals aloud—one after the other from start to finish—she is very dogmatic."

4. "Gift."

5. "He was not faithful to the history." The story of Inês de Castro appears in the epic *Os Lusíadas* [The Portuguese] (1572), by Portuguese poet Luis Vaz de Camões (1524–80).

6. See 13 May 1818.

7. Thomas Medwin (1788–1869), author, was Shelley's second cousin. Medwin was born and raised at Horsham, two miles from Shelley's family home at Field Place, and the cousins were childhood friends. Like Shelley, Medwin had early literary aspirations, and he collaborated with Shelley on a Gothic tale (now lost) in 1809–10. After giving up his study of law, Medwin became first a cornet (1812) and then a lieutenant (1813) in the 24th Light Dragoons (these were purchased positions; Medwin had had no previous military training). He served in India from 1813 to 1818 and then returned to England. In September 1819 Medwin was at Geneva and from there wrote to Shelley. On 21 October 1820, in Pisa, Medwin and Shelley were reunited after a seven-year separation. At first pleased with Medwin, Shelley soon came to find him a bore (*seccatura*). Through Medwin the Shelleys met Edward and Jane Williams (see below, n. 8) and Trelawny (see 9 February 1822). Shelley introduced Medwin to Byron at Pisa on 21 November 1821. Medwin's brief association with Byron formed the basis of his *Conversations*, which was attacked by Byron's closest friends and associates as unauthentic and caused great public controversy (see 10 November [1824]; 19 February [1825]). He also wrote "Memoir of Shelley," for the *Athenaeum* (1832); "Shelley Papers," *Athenaeum* (1832–33), republished as *The Shelley Papers. Memoir of Shelley* (London: Whittaker, Treacher & Co., 1833); and *The Life of Percy Bysshe Shelley* (cited herein as Medwin, *Shelley*), which Mary Shelley regarded as an attempt to blackmail her. Although Medwin was often inaccurate, his works demonstrate loyalty to Byron and especially to Shelley and remain a valuable source of information (Lovell, *Medwin*. White, *Shelley*, I, 19, 55; II, 228–29, 336–37, 400).

8. Lieutenant Edward Ellerker Williams (1793–1822) served with Medwin in India. While there, Williams met Jane Cleveland Johnson (1798–1884), who was separated from her husband, John Edward Johnson, and living with her brother, John Wheeler Cleveland (1791–1883), who in 1868 became a general. She and Williams formed a common-law marriage and returned to England; in July 1819 they went to the Continent (see 28 July [1824]). At Geneva they met Williams's former comrade Medwin and rented a house with him. The Williamses named their first child, born at Geneva on 7 February 1820, Edward Medwin Williams. Williams's interest in Shelley was excited by Medwin, and the Williamses readily accepted Medwin's invitation to come to Pisa, arriving on 16 January 1821 (White, *Shelley*, II, 282–83; Williams, *Journals and Letters*, 11–13).

9. "Make friends with." Perhaps Mary Shelley is referring to the same Eliza mentioned—but unidentified—in Claire Clairmont's *Journal* (pp. 48, 51, 52).

To Claire Clairmont — Jan. 21 (24) 1821—Pisa

My dear Claire

I have no adventures to record or story to tell in this letter, but as you may be somewhat curious about our new friends[1] I will tell you the little

I have observed about them. Jane is certainly very pretty but she wants animation and sense; her conversation is nothing particular, and she speaks in a slow monotonous voice: but she appears good tempered and tolerant. Ned seems the picture of good humour and obligingness, he is lively and possesses great talent in drawing so that with him one is never at a loss for subjects of conversation—He seems to make all he sees subjects of surprize & pleasure—cannot endure Miss Edgeworth's novels & is the opposite of a prude in every way. (and di piu has a soft harmonious voice infinitely pleasing) Of course they have somewhat helped from our shoulders the burthen of Tom[2] which was beginning to be very heavy. Pacchiani has helped off another piece—M. has no sympathy with our tastes or conversation—he is infinitely common place and is as silent as a fireskreen but not half so useful; except that he sometimes mends a pen.

You should hear Williams's account of his friend Captain Bowen who has spent £1100 of prize money in shewing two sisters Italy—A rough English sailor who while the young ladies say—What a charming picture —really that statue if one knew what it meant would be very pretty—stands with one of them hanging on each arm with his thumbs in his pockets whistling & looking another way—When they were at Florence they had several letters of introduction to Italian ladies—But you know, John, said they—we cannot go & visit these ladies without knowing what their characters are!—What, damn it, said he, would you have me go to the husbands & ask what their wives characters are—but unable to persuade them—Poor devils I could not leave them alone a whole evening so there we went tow row to the Opera.—At Leghorn he is was infinitely delighted but his sisters said—There, John, now you have brought us to a place where we dont know a soul."—An Old lady asked his advise for her route from Florence to Naples—standing with anxious care tracing her way on the map with her finger—From Narni to Rome—then from Rome to Albano, from Albano to Velletri, from Velletri to Terracina"—"There Madam you will to a certainty have your throat cut."—"Lord, sir, (and the old lady lifted up both her eyes & her tracing finger(you dont say so! but how?"—"The robbers, Madam, the robbers"—"But sir the robbers—they only want ones money—and though its disagreable to lose ones money I would give them all mine with pleasure rather than"—"Ah you're deceived—you would most assuredly have your throat cut—to be sure they might shoot you"—"Oh pray Dont talk about it Captain Bowen, I would not go to Naples on any account to be robbed & have my throat cut half way"—

The old lady came to Williams saying—"To be sure I am much obliged to you, Sir, for having introduced me to Captain Bowen—Else I might have gone to Naples & have been robbed & murdered by the way—Bless me! What a very shocking road it must be.

(Jan 23) I had intended to finish this letter at my ease & to dispatch it with Sgricci on his return to Florence but since Shelley neglected to send the enclosed Bulletin in his letter I write to send it—In the mean time I will fill my paper with what gossip I may.

Pacchiani's crime which I thought concealed is I find tolerably well known I do not scruple therefore to confide it to you. You know the many compliments he has received on account of his goodness to Æsop[3]—Well not only does this poor youth serve him for servant secretary &c &c & is in truth a hardly used slave, but P. appropriates for his own use the money Æsop gets from his scholars, half starving the poor fellow and doling him out grazia per grazia when he want to be shaved &c—When P. accompanied you to Florence he took with him 20 crowns of EAsops earnings & when he returned he went round and got money from his pupils in advance—Being necessitated to pay a debt yesterday he made Æsop go and get 6cr in advance from Prince Codarto although the prince had before advanced two months pay to him. He said to the V. [*Viviani*] the other day—questo Esops e un sciocco, un balordo,[4] how will he ever get on if he goes among the English so shabbily dressed—but Pacchiani must do everything—I went to Ghiri & cut off a coat waist coat & pantaloons—it cost me 200 lircs which I can ill spare ma bisogna fare bene al prossimo questo e il mio massimo per questo non son ricco[5]—Emilia was pleased with this small justice of Pacchiani but on enquiry of Æsop she found that his charity had amounted to his having run a bill up for the poor fellow at Ghiri's—for he took the clothes & had them put down to Campetti's name. You may easily believe that were it not for Emilia we would never see this rascal again. When we paid him for our legno[6] for Lucca we insisted on paying the whole charge—he refused with much vociferation & magnanimity when—suddenly stopping short he said—Yes I take them for Æsop. So besides thieving from him his honest gains he makes him appear a beggar & to finish the picture treats him with a tyranny and harshness that breaks the poor fellow's spirit

Upon the occasion of Sgci's second Academia he wished this latter to give him 200 tickets to distribute among the poor scolars to fill the pit—(I have not the smallest portion of a doubt that he intended to sell them at a paul or ½ a paul a piece) S. [*Sgricci*] refused to mendicare con i lodi[7] in consequence this excellent friend did not attend his Academia yesterday night[8]—We went as you may suppose & after much deliberation & consultation we agreed that the best way would be to give a sum at the door as is the custom for the friends of the Actor or Poet to do—Accordingly we left 10 sequins—a small sum but as you know as much as we could afford—Hardly had we entered our box—keeping ourselves for a while in the obscurest part of it than we heard it announced in the pit that dei Inglesi hanno last lascriarti dieci zechini all'uscio[9]—the words were repeated again & again—I sat in the greatest fear I ever felt you could not have watched & doubted more the shaking posts of our carriage windows than I feared (not then knowing that P. was not in the house) that he or others would find us out & that the scolari ever in search of amusement & most riotous in carnival time should treat us with some of their sonorous approbation— But our Black Genius not being there the sound of the zechini died away from the voice of man & we heard no more

The subject of the Tragedy was the Death of Hector. S. [*Sgricci*] was in excellent <u>inspiration</u>, his poetry was brilliant flowing & divine—a hymn to Mars & another to Victory were wonderfully spirited & striking—Achilles foretold to Hector that he (Achilles) was the master spirit who would destroy & vanquish him—Victory, he said, sits on the pummel of my sword & the way is short from thence to the point. The madness of Cassandra was exquisitely delineated—and her prophesies wondrous & torrent like—they burst on the ear like the Cry Trojans cry—of Shakespear and music eloquence & poetry were combined in this wonderful effort of the imagination —or rather shall I say of the inspiration of some wondrous deity.

(24) I was interrupted last night in my letter by the entrance of Prince Mauro[10]—On the day before the Williams and Medwin (the latter to our infinite joy & good fortune for he threatened us with his seca presenza at the theatre) went to Livorno & yesterday S. went to join them so I was alone. Prince Mauro is a man much to my taste gentlemanly—gay learned and full of talent & enthusiasm for Greece—he gave me a greek lesson & staid until 8 o'clock—about half an hour after Sgricci came & we had a tête a tête for two hours until Shelleys return. I was extremely pleased with him he talked with delight of the inspiration he had experienced the night before, which bore him out of himself and filled him as they describe the Pythyness[11] to have been filled with divine & tumu[l]tuous emotion— especially in the part where Cassandra prophesies he was as over come as she could { } & he poured forth prophecy as if Apollo had also touched his lips with the oracular touch. He talked about many things as you may guess in that time—with a frankness & gentleness beyond what I have before seen in him & which was the best and a conclusive answer to what has been said of his irregular life.

One word more of our Black Genius—A rich Englishman here—a natural philosopher bought at Leghorn a box of Elba minerals—worth at the very most 20 crowns—Pacchiani joined with the seller & together they made this poor fellow pay £70—This is well known all over Leghorn—where Pacchiani exults & revels with this well got cash.

Emilia is at present in much better spirits than I have seen her for a long time—Pacchiani brings her many visitors—She says she does not like this but at least it makes pass the time & gives her something else to think of than the dreary cells & high walls of her convent.

Adieu—I will write to you soon again—Sgricci conveys this to you. I am sorry that he is going—yet in some sort glad for Florence is better suited to him than Pisa—He talks of giving an Acedemia there in the Quaresima

Ever yours M.

ADDRESS: Miss Clairmont. PUBLISHED: Jones, #110. TEXT: MS., Pforzheimer Library (p. 4 contains two unpublished lines in Italian cross-written by Shelley).

1. Jane and Edward Williams (see [14–15] January 1821, n. 8).
2. Thomas Medwin (see [14–15] January 1821, n. 7).
3. Esopo Campetti, a young teacher exploited by Pacchiani.
4. "This Esops is a fool, a simpleton."
5. "It is necessary to do good for the next man, this is my maxim—for this reason I am not rich."
6. "Carriage."
7. "Beg for praises."
8. Mary Shelley recorded in her Journal for 22 January 1821: "Accademia in the evening—the subject the Quattro Etade & of the tragedy la morte d'ettore—He visits our box after the end of the tragedy."
9. "Some Englishmen have lost ten sequins at the door."
10. See 29 [?30] December [1820].
11. The priestess of Apollo, believed to have powers of prophecy.

To Maria Gisborne — Casa Galetti Pisa [c. 14] Feby 1821[1]

My Dear Mrs G—

I send you the books, which I have been some time in collecting; but I hope you were not in furia—I send you a packet of newspapers—be so kind as to return them as soon as you have done with them.

Shelley is tolerably well—The sunshine, however cold the air may be, agrees with me. I hope Mr G— [*Gisborne*] is now quite recovered—Do you not envy my luck, that having begun Greek, an amiable, young, agreeable and learned Greek prince[2] comes every morning to give me a lesson of an hour and a half. This is the result of an acquaintance with Pacchiani —so you see, even the Devil has his uses. P— [*Pacchiani*] himself has now been a fortnight at Florence[3]—I dread his return—

No news from or of Naples—

I wish you could find a letter from my father in the Leghorn Post office, for I have surely lost one.

I hope you are well—Addio

Ever Your's
Mary WS

PUBLISHED: Jones, #111. TEXT: John Gisborne Notebook No. 2, Abinger MS., Bodleian Library.

1. Dated "middle of Feby 1821" in John Gisborne's Notebook.
2. Alexander Mavrocordato (see 29 [?30] December [1820]).
3. Pacchiani had gone to Florence on 29 January (*MWS Journal*).

To Maria Gisborne — Casa Galetti Pisa Feb. 21—1821

My dear Mrs Gisborne

Shelley will take the opportunity of a letter he intends to write to Ollier in a few days to bid him fulfil Mr G's [*Gisborne's*] request concerning the books for his sister.[1]

Would you have the kindness to pay a debt or two that we have at Leghorn—& when you tell me the amount I will forward the sum to you immediately by Pepi—there are 20 livres to Terazzi—some such sum to Prinoth (where I bought my work box) and a bill to our old shoemaker—he whom you recommended to me—be so kind (having paid it) to forward me the bill of the latter for part of the account, how much I know not is Mrs Masons. This man deserves an excessive scolding—When at Leghorn last summer I ordered 6 P. of walking shoes & he has made them of such vile leather that I can only wear them a few times—I shall have no more from him—

Be so kind as to send the Sophocles by Pepi & Zenophon's Anabases if you can find it among our books. I hope this fine weather does you all good—I work hard at Greek & sh^d^ get on were it not for the intolerable grammar—We are promised soon several boxes from England—containing (one of them) Papa's answer to Malthus[2] which perhaps you are curious to see—

I have had a letter from him[3] which contains the agreable news that William has obtained without any advance of money a seat in the house of Nash[4] the kings Architect whom of course—Henry will well remember—

Adieu—

Yours Ever

Mary W. Shelley

I find that Prinoth has been paid—so Terrazi & the shoemaker are our only creditors.—w^d^ you ask the former if he has any, & the price of some very fine cambric pocket handkerchiefs taking a dozen of them—

ADDRESS: Alla Signora / La Signora Maria Gisborne / Casa Ricci / All' Origine / Fuore della Porta Pisa / Livorno. PUBLISHED: Jones, #112. TEXT: MS., Bodleian Library (MS., Shelley, c. 1, ff. 466–67).

1. See *PBS Letters*, #611.

2. *Of Population* (see 26 July 1818, n. 3).

3. Godwin's letter to Mary Shelley dated 30 January 1821 mentions that both he and Peacock are in the process of sending boxes to the Shelleys, Godwin's to include his *Of Population*, as well as a number of other books that Mary Shelley requested in her letter of 20 December 1820. Godwin's letter is of particular interest because it discusses matters about which Mary Shelley had written him in her letters of 20 December 1820 and 6 January 1821, both of which are unlocated to date. Godwin answers her specific inquiry about the career and character of William Godwin, Jr., who is about to become an apprentice architect (a career he did not pursue because of an injury). Godwin also writes, "You ask me about politics; but I am an ill hand at satisfying inquiries on that head." He goes on, however, to mention a number of political matters, including the situation of Caroline of Brunswick and the "Oppression of Debts and Taxes." Apparently Mary Shelley had also written to him of the misunderstanding between the Shelleys and the Gisbornes but had not given Godwin details, since he comments that he "would be glad to hear particulars" (*S&M*, III, 580A–580C).

4. John Nash (1752–1835), architect, best known for Regent's Park, Regent Street and the Brighton Pavilion. William Godwin, Jr., had begun his apprenticeship on 28 December 1820.

To Maria Gisborne [Pisa] 1 March 1821

My Dear M^rs^ G—

Forgive my delay about the money—the handkerchiefs must be bargained for. They are too dear.

We received yesterday a letter from Henry, most interesting and well written, who begs us to tell you that he and his red neckcloth have escaped safe and sound from the buffaloes,[1] and are well lodged at Elba—I hope you are all well—

Your's &c—

PUBLISHED: Jones, #113. TEXT: John Gisborne Notebook No. 2, Abinger MS., Bodleian Library.

1. On 20 February 1821 Henry Reveley had written Shelley a narrative of his journey from Leghorn to Elba, describing the habits of the wild buffaloes encountered en route and their particular attraction to his red cravat (Gisborne, *Journals and Letters*, pp. 67–70).

To Maria Gisborne Pisa. Casa Aulla.[1] [c. 21 March] 1821[2]

My Dear M^rs^ G—

I send you a few papers which you will be so kind as to return when done with—What think you of that unfortunate lady Charlotte Harley—Mr Aston was married, and the very morning after his death (he poisoned himself) the news of his wife's death arrived. He was neither an amiable or good man.[3]

I wish you would get me from Arbib's a scarf of China crape. I want it a light pretty colour—lilac, or blue, but not pink—I believe they ask the English six monete for them, but I should think you could get it for four, or for thirty livres—You would much oblige me by sending it as soon as you conveniently can. We are all well I have finished the two Œdipi with my Greek,[4] and am now half way through the Antigone. He is also my pupil in English, though not very regular—He is exceedingly clever as you will judge when I tell you that he has learned English {in} only four months—he can read any prose—poetry with very little help, and writes it very tolerably—and indeed he could do all this two months ago—How does your pupil and master go on?

We understand that two parcels have been shipped for us—One by Peacock directed to you—We do not know either the name of the ship or Captain, but have written to learn. The other by Papa—the Amy, Capt. Bloomfield—

Shall we have the pleasure of seeing you before we retreat to the mountains for our summer quarters? Is Henry returned safe and sound? Adieu.

Ever truly your's
Mary WS

PUBLISHED: Jones, #114. TEXT: John Gisborne Notebook No. 2, Abinger MS., Bodleian Library.

1. The Shelleys had moved to Casa Aulla on 5 March 1821.

2. Although John Gisborne's Notebook dates this letter "April or May 1821," Mary Shelley's postscript to Shelley's letter of 21 March mentions the completion of the *Œdipi* and the partial completion of *Antigone*, about which she also writes in this letter. Moreover, her *Journal* indicates that she completed *Antigone* on 26 March.

3. The scandal involving Charlotte Harley and H. Harvey Aston reached the English press. The *Times* (London) of 22 February reported that "the nephew of a Peer" had seduced two sisters, "who both proved pregnant"; as a result, he "terminated his existence with a pistol." Two days later, the *Times* printed a letter from J. Stirling, British Consul at Genoa, who stated that Aston had died of apoplexy and that the story of the pregnancies was entirely false. According to Stirling, Aston could be faulted only for attempting to elope with one of the young ladies against her family's wishes. Mary Shelley most likely read of the incident in *Galignani's Messenger*.

4. Prince Mavrocordato.

SHELLEY TO THOMAS LOVE PEACOCK[1] — Pisa, March, 21. 1821

[*Postscript by Mary Shelley*] also, if you will be so kind. 4 skeins of white netting silk. 2 green & 2 crimson—all of a size fit for purses. You will send them to Ollier with the seals[2] &c if his parcel is not yet dispatched—if it is have the goodness to send them as soon as you can by some other opportunity

Am I not lucky to have got so good a master. I have finished the 2 Œdipi —and very soon the Antigone—the name of the Prince is *Αλεξανδρος Μαυροcορδατος* he can read English perfectly well.

ADDRESS: T. L. Peacock Esqr / India House / London / Angleterre / via Francia. POSTMARKS: (1) PISA; (2) FPO / AP. 5 / 1821. PUBLISHED: Jones, #115. TEXT: MS., Bodleian Library (Dep. b. 214).

1. *PBS Letters*, #615.

2. Shelley asked Peacock to obtain two letter seals, both bearing the device of a dove with outspread wings and the motto: Μάντις ἔιμὶέσθλῶν ἀγώνων ("Prophet I am of noble combats" [Sophocles *Oedipus Coloneus*, line 1080]). Dowden suggests that these may have been given by the Shelleys as gifts to Mavrocordato (*Shelley*, II, 444). Mary Shelley and Mavrocordato had read *Oedipus Coloneus* together (see [c. 21 March] 1821 to Maria Gisborne); and Mavrocordato prefixed the same quoted line as a motto in a letter dated Pisa, 2 April 1821, that he wrote to friends in Paris (Huscher, "Alexander Mavrocordato," p. 30).

TO CLAIRE CLAIRMONT — [Pisa] April 2—1821

"ΥΨιΛὰντι
† "ΥΨιΛὰντι[1]

My dear Claire,

Greece has declared its freedom![2] Prince Mavrocordato had made us expect this event for some weeks pas{t}. Yesterday he came rayonnant de joie

—he had been ill for some days but he forgot all his pains—Ips̊elanti, a greek General in the service of Russia, has collected together 10,000 Greeks & entered Wallachia declaring the liberty of his country—The Morea—Epirus—Servia are in revolt. Greece will most certainly be free. The worst part of this news for us is that our amiable prince will leave us—he will of course join his countrymen as soon as possible—never did Man appear so happy—yet he sacrifices family—fortune every thing to the hope of freeing his country—Such men are repaid—such succeed. You may conceive the deep sympathy that we feel in his joy on this occasion: tinged as it must be with anxiety for success—made serious by the knowledge of the blood that must be shed on this occasion. What a delight it will be to visit Greece free.

April has opened with a weather truly heavenly after a whole week of libeccio—rain & wind it is delightful to enjoy one of those days peculiar to Italy in this early season—the clear sky animating sun & fresh yet not cold breeze—Just that delicious season when pleasant thoughts bring sad ones to the mind—when every sensation seems to make a double effect—and every moment of the day is divided, felt, and counted. One is not gay—at least I am not—but peaceful & at peace with all the world—

I write you a short letter today but I could not resist the temptation of acquainting you with the changes in Greece the Moment P[ce] Mavrocordato gave us leave to mention it.

I hope that your spirits will get better with this favourable change of weather—Florence must be perfectly delightful send the white paint as soon as you can & two strisce's[3] for me—

Shelley says that he will finish this letter[4]—We hear from no one in England

Ever yours
MWS

ADDRESS: Miss Clairmont / presso al Profe Bojti / dirimpetto Palazzo Pitti / Firenze. PUBLISHED: Jones, #116. TEXT: MS., Pforzheimer Library.

1. "Ipselanti, Ipselanti." Note the cross here and over *Ipselanti* in line four in the text of the letter.

2. On 6 March 1821 Greek rebels led by Prince Alexandros Ypsilanti rose against the Turks in Wallachia (now Rumania) but were defeated. On or about 25 March new uprisings broke out in the Morea, in Roumeli, and on several islands, beginning a period of war between Greek and Turkish forces (with England, France, and Russia aiding Greece at various times) that culminated in Greek independence in 1832. On 3 April Mavrocordato wrote to Mary Shelley telling her that he was writing a small article supporting Greek liberty, which Shelley had promised to have inserted in an English newspaper (Abinger MS.).

3. "Strips."

4. See *PBS Letters*, #617.

To Maria Gisborne [Pisa] Thursday 5 April [1821]

My dear Mrs Gisborne

I ought to have answered your letter before but I waited until I could send you a few papers. I have now other news to communicate to you which must needs interest you greatly—This is no less than that Greece has declared its Liberty—has declared the war of the cross against the Crescent. Alexander Ipsilanti—a Greek General in the Russian service and an Aidde-camps of the Emperor Alexander has advanced as far as Buchareste with 10,000, Greeks, collected from the Russian service, has issued an eloquent & Beautiful Cry of War to his countrymen & is hastening to Join the Sulliotes, Servians, Epirotes & the people of the Morea who have all revolted—My Master, the Prince Mavrocordato, is hastening to join the army[1] —while the Greeks of rank here, Prince Caraja, the former Ospadaro of Wallachia & his daughter the Princess Argiropoli & her husband[2] are about to sell their worldly goods here & to return to their country—It is believed that The Russians will help the Greeks being bribed thereto by the gift of the provinces of Moldavia & Wallachia. Did you ever hope that Greece would ever free itself in your day?—They do not intend to attempt Constantinople unless the Turks should think of a massacre & then they hope to be prepared for them.

I am sorry you did not so arrange you affairs as to be able to pay us a visit here—It is now a very long time since I have had the pleasure of seeing you nor can I guess how much more time you will allow to elapse before you visit us.

Shelley would answer Henry's letter if he knew whether he were returned—And will you request him to have the kindness to look to the two saddles of ours that are at your house & to get them cleaned for us & put in order—as Shelley thinks of going over to Leghorn in a few days & he wants to bring them back with him.

Have you any news {from} abroad in your part of the world—There has been a report current that our king was dead which arose from a Miss Campbell sending a note to a Miss Wilson with this intelligence on the first of April & she had the pleasure of making some dozens of April fools.

Adieu kind remembrances to Mr G. [*Gisborne*] & Henry I hope the latter will get better as the season advances—do you return to England this Spring—

What news of our boxes we wait anxiously for intelligence concerning them—

Ever yours MWS.

[*P. 1, top*] Hunt has been very ill of a kind of nervous fever—we had a letter from him yesterday—he is better though still far from well. Keats they say is dying at Rome[3]—

ADDRESS: Mrs. Gisborne. PUBLISHED: Jones, #117. TEXT: MS., Bodleian Library (MS., Shelley, c. 1, ff. 463, 465).

1. See 2 April 1821.

2. Princess Ralou Argiropoulo, Mavrocordato's cousin, the daughter of Prince John Cardja, former Hospodar of Wallachia. Mavrocordato had aided in the administration of Wallachia but had fled with the Hospodar and his family when the Hospodar's life was threatened in 1818; eventually they had traveled to Pisa. The Princess and her husband, George Argiropoulo, were active Greek patriots. They, too, were introduced to the Shelleys by Pacchiani and became frequent callers (Huscher, "Alexander Mavrocordato," pp. 30, 32).

3. See 17 April 1821.

*TO LEIGH HUNT

Pisa—April 17—1821

My dear Hunt; I do not know whether you [ ]itte think the above story[1] fit for your Indicator. It appears to me that the whole story terminating with {the} last visit of Marietta to Lodovico would be a moving tale under your pen. I have another Itali[a]n story for you of the present day; which I will relate to you as I heard it if you like.

It is a curious circumstance that the seige of Florence was being carried on with the greatest vigour at that time; a seige which ended by the family of the Medici being forced by the Imperial arms & treason on the Florentines[2]—It is strange therefore that Lodovico should have his portrait in the Gallery of the Grand dukes since he was their enemy. The Prince of Orange was the Leader of the Imperial army against Florence.

I send you the latest news from Greece—you see what a pretty part We English are acting[3]—but we are so moral & religious that there can be no wonder that we help Turks & Tyrants against Xtians & the Would-be-free.

We have been much shocked to hear of Keats' death—and sorry that it was in no way permitted us to be of any use to him since his arrival in Italy.[4] I hope your health my dearest friend is now tolerably re-established; ask Marianne why she does not write. I wait for a letter from her with great anxiety.

All is at peace now in Piedmont;[5] such a peace as Moore says—Like the Lords passeth all Human Understanding. Russia & Austria have both joined in a declaration that they disapprove of the Revolt of the Greeks—Austria would if she dared declare openly for the Turks—as it is she refuses passports to allow the Greeks dispersed in Europe to pass through her territories to Wallachia—They must therefore wait until the army of Ipsilanti coming south the whole of Greece [ ] so that Prince Mavrocordato is not yet gone, & the poor Ex-Ospodaro here who thought to return not to his principality but to his estates in Wallachia is obliged to wait. They stop all letters also—Thus at once avowing their wicked hypocrisy with regard to religion, and as their own policy suits them declaring for the crescent against the Cross—Why I am a better Xtian than they.

However Naples has shamefully fallen & Piedmont is but a step behind her—however the seed may be now sown the fruit of which we may reap some years hence—

How are the Lambs & other common friends remember me to them—particularly to Miss L. [*Lamb*] Adieu, my dear Hunt; let us hear of your returning health

Ever affectionately Yours. Marina

[*Enclosure*]

Duello Formale di due de' Fiorentini

Lodovico di Giovanfrancesco Martelli, giovane di grandissimo cuore, avendo secreta nemista con Giovanni Bandini per le cagioni, chè di sotto si vedranno,* preso una bellissima e favorevole occasione di voler combattere o morir bisognando per l'amor della Patria, e che glielo voleva provare coll'arme in isteccato à corpo à corpo, concendendogli l'elezione così del campo, come dell'arme, o volesse a piè, o volesse a cavallo: alcuni altri dicono Ludovico aver mentito per la gola Giovanni, per aver egli detto, che la Milizia Fiorentina era pro forma.† Giovanni, al quale non mancava l'animo, e abbondava l'ingegno, cercando di sfuggire il combattere sì brutta querela, gli rispose con maggior prudenza che verità, se non esser nel campo de' nemici per venir contro la Patria, la quale egli amava così bene quant'-alcun altro; ma per vedere e visitare certi suoi amici; la qualcosa, o vera, o falsa che si fosse poteva, anzi doveva bastare a Ludovico; ma egli che voleva cimentarsi con Giovanni in ogni modo, rispose in guisa, che bisognò che Giovanni per non mancare all'onor del Gentiluomo, del che egli faceva particolar professione, accettasse; e convennero che ciascuno di loro s'eleggesse un compagno a sua scelta. Giovanni, avendo Pandolfo Martelli e alcuni altri Fiorentini, i quali erano nel campo ricusato, secondo il volgo con poco onor loro, ma secondo gl'intendenti con molta prudenza di voler venire a cotal cimento, s'elesse Bettino di Carlo Aldobrandini. Era Bettino giovanetto di prima barba, allievo di Francesco, altrimenti Cecchino‡ del Piffero, fratello di Benvenuto Cellini, orafo in quel tempo di grandissimo nome, e di maggior speranza; il qual Cecchino avezzo tra le Bande nere§, e non conoscendo paura nessuna, era stato morto in Pisa dalla famiglia del Bargello, mentrechè egli solo voleva con molto ardire mà poca prudenza combattere con tutti. Lodovico prese per suo compagno Dante di Guido da Castiglione, il qual solo si messe a cotal rischio, veramente per l'amor della Patria, come quegli che era Libertino, e di gran coraggio.—Partironsi dunque Lodovico e Dante di Firenze agli undici di Marzo dalla Piazza di S. Michele Bertoldi, in questa maniera. Eglino avevano innanzi 2 Paggi, ovvero ragazzi vestiti di rosso e bianco sopra due cavalli bardati di corame bianco. e poi 2 altri, o ragazzi o paggi sopra 2 corsieri grossi da lancia, vestiti nel medesimo modo; dietro a questi eran 2 trombetti, uno del Principe (d'Oranges) ed uno di Malatesta (Malatesta Baglioni, Generale delle armi Fiorentini) i quali andavano sonando continuamente. Dopo questi venivano il Capitan Giovanni da Vinci, Giovane di fatezze straordinarie, Patrino di Dante, e Paolo Spinelli Cittadino e soldato vecchio di grandissima sperienza, Patrino di Lodovico, e Messer Vi[tello Vi]telli Patrino d'amendue se per sorte gli avversarii avessero eletto di voler combattere a cavallo. Dopo questi seguivano i due combattenti sopra due Cavalli Turchi di maravigliosa bellezza e salute.

Avevano in dosso ciascuno una casacca di raso rosso colla manica medesimamente squartata di teletta; avevano le calze di raso rosso filettate di teletta bianca, e soppannate di teletta d'argento, e in capo un berrettino di raso rosso con un cappelletto di seta rosso, con uno spennacchio bianco. A piedi di ciascuno camminavano per istaffieri sei servitori vestiti in quel medesimo modo di quegli che eran a cavallo. Dietro di loro eran parecchi Capitani, e valorosi soldati con molti della Milizia Fiorentina, i quali avendo desinato con essi la mattina tennero loro compagnia infino alla Porta dove si fece diligente guardia che alcuno non uscisse di Fiorentini, eccetto il Sordo delle Calvane, che aveva il braccio al collo per un'archibussata, che in scaramucciando vi aveva tocco. e Jacopo, chiamato Jacopino Pucci. Fecero la via di Piazza, per Borgo Santo, Apostolo, per Parione, e passato il ponte alla Carraia andarono alla Porta di S. Friano, dove erano i carriaggi, che furono muli ventuno, carichi di tutti e di ciascheduna di quelle cose, che loro bisognavano, così al vivere come all'armare, tanto di piè quanto a cavallo: perchè per non avere a sevirsi d'alcuna cosa de' nemici, portavano con esso seco pane, vino, biade, paglia, legne, carne d'ogni sorte, uccelami d'ogni ragione, pesci d'ogni qualità, confezioni di tutte maniere padiglioni con tutti i fornimenti, e con tutte le masserizie di qualsivoglia sorte, che potessero venir loro a bisogno, infino all'acqua: menarono Prete, Medico, Barbiere, Maestro di Casa, Cuoco, e Guattero. Uscirono fuori della Porta con tutta questa salmeria dietro, a andarano lungo la mura infino presso alla porta a S. Pier Gattolini, dove attraversarono nella man ritta, e calati alla fonte del Borgo della medesima Porta, presero la via per traverso della Casa del Cappone, dove era il fine delle trincee de nemici, e quindi si condussero a Baroncelli, correndo tutto il campo a vedergli; che s'era convenuto, che infino non fussero davanti al Principe d'Oranges, non si dovesse trarre artiglierie nè grosse, nè minute da nessuna delle parti, e così fu osservato.

Agli dodici, il giorno di San Gregorio, che venne in Sabato, combatterono in due steccati l'uno avanti all'altro tramezzati solamente da una cordo,|| serrati intorno per guardia del campo il quale aveva circondato Orange di Tedeschi, Spagnoli, e Italiani, tanti degli uni quanti degli altri. Combatterono in camicia, cioè calze e non giubbone, e la manica della camicia della mano destra tagliata fino al gomito, [con] una spada, e un guanto di maglia corta nella mano della spada, senza niente in testa. Fu quest'arme elette da Giovanni per rimuovere un opinione, che s'aveva in Firenze di lui, ch'egli fosse più cauto che valente, e procedesse più con astuzia che valore. Dante fattasi radere la barba, la quale di color rosso gli dava quasi al bellico, venne alle mani col Bettino, e toccò in sulla prima giunta una ferita, nel braccio ritto, e una stoccata ma leggiera in bocca, ed era assalita dal nemico con tanta furia, che senza poter riperarsi ebbe tre ferite in sul braccio sinistro, una buona, e due leccature; ed era a tal condotto, che se Bettino si fosse ito trattenendo, come doveva, bisognava che s'arendesse perchè non poteva piu reggere la spada con una mano sola, la prese però con tutte e due, ed osservandosi con gran riguardo quello che faceva il nemico, e vedutolo colla medesima furia e inconsiderazione sua venir alla volta di lui, come quelli che [quale] era giovane e troppo volonteroso, gli si fece incontro, e distendendo ambo le braccia gli ficcò la spada in bocca tra la lingua e la gola, talmentechè subito gli enfiò l'occhio destro; ed egli, ancorchè aveva promesso baldanzosamente prima di morire mille volte che mai arrendersi una, o vinto dalla forza del dol ore, avendogli Dante date alcune altre ferite nel petto, o per essere uscito di se, con grandissimo dispiacere del Principe, e del Conte di San Secondo, il quale nello steccato stette con un'alabarda in mano, e lo favorì contra al tenore del Bando colle parole, s'arrendè, e la notte seguente si morì a sei ore. Dante allora per animare il compagno gridò forte due volte Vittorice, non lo potendo per la legge tra loro posta altramente aiutare.

Lodovico, dato che fu nella tromba, andò ad affrontare Giovanni con incredibile ardore: ma Giovanni, il quale ben teneva l'arme in mano, e non si lasciava vincere dall'ira altra passione, gli diede una ferita sopra le ciglia, il sangue della quale cominciò a imperdirgli la vista; onde egli piu che animosamente andò tre volte per pigliare la spada colla mano stanca, e pigliolla; ma Giovanni avvolgendola, e tirandola fortemente a se, gliela cavò sempre di mano, e lo feri in tre luoghi della stessa mano sinistra; onde egli quanto più brigava di nettarsi gli occhi dal sangue colla mancina per veder lume, tanto più gl'instrattava, e nondimeno colla destra tirò una terribile toccata a Giovanni la quale lo passò di là di più d'una spanna, e non gli fece altro male, che una sgraffiatura sotto la poppa manca; allora Giovanni gli menò un mandritto alla testa, ed egli non potendo schivare altramente parò la man sinistra così ferita per veder di pigliarli un'altra volta la spada; il che non gli riuscendo, anzi restando gravamente ferito, pose ambele mani agli elsi, e appogiato il pomo al petto corse verso Giovanni per investirlo; ma egli il quale non era men destro, che balioso, salto indietro, e menògli nel medesimo instante una coltellata alla testa, dicendo: "se non vuoi morire arrenditi a me!—Ludovico non veggendo più lume, e avendo adosso parecchie ferite, disse, "Io m'arrend al Marchese del Guasto;"—Ma avendo Giovanni fatta la medesima proposta, arrendè a lui.—Dante e Lodovico essendosi fatto cambio e barattati i prigioni, se ne tornarono la sera stessa per la medesima porta, e in sull'un'ora in Firenze con tutti loro

La legge della storio me [sforza] a dire quello, che io volentieri [taciuto] avrei, e ciò è che il rancore tra Lodovico e Giovanni era nato per cagione d'una donna, la quale essendosi mostrata più favorevole a Giovanni che a Lodovico, lo mosse a far quello che fece, per dimostrarle, che ne anco nelle arme non era meno del suo rivale, come ella per aventura il teneva. Gli amici di Lodovico, credendosi di dargli contento, operarono sì co' parenti della donna amata (Una Marietta Ricci, moglie di Niccolò Benintendi) che ella con licenza del marito l'andò a visitare, della qual cosa egli prese si fatta tristezza, che egli più di quel dispiacere, che delle ferite si morì, dopo ventiquattro giorni, che egli combattuto aveva.

* Qualunque altro motivo segreto avesse il Martelli di sfidare in duello il suo nemico, egli è però certo ch'ei lo colorì bastantemente col desio di far le vendette della Patria contro un cittadino, qual'era Giovanni Bandini, fattosi ribelle, e mescolatosi tra le armi Imperiali, allorchè queste vennero ad assediar Firenze nel 1530. Con questo titolo potè Ludovico essere noverato trai Cittadini Illustri per l'amor della Patria, ed aver il suo ritratto nelle Volte della Real Galeria.

† Ad questo duello adunque, che veramente era mosso da privata inimicizia, si diede tutto il colore di uno di quegli esperimenti, chiama ne' tempi barbaraci Giudizi di Dio.

‡ Cecchino il nickname di Francesco

§—Uno bando dei Condottieri così chiamato nero dopo la morte del loro duca Ludovico di Medici chi aveva il sopranome dell'Invitto. Fù egli scendente del fratello di Cosimo Padre della Patria avo di Lorenzo il Magnifico—e fù padre del stirpe ducale dei Medici

|| cioè a dire il campo fu diviso in due parti nel uno de quali doveva combattere Giovanni e Ludovico—nell'altro Dante e Bettino

[*Translation*]

Formal Duel of Two of the Florentines

Lodovico di Giovanfrancesco Martelli, a youth with a very big heart, having a secret enmity with Giovanni Bandini for reasons which will be seen below,* seized a most beautiful and favorable occasion to decide to battle him for the love of his country or to die wanting to, and he wished to test him with weapons while fighting in an encampment, hand to hand, leaving to him the choice of the field, the choice of the weapons, and whether to be on foot or on horseback. Some people say that Lodovico told Giovanni gross lies when he said that the assembling of the Florentine army was a formality.† Giovanni, who was not lacking in spirit and had plenty of talent, trying to avoid fighting such an ugly battle, replied to him with more caution than truth that he was not in the enemy's camp in order to fight against his homeland, which he loved as well as any other man, but in order to see and visit certain of his friends. Whether this was true or false, it should have been enough for Lodovico. But he was determined to compete with Giovanni in any case and replied in such a way that it became necessary for Giovanni to accept in order not to appear lacking in his honor as a gentleman, of which he made a special profession; and they agreed that each of them should appoint a companion of his choice. Giovanni, who had Pandolfo Martelli and several other Florentines who had been rejected from the camp—with dishonor, according to the populace, but according to those knowledgeable of the situation, with great care in wanting to come to such a hazardous trial—chose Bettino di Carlo Aldobrandini. Bettino was a youth, a student of Franceso, otherwise known as Cecchino‡ del Piffero, a brother of Benvenuto Cellini, at that time a goldsmith of great fame and even greater expectations. This same Cecchino was trained among the black Bands,§ and not knowing any fear, he had been killed by the Bargello family at Pisa, where only he—with great courage but little caution—had been willing to do battle with all. Lodovico chose for his companion Dante di Guido da Castiglione, who only placed himself at such a risk for true love of his country, like the former was a Libertine and of great courage. Well then, Lodovico and Dante departed from Florence on the eleventh of March from the Piazza of San Michele Bertoldi, in the following manner. They had ahead of them two pages, or rather boys, dressed in red and white, upon two horses harnessed with white stamped leather. And then came two others, youths or pages, astride two large steeds, in the manner of lancers, dressed in the same way. Behind them were two trumpeters—one of the Prince (of Oranges) and the other of Malatesta (Malatesta Baglioni, general of the Florentine troops)—who played continuously as they went. Behind them came Captain Giovanni da Vinci, a youth of extraordinary features, the second of Dante, and Paolo Spinelli, citizen and old soldier of the greatest experience, the second of Lodovico, and Master Vi[tello Vi]telli, a second of them both if by chance the adversaries should choose to do battle on horseback. After them followed the two combatants upon two Turkish horses of marvelous beauty and health. Each one wore a jacket of red satin with the sleeves quartered in the same way with buckram; they had stockings of red satin adorned with white buckram and lined with silver buckram; and on their heads they wore a little hat of red satin with a cap of red silk and a white plume. At the foot of each, six servants walked as footmen, dressed in the same way as those on horseback. Behind them were numerous captains and gallant soldiers, as well as many from the Florentine troops who had breakfasted with them that morning and kept them company as far as the gate, where a careful watch was kept in order that none of the Florentines might leave, excepting the deaf man of the Calvane, who had his arm in a sling because of an arquebus wound that had hit him while skirmishing, and Jacopo, called Jacopino Pucci. They took the road of the Piazza to Borgo Santo, Apostolo, to Parione, and passing the bridge of the Carraia, they went to the Gate of San Friano, where the wagons were, and twenty-one mules, loaded with each and every one of those things that they might need for living, as well as for arming themselves; for going on foot, as well as on horseback. In order not to have to make use of anything belonging to the enemy, they brought with them bread, wine, crops, straw, firewood, meat of every sort, fowl of every description, fish of every kind, clothing of every fashion, tents with all the furnishings and with all the kitchen utensils of whatever type they might have needed, down to water. They brought a priest, a doctor, a barber, a house steward, a cook, and a scullery boy. They departed through the gate with this baggage train behind, and they proceeded along the wall until they approached the gate at San Pier Gattolino, where they passed through on the right-hand side and descended at the beginning of the street of this same gate and took the road across to the House of the Cappone, where the last of the enemy entrenchments were; and from here they were directed to the Baroncelli, running the whole field to see him. It had ben agreed that until they were before the Prince of Oranges, they would not draw their weapons from any part, large nor small—and this agreement was observed.

At twelve o'clock on the day of San Gregorio, which fell on a Saturday, they battled in two stockades, one in front of the other, separated only by a rope,|| and enclosed on every side by the guard of the camp, which surrounded Orange with Germans, Spaniards, and Italians, as many of one as of the others. They fought in shirt-sleeves, that is to say, in trousers but without a coat, and the right shirt-sleeve was cut up to the elbow, this hand holding the sword and wearing a short knit glove, wearing nothing on their heads. These arms were chosen by Giovanni to counteract an opinion they had of him in Florence, that he was more cautious than able and acted more with cunning than bravery. Dante, having had his beard shaven, whose red color made him look almost warlike, came to blows with Bettino, immediately struck a wound in his right arm and a light stab in the mouth, and was then attacked by the enemy with so much fury that without being able to shelter himself, he had three wounds in his left arm—one serious and two just grazing. If Bettino had gone and restrained him at this point, as he should have, it would have been necessary for Dante to surrender, since he could no longer hold the sword with just one hand. He took it, however, with both hands, and watching very carefully what his enemy was doing, and seeing him come at his face with the same fury and rashness as one who was young and too eager, he went and met him; and extending both his arms, he thrust the sword into his mouth between the tongue and the throat, to such an exent that the right eye immediately became swollen. And although he had boldly promised to die a thousand times before he would ever surrender once—whether overcome by the fierceness of the pain (Dante having also wounded him in the chest) or whether beside himself with the great displeasure of the Prince and of the Count of San Secondo, who was in the stockade with a halberd in his hand and encouraged him with words against the manner of the crowd—he surrendered, and the following night at six o'clock he died. Then Dante, in order to encourage his comrade, loudly shouted two times that he was victorious, since the rules set down by the opponents did not allow him to help otherwise.

Lodovico, considering that he was failing, went to confront Giovanni with incredible ardour; but Giovanni kept his weapon firmly in his hand and did not allow his rage to overcome his other interests and wounded

Lodovico above his eye, the blood from which began to impede his vision. And so, Lodovico very courageously went three times to take up his sword with his tired hand, and he did seize it; but Giovanni, entangling it and strongly drawing it towards him, pulled it out of his hand and wounded him in three places on this same left hand—whereby, however much he attempted to cleanse his eye of the blood with his left hand in order to see the light, the more he beclouded it. Nonetheless, with the right hand, he cast a terrible blow to Giovanni that passed across his body for a span but did him no other harm than to give him a scratch beneath the left breast. Then Giovanni landed a right hand to the head, and Lodovico not being able to avoid it otherwise, stretched out his wounded right hand to try to take up his sword another time. Not succeeding at this—and in fact being seriously wounded—he placed both hands on the helm, and leaning the pommel against his breast, he ran towards Giovanni to attack him. But Giovanni, not being less skillful than bold, jumped backwards and in the same instant dealt him a blow to the head, saying: "If you do not wish to die, surrender to me!"—Lodovico, no longer able to see, and being wounded all over, said, "I surrender myself to the Marchese del Guasto"; but since Giovanni made the same proposal, he surrendered to him. Dante and Lodovico, having been exchanged for the prisoners, returned that same evening through the same gate, and in about an hour they were in Florence with all of their supporters.

The legend of the story [bids] me to tell that which I do willingly—and that is, that the rancour between Lodovico and Giovanni arose because of a woman, who, having shown herself to be more favorable to Giovanni than to Lodovico, caused him [Lodovico] to do that which he did in order to show her that even with weapons he was not less able than his rival, as she perhaps considered him to be. Lodovico's friends, believing it would make him happy, operated in such a way with the family of the beloved woman (a Marietta Ricci, wife of Niccolò Benintendi) that she, with the permission of her husband, went to visit him, from which visit he became so unhappy that more from this displeasure than from his wounds, he died twenty-four days after doing battle.

* Whatever other secret motive Martelli may have had for challenging his enemy to a duel, it is certain that he was largely influenced by the desire to take revenge on behalf of his country against a citizen such as Giovanni Bandini, who had turned rebel and mingled with the imperial armies when they came to besiege Florence in 1530. With this to his credit, Lodovico could have been numbered amongst the citizens renowned for the love of their country and had his portrait in the vaults of the Real Gallery.

† This duel, therefore, which was really motivated by personal enmity, took on all the color of the trials, which in barbaric times were called ordeals.

‡ Cecchino is the nickname for Francesco.

§ A band of Condottieri, called black after the death of their duke Lodovico di Medici, who had the nickname of "The Invincible." He was a descendent of the brother of Cosimo—Father of the Nation, grandfather of Lorenzo the Magnificent—and he was the father of the ducal branch of the Medici family.

|| that is to say, the field was divided into two parts—in one, Giovanni and Lodovico were to fight; in the other, Dante and Bettino

ADDRESS: Leigh Hunt Esq / Vale of Health / Via Francia / Hampstead / near London / Inghilterra / Londres. POSTMARKS: (1) FPO / MY. 7 / 1821; (2) 4 o'Clock / MY. 7 / 1821 EV. UNPUBLISHED. TEXT: Harkness Collection, New York Public Library. TRANSLATION: Ricki B. Herzfeld.

1. Mary Shelley copied the "Duello Formale di due de' Fiorentini" from Marco Lastri, *L'Osservatore Fiorentino* (3d ed., 8 vols. [Florence, 1821], I, 183–92), which she was reading in April (*MWS Journal*, pp. 151–52). Here the text of the story follows, although in the original manuscript the story was transcribed before the letter. Words torn from the manuscript have been supplied in square brackets from the printed text. Mary Shelley's transcription is accurate, with the exception of some minor errors. *L'Osservatore Fiorentino* is also the source of Shelley's *Ginevra*. Hunt responded on 11 July 1821: "How I regretted I could not use the story which Marina sent me; but it was a cordial sent to a dead man—the *Indicator* had long expired" (Hunt, *Correspondence*, I, 165–66).

2. Emperor Charles V sent an imperial army of Germans and Spaniards to suppress the Florentine republic; this resulted in a siege of Florence from October 1529 to August 1530, which restored Medici rule.

3. At the outset of the Greek war of independence, England, France, and Austria proclaimed a policy of neutrality. Subsequently both England and France aided the Greek cause.

4. The news of Keats's death (on 23 February) was contained in Horace Smith's letter to Shelley of 28 March, received on 11 April (*Shelley Memorials*, p. 167). On 27 July 1820 Shelley, having heard of Keats's poor health, had written to invite Keats to join them at Pisa. Keats had accepted the invitation, health permitting. In February 1821 Shelley had repeated his invitation (*PBS Letters*, #579, #610; *SC*, V, 412–15).

5. On 10 March, in Turin, Piedmontese constitutionalists had staged a successful rebellion to overthrow Victor Emmanuel I, but on 8 April they were defeated by the Austrians near Novara (approximately forty miles from Turin).

TO MARIA GISBORNE — Casa Aulla [Pisa] 19 April [1821]

My dear Mrs Gisborne

Shelley has brought home the Good news that you intend to visit us early next week.[1] I am very glad to hear this; since it is now I fancy about six months since I last saw you. We have plenty of room for you; so I hope that you do not intend to pay us one of your little skinny visits—but one of regular length breadth & thickness. Will you not?

Let me remind Henry of my saddle. I believe that Williams told him about the new saddle tree & all else that it required.

Henry will have told you perhaps that poor Keats is dead—at Rome.[2] I fancy that we shall pass this summer at the Baths of Pisa.

Expecting soon to see you I write no more at present—I hope that your eyes are well—& that Mr Gisborne does not any longer suffer from his rhumatism

Ever most sinc{ere}ly yours
MaryWS.

ADDRESS: Alla Ornatissima Signora / La Signora Maria Gisborne / Livorno. POSTMARKS: (1) PISA; (2) 20 Aprile. ENDORSED: Recd. 22nd April 1821. PUBLISHED: Jones, #120. TEXT: MS., Bodleian Library (MS., Shelley, c. 1, ff. 422–23); p. 1 from Shelley to Henry Reveley, *PBS Letters*, #623.

1. The Gisbornes visited the Shelleys from 26 to 30 April (*MWS Journal*).

2. See 17 April 1821, n. 4.

TO MARIA GISBORNE — Pisa. Casa Aulla. [c. 20] April 1821[1]

My Dear Mrs G—

You see the fine weather is come, doubly fine if it bring friendship with it. So we may expect you.

I have only time to say this word, and to enquire concerning the convalescence of the boat. When it is quite well let me know, since S. wishes to convoy the delicate young lady[2] here himself

Ever your's

PUBLISHED: Jones, #118. TEXT: John Gisborne Notebook No. 2, Abinger MS., Bodleian Library.

1. On 16 April Henry Reveley purchased a ten-foot, flat-bottomed boat for Shelley at Leghorn. Shelley, Williams, and Reveley then proceeded to sail it along the canal from Leghorn to Pisa, but Williams stood up, causing the boat to capsize. Shelley and Williams returned to Pisa, while Reveley took the boat back to Leghorn for repairs. From 26 to 30 April the Gisbornes visited the Shelleys at Pisa, and on 30 April Reveley brought the boat to Pisa (Dowden, *Shelley*, II, 398–400; Gisborne, *Journals and Letters*, pp. 70–71; *PBS Letters*, #622, #623). John Gisborne dates this letter April or May 1821. We may date this letter c. 20 April in light of the events concerning the boat, Mary Shelley's letter of 19 April regarding the Gisbornes' visit, and Mary Shelley's *Journal* entries noting fine weather beginning on 20 April.

2. The "convalescent" boat.

TO MARIA GISBORNE — Pisa [c. 30] April [1821][1]

My Dear Mrs G—

Your Captain is too dear. Miss Field[2] had heard of him before: but he asks two hundred Crowns, and the passenger to provide bed. I must absolutely have pocket handkerchiefs, so be so kind as to get them (a dozen) as I mentioned, without delay.

I hope Mr G— [*Gisborne*] did not suffer from his visit here, and that this fine weather does him good.

There has been some cutting off of heads at Constantinople among some friends and relations of the Ospodar[3] and of Prince Mauro Cordato—There is a report of a tumult there, successful for the Greeks, but it wants confirmation—

You will see Ulysses and his friend soon, but be neither Calypso nor Circe, but send him back au plus vite—

Adieu—

Ever your's M. WS

The Catholic question has been lost in the house of Lords by a majority of 39[4]—

PUBLISHED: Jones, "New Letters," p. 59. TEXT: John Gisborne Notebook No. 2, Abinger MS., Bodleian Library.

1. Although John Gisborne's Notebook dates this letter "about the end of April 1820," Jones assigns a date of 14–23 April 1820, arguing that the Gisbornes' intended visit to the Shelleys, mentioned in the letter, took place between those dates. A closer look at the contents of the letter, however, indicates that it was written in 1821, not in 1820. The Shelleys first met Mavrocordato in December 1820, and the events at Constantinople (reprisals by the Turks, including the hanging of the patriarch, Gregorios) occurred in April 1821. As the visit of the Gisbornes took place between 26 and 30 April, this letter could have been written the evening of 30 April 1821 at the earliest.

2. Matilda Field, an English schoolmistress who lived with the Masons from May 1820 through May 1821 (*CC Journals*, pp. 149, 233). This information must refer to the Gisbornes' preparations for returning to England permanently.

3. Prince John (Ionnes) Caradja, Mavrocordato's uncle and former Hospodar of Wallachia (see 5 April [1821], n. 2).

4. From 28 February through 16 April 1821 Parliament debated a bill intended to give Roman Catholics "certain offices, franchises, and civil rights." The bill was defeated in the House of Lords, 159 to 120 (*Annual Register*, 1821, pp. 29–43).

To Amelia Curran

Pisa[1] 14 May—1821

My dear Miss Curran

I am very glad to believe, since your letter contains nothing to the contrary, that you have recovered from Your illness of last year—You do not talk of going to England Nor do you mention painting—I wish you would let me hear somthing of both these things—

Here we are for the present; and it would be a great addition to this town if it could boast you among its inhabitants—and we you among our visitors—Do you seriously think of coming?—Our affairs, like all human affairs, and ours most particularly, are very uncertain.—A friend has tried to persuade us to make a trip to Como during the summer months—the distance & Northern direction of this town has made us hesitate—However we count entirely on a visit to Rome during the ensueing winter—If therefor our unsettled state does not permit us, as we so much desire, to say, come to us, this summer at least we shall have the pleasure of enjoying much of your society during the winter months at your Divine City.[2]

Shelley is somewhat but not much better than when you saw him—he goes on much in the same way—I and Claire are well and my little Percy flourishing.

I am delighted when I think that I shall visit Rome next winter—if we do come, and you are still there, I dare say that you would have the kindness to secure lodgings for us before hand—as the saving of such an expence to us would more surely ensure our journey.

Pray let me hear from you soon again And believe me ever Most since{re}ly yours—

Mary W Shelley

Shelley desires his very kindest remembrances.

PUBLISHED: Jones, #122. TEXT: MS., Bodleian Library (MS., Shelley, c. 1, f. 468).

1. This letter was probably written from the Bagni di San Giuliano (also called Bagni di Pisa, about five miles from Pisa), where the Shelleys had moved on 8 May. Shelley wrote to Claire Clairmont on 8 June: "Miss Curran wrote the other day inviting herself to spend the summer with us; but Mary sent an excuse" (*PBS Letters*, #630). Mary Shelley's excuse was quite likely motivated by her fear that Amelia Curran had not fully recovered from malaria and might expose Percy to the disease.

2. Shelley wrote to Claire Clairmont on [16 June]: "I think of spending next winter at Florence, Mary talks of Rome" (*PBS Letters*, #634).

TO MARIA GISBORNE — Baths of San Giuliano 28 May 1821

My Dear Mrs Gisborne—

We have heard that the Amy is arrived, and as its contains a most interesting Box for us, let me intreat you to send it, (the parcel, not the Amy) directed to Casa Silva, as quickly as you can—Mrs Mason says that she cannot afford more than 120 Sequins for the Piano. She has your Catalogues, and I fancy will buy some of your music. We have a wish for your maps,[1] if you will be so kind as to tell us what they are. If also you wish to <u>debarasser</u> yourself of some of your linen, I would like to have 2 Table clothes, a dozen table napkins, and ½ dozen towels, as I must buy them new else—these things are so cheap in England that it might lighten your luggage, and do you no harm.[2]

When shall we see you again?[3] I pity your trouble and fatigue most extremely, and how sincerely do I pray that England may repay your toils—

The Greeks are getting on finely, except that the Patriarch and four Bishops, and some Princes have been decapitated in Constantinople, but in Greece they conquer and cut to pieces the forces sent against them, and their fleet of 120 Sail is expected to hinder the debarkation of Turkish troops, since the Turkish fleet, almost entirely manned by Greeks, is now nearly useless through desertion[4]—

I have not heard from Papa this age. Pray enquire if there are letters for us at the Leghorn Post Office—

Shelley desires his best remembrances. Percy is quite well. S—, after the interval of a few days, is again horridly tormented by a pain in his side. If you would come, I would read you the first volume of my book.[5] Adieu—my dear Friend

Ever your's
M. WS—

PUBLISHED: Jones, #123. TEXT: John Gisborne Notebook No. 2, Abinger MS., Bodleian Library.

1. The Gisbornes sent their maps to the Shelleys as a gift, in exchange for which Shelley sent them a copy of *Adonais: An Elegy on the Death of John Keats, Author of Endymion, Hyperion etc.*, then being printed at Pisa (*PBS Letters*, #640).

2. The Gisbornes wished to sell a number of their possessions before their departure for England. For more about the piano and other items they wished to sell, see *PBS Letters*, #628.

3. The Gisbornes visited the Shelleys from 26 to 29 July and then departed on their journey to England. Shelley accompanied them as far as Florence (*MWS Journal*, p. 158).

4. The details of the Greek uprising were sent by Mavrocordato to Mary Shelley on 20 May (*S&M*, III, 626–28).

5. *Valperga*. See 30 June 1821 for Mary Shelley's account of the writing of *Valperga*. On [13 July] Shelley informed the Gisbornes that Mary Shelley was "on the verge of finishing her Novel; but it cannot be in time for you to take to England" (*PBS Letters*, #640). *Valperga* was completed by the end of August and Mary Shelley copied it through November; on 30 November and 1 December, she corrected it (*MWS Journal*). Towards the end of July Shelley approached Ollier about publishing *Valperga* (*PBS Letters*, #645). Shelley's third letter to Ollier on the subject of publication contains his highly laudatory appraisal of the work (*PBS Letters*, #663). Mary Shelley intended the money earned from *Valperga* to go to Godwin and tried to get advance payment, which Ollier refused (Gisborne, *Journals and Letters*, pp. 73–74). After months of waiting for a response from Ollier, and before receiving word from Gisborne about Ollier's decision, Shelley wrote on 11 January 1822 (coincidentally, Gisborne wrote to Shelley about Ollier the same day) that the novel had ben sent directly to Godwin "with liberty to dispose of it to the best advantage" (see [?20 December–] 21 December [1821]; *PBS Letters*, #675).

TO MARIA GISBORNE — Baths of San Giuliano June 1 1821

My Dear M[rs] Gisborne—

Perhaps by this time our parcel from the Amy is on its way to us—but we have yet heard nothing about it, and are anxious to see it. If Shelley were well enough he would come and hear more of Faust; but he really suffers a great deal—more than he ought this fine weather. I hope that you are all better, and not quite Killed by bustle. Pray write, and come as soon as you can—If Henry should not be returned—could you not try to get the pistol-case arranged, as S— mentions, and let us have it back as soon as possible.

Adieu!

Ever your's
M. WS

PUBLISHED: Jones, "New Letters," p. 69. TEXT: John Gisborne Notebook No. 2, Abinger MS., Bodleian Library.

TO JOHN TAAFFE[1]

Teusday evening Baths of St. Giuliano
[5 June 1821]

My dear Sir

I send my servant for the Guinea Pigs,[2] and am extremely obliged to you for the book.

The Williams' are very well and desired regards if I should see you; but I am afraid that this tempo matto does not accord with you or your little horse.

Shelley will be very glad to receive the next proof.

Your Obedient Servant
Mary Shelley

I send you some lists of articles that some friends of ours going to England wish to sell. Perhaps you will have the kindness to shew them to any of your friends. Mad[me] Regny[3] might like to buy some of the music for Ida. Those marked with a cross are already sold

ADDRESS: John Taaffe Esq / Casa Mostardi / Pisa. PUBLISHED: Jones, #124. TEXT: Humanities Research Center, University of Texas at Austin.

1. Count John Taaffe (c. 1787–1862), an Irishman, was introduced to the Shelleys and Claire Clairmont at about the same time as Pacchiani, Sgricci, Viviani, and Mavrocordato, that is, November–December 1820 (*CC Journals*, 28 November 1820). Regarded by the Shelleys and Byron as a bore but "a good fellow," he considered himself to be the poet laureate of Pisa. Although the Shelleys and Byron derided his poetry, they attempted to help him publish his translation of *The Divine Comedy*, thinking his commentary of some value. Ollier declined Shelley's suggestion of publication, but Byron succeeded with John Murray, who published the first volume in 1822. (Shelley read proof of the translation, which was printed at Pisa in 1821.) No further volumes were published (Cline, *Pisan Circle*, pp. 16–25, 64, 68–69; Dowden, *Shelley*, II, 363–65).

2. Shelley wrote to Claire Clairmont on 8 June: "Mr. Taaffe comes sometimes, & on an occasion of sending two Guinea pigs to Mary wrote this at the end of his letter. O, that I were one of those Guinea pigs that I might see you this morning!" (*PBS Letters*, #630).

3. Artemisia Castellini Regney was "a woman of unusual culture and personal charm" and "a painter of ability." Through his friendship with her, Taaffe became acquainted with painters, intellectuals, and "the first society of Pisa, Lucca, and Florence" (Cline, *Pisan Circle*, pp. 19, 225).

TO MARIA GISBORNE

Baths of S. Giuliano June 25th 1821

My Dear M[rs] Gisborne

Would you have the kindness to get the enclosed delivered immediately to its address? Pardon me for troubling you with this, and pray let it be sent without any delay—You will hear of the Prince at M. Constantin

Argyropoli, a merchant at Leghorn. If he has sailed,[1] then let the letter be sent back to me—Would you also tell your Messenger to ask whether the Prince sailed for Marseilles, as I wish to know whether he touches there before he goes elsewhere—

How do you get on? However I shall hear all your news from Shelley when he returns[2]—Most truly Your's

Mary WS.

If your Messenger finds the Prince, let him wait for a reply.

PUBLISHED: Jones, "New Letters," p. 70. TEXT: John Gisborne Notebook No. 2, Abinger MS., Bodleian Library.

1. On 26 June Mavrocordato left Italy for Greece to become one of the leaders of the revolution against the Turks.

2. Shelley was at Leghorn on 24 and 25 June (*MWS Journal*).

TO MARIA GISBORNE Baths of St. Giuliano June 30th 1821

My dear Mrs Gisborne

Well how do you get on? Mr Gisborne says nothing of that in the note which he wrote yesterday, and it is that in which I am most interested. I pity you exceedingly in all the disagreable details to which you are obliged to sacrifice your time & attention—I can conceive no employment more tedious; but now I hope it is nearly over, and that as the fruit of its conclusion you will soon come to see us.

Shelley is far from well—he suffers from his side & nervous irritation. The day on which he returned from Leghorn he found little Percy ill of a fever produced by teething—he got well the next day—but it was so strong while it lasted that it frightened us greatly. You know how much reason we have to fear the deceitful appearance of perfect health—

You see that this your last ⟨winter⟩ summer in Italy is manufactured on purpose to accustom you to the English seasons—It is warmer now, but we still enjoy the delight of cloudy skies—The cicala has not yet made himself heard—

I get on with my occupation[1] & hope to finish the rough transcript this month—I shall then give about a month to corrections & then I shall transcribe it—It has indeed been a child of mighty slow growth, since I first thought of it in our library at Marlow. I then wanted the body in which I might embody my spirit—The materials for this I found at Naples —but I wanted other books—nor did I begin it until a year afterwards at Pisa—it was again suspended during our stay at your house & continued again at the Baths—All the winter I did not touch it—but now it is in a state of great forwardness since I am at page 71 of the 3rd Vol. It has indeed been a work of some labour since I have read & consulted a great many books—I shall be very glad to read the first Vol to you that you may give me your opinion as to the conduct and interest of the story.

June is now at its last gasp—you talked of going in August—I hope therefore that we may soon expect you.

Have you heard any thing concerning the inhabitants of Skinner St.[2] It is now many months since I received a letter—& I begin to grow alarmed.

Adieu
Ever sincerely yours
MaryWS.

[*Postscript by Shelley*] I have got an offer of 5 crowns for the Microscope.—You may accept it, if you cannot get a better.—

ADDRESS: Alla Signora Maria Gisborne / Livorno. POSTMARKS: (1) PISA; (2) 1 LUGLIO. ENDORSED: Recd. 1st July 1821. Ansd. PUBLISHED: Jones, #126. TEXT: MS., Bodleian Library (MS., Shelley, c. 1, ff. 469–70).

1. Writing *Valperga.*
2. The Godwins.

TO SHELLEY[1] [Pisa] Friday [10 August 1821]

My dear Shelley

Shocked beyond all measure as I was I instantly wrote the enclosed—if the task be not too dreadful pray copy it for me I cannot—

send that part of you letter—which contains the accusation—I tried but I could not write it—I think I could as soon have died—I send also Elise's last letter[2]—enclose it or not as you think best.

I wrote to you with far different felings last night—beloved friend—our bark is indeed tempest tost but love me as you have ever done & God preserve my child to me and our enemies shall not be too much for us.

Consider well if Florence be a fit residence for us[3]—I love I own to face danger—but I would not be imprudent—

Pray get my letter to M^{rs} H [*Hoppner*] copied for a thousand reasons

Adieu dearest take care of yourself all yet is well—the shock for me is over and I now despise the slander—but it must not pass uncontra{di}cted—I sincerly thank Lord Byron for his kind unbelief[4]

affectionately yours
MaryWS.

Do not think me imprudent in mentioning Clares illness at Naples[5]—It is well to meet facts—they are as cunning as wicked—I have read over my letter it is written in haste—but it were as well that the first burst of feeling sh^{d} be expressed—No letters—

PUBLISHED: Jones, #127. TEXT: MS., Bodleian Library (MS., Shelley, c. 1, f. 471).

1. When Shelley returned from Florence on 2 August, he found waiting for him a letter from Byron asking that he come at once to Ravenna, since Byron intended to leave there shortly. Concerned about Byron's plans for Allegra, Shelley departed from the Baths of Pisa on 3 August, spent 4 August at Leghorn with Claire Clairmont (who on 19 June had gone "to bathe at Livorno for an Aneurism of the heart" [*CC Journals*]), and arrived at Ravenna on 6 August. Shelley's letter to Mary

Shelley of 7 August informed her that Elise Foggi had told the Hoppners that Claire Clairmont had given birth to Shelley's child at Naples (see 18 June 1820, n. 1). The accusation was repeated by Hoppner in his letter of 16 September to Byron: "You must know then that at the time the Shelleys were here Clare was with child by Shelley: you may remember to have heard that she was constantly unwell, and under the care of a Physician, and I am uncharitable enough to believe that the quantity of medicine she then took was not for the mere purpose of restoring her health. I perceive too why she preferred remaining alone at Este, notwithstanding her fear of ghosts and robbers, to being here with the Shelleys. Be this as it may, they proceeded from here to Naples, where one night Shelley was called up to see Clara who was very ill. His wife, naturally, thought it very strange that he should be sent for; but although she was not aware of the nature of the connexion between them, she had had sufficient proof of Shelley's indifference, and of Clara's hatred for her: besides as Shelley desired her to remain quiet she did not dare to interfere. A Mid-wife was sent for, and the worthy pair, who had made no preparation for the reception of the unfortunate being she was bringing into the world, bribed the woman to carry it to the Pietà, where the child was taken half an hour after its birth, being obliged likewise to purchase the physician's silence with a considerable sum. During all the time of her confinement Mrs. Shelley, who expressed great anxiety on her account, was not allowed to approach her, and these beasts, instead of requiting her uneasiness on Clara's account by at least a few expressions of kindness, have since increased in their hatred to her, behaving to her in the most brutal manner, and Clara doing everything she can to engage her husband to abandon her. Poor Mrs. Shelley, whatever suspicions she may entertain of the nature of their connexion, knows nothing of their adventure at Naples, and as the knowledge of it could only add to her misery, 'tis as well that she should not. This account we had from Elise, who passed here this summer with an English lady who spoke very highly of her. She likewise told us that Clara does not scruple to tell Mrs. Shelley she wishes her dead, and to say to Shelley in her presence that she wonders how he can live with such a creature" (*PBS Letters*, #650, n. 5).

2. See 10 August 1821 to Isabella Hoppner, n. 4.
3. Claire Clairmont made her home at Florence.
4. Byron believed the Hoppners' report at least through March 1821 (Byron, *Works*, V, 500–501). On 8 October 1820 he had written to Hoppner: "The Shiloh story is true no doubt, though Elise is but a sort of Queen's evidence. You remember how eager she was to return to them, and then she goes away and abuses them. Of the facts, however, there can be little doubt; it is just like them. You may be sure that I keep your counsel . . ." (Byron, *Works*, V, 86).
5. *Mary Shelley's Journal* of 27 December 1818 records: "Claire is not well."

To Isabella Hoppner[1] — Pisa. August 10th 1821

My dear Mrs Hoppner—

After a silence of nearly two years I address you again, and most bitterly do I regret the occasion on which I now write. Pardon me that I do not write in french; you understand English well, and I am too much impressed to shackle myself in a foreign language; even in my own, my thoughts far outrun my pen, so that I can hardly form the letters. I write ⟨in⟩ to defend[2] ⟨of⟩ him to whom I have the happiness to be united, whom I love and esteem beyond all creatures, from the foulest calumnies; and to you I write this, who were so kind, to Mr Hoppner; to both of whom I indulged the pleasing ⟨hope⟩ idea that I have every reason to feel gratitude. This is indeed a painful task.

⟨M^{r}⟩ Shelley is at present on a visit to Lord Byron at Ravenna and I received a letter[3] from him today containing accounts that make⟨s⟩ my hand tremble so much that I can hardly hold the pen. It tells me that Elise wrote to you relating the most hideous stories against him, and that you have believed them. Before I speak of these falsehoods permit {me} to say a few words concerning this miserable girl. You well know that she formed an attachment with Paolo when we proceeded to Rome, & at Naples their marriage was talked of—We all tried to dissuade her; we knew Paolo to be a rascal and we thought so well of her that we believed him to be unworthy of her. An accident led me to the knowledge that without marrying they had formed a connexion; she was ill we sent for a docter who said there was danger of a miscarriage—I w^{d} not turn the girl on the world without in some degree binding her to this man—we had them married at Sir W. A'Courts—she left us; turned catholic at Rome, married him & then went to Florence. After the disastrous death of my child we came to Tuscany—we have seen little of them; but we have had knowledge that Paolo has formed a scheme of extorting money from Shelley by false accusations—he has written him threatning letters saying that he w^{d} be the ruin of him &c—we placed these in the hands of a celebrated lawyer here who has done what he can to silence him. Elise has never interfered in this and indeed the other day I received a letter[4] from her entreating with great professions of love that I w^{d} send her money—I took no notice of this; but although I knew her to be in Evil hands I w^{d} not believe that she was wicked enough to join in his plans without proof.

And now I come to her accusations—and I must indeed summon all my courage while I transcribe them; for tears will force their way, and how can it be otherwise? You knew Shelley, you saw his face, & could you believe them? Believe them only on the testimony of a girl whom you despised? I had hopes that such a thing was impossible, and that although ⟨stange⟩ strangers might believe the calumnies that this man propogated, that none who had ever seen my husband could for a moment credit them.

She says Claire was Shelley's ⟨miss⟩ mistress, that—Upon my word, ⟨I vow by all that I hold⟩ I solemnly assure you that I cannot write the words, I send you a part of Shelleys letter that you may see what I am now about to refute—but I had rather die that [*than*] copy any thing so vilely so wickedly false, so beyond all imagination fiendish.

I am perfectly convinced, in my own mind that Shelley never had an improper connexion with Claire—At the time specified in ⟨Claires⟩ Elise's letter, the winter after we quited ⟨Nap⟩ Este, I suppose while she was was with us, and that was at Naples, we lived in lodgings where I had momentary entrance into every room and such a thing could not have passed unknown to me. The malice of the girl is beyond all thought—I now do remember that Claire did keep her bed there for two days—but I attended on her—I saw the physician—her illness was one that she had been accustomed to for years—and the same remedies were employed as I had before ministered to her in England.

Claire had no child—the rest must be false—but that you should believe it—⟨I th⟩ That my beloved Shelley should stand thus slandered in your minds—⟨He⟩ He, the gentlest & most humane of creatures, is more painful to me, oh far more painful than any words can express.

It is all a lie—Claire ⟨if anything⟩ is timid; she always shewed respect even for me—poor dear girl! she has ⟨many⟩ some faults—you know them as well as I—but her heart is good—and if ever we quarelled, which was seldom, it was I, and not she, that was harsh, and our instantaneous reconciliations were sincere & affectionate.

Need I say that the union between my husband and ⟨hims⟩ myself has ever been undisturbed—Love caused our first imprudences, love which improved by esteem, a perfect trust one in the other, a confidence and affection, which visited as we have been by severe calamities (have we not lossed two children?) has encreased daily and knows no bounds.

I will add that Claire has been seperated from us for about a year[5]—She lives with a respectable German family at Florence—The reasons of this were obvious—her connexion with us made her manifest as the Miss Clairmont, the Mother of Allegra—besides we live much alone—she enters much into society there—and solely occupied with the idea of the welfare of her child, she wished to ⟨be⟩ appear such that she may not be thought in after-times to be unworthy of fulfilling the maternal duties—you ought to have paused before you tried to convince the father of her child of such unheard of atrocities on her part—If his generosity & knowledge of the world had not made him reject the slander with the ridicule it deserved ⟨of⟩ what irretrievable mischief you would have occasioned her.

Those who know me ⟨we⟩ well believe my simple word—it is not long ago that my father said in a letter to me, that he had never known me utter a falsehood—but you, easy as you have been to credit evil, who may be more deaf to truth—to you I swear—by all that I hold sacred upon heaven & earth by a vow which I should die to write if I affirmed a falsehood—I swear by the life of my child, by my blessed & beloved child, that I know these accusations to be false—

Shelley is as incapable of cruelty as the softest woman—To those who know him his humanity is almost as a proverb.—He has been unfortunate as a father. the laws of his country & death has cut him off from his dearest hopes—⟨But⟩ His enemies have done him incredible mischief—but that you should believe such a tale coming from such a hand, is beyond all belief, a blow quite unexpected, and the very idea of it beyond words shockings—

But I have said enough to convince you And are you not convinced? Are not my words the words of truth? Repair—I conjure you the evil you have done by retracting you confidence in one so vile as Elise, and by writing to me that you now reject as false every circumstance of her infamous tale.[6]

You were kind to us, and I shall never forget it; now I require justice; You must believe me, and do me, I solemnly entreat you, the justice to confess that you do so.

Mary W. Shelley

I send this letter to Shelley at Ravenna, that he may see it. For although I ought, the subject is too odious to me to copy it. I wish also that Lord Byron should see it—He gave no credit to the tale, but it is as well that he should see how entirely fabulous it is. 〈, and I〉

ADDRESS: A Madame / Madme Hoppner. PUBLISHED: Jones, #128. TEXT: MS., John Murray.

1. The text of this letter has heretofore been published from the original, with minor omissions and editorial emendations of spelling and punctuation (Byron, *Correspondence*. II, 185–88), or from Lady Shelley's copy, which omitted passages and was otherwise imperfect (*S&M*, III, 710–13, from which Jones took his text). The original, now available, permits a transcription of the letter as written, including significant deletions.

2. The final *d* is written over *ce*, making Mary Shelley's original phrase "in defence of."

3. *PBS Letters*, #650.

4. Elise Foggi's letter is written in highly imperfect French. In an attempt to keep the character of the original, I give here an idiomatic translation based on a transcription and literal translation by Linette F. Brugmans (MS. of Elise Foggi letter, John Murray):

Dear and kind madam

I have not had the pleasure of getting dear news from you in more than 20 months: I wrote you at livorno and pisa without ever having received an answer and I cannot understand what has prevented me from getting a dear letter from you and to know how your dear little passett is as well as the rest of your kind family. I heard from my doctor that monsieur was still in very poor health which pains me very much to know that he has remained ill for such a long time, but I think he will get better and that you, madam are always in good health as well as your little one.

I must tell you that I have given birth to a pretty little girl who is very fat and very cheerful she will be 6 months old on the 3rd of the coming month I am still nursing her and as I said she is coming along very well but I will soon have to wean her since for the past 10 months I have earned nothing and especially for almost the last 3 months I find myself in critical circumstances and if it were only possible for me to find a position as wet-nurse, as I have a lot of milk, or as a chamber maid to support my dear little girl for without the help of one or the other it is impossible to live.

my dear madam as I know your kind heart and your affection for me in view of the confidence my dear mistress always had in me I believe that you will be willing to have the kindness to protect me always and if you need anyone you will give me preference if it is not imposing too much on your kindness to ask you if it is possible to lend me some money for which I will give you a note and when I have a position I will pay you back: I know my dear kind madam that your heart is always open to the voice of nature and always so charitable that you will not refuse to help a mother who beseeches you and will always be grateful to you and will repay you as soon as she has a position believe me my dear lady it is only

great need that makes me beg this favor of you since my little one is teething and it will take me another 3 months to wean her because she suffers so much I beg you to excuse my boldness but so kind a soul as you will pardon me please do me the favor of an answer as soon as possible you will oblige your devoted servant and I am for life your Elise Foggi
florence 26 July 1821
via maggio 1927

5. Claire Clairmont had gone to live with the Bojti family on 20 October 1820 (*CC Journals*).

6. Shelley wrote to Mary Shelley on 16 August that he had given her letter to Mrs. Hoppner, that is, "to Lord Byron, who has engaged to send it with his own comments to the Hoppners" (*PBS Letters*, #656). After Byron's death, Mary Shelley's letter to Mrs. Hoppner was found among his papers, and to date there is no clear evidence to settle the question of whether Byron forwarded it to the Hoppners, as requested (and had it returned), or never sent it. Nor is there any evidence that Mary Shelley ever received a response from Mrs. Hoppner. In 1843 Mary Shelley met Mrs. Hoppner in Florence and deliberately snubbed her (unpublished letter from Mary Shelley to Claire Clairmont, 20 February 1843, Pforzheimer Library).

To Maria Gisborne

Pisa Nov. 30th 1821[1]

My Dear Mrs Gisborne—

Although having much to do be a bad excuse for not writing to you, yet you must in some sort admit this plea on my part—Here we are in Pisa, having furnished very nice apartments for ourselves, and what is more paid for the furniture out of the fruits of two year's economy. We are at the top of the Tre Palazzi di Chiesa—I daresay you know the house, next door to la Scoto's house on the North side of Lung' Arno: but the rooms we inhabit are South, and look over the whole country towards the Sea, so that we are entirely out of the bustle and disagreeable puzzi &c—of the town, and hardly know that we are so envelopped until we descend into the street. The Williams's have been less lucky, though they have followed our example in furnishing their own house, but renting it of Mr Webb, they have ben treated scurvily.—So here we live, Lord B just opposite to us in Casa Lanfranchi[2] (the late Sigra Filicchi's house)—So Pisa you see has become a little nest of singing birds—You will be both surprised and delighted at the work just about to be published by him.—his Cain[3]—which is in the highest style of imaginative Poetry. It made a great impression upon me, and appears almost a revelation from its power and beauty—Shelley rides with him—I, of course, see little of him. The lady, whom he serves, is a nice pretty girl, without pretensions, good-hearted and amiable[4]—her relations were banished {from} Romagna for Carbonarism.

Do you hear any thing of Shelley's Hellas?[5] Ollier treats us abominably—I should much like to know when he intends to answer S—'s last letter concerning my affair.[6] I had wished it to come out by Christmas—now there is no hope—We are warned on all hands not to trust him, and more to secure his attention and care than for any other reason, I wish to be sure of the money before he gets the book. I should not be sorry that we broke with him, although it would be difficult to bargain with another bookseller, at the distance we are. What do you know of Hunt? About two months ago he wrote to say that on the 21st October he should quit England,[7] and we have heard nothing more of him in any way. I expect that some day he and six children[8] will drop in from the clouds—trusting that God will temper the wind to the shorn lamb. Pray when you write tell us every thing you know concerning him. Do you get any intelligence of the Greeks —Our worthy Countrymen take part against them in every possible way, yet such is the spirit of freedom, and such the hatred of these poor people for their oppressors, that I have the warmest hopes—*μάντις εἴμ' ἐσθλῶν ἀγώνων*.[9]—Mavro cordato is there justly revered for the sacrifice he has made of his whole fortune to the cause, and besides for his firmness and talents. If Greece be free, Shelley and I have vowed to go, perhaps to settle there, in one of those beautiful islands where earth, ocean, and sky form the Paradise—

You will, I hope, tell us all the news of old friends when you write—I see no one that you knew. We live in our usual retired way, with few friends, and no acquaintances—Claire is returned to her usual residence, and our tranquillity is unbroken in upon, except by those winds, scirocco or tramontana, which now and then will sweep over the ocean of one's mind, and disturb or cloud its surface.

Since this must be a double letter, I save my self the trouble of copying the enclosed, which was a part of a letter written to you a month ago, but which I did not send—Will you attend to my requests—Every day increases my anxiety concerning the desk—Do have the goodness to pack it off as soon as you can.

How do you all get on? Have you yet embarked, and what is Henry about? I need not tell you how anxious we are to have these questions answered. I hope that you do not regret your journey to England, and that neither the climate, nor its more freezing accompaniments make you regret dear Italy. For this last month we have been enjoying a warm scirocco, which has rendered fires unnecessary—sometimes the days are surpassingly fine, and the burning sun of winter drives us to seek the shade.

Shelley was at your hive yesterday[10]—it is as dirty and busy as ever, so people live in the same narrow circle of space and thought, while time goes on, not as a race-horse, but "a six-inside dilly,"[11] and puts them down softly at their journey's end; while they have slept and ate, and "ecco tutto"—with this piece of morality, Dear Mrs G—, I end. Shelley begs every remembrance of his to be joined with mine to Mr G— [*Gisborne*] and Henry. Ever your's. Mary WS.

And now, my Dear Mrs Gisborne, I have a great favour to ask of you—Ollier writes to say that he has placed our two desks in the hands of a merchant of the City, and that they are to come—God knows when! Now as we sent for them two years ago, and are tired of waiting, will you do us the favour to get them out of his hands, and to send them without delay—If they can be sent without being opened, send them in statu quo; if they must be opened, do not send the smallest, but get a key (being a patent lock, the key will cost half a guinea) made for the largest and send it, and return the other to Peacock—If you send the desk, will you send with it, the following things—a few Copies of all Shelley's works, particularly of the 2nd edition of the Cenci—my mother's posthumous works, and letters from Norway[12]—from Peacock, if you can, but do not delay the box for them—then get money from Ollier to buy a good pen-knife with several blades—needles in a case, pins, minnikin pins, sealing wax, scissors, a dozen skeins of white netting silk, not too fine for purses, a tortoise shell comb for combing out the hair—half a dozen ditto such as you gave me—a good spy-glass set in a gold rim for short sight, one to suit Papa, or any person of your acquaintance of the like sight—N° 10 I think they call it. Ask Peacock if he have any thing to send us—new books we hardly want, since we get them from Ld B Doing this, particularly in sending us the desk, you would do us a real service, for I have long waited in vain for it—You might also send me a doz. pair of stockings for a child of 3 years old—some of the best vellum drawing paper for miniatures—½ doz. Brookman and Langdon's pencils, marked H.B. and a cake of carmine from Smith's and Warner's. If you could get the money from Ollier, I should like very much a cornelian seal with S—'s coat of arms—

PUBLISHED: Jones, #129. TEXT: John Gisborne Notebook No. 2, Abinger MS., Bodleian Library.

1. The Shelleys had moved to the Tre Palazzi di Chiesa in Pisa on 25 October (*CC Journals*; Williams, *Journals and Letters*). Although in this letter Mary Shelley states that their new home was on the north side of the Arno, it was actually on the south side.

2. Byron had arrived in Pisa on 1 November.

3. Published by John Murray on 19 December 1821.

4. Countess Teresa Guiccioli, née Gamba (c. 1800–73), was married to Count Alessandro Guiccioli, forty years her senior. She and Byron became lovers in 1819 and continued their relationship until Byron's death (see Origo, *The Last Attachment*, for a study of the Byron-Guiccioli relationship. See also Countess Teresa Guiccioli, *My Recollections of Lord Byron*, trans. Hubert E. H. Jerningham, 2 vols. [London: Richard Bentley, 1869]; and Marchand, *Byron*).

5. Shelley had completed *Hellas* in late October. From 6 to 10 November Edward Williams (who had suggested its title on 25 October) made a fair copy of it (Williams, *Journals and Letters*, pp. 106, 110–11). On 11 November Shelley sent it to Ollier, who published it in February 1822.

6. The publication of *Valperga*.

7. While Shelley was at Ravenna, he and Byron agreed to establish a liberal periodical. It was to be owned by Byron and Hunt; and Byron, Hunt, and Shelley would contribute (*PBS Letters*, #660). Hunt accepted the proposal, which included the plan for the Hunts to go to Italy. Inclement weather and illness delayed their arrival until 15 June 1822 at Genoa and 1 July 1822 at Leghorn. Four issues of

The Liberal, Verse and Prose from the South were published, between October 1822 and July 1823 (Marshall, *The Liberal*, pp. 21–28, 50, 81, 196).

8. Thornton, John, Mary, Swinburne, Percy, and Henry.

9. See 21 March 1821 to Peacock, n. 2.

10. Shelley and Williams were at Leghorn on 29 November (*MWS Journal*).

11. A quotation from Thomas Moore's *Fudge Family in Paris*:

> Beginning gay, desperate, dashing down-hilly;
> And ending as dull as a six-inside Dilly (letter 10, line 35).

Dilly was the familiar name for a diligence, or public stagecoach.

12. *Posthumous Works* and *A Short Residence.*

To Maria Gisborne

[Pisa ?20 December–]
(December 21) [1821]

My dear Mrs Gisborne

Since writing my last letter we have heard of the departure of Hunt,[1] and now anxiously await his arrival. He will be more comfortable than he dreams of now. For Lord Byron has furnished the pian terreno of his own house for him, so that more lucky than the rest of the œconomical English who come here, he will find clean and spacious apartments, with every comfort about him.—And a climate—such a climate—we dine in a room without a fire with all the windows open;—a tramontano reigns, which renders the sky clear and the warm sun pours into our apartments. It is cold at night—but as yet not uncomfortably so, and it now verges towards Christmas day. I am busy in arranging Hunt's rooms since that task devolves upon me.

(December 21) Since I wrote the above we have had some high wind and rain. The wind I hope and trust is in Hunt's favour so now we expect them anxiously and daily—I am so happy to think that we shall stow them comfortably when they do come and feel much gratitude towards L. B. for his unpretending generosity on this occasion. My lord is now living very sociably, giving dinners to his male acquaintance and writing divinely; perhaps by this time you have seen Cain and will agree with us in thinking it his finest production—To me it sounds like a revelation—of some works one says—one has thought of such things though one could not have expressed it so well—It is not thus with Cain—One has perhaps stood on the extreme verge of such ideas and from the midst of the darkness which has surrounded us the voice of the Poet now is heard telling a wondrous tale.

To come to my own poor penmanship—Ollier does not answer our letter I suppose that he never will and I consider this long delay as freeing us from any engagement with him though I cannot guess what we shall do next.[2]

Our friends in Greece are getting on famously—All the Morea is subdued and much treasure was aquired with the capture of Tripoliza[3]—Some cruelties have ensued—But the oppressor must in the end buy tyranny with blood—such is the law of necessity. The young Greek Prince[4] whom you saw at our house is made the head of the Provisional Government in Greece — He has sacrificed his whole fortune to his country, and heart and soul is bent upon her cause.

It is an age since we have heard from you I hope that you have received my last letter sent through Ollier—I am anxious concerning your answer, I want to hear of your own affairs much—You have entered on a shoreless sea—but is not your wind favourable?

And my desk too—pray at any rate get it out of Ollier's clutches and send it to me—send also with it if it be not yet shipped—some of the finest hot Bristol pressed paper but I think I mentioned that before, with a cake of Carmine from Smith & Warners—I do not think that I want any thing else except those things which I m[entioned] in my last letter.

You will be glad to hear that Shelley's health is much improved this winter—he is not quite well but he is much better—The air of Pisa is so mild and delightful and the exercise on horseback agrees with him particularly—Williams also is quite recovered—We think that we may probably spend next summer at La Spezia—at least I hope that we shall be near the sea.

How is my father? how are all our friends? How is Henry and his little bevy of admired maidens? Pray tell us how you get on

The clock strikes twelve. I have taken to sit up rather late this last month —When all the world is in bed or asleep a [*I*] find a little of that solitude, one cannot get in a town through the day—I may fancy myself in a hermitage *ἄιτη, ἄπνστη*[5] (there is a little greek for you) yet daylight brings with it all the conveniences of a town residence, & all the delights of friendly and social intercourse—few of the pains—for my horizon is so contracted that it shuts most of those out.

Most sincerely yours,
MaryW.S.

an inch is left for me just to edge in "The Compliments of the Season." We intend to make mince pies, a letter came today from Hunt—so we need not expect him this long time—Send all S's works, a box of ivory letters and some picture books for Percy, and the Fudge Family in Italy.[6]

ADDRESS: (To be forwarded immediately) / Mrs. Gisborne / To the care of Mess. Ollier / Booksellers / Vere St. Bond Street / Inghilterra / London / Londres. [*Redirected to*] 33 King St. / Montague Sq. POSTMARKS: (1) PISA; (2) FPO / JA. 10 / 1822; (3) 12 o'Clock / JA. 11 / 1822 Nn. PUBLISHED: Jones, #130. TEXT: MS., Bodleian Library (MS., Shelley, c. 1, ff. 478–79).

1. The Hunts sailed from London on 15 November but were forced back by bad weather (Hunt, *Correspondence*, I, 174–76).

2. See 28 May 1821, n. 5.

3. This news was given by Prince Argiropoulo on 11 November (Williams, *Journals and Letters*, p. 111; *MWS Journal*).

4. Prince Mavrocordato.

5. I am indebted to Bruce Barker-Benfield for the suggestion that this is probably Mary Shelley's attempt to translate into the feminine gender the Homeric phrase meaning "out of sight, out of hearing," said by Telemachus of the lost Odysseus (*Odyssey* 1. 242).

6. The many imitations of *The Fudge Family in Paris* did not include one of the family in Italy.

To Maria Gisborne — Pisa Jan^y [?-] 18 1822

My Dear Mrs Gisborne:

Many thanks for your long letter, and so you see I am going to follow your example, and begin in a small hand at the very top of my paper. First, let me tell you that the Hunts are not come. We wait anxiously for them, still more anxiously after having heard the wind whistle, and the distant sea roar; but I am sure they are safe—it is but hope delayed—Pisa today ha cambiato viso;[1] all was allegrezza,[2] the Court here, balls &c—when a brother of the Dutchess, a promising young man, has suddenly died of a mal maligno, so the Court has left us. The ladies look in despair at their new gowns, the gentlemen, among them Medwin,[3] sigh to think of the wal{t}zing they might have had—Oh plaisirs! un long adieu!—You know us too well not to know that we have not lost any thing by this change—I had thought of being presented, mais J'ai beau faire—Shelley would not take the necessary steps, and so we go on in our obscure way—the Williams's lead the same life as us, and without a sigh, we see Medwin depart for his evening assemblies—Yet though I go not to the house of feasting, I have gone to the house of prayer—In the piano sotto di nos there is a Reverend Divine who preaches and prays, and sent me so many messages that I now make one of his congregation, and that from a truly Christian motive—Vaccà reported that this Doct^r Nott[4] said in Society that Shelley was a scelerato[5]—We told Taaffe and the little gossip reported it to all the world. Doct^r Nott heard of it, and sent a message by Medwin to deny it, and put our absence from Church on the score of this report, so to prove that I forgave or disbelieved, I went once, and then that I might not appear to despise his preaching, I went again and again—

What think you of Cain?[6] Is it not a wonderful work? It appears to me to be his finest, and that which he has written since, though beautiful, has not the sublimity of Cain. He is, at present employed in writing another Tragedy[7]—Do you remember some newspaper verses of Lord Carlisle, addressed to Lady Holland, begging her not to accept Napoleon's Snuff-box? Lord Byron began a parody on it, of which this is the first verse,

> Lady! accept the Box the Hero wore,
> In spite of all this elegiac stuff;
> Nor let seven Verses written by a Bore,
> Prevent your Ladyship from taking snuff.[8]

By the bye—Has Hogg yet got over his dislike of Lord B—I do not see much of him; but he is very amiable when we do meet—he knows that I am a great admirer of his poetry—We see a good { } of La Guiccioli

—She is a good amiable girl, and her brother Pierino[9] is one of the most gentlemanly Italians I have met with. You know the Italian manieres de compagnie—when Williams first saw this lady, they made him almost mad, and in vain do I try to drub into him a few of the expressions which fill up an Italian visit. I wrote them down, but he would not learn them; "ora la levo l'incomodo." "Incomodo! no, anzi è un piacare."[10]—the answer alone makes him mad; but reply follows reply "Il piacare è tutto mio" "bontà sua", and some dozen more.[11]

I am vexed to hear that you do not get on as you hoped; but I have better hopes than you—such undertakings always look desparingly at the beginning; but lay ever so small a foundation, and you will see the edifice rise of itself—You do not mention Henry's employments—however, since Mr Gisborne has regained his health, I look upon your removal to England as a great advantage to you. You talk of a sea-coal fire—We dined today in a room without a fire, with all the windows open—To be sure, that will not do for any time—and besides these are the first sunny days after a series of rain, which so caused the Arno to rise that the upper bridge was nearly choked up.

Jan. 18. So far we are advanced in 1822—yet the Hunts are not arrived—The Storms have been horrible and universal. At Genoa, forty ships were cast away, and 125 Souls lost; but I will not augur ill. And in a very few days I hope the memory will be all that will remain to them of their tedious and stormy sea-voyage—

Shelley is better this winter than he has been a long, long time—I have suffered from rheumatism in the head, very much indeed. It has been a sort of epidemic in Pisa. Percy is quite well. "Galliardo e sano, se Dio vuole"[12]—I hope, by this time, my desk[13] is en route—I own I am anxious to hear that it is safe out of Ollier's hands, who treats us infamously in every way. Now you are in England, we have some hope of hearing really something about his literary affairs—I hear that he is talked of. The Cenci most—I hope Charles the 1st[14] which is now on the anvil, will raise his reputation—I long to see Sardanapalus,[15] which I hear praised. You may soon expect other deeds from the same pen—His poetry is an overflowing river, without argini,[16] which makes a continual piena.[17] Sometimes it only floods a field—sometimes it is as a Cataract—Do you know, as a last Commission, if my desk be not sent, and you could get the money from Ollier, I should like a few large damask table-clothes, and napkins—The table Cloths 3 ½ braccia wide and long as the last, last Codicil, send a few quires of gilt-edged note-paper; it will be very useful to me—Be sure to ask Peacock if he has anything to send. Do you remember what I wrote about Matilda[18]—

Pray write often and fully—My Compliments to Emma Clementi.[19] All the time I write, a duo of Rossini's is running in my head, now singing at the Opera—Sinclair[20] sings one part, and cuts an amazingly fine figure among them. It is hummed about as much as merivedone was, Do you know it? "Nati in ver noi siamo"—Adieu. Success attend you. Ever your's,

MWS. Send an address for your letters. I do not wish to send any more through Ollier—

PUBLISHED: Jones, "New Letters," pp. 70–74. TEXT: John Gisborne Notebook No. 2, Abinger MS.; Bodleian Library.

1. "Changed its expression."

2. "Cheerfulness."

3. Medwin had returned to Pisa on 14 November 1821 (*MWS Journal*).

4. George Frederick Nott (1767–1841), cleric and author. Dr. Nott lived on a lower floor of the Tre Palazzi and conducted chapel services on Sundays for a small English congregation (Cline, *Pisan Circle*, p. 70). Mary Shelley attended on 9 and 16 December 1821; 24 February and 3 March 1822. On 30 December 1821 Dr. Nott had christened Rosalind Williams, the Williamses' second child (born on 16 March), to whom Mary Shelley was godmother (Williams, *Journals and Letters*, pp. 103, 121; *MWS Journal*, 16 March 1821).

5. "Scoundrel."

6. See 30 November 1821.

7. *Werner, A Tragedy* (London: John Murray, 1823), which Mary Shelley was copying for the printer (Marchand, *Byron*, III, 965).

8. Thomas Medwin wrote the following account of Byron's verse to Lady Holland: " 'I [Lord Byron] observe, in the newspapers of the day, some lines of his Lordship's, advising Lady Holland not to have any thing to do with the snuff-box left her by Napoleon, for fear that horror and murder should jump out of the lid every time it is opened! It is a most ingenious idea—I give him great credit for it.' He then read me the first stanza, laughing in his usual suppressed way,—'Lady, reject the gift,' &c. and produced in a few minutes the following parody on it:

> Lady, accept the box a hero wore,
> In spite of all this elegiac stuff:
> Let not seven stanzas, written by a bore,
> Prevent your Ladyship from taking snuff!

(Medwin, *Conversations*, pp. 234–35). Ernest J. Lovell, Jr., points out that these lines are a parody of Carlisle's first stanza:

> Lady, reject the gift! 'tis tinged with gore!
> Those crimson spots a dreadful tale relate;
> It has been grasp'd by an infernal Power;
> And by that hand which seal'd young Enghein's fate.

9. Count Pietro Gamba (?1801–27) was an activist in the cause of Italian liberty in Ravenna and a leader of the revolutionary society of the Carbonari (Marchand, *Byron*, II, 780). He accompanied Byron to Greece in 1823, and in 1825 he expressed his friendship and admiration for Byron in his book, *A Narrative of Lord Byron's Last Journey to Greece* (London: John Murray, 1825) (see [?24–31] May [1824]; 19 February [1825]). In 1825 he returned to Greece, where he died in 1827 (see [6 March 1825]; 20 August 1827).

10. "Now I'll annoy her no longer." "Annoy! no, rather it's a pleasure."

11. "The pleasure is all mine"; "your goodness."

12. "Strong and healthy, if God wills."

13. Mary Shelley's lap desk had been left behind at Marlow in 1818, and for two years she had been trying to recover it. It finally arrived at Albaro on 7 October 1822 (*MWS Journal*).

14. *Charles the First*, a drama Shelley did not complete.

15. Byron's *Sardanapalus* was published with *Cain* and *The Two Foscari* by John Murray on 19 December 1821.

16. "Riverbanks."

17. "Fullness."

18. The Gisbornes had taken Mary Shelley's novella to England in May 1820 and left it with Godwin. In her letter of 9 February 1822, which answers many points of this letter by Mary Shelley, Maria Gisborne wrote: "With regard to Mathilda (another impediment), as your father has put a stop to all intercourse between us, I am at a loss what step to take" (Gisborne, *Journals and Letters*, p. 76). *Matilda* was first published in 1959 (see 5 March 1817 to Leigh Hunt, n. 4).

19. See 19 July 1820.

20. John Sinclair (1791–1857), English tenor.

Shelley to Leigh and Marianne Hunt[1] — Pisa, Jan. 25. 1822
[*Postscript by Mary Shelley*]

Dearest Children

I fill up a little empty space of blank paper with many wishes, regrets and &c's—Stay no longer, I beseech you in your cloudenvironed isle—as cloudy for the soul as for the rest of it—Even friends there are only to be seen through a murky mist which will not be under the bright sky of dear Italy—My poor Marianne will get well[2] and you all be light hearted & happy—Come quickly

Affectionately yours
Mary S.

ADDRESS: Leigh Hunt Esq. / Post Office / Dartmouth / England. [*Redirected to*] M[iss] Hunt / 72 St. Paul's Church Yrd / London. POSTMARKS: (1) Pisa; (2) FPO / FE. 7 / 1822; (3) FE / 11 / 1822. PUBLISHED: Jones, #131. TEXT: MS., Bodleian Library (MS., Shelley, c. 1, ff. 484–87).

1. *PBS Letters*, #679.

2. On 6 January Hunt had written to inform the Shelleys of the further delay of their voyage, caused first by bad weather and then by Marianne Hunt's severe illness (Hunt, *Correspondence*, I, 174–76).

To Maria Gisborne — Pisa Feb 9. 1822

My dear Mrs Gisborne

Not having heard from you I am anxious about my desk[1]—It would have been a great convenience to me if I could have received it at the beginning of the winter But now I should like it as soon as possible—I hope that it is out of Ollier's hands—I have before said what I would have done with it—if both desks can be sent without being opened let them be sent—if not give the small one back to Peacock—get a key made for the larger & send it I entreat you by the very next vessel. This key will cost half a guinea & Ollier will not give you the money—but give me credit for it I entreat you—& pray let me have the desk as soon as possible.

Shelley is now gone to la Spezia to get houses for our Colony for the summer[2]—It will be a large one—too large I am afraid for unity—yet I hope not—there will be Lord Byron who will have a large & beautiful boat built on purpose by some English navy officers at Genoa[3]—There will be the Countess Guiccioli and her brother—The Williams', whom you know—Trelawny[4]—a kind of half Arab Englishman—whose life has been as changeful as that of Anastatius[5] & who recounts the adventures of his youth as eloquently and well as the imagined Greek—he is clever—for his moral qualities I am yet in the dark he is a strange web which I am endeavouring to unravel—I would fain learn if generosity is united to impetuousness—Nobility of spirit to his assumption of singularity & independence—he is six feet high—raven black hair which curls thickly & shortly like a Moors dark, grey—expressive eyes—overhanging brows upturned lips & a smile which expresses good nature & kindheartedness—his shoulders are high like an Orientalist—his voice is monotonous yet emphatic & his language as he relates the events of his life energetic & simple—whether the tale be one of blood & horror or of irrisistable comedy His company is delightful for he excites me to think and if any evil shade the intercourse that time will unveil—the sun will rise or night darken all.—There will be besides a Captain Roberts[6] whom I do not know—a very rough subject I fancy—a famous angler—&c—We are to have a smaller boat[7] and now that these first divine spring days are come (you know them well) the sky clear—the sun hot—the hedges budding—we sitting without a fire & the window open—I begin to long for the sparkling waves the olive covered hills & vine shaded pergolas of Spezia—however it would be madness to go yet—yet as ceppo[8] was bad we hope for a good Pascua[9] and if April prove fine we shall fly with the swallows

The Opera here has been detestable—The English Sinclair is the primo tenore & acquits himself excellently—but the Italians after the first have enviously selected such operas as give him little or nothing to do—We have English here & some English balls & parties to which I (mirabile dictú!) go sometimes. [We][10] have Taaffe who bores us out of our [senses][11] when he comes & writes complimentary verses telling a young lady that her eyes shed flowe{r}s why therefore should he send any

> Lovely flowers from heavenly bowes
> Love & friendship are what are due.

I have sent my novel[12] to Papa—I long to hear some news of it—as with an authors vanity I want to see it in print & hear the praises of my friends—I should like as I said when you went away—a Copy of Matilda—it might come out with the desk.

I hope as the town fills to hear better news of your plans—We long to hear from you—What does Henry do—how many times has he been in love—

Ever Yours MaryWS.

Shelley w^{d} like to see the review of the Prometheus in the Quarterly[13]

ADDRESS: Mrs. Gisborne / 33 King Street West / Bryanstone Square / Inghilterra London / Londres. POSTMARKS: (1) PISA; (2) FPO / FE. 23 / 1822; (3) 12 o'Clock / FE. 23 / 1822 Nn. ENDORSED: Recd. 23rd Feb. 1822. PUBLISHED: Jones, #132. TEXT: MS., Bodleian Library (MS., Shelley, c. 1, ff. 511, 513).

1. On 9 February Maria Gisborne wrote: "We applied too late to get your desk out of this man's rapacious clutches; he assured us that he had sent it off" (Gisborne, *Journals and Letters*, p. 75).

2. Shelley and Williams were house-hunting from 7 to 11 February but found only one suitable house. On 17 April Shelley and Williams again looked; and from 23 to 25 April Williams, Jane Williams, and Claire Clairmont looked for summer residences for the colony. The unavailability of appropriate housing caused them to give up their plan, and the Shelleys and Williamses ended up sharing the same house, Casa Magni, at San Terenzo, near Lerici (see 2 June 1822, n. 5).

3. The *Bolivar*, completed in June and delivered to Byron shortly after 18 June (Williams, *Journals and Letters*, pp. 154–55).

4. Edward John Trelawny (1792–1881), the younger son of a retired lieutenant colonel, was enrolled by his family as a volunteer first class in the Royal Navy. He served from 1805 to 1812 but left without achieving a commission. Unhappy at home, at school (he was expelled at the age of ten), in the navy, and in marriage, he found refuge in an expansive fantasy life, in which he amplified his experiences as a midshipman into the imaginary adventures of a corsair. After his divorce in 1819, Trelawny went to live in Paris and then Switzerland, supported by an annual allowance of £300 provided by his father. At Geneva in 1820 he became friends with the Williamses and Medwin, and at their invitation he went to Pisa on 14 January 1822 to join them and to meet Byron and Shelley, whose works he greatly admired. Trelawny was welcomed into the Pisan circle and became the particular friend of the Shelleys, who were taken with his unconventional character and tales of adventure. After the deaths of the poets, Trelawny's written and spoken accounts of Byron and Shelley brought him attention throughout his long life as their special friend. Trelawny's accounts of himself and others, present a decided problem, for they entangle truth and fiction to an almost indistinguishable degree (see Trelawny, *Recollections*, revised, and reissued as *Records of Shelley, Byron, and the Author* [Trelawny, *Records*]; St. Clair, *Trelawny*; *SC*, V, 37–81).

5. *Anastasius* (1819), a picaresque novel in autobiographical form by Thomas Hope (?1770–1831). The central figure is a courageous but unscrupulous Greek who has numerous extraordinary adventures in Greece, Constantinople, Egypt, Smyrna, and Arabia.

6. Captain Daniel Roberts, Trelawny's friend, built both the *Bolivar* and Shelley's boat, the *Don Juan*.

7. The *Don Juan* was delivered to Shelley on 12 May (Williams, *Journals and Letters*).

8. "Christmas."

9. "Easter."

10. Word taken from John Gisborne Notebook No. 4, Abinger MS., Bodleian Library.

11. Word taken from John Gisborne Notebook No. 4, Abinger MS., Bodleian Library.

12. *Valperga*.

13. A foolish review by William Sidney Walker (1795–1846) in the *Quarterly Review* 26 (October 1821): 168–80, which appeared in December 1821 (Reiman, *The Romantics Reviewed*, II, 780–86).

To CLAIRE CLAIRMONT [Pisa] Wednesday 20th Feb [1822][1]

My dear Claire

I have this moment received your letter which both surprizes & grieves me greatly—Come here directly—S. will return with you to Florence—but in every way it is best that you come here—take your place and come tomorrow[2] morning. You ought and must see Mrs. Mason before you leave Italy, if you do. I think in every way it would make you happier to come here,—and when here, other views may arise,—at least discuss your plans in the midst of your friends before you go. This letter you will have, I hope, by an express to-night.

Yours affecly,
Mary.

PUBLISHED: Jones, #133. TEXT: *The Athenæum*, 5 April 1879, p. 438; Sotheby Catalogue, 25 July 1978, lot 458.

1. On 19 February Claire Clairmont sent letters to Charles Clairmont, Shelley, Mary Shelley, and Mrs. Mason announcing her intention of leaving Italy for Vienna. Mary Shelley responded with this note, and on 21 February Claire Clairmont went to Pisa, where conversations with her friends changed her intentions. On 25 February she returned to Florence (*CC Journals*).

2. The text up to this point was taken from a photocopy in the Sotheby Catalogue. The present owner of the letter has refused to allow a transcription from the original.

To MARIANNE HUNT [Pisa] 5th March, 1822

My dearest Marianne—I hope that this letter will find you quite well, recovering from your severe attack, and looking towards your haven Italy with best hopes. I do indeed believe that you will find a relief here from your many English cares, and that the winds which waft you will sing the requiem to all your ills. It was indeed unfortunate that you encountered such weather on the very threshold of your journey, and as the wind howled through the long night, how often did I think of you! At length it seemed as if we should never, never meet; but I will not give way to such a presentiment. We enjoy here divine weather. The sun hot, too hot, with a freshness and clearness in the breeze that bears with it all the delights of spring. The hedges are budding, and you should see me and my friend Mrs. Williams poking about for violets by the sides of dry ditches; she being herself—

A violet by a mossy stone
Half hidden from the eye.[1]

Yesterday a countryman seeing our dilemma, since the ditch was not quite dry, insisted on gathering them for us, and when we resisted, saying that we had no quattrini (i.e. farthings, being the generic name for all money), he indignantly exclaimed, Oh! se lo faccio per interesse![2] How I wish you were with us in our rambles! Our good cavaliers flock together, and as they do not like fetching a walk with the absurd womankind,[3] Jane (i.e. Mrs. Williams) and I are off together, and talk morality and pluck violets by the way. I look forward to many duets with this lady and Hunt. She has a very pretty voice, and a taste and ear for music which is almost miraculous. The harp is her favourite instrument; but we have none, and a very bad piano; however, as it is, we pass very pleasant evenings, though I can hardly bear to hear her sing "Donne l'amore"; it transports me so entirely back to your little parlour at Hampstead—and I see the piano, the bookcase, the prints, the casts—and hear Mary's far-ha-ha-a!

We are in great uncertainty as to where we shall spend the summer. There is a beautiful bay about fifty miles off, and as we have resolved on the sea, Shelley bought a boat. We wished very much to go there; perhaps we shall still, but as yet we can find but one house; but as we are a colony "which moves altogether or not at all,"[4] we have not yet made up our minds. The apartments which we have prepared for you in Lord Byron's house will be very warm for the summer; and indeed for the two hottest months I should think that you had better go into the country. Villas about here are tolerably cheap, and they are perfect paradises. Perhaps, as it was with me, Italy will not strike you as so divine at first; but each day it becomes dearer and more delightful; the sun, the flowers, the air, all is more sweet and more balmy than in the Ultima Thule[5] that you inhabit.

M. W. S.

PUBLISHED: Jones, #134. TEXT: Marshall, *Mary Shelley*, I, 332–33.

1. Wordsworth, "She Dwelt Among the Untrodden Ways."
2. "Oh! as if I do it for my own advantage."
3. Byron often quoted the phrase "absurd womankind," used by Monkbarns in Scott's *Antiquary* (Marchand, *Byron*, III, 1062).
4. Wordsworth, "Resolution and Independence," line 77, paraphrased.
5. Among the ancients, the northernmost region of the world.

To Maria Gisborne [Pisa] March 7th 1822

My dear Mrs Gisborne

[*Cross-written*] I am very sorry that you have so much trouble about my commissions, and vainly too! Ma che vuole![1] Ollier will not give you the money and we are, to tell you the truth too poor at present to send you a cheque upon our Banker; two or three circumstances have caused

—that climax of all human ills;
The inflamation of our weekly bills[2]

But far more than that we have not touched a quattrino of our Xmas quarter, since debts in England and other calls swallowed it entirely up.[3]— For the present therefore we must dispense with those things that I asked you to get. As to the desk, we received last post from Ollier (without a line) the bill of lading that he talks of, & se dio vuole[4] we shall receive them safe, the vessel in which they were shiped is not yet arrived. The worst of keeping on with Ollier[5] (though it is the best I believe after all) is that you will never be able to make anything of his accounts until you can compare the number of copies in hand with his account of their sale—As for my novel, I shipped it off long ago to my father, telling him to make the best of it, & by the way in which he answered my letter I fancy that he thinks he can make something of it; this is much better than O. [*Ollier*] for I should never have got a penny from him & moreover he is a very bad bookseller to publish with—Ma basta poi with all these secaturas. Poor dear Hunt you will have heard by this time of the disastrous conclusion of his second embarkment—He is to try it a third time in April & if he do not succeed then—we must say that the sea is un vero precipizio, & let him try land. By the bye why not consult Varley[6] on the result; I have tried the sors Homeri and the sors Virgilia; the first says (I will write this Greek better, but I thought that Mr G. [*Gisborne*] could read the Romaic writing, & I now quite forget what it was)—

'Ηλώμην, τείως μοι ἀδελῳεὸν αλλος ἔπεῳνε
ὡς δ' ὁπότ' 'Ιασίωνι ἐΰχλόκαμος Δημήτηρ
Δουράτεον μέγαν ἵππον, ὅϑ' ἕιατο πάχτες ἄριστοι[7]

which first seems to say that he will come though his brother may be prosecuted for a libel in the meantime—of the 2nd I can make neither head or tail.

And the third is as oracularly obscure as one could wish, for who these great people are who sat in a wooden horse chi lo sa? I should think it were a hobby—and who best or worst but has that? but then folks ride on & not in a hobby. Virgil, except the first line which is unfavourable is as enigmatical as Homer

Fulgores nunc terrificos, sonitumque, metumque
Jam leves calamos, et rasæ hastilia virgæ
Connexosque angues, ipsamque in pectore divæ[8]

But to speak of predictions or antedictions some of Varley's are curious enough. Ill-fortune in May or June 1815. No. it was then that he arranged his income—there was no ill except health, al solito,[9] at that time—the particular days of the 2nd 14 June 1820 were not ill, but the whole time was disastrous—it was then that we were alarmed by Paolo's attack—disturbance about a lady in the winter of last year enough God knows[10]—nothing particular about a bouncing fat lady at 10 at night—& indeed things got more quiet in April—in July 1799. S. was only seven years of age—a great blow up every seven years—S. is not at home when he returns I will ask him what happened when he was fourteen—in his 22nd year we made our scapatina[11] At 28–9—a good deal of discomfort on a certain point but it hardly amounted to a blow-up. Pray ask Varley also about me.—

So Hogg is shocked that for good neighborhoods sake I visited the piano di sotto[12]—let him reassure himself, since [*end of cross-writing*] instead of a weekly it was only a monthly visit—in fact after going 3 times I staid away until I heard he was going away—he preached against Atheism—& they said against S. as he invited me himself to come this appeared to me very impertinent so I wrote to him to ask him whether he intended any personal allusion, but he denied the charge most entirely—this affair as you may guess among the English at Pisa made a great noise—the gossip here is of course out of all bounds, some people have given them something to talk about—I have seen little of it all but that which I have seen makes me long most eagerly for some sea girt isle where with Shelley, my babe, my books & horses we may give the rest to the winds. This we shall not have. For the present S. is entangled with Lord B. who is in a terrible fright lest he should desert him—We shall have boats & go somewhere on the sea coast where I dare say we shall spend our time agreably enough for I like the Williams' exceedingly—though there my list begins & ends. Emilia married Biondi[13]—we hear that she leads him & his mother (to use a vulgarism) a devil of a life—The conclusion of our friendship a la Italiana puts me in mind of a nursery rhyme which runs thus—

As I was going down Cranbourne lane,
Cranbourne lane was dirty,
And there I met a pretty maid,
Who dropt to me a curt'sey;
I gave her cakes, I gave her wine,
I gave her sugar candy,
But oh! the little naughty girl!
She asked me for some brandy

Now turn Cranbourne lane into Pisan acquaintances, which I am sure are dirty enough, & brandy into that wherewithall to buy brandy (& that no small sum pero)[14] & you have [the][15] whole story of Shelley['s][16] Italian platonics. We now know indeed few of those whom we knew last year. Pacchiani is at Prato—Mavrocordato in Greece—the Argyropulo's in Florence—& so the world slides—Taaffe is still here—the but{t} of Lord B's quizzing & the poet laureate of Pisa—on the occasion of a young ladys birthday he sent her the following verses

Eyes that shed a thousand flowers
Why should flowers be sent to you
Sweetest flowers of heavenly bowers,
Love & friendship are what are due.

then he wrote an elegy on the death of a saxon Prince beginning Woe! woe! but he put in another woe! lest woe should be read whoo! & that at the beginning of his poem was too great a kindness to bestow on his readers, it ought to have been geho!

[*Cross-written*] Well what more news have I for you: None I think—could you not in any way write for Matilda?—I want it very much. I hope you will succeed in your new plan, you ought at least—And I hope your next letter will bring some good news. Your healths are all good I hope. After some divine Italian weather we are now enjoying some <u>fine English weather cioè</u>—it does not rain—but not a ray can pierce the web aloft

Most truly yours
MaryWS.

ADDRESS: Mrs. Gisborne / 33 Kings Street West / Bryanstone Square / London / Inghilterra / Londres. POSTMARKS: (1) PISA; (2) FPO / MR. 21 / 1822; (3) 12 o'Clock / MR. 21 / 1822 Nn. PUBLISHED: Jones, #135. TEXT: MS., Bodleian Library (MS., Shelley, c. 1, ff. 514–15). Pages 1 and 2 contain a cross-written letter from Shelley to John Gisborne (*PBS Letters*, #690).

1. "Not at all what I wanted."

2. *Don Juan* 3. 35.

3. They were particularly pressed because Shelley supplied Hunt with £150 in January 1822 (*PBS Letters*, #679, #680).

4. "God willing."

5. Because Ollier had not answered their inquiries about Shelley's *Adonais*, *Hellas*, and *A Defence of Poetry* and Mary Shelley's *Valperga* for six months, the Shelleys considered breaking with him. The Gisbornes and Hogg advised the Shelleys to continue to deal with Ollier (Gisborne, *Journals and Letters*, pp. 75, 79–81).

6. John Varley (1778–1824), landscape painter, art teacher, and astrologer. Maria Gisborne's letter of 9 February tells of inviting Varley (who was married to John Gisborne's sister) to meet Hogg and of Varley's auguries concerning Shelley: "We talked of Shelley without mentioning his name; Varley was curious, and being informed by Hogg of his exact age, but describing his person as short and corpulent, and himself as a *bon vivant*, Varley amused us with the following remarks. Your friend suffered from ill fortune in May or June, 1815. Vexatious affairs on the 2nd and 14th of June, or perhaps latter end of May, 1820. The following year disturbance about a lady. Again, last April, at ten at night, or at noon, disturbance about a bouncing stout lady, and others. At six years of age, noticed by ladies and gentlemen for learning. In July, 1799, beginning of charges made against him. In September, 1800, at noon, or at dusk, very violent charges. Scrape at 14 years of age. Eternal warfare against parents and public opinion, and a great blow-up every seven years till death, &c., &c. Is all this true?" (Gisborne, *Journals and Letters*, p. 77).

7. The *Sortes Homericæ* used the same method as the *Sortes Vergilianæ*, but with a text of Homer (see 18 June 1820). The transcription and translation of these lines was provided by Bruce Barker-Benfield: *Odyssey* 4. (line 1) ἠλώμην, τηός μοι ἀδελφὸν ἄλλος ἔπεφνεν (*Odyssey* 4. 91): "I wandered; meanwhile another slew my brother"; (line 2) ὣς δ'ὁπότ' Ἰασίωνι εὐπλόκαμος Δημήτηρ (*Odyssey* 5. 125): "Thus when Demeter of the beautiful hair [made love to] Iasion"; (line 3) δουράτεον μέγαν ἵππον, ὅθ' ἥατο πάντες ἄριστοι (*Odyssey* 8. 512): "[for it was their fate to perish when their city should enclose] the great horse of wood, wherein were sitting all the best men [of the Argives . . .]."

8. Identification of these three lines was provided by Richmond Y. Hathorn: (line 1) "terrifying flashes, crash, and panic" (*Aeneid* 8. 1. 321); (line 2) "now smooth reeds, shafts of the peeled stalk" (*Georgics* 2. 358); (line 3) "intertwining serpents and [the Gorgon] itself on the goddess's chest" (*Aeneid* 8. 437).

9. "As usual."

10. Emilia Viviani.

11. Their elopement on 28 July 1814.

12. In her letter of 9 February Maria Gisborne had reported that Hogg was "molto scandalizzato" because Mary Shelley attended Dr. Nott's services (Gisborne, *Journals and Letters*, p. 78).

13. Emilia Viviani had married Luigi Biondi on 8 September 1821.

14. Shortly before her marriage, Emilia Viviani had requested a substantial sum from Shelley purportedly to aid a friend. White conjectures that Shelley probably did not comply because he had no considerable sum then at his disposal (White, *Shelley*, II, 323–25, 484–85). For Mary Shelley's fictionalized account of Emilia Viviani, see 3 December 1820 to Leigh Hunt, n. 5; 2–5 October [1823], n. 17.

15. Taken from John Gisborne Notebook No. 4, Abinger MS., Bodleian Library.

16. See above, n. 15.

Mary Shelley and Shelley to Claire Clairmont[1] — [Pisa 20 March 1822]

My dear Claire

Shelley and I have been consulting seriously about your letter received this morning, and I wish in as orderly a manner as possible to give you the result of our reflections. First as to my coming to Florence; I mentioned it to you first, it is true, but we have so little money, and our calls this quarter for removing &c will be so great that we had entirely given up the idea. If it would be of great utility to you, as a single expence we might do it—but if it be necessary that others sh^d follow, the crowns w^d be minus. But before I proceed further on this part of the subject let me examine what your plans appear to be. Your anxiety for A's [*Allegra's*] health is to a great degree unfounded; Venice, its stinking canals & dirty streets, is enough to kill any child; but you ought to know, & any one will tell you so, that the towns of Romagna situated where Bagnacavallo[2] is, enjoy the best air in Italy—Imola & the neighbouring paese are famous. Bagnaca{va}llo especially, being 15 miles from the sea & situated on an eminence is peculiarly salutary. Considering the affair reasonably A. is well taken care of there, she is in good health, & in all probability will continue so.

No one can more entirely agree with you than I in thinking that as soon as possible A. ought to be taken out of the hands of one as remorseless as he is unprincipled. But at the same time it appears to me that the present moment is exactly the one in which this is the most difficult—time cannot add to these difficulties for they can never be greater. Allow me to enumerate some of those which are peculiar to the present instant. A. is in a convent, where it is next to impossible to get her out, high walls & bolted doors enclose her—& more than all the regular habits of a convent, which never permits her to get outside its gates & would cause her to be missed directly. But you may have a plan for this and I pass to other objections. At your desire Shelley urged her removal to LB. and this appears in the highest degree to have exasperated him—he vowed that if you annoyed him he would place A. in some secret convent, he declared that you sh^d have nothing to do with her & that he w[d] move heaven & earth to prevent your interference. LB is at present a man of 12 or 15 thousand a year, he is on the spot, a man reckless of the ill he does others, obstinate to desperation in the pursuance of his plans or his revenge. What then would you do—having A. on the outside of the convent walls? w[d] you go to America? the money we have not, nor does this seem to be your idea. You probably wish to secret yourself. But LB would use any means to find you out—& the story he might make up—a man stared at by the Grand Duke[3]—with money at command— above all on the spot to put energy into every pursuit, w[d] he not find you? If he did not he comes upon Shelley—He taxes him; Shelley must either own it or tell a lie{.} in either case he is open to be called upon by LB to answer for his conduct—and a duel—I need not enter upon that topic, your own imagination may fill up the picture.

On the contrary a little time, a very little time, may alter much of this. It is more than probable that he will be obliged to go to England within a year—then at a distance he is no longer so formitable—What is certain is that we shall not be so near him another year—He may be reconciled with his wife, & though he may bluster he may not be sorry to get A. off his hands; at any rate if we leave him perfectly quiet he will not be so exasperated, so much on the qui vive as he is at present—Nothing remains constant, something may happen—things cannot be worse. Another thing I mention which though sufficiently ridiculous may have some weight with you. Spring is our unlucky season. No spring has passed for us without some piece of ill luck. Remember the first Spring at M[rs] Harbottles.[4] The second when you became acquainted with LB. the Third We went to Marlow—no wise thing at least—The fourth our uncomfortable residence in London—The fifth our Roman misery—The sixth Paolo at Pisa—the seventh a mixture of Emilia & a Chancery suit[5]—Now the aspect of the Autumnal Heavens has on the contrary been with few exceptions, favourable to us—What think you of this? It is in your own style, but it has often struck me. W[d] it not be better therefore to wait, & to undertake no plan until circumstance bend a little more to us.

Then we are drearily behind hand with money as present Hunt[6] & our furniture has swallowed up more than our savings. You say great sacrifices will be required of us. I would make many to extricate all belonging to me from the hands of LB, whose hypoccrisy & cruelty rouse one's soul from its depths. We are of course still in great uncertainty as to our summer residence—we have calculated the great expence of removing our furniture for a few months as far as Spezia, & it appears to us a bad plan—to get a furnished house we must go nearer Genoa, probably nearer LB. which is contrary to our most earnest wishes. We have thought of Naples.[7]

ADDRESS: A Mademoiselle / Madlle de Clairmont / Chez M. le Professeur Bojti / Florence. POSTMARK: PISA. PUBLISHED: Jones, #121. TEXT: MS., Humanities Research Center, University of Texas at Austin.

1. See *PBS Letters*, #691. Jones corrected his dating and all previous datings of

this letter in "A Shelley and Mary Letter to Claire," *Modern Language Notes* 65 (1950): 121–23.

2. On 15 March Claire Clairmont was greatly agitated by information from Shelley and Mary Shelley that Byron had placed the four-year-old Allegra in the Convent of St. Anna at Bagnacavallo (*CC Journals*). (For Byron's justification for placing Allegra in the convent, see Byron, *Works*, V, 262–64; for Shelley's response to Byron on hearing that Allegra was in the convent, see *PBS Letters*, #621.)

3. On 8 July 1827 Mary Shelley told Thomas Moore about "the Grand Duke of Tuscany and his family walking past Byron's house at Pisa to get a glimpse of him . . ." (Moore, *Memoirs*, V, 189–90).

4. A reference to the death of the Shelleys' first baby on 6 March 1815.

5. Chancery proceedings were brought against Shelley—and Shelley was given no notice—by Dr. Thomas Hume, guardian of Ianthe and Charles Shelley, when he did not receive the quarterly allowance for the children's keep. Because of this, Shelley's allowance was stopped (*MWS Journal*, 11 April 1821). Horace Smith, acting on Shelley's behalf, quickly clarified the matter, and Shelley's allowance was reinstated. The suit was unnecessary, for the money was available all the while, and a direct inquiry to Shelley would have resolved the problem (White, *Shelley*, II, 284–85, 610 n. 57).

6. Leigh Hunt, ill for months, had given up the *Indicator* and contributed almost nothing to the *Examiner*. On 24 January 1821 Marianne Hunt had written of their plight to the Shelleys, asking them to bring the Hunts to Italy (*S&M*, III, 578–79). Shelley responded by sending the Hunts whatever money he could manage (White, *Shelley*, II, 284).

7. Letter completed by Shelley (see above, n. 1).

To Maria Gisborne

Pisa April 6th April 10th 1822

My Dear Mrs Gisborne—

Not many days after I had written to you concerning the fate which ever pursues us at spring-tide, a circumstance happened which shewed that we were not forgotten this year. Although, indeed, now that it is all over, I begin to fear that the King of Gods, and men will not consider it a sufficiently heavy visitation, although for a time it threatened to be frightful enough—Two Sundays ago[1] Lord Byron, Shelley, Trelawney, Captn Hay,[2] Count Gamba, and Taaffe were returning from their usual Evening ride, when near the Porta della Piaggia, they were passed by a soldier, who gallopped through the midst of them, knocking up against Taaffe—This wise little gentleman exclaimed, "Shall we endure this man's insolence?"—Lord Byron replied, "No! we will bring him to an account"—And Shelley (whose blood always boils at any insolence offered by a soldier,) added, "as you please!" So they put spurs to their horses, (i.e. all but Taaffe, who remained quietly behind,) followed and stopped the man, and fancying that he was an Officer, demanded his name, and address, and gave their Cards—The man who, I believe, was half drunk, replied only by all the oaths, and abuse in which the Italian language is so rich—He ended, by saying, If I liked, I could draw my sabre and cut you all to pieces, but as it is, I only arrest you, and he called out to the guards at the gate, "arrestateli"—Lord B. laughed at this, and saying, "arrestateci pure," gave spurs to his horse, and rode towards the gate, followed by the rest—Lord B—and Gamba passed, but before the others could get through, the soldier got under the gate-way, called on the guard to stop them, and, drawing his sabre, began to cut at them—It happened that I, and the Countess Guiccioli were in a carriage close behind, and saw it all, and you may guess how frightened we were, when we saw our Cavaliers cut at, They being totally unarmed. Their only safety was, that the field of battle being so confined, they got close under the man, and were able to arrest his arm—Capt. Hay was, however, wounded in the face, and Shelley thrown from his horse. I cannot tell you how it all ended, but after cutting and slashing a little, the man sheathed his sword and rode off; while the others got from their horses to assist poor Hay, who was faint from loss of blood—Lord B—, when he had passed the gate, rode to his own house, got a sword-stick from one of his servants, and was returning to the gate Lung' Arno, when he met this man, who held out his hand, saying "siete contento?" Lord B—replied, "No"! I must know your name, that I may require satisfaction of you—The soldier said, "Il mio nome é Masi, sono sargente maggiore" &c &c—while they were talking, a servant of Lord B— came, and took hold of the bridle of the serjeant's horse—Lord B— ordered him to let it go, and immediately the man put his horse to a gallop, but, passing Casa Lanfranchi, one of Lord B—'s servants[3] thought that he had killed his master, and was running away, determining that he should not go scot-free, he ran at him with a pitch-fork, and wounded him—the man rode on a few paces, cried out, "sono ammazzato," and fell, was carried to the hospital, the misericordia bell ringing—We were all assembled at Casa Lanfranchi, nursing our wounded man, and poor Teresa, from the excess of her fright, was worse than any, when, what was our consternation, when we heard that the man's wound was considered mortal—Luckily none but ourselves knew who had given the wound; it was said by the wise Pisani to have been one of Lord B—'s servants, set on by his padrone, and they pitched upon a poor fellow,[4] merely because, "aveva lo sguardo fiero," quanto un' assassino"[5]—For some days, Masi continued in great danger, but he is now recovering—As long as it was thought he would die, the government did nothing: but now that he is nearly well, they have imprisoned two men, one of Lord B—'s servants, (the one with the sguardo fiero), and the other, a servant of Teresa, who was behind our carriage, both perfectly innocent, but they have been kept "in segreto," these ten days, and God knows when they will be let out. What think you of this? Will it serve for our spring adventure? It is blown over now, it is true, but our fate has, in general, been in common with dame Nature, and March winds, and April showers have brought forth may flowers—You have no notion what a ridiculous figure Taaffe cut in all this—he kept far behind, during the danger, but the next day he wished to take all the honour to himself, vowed that all Pisa talked of him alone, and coming to Lord B— said, "My Lord, if you do not dare ride out today,

I will alone"—But the next day he again changed—he was afraid of being turned out of Tuscany, or of being obliged to fight with one of the officers of the Serjeant's regiment, of neither of which things there was the slightest danger, so he wrote a declaration to the Governor to say that he had nothing to do with it, so embroiling himself with Lord B—, he got between Scylla and Charybdis, from which he has not yet extricated himself,[6]—for ourselves, we do not fear any ulterior consequences—

April 10th—We received Hellas[7] today, and the Bill of Lading. S— is well pleased with the former, though there are some mistakes. The only danger would arise from the vengeance of Masi, but the moment he is able to move, he is to be removed to another town—he is a "pessimo soggetto,"[8] being the crony of Soldaini, Rosselmini and Anguistini, Pisan names of evil fame, which, perhaps, you may remember. There is only one consolation in all this, that, if it be out fate to suffer, it is more agreeable, and more safe to suffer in company with five or six, than alone—

Well! after telling you this long story, I must relate our other news—And first the Greek—Ali Pashaw is dead,[9] and his head sent to Constantinople—the reception of it was celebrated there by the massacre of four thousand Greeks—The latter however get on—The Turkish fleet of 25 Sail of the line of war-vessels, and 40 Transports endeavoured to surprise the Greek fleet in its winter quarters—finding them prepared they bore away for Zante, and, pursued by the Greeks, took refuge in the bay of Naupacto—Here they first blockaded them, then fought them, and obtained a complete victory—All the soldiers on board the transports, on endeavouring to land, were cut to pieces, and the fleet taken or destroyed—I heard something about Hellenists, which greatly pleased me—When any one asked of the peasants of the Morea—what news there is? and if they have had any victory; they reply, "I do not know, but for us it is, ἤ Tὰν, ἤ εωι Tηs," being their Doric pronunciation of ἤ Tαν, ἤ εωὶ Tῆs, the speech of the Spartan mother, on presenting his shield, to her son—"with this, or on this"—

I wish, my Dear M^rs G— that you would send the first part of this letter, addressed to Mr W. Godwin, at Nash's Esqre Dover Street[10]—I wish him to have an account of the fray, and you will thus save me the trouble of writing it over again, for what with writing and talking about it, I am quite tired—In a late letter of mine to my father, I requested him to send you Matilda—I hope that he has complied with my desire, and, in that case, that you will get it copied, and send it to me by the first opportunity, perhaps by Hunt, if he comes at all—I do not mention commissions to you, for although wishing much for the things, about which I wrote, for the present {   } no money to spare. We wish very much to hear from you again, and to learn if there are any hopes of your getting on in your plans, what Henry is doing, and how you continue to like England—The months of February and March were, with us, as hot as an English June—the first days of April we have had some very cold weather; so that we are obliged to light fires again—S— has been much better in health this winter than any other since I have known him. Pisa certainly agrees with him exceedingly well, which is it's only merit, in my eyes. I wish fate had bound us to Naples instead. Percy is quite well—he begins to talk—Italian only now, and to call things bella and buono, but the droll thing is, that he is right about the genders—a silk vestito is bello, but a new frusta is bella—He is a fine boy—full of life, and very pretty—Williams is very well, and they are getting on very well—M^rs^ W— [*Williams*] is a miracle of economy, and, as M^rs^ G— [*Godwin*] used to call it, makes both ends meet with great comfort to herself and others. Medwin is gone to Rome; We have heaps of the gossip of a petty town this winter, and { } been just in the coterie where it was all carried on—but now, Grazie a Messer domenedio,[11] the English are almost all gone, and we, being left alone, all subjects of discord and clacking cease—You may conceive what a bisbiglio[12] our adventure made.—The Pisans were all enraged because the maledetti Inglesi were not punished—yet when the gentlemen returned from their ride the following day (being festa) an immense crowd was assembled before Casa Lanfranchi; and they all took off their hats to them. Adieu. State bene e felice—best remembrances to Mr Gisborne, and Comp^ts^ to Emma. Henry, who will remember Hay as one of the Maremma hunters; he is a friend of Lord B—

Yours ever truly Mary WS.

PUBLISHED: Jones, #136. TEXT: John Gisborne Notebook No. 4, Abinger MS., Bodleian Library.

1. The altercation between the Shelley-Byron party and Sergeant Major Stefano Masi occurred on 24 March. Further details of the events are provided in *MWS Journal* and Williams, *Journals and Letters.* (A full account is found in Cline, *Pisan Circle*, pp. 91–154. See also Dowden, *Shelley*, II, 478–81; Marchand, *Byron*, III, 980–87, 989–90; and White, *Shelley*, II, 351–54.)

2. Captain John Hay was an old friend of Byron's and was very distantly related to him (Cline, *Pisan Circle*, pp. 86–89). On 3 April he departed for England (Williams, *Journals and Letters*).

3. Byron's coachman, Vincenzo Papi (Marchand, *Byron*, III, 986).

4. Byron's servant Giovanni Battista "Tita" Falcieri. Tita, who was innocent, and Vincenzo Papi were both arrested on 27 March. On 28 March Papi was released, but Teresa Guiccioli's servant Antonio Maluccelli was arrested. Tita was released at the end of April, and by 3 May he was with the Shelleys at Casa Magni. Maluccelli was held prisoner until 2 June, when he was ordered exiled from Tuscany along with Pietro Gamba and others of their party (Marchand, *Byron*, II, 741; III, 997, 1007).

5. "He had a fierce look, like a murderer."

6. Williams's *Journal* entry for 3 April noted that Byron was "willing to give his hand to Taaffe as usual—all right again" (Williams, *Journals and Letters*).

7. On 10 April Shelley wrote to John Gisborne acknowledging receipt of *Hellas*, "which is prettily printed, & with fewer mistakes than any poem I ever published." On 11 April Shelley sent Ollier an errata list (*PBS Letters*, #697).

8. "Very unhappy subject."

9. Ali Pasha was killed on 5 February by men who served Mahmud II (see 29 December 1820–1 January 1821, n. 12).

10. William Godwin, Jr. (see 21 February 1821, n. 3).

11. "Thanks to Sir God."
12. "Whisper."

*To Lord Byron [Pisa] one o'clock [12 April 1822][1]

I understand that Your Lordship wishes that Hunt should have a detailed account of your zuffa:[2] and Shelley (who is gone to Livorno) wished to send a copy of the report presented to the Governor here; could your secretary furnish me with a copy written small on thin paper.

We had a letter from Hunt today; he has engaged another passage & hopes to sail in the course of the present month. He has sent Fletcher's letter to his wife[3] with directions what to do.

I had a note from Mrs Beauclerk[4] today who says that she has only heard praises of your Lordship's conduct in the late affair both from Mr Dawkins[5] & the court; Excuse this annoyance from womankind[6] & allow me to hope that it will not be long before you employ me on my usual interesting task. Is there any hope of our ever getting a copy of the Vision of Judgement?[7]

truly Yours,
Mary Shelley

Unpublished. Text: MS., John Murray.

1. Mary Shelley's *Journal* records that on 12 April Shelley went to Leghorn and on 13 April she wrote to Hunt. Her letter to Hunt contained the account she requested of Byron in this letter.

2. "Altercation."

3. William Fletcher, hired by Byron in 1804 as a groom, became Byron's valet and remained with him until Byron's death (Moore, *Accounts Rendered*, p. 56). In Hunt's letter of 26 March 1822, informing the Shelleys that the Hunts would sail on the *David Walter* in a fortnight, he indicates that Mrs. Fletcher will be sailing with them and they will "attend to her comforts in every respect" (Hunt, *Correspondence*, I, 178).

4. Mrs. Beauclerc, daughter of the Duchess of Leinster, had seven daughters. At Pisa she gave frequent entertainments, which the Shelleys occasionally attended (Dowden, *Shelley*, II, 447). One of the daughters, Georgianna (called Gee in the *MWS Journal*), became Mary Shelley's close friend in England (*CC Journals*, pp. 240–41). Mrs. Beauclerc had left Pisa for Florence on 4 April 1822 (Cline, *Pisan Circle*, p. 129).

5. Edward Dawkins was Secretary to the Legation in Tuscany. Later he assisted Mary Shelley in making arrangements for Shelley's burial (see 21 August 1822).

6. See 5 March 1822, n. 3.

7. Byron's *The Vision of Judgment*, a satire of Southey's *A Vision of Judgment*, was written at Ravenna in September and October 1821 and published in the first issue of the *Liberal*, on 15 October 1822 (Marshall, *The Liberal*, pp. 53–55).

To Thomas Medwin Pisa. April 12th 1822

Dear Medwin

Excuse me that I write instead of Shelley, who you know is a very bad correspondent. At Lord Byron's desire I send you the copies of some of the documents concerning the row that took place a fortnight ago. You see what a goose Taaffe makes of himself; Lord B. says that the words he used were, "Shall we endure this man's insolence?" Lord B. replied, "No, we will bring him to an account." Masi after having been in great danger is now recovering & is to be removed from Pisa, as he vows deadly revenge; the Police here have imprisoned Tita & the Countess Guiccioli's servant, as suspected of having wounded the sergeant, they have been there a fortnight and one can guess when they will be let out: they are both perfectly innocent. It so happened that Mad[me] Guiccioli & I were in the carriage ten paces behind and saw the whole zuffa, and as you may suppose were not a little frightened. No measures have been taken except with these two men; no other person, more particularly none of the Gentlemen have been in any degree molested, but have ridden out as usual every day since. I say this because I hear that various reports have been circulated at Rome concerning the arrest of Lord B. all utterly devoid of foundation. You cannot conceive the part Taaffe played; as you may guess from his affidavit and as I saw with my own eyes, he kept at a safe distance during the row, but fearing to be sent out of Tuscany, he wrote at first such a report as embroiled him with Lord Byron, and what between insolence and dastard humility (a combination by no means uncommon in real life) kept himself in hot water when in fact he had nothing to fear.

You have of course heard that M[rs] Beauclerk has removed to Florence; Pisa is fast emptying of strangers. Lord B. will, I believe pass the summer in the vicinity of Livorno; but in all probability the W's [*Williamses*] & we shall be at la Spezia. During the last week we have suffered greatly from the cold; winter returned upon us, doubly disagreable from our having fostered the agreable hope that we had said a last rivederla. The country is however quite green, the blossoms are fading from the fruit trees, and if the wind change we shall feel summer at last.

Shelley has received Hellas from England; it is well printed & with not many faults. Lord B. seems pleased with it. His Lordship has had out from England a volume of poems entitled "Dramas of the Ancient World"[1]—and by a strange coincidence, the author (one David Lindsey) has chosen three subjects treated by Lord Byron; Cain, the Deluge and Sardanapalus. The two first are treated quite differently. Cain begins after the death of Abel & is entitled the Destiny & death of Cain. I mention them because they are works of considerable talent, and strength of poetry & expression; although of course in comparison with Lord Byron as unlike as Short life and Immortality. This is all the literary news I have for you.

I am afraid that you will be frightened at the immensity of the packet I send; but the papers were consigned to us by Lord B., and his name must be our excuse. The affidavits being in Italian will be an exercise for you, especially Taaffe's who has used I think all the many adverbs with which the Italian language is enriched withal. I could not prevail on myself to undertake the task of translating & tra{n}scribing such a rigmarole; especially as I am heartily tired of the whole subject; it flooded us at first, but the tide has now made its reflux, leaving the shingles of the mind as dry as ever. With the exception of some anxiety on the score of the two prisoners.

Edward is quite well; Jane I fancy will soon write to you. Our little Percy is as blooming as ever. I hope we shall be favoured with a visit on your return Northward; Shelley desires his best remembrances

Truly Yours
Mary W. Shelley

ADDRESS: Thomas Medwin Esq. PUBLISHED: Jones, #138. TEXT: MS., Keats-Shelley Memorial House, Rome.

1. Edinburgh, 1822. David Lyndsay was the pseudonym of Mary Diana Dods, who later became Mary Shelley's friend (see 30 October [1826] to Alaric A. Watts; [?30 October 1826] to Henry Colburn). On 9 April Williams also commented on the coincidence of Lyndsay's and Byron's subjects (Williams, *Journals and Letters*, p. 142).

To Leigh Hunt [Pisa 13 April 1822][1]

My dear Hunt

Shelley sends the enclosed order on Brooks although he hopes there is no necessity for it. This order was addressed to Brooks & you could not have the money until {this} past Lady Day.[2]

You will wonder what the enclosed is—If you read the first page you will find that it is an account of a brawl between the 5 gentlemen whose name are subjoined and a soldier here—It made a great noise, for the man (as you will find by the last affidavit) was wounded by a pitchfork & his life despaired of for some days. He was wounded, as is asserted, by a servant of Lord Byrons, and two of them are still imprisoned on suspicion though we know that those two in particular are perfectly innocent. The mode of conducting the judicial part of the affair is a specimen of their law here. While {the} Man was in danger not a single step was taken, & the man who wounded him had every opportunity to evade; as he got better they imprisoned these 2 men on suspicion, & they have been kept a fortnight on jail allowance without being allowed to see any friends, not even their wives, or to receive any assistance or even change of linen from their friends. The second paper is Taaffes affidavit—I think that before now I have had occasion to mention this wise little gentleman—he was riding with Lord B. at the time—& when he saw his friends in danger prudently kept out of the way: was afterwards terribly afraid of being implicated & turned out of Tuscany & so wrote the enclosed to justify himself. Of course if none of the public papers take notice of this affair do you not in your Examiner for there is no great glory attached to such a row; if however any garbled accounts get current, I should think you might manufacture from these documents, which are the judicial ones, a true statement. I ought not to omit that a lady writes to me from Florence[3] to say—that she hears nothing but praise of Lord Byron's & his friends' conduct on this occasion both from the English Minister, Mr. Dawkins & the Tuscan Court.

So much, my dear Friend, for this business to which Lord Byron attaches considerable importance, although to us, ever since the convalescence of the soldier it has been a matter of perfect indifference. Tell poor dear Marianne not to teaze her spirits by writing, but to nurse herself so that she may come safely and well. It appears to me a dream that you will ever reach these Tuscan shores—One begins to distrust every thing after so many disappointments. You will find Shelley in infinitely better health; indeed he has got over this winter delightfully. Pisa is a Paradise during that season for invalids, although I fear that Marianne will find it rather hot in the summer—but once here, I doubt not but that in some way all will go well.

You do not mention your health in the last letter, but I do not doubt that it is improved [in] exact proportion to the number of miles you are distant from London; God knows when I shall again see that benedetto luogo—but even at this distance it sometimes strikes me with sudden fright to think that any chain binds me to it.

My love to Marianne; I hope to have no answer to this letter but that you will in person acknowledge it—My dear Hunt

Affectionately yours
MaryWS.

The Gisbornes have my account of the zuffa; if you w[d] like to see it.

By the note to Taaffe's giuramento you will see that he is a bad horseman & that Lord Byron is accustomed to joke him on the many falls which he has had—while Taaffe always vows it was only salti del cavallo—that "come di entrare nel fosso[4] was a very famous affair.{"}

ADDRESS: Leigh Hunt, Esq. / Stone House / Near Plymouth / Inghilterra, Devon. / Angleterre. POSTMARKS: (1) PISA; (2) FPO / AP. 27 / 1822; (3) AP / 27 / 1822. PUBLISHED: Jones, #137. TEXT: MS., Bodleian Library (MS., Shelley, c. 1, ff. 516–17).

1. For date, see [12 April 1822] to Byron, n. 1.

2. The twenty-fifth of March, the feast of the Annunciation, one of the four dates on which Shelley received his quarterly payments. The other dates were 24 June, 29 September, and 25 December (*PBS Letters*, #288; for more information about Shelley's order, see *PBS Letters*, #696, #700).

3. See [12 April 1822] to Byron, n. 4.

4. "Jumps of the horse"; "how he entered the ditch."

TO MARIA GISBORNE — Casa Magni, presso a Lerici June 2nd 1822[1]

My Dear M[rs] Gisborne

We received a letter from M[r] G— [*Gisborne*] the other day, which promised one from you—It is not yet come, and although I think that you are two or three in my debt, yet I am good enough to write to you again, and thus to increase your debit—nor will I allow you, with one letter, to take advantage of the Insolvent act, and thus to free yourself from all claims at once. When I last wrote, I said, that I hoped our spring visitation had come and was gone—but this year we were not quit so easily—however, before I mention anything else, I will finish the story of the Zuffa, as far as it is yet gone. I think that in my last I left the Serjeant recovering; one of Lord B—'s and one of the Guiccioli's servants in prison, on suspicion, though both were innocent. The Judge or Advocate, called a Cancelliere, sent from Florence to determine the affair, disliked the Pisans, and having poca paga,[2] expected a present from Milordo, and so favoured our part of the affair, was very civil, and came to our houses to take depositions, against the law.[3] For the sake of the Lesson, Hogg should have been there, to learn to cross question The Cancelliere, a talkative buffon of a Florentine, with "mille scuse per l'incomodo," asked, "Dove fu lei la sera del 24 Marzo"? "Andai a spasso in carozza, fuori della Porta della Piaggia—"[4] A little clerk, seated beside him, with a great pile of papers before him, now dipt his pen in his Ink-horn—and looked expectant, while the Cancelliere, turning his eyes up to the ceiling repeated, "Io fui a spasso &c" This scene lasted two, four, six hours, as it happened—In the span of two months, the depositions of fifteen people were taken—and finding Tita (Lord B—'s servant) perfectly innocent, the Cancelliere ordered him to be liberated, but the Pisan Police took fright at his beard—they called him "il barbone," and although it was declared that on his exit from prison he should be shaved, they could not tranquillize their mighty minds, but banished him—We, in the meantime were come to this place, so he has taken refuge with us. He is an excellent fellow, faithful, courageous and daring—How could it happen that the Pisans should not be frightened at such a mirabile mostro of an Italian, especially as the day he was let out of secreto, and was a larga in prison, he gave a feast to all his fellow prisoners, hiring chandeliers and plate—But poor Antonio, the Guiccioli's servant, the meekest hearted fellow in the world is kept in secret, not found guilty, but punished as such—e chi sa when he will be let out—so rests the affair—

About a month ago Claire came to visit us at Pisa, and went, with the Williams's to find a house in the Gulph of Spezia; when, during her absence, the disastrous news came of the death of Allegra[5]—She died of a typhus fever, which had been raging in the Romagna; but no one wrote to say it was there—she had no friends, except the nuns of the Convent, who were kind to her, I believe, but you know Italians—If half of the Convent had died of the plague, they would never have written to have had her removed, and so the poor child fell a sacrifice. Lord B— felt the loss, at first, bitterly—he also felt remorse, for he felt that he had acted against every body's councils and wishes, and death had stamped with truth the many and often urged prophecies of Claire, that the air of the Romagna, joined to the ignorance of the Italians, would prove fatal to her. Shelley wished to conceal the fatal news from her, as long as possible, so when she returned from Spezia, he resolved to remove thither without delay—with so little delay, that he packed me off with Claire and Percy the very next day. She wished to return to Florence, but he persuaded her to accompany me—The next day, he packed up all our goods and chattels, (for a furnished house was not to be found in this part of the world) and like a torrent, hurrying every thing in it's course, he persuaded the W's [*Williamses*] to do the same.—They came here—but one house was to be found for us all—It is beautifully situated on the sea shore, under a woody hill.—But such a place as this is! The poverty of the people is beyond anything—Yet, they do not appear unhappy, but go on in dirty content, or contented dirt, while we find it hard work to purvey, miles around for a few eatables—We were in wretched discomfort at first, but now we are in a kind of disorderly order, living from day to day as we can—After the first day or two, Claire insisted on returning to Florence—so S— was obliged to disclose the truth—You may judge of what was her first burst of grief, and despair—however she reconciled herself to her fate, sooner than we expected; and although of course, until she form new ties, she will always grieve, yet she is now tranquil—more tranquil than, when prophesying her disaster, she was forever forming plans for getting her child from a place she judged, but too truly, would be fatal to her. She has now returned to Florence, and I do not know whether she will join us again. Our colony is much smaller than we expected, which we consider a benefit—Lord B— remains with his train at Monte Nero—Trelawny is to be the commander of his vessel, and, of course, will be at Leghorn—He is, at present at Genoa, awaiting the finishing of this boat—Shelley's boat is a beautiful creature. Henry would admire her greatly—though only 24 feet by 8, she is a perfect little ship, and looks twice her size—She had one fault—she was to have been built in partnership with Williams and Trelawny—T—y chose the name of the Don Juan, and we acceded; but when Shelley took her entirely on himself, we changed the name to the Ariel—Lord B— chose to take fire at this, and determined she should be called after the poem—wrote to Roberts to have the name painted on the mainsail, and she arrived thus disfigured—for days and nights full twenty one did Shelley and Edward ponder on her anabaptism, and the washing out the primeval stain. turpentine, spirits of wine, buccata, all were tried, and it became dappled and no more—at length the piece has been taken out, and reefs put, so the sail does not look worse. I do not know what L^d B— will say, but Lord and poet as he is, he could not be allowed to make a coal-barge of our boat.[6] As only one house was to be found habitable in this gulph, the W's's have taken up their abode with us, and their servants and mine quarrel like cats and dogs; and besides you may imagine how ill a large family agrees with my laziness, when accounts and domestic concerns come to be talked of.—"Ma pazienza"—after all, the place does not please me—the people are rozzi,[7] and speak a detestable dialect.—and yet it is better than any other Italian sea-shore north of Naples —the air is excellent, and you may guess how much better we like it than

Leghorn, where besides we should have been involved in English Society, a thing we longed to get rid of at Pisa. M[r] G— talks of your going to a distant country. Pray write to me in time before this takes place, as I want a box from England first, but cannot now exactly name its contents. I am sorry to hear you do not get on; but perhaps Henry will, and make up for all. Percy is well and S— singularly so, his incessant boating does him a great deal of good. I had been very unwell for some time past, but am better now.

I have not even heard of the arrival of my novel; but I suppose, for his own sake, Papa will dispose of it to the best advantage[8]—If you see it advertized, pray tell me—also its publisher &c &c. We have heard from Hunt the day he was to sail, and anxiously and daily now await his arrival—S— will go over to Leghorn to him, and I also, if I can so manage it—We shall be at Pisa next winter, I believe—fate so decrees—Of course you have heard that the lawsuit went against my father.—this was the summit and crown of our spring misfortunes—but he writes in so few words, and in such a manner, that any information that I could get, through anyone, would be a great benefit to me.[9]

Adieu—Pray write now, and at length—remember both S— and I to Hogg—Did you get Matilda from Papa?

Your's ever,
Mary W. Shelley.

Continue to direct to Pisa

PUBLISHED: Jones, #139. TEXT: John Gisborne Notebook No. 4, Abinger MS., Bodleian Library.

1. The Shelleys had moved to Casa Magni at San Terenzo, near Lerici, on the Gulf of Spezia on 30 April (*MWS Journal*).

2. "Small salary."

3. Byron's courier was questioned on 18 April; Mary Shelley and Teresa Guiccioli were questioned on 19 April; on 20 April further depositions were taken at Byron's house, and Williams wrote: "It is singular enough that suspicion should fall on me as the murderer" (Williams was not present at the affray); on 22 April Trelawny was questioned; and on 26 April Williams was questioned (Williams, *Journals and Letters*, pp. 144–45).

4. "A thousand apologies for the inconvenience" . . . "Where were you on the night of the 24th of March?" . . . "I went for a diversion in a carriage, outside the Porta della Piaggia."

5. Claire Clairmont arrived at Pisa on 15 April. On 23 April she and the Williamses went to Spezia to seek summer quarters. On the same day, news came of Allegra's death at Bagnacavallo on 19 April. Anxious that Claire Clairmont not learn of the death while in the vicinity of Byron, Shelley rushed Claire Clairmont, Mary Shelley, and Percy to Spezia on 26 April, and he and the Williamses followed the next day. On 1 May the Williamses, unable to find other accommodations, moved in with the Shelleys at Casa Magni. On 2 May Claire Clairmont was told of Allegra's death. She returned to Florence on 21 May, but on 7 June she rejoined the Shelleys and the Williamses (Williams, *Journals and Letters*; Marchand, *Byron*, III, 991–96; *PBS Letters*, #702, #703).

6. Although Shelley had wanted to change the name of his boat to the *Ariel*, he

accepted the name *Don Juan* (see 16 September 1822); however, he objected to its name being painted in large letters across the mainsail (*MWS Letters*, I, #139, n. 3; White, *Shelley*, II, 366).

7. "Coarse."

8. Shelley's letter of 29 May to Mrs. Godwin indicates that Godwin had written to Mary Shelley about *Valperga*. The information about the novel, however, was in one of many letters from Godwin outlining his dire financial situation as a result of the Skinner Street-rent lawsuit decision given against him. By the end of May Mary Shelley was approximately three months pregnant. Because Godwin's letters seriously upset her already poor health, it was agreed by the Shelleys that Godwin's letters to Mary Shelley would be received and read by Mrs. Mason, who would then send all or parts of the letters to Shelley, who would then relate to Mary Shelley whatever information he thought appropriate. From Shelley's letter of 29 May we learn that Godwin intended to withhold *Valperga* from publication for fear that booksellers might give him less than its worth because of his publicized financial distress. Shelley must have suppressed this information, knowing Mary Shelley's interest in having her novel published and perhaps concerned that *Valperga*, like *Matilda*, might come to nought in Godwin's hands (*PBS Letters*, #709, #710, #711; Mrs. Mason to Shelley, *S&M*, III, 800–802).

9. Godwin's letters of 19 April and 3 May and William Godwin, Jr.'s letter of 24 June, published together with Shelley's 29 April letter to Mrs. Godwin, his c. 21 May letter to Horace Smith, and Smith's 5 June response to Shelley, offer many details of the pressure exerted on the Shelleys by Godwin, as well as details of the Shelleys' efforts on Godwin's behalf (*PBS Letters*, #708, #710).

To Leigh Hunt [Casa Magni c. 30 June 1822][1]

My dear Friend—

I know that S. has some idea of persuading you to come here I am too ill[2] to write the reasonings only let me entreat you let no persuasions induce you to come, selfish feelings you may be sure do not dictate me—but it w[d] be complete madness to come—

I wish I c[d] write more—I wish I were with you to assist you—I wish I c[d] break my chains & leave this dungeon[3]—adieu—I shall { } about you & Marianne's health from S—

Yor fn
M.

ADDRESS: Leigh Hunt Esq. PUBLISHED: Jones, #140. TEXT: MS., Princeton University Library.

1. The Hunts had arrived at Genoa on 15 June. On 1 July they reached Leghorn, and on the same day, Shelley and Williams sailed from Casa Magni to Leghorn to welcome them and escort them to their residence at Casa Lanfranchi at Pisa. This letter, which bears no postmark, was probably carried by Shelley to Hunt.

2. On 16 June Mary Shelley had suffered a near-fatal miscarriage (see 15 August 1822).

3. The crowded conditions at Casa Magni, its remoteness, and the rusticity of the local populace greatly distressed Mary Shelley, who urged Shelley to find a less desolate place for the remainder of the summer (see 3 July 1822).

*To [Shelley][1] [Casa Magni] 3 Luglio [*July*] 1822

[ ]r order & cleanliness w^d under
[ ]alk to her also about Claire
[ ]o not understand—& ask for my

that have more
[?] the paper with
Remember me to the
[Tr]elawny a kiss from
[ ]r & so farewel

Yours Entirely
MaryWS

Retta[2]
[?place] all [o]ur own

Unpublished. Text: MS., Bodleian Library (MS., Shelley, Adds., c. 12, f. 78). One-page, damaged fragment, 8″ × 5″; wove paper; watermark: [BENEDETTO PAR]ODI. Letters dated 29 July 1822 and [c. 27 August 1822] were also written on wove paper bearing the watermark BENEDETTO PARODI. Since they were on paper measuring 10 1/16″ × 7½″, we may estimate that more than 2 inches are missing from the left side of the fragment and up to 2½ inches may be missing from the bottom.

1. The signature on this badly damaged fragment makes clear that the letter was written to Shelley. On 4 July Shelley wrote Mary Shelley that he had received both of her letters and would attend to the instructions in them. Shelley also informed her that he had not yet looked into the possibility of houses available near Pugnano and concluded with an expression of concern for her health and the hope that she was "more reconciled to staying at Casa Magni at least during the summer" (*PBS Letters*, #720). On 4 July Shelley also wrote to Jane Williams reflecting that the Williamses' and the Shelleys' happy days at Casa Magni might be over forever (*PBS Letters*, #721). Jane Williams understood Shelley's "melancholy lines" as a prediction of his death or hers (Williams, *Journals and Letters*, pp. 160–61). It is quite possible, however, that Shelley was referring to Mary Shelley's unhappiness in the cramped quarters of Casa Magni and her desire to remove from there, a desire Shelley clearly did not share (see 15 August 1822).

Having settled the Hunts at Pisa, Shelley returned to Leghorn on 7 July. On 8 July Shelley, Williams, and Charles Vivian (a sailor-boy who assisted in working the boat) sailed for San Terenzo. Caught in a sqall off the coast of Viareggio that capsized their boat, they were drowned. Mary Shelley's letter of 15 August to Maria Gisborne gives a detailed account of the events before and including the drowning, ending on the day Trelawny sailed to meet Hunt and Byron in order to cremate the remains of Shelley and Williams.

The circumstances and physical condition of this letter suggest that it may have been among Shelley's papers on the *Don Juan* and was returned to Mary Shelley along with other•articles recovered (see 16 September 1822; 17–20 September 1822).

2. "Attention."

To THE POSTMASTER AT SARZANA [Casa Magni 15 July 1822][1]

Monsieur,

Je vous prie d'avoir la bonté de m'expedier mes lettres le moment qu'elles arrivent ou que ce soit par nuit ou par jour, car il est absolument necessaire dans le moment actuel, que je les recois aussi-tot que possible. Pardonnez, je vous prie, Monsieur, la peine que je vous coute et recevez mes remercimens pour tous les attentions que vous avez eu pour nous. Je suis

Villa Magni—Lerici

&. &.
M. SHELLEY

[*Translation*]

Sir

Would you have the kindness to send me my letters the moment that they arrive whether it be at night or day, because it is absolutely necessary just now that I receive them as soon as possible. Please, Sir, excuse the trouble that I cause you and accept my thanks for all the care you have shown us. I am

Villa Magni—Lerici

&. &.
M. SHELLEY

ADDRESS: A Monsieur / Monsieur le Directeur de la Poste / a Sarzana. PUBLISHED: Ubaldo Mazzini, "Lettera inedita di Maria Shelley," *La Spezia a P. B. Shelley* (Spezia, 27 October 1907), p. 18. TEXT: *La Spezia a P. B. Shelley*, copy at Keats-Shelley Memorial House, Rome.

1. Mazzini conjectures the date of this letter to be 15 July, since the postmaster endorsed the letter as received on the sixteenth ("Lettera inedita di Maria Shelley," p. 18). Until 19 July, when Trelawny informed Mary Shelley and Jane Williams that Shelley's and Williams's bodies had been found, the two women sought information (see 15 August 1822).

To AMELIA CURRAN Pisa July 26th 1822[1]

My dear Miss Curran

You will have received my letter concerning the pictures[2] and now I have another request to make. Your kindness to us when we were both so unhappy, your great kindness, makes me do this without that feeling of unwillingness which I have in asking favours of any other person. Besides you are unhappy, and therefore you can better sympathize with and console the miserable.

You w[d] greatly oblige me if you w[d] get me from one of those shops in the Piazza di Spagna two mosaic stones about as large as on one I wish an heart's ease to be depicted they call these flowers in Italian—Tocera, Nuora or Viola farfalla Viola regolina—or Viola una jola—on the other (I think I have seen such an one) a view of the tomb of Cestius.[3] I remember also that in one of your rooms there was a view of this place & the people of the house might part with it—or a modern artist at Rome might make one for me which would give me great pleasure—The difficulty is to pay you for these things—but I will take care—as soon (if you have the extreme kindness to fulfill my requests) as I know what money you spend for me I will take care that it shall be remitted to you without delay.

Will you indeed, my dear Miss Curran, do as I ask you—alas these trifles (not the picture that is no trifle) serve as a kind of vent for those sentiments of personal affection & attentions which are so cruelly crushed for ever—In a little poem of his are these words—pansies let my flowers be pansies are hearts ease—and in another he says that pansies mean memory[4] —so I would make myself a locket to wear in eternal memory with the representation of his flower & with his hair—such things now must do instead of words of love & the dear habit of seeing him daily—Pity me then & indulge me.

In my last letter I was so selfish that I did not ask after your welfare—pray write to me—I must ever be grateful to you for your kindness to us in misfortune & how much more now when through your talents & your goodness I shall possess the only likeness there is of my husband's earthy form.

My little Percy is well—not so beautiful as William—though there is some resemblance

Your's ever truly
MaryWShelley

I would add that several reasons make me entreat you to send these things speedily as I shall soon leave Italy—heat does not agree with my boy—nor w[d] I not have risked this summer had not I seen S. getting better & better under the influence of the climate—When I say soon I mean perhaps a month or 6 weeks—before the snows cover the alps—

ADDRESS: Miss Curran / 64 Via Sistina / all'arco della Begina / Terzo Piano—Roma. POSTMARKS: (1) PISA; (2) 1 AGOSTO; (3) FPO / AU. 20 / 1822; (4) CHAMBERY; (5) 9 SETTEMBRE. PUBLISHED: Jones, #141. TEXT: MS., Bodleian Library (MS., Shelley, c. 1, ff. 518–19).

1. On 20 July Mary Shelley, Jane Williams, and Claire Clairmont had returned to Pisa, where they lived together until 11 September.

2. Amelia Curran's response of 6 October, written from Paris, makes clear that she had not received Mary Shelley's first letter, obviously written shortly after Shelley's death. Of the pictures requested, she wrote: "Your picture and Clare's I left with him [Mr. Brunelli] to give you, when you should be at Rome, as I expected, before you returned to England. The one you now write for I thought was not to be inquired for; it was so ill done, and I was on the point of burning it with others before I left Italy. I luckily saved it just as the fire was scorching it, and it is packed up with my other pictures at Rome; and I have not yet decided where they can be sent to, as there are serious difficulties in the way I had not adverted to. I am very sorry indeed, dear Mary, but you shall have it as soon as I possibly can" (*S&M*, III, 886). The portrait was the topic of correspondence between Mary Shelley and Amelia Curran for the next few years. To Mary Shelley's letter of 2

January [1825], Amelia Curran responded on 19 April 1825: "I waited to write to you until I could say that, at last, I had found an opportunity of sending the picture you are so anxious about. I fear it will disappoint you. You condemned it at first, I recollect. If you can get anything done from it that you think better, pray keep the original for me. I should have made another sketch of the head, had I painted since my return. It is enclosed in a small case of pictures to Edgell Wyatt-Edgell, Esq., care of Messrs. Calron, Wine Merchants, St. Mary's Hill, Fenchurch Street, London. If the duty on pictures has not been taken off, as we hear, you will have to pay it. The picture is to be delivered expenses paid; it is the best I could do to forward it to you. The sketch of my little favourite William I could not send you at present, but you shall have it another time, or when you come" (*S&M*, IV, 1062). Mary Shelley finally received the portrait on 7 September 1825 and recorded in her Journal: "Thy picture is come, my only One—thine those speaking eyes that mild yet animated look—Unlike aught earthy wert thou ever & art now . . ." (see 25 February [1826]).

3. In December 1818, Shelley had sent Peacock the following description of the burying ground: "The English bur[y]ing place is a green slope near the walls, under the pyramidal tomb of Cestius, & is I think the most beautiful & solemn cemetery I ever beheld. To see the sun shining on its bright grass fresh when we visited it with the autumnal dews, & hear the whispering of the wind among the leaves of the trees which have overgrown the tomb of Cestius, & the coil which is stirring in the sunwarm earth & to mark the tombs mostly of women & young people who were buried there, one might, if one were to die, desire the sleep they seem to sleep. Such is the human mind & so it peoples with its wishes vacancy & oblivion" (*PBS Letters*, #488).

4. "Remembrance," line 20; and "An Ode Written October, 1819, Before the Spaniards Had Recovered their Liberty," lines 34–35. See also the example of the pansy in *Adonais* 33. 1.

To Thomas Medwin [Pisa] July 29th 1822

Dear Medwin

At Jane's request I inclose you this letter—Of course the horse is useless to her, nor cd she keep it in any way nor can she in her state of mind attend to it—If nothing else can be done with it you can sell it to pay its expences—but you will be so kind as to attend to the affair yourself.

I ought to say something more about that which has left us in desolation—but why should I atrister you with my despair. I will only mention Jane, since you will be interested & anxious perhaps—She is not well—she does not sleep—but I hope with care she may get better—God knows!—she must have struggles & no one is more unfit for them—no woman had ever more need of a protector—but we shall be together & until she joins either her Mother or Edwards brother[1] who is expected next year I shall be with her. Seven or ⟨Six⟩ weeks ago—just three weeks before this blank moral death visited me I was very ill—near dying—but I have got through it all—I had not been out of the house from illness when Jane & I posted to Leghorn from Lerici to get intelligence of them & without intelligence—without rest we returned—to wait ten days for the confirmation of our sentence of a life of eternal pain—Yet not eternal—I think we are all short lived—but for my child I would take up my abode at Rome—Rome is a good nurse & soon rocks to a quiet grave those who seek death

I scrawl all this nonsense I know not why—I intended to have written two words only—but grief makes my mind active & my pen in my hand I run on by instinct I could do so for sheets.

Adieu—I hope you will be happy—

Yours very truly
MaryWShelley

S. & I were united exactly 8 years ago yesterday—on the 4th of August he w^{d} have been 30—Except that his health was getting better & better I w^{d} not selfishly desire that his angelic spirit sh^{d} again inhabit that frame which tormented it—he is alive & often with me now—Every one feels the same, all say that he was an elemental spirit imprisoned here but free & happy now—I am not now—one day I hope to be worthy to join him—my life is chalked out to me—it will be one of study only—Except for my poor boy—

The children are in excellent health—

ADDRESS: A Monsieur / Monsieur Medwin / Poste Restante / Geneve. POSTMARK: Pisa. PUBLISHED: Jones, #142. TEXT: MS., Keats-Shelley Memorial House, Rome.

1. Captain John Williams (see 7 March 1823, n. 11).

TO AMELIA CURRAN — Pisa. August 14th 1822

My dear Miss Curran

I have written two letters to you, requesting that favour now nearer my heart than any other earthly thing—the picture of my Shelley.—Perhaps you have been at Gensano[1] & that delays your reply, perhaps you have altered your residence and have not received my letters. I write to you now through the medium of Torlonia[2] to tell you this—the letters were directed 64 Via Sistina—

I am well so is my boy—We leave Italy soon so I am particularly anxious to obtain this treasure, that I am sure you will give me, as soon as possible. I have no other likeness of him—& in so utter a desolation how invaluable to me is your picture? Will you not send it? Will you not answer me without delay?—Your former kindness bids me hope everything.

Very sincerely yours,
MWShelley

PUBLISHED: Jones, #143. TEXT: MS., Bodleian Library (MS., Shelley, c. 1, f. 520).

1. Gensano is about twenty miles southeast of Rome.

2. In Rome Shelley had banked with Messrs. Torlonia & Co., a banking empire founded by Giovanni-Raimondo Torlonia (1775–1829), Duke of Bracciano (*SC*, VII, 801).

To Maria Gisborne — Pisa August 15th 1822

I said in a letter to Peacock, my dear Mrs Gisborne, that I would send you some account of the last miserable months of my disastrous life. From day to day I have put this off, but I will now endeavour to fulfill my design. The scene of my existence is closed & though there be no pleasure in retracing the scenes that have preceded the event which has crushed my hopes yet there seems to be a necessity in doing so, and I obey the impulse that urges me. I wrote to you either at the end of May or the beginning of June. I described to you the place we were living in:—Our desolate house, the beauty yet strangeness of the scenery and the delight Shelley took in all this—he never was in better health or spirits than during this time. I was not well in body or mind. My nerves were wound up to the utmost irritation, and the sense of misfortune hung over my spirits. No words can tell you how I hated our house & the country about it. Shelley reproached me for this—his health was good & the place was quite after his own heart—What could I answer—that the people were wild & hateful, that though the country was beautiful yet I liked a more countryfied place, that there was great difficulty in living—that all our Tuscans would leave us, & that the very jargon of these Genovese was disgusting—This was all I had to say but no words could describe my feelings—the beauty of the woods made me weep & shudder—so vehement was my feeling of dislike that I used to rejoice when the winds & waves permitted me to go out in the boat so that I was not obliged to take my usual walk among tree shaded paths, allies of vine festooned trees—all that before I doated on—& that now weighed on me. My only moments of peace were on board that unhappy boat, when lying down with my head on his knee I shut my eyes & felt the wind & our swift motion alone. My ill health might account for much of this—bathing in the sea somewhat relieved me—but on the 8th of June (I think it was) I was threatened with a miscarriage, & after a week of great ill health on sunday the 16th this took place at eight in the morning. I was so ill that for seven hours I lay nearly lifeless—kept from fainting by brandy, vinegar eau de Cologne &c—at length ice was brought to our solitude—it came before the doctor so Claire & Jane were afraid of using it but Shelley overuled them & by an unsparing application of it I was restored. They all thought & so did I at one time that I was about to die—I hardly wish that I had, my own Shelley could never have lived without me, the sense of eternal misfortune would have pressed to heavily upon him, & what would have become of my poor babe? My convalescence was slow and during it a strange occurence happened to retard it. But first I must describe our house to you. The floor on which we lived was thus

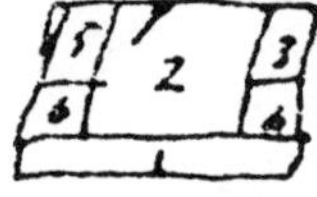

1 is a terrace that went the whole length of our house & was precipitous to the sea. 2 the large dining hall —3, a private staircase. 4 my bedroom 5 M^{rs} [*Wil-*

liams's] bedroom, 6 Shelleys & 7 the entrance from the great staircase. Now to return. As I said Shelley was at first in perfect health but having over fatigued himself one day, & then the fright my illness gave him caused a return of nervous sensations & visions as bad as in his worst times. I think it was the saturday after my illness while yet unable to walk I was confined to my bed—in the middle of the night I was awoke by hearing him scream & come rushing into my room; I was sure that he was asleep & tried to waken him by calling on him, but he continued to scream which inspired me with such a panic that I jumped out of bed & ran across the hall to M^rs^ W's room where I fell through weakness, though I was so frightened that I got up again immediately—she let me in & Williams went to S. who had been wakened by my getting out of bed[1]—he said that he had not been alseep & that it was a vision that he saw that had frightened him—But as he declared that he had not screamed it was certainly a dream & no waking vision—What had frightened him was this—He dreamt that lying as he did in bed Edward & Jane came into him, they were in the most horrible condition, their bodies lacerated—their bones starting through their skin, the faces pale yet stained with blood, they could hardly walk, but Edward was the weakest & Jane was supporting him—Edward said—Get up, Shelley, the sea is flooding the house & it is all coming down." S. got up, he thought, & went to the his window that looked on the terrace & the sea & thought he saw the sea rushing in. Suddenly his vision changed & he saw the figure of himself strangling me, that had made him rush into my room, yet fearful of frightening me he dared not approch the bed, when my jumping out awoke him, or as he phrased it caused his vision to vanish. All this was frightful enough, & talking it over the next morning he told me that he had had many visions lately—he had seen the figure of himself which met him as he walked on the terrace & said to him—"How long do you mean to be content"—No very terrific words & certainly not prophetic of what has occurred. But Shelley had often seen these figures when ill; but the strangest thing is that Mrs W. saw him. Now Jane though a woman of sensibility, has not much imagination & is not in the slightest degree nervous—neither in dreams or otherwise. She was standing one day, the day before I was taken ill, at a window that looked on the Terrace with Trelawny—it was day—she saw as she thought Shelley pass by the window, as he often was then, without a coat or jacket—he passed again—now as he passed both times the same way—and as from the side towards which he went each time there was no way to get back except past the window again (except over a wall twenty feet from the ground) she was struck at seeing him pass twice thus & looked out & seeing him no more she cried—"Good God can Shelley have leapt from the wall? Where can he be gone?" Shelley, said Trelawny—"No Shelley has past—What do you mean?" Trelawny says that she trembled exceedingly when she heard this & it proved indeed that Shelley had never been on the terrace & was far off at the time she saw him. Well we thought {no} more of these things & I slowly got better. Having heard from Hunt that he had sailed from Genoa, on Monday July 1st S., Edward & Captain Roberts (the Gent. who built our boat) departed in our boat for Leghorn to receive him—I was then just better, had begun to crawl from my bed-room to the terrace; but bad spirits succeded to ill health, and this departure of Shelley's seemed to add insuferably to my misery. I could not endure that he should go—I called him back two or three times, & told him that if I did not see him soon I would go to Pisa with the child—I cried bitterly when he went away. They went & Jane, Claire & I remained alone with the children—I could not walk out, & though I gradually gathered strength it was slowly & my ill spirits encreased; in my letters to him I entreated him to return—"the feeling that some misfortune would happen," I said, "haunted me": I feared for the child, for the idea of danger connected with him never struck me—When Jane & Claire took their evening walk I used to patrole the terrace, oppressed with wretchedness, yet gazing on the most beautiful scene in the world. This Gulph of Spezia is subdivided into many small bays of which ours was far the most beautiful—the two horns of the bay (so to express myself) were wood covered promontories crowned with castles—at the foot of these on the furthest was Lerici on the nearest Sant Arenzo—Lerici being above a mile by land from us & San Arenzo about a hundred or two yards—trees covered the hills that enclosed this bay & then beautiful groups were picturesquely contrasted with the rocks the castle on [*and*] the town—the sea lay far extended in front while to the west we saw the promontory & islands which formed one of the extreme boundarys of the Gulph—to see the sun set upon this scene, the stars shine & the moon rise was a sight of wondrous beauty, but to me it added only to my wretchedness—I repeated to myself all that another would have said to console me, & told myself the tale of love peace & competence which I enjoyed—but I answered myself by tears—did not my William die? & did I hold my Percy by a firmer tenure?—Yet I thought when he, when my Shelley returns I shall be happy—he will comfort me, if my boy be ill he will restore him & encourage me. I had a letter or two from Shelley mentioning the difficulties he had in establishing the Hunts,[2] & that he was unable to fix the time of his return. Thus a week past. On Monday 8th Jane had a letter from Edward, dated saturday, he said that he waited at Leghorn for S. who was at Pisa That S's return was certain, "but" he continued, "if he should not come by monday I will come in a felucca, & you may expect me teusday evening at furthest."[3] This was monday, the fatal monday, but with us it was stormy all day & we did not at all suppose that they could put to sea. At twelve at night we had a thunderstorm; Teusday it rained all day & was calm—the sky wept on their graves—on Wednesday—the wind was fair from Leghorn & in the evening several felucca's arrived thence—one brought word that they had sailed monday, but we did not believe them—thursday was another day of fair wind & when twelve at night came & we did not see the tall sails of the little boat double the promontory before us we began to fear not the truth, but some illness—some disagreable news for their detention. Jane got so uneasy that she determined to proceed the next day to Leghorn in a boat to see what was the matter—friday came & with it a heavy sea & bad wind—Jane however resolved to be rowed to Leghorn (since no boat could sail) and busied herself in preparations—I wished her to wait for letters, since friday was letter day—she would not—but the sea detained her, the swell rose so that no boat would venture out—At 12 at noon our letters came—there was one from Hunt to Shelley, it said—"pray write to tell us how you got home, for they say that you had bad weather after you sailed monday & we are anxious"—the paper fell from me—I trembled all over—Jane read it—"Then it is all over!" she said. "No, my dear Jane," I cried, "it is not all over, but this suspense is dreadful—come with me, we will go to Leghorn, we will post to be swift & learn our fate." We crossed to Lerici, despair in our hearts; they raised our spirits there by telling us that no accident had been heard of & that it must have been known &c—but still our fear was great—& without resting we posted to Pisa It must have been fearful to see us—two poor, wild, aghast creatures—driving (like Matilda)[4] towards the sea to learn if we were to be for ever doomed to misery. I knew that Hunt was at Pisa at Lord Byrons' house but I thought that L. B. was at Leghorn. I settled that we should drive to Casa Lanfranchi that I should get out & ask the fearful question of Hunt, "do you know any thing of Shelley?" On entering Pisa the idea of seeing Hunt for the first time for four years under such circumstances, & asking him such a question was so terrific to me that it was with difficulty that I prevented myself from going into convulsions—my struggles were dreadful—they knocked at the door & some one called out "Chi è?" it was the Guiccioli's maid L.B. was in Pisa—Hunt was in bed, so I was to see LB. instead of him—This was a great relief to me; I staggered up stairs—the Guiccioli came to meet me smiling while I could hardly say—"Where is he—Sapete alcuna cosa di Shelley"—They knew nothing—he had left Pisa on sunday—on Monday he had sailed—there had been bad weather monday afternoon—more they knew not. Both LB & the lady have told me since—that on that terrific evening I looked more like a ghost than a woman—light seemed to emanate from my features, my face was very white I looked like marble—Alas. I had risen almost from a bed of sickness for this journey—I had travelled all day—it was now 12 at night—& we, refusing to rest, proceeded to Leghorn—not in despair—no, for then we must have died; but with sufficient hope to keep up the agitation of the spirits which was all my life. It was past two in the morning when we arrived—They took us to the wrong inn—neither Trelawny or Cap^{n} Roberts were there nor did we exactly know where they were so we were obliged to wait until daylight. We threw ourselves drest on our beds & slept a little but at 6 o'clock we went to one or two inns to ask for one or the other of these gentlemen. We found Roberts at the Globe. He came down to us with a face which seemed to tell us that the worst was true, and here we learned all that had occurred during the week they had been absent from us, & under what circumstances they had departed on their return.———— Shelley had past most of the time a[t] Pisa—arranging the affairs of the Hunts—& skrewing LB's mind to the sticking place[5] about the journal. He had found this a difficult task at first but at length he had succeeded to his heart's content with both points. Mrs Mason said that she saw him in better health and spirits than she had ever known him, when he took leave of her sunday July 7th His face burnt by the sun, & his heart light that he had succeeded in rendering the Hunts' tolerably comfortable. Edward had remained at Leghorn. On Monday July 8th during the morning they were employed in buying many things—eatables &c for our solitude. There had been a thunderstorm early but about noon the weather was fine & the wind right fair for Lerici—They were impatient to be gone. Roberts said, "Stay until tomorrow to see if the weather is settled; & S. might have staid but Edward was in so great an anxiety to reach home—saying they would get there in seven hours with that wind—that they sailed! S. being in one of those extravagant fits of good spirits in which you have sometimes seen him. Roberts went out to the end of the mole & watched them out of sight—they sailed at one & went off at the rate of about 7 knots—About three—Roberts, who was still on the mole—saw wind coming from the Gulph—or rather what the Italians call a temporale anxious to know how the boat wd weather the storm, he got leave to go up the tower & with the glass discovered them about ten miles out at sea, off Via Reggio, they were taking in their topsails—"The haze of the storm," he said, "hid them from me & I saw them no more—when the storm cleared I looked again fancying that I should see them on their return to us—but there was no boat on the sea."—This then was all we knew, yet we did not despair—they might have been driven over to Corsica & not knowing the coast & Gone god knows where. Reports favoured this belief.—it was even said that they had been seen in the Gulph—We resolved to return with all possible speed—We sent a courier to go from tower to tower along the coast to know if any thing had been seen or found, & at 9 AM. we quitted Leghorn—stopped but one moment at Pisa & proceeded towards Lerici. When at 2 miles from Via Reggio we rode down to that town to know if they knew any thing—here our calamity first began to break on us—a little boat & a water cask had been found five miles off—they had manufactured a piccolissima lancia of thin planks stitched by a shoemaker just to let them run on shore without wetting themselves as our boat drew 4 feet water.—the description of that found tallied with this—but then this boat was very cumbersome & in bad weather they might have been easily led to throw it overboard—the cask frightened me most—but the same reason might in some sort be given for that. I must tell you that Jane & I were not now alone—Trelawny accompanied us back to our home. We journied on & reached the Magra about ½ past ten P.M. I cannot describe to you what I felt in the first moment when, fording this river, I felt the water splash about our wheels—I was suffocated—I gasped for breath I thought I should have gone into convulsions, & I struggled violently that Jane might not perceive it—looking down the river I saw the two great lights burning at the foce—A voice from within me seemed to cry aloud that is his grave. After passing the river I gradually recovered. Arriving at Lerici we {were} obliged to cross our little bay in a boat—San Arenzo was illuminated for a festa—what a scene—the roaring sea—the scirocco wind—the lights of the town towards which we rowed—& our own desolate hearts—that coloured all with a shroud—we landed; nothing had been heard of them. This was saturday July 13. & thus we waited until Thursday July 25th[6] thrown about by hope & fear. We sent messengers along the coast towards Genoa & to Via Reggio— nothing had been found more than the lancetta; reports were brought us—we hoped—& yet to tell you all the agony we endured during those 12 days would be to make you conceive a universe of pain—each moment intolerable & giving place to one still worse. The people of the country too added to one's discomfort—they are like wild savages—on festa's the men & women & children in different bands—the sexes always separate—pass the whole night in dancing on the sands close to our door running into the sea then back again & screaming all the time one perpetuel air—the most detestable in the world—then the scirocco perpetually blew & the sea for ever moaned their dirge. On thursday 25th[7] Trelawny left us to go to Leghorn to see what was doing or what could be done. On friday I was very ill but as evening came on I said to Jane—"If any thing had been found on the coast Trelawny would have returned to let us know. He has not returned so I hope." About 7 o'clock P.M. he did return—all was over—all was quiet now, they had been found washed on shore—Well all this was to be endured.

Well what more have I to say? The next day we returned to Pisa[8] And here we are still—days pass away—one after another—& we live thus. We are all together—we shall quit Italy together. Jane must proceed to London —if letters do not alter my views I shall remain in Paris.—Thus we live—Seeing the Hunts now & then. Poor Hunt has suffered terribly as you may guess. Lord Byron is very kind to me & comes with the Guiccioli to see me often.

Today—this day—the sun shining in the sky—they are gone to the desolate sea coast to perform the last offices to their earthly remains.[9] Hunt, LB. & Trelawny. The quarantine laws would not permit us to remove them sooner— & now only on condition that we burn them to ashes. That I do not dislike—His rest shall be at Rome beside my child[10]—where one day I also shall join them—Adonais is not Keats's it is his own elegy—he bids you there go to Rome.—I have seen the spot where he now lies—the sticks that mark the spot where the sands cover him—he shall not be there it is too nea[r] Via Reggio—They are now about this fearful office—& I live!

One more circumstance I will mention. As I said he took leave of Mrs

Mason in high spirits on sunday—"Never," said she, "did I see him look happier than the last glance I had of his countenance." On Monday he was lost—on monday night she dreamt—that she was somewhere—she knew not where & he came looking very pale & fearfully melancholy—she said to him—"You look ill, you are tired, sit down & eat." "No," he replied, "I shall never eat more; I have not a soldo left in the world."—"Nonsense," said she, "this is no inn—you need not pay—"—"Perhaps, he answered, "it is the worse for that." Then she awoke & going to sleep again she dreamt that my Percy was dead & she awoke crying bitterly ⟨—so bitterly th⟩ & felt so miserable—that she said to herself—"why if the little boy should die I should not feel it in this manner." She [was] so struck with these dreams that she mentioned them to her servant the next day—saying she hoped all was well with us.

Well here is my story—the last story I shall have to tell—all that might have been bright in my life is now despoiled—I shall live to improve myself, to take care of my child, & render myself worthy to join him. soon my weary pilgrimage will begin—I rest now—but soon I must leave Italy —& then—there is an end of all despair. Adieu I hope you are well & happy. I have an idea that while he was at Pisa that he received a letter from you that I have never seen—so not knowing where to direct I shall send this letter to Peacock—I shall send it open—he may be glad to read it—

Your's ever truly Mary WS.—Pisa

I shall probably write to you soon again.

I have left out a material circumstance—A Fishing boat saw them go down—It was about 4 in the afternoon—they saw the boy at mast head, when baffling winds struck the sails, they had looked away a moment & looking again the boat was gone—This is their story but there is little down [*doubt*] that these men might have saved them, at least Edward who could swim. They c^{d} not they said get near her—but 3 quarters of an hour after passed over the spot where they had seen her—they protested no wreck of her was visible, but Roberts going on board their boat found several spars belonging to her.—perhaps they let them perish to obtain these.[11] Trelawny thinks he can get her up, since another fisherman things [*thinks*] that he has found the spot where she lies, having drifted near shore. T. does this to know perhaps the cause of her wreck—but I care little about it

ADDRESS: [*by Mary Shelley*] Mrs. Gisborne / [*by Peacock*] 33 King Street West / Bryanstone Square / London. ENDORSED: [*by Peacock*] Combe near Wendover, Bucks; Septr. 2. 1822. / T.L.P.; [*by Mrs. Gisborne*] rec. 3rd Sept / 1822 / Ans. POSTMARKS: (1) WENDOVER; (2) [ ] / 3 SE 3 / 1822. PUBLISHED: Jones, #144. TEXT: MS., British Library (Ashley 5022).

1. Williams's *Journal* for 23 June records: "During the night Shelley sees *spirits* and alarms the whole house" (*Journals and Letters*, p. 155).

2. *PBS Letters*, #720.

3. Williams, *Journals and Letters*, p. 163.

4. The heroine of Mary Shelley's novella *Matilda*, in an unsuccessful effort to

prevent her father's suicide, desperately follows his rush "towards the sea" (MWS, *Matilda*).

5. *Macbeth* I. 60.
6. An error for Thursday, 18 July.
7. See n. 6.
8. On 20 July.
9. On 15 August Trelawny, Hunt, and Byron gathered at the beach a distance from Viareggio where the bodies of Shelley and Williams had been temporarily interred in limestone. They disinterred and cremated Williams's remains on 15 August. The next day they disinterred and cremated Shelley's remains. Trelawny left more than ten detailed accounts of the cremations (Trelawny, *Letters*, pp. 2–14; for a discussion of Trelawny's many accounts, see Leslie A. Marchand, "Trelawny on the Death of Shelley," *Keats-Shelley Memorial Bulletin* 4 [1952]: 9–34).
10. Shelley was not buried beside William, for the child's remains could not be found (see 7 September 1822, n. 2).
11. See 17–20 September 1822 for further discussion of the sinking of the *Don Juan*.

*TO EDWARD DAWKINS Pisa 21 Aug. 1822

Sir

Permit me on the present occasion to return you my most grateful thanks for the kindness with which you have attended to the many applications of Mr Trelawny on my account,[1] and to express my sorrow that we were obliged thus to annoy you. Mine indeed is a fate which may awaken the sympathy of a stranger; but the very affliction that causes that sympathy, renders me more sensible of the obliging attentions of others.

May I trouble you once more? I am ashamed to do so, but you will I trust forgive my importunity from its cause. It is my intention to forward the remains of him I have lost to Rome, to be buried there beside a darling boy whom we lost three years ago, near whom he always desired to be placed. Having no friend in that city, you would perhaps have the kindness to send me a letter for the consul there,[2] who thus called upon would be induced to see that my intentions are fulfilled, that the last honours are paid to him, and above all that he should really be placed close to our child; a tomb over him marks the spot.

Again I must apologize for my new intrusion, and thank you for your attention to my past. I have the honour to be,

Sir,
Your obliged humble servant
Mary Shelley

ADDRESS: To His Excellency / Edward Dawkins Eq / Envoy Extraordinary of H.R.M. to the court of Tuscany / Florence. POSTMARKS: (1) PISA; (2) 22 / AGOSTO. UNPUBLISHED. TEXT: MS., Pforzheimer Library.

1. Edward Dawkins, Secretary to the Legation in Tuscany, who had assisted Byron in his exertions to free his servant Tita (see [13 April 1822]), made the arrangements with the Lucchese and Tuscan governments to permit the disinterment

and cremation of Shelley and Williams (Trelawny, *Letters*, pp. 2–3; Cline, *Pisan Circle*, pp. 181–87).

2. The English Consul at Rome was John Parke. On 22 August Dawkins replied to Mary Shelley:

"According to your wishes I have written a letter to our Consul at Rome which will, I hope, remove every difficulty in the performance of your most melancholy duty.

"Should it be the intention of those who advise you on this occasion to carry this letter by land, I will request Mr Parke to send a Lascia passare to the frontier of the Roman States, which will prevent all enquiries at the Custom House—

"I am much flattered, Madam, by the expression of your thanks; but I am not conscious of having deserved them—I have simply done my Duty; which, owing to the Laws of this Country, has not been so effective as I could have wished" (Abinger MS.).

After the cremation Shelley's ashes were put in an oak coffer and conveyed on the *Bolivar* to Leghorn, where they were consigned to an English merchant named Grant, who then consigned them to his correspondent at Rome, John Freeborn (H. Nelson Gay, "The Protestant Burial-Ground in Rome," *Keats-Shelley Memorial Bulletin* 2 [1913], pp. 52–54). Although John Parke was British Consul, he did not live in Rome, and John Freeborn served as his consular agent there (*MWS Letters*, I, #146, n. 1).

To Maria Gisborne [Pisa c. 27 August 1822]

And so here I am! I continue to exist—to see one day succeed the other; to dread night; but more to dread morning & hail another cheerless day. My boy too is alas! no consolation; when I think how He loved him, the plans we had for his education, his sweet & childish voice strikes me to the heart. Why should he live in this world of pain and anguish? And if he went I should go too & we should all sleep in peace. At times I feel an energy within me to combat with my destiny—but again I sink—I have but one hope for which I live—to render myself worthy to join him—such a feeling sustains one during moments of enthusiasm, but darkness & misery soon overwhelms the mind when all near objects bring agony alone with them. People used to call me lucky in my star You see now how true such a prophecy is—I was fortunate in having fearlessly placed by destiny in the hands of one, who a superior being among men, a bright planetary spirit enshrined in an earthly temple, raised me to the height of happiness—so far am I now happy that I would not change my situation as His widow with that of the most prosperous woman in the world—and surely the time will at length come when I shall be at peace & my brain & heart be no longer alive with unutterable anguish. I can conceive but of one circumstance that could afford me the semblance of content—that is the being permitted to live where I am now in the same house, in the same state, occupied alone with my child, in collecting His manuscripts—writing his life, and thus to go easily to my grave. But this must not be. Even if my circumstances did not compel me to return to England, I would not stay another summer in Italy with my child.—I will at least do my best to render him well & happy—& the idea that my circumstances may at all injure him is {the} fiercest pang my mind endures.

I wrote you a long letter containing a slight sketch of my sufferings I sent it directed to Peacock at the India House, because an accident led me to fancy that you were no longer in London. I said in that, that on that day (August 15) they had gone to perform the last offices for him—however I erred in this, for on that day those of Edward were alone fulfilled & they returned on the 16th to celebrate Shelley's. I will say nothing of the ceremony since Trelawny has written an account of it to be printed in the forthcoming journal[1]—I will only say that all except his heart (which was unconsumable)[2] was burnt, and that two days ago I went to Leghorn and beheld the small box that contained his earthly dress—that form, those smiles—Great God! No he is not there—he is with me, about me—life of my life & soul of my soul—if his divine spirit did not penetrate mine I could not survive to weep thus.

I will mention the friends I have here that you may form an idea of our situation. Mrs Williams Claire & I live all together, we have one purse, & joined in misery we are for the present joined in life. She poor girl, withers like a lily—she lives for her children, but it is a living death. Lord Byron has been [*several words canceled*] very kind—[*half-line canceled*] but the Guiccioli restrains him perhaps—she being an Italian is capable of being jealous of a living corpse such as I. Of Hunt I will speak when I see you. But the friend to whom we are eternally indebted is Trelawny. I have of course mentioned him in my letters to you—as one who wishes to be considered eccentric but who was noble & generous at bottom. I always thought so even when no fact proved it, & Shelley agreed with me, as he always did, or rather I with him. We heard people speak against him on account of his vagaries, we said to one another—"Still we like him—we believe him to be good." Once even when a whim of his led him to treat me with something like impertinence I forgave him, & have now been well rewarded. In my outline of events, you will see how unasked he returned with Jane & I from Leghorn to Lerici, how he staid with us miserable creatures twelve days there endeavouring to keep up our spirits—how he left us, on thursday, & finding our misfortune confirmed then without rest returned on friday to us, & again without rest returned with us to Pisa on saturday. These were no common services—Since that he has gone through by himself all the annoyances of dancing attendance on consuls & governors for permissions to fulfil the last duties to those gone, & attending the ceremony himself, all the disagreable part & all the fatigue fell on him—as Hunt said—"He worked with the meanest and felt with the best." He is generous to a distressing degree. But after all these benefits towards us what I most thank him for is this. When on that night of agony, that friday night he returned to announce that hope was dead for us—when he had told me that his earthly frame being found, his spirit was no longer to be my guide, protector & companion in this dark world—he did not attempt to console me, that would have been to{o} cruelly useless; but he launched forth into as it were an overflowing & eloquent praise of my divine Shelley—until I almost was happy that I was thus unhappy to be fed by the praise of him, and to dwell on the eulogy that his loss thus drew from his friend.

Of my friends I have only M[rs] Mason to mention. Her coldness has stung me—yet she felt his loss keenly, & would be very glad to serve me—but it is not cold offers of service that one wants—one's wounded spirit demands a number of nameless & slight but dear attentions that are a balm & wanting them one feels a bitterness which is a painful addition to one's other sufferings.

God knows what will become of me! My life is now very monotonous as to outward events—yet how diversified by internal feeling—How often in the intensity of grief does one instant seem to fill & embrace the universe. As to the rest, the mechanical spending of my time; of course I have a great deal to do preparing for my journey—I make no visits except one once in about ten days to M[rs] Mason—I have not seen Hunt this nine days. Trelawny resides chiefly at Leghorn since he is captain of LordB.'s vessel, the Bolivar, he comes to see us about once a week; & LordB. visits me about twice a week, accompanied by the Guiccioli. But seeing people is an annoyance which I am happy to be spared. Solitude is my only help & resource; accustomed even when he was with me to spend much of my time alone, I can at those moments forget myself—until some idea, which I think I would communicate to him, occurs & then the yawning & dark gulph again displays itself unshaded by the rainbows which the imagination had formed. Despair, energy, love, despondency & excessive affliction are like clouds, driven across my mind, one by one, until tears blot the scene, & weariness of spirit consigns me to temporary repose.

I shudder with horror when I look on what I have suffered; & when I think of the wild and miserable thoughts that have possessed me, I say to myself "Is it true that I ever felt thus?"—And then I weep in pity of myself. Yet each day adds to the stock of sorrow & death is the only end. I would study, & I hope I shall—I would write—& when I am settled I may—But were it not for the steady hope I entertain of joining him what a mockery all this would be. Without that hope I could not study or write, for fame & usefulness (except as far as regards my child) are nullities to me—Yet I shall be happy if any thing I ever produce may exalt & soften sorrow, as the writings of the divinities of our race have mine. But how can I aspire to that?

The world will surely one day feel what it has lost when this bright child of song deserted her—Is not Adonais his own Elegy—& there does he truly depict the universal woe wh[ich] should overspread all good minds since he has ceased to be [their] fellow labourer in this worldly scene. How lovely does he [ ] paint death to be and with what heartfelt sorrow does one repeat that line—"But I am chained to time & cannot thence depart."[3] How long do you think I shall live? as long as my mother? then eleven long years must intervene—I am now on the eve of completing my five & twentieth year—how drearily young for one so lost as I! How young in years for one who lives ages each day in sorrow—think you that those moments are counted in my life as in other people's?—oh no! The day before the sea closed over mine own Shelley he said to Marianne—"If I die tomorrow I have lived to be older than my father, I am ninety years of age." Thus also may I say—The eight years I passed with him was spun out beyond the usual length of a man's life—And what I have suffered since will write years on my brow & intrench them in my heart—surely I am not long for this world—most sure should I be were it not for my boy—but God grant that I may live to make his early years happy.

Well adieu—I have no events to write about & can therefore can only scrawl about my feelings—this letter indeed is only the sequel of my last—In that I closed the history of all of event that can interest me. That letter I wish you to send my father[4]—the present one it is best not.

I suppose I shall see you in England some of these days—but I shall write to you again before I quit this place—Be as happy as you can, & hope for better things in the next world—by firm hope you may attain your wishes—again adieu

Affectionately yours
MWS

Do not write me again here. or at all until I write again

ADDRESS: Mrs. Gisborne / 33 King's Street West / Bryanstone Square / Inghilterra London / Londres. POSTMARKS: (1) PISA; (2) FPO / SE. 10 / 1822; (3) SE. 10 / 1822 Nn; (4) [ ] Clock / SP. 10 / 1822 Nn. ENDORSED: Recd. 10th Sept. 1822. PUBLISHED: Jones, #145. TEXT: MS., Bodleian Library (MS., Shelley, c. 1, ff. 521–23).

1. Trelawny's account was not published in the *Liberal*, but it was incorporated, in an altered form, into Hunt's *Lord Byron and Some of His Contemporaries* (Marshall, *The Liberal*, p. 75).

2. Shelley's heart, taken from the flames by Trelawny, was first given to Hunt, who intended to keep it. Mary Shelley's wish to have the heart precipitated a quarrel with Hunt. On 17 August he wrote:
"I am sorry after what I said to you last night, that you should have applied to Lord B. on this subject & in this manner. It is not that my self-love is hurt, for that I could have given up, as I have long [?learnt] to do; but it is my love,—my love for my friend; and for this to make way for the claims of any other love, man's or woman's, I must have great reasons indeed brought me—I do not say it is impossible for such reasons to be brought; but I say that they must be great, unequivocal, & undeniable. In his case above all other human beings, no ordinary appearance of rights, even yours, can affect me. . . . I begged it at the funeral pile; I had it; & his Lordship who happened to be at a distance at the momnt, knew nothing of the matter till it was in my possession" (*MWS Letters*, I, #145, n. 2). According to John Gisborne, Jane Williams's intercession, which stressed the bitterness between Mary Shelley and Hunt that resulted from his unwillingness to give Mary Shelley the heart, finally persuaded Hunt to relent (Gisborne, *Journals and Letters*, pp. 88–89). When Mary Shelley died, the heart, dried to dust, was discovered in a copy of *Adonais*. In 1889 Sir Percy Florence died, and the relic of the heart was buried with him in

the vault that also contained the remains of Mary Shelley, William Godwin, and Mary Wollstonecraft, in St. Peter's Churchyard, Bournmouth (White, *Shelley*, II, 635).

In "Shelley's Heart," *Journal of the History of Medicine*, 10 (January 1955): 114, Arthur M. Z. Norman offers the following reason for the heart's impregnability to fire, as well as reasons for other physical discomforts Shelley suffered during his life: "It seems very probable that Shelley suffered from a progressively calcifying heart, which might well have caused diffuse symptoms with its increasing weight of calcium and which indeed would have resisted cremation as readily as a skull, a jaw, or fragments of bone. Shelley's heart, epitome of Romanticism, may well have been a heart of stone."

3. *Adonais* 26. 9.

4. On 6 August Godwin had written Mary Shelley that he had heard "the most afflicting intelligence to you, & in some measure to all of us, that can be imagined, the death of Shelley on the 8th ult" through Hunt's letter of 20 July to Bessy Kent (Hunt, *Correspondence*, I, 189–91). Godwin offered his condolences and his assistance and requested direct word from her. Before sending his letter, he received an undated letter from Mary Shelley, and he added a postscript to note its receipt, delayed "some hours by being directed to the care of Monro, for which I cannot account. William wrote to you on the 14th of June & I on the 23rd of July. I will call on Peacock & Hogg, as you desire. Perhaps Williams letter, & perhaps others, have been kept from you. Let us now be open & unreserved in all things" (Abinger MS.). Godwin had obviously forgotten his instructions to Mary Shelley of 3 May 1822, the day the Godwins were "compelled by summary process, to leave the house we live in," to direct her letters, until further word, "to the care of Mr Monro" (Abinger MS.). For Godwin's remarks about letters kept from Mary Shelley, see 2 June 1822. Since Mary Shelley was already in direct touch with Godwin, her request to show the 15 August letter to him was no doubt an expedient way of giving him a detailed account of events before and after Shelley's death, just as she had left the 15 August letter open for Peacock to read before he sent it on to Maria Gisborne.

To John Parke

Pisa—September 7th 1822

Sir

This letter will be delivered to you conjointly with one from Mr Dawkins, Secretary to the English Legation at Florence, which will I believe explain to you the circumstances which induce me to trouble you.[1] If there had been a resident Clergyman at Rome, I should have consigned to his care that which I now take the liberty of entrusting to yours. You will receive with this letter a case containing the ashes of my late husband which I wish to be buried at the English Burying Ground at Rome.[2] Among the tombs there, you will find one to the memory of our boy, William Shelley, and I wish the ashes I send to be interred if possible in the same grave, or close to it. If there is an English Clergyman at Rome, he will perhaps have the goodness to superintend the interment, if there is not you will be so kind as to see it executed in the most decorous manner the circumstances will permit. Mr Grant of the House of Grant Pellan & Co at Leghorn has kindly interested himself in removing my difficulties on the present occasion, and has the goodness to authorize me to desire you to draw on his correspondant at Rome, Mr Freeborn, for money to meet all the expences attendant. I wish also a plain stone to be placed to cover the grave (which you will oblige me by allowing to be very deep) inscribe with the same words as those on the brass plate on the case.

I beg you will pardon the liberty I take in thus intruding upon you; but having no friend at Rome, and encouraged by Mr Dawkins' polite assurances I have ventured to address myself to you, and I assure myself that you will kindly undertake the fulfilment of my melancholy duty.

I have the honour to be, Sir,
Your Obedient Servant
Mary Shelley

ADDRESS: John Parke Esq. / Consul to H.B.M. at Rome. PUBLISHED: Jones, #146. TEXT: MS., Bodleian Library (MS., Shelley, c. 1, ff. 524–25).

1. See 21 August 1822.

2. Interment in the old Protestant burial ground where William Shelley was buried was then forbidden by Papal authorities, and Shelley's ashes remained for some months in Freeborn's wine cellar. Joseph Severn (1793–1879), Keats's devoted friend, was called on to expedite matters. Because of the Papal decree, it was decided to disinter William's remains and rebury him together with Shelley in the new enclosure. On 21 January 1823 the child's grave was found to hold the skeleton of an adult, and Shelley's ashes alone were buried in the new ground (Gay, "The Protestant Burial-Ground in Rome," pp. 52–54; William Sharp, *The Life and Letters of Joseph Severn* [London: Sampson Low, Marston & Co., 1892], pp. 122–23).

To Thomas Jefferson Hogg

Pisa. Septr 9th 1822

My dear Hogg

This letter will be delivered to you by Mrs Williams,[1] the widow of the dear friend who was lost with mine own Shelley. You will find in her the friend whom he saw daily for nearly two years, to whom he was affectionately attached, & who more than any person can describe to you the last actions & thoughts of your incomparable friend. If you still retain the affection you once had for him, and think of him with that kindness which he always felt for you, her company will be invaluable to you—although you can in part repay her by talking of the former years of the life of one whom she loved, esteemed & admired beyond all her other friends.

You did not know Edward, & cannot tell what she has lost in losing him. They were enthusiastically attached to each other, and he by his talents, angelic disposition, his gentle, brave & generous nature fully merited all the tenderness which she, the model of all gentleness, ⟨& elegance⟩ and grace, bore him. If my own unhappiness had not penetrated my heart so entirely I could never have endured to see her divided from one she loved so well; and you who used to be a fervent admirer of that devotion which distinguishes the sentiment of love in a woman, will appreciate her virtues, although they are repaid, as all earthly virtue is, by desolation & misery.

I would say do all in your power to be of use to her, but to know her is sufficient to make the desire of serving her arise in an unselfish mind. Do what little you can to amuse her.

By the time you receive this you will probably have heard from me by the post, so I say nothing of such a nullity as I now am—Adieu

Truly yours
MaryW. Shelley.

ADDRESS: Jefferson Hogg Esq / 1 Garden Court & Temple. PUBLISHED: Donald H. Reiman, "Shelley's 'The Triumph of Life': The Biographical Problem," *Publications of the Modern Language Association* 78, no. 5 (December 1963): 542–43. TEXT: MS., Abinger MS., Bodleian Library.

1. Jane Williams left Italy for England on 17 September (see 17–20 September 1822; 18 September 1822).

TO CLAIRE CLAIRMONT Pisa. [error for Genoa][1] Septr 15 1822

My dear Claire

I do not wonder that you were & are melancholy—or that the excess of that feeling should oppress you. Great God! What we have gone through—what variety of care and misery, all closed now in blackest night. And I—am I not melancholy?—here in this busy hateful Genoa where nothing speaks to me of him, except the sea, which is his murderer.—Well I shall have his books & manuscripts & in those I shall live & from the study of those I do expect some instants of content. In solitude my imagination & ever moving thoughts may afford me some seconds of exaltation that may render me both happier here & more worthy of him hereafter. Such as I felt walking up a mountain by myself at sunrise during my journey—when the rocks looked black about me & a white mist concealed all but them—I thought then that thinking of him and exciting my mind my days might pass in a kind of peace—but these thoughts are so fleeting—& then I expect unhappiness alone from all the worldly part of my life—from my intercour{s}e with human beings—I know that that will bring nothing but unhappiness to me. If indeed I except Trelawny who appears so truly generous & kind.

But I will not talk of myself. You have enough to annoy & make you miserable—& in nothing can I assist you But I do hope that you will find Germany better suited to you in every way than Italy—& that you will make friends—& more than all, become really attached to some one there.

I wish when I was in Pisa that you had said that you thought you should be short of money & I would have left you more—but you seemed to think 150 francesconi plenty.—I would not go on with Goëthe[2] except with a fixed price per sheet to be regularly paid—& that price not less than five guineas—Make this be understood fully through Hunt before you go. & then I will take care that you get the money—but if you {do} not fix it, then I cannot manage so well.

You are going to Vienna, how anxiously do I hope to find peace—I do not hope for it here—Genoa has a bad atmosphere for me I fear, & nothing but the horrow [*horror*] of being a burthen to my family prevents my accompanying Jane—If I had any fixed income I would go at least to Paris —& I shall go the moment I have one.

Adieu my dear Claire—write to me often as I shall to you

Affectionately Yours
MaryWS.

I cannot get your German dictionary now since I must have packed it in my great case of books—but I will send it by the first opportunity

PUBLISHED: Jones, #148. TEXT: MS., Berg Collection, New York Public Library.

1. On 11 September Mary Shelley and Jane Williams had left Pisa for Genoa. They lodged at the Croix de Malthe while Mary Shelley looked for a house, which she and the Hunts would share. By 2 September Counts Ruggero Gamba (Teresa Guiccioli's father) and Pietro Gamba had already rented the Casa Saluzzo at Albaro, a suburb of Genoa, for Byron and his party (Marchand, *Byron*, III, 1027). Mary Shelley rented the Casa Negroto, about one mile from Casa Saluzzo, which Hunt reported cost less than £20 a year "for about forty rooms" (*Correspondence*, I, 192).

2. When Byron had expressed his willingness to pay for a translation of Goethe's *Memoirs*, Shelley had arranged for Claire Clairmont to do the translation but had told Byron that the work was being done in Paris. Claire Clairmont began the translation on 9 March 1822. Shelley's letter to her of 31 March indicates that Claire Clairmont had expected Shelley to tell Byron who his translator was, but Shelley had refused (*PBS Letters*, #692, #694; *CC Journals*). Claire Clairmont's letter of 11 September to Mary Shelley indicates that Byron had by that time been informed of the identity of his translator: "You may remember what Lord Byron said about paying for the translation—now he has mumbled & grumbled and demurred and does not know whether it is worth it and will only give forty crowns so that I am afraid I shall not be overstocked when I arrive at Vienna, unless indeed God shall spread a table for me in the wilderness" (Abinger MS.). Claire Clairmont left Pisa on 20 September to join her brother, Charles Clairmont, at Vienna.

TO THE AUTHORITIES OF VIA REGGIO

Genova—
16 Settbre [September] 1822

Io, sottascritta, prego le Autorità di Via Reggio o Livorno di consegnare al Signore Odoardo Trelawny, Inglese, la Barca nominata Il Don Juan e tutta la sua ⟨roba⟩ carica,[1] appartenenda al mio Marito, per essere alla sua dispozizione.

Maria Shelley

[*Translation*]

I, the undersigned, request the authorities of Via Reggio or Livorno to consign to Mr. Edward Trelawny, Englishman, the boat named The Don Juan, and all its ⟨goods⟩ cargo,[1] belonging to my husband, to be at his disposal.

PUBLISHED: Jones, #149; Palacio, *Mary Shelley*, p. 602. TEXT: MS., Jean de Palacio.

1. Mary Shelley wrote to Maria Gisborne on 17 September: "That miserable boat has been found & drawn up from the bottom of the sea with everything in her."

To Maria Gisborne Genoa. Sept[r] 17 September 20th 1822

I am here alone in Genoa; quite, quite alone! Jane has left me to proceed to England, & except my sleeping child, I am alone. Since you do not communicate with my father you will perhaps be surprised after my last letter, that I do not come to England. I have written to him a long account of the arguments of all my friends to dissuade me from that miserable journey;[1] Jane will detail them to you; & therefore I merely say now, that having no business there (for the will can in no way be acted upon until Sir T.'s [*Timothy Shelley's*] death, & an allowance from him can be procured as well in my absence) I have determined not to spend that money which will support me nearly a year here, in a journay the sole end of which appears to me the necessity I should be under, when arrived in London, of being a burthen to my father. After my crowns are gone, if Sir T. behaves ill, I hope to be able to support myself by my writings & mine own Shelley's Mss. At least during many long months I shall have peace as to money affairs & one evil the less is much to one whose existence is suffering alone. LB. has a house here & will arrive soon;[2] I have taken a house for Hunt & myself, outside one of the Gates—it is large and neat with a poderè attached, we shall pay about 80 crowns between us, so I hope that I shall find tranquillity from care this winter, though that may be the last of my life so free. Yet I do not hope it, though I say so; I expect nothing but ill for me—hope is a word that belongs not to my situation; He, my own beloved, the exalted & divine Shelley, has left me alone in this miserable, hateful world;—on this earth which bears grass only that it may perish again & again—this earth canopied by the eternal starry heaven—where he is—where, Oh my God! yes—where I shall one day be.

Claire goes to Vienna to Charles—she is no longer with me. Jane quitted me this morning at four. After she left me I again went to rest & thought of Pugnano,[3] its halls, its cypresses—the perfume of its mountains & the gaiety of our life beneath their shadow. Then I dozed awhile and in my dream saw dear Edward most visibly; he came, he said, to pass a few hours with us, but could not stay long. Then I woke & the day began. I went out—took Hunt's house—but as I walked I felt that which is with me the sign of unutterable grief. I am not given to tears; & though my most miserable fate has often turned my eyes to fountains—yet oftener I suffer agonies unassuaged by tears. But during these last sufferings I have felt an oppression at my heart I never felt before—It is not a palpitation but a stringemento[4] which is quite convulsive & did I not struggle greatly would cause violent hysterics—Looking on the sea or hearing it's roar—his dirge, it comes upon me. But these are corporeal sufferings that I can get over, but that which is insurmountable is the constant feeling of despair that shadows me; I seem to walk on a narrow, dark path with fathomless precipieces all around me. Yet where can I fall? I have already fallen, and all that comes of bad or good is a mere mockery.

Those about me have no idea of what I suffer; for I talk, aye & smile as usual—& none are sufficiently interested in me to observe that though my lips smile, my eyes are blank, or to notice the desolate look that I cast up towards the sky in anger—that I have smiled. And if I talk not to those about me of my sufferings why should I make you unhappy with an account of them? Pardon, dear friend, this selfishness. There are moments when the heart must sfogare[5] or be suffocated; & such a moment is this—when quite alone, my babe sleeping, my dear Jane having just left me, it is with difficulty I prevent myself from flying from mental misery by bodily exertion—when to destroy every thing around me & to run in to that vast grave (the sea) until fatigued I sunk to rest would be a pleasure to me. And instead of this I write, & as I write I say Oh God! have pity on me!—At least I will have pity on you. Good night—I will finish this letter when people are about me & I am in a more cheerful mood—Goodnight—I will go look at the stars, they are eternal; so is he—so am I.

September 20th

You have not written to me since my misfortune. That is to say since Mr G.'s [*Gisborne's*] first short letter. I understand this; you first waited for a letter from me & that letter told you not to write. But answer this as soon as you receive it; talk to me of yourselves—and also of my English affairs. I am afraid that they will not go on very well in my absence, but it wd cost more to set them right than they are worth. I will however let you know what I think that my friends ought to do, that when you talk to Peacock he may learn what I wish. The will cannot be acted upon until Sir Timothy's death, & I am convinced that it is for my interest that nothing should be said about it until then—but that a claim should be made on the part of Shelley's executors for a maintainance for my child & myself from Sir T. LB. is ready to do this or any other service for me that his office of executor demands from him. But I do not wish it to be done seperately by him, and I wait to hear from England before I ask him to write to Whitton on the subject. He will write the moment I ask him. Secondly Ollier ought to be looked to—all Mss. taken from him, and some plan be reflected on for the best manner {of} republishing S's works as well as the writings he has left be[hind]. Who will allow money to Ianthe & Charles?[6]—

As for you, my dear friends, I do not see what you can do for [me] except to send me the originals or copies of Shelley's most interesting letters to you. I have given Jane a list of the things I wish her to get me she will bring them to you, I shall write to Peacock & my father for what other {things} I wish to be sent out to me, & you who see Peacock will arrange the sending them together with the things Jane gets for me. If Jane has any money left of mine I wish you would get painted on velvet for me two things. I wish each piece of velvet to be about the size of this page of paper.[7] On one I wish a pansey (that is heart's ease—not a single flower but a plant) the natural size to be painted & under it to be written these words—"The Pansey let my flower be!"[8] on the other let a shell be painted of the kind of S's arms—in this shape [drawing] I can not draw it—the shoulder of mutton shape—but let it be the copy of a large & beautiful Indian shell. round it thus [drawing] let it be written those words of Ariel in the Tempest—"We will all suffer a sea change"—& in a strait line under—"But I am chained to time & cannot thence depart."[9] Perhaps Mr Fielding[10] can do these—you know they must not cost much though I wish them to be well done—but I believe painting on velvet is not dear.

My Percy is well—he is a very good boy which is great consolation to me. I hope soon to get into my house with Hunt, where writing, copying S's Mss. walking & being of some use in the ⟨management⟩ education of Marianne's children will be my occupations. Hunt was to depart from Pisa either yesterday or will depart tomorrow—if Marianne be not ill he will arrive in 4 days—his furniture will be sent the day of his departure & will come in 2—so in the beginning of next week I hope to settle myself.—Here is a long letter all about myself—but though I cannot write I like to hear of others, so tell me all your plans—All that I do not inform you of myself Jane can explain when you see her. Adieu, dear friends, Your sincely attached

MaryW S.

[*P. 4, cross-written*] Where is that letter in verse S. once wrote to you?[11] let me have a copy of it. Since writing this. I have thought that there is one thing you might do for me better than any one else—that is Mr. G. but let him judge. I have Shelley's perfect translation of the Theologico Polical tract of Spinoza[12]—perhaps you cd. dispose of this for me to some Bookseller—Longman or some one else.

Is not Peacock very lukewarm & insensible in this affair?—Tell me what Hogg says & does—& my father also if you have an opportunity of knowing

[*P. 1, top*] That miserable boat has been found & drawn up from the bottom of the sea with everything in her. she did not upset, but filled & went down.[13] S certainly did not suffer except one pang which thank God we must all feel. But Jane will instruct you in every particular. She will call on you on her arrival. [drawing] That is more the shell's shape. [drawing]

ADDRESS: Mrs. Gisborne / 33 King's St. West / Bryanstone Square / Inghilterra London. POSTMARKS: (1) GENOVA; (2) FPO / OC. 3 / 1822 Nn; (3) 12 o'Clock / OC. 3 / 1822 Nn. ENDORSED: 3rd Oct. Ansd. 8th Oct. PUBLISHED: Jones, #150. TEXT: MS., Bodleian Library (MS., Shelley, c. 1, ff. 527–28).

1. On 10 September Byron had written to Mary Shelley regarding her future plans: "Upon the subject of your journey, I do not like to give any positive opinion; but I cannot see the immediate advantage, or even future, from such a step, just now. The will is known to exist; it cannot be altered, or made away with; but you can consult Mrs. Mason, and regulate yourself by the mechanism of 'Clare's Minerva.' As to sharing Mrs. Godwin's small estate, I rather suspect that 'tis your own which

the means. At any rate, write to Godwin to take a copy of the will to my solicitors, John and Charles Hanson . . ." (*S&M*, III, 869–70).

2. See 18 September 1822.

3. The Williamses had lived at Pugnano, about seven miles from Pisa, from May through October 1821.

4. "Pressing, squeezing."

5. "Pour forth."

6. Shelley had been providing £200 per year to Dr. Thomas Hume for their care. Sir Timothy Shelley continued this allowance until the middle of 1823, when he was appointed guardian of Charles, and Eliza Westbrook Beauchamp and her father were appointed guardians of Ianthe (Ingpen, *Shelley in England*, p. 512).

7. The page measures 9 13/16" × 7 15/16".

8. See 26 July 1822.

9. Ariel's Song, *The Tempest* I. 2. 399–401 ("Nothing of him that doth fade, / But doth suffer a sea-change / Into something rich and strange"); and *Adonais* 26. 9. Trelawny had the quotation from *The Tempest* carved on Shelley's tombstone. The particular significance of the lines is explained in Mary Shelley's letter to Maria Gisborne of 3–6 May [1823] (see also 22 November 1822).

10. Probably the painter Copley Fielding, whose sister married Henry Reveley in 1824 (Gisborne, *Journals and Letters*, p. 11).

11. Shelley's *Letter to Maria Gisborne*, written while the Shelleys occupied Casa Ricci, the Gisbornes' house, during the Gisbornes' stay in England in the summer of 1820. On 8 October Maria Gisborne responded that they would transcribe the poem for her (Gisborne, *Journals and Letters*, p. 92).

12. *Tractatus Theologico-Politicus* (see *MWS Journal*, pp. 85, 127–28, 130–32, 134, 161; Williams, *Journals and Letters*, pp. 112, 114).

13. The *Don Juan* had been located and raised by two fishing smacks owned by Stefano Baroni, of Viareggio, shortly before 12 September. The boat was brought to Leghorn, where Captain Roberts inspected it; he wrote to Mary Shelley on 14 September. On 16 September the boat and its contents were auctioned off, and Roberts purchased its shell. Mary Shelley's description in this letter of the sinking of the *Don Juan* agrees with Captain Roberts's letter of 14 September (Cameron, *The Golden Years*, p. 101). Trelawny, however, believed that a fishing boat had run down the *Don Juan* in order to plunder it. Roberts came to hold Trelawny's view, as did, for a while, Mary Shelley. For details of the recovery of the *Don Juan*, see Guido Biagi, *The Last Days of Percy Bysshe Shelley* (London: T. Fisher Unwin, 1898), pp. 140–49, 163–64; and Cameron, *The Golden Years*, pp. 100–108. Cameron, in assessing all the evidence surrounding the sinking of the *Don Juan*, argues persuasively that the *Don Juan* was "a nautical monstrosity" that had been "swamped by a heavy sea" and that the "running-down theory" helped alleviate the consciences of Trelawny and Roberts, both of whom were responsible for the design and building of the *Don Juan*.

*To Jane Williams — Genoa. Sept[t] 18th 1822

You write to me from this place—that is to say from Gene{v}a Dearest Jane, do you not? You write to tell me that you still live & are so far on your journey. Ever since you quitted me I am overpowered by a melancholy & misery no human words can describe and no human mind long support. I am irritated against all I feel, or see or hear, this must end soon, & probably when utterly exhausted by grief I shall sink into lethargy—but now I repeat only—"Pain, pain, ever & forever pain!"[1]—& my heart is full to bursting.

Well, my best girl I will not irritate your many sorrows by talking of mine. You are gone, the last link of a golden chain leaving me bound by a leaden one alone. You the Eve of a fair Paradise—Now through Eden take your solitary way. I was never the Eve of any Paradise, but a human creature blessed by an elemental spirit's company & love—an angel who imprisoned in flesh could not adapt himself to his clay shrine & so has flown & left it—& I feel as poets have described those loved by superhuman creatures & then deserted by them—Impatient, despairing—& resting only on the moment when he will return to me.

Well—of my worldly affairs—I have taken a large neat pleasantly situated house—& remain in this inn until the furniture arrives which will—be Monday I hope.[2] I am much afraid of the life I am about to lead—for I see some new points in Hunt's character which leads me to think that he will not allow things to go smoothly—but I shall keep much to myself, & lead him to expect little from me that he may not accuse me of disappointing him.

I have seen Mrs Wright[3] & made the best bargain I cd to get out of the dilemma into which Trelawny's thoughtlessness brought me. I am come to a resolution about that lady, to see & know her as little as I well can. She will not like any one who will not assist her in her intrigue—now this is not only against my interests but my principles—I hate & despise the intrigues of married women, nor in my opinion can the chains which custom throws upon them justify them in conducting themselves with deceit & falsehood—it may render them pardonable—but despicable at the same time. Truth is the only thing of any worth ⟨to me now⟩ in ones intercourse with one's fellows—& where there is not that, vice must follow

Forgive this moral discourse, I have indulged myself in the expression of my sentiments to you as they may reassure you as to any danger you may think I run in my acquaintance with this lady. It is an acquaintance & so it shall remain

dearest Jane, How are you? What are you doing & suffering? I expect a letter from you with great impatience—Take care of yourself, for your little ones' sake—remember that the loss of a mother can never be compensated—& that in your especial case you are invaluable to your babes. Remember however in your will to mame [*name*] me the guardian of your girl—& be assured that if I survive you I will as far as I can be a Mother to her. Poor thing, she is so like Edward that that alone is sufficient to excite all my tenderness for her, were she not also your child—& thus has double claims.

We meet again I hope soon—think of me with affection—& although you say "you would not be surp[rized] at any thing that happens in this world"—remember that I consider myself as much married as when he was here & that my faith is vowed to him in life & death. After loving him I could only love an angel like him—but I could not even love another angel loving him alone.

Adieu my best, dearest, only friend

Your affectionate
MaryW. Shelley.

ADDRESS: A Madame / Madme Williams / Poste Restante / Genêve / La Suisse. POSTMARK: GENOVA. UNPUBLISHED. TEXT: MS., Abinger MS., Bodleian Library.

1. Variant quotation of *Prometheus Unbound* I. 23.

2. Marianne Hunt kept a diary from 18 September through 24 October 1822. In it she indicates that the Hunts expected to leave for Genoa on 18 September but did not leave until 27 September and arrived at midnight on 4 October (H. Nelson Gay, "Unpublished Diary of Mrs. Leigh Hunt [Pisa, September 18, 1822—Genoa, October 24, 1822]," *Keats-Shelley Memorial Bulletin* 2 [1910]: 71–76). Mary Shelley's Journal for 5 October 1822 confirms their arrival: "Well they are come—& it is all as I said. I awoke as from sleep & thought how I had vegetated these last days." Byron and Teresa Guiccioli arrived on 3 October (Marchand, *Byron*, III, 1036). Sailing the *Bolivar* to Genoa, Trelawny kept pace with Byron's schedule and arrived the same day (Trelawny, *Records*, II, 51).

3. Gabrielle Wright, with whom Trelawny was having an affair, was the wife of the boatbuilder at Genoa who built the *Bolivar* and the *Don Juan* (*SC*, V, 49). Writing to Mary Shelley from Geneva, Jane Williams commented: "I am very uneasy about Trelawny, and have a strange presentiment something will happen to him. Pray urge him to leave Genoa before W[right] returns: the affair is more public than he imagines" (Williams, *Journals and Letters*, p. 164).

*TO THOMAS LOVE PEACOCK

Casa Negroto, Crosa di San Nazaro,
Albaro,—fuore delle[1] Porte all'Arco.
Genova September 29th 1822

My dear Friend

Before you receive this letter you will have seen my father, who will have acquainted you with the change in my plans. I do not return to England. I thought this journey perfectly necessary at first but Lord Byron, & afterwards all my friends, combined to shew me the inexpediency of such a step. What have I to do there? If Sir Timothy allows me nothing,[2] I should be a burthen to my father, and have expended on a fruitless journey that money which will maintain me & my child a long time here. If he allows me any thing it will be so small a sum that I should live miserably in your dear country; while however small, I am sure it would maintain me comfortably here. As to the will, I am convinced that nothing can be done with it until after Sir Timothys death. How can I give it up?—if it is not valid I can only give it up to the heir at law, who is Charles Bysshe, & he is under the Chancellor's & the Westbrooks protection, & has no interests in common with his paternal grandfather. All that can be done now is, to be silent concerning the will, & that you (in your own & Lord Byron's name) should apply to Sir Timothy through Whitton, for a maintainance for me & my child. Lord Byron is very kind to me, promises to Do his duty as executor,

& really appears interested in my fate. If it be judged expedient he will write to Whitton himself—or take any other step to secure me a fitting allowance, which you should point out as proper to be taken.

In the mean time {I} remain here with the Hunts, spending little & passing the miserable hours as I can: better here than in England: I shall spend little, occupy myself in literature, take care of my child and even be useful to the Hunts. I have taken with them an unfurnished house in the outskirts of this town, it is large, pleasantly situated, neat & very cheap—my share in the rent is about 30 crowns a year. Can I do better in the present moment than make the resources I have in hand last as long as possible? I hope Sir Timothy will allow me something or at the end of some months my situation will become very disagreable, but I trust that he will; I am sure, my dear Peacock, that you will exert your utmost to induce him;—a maintainance, An Italian Maintainance is all that I require.

I must explain to you more fully about this bill. It is for the June & not for the September quarter.[3] In the middle of June I saw a letter of Shelley's to B. & D. [*Brooks & Dixon*] ordering to pay the June quarter into the hands of Guebhard. B. & D. wrote to Guebhard in reply, that they were ready to honour a bill for the amount. Guebhard's answer to this was this very bill drawn July 8th. I believe therefore that this bill is already honoured, since B. & D. say that they have paid the June quarter; but if ⟨it is nece⟩ on the contrary they dishonour it you must learn particularly from them in what form they remitted the June quarter to Shelley. I am convincd from having read his letters, that he never received it, except as this bill of July 8th is paid. His letter to B. & D. asking them to advance his next quarter's annuity had nothing in common with this bill. This request was made only in consequence of our having taken up our abode at Lerici, where it was difficult to get bills remitted to us, and he wished to have ready money in his hands. As I have said, this bill of July 8th, is I doubt not honoured with the funds accrueing from the June quarter; if not, pray let me know very particularly in what form the June quarter was remitted to Shelley, that I may endeavour to fathom this mystery. If all this goes well, as I trust it will, and B. & D. receive in addition the September quarter, I shall get on very well for the present; if it be so, let the money be remitted to me instantly here

You would oblige me by communicating this letter to my father; if your time should be so much taken up that you cannot give sufficient attention to what is indeed life & death to me, I am sure that he will exert himself to be become master of the true state of the affair. Tell him I will write to him very soon, very soon indeed.

I am impatient for the papers I mentioned.[4] If you get all our Mss. from Maddocks let them all be sent to me. I wish particularly also for my two journal books—(one a green covered book & the other a little one bound with red leather). I shall not be easy until I get all the books from Maddocks' hands—& the moment my affairs are at all arranged I shall endeavour to obtain them. M[rs] Williams, the widow of dear, lost Edward, is on her way to England. I have asked her to [*cross-written*] procure several things for me which she will give to the Gisbornes'; add to these the Mss. you have—& some others that I shall ask my father to send you, & making a case for all, send them to me here, forwarding me the bill of lading.

I have written you a letter entirely about business, when I hold a pen in my hand my natural impulse is to express the feelings that overwhelm me; but resisting that impulse I dare not for a moment stray from my subject or I should never find it again. I have written to the Gisbornes twice since that letter which I enclosed to you, they can tell you what the real current of my mind is.—Alas! find in the whole world so transcendant a being as mine own Shelley—& then tell me to be consoled & it is not he alone I have lost, though that misery, swallowing up every other, has hitherto made me forgetful of all others—my best friend, my dear Edward, whom next to S. I loved—& whose virtues were worthy of the warmest affection he also is gone—Jane (i.e. M[rs] Williams) driven by her cruel fate to England, has also deserted me, What have I left? Not one that can console me—not one that does not shew by comparison how deep & irremediable my losses are. Trelawny is the only quite disinterested friend I have here, the only one who clings to the memory of my loved ones, as I do myself—but he alas! is not as one of them, though he is really good & kind. Adieu my dear Peacock, be happy with your wife & child—I hear that the first is deserving of every happiness & the second a most interesting little creature I am glad to hear this, desolate as I am I cling to the idea that some of my friends at least are not like me. Again adieu

Your attached friend
MaryW. Shelley

ADDRESS: Thomas L. Peacock Esq / India House / London / Inghilterra / Londres. POSTMARKS: (1) GENOVA; (2) FPO / OC. 12 / 1822. UNPUBLISHED: a paragraph in Jones, #151. TEXT: MS., Pforzheimer Library.

1. "Outside the."

2. Shelley's allowance ceased with his death. Through the intercession of Peacock and Byron, Mary Shelley was attempting to receive a maintenance from Sir Timothy Shelley for herself and Percy. On 6 August, in a letter informing Timothy Shelley of his son's death, Peacock wrote: "He had not insured his life, and his widow and her infant son are left without any provision" (Peacock, *Works*, VIII, 229). On 18 October Peacock wrote to Mary Shelley: "Your Father has communicated to you his opinion that a personal application from Lord Byron's solicitor to Whitton on the subject of a permanent provision for you and your child will be the most advisable course . . ." (Peacock, *Works*, VIII, 232). Shelley had appointed Byron and Peacock as joint executors of his will.

3. Peacock's response to Mary Shelley's inquiries about the June quarter are of particular interest, since he refers to three letters from Mary Shelley, two of which have not been located; the third is Mary Shelley's letter of 15 August to Maria Gisborne. On 2 September Peacock had written: "I write from a cottage in the Chiltern Hills, in which I am lodging with my wife and child. I shall return to London on the 16th. Before I left town I received your letter, with the certificate of your little boy's baptism, with which I did as you requested. I have now received

two more letters from you, the first relating to Guebhard's bill of 220l., the second enclosing one for Mrs. Gisborne. . . . Brooks and Dixon have already fully explained to me the state of affairs between them and Shelley. They have paid the whole of his June quarter, with the exception of 8l., which they have still in hand. The bill of 220l., which was drawn on the 8th of July, must be for the September quarter, which he had requested them, and which they had refused, to advance. I understand it is customary, in cases of life annuity, to pay the full amount of the quarter in which an annuitant dies; therefore, I presume the quarter's annuity will be paid at Michaelmas; but Brooks and Dixon will not honour the bill unless, or until, they receive the money; and whether they will receive it or not cannot be known till the time arrives. I will do all that I can do in the matter when I return to town. I have been to Marlow, and have seen Maddocks. I am not yet in possession of the papers, but have no doubt that I shall be in about three weeks. I will procure the manuscripts from Ollier. I have the *Defence of Poetry*. Ollier lent it to me, and was to send for it when he wanted it for publication. He did not continue the *Miscellany*, and never applied for the manuscript. I have read your letter to Mrs. Gisborne with deep and painful interest. I forward it by this post. Her address is 33, King Street West, Bryanstone Square" (Peacock, *Works*, VIII, 230–31). In response to Mary Shelley's letter of 29 September, Peacock again saw Brooks and Dixon and found that Guebhard's bill was for the June quarter, that it had been accepted and would be paid by them. For the September quarter, however, it was necessary that application be made to Whitton, and Peacock suggested that Byron's solicitor should intercede (Peacock, *Works*, VIII, 231–32).

4. On 15 April 1823 Peacock sent Mary Shelley all the items she had requested, with the exception of the papers at Marlow (Peacock, *Works*, VIII, 232–34).

*To Martin Stow[1] Casa Negroto, Crosa di San Nazaro. Albaro.
Sunday Evening. [29 September 1822][2]

Dear Sir

I have left the Croix de Malthe and am now residing at this house. Whenever you find it convenient to take so long a walk to visit a very melancholy person I shall be very happy to see you.

Leigh Hunt is not yet arrived. I expect him tomorrow or Teusday. I have not heard from Captain Roberts, & know nothing either of him or my desk. Do you expect him soon?

You have had a grand procession today, have you not? I hope you were amused—

Your obedient Servant
Mary Shelley

[*P. 1, top*] Perhaps you would have the kindness to lend me a book to amuse me. Mine are all in durance. It would be a charity.—

Address: The Reverend Martin Stow / Carmine. Unpublished. Text: MS., Pforzheimer Library.

1. Perhaps the Rev. Martin Stow of Surrey (1793–1825), who took his B.A. at New College, Oxford (1815), and became chaplain to the bishop of Calcutta (*Alumni Oxonienses*, IV, 1362).

2. Mary Shelley's letter of 15 October explains that she moved to Casa Negrotto one week after her 18 September letter to Jane Williams, that is, c. 25 September. The only remaining Sunday in September 1822 was 29 September.

Percy Bysshe Shelley

Portrait by Amelia Curran, 1819, courtesy of the National Portrait Gallery, London

William Godwin

Portrait by James Northcote, 1802, courtesy of the National Portrait Gallery, London

Mary Wollstonecraft Godwin

Portrait by John Opie, 1797, courtesy of the National Portrait Gallery, London

William Shelley

Portrait by Amelia Curran, 1819, courtesy of
The Carl H. Pforzheimer Library

Claire Clairmont

Portrait by Amelia Curran, 1819, courtesy of the Nottingham Public Libraries

Leigh Hunt

Engraving by Henry Meyer from a drawing by John Hayten

Lord Byron

Portrait by Thomas Phillips, 1814, courtesy of Newstead Abbey, Nottingham Museums

Edward John Trelawny

From a sketch by Seymour Kirkup

Jane Williams

Portrait by George Clint, courtesy of the Bodleian Library

Edward Ellerker Williams

Portrait by George Clint, courtesy of
the Bodleian Library

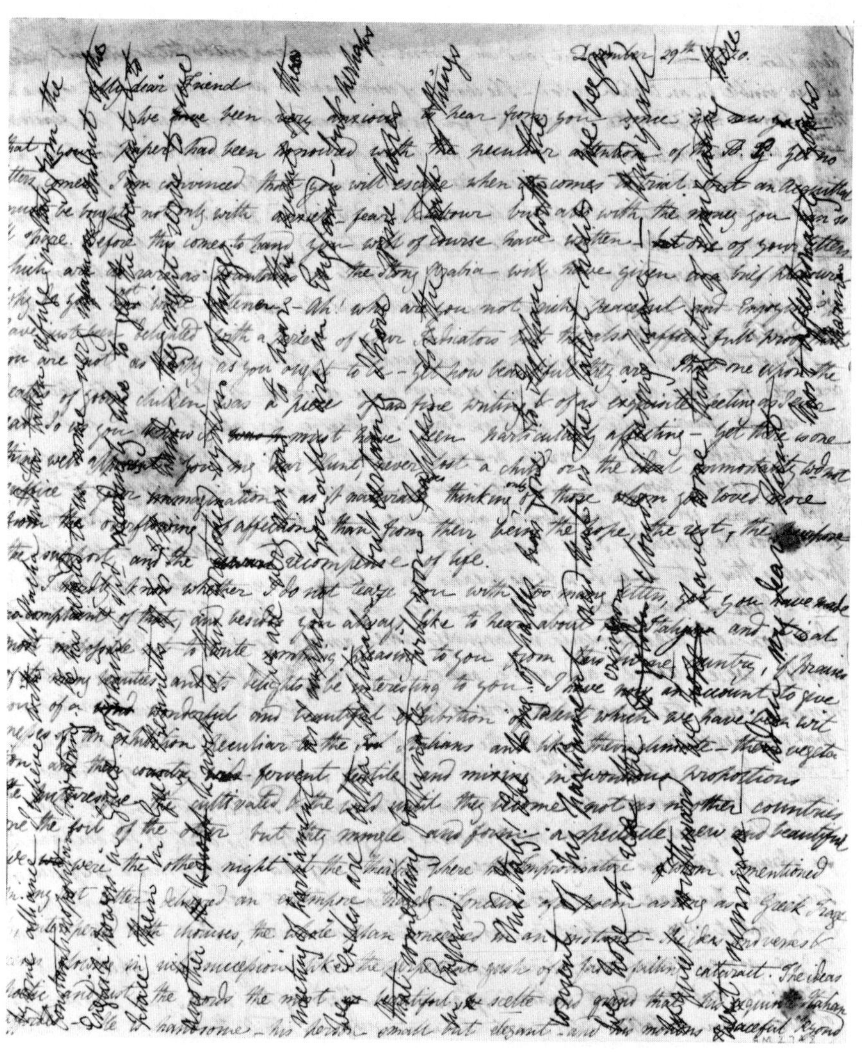

Letter from Mary Wollstonecraft Shelley to Leigh Hunt, 29 December 1820. An example of cross-writing, courtesy of the Huntington Library.

is on her way to England – I have asked her [illegible] which she will give to the Gisbornes; add to these [illegible] that I shall ask my father to send you, & making [illegible] here forwarding me the bill of lading.

I have written you a letter [illegible] my hand my natural impulse is to [illegible] but resisting that impulse I dare not [illegible] subject or I should never find it again. I have written [illegible] since that letter which I enclosed to you, they can tell you [illegible]

Thomas L. Peacock Esq
India House
London
Inghilterra

Londres.

F P O
OC 12
1822

real current of my mind is — alas! find in the whole world [illegible] ardent a being as mine own Shelley – & then tell me to be [illegible] & it is not he alone I have lost, though that misery, swallowing [illegible] other, has hitherto made me forgetful of all others – my best friend, [illegible] whom next to S. I loved – & whose virtues were worthy of the warmest [illegible] is gone – Jane (i.e. Mrs Williams) driven by her cruel fate to England, has also [illegible] What have I left? Not one that can console me – not one that [illegible]

Letter from Mary Wollstonecraft Shelley to Thomas Love Peacock, 29 September 1822. An example of cross-writing, with address, courtesy of The Carl H. Pforzheimer Library.

*To Jane Williams Genoa Oct 15th 1822

This letter will find you, dearest Jane, not only arrived in England, but I hope, somewhat reposed from your fatigue and from the agitation of your first arrival. It will find you in the midst of those friends, with whom your & dear Edward's lively descriptions have made me well acquainted. I anxiously wait to hear from you, my best girl, to sympathize in your sorrows, and yet in the mean time to hope the best for you. I know that you are so beloved by all that know you that I trust you find some consolation in your present society. As for me, dreadful as the idea of going to England was to me, I sometimes now think that I should be less miserable there than here; & yet I should not.—I wrote to you, my dear girl, from the Croce di Malta where I remained a week longer & then I removed (that change at least was for the better) to this house; where for another week I enjoyed tranquillity & perfect solitude. Enjoyed, I say; that is, each night was marked by tears & each day by a miserable & intolerable impatience which goaded me almost to madness. At the end of this week Pietro[1] & I began both of us to be somewhat uneasy at the non arrival of any of our friends whom we knew had left Pisa 8 days ⟨ago⟩ before.—Nor was the cause of this delay an agreable one, since Lord Byron had been confined to his bed at Lerici for four days by a rhumatic fever which made him suffer very much. Imagine He & train & the Hunts all at that most horrible place.—Since their arrival my mode of life has changed very litle. The Hunts live in the same house with me & I generally spend the evening with them, & often walk to Genoa with him. I have no cause to complain of either of them—Marianne is sick & goodtempered Motherly & industrious. Hunt taken up chiefly with his own thoughts, yet he has not annoyed me in any way. I hope I have not them; I know that neither of them would be indulgent to me if I did—I think of the life I lead with them and I weep to remember Pugnano.[2] Do you remember him, my best girl, as he scrambled up the hills or listened to your music, do you remember your own Edward, how we used, like children, to play in the great hall or your garden & then sit under the cypresses & hear him read his play?[3]—do you remember your own sweet self—breathing love & shedding happiness around you—nay you weep now—& so do I.—Three dear, beloved beings!—I am deserted by you all—but I must live—dearest, we may not rest.

—Well to the other personages of my uninteresting drama. I see nobody at all—Not even Trelawny—I wished to warn him away from Genoa,[4] but I have only seen him 3 times since his return here. Once for half an hour the day after—once at his lodgings with Hunt—& once he came in the evening here with Gabrielle. I do not lament his absence for myself alone—perhaps not at all on that account; I know indeed that he is the only one in Italy who has a sincere affection for me, perhaps his society might amuse me; but I cannot take the trouble of wishing for any thing, life must run on in its course, I will not as formerly be at the pains of decorating its banks—

it runs to its sea of repose—Eternity or the real sea—it is the same thing, & may be as dark & sullen as it will. But I cannot help lamenting the life he leads. He is at the Croce di Malta; Gabrielle sees him every day—generally dines with him there, & what will become of him when W. [*Wright*] comes home?—I have only seen LB. once & that by accident—his rhumatism has left him but has left him as the G— [*Guiccioli*] told me, very bilious, cross & sleepy. He was very complaisant to me however, after having teazed me about my having taken back one or two articles of the furniture I sold him.[5] I have copied for him the 10th Canto of Don Juan[6] It is not in his fine style, but there are some beautiful & many witty things in it—He calls Sir W. Curtis—"The witless Fallstaff of a hoary Hal"—the most severe satire I ever read—what is Fallstaff without his wit but a thing an old play must give a name to—and Hal without his youth but an unpardonable rake.—I have seen the G—i twice. This then is the whole history of my acquaintance & my life consequently would be sufficiently monotonous were it not for the endless change of thought & feeling which varies every hour of the day. I have chosen this as one of my best days to write to you: for being yesterday night teazed with the toothach I took a little laudanum which has quieted also a nervousness which preyed on me for a week, rendering every action of my life an act of pain. I rise about eight—copy S's Mss. work or read until 2. Dine and if I do not walk spend the afternoon as I spent the morning—and I pass the evening with the Hunts—Thus the sun rises & sets, but my days are no longer Italian days, cloudless & the same—look at your succession of fogs—rain—winds clouds—& now & then a ray, the memory of better times, to paint a rainbow—and this is my life.—

The Don Juan was sold—The Captain of the Palute at Via Reggio made the bargain that her finders shd have a third—the men came to Roberts to say that they had heard that half had been promised—R. [*Roberts*] sent them to LB. & LB said they shd have half. As Trelawny had given out at Leghorn that whoever found her shd have half I shd not have repined at this; but the men finding so ready an acquiescence to their demand, made a further one for their expences, which LB. also granted—so they got more than two thirds & from more than 400 cr. I only got 97.[7] the greater part of this (since Trelawny refuses every payment) belongs to you, dear Jane, & when I hear from you concerning Medwin I will see about the best way of letting you have it. Trelawny found the whole affair disposed of & finished when he arrived—most of the things were sold—some however were preserved though I have not yet received them & do not exactly know what. I have only the Mss. among them Ned's journal book. Trelawny made no enquiry about your things at Leghorn but as the journal book is with me I do not know how to send it to you: it is in excellent preservation nothing but the covers being destroyed. I copy for you all that he wrote after his departure from Lerici—it is short but as I cannot tell how to send the whole I am sure you wd like to see it. What, my dear Jane am I to do about it?—You may be sure that I will seize the first very safe opportunity of sending it to you—& I will let no one have it, not even Medwin if he comes.—"Monday July 1st calm & clear; Rose at four to get the topsails altered. At 12 a fine breeze from the westward tempted us to weigh for Leghorn; at 2 stretched across to Lerici to pick up Roberts, & ½ past found ourselves in the offing with a side wind. At ½ 9 arrived at Leghorn. A run of 45 to 50 miles in 7 hours & ½. Anchored astern of the Bolivar, from whom we procured cushions & made for ourselves a bed on board, not being able to get ashore after sunset; on account of health office shutting up at that hour. Teusday, July 2nd Fine weather. We heard this mg. [*morning*] that the Bolivar was about to sail for Genoa, & that Lord B was quitting Tuscany on account of Count G's [*Gamba's*] family having again been exiled thence. This on reaching the shore, I fo[und] really to be the case for they had just left the Police office, having there received their sentence. Met Lord B. a[t Dunns][8] & took leave of him. Was introduced to Mr Leigh Hunt & called on Mrs H. shopped & strolled about all day. Met L[t.] Marsham of the Rochfort, an old school fellow & shipmate.—Wednesday. July 3rd Fine. Strong sea breeze. called on Degough & red from him 220 crowns 3 p. 5 for a bill on Harvey for £50. drew on H for £25 more—on Paxtons for £50 and on Allat for £35. Wrote to each this day. Thursday—July 4th Fine. Processions of priests & religisi have for several days past been active in their prayers for rain—but the Gods are either angry or nature is too powerful."—And this, dear Jane, is all.

The Don Juan was found her topsails down and her other sails fast. Trelawny tells me that in his, Roberts & every other sailor's opinion that she was run down; of course by that Fishing boat—which confessed to have seen them. When I see Roberts I shall talk to him on this subject & tell you all he says—for I know that however painful you will wish to hear all. It may add a most bitter pang to know that they might have been saved—but so many circumstances have concurred to rob us of all we loved, that we can hardly put our finger on one solitary one & say that was it—a feather might have checked the progress of the chain—formed, no giant could break it.

As probably sometime will elapse before you can send me the things I asked for, will you in your next letter send me a drawing or description of Shelley's crest—a drawing it must be as I want to get it cut here on a stone I have: but it must be done by one who understands heraldy—it may be as small as possible, but pray send it in your next letter.

My little Percy is quite well and good—How are your children—how are you write often my dear Jane. I would not that the chain that binds us shd be snapped We may draw closer one day—soon perhaps—may we not?—Claire left Pisa on the monday she mentioned—T. [*Trelawny*] consequently did not see her. I have had a letter from her brother. Madme Hennikstein[9] is to receive her at her home. Gabrielle says that both Madme H & Madme Schwalb (the lady who wd have received her if Madme H. had not) are friends of hers, highly respectable people.—Good night—God bless my sorrowing Jane—I will add another word before I close my letter. Do you sleep now? it is 11 o'clock.

I have received my desk[10]—with several letters in it from me to mine own S. when he left me at Marlow to go to London for a few days—they are full of William—Clara & Allegra—I was in another world while I read them—when I had done even my Percy seemed a dream—for they were here—warm & living as he—& I am still here but they are not—My diamond cross was there too—the pledge of his safety who is no longer safe. The desk had been sent to LB. He read the letters—Ma che vuole che la dico?[11] There were some things a little against him—& others in praise of his writings—there was a lock of my S's hair & one of my Clara's—There is a fearful agony in that name for me—she was like him—But long, long ago I was destined to be the most miserable of living beings Percy w[d] go too, only then I sh[d] no longer be chained to time but sh[d] depart[12]—without self violence (which I wd never use) I know that I sh[d] then die. I have assurance of that and it renders me very tranquil sometimes in the midst of despair.—I have written to Miss Curran & I hope you will hear from her—Adieu, dear Jane—Affectionately Y[s] MaryW. Shelley

ADDRESS: Mrs. Williams / Mrs. Cleveland / 24 Alsop's Buildings / New Road—Marybone / Inghilterra—London. POSTMARKS: (1) GENOVA; (2) FPO / OC. 29 / 1822; (3) 12 o'Clock / OC. 29 / 1822 Nn. UNPUBLISHED. TEXT: MS., Pforzheimer Library.

1. Pietro Gamba awaited the Byron party at the Casa Saluzzo.
2. See 17–20 September 1822.
3. See [20 May 1825].
4. See 18 September 1822, n. 3.
5. For discussion of items Byron bought from Mary Shelley and Jane Williams, see Moore, *Accounts Rendered*, pp. 350–51, 495–97; Byron, *Works*, VI, 119–20.
6. On 9 October Byron wrote to Murray that Canto 10 was finished but not yet transcribed and Canto 11 was begun. By 24 October both cantos had been transcribed. Byron paid Mary Shelley to make copies of his work (Byron, *Works*, VI, 121, 130; Marchand, *Byron*, III, 1042).
7. Also retrieved from the *Don Juan* were "ninety and odd crowns" that Shelley was taking to Casa Magni. This sum also was turned over to Mary Shelley (Byron, *Works*, VI, 119).
8. From printed text of Williams, *Journals and Letters*.
9. Jeannette de Henickstein, whom Claire Clairmont had known in Pisa, became her good friend in Vienna (*CC Journals*, pp. 293, 359).
10. On 7 October (*MWS Journal*).
11. "But what can I say?"
12. Variant of *Adonais* 26. 9.

TO LORD BYRON [Genoa] Monday [21 October 1822]

My dear Lord Byron

The letters that I received today were from Jane, Claire, & M[rs] Gisborne,[1] nothing about business in any of them; indeed I do not expect to hear from my father before the expiration of a week. Mrs Gisborne saw him; she says—"I saw him alone, we spoke of you & of the ever to be lamented catastrophe without any expression or outward sign of sorrow. I thought that he had erred in his memorable assertion & that we human beings really were 'stocks & stones.' When Peacock called upon me, a tear did force itself into my eye in spite of all my struggles."

—But I do not write to your Lordship to tell you this, but to mention another subject in her letter. She says—"When Mr Gisborne went to Harrow, to accompany a son of Mr Clementi's who is placed in the Harrow school, he saw the grave of poor Allegra. This was precisely the day your father called on me, the funeral had taken place the day preceding. There was a great outcry among the Ultra priests on the occasion, and at the time they seemed resolved that the inscription intended by her father, should not be placed in the church. These Gentlemen would willingly cast an eternal veil over King David's infirmities & their own, but the world will peep through, even though poor Allegra should be without the honours of her inscription."[2]

Would you tell me the Book, Chapter & verse of this ⟨inscription⟩ quotation for the Epitaph.

I send you Lordship two letters from Hunt—he says that—"there appears some mistake about the Preface to the "Vision," but he hopes the realizations on the 7,000 will compensate for all defects."[3]

Jane writes from Paris—She has been very ill, but intends proceeding to England without delay. She desires to be remembered to you & begs me to remind you of your promise of bidding Murray send her your works.

This then is all my news.—Teresa's visit caused me to be out yesterday when you called, otherwise I am always at home at that hour & when you feel inclined to prolong your ride to this house you will be sure to find me.

I have nearly finished copying your savage Canto[4]—You will cause Milman to hang himself—"non c'è altro rimedio"—I was much pleased with your notice of Keats—your fashionable World is delightful—& your dove—you mention eight years—exactly the eight years that comprizes all my years of happiness—Where also is he, who gone has made this quite, quite another earth from that which it was?—There might be something sunny about me ⟨now⟩ then, now I am truly cold moonshine.[5]

Adieu, Truly yours,
Mary Shelley

PUBLISHED: Jones, #153. TEXT: MS., John Murray.

1. Maria Gisborne's letter of 8 October is Italian postmarked 21 October (Abinger MS.; Gisborne, *Journals and Letters*, pp. 89–93).

2. The result of the objection by the churchwarden and some parishioners was that no tablet or monument was erected in memory of Allegra, who was buried just inside the church door on 10 September 1822 (Marchand, *Byron*, III, 1001). Byron had asked John Murray to have inscribed on a marble tablet: "In memory of / Allegra, / daughter of G. C. Lord Byron, who died at Bagnacavallo, in Italy, April 20th, 1822, / aged five years and three months. / 'I shall go to her, but she shall not return to me.' 2d Samuel, xii. 23" (Byron, *Works*, VI, 70–72).

3. Seven thousand copies of the first issue of *The Liberal* (dated 15 October 1822) were printed. Byron's preface, explaining that *The Vision of Judgment* was aimed at Robert Southey and not at George III, was not published with the poem because John Murray failed to give it to John Hunt. The preface was printed in the second issue of *The Liberal*, 1 January 1823 (Marshall, *The Liberal*, pp. 53–54, 72–73, 78, 238). On 22 October Byron wrote John Murray an angry letter remonstrating with him for this omission (Byron, *Works*, VI, 126–27).

4. Canto 11 of *Don Juan*.

5. An identification of herself and the "cold chaste moon" of Shelley's poem *Epipsychidion* (line 281). In Mary Shelley's Journal entries of 5 and 10 October 1822 she refers to herself as "moonshine," not in a self-deprecating way but rather as a metaphor for her reflection of Shelley's sunshine and her commitment to "endeavour to consider my self a faint continuation of his being." A pertinent reference to Mary Shelley's seeming coldness appears in Emilia Viviani's letter to her of 24 December 1820: "Tu mi sembri un poco fredda, talvolta, e mi dai qualchè soggezione; ma conosco che tuo Marito disse bene, allorchè disse: che la tua apparente freddezza non è che la cenere che ricuopre un cuore affettuoso" (*S&M*, III, 559) ("You seem to me a little cold sometimes, and that causes me an uncomfortable feeling; but I know that your husband said well when he said that your apparent coldness is only *the ash which covers an affectionate heart*" [White, *Shelley*, II, 476]). The accusation of coldness troubled Mary Shelley throughout her life (see, for example, *MWS Journal*, 11 November 1822).

*To Lord Byron [Albaro] Wednesday [30 October 1822][1]

I asked Hunt to shew your Lordship Peacock's letter that you might see that in complying so kindly with my request the other day, you did that which appears to every one the best thing that can be done in the present state of my affairs.

You could not have sent me a more agreable task than to copy your drama,[2] but I hope you intend to continue it, it is a great favourite of mine.

Truly yours
Mary Shelley

ADDRESS: Rt. Honble Lord Byron / &c &c &c. UNPUBLISHED: summary in Jones, #154. TEXT: MS., John Murray.

1. On 23 October Byron had written to John Hanson, his solicitor, requesting that he contact Sir Timothy Shelley's solicitor on Mary Shelley's behalf (Byron, *Works*, VI, 127–28). Peacock's letter of 18 October advised just such action (see 29 September 1822 to Peacock). The first Wednesday Peacock's letter could have arrived at Genoa was 30 October, since mail from England to Genoa generally took from twelve to fourteen days.

2. *The Deformed Transformed*.

To Edward John Trelawny [Albaro] Saturday [November 1822][1]

My dear Trelawny

I called on you yesterday but was too late for you.

I was much pained to see you so out of spirits the other night—I can in no way make you better I fear, but I should be glad to see you—Will you dine with me monday after your ride—If Hunt rides as he threatens with Lord Byron he will also dine late, & make one of our party. Remember you will also do Hunt good by this, who pines in this solitude.

You say that I know so little of the world, that I am afraid that I may be mistaken in imagining that you have a friendship for me; especially after what you said of Jane the other night—but besides the many other causes I have to esteem you I can never remember without the liveliest gratitude all you said that night of agony when you returned to Lerici. Your praises of my lost Shelley were the only balm I could endure—& he also always joined with me in liking you from the first moment we saw you.

Adieu

Your attached friend

MWS

Have you got my books on shore from the Bolivar? If you have pray let me have them—for many of them are odd volumes, & I wish to see if they are to{o} much destroyed to rank with those I have.[2]—

PUBLISHED: Jones, #158. TEXT: MS., The Robert H. Taylor Collection, Princeton.

1. Trelawny's response to this letter, dated November 1822, is published in Trelawny, *Letters*, pp. 26–27.

2. Books retrieved from the *Don Juan* (Trelawny, *Records*, II, 46–47).

To Maria Gisborne

Albaro. Nov. 6th 1822

This, my dear Friend, will I believe only be an excuse for a letter; I have determined to write every day since I received yours, but yet I have never been able to prevail on myself so to do—First I have been occupied by writing an article for the Liberal[1]—& then I have been out of spirits—out of all desire to exert myself—I write now more for business than aught else—

I have not heard of Jane's arrival in England & am very anxious—I fear she is ill—for she wrote from Paris as if she were ill—I have heard from Miss Curran who is at Paris—My own Shelley's picture is at Rome, so nothing can be done about that. As soon as Jane writes to me—I shall see about her getting the money for my other commissions—and then pray send the things I asked for as quickly as possible.

Peacock says that he has got Shelleys—"Defence of Poetry." I wish him to send it to Mr John Hunt at the Examiner office[2]—Will you let him know that.

I am well—but very nervous—My poor child is quite well—My excessive nervousness (how new a disorder for me—my illness in the summer is the foundation of it) is the cause I do not write—& even now that I do I am in a state of excessive irritation. Well forgive me—I will seize my first <u>best</u> moment to scribble to better purpose than this scrawl—let me have long & frequent letters from you I pray.

I asked Jane to get for me, but if she be not arrived pray do you get &

send in your next letter, a drawing of Shelley's crest that I may get it engraved on a seal—do not confound the two baronatages Sir John & Sir Timothy—pray do this as it will be very easy to get a book with the Baronatage—the crest is all I want—but let it be well drawn that the people here may understand it—

I live as comfortably as I can—I do not wish for any change—except that I do not like Genoa ma pocca mi cale[3]—I am so thankful to Lord B. that he prevented my journey to England how miserable I should have been there—We have here the most divine Italian skies—having first had a meteora cioè a rovina d'Acqua[4]—that forced all the torrents from their beds & did infinite guasto near us—but we are at the top of the {h}ill & so did not suffer. Houses were thrown down & many walls—which is good —for the type of Genoa is a lane 10 feet wide between 2 stone walls each 20 feet hig[h][5] There is one pretty walk—Mrs Hunt is not I h[ope][6] worse than the season renders reasonable that she should be[7]—

This as I said is only an excuse for a letter—I write principally that Mr John Hunt may get the defence of poetry & that you may hear that I am well—so adieu—If I could get over the intense hatred I feel to every thing I think, do, or see I might get on—but day after day I long only more & more to go where all I love are save my poor boy who chains me here—

Adieu

Affectionately yours,
Mary W. Shelley

Will you add to the things sent out to me a bottle of lavender water?

ADDRESS: Mrs. Gisborne / 33 Kings Street West / Bryanstone Square / Inghilterra London. POSTMARKS: (1) GENOVA; (2) FPO / NO. 23 / 1822; (3) 12 o'Clock / No. 23 / 1822 Nn. ENDORSED: Recd. 23rd Nov. 1822 Ans. PUBLISHED: Jones, #155. TEXT: MS., Bodleian Library (MS., Shelley, c. 1, ff. 529–30).

1. On 10 November Mary Shelley recorded in her Journal: "I have made my first probation in writing & it has done me great good, & I get more calm." Mary Shelley's contribution to the second number of the *Liberal* was "A Tale of the Passions," a short story that, according to Elizabeth Nitchie, bears an endorsement of Shelley's and thus must have been written prior to Shelley's death (Nitchie, *Mary Shelley*, p. 156). On 5 December Mary Shelley informed Jane Williams that she had written "an Article (a Tale)" for the next *Liberal*. The location of the manuscript of "A Tale of the Passions" is presently unknown.

2. By 22 November Mary Shelley had received word that Peacock had given John Hunt the manuscript of *A Defence of Poetry* for inclusion in the second issue of the *Liberal* (see 22 November 1822). It remains unclear why it was not included in that issue or in either of the final two issues (Marshall, *The Liberal*, pp. 141–42).

3. "But it doesn't matter much to me."

4. "Meteor, that is, a heavy downpour."

5. Taken from John Gisborne Notebook No. 4, Abinger MS., Bodleian Library.

6. See n. 5.

7. Marianne Hunt was severely ill when she arrived in Italy. Vaccà who was consulted immediately after the Hunts' arrived at Pisa, misjudged her condition as hopeless (*PBS Letters*, #720).

TO LORD BYRON [Albaro] Saturday Morning. [16 November 1822][1]

I am induced to say a few words to your Lordship on this affair of Hunt's. I wish indeed that I could say them, as these things are always better said; but I will not venture on a second intrusion & dare not inflict upon you the pain of paying me a visit. Hunt did not send those letters to his nephew that he sent for you to read, and this delay has made him reflect. Indeed, my dear Lord Byron, he thinks much of this & takes it much to heart. When he reflects that his bread depends upon the success of this Journal, & that you depreciate it in those circles where much harm can be done to it; that you depreciate him as a coadjutor, making it his { } appear (pardon the quotation) that his poverty & not your will consents[2]—all this dispirits him greatly. He thinks that an explanation would come ungracefully from him, but that it would come gracefully from you. He is very much vexed that his Nephew noticed these reports, but they are noticed, Murray may publish, or give free circulation to your letter, and that places him in a kind of degrading point of view. For "his sick ⟨children⟩ wife & six children" are alledged—not your friendship for him. He said this evening that he thought of writing to you about this, but I offered to write instead, to spare him a painful task. He does not see my letter.

Consider that however Moore may laugh at Rimini-pimini, that Hunt is a very good man. Shelley was greatly attached to him on account of his integrity, & that really your letter does place him in an awkward situation. The Journal is now a work of charity—a kind of subscription for Hunt's family—this must hurt the work. Do not you then think that a few words from you in explanation or excuse such as could appear, are due to your literary companionship with him? It would be a goodnatured thing—& a ⟨friend⟩ prudent thing—since you would stop effectually the impertinence of Murray, by shewing him that he has no power to make you quarrel with your friend, & that you do not fear his treason.

It is a painful thing to me to put forward my own opinion. I have been so long accustomed to have another act for me; but my years of apprenticeship must begin. If I am awkward at first, forgive me. I would, like a dormouse, roll myself in cotton at the bottom of my cage, & never peep out. But I see Hunt annoyed in every way. Let us pass over his vanity. What if that has been pampered—little else about him has—& qualms have visited him even upon that tender point. But here even the independance of his character is in some measure staked—Besides the success of his Journal—& consequently his very existence. So I would fain do a little to make him easy again. You asked me the other evening, why I had not sent you a note about it; I do so now. So do not think me impertinent; if you do not know that I am timid, yet I am so;—it is a great effort to me to intrude with my writing upon you. But if I can make Hunt have less painful feelings by inducing you to soften the effect that your letter must have had in London, why for that I will even risk being impertinent.[3]

I have copied your MSS.[4] The "Eternal Scoffer" seems a favourite of yours. The Critics, as they used to make you a Childe Harold, Giaour, & Lara all in one, will now make a compound of Satan & Cæsar to form your prototype, & your 600 firebrands in Murray's hands will be in costume. I delight in your new style more than in your former glorious one, & shall be much pleased when your fertile brain gives my fingers more work.

Any news of Douglass Kinnaird?[5] May I ask you to answer this letter soon as Hunt's letters for England will not be written until it arrives, & really another post ought not to be lost.

Again I beg your Lordship to excuse my annoying you—

Truly Yours
Mary Shelley.

ADDRESS: To the Right Honble. / Lord Byron. PUBLISHED: Jones, #156. TEXT: MS., John Murray.

1. Byron's letter of 9 October 1822 to John Murray expressed discontent with the *Liberal* and with the Hunts (Byron, *Works*, VI, 123–24). John Murray circulated Byron's letter, and word of it reached John Hunt and his son, Henry Hunt. The latter dared Murray to publish Byron's letter in the *Examiner* of 27 October 1822 and suggested that it was a forgery. The younger Hunt also sent word of the affair and the published dare to Leigh Hunt, who was greatly distressed by it. The earliest this letter could have arrived was 8 November. Byron, regarding Murray's behavior as "indiscreet," mildly reproved him and assured Hunt of his good will (Byron, *Works*, VI, 138, 174). In an 11 November letter to Byron that demonstrates that his feelings were somewhat pacified, Hunt told Byron that he would write to his nephew by "return of post, and shew you, as usual what I write" (Brewer, *The Holograph Letters*, p. 122). Hunt's letter to his nephew is dated 14 November (Brewer, *The Holograph Letters*, p. 157). In accordance with his word, Hunt sent the letter to Byron to read and on the same day (14 November), Byron wrote Mary Shelley that "the letter is all very well" and went on to reiterate his positive appraisal of Hunt's character (unpublished MS., University of Iowa). In the same letter, Byron sent Mary Shelley the completion of the first part of *The Deformed Transformed.* Since Mary Shelley's letter indicates that she was writing on a Saturday after Byron had read Hunt's letter to his nephew and also that she had copied Byron's MS. (and refers to other details of Byron's letter of 14 November, including Kinnaird's health [see below, n. 5]), we may conclude that Mary Shelley's letter was written on 16 November.

2. *Romeo and Juliet* 5. 1. 75: "My poverty but not my will consents."

3. For Byron's response to Mary Shelley's letter, see Byron, *Works*, VI, 174–75 (undated).

4. See above, n. 1.

5. Douglas James Kinnaird (1788–1830), Byron's trusted friend and adviser.

To Lord Byron [Albaro] Saturday [16 November 1822]

Hunt does not feel so lightly as your Lordship does as to what the world will say, & he has a deeper stake than you in it. I have read to him the principal part of your letter[1] & will write word for word his answer. I will add nothing—for really I have nothing to say—except that Murray is a troublesome fellow & his first firebrand would have been more agreable if like the Widow's it, had been hid under a bushell. Hunt says—"That he thinks something better might have been done, but that these are matters of taste, which it is not to be supposed that any body can alter at a moment's notice, even if they ought. And that with regard to friendship, he feels that his friendship, in the sense in which you speak of it, is in the other world."—

Certainly if you did not feel any for one of such transcendant merit, & whose merit you so freely acknowledged & praised, as Shelley, he cannot complain. For your pursuits & tastes were far more congenial—& then none of that delicasy you mention, which is the death of all sentiment, had existence between you. I do not think that his poverty in any degree enters into your consideration, unless to make you hold your hand—for I believe that talents & genius would at any time in your mind outweigh the [ ] Pens. He sees this somewhat differently & talks about your being a Lord, he is quite in the wrong—it is Rimini-pimini-follage & all that,[2] which makes you dislike entering into the journal, although his talents of another kind have caused you to enter into it.

You cannot tell how I have been pained in entering into this subject [with] you.—But I shall annoy you no more—

Ever your's obliged,
Mary Shelley

ADDRESS: To the Right Honble / Lord Byron. PUBLISHED: Jones, #157. TEXT: MS., John Murray.

1. Mary Shelley wrote this letter in response to Byron's answer to hers of that morning (see Saturday Morning. [16 November 1822]).

2. Hunt's *Story of Rimini* (1816), dedicated to Byron, and *Foliage* (1818) provoked a number of hostile reviews, particularly critical was a series by John Gibson Lockhart in *Blackwood's Edinburgh Magazine* (see Reiman, *The Romantics Reviewed*, Part C, I, 49–53, 80–89, 111–17).

TO MARIA GISBORNE

Albaro near Genoa. Nov. 22nd 1822

My dear Friend

No one ever writes to me. Each day, one like the other, passes on and if I were where I would that I were methinks I could not be more forgotten. I cannot write myself, for I cannot fill the paper always with the self same complaints—or if I write them, why send them, to cast the shadow of my misery on others. What I have endured is not to be alleviated by time; for every new event & thought brings more clearly before me the fearful change. My ideas wanting their support, fall—wanting their mate, they pine—& nothing the earth contains can alleviate that. I see no one who did not know him & thus I try to patch up the links of a broken chain. I see consequently only the Hunts, Lord Byron & Trelawny. But although Hunt knew him, he did not know him lately, my freshest impressions are void for him, & he did not know Edward, who after My Lost One I loved best. Lord Byron reminds me most of Shelley in a certain way, for I always saw them together, & when LB. speaks I wait for Shelley's voice in answer as the natural result[1]—but this feeling must wear off—& there is so little resemblance in their minds, that LB. seldom speaks to me of him without unwittingly wounding & torturing me. With Trelawny I can talk & do talk for hours unwearedly of both, but he is about to leave us[2] & then I shall be thrown on my own mind to seek in its frightful depths for memories & eternal sorrow.

Pardon me, my dear Mrs Gisborne, that I still write to you in this incoherent and unletterlike manner. But I strive in vain to do better My last letter is a proof of how I succeed for when I curb myself to the relation of facts alone, or determine so to curb myself, I put off writing from day to day endeavouring to catch the moment when I shall feel less, but the pen in my hand the same spirit guides it, & one only thought swells the torrent of words that is poured out. Perhaps it would be better not to write at all; but the weakness of human nature is to seek for sympathy:—I think but of one thing—my past life—while living (do I live now?) I loved to imagine futurity, & now I strive to the same—but I have nothing desirable to imagine, save death; & my fancy flags or sleeps or wanders when it endeavours to pursue other thoughts.—I imagine my child dead & what I should do then—never does the idea of peaceful futurity intrude itself—I feel that my whole life is one misery—it will be so—mark me—I shall never know peace:—my only safeguard is in not seeking it, for so surely as I do shall I be cast wounded, helpless & lacerated on the barren rocks of my most cheerless life

Again why do I write this. Let me say something else. The Hunts are getting on well—Marianne is not better but she is not worse—Hunt writes—& he turns over the pages of books & he makes puns—& save the same want of tact which he ever had, he is good & kind. We often see Trelawny of an evening—Hunt likes him very much, & for me I feel so deep a gratitude towards him that my heart is full but to name him. He supported us in our miseries, my poor Jane & I.—But for him menials would have performed the most sacred of offices—& when I shake his hand I feel to the depth of my soul that those hands collected those ashes—Yes—for I saw them burned & scorched from the office—no fatigue—no sun—or nervous horrors deterred him, as one or the other of these causes deterred <u>all</u> others—he stood on the burning sands for many hours beside the pyre—if he had been permitted by the soldiers he would have placed him there in his arms—I never—never can forget this—And now he talks of little else except my Shelley & Edward.—

I am very anxious to hear from Jane—It must be more than a month since I had a letter from her dated Paris. I wish to hear of her safe arrival at least—And next to that I wish for the papers Peacock is to send out to me. I wish <u>all</u> Mss. to be sent without any exception & that as soon as possible. I have heard from Miss Curran, she is in Paris, & My Shelley's picture is at Rome—nothing can be done therefore with regard to that—

so pray let me have the Mss. without any delay. If you shd receive a packet from Miss Kent directed to me pray send it with them. But let me entreat you, as you love me, to wait f[or][3] nothing—but the very moment the Mss. are obtained from P[eacock][4] to send them to me—sending me the bill of lading. This is of more consequence to me than you think.

I wish you would enter into an unbreakable engagement to me to write to me once a month. Your letter may be the work of several hours scattered over the month; but put a long letter into the post for me the first day of every month. I want some object, some motive, great or small—I should look forward to your letter as a certain thing, & it would be something to expect. Never mind what you write about—let it be about his friends—some facts—it would be a great solace to me indeed it would. If you see Jane, there will be plenty to say about her.

Well Good night—for tonight I will write no more—as usual all are in bed except me—my restless thoughts, homeless in this world, if they do not steal to the bed side of my sleeping babe, & then I tremble, wander to seek him who lives—& gives me strength to grieve eternally—Good night!—

Percy is quite well. After all there is something about him that seems of this world—I know not what. But I think the new soul tries to amalgamate itself with its stubborn shrine—& if it be too finely tempered it cannot succeed—if it does a certain something—earthly thought [*though*] good, seems to announce the decision of Nature. So it is with Percy—the crisis was last summer—how I trembled for him then—& now it is not reason but habit that makes me shudder

I hear through Hunt's nephew that Peacock has given the "Essay on Poetry" to be published for the Liberal & Peacock added that he had other Mss. of Shelleys—which says Young Hunt—"We will procure"—now I am convinced there is nothing perfect and I wish all to be sent to me without delay,[5] & nothing but this "Essay on poetry" to be given to the Liberal. Pray let all Mss. of whatever kind—letters &c be sent to me immediately. A Miss Hitchener[6] has some Mss. of Shelley. She is dead, but they may be in the hands of her Executor & you would afford me the greatest consolation I am capable of having & d[o me an act][7] of real, real friendship if you wd stir yourselves to get them. Hogg or Peacock wd tell you about her place of abode. Miss Westbrook, Harriets sister, now I see married to Mr Beauchamp[8] has a quantity of Mss.—now I fear it would be utterly useless to endeavour to get them from her. But she being married—God knows—the thing might be tried, & the pleasure done to me immense.

Pray write soon. Post after post & I hear nothing from any body.

The quotation I sent from Shakespear for the velvet was wrong—the words are I believe—"There is nothing in us but must suffer a sea change"[9] —I have not a Shakespear to refer to—but will you look at the Tempest & if it be not too late get it written rightly. Adieu.

Affectionately yours
MaryW. Shelley

I hear that Jane is arrived through Miss Kent.—I am glad of that at least, for I began to be anxious.

[*P. 1, top*] Would you send a box of letters for Percy?

ADDRESS: Mrs. Gisborne / 33 King's Street West / Bryanstone Square / Inghilterra London / Londres. POSTMARKS: (1) GENOVA; (2) FPO / DE. 9 / 1822; (3) 12 o'Clock / DE. 9 / 1822 Nn. PUBLISHED: Jones, #159. TEXT: MS., Bodleian Library (MS., Shelley, c. 1, ff. 531–32).

1. Mary Shelley wrote of the melancholy effect that Byron's voice had on her in her *Journal* entry of 19 October 1822.

2. By 20 December Trelawny had left Genoa for Leghorn. He then went to the Maremma to hunt and then to Rome and Florence before returning to Genoa in mid-June (Trelawny, *Letters*).

3. Taken from John Gisborne Notebook No. 4, Abinger MS., Bodleian Library.

4. See n. 3.

5. See 29 September 1822 to Peacock.

6. Elizabeth Hitchener (?1782–1822) became Shelley's "disciple" in 1811. By 1812 Shelley referred to her as "the Brown Demon," and she, in turn, wrote bitter letters about him to their mutual friends. She died shortly before 8 March 1822, and a number of her letters from Shelley, in the care of her executor, H. Holste, eventually went to the British Library (David Booth and Elizabeth Hitchener, *Evra and Zephyra, The Fire-side Bagatelle, The Weald of Sussex*, with an introduction by Donald H. Reiman [New York: Garland Publishing, 1978], pp. i–iv).

7. See above, n. 3.

8. Elizabeth Westbrook married Robert Farthing Beauchamp. Maria Gisborne responded that Godwin might be the appropriate person to approach the Westbrook family. Ianthe Shelley eventually inherited Shelley's notebook, now known as the *Esdaile Notebook* (Ianthe Shelley married Edward Jeffries Esdaile in 1837) (Shelley, *The Esdaile Notebook*, ed. Kenneth Neill Cameron [London: Faber and Faber, 1964], pp. vi–vii).

9. See 17–20 September 1822.

To Lord Byron

Casa Negroto Wednesday
[27 November 1822][1]

My Dear Lord Byron

I have received a letter this morning from my father.—He says: "—I saw young Hanson today. His father has not yet seen Whitton. He is over head & ears in an unlucky business of his own respecting his daughter the Countess of Portsmouth.[2] This business is now almost every day before the L. [*Lord*] Chancellor. The young man however has promised me an interview with his father in a day or two. I told him I was writing this day to Italy. You shall hear from me the moment I know any thing material on the subject."—I have plenty of patience in all this, and yet one way or another I shall be very glad when I come to a certainty on my affairs. However thanks to your Lordship's having prevented my journey to England, I can wait without any inconvenience for some time longer.

I have had also a letter from Jane. She is arrived, is in good health & is at present residing with her Mother. She desires to be kindly remembered to you.

This is all my news. Except that both my father & Jane say that Peacock does not appear lukewarm but assiduous in my affairs. This is indeed of much consequence as he is on the spot. Besides that it is always a pleasant thing to receive kindnesses; and I need not say how truly I thank you for those that you have shewn me. I am quite of the old school with regard to gratitude & I feel it very deeply whenever my friends are good enough to shew affection for me and I am not afraid of being misinterpreted when I express it—

Truly yours
Mary Shelley.

PUBLISHED: Jones, #160. TEXT: MS., John Murray.

1. Godwin's letter, dated 15 November, is Italian postmarked 27 November (Abinger MS.).

2. John Hanson's eldest daughter, Mary Anne, had married Lord Portsmouth on 7 March 1814. A commission of lunacy was taken against Lord Portsmouth in 1822 by his nephew and next heir, Henry Wallop Fellowes. Byron, who had given the bride away, signed an affidavit affirming Portsmouth's sanity at the time of the marriage. In February 1823 a jury declared Portsmouth insane since 1809. Byron commented: ". . . but I could not forsee that a man was to turn out mad, who had gone about the world for fifty years, as competent to vote, and walk at large; nor did he seem to me more insane than any other person going to be married" (see Byron, *Works*, VI, 177).

Whitton and Hanson were in correspondence between 22 and 27 November, but on 17 December Whitton declined to discuss the matter with Hanson and requested instead a written application. On 20 December Whitton sent Hanson an unfavorable response (Ingpen, *Shelley in England*, p. 562).

*To Jane Williams — Genoa Decr 5th 1822

Your letter, my best Jane, was exceedingly welcome to me. I had been under some anxiety concerning your safe arrival; but Miss Kent had relieved that the day before by mentioning having seen you. You are then now, my poor girl, surrounded by all that can most painfully remind you of the past; cheer up, our journey is not yet over but some day all this will be only a very frightful dream, at least we are hardly used indeed if being placed here only to suffer we do not reap hereafter sweet fruit from the bitter tree of life. I was much surprized to hear of Spencer's death, but not {at} all at the brutality of M^rs W's [*Williams's*] conduct,[1] it is in entire keeping with all that I have ever heard of her; but she is too miserable a creature to wound more than all sensitive natures must be wounded by the near contact of evil. I hope she can do you no real harm, and that very soon you will be out of the reach even of her annoyances.

Not the slightest change has taken place in my circumstances or mode of life since I last wrote to you. About a month ago I had a letter from my father saying that no application had been made to Sir Timothy and that he wish LB. to request his Solicitor Hanson to make it. LB instantly by return of post wrote to Hanson directing him so to do, by a letter received from my father by the same post as yours it appears nothing had yet been done. LB is to me as kind as ever; I hardly ever see him, manco male;[2] but he is all profession & politeness & in the only instance (that of writing to Hanson) that I called on him for action he complied with my request in the kindest or fullest manner. I do not suppose any miracle worked in my favour, or that his defect would not touch me if I touched it, but his purse-strings are yet undrawn by me & will remain so, & that you know is the tender point. He is kept in excellent order, quarelled with & hen-pecked to his hearts content—but mention none of this gossip I entreat you to another—He has done himself with T—y. [*Trelawny*] & overdone himself with R—ts. [*Roberts*] on account of some old clothes, quite in the auctioneering taste, & this defect of his grows & grows until his whole character is overshadowed by its virtue killing shade.[3]—T—y. is a great contrast to him. He never was more amiable or generous than now. W.[4] has returned; he only suspects platonism & shuts G. [*Gabrielle*] up; & T—y ought to go & as soon as fine weather comes will I believe certainly go—to shoot in the Maremma with R—ts—but as he intends going on horseback a long continuation of tempo il più patetico[5] render his journey just now impracticable. He passes nearly every evening with the Hunts & me; Hunt likes him very much; his situation with us all has caused him to cast aside that indelicasy of manner & speech that often annoyed Ned & us—and he is so truly generous that when he allows that part of him to be uppermost he must be liked—I have many reasons for being attached to one who was our chief support in our excessive misery; & now he is the only person to whom I can talk of Ned, and we do talk of him for hours together, of both indeed as you may guess.

I do not know what to say to you of Marianne's health, for I do not know what to think of it myself. She ought to have remained at Pisa for this is a frightful climate, cold & rainy. She is not worse than one might have expected—but she is very ill—This winter & spring will be very critical to her, but I am not without hopes. What a detestable place this is! We are in a good home out of the town—but the sea, though I seldom look at it, is near, & when the dull scirocco, windless but coming up from the sea, reigns here its hateful roar comes on me in the silence of night & almost drives me mad—How very glad I shall be to get away—I have thought a great deal about what I had better do, and with my prospects yet so uncertain, I also must be very undecided. If things go well with me I think that I shall make my future residence at Florence, for that is a large town, and it is probable that the Hunts will go there also.—There is something inexpressibly dispiriting & miserable in looking forward to what I had better Do—for there is only a choice of evils for me, & so very lately I had such bright prospects—but I must look forward for I can never decide on any thing at the moment, but must make up my mind long before, and I hate Genoa so cordially that I would not stay here longer than is necessary to me for the world. It is folly to look forward if it be to dwell on happiness, but it is only prudence in me to endeavour to fix my very wavering mind, although when I have resolved on any thing, it will probably be just the thing I cannot do. I hope to be quiet, for forced to study, & even desiring to study and understand my nature, I am more & more convinced that blank as my future life must be, it is only in books and literary occupation that I shall ever find alleviation. Friendship can do little more than remind me of what I have lost. After having written an Article (a Tale)[6] for the ensueing number of the Liberal I am employed in copying my Shelleys Mss. I do not know what I shall make of this as yet—for there are not many things—however I shall write to Peacock for his advice, & I must employ some time in arranging them as I cannot conclude without receiving those now in England.

I have heard from Miss Curran (she does not mention her marriage)[7] she is in Paris; the picture is in Rome to which place she expects to return next spring when I am to have it—I have told her that you will send her for me a copy of Ned's picture of S. will you do this as she has much talent and may be able to make a good picture from both together.[8] You know, my dear Jane, that I intended through Medwin not only to provide you funds for my commissions but to repay you the balance of what I owe you from the money got up from the bottom of the sea—(to shew us the truth of LB's remark—that all in nature is more durable than the divine form of man—and to contradict a remark of Plato's that I copied from one of my Shelley's Mss books—also got up from the same place, that that which is most perfect is most durable, if so, my unhappy girl, we should still be with the two most perfect creatures this earth contained,)—but of the money; St Aubyn[9] writes to Try [*Trelawny*] that Medwin is married, but yet I cannot prevail on myself to ask for the crowns.[10] LB. offered to write to him as executor—I refused then but perhaps I shall request that he will—in the mean time, never mind, or think of my commissions until I send you money, unless you are able to send me a copy of dearest Edward's picture of himself.—In the mean time I am very anxious for the papers that Peacock is to send me, & if you can at all hasten them, I know you will, as in a thousand ways they are of consequence to me. Let the box be directed to me or Hunt not to LB. who would open the box & read all the papers, letters particularly, before he sent them to me.—You have then seen my father. Until I knew Shelley I may justly say that he was my God—& I remember many childish instances of the excess of attachment I bore for him. This is past—all good is past for me, and all feelings except painful ones are far less vivid within me since life has become the solitude for me.

I have had only one letter from Claire from Vienna. Ty has had several long ones, he has not shewn them to me, he has at least had that delicasy, nor would I have read them.[11] He is however very discontented with her because she sent him an untimely & undeserved scolding for not having written to her, when as he says he went to Leghorn merely to see her—however he praises her after all. You will have seen her mother—and perhaps William also; I should like to know your unreserved opinion of the latter; having hardly ever seen him during the last eight years, my wishes more than my affections are interested in him, & I really wish to know the truth about him. I have written to my father for his advice concerning the publication of the marriage[12]—but in any case, Hunt says that an article upon my lost one (including I believe a part of T—ys Mss—but I do not know how much since both H. & Marianne loudly exclaimed against its horror & impropriety—so preserve the original & send me a copy if you can by box) will appear in the 3 number of the Liberal. ⟨I am very⟩ & then something will be said to put the matter to rest.

This place is almost as unlike Pisa as England can be—We have a succession of rains, storms & wind, such as I never before witnessed in Italy. I hope—& if I dare speak so—am determined never to pass another winter here. But I have no right to complain—I am quiet— & the Hunts kind—Hunt indeed the other day shewed a delicasy of kindness for which I am deeply grateful—& pardon all the past—if he pardons it—Indeed I was not then responsible for what I did—and the agony I suffered in that coach was a sufficient punishment if I did wrong.

So I write & read—& am again transformed into the silent Mary. During later years, and particularly after your & Edward's gaiety of character had given to my mind the spring it wanted, I was no longer the silent and the serious—but I am so again—& then I am that which before this fatal summer, I never was—nervous to a degree that borders on insanity sometimes—You will think that I make up for my silence in speech by my garullity on paper—& so indeed it is—I can speak of nothing but the one train of feeling which engrosses me—I cannot speak of that—but I can write, & so I scrible—But good Night, my beloved Jane—God bless you! This {is} not a mere word—God has still one blessing for you & me—the hope—the belief of se{e}ing them again, & may that blessing be as entirely yours as it is mine.

The Hunts send their kindest love. A series of very bad weather has prevented our seeing Ty for several days or I am sure he w^{d} return with interest your affectionate messages

Percy is quite well—And I am very glad to hear of the health of yours kiss them both—particularly my little God-daughter for me, & teach her to think of her God-mother in Italy—

Adieu, my best girl—misfortune has both united & seperated us—but the union is the strongest power of the two, so until death I am

Affectionately Yours
Mary W. Shelley

ADDRESS: Mrs. Williams / Mrs. Cleveland / 24 Alsop's Buildings / New Road / Londres Marybone / Inghilterre. POSTMARKS: (1) GENOVA; (2) FPO / DE. 23 / 1822; (3) [ ] o'Clock / DE. 23 / 1822 Nn. UNPUBLISHED: TEXT: MS., Abinger MS., Bodleian Library.

1. Jane Williams's letter of 13 November begins: "You will not have been more

anxious to hear from me than I to write to you my dear Mary; but I have delayed doing so from time to time, in the hope of being able to give you some account of my affairs; a fortnight has now elapsed since I began to put them in train, and it was only yesterday I heard that it was probable letters of administration would be granted me; as Mr Spencer the Executor has been some time dead; it will be an advantage to me I am told, but in what way I know not; and this is all I can tell you at present on this subject, which is one of the greatest interest at this moment to my friends—

"Behold me my dear Mary in this land of tyranny and misery! You know I always hailed my arrival here with all the evil forebodings of prophetic truth and they are realized to the full extent—On my arrival my Mother had just received the following note from Mrs. Williams. 'Madam I desire you will send by the bearer the remains of my lamented Edward as I have prepared a vault for them at Millbrook.' This delicate and feeling appeal was sent by an undertaker at seven in the morning my Mother of course declined any conference on the subject. Mrs W. then sent a message by Mr Spencer's brother saying she wished to settle her affairs and would educate my children provided I would yield all claim to them; as she would by no means suffer my interference or controul in any thing that regarded them—To this I made a suitable reply—" (Abinger MS.).

Jane Williams's anxieties about her right to Edward Williams's estate and the actions of Williams's stepmother, Mary Ann Williams (see 9–11 September [1823], n. 14), stemmed from the fact that she and Williams had not been legally married because she was already married (see [14–15] January 1821). In her letter of 13 November she informed Mary Shelley that "her legal tyrant" was then in London (see also Lovell, *Medwin*, pp. 136–39).

2. "So much the better."

3. Byron gave two crew members of the *Bolivar* the clothes he had bought for them but denied the clothes to two others he believed dishonest, and Roberts tried to change Byron's mind (Byron, *Works*, VI, 142, 144–46).

4. Gabrielle Wright's husband.

5. "Melancholy weather."

6. See 6 November 1822.

7. Jane Williams had informed Mary Shelley that Amelia Curran had been married for two years.

8. Jane Williams's letters discuss both the portrait of Shelley by Amelia Curran and a drawing of Shelley by Edward Williams. Jane Williams's letter of 13 November 1822 informed Mary Shelley that as yet she had been unable to locate Amelia Curran, whom she believed to be married and, according to Godwin, living in Paris. On 22 December 1822, Jane Williams wrote of Williams's drawing: "I am in hopes of getting a good picture of our Shelley I have given it to a lady of great talent who has promised to make the alterations I suggested and if it is a good likeness I think I can make interest to get it engraved. I am also endeavouring to get a front likeness of my Angel the moment I succeed with either you shall have copies." On 12 February 1823 Jane Williams reported that the artist engaged to do the alterations had changed her mind: "I think you had better get Miss Currans and see what can be made of it and I will in the meantime seek another person to copy Edward's drawing of our Shelley" (Abinger MS.). For a lengthy discussion of Williams's portraits of Shelley and reproductions of the portraits, see White, *Shelley*, I, frontispiece; II, 518–19, 523–30.

9. Sir John St. Aubyn (1758–1839), a former M.P. with an annual income said to be £76,000, was described by Trelawny as "well read, and polished by long intercourse with intelligent men of many nations . . . his dining hall was open to his friends" (Lovell, *Medwin*, p. 66). Medwin regarded St. Aubyn as a cherished friend.

10. It was Mary Shelley's understanding that the crowns Shelley gave Medwin on 10 March 1822 were a loan, but it is possible that Shelley gave them as a gift (Lovell, *Medwin*, p. 110).

11. Trelawny, declaring his love to Claire Clairmont, had tried to prevent her from going to Vienna (*CC Journals*, pp. 284–85).

12. Jane Williams had written: "Your marriage should be made public: it is neither known nor believed; and was absolutely denied in one of the papers the other day."

*To Lord Byron [Albaro] Saturday. [?14 December 1822][1]

Your Lordships MS. was very difficult to decypher, so pardon blunders & omissions

I like your Canto extremely; it has only touches of your highest style of poetry, but it is very amusing & delightful. It is a comfort to get anything to gild the dark clouds now my sun is set.—Sometimes when very melancholy I repeat your lyric in "The Deformed", & that for a while enlivens me:—But—

But I will not scrawl nonsense to you

Adieu Yours MaryS.

Address: To the Rt Honble / Lord Byron. Unpublished. Text: MS., John Murray.

1. By 24 October Mary Shelley had copied Canto 11. She copied Canto 12 between 7 and 14 December, and Cantos 13 through 16, as well as further scenes from *The Deformed Transformed*, before 21 May 1823 (Steffan, *Byron's Don Juan*, I, 307, 308–9). This letter is placed at its earliest possible date.

To Claire Clairmont [Albaro 19 December–] Decr 20th 1822

My dear Claire

I have delayed writing to you so long for two reasons. First, I have every day expected to hear from you, and secondly I wished to hear something decisive from England to communicate to you. But I have waited in vain for both these things. You do not write—and I begin to despair of ever hearing from you again. A few words will tell you all that has been done in England. When I wrote to you last I think that I told you that LB. had written to Hanson bidding him call upon Whitton. Hanson wrote to Whitton desiring an interview which W. declined requesting H. to make his application by letter; which H. has done—& I know no more. This does not look like an absolute refusal—but Sir T. [*Timothy*] is so capricious that we cannot trust to appearances.

And now the chapter about myself is finished, for what can I say of my present life. The weather is bitterly cold with a sharp wind—very unlike dear—Carissima Pisa—but soft airs and balmy gales are not the attributes of Genoa—which place I daily & duly join Marianne in detesting. There is but one fire place in the house—& although people have been for a month putting up a stove in my room, it smokes too much to permit of its being lighted. So I am obliged to pass the greater part of my time in Hunt's sitting room, which is as you may guess the annihilation of study—& even of pleasure to a great degree. for after all Hunt does not like me;[1] it is both our faults & I do not blame him, but so it is. I rise at nine. breakfast work read and if I can at all indure the cold, copy my Shelleys Mss. in my own room & if possible walk before dinner—after that I work—read Greek &c till ten when Hunt & Marianne go to bed. Then I am alone. Then the stream of thought which has struggled against its argine[2] all through the busy day, makes a piena,[3] and sorrow, & memory and imagination—despair—& hope in despair are the winds & currents that impel it. I am alone & myself—And then I begin to say—as I ever feel—"How I hate life! What a mockery it is to rise, to walk, to feed & then go to rest & in all this a statue might do my part. One thing alone may or can awake me, & that is study the rest is all nothing."—And so it is!—I am silent & serious. Absorbed in my own thoughts—What am I then in this world, if my spirit live not to learn & to become better—that is the whole of my destiny, I look to nothing else. For I dare not look to my little darling other than as—not the sword of Damocles—that is a wrong simile—or to a wrecked seaman's plank—true he stands, & only he, between me & the sea of eternity but I long for that plunge—no I fear for him, pain disappointment—all—all fear.

You see how it is—It is near eleven & my good friends repose—this is the hour when I can think unobtruded upon and these thoughts, malgré moi will stain this paper. But then, my dear Claire, I have nothing else except my nothingless self to talk about. You have doubtless heard from Jane & I have heard from no one else. I see no one. The Guiccioli and LB. once a month. Trelawny seldom, & he is on the eve of his departure for Leghorn. All as yet wears a tranquil appearance with regard to Gabrielle. W. [*Wright*] is still here—& they go out no where. This is the list of my outdoor acquaintances, I see no other human face.

Marianne suffers during this dreadfully cold weather, but less than I should have supposed. The children are all well. So also is my Percy—poor little darling—they all scold him because he speaks loud a l'Italien—people love to, nay they seem to exist on, finding fault with others—but I have no right to complain—& this unlucky stove is the sole source of all my dispiacere; if I had that I shou[ld] not teaze any one or any one me, or my only one—but after all these are trifles; I have sent for another Engeniere and I hope before many days are elapsed to retire as before to my hole.

I have again delayed finished [*finishing*] this letter waiting for letters from England—that I might not send you one so barren of all intelligence—but I have had none. And nothing new has happened except Trelawny's departure for Leghorn so that our days are more monotonous than ever. The ⟨day⟩ weather is drearily cold & an eternal north east whistles through every crevice. Percy however is far better in this cold than in summer—he is warmly clothed—& gets on.

Adieu Pray Write. My love to Charles—I am ashamed that I do not write to him but I have only an old story to repeat—& this letter tells that

Affectionately yours
MaryShelley

ADDRESS: A Mademoiselle / Madlle de Clairmont / Chez Madame / Madme Jeanette de Henneikstein / a Vienne (Wien) / L'Autricke. POSTMARKS: (1) GENOVA: (2) SAR[ ]. PUBLISHED: Jones, #162. TEXT: MS., Pforzheimer Library.

1. Hunt's behavior towards Mary Shelley resulted from his belief that she had been a source of unhappiness to Shelley. His information about the Shelleys' relationship came from comments Shelley made to him at Pisa, supplemented by reports by Jane Williams. In Jane Williams's letter of 28 April 1824, she quotes Hunt as saying: "The truth is she [*Jane Williams*] perplexed me very much in my intercourse with Mrs. S. by giving me accounts which exceedingly embittered it and made me cold and almost inhospitable." Jane Williams defended herself by saying she had not told Hunt anything he had not observed on his own (Williams, *Journals and Letters*, p. 165). By July 1823 the friendship between Mary Shelley and Hunt was fully reestablished.

2. "Dam."

3. "Overflow."

To Lord Byron [Albaro] Teusday [7 January 1823]

My dear Lord Byron

Your letter is very good,[1] & I cannot express to you how obliged I am by your kindness—You have been & are very kind to me now that I have so few friends that I feel it & want it most.

You have not mentioned in your letter that you enclose by my desire the certificates My father mentioned[2]—but as those must be got in England I think it is best as it is.

When you send to the post—will you have the kindness to send Lega[3] to me for letters.

Most truly yours obliged
MaryShelley

[*P. 1, top*] Have you the Posthumous Works of Gibbon & could you lend me them?

ADDRESS: To the Rt Honble / Lord Byron. PUBLISHED: Jones, #164. TEXT: MS., John Murray.

1. On 7 January Byron wrote directly to Sir Timothy Shelley requesting a "simple provision" for Mary Shelley and Percy. Although the elder Shelley had confided to Whitton, his attorney, that he might allow £160, his response to Byron of 6 February declined any provision for Mary Shelley and offered support for Percy only if Mary Shelley would relinquish custody of Percy and if he were to live in England (Ingpen, *Shelley in England*, pp. 563–67. See [30 October 1822]; [27 November 1822]; Tuesday— [25 February 1823]; Tuesday ½ past 2 P.M. [?25 February 1823]).

2. The certificates of the Shelleys' marriage and Percy's baptisim. On 8 August

Sir Timothy Shelley commented to Whitton: "I have no doubt but you will find both the marriages correct. He was particular in that respect—I suppose there will require some arrangement when matters are understood" (Ingpen, *Shelley in England*, p. 551).

3. Lega Zambelli, Byron's steward.

To Edward John Trelawny — Albaro. Jan. 7th [1823]

A letter, my dear Trelawny, from this solitary & wind striken hill of Albaro—may well appear to you a letter from the dead to the living. And shut out as I am from all communication with life I feel as if a letter from you would be to me a token sent from a world of flesh & blood to one of shadow. Here I am just as you left me—the wind whistling, & myself as comfortless as then. Forgotten by every body I cannot forget them & much less you—since the scenes that are ever present to my memory are those in which you bore a principal part, & cold as my heart is it warms then with gratitude—What should we, poor Jane & I, wild & desolate as we were, have done without you. We saw sorrow in other faces but we found help only from you.

I would not make you sorrowful by recalling those heavy hours but I have nothing so near my heart—and when I write that subject seems by right to tyrannize over my pen & to force me to write concerning it. I will conclude all allusion to it however by mentioning that soon after your departure Hunt had a letter from Mr Brown[1] at Pisa telling him that he had received a letter from Mr Severn (Keats' friend) at Rome who said that he was about to fulfill the last scene of misery for me by—by doing that which was to be done for me in that city—You understand me—so all the difficulties seem to be surmounted though I anxiously wait for the letter which will say that all is done.

What are you doing? And does the wind blow as bleakly & is the weather as cruelly sharp with you as with us? I can go no where & have not been to Genoa once since you left us. The only thing that could take me there, would be my desire to call on Mrs Thomas[2] to learn news of you (if she is more lucky than I in having heard from you) & of G.W. [*Gabrielle Wright*] & the first day that the sun shines I shall certainly go. I hate this place more than ever and shall be delighted to get away—for indeed I shall be wretched until then but I must stay with Marianne for some months,[3] & besides Sir T. Shelley has declined giving any answer to the application made to him for an allowance for me. LB. is now writing to him directly for a decisive answer—until that is decided I must be very economical, although as yet my money is far from being expended, & I expect to receive some also from the Liberal[4]

I do not mention any thing of Claire's affairs since she says in a letter I received from her yesterday that she has written to you directed to the Post office of Leghorn. I have not heard from Jane. And the only news I have is that the 2nd number of the Liberal was published the 1st of this month & promises to be a good number. There is in it the "Heaven & Earth" of LB. Shelley's Defence of Poetry—2 articles by Hazlitt 1 by Hogg —1 of mine &c[5]—Will you have the kindness to lend your copy of the 1st number to Mrs Mason[6]—if you direct it to her Casa Silva, Pisa, Dunn can send it—& I promise you that it will be speedily & safely returned.

Just this time last year, my dear Friend, you left Genoa to find us happy & enjoying all the goods of life at Pisa. You found two who have now deserted us—You found me, so full of spirits & life that methinks when you first saw me you must have thought me even a little wild—now all is changed & surely he who is now beside my beloved boy at Rome is n[ot] more altered than I. I desire only solitude—I live only [ ] sorrow & my imagination then so fond of sharring with [ ] the shores of the sweet waters of life now only dwells under funereal shades—unless it peep beyond them to something that will be when I am not here. But may you long enjoy that delight which the stirring of one's warm blood—& the sense of life & the emotions of love may & do bestow—You deserve every happiness & I trust that { } do enjoy a part at least

Adieu—trust to the feelings of gratitude & affection with which I am yours & when you are too melancholy to do any thing else write to

Mary Shelley

I have received a letter from Jane—she is well & enquires kindly after you —She is in low spirits & longs for Italy.

ADDRESS: Edward Trelawny Esq. / Presso al Signor Dunn / Via Grande / Livorno. POSTMARKS: (1) GENOVA; (2) 10 GENNAIO. PUBLISHED: Jones, #163. TEXT: MS., Bodleian Library (MS., Shelley, Adds., c. 6, ff. 1–2).

1. See 7 September 1822. Charles Armitage Brown (1787–1842) was a friend of Hunt, Joseph Severn, and Keats. He arrived in Pisa at the end of August 1822 and he met Byron through Hunt. His correspondence with Severn indicates that he played an intermediary role between Mary Shelley and Severn in the arrangement of Shelley's funeral. In Brown's letter of 23 September 1822 to Severn he wrote: "I will also mention your offer concerning Shelley's grave" (Brown, *Letters*, pp. 102–6, 111, 119–20).

2. It is quite likely that Mary Shelley met Mrs. Thomas through John Taaffe, who had asked Shelley to read Mrs. Thomas's verses in 1821—Shelley called them "insufferable trash" (*PBS Letters*, #600). Mrs. Thomas tended to several commissions on Mary Shelley's behalf, and Mary Shelley gave her copies of the *Liberal* and an autographed copy of *Frankenstein* that contains corrections and additions for a second edition (Cline, *Pisan Circle*, pp. 22, 226). On the title page of her copy of *Frankenstein*, Mrs. Thomas wrote: "My Acquaintance with this very interesting Person—arose from her being introduced to Me under Circumstances of so Melancholy a Nature (which attended her Widowhood)—that it was impossible to refuse the Aid Asked of me—I gave her All I could and Passed Many delightful hours with her at Albaro—She left Genoa in a few Months for England I called on her in London in 1824—but as My friends disliked her Circle of Friends—and Mrs Shelley was then No longer in a Foreign Country helpless, Pennyless, and broken hearted—I Never Returned Again toher but I preserve this Booke and her Autograph Notes to me—as at some future day they will be literary Curiosities—" (Pierpont Morgan Library).

On 4 October 1823 Marianne Hunt wrote a letter to Mary Shelley complaining about Mrs. Thomas: "Mrs. Thomas has sent for your direction I paid her as you desired or at least she paid herself for she stopt 6 or 7 crowns for freight of boxes &c out of what Mr. Saunders was to send us. I mention it that you may know how to deal with such a lady and if it may please you to unite voices. She has done for herself in Mr. Hunt's good graces; I don't know if that was the cause or no" (*MWS Letters*, I, 214, n. 3; see 28 July [1824]).

3. Mary Shelley had promised to stay with Marianne Hunt through her confinement with her seventh child, expected in June.

4. See 31 January [1823], n. 3.

5. The second issue of the *Liberal*, published on 1 January 1823, included Byron's "Heaven and Earth"; Hazlitt's "On the Spirit of Monarchy" and "On the Scotch Character"; Hogg's "Longus"; and Mary Shelley's "A Tale of the Passions." For *A Defence of Poetry*, see 6 November 1822; and Marshall, *The Liberal*, pp. 135–63.

6. On 14 January Mrs. Mason wrote to Mary Shelley: "No letter from Mrs G [*Godwin*]—I suppose she waits to tell me that the Novel [*Valperga*] is out—I shall be very anxious to hear of its success—Have you begun another? Or does the Liberal prevent you from thinking of any other occupation? Mr. T— does not obey your orders about the first number—pray remind him of it—I will return it safe & speedily you may be sure" (Abinger MS.).

*TO JANE WILLIAMS Albaro. Jan[ry] 12th [1823]

A letter from you, dearest Jane, although a melancholy one, is the source of great delight to me. I live in a state of such complete isolation that the voice of affection comes to me like the sounds of remembered music. I am indeed alone. You, my best girl, have some two or three, I hope many more, who love you; who sympathize in your sorrows & to whom you can speak of them. I have none; and the feeling of alienation which seems to possess the very few human beings I see, causes a kind of humiliating depression that weighs like a fog about me. Yet I ought not to complain. God knows that except yourself & now & then Trelawny I wish to see none but those I do see. And those are three. LB. is all kindness—but there is more of manner than heart, or to speak more truly, I am satisfied with the little he bestows—It is much & it is nothing. It is much in the way of what is called essential service, in that way it is every thing I can desire—It is nothing for my heart, but then that restless piner seeks nothing from him. Marianne is very good. She does all she can to make me comfortable—but her heart is not an universe—it has received within itself her husband & children, & the gates are closed. Is Hunt then the object of my complaint. This is too bad; but he does not like me—I feel & know this; he has never forgiven my resistance to his intolerable claims at Pisa[1]—He avoids walking with { }, nor does he refrain at times from saying bitter things. I am a coward—I hate contention & I disdain the victory—I wish only to fly—I am enthrawled & feel my chains & bolts.

Yet this after all is nothing. Sometimes he stirs my torpid blood, & when I am very miserable, will cause my tears to flow—Yet now when at night all is quiet and my thoughts resume their usual train—it seems nothing.

For in truth I live little in this world—I live on the past & future and the present, day by day, fades like the figures on a lantern.[2] I dare not look on it; I hate every thing about me, all my feelings—the air—the light; I desire death & it comes not; I look on my poor boy, & for worlds I would not die to leave him; every sentiment I have contends one with the other—& I have no refuge. The cup is very deep from which I drink, and all its ingredients are bitter.

So, my own Jane, we two poor creatures compare notes of misery. And like you, I also hate the place of my abode. We have had dreadful weather, snow & a biz[3] (it is worse than any biz) that has endured uninterruptedly for two months. Even in fine weather this place is odious to me. All the walks are between two stone walls so high that you see only the sky above them. I do not wonder at this. In England hedges are enough to protect the fields, but all being here on a declivity the floods & winds would swiftly sweep the whole soil into the waters did not they build walls which resemble in heigth [*height*] length & thickness the Great Wall of China—they say, I think this Great Wall is divided & you can walk between it—& such is Albaro. And if you see any opening it is but to behold that murderous element, which girts me as a hissing and howling serpent, so that I would that the walls were endless—Oh! how very miserable that wretched sight makes me—I long to enclose myself with the solid rock—& again I would run to it & bid it swallow its prey—but I pause & tremble—I have never seen it nearer than from our windows—& I seldom approach them that I may not see it; the gorgeous sunsets, and rosy tinged Mountains of the West are lost to me, I feel its presence for ever—& desire annihilation to be rid of it.

You see how selfish I am and that I talk only of myself. Yet I think of you & my heart is with you in your ruined sanctum. Your children must employ you somewhat, & I hope you read, for in books we live in a peaceful world; & save that to which the imagination carries us to among the dead, the best the earth affords. If you can get it pray read Sir Philip Sidney's "Arcadia"—It is a beautiful book; its exquisite sentiments and descriptions would have delighted you in happier days, perhaps they will now. It is pleasant to me to think that we both turn our eyes to the same spot for our place of rest. Come to Florence, my dear Jane, & let us see if mutual affection will not stand us in some stead in our calamities—Our fate is one, so ought our interests here to be; we can talk eternally to each other of our lost ones, and surely they would be best pleased to find us together. I will deserve your love—if love can buy its like; and with me—perhaps you may attain the peaceful state you desire—I might ease you of some of your cares—& your affection to me would be a treasure. These may be dreams You are in England, I imprisoned at Albaro—Sir T.S. [*Timothy Shelley*] seems resolved that I shall not be independant through his means—& even if this difficulty were overcome I must remain for the present near Marianne. Her state is now critical, for she is pregnant—& the fear of a miscarriage haunts us all—she hopes for the best, & she is not worse as to her complaint than when you saw her, which considering the season she has encountered can only be attributed to her situation. Her time is in June, and I shall continue near her until then.

Claire's situation appears precarious. I will however confide to you a secret about her, which remember I do in the perfect confidence that you will mention it to no one,[4] & above all not to her. Mrs Mason seeing the extremities to which this exile might reduce her applied to LB. calling on him for an allowance such as she thought was justly due to poor C— LB. has complied with her request[5]—he has not yet I believe made up his mind as to the amount, but by this means she will will be put out of the fea[r] want. As Mrs M. has begun the affair she of course will arrange the m[anner] in which C— will receive it—I entreat you not to tell her—or to suffer compassion or any other feeling to cause you to reveal it to her Mother.—C— & T—y [*Trelawny*] have been scratching by letter, as he told me; so hasty & ill formed a junction cd not end well. I have not heard from him since he left us a month ago. He went he said to Leghorn. His affair with G.W. [*Gabrielle Wright*] was ended by W's [*Wright's*] return—who behaved very well—& she very ill, as she shewed & still shews herself ready to sacrifize all—even her lover's safety, to her wilful desires.

As I said before do not think of my commissions until I send you money. They say that the Banker has £8. could this be applied to my use? Not that I wish you to get any thing else except the picture,[6] & that My father shd without expence to himself send me Mrs Barbauld's lessons for children, My mother's early lessons[7]—a spelling book—& other books of the same kind for my little fellow—who now knows his letters & will read as soon as he has learned English which he is picking up by slow degrees among the Hunts. The youngest is his favourite.—I shall be delighted to have dear, dear Edwards picture[8]—& also a copy of his play[9] & poems—& if I be not indiscreet, a copy of one or two of his best letters to you. As to Medwin—I shall not ask for my crowns in any case. Though if he pleases you may gain some—since I am sure they would be glad to insert in the Liberal a good translation of the Mss. he read to us at Pisa[10]—All will be as you wish about the Mss. you mention, which, altered by Hunt will appear in the next No.[11]

LB. was much pleased by your message to him. He said—I love Janey very much—Not that I shd have been in love with her—but I should like her as a sister—rather an unlucky phrase for me—but I mean a quiet love —I will send her a letter to Murray, & write her a nice sentimental one myself. The G. [*Guiccioli*] & he are as ill together as may be.

I intend to publish my Shelley's Mss. in the Liberal. First—being out of England & Ollier behaving so ill it is almost impossible to do it in any other way.—I think also that they will do good to the work & that would best please him—Then when I am rich enough I will make an edition of all he has written—& his works thus appearing at intervals will keep him alive in the minds of his admirers. The Witch of Atlas will appear in the next number.[12]

—Last night, dear Jane I dreamt of them. He was looking well & happy [*p. 1, cross-written in pencil*] & I was transported to see him—I asked Ned if the men in the fishing boat could not have saved them—he replied no—for though they appeared near the high waves rendered it impossible for them to approach—Had you not a dream, where the same answer was given. Would that I could dream of them thus every night & I would sleep for ever

Kiss your Children for me, & teach my little God-daughter that there is one in Italy who loves her.

Your very Affectionate
Mary W. Shelley

Among the books I have mentioned that I wish my father to send for Percy I wish books with pictures of animals to be included. If my box with the papers be gone—if he send a parcel to Mr John Hunt of the Examiner Office begging him to forward it to me it will be sent—As you see the Godwins occasionally would you mention it.

[*P. 4*] You know, do you not that LB. wrote slightingly to Murray of Hunt—& H. has heard of this—he never can or will forgive LB. & is very sore at any praise of him you will have Mrs Mason's book.[13]—Is not the end of mine wondrous—the fate—the shore—how miserably foretold—it is very strang[e][14]

ADDRESS: Mrs. Williams / Mrs. Cleveland / 24 Alsop's Buildings / New Road / Inghilterra London / Londres. POSTMARKS: (1) GENOVA; (2) FPO / JA. 27 / 1823; (3) 12 Noon 12 / JA. 27 / 1823. UNPUBLISHED. TEXT: MS., Abinger MS., Bodleian Library.

1. See [c. 27 August 1822], n. 2.
2. An optical instrument, first made in England around 1808, by means of which a magnified image of a picture on glass is projected onto a screen in a darkened room.
3. "Northeast wind."
4. Jane Williams revealed this secret to Hogg (see Norman, *After Shelley*, p. 10).
5. Claire Clairmont's financial problems at Vienna resulted from the government's refusal to grant her a license to teach. In addition, she fell severely ill. Unknown to her, Mrs. Mason wrote to Lord Byron on 28 December 1822 asking him to provide funds for Claire Clairmont. Although this letter suggests that Byron gave Mary Shelley the impression that he was willing to comply, by 13 January Mrs. Mason had received his refusal with "a sting in its tail" (*CC Journals*, pp. 294–96; Marchand, *Byron*, III, 1049–50; McAleer, *The Sensitive Plant*, pp. 173–77).
6. See 5 December 1822, n. 8.
7. Anna Laetitia Barbauld, *Lessons for Children* (Dublin, 1779), revised and republished in four parts by Joseph Johnson & Co., London, in 1812; Mary Wollstonecraft, *Original Stories from Real Life* . . . (London: Joseph Johnson, 1788), with plates by William Blake.
8. See 5 December 1822, n. 8.
9. See 15 October 1822; [20 May 1825].
10. Medwin had read his translations of Dante to the Shelleys at Pisa (see [14–

15] January 1821). In his letter to Byron of 8 December 1822 Medwin had enclosed a translation from Ariosto that he wished the Hunts to consider for the *Liberal* (Lovell, *Medwin*, p. 133). No work by Medwin appeared in the *Liberal.*

11. In Jane Williams's letter of 22 December she had asked Mary Shelley to send her "a copy of Shelleys words to the Indian Air 'I arise from dreams of thee'" (Abinger MS.). "The Indian Girl's Song" was published in the second number of the *Liberal.*

12. "Lines to a Critic" was published in the second number of the *Liberal,* but *The Witch of Atlas* was first published by Mary Shelley in the 1824 *Posthumous Poems.*

13. *Advice to Young Mothers on the Physical Education of Children* (London, 1823). Mrs. Mason's book on nursery, diet, exercise, fresh air, preventive medicine, and child psychology was well received and went through a number of editions. On 4 March Mrs. Mason wrote Mary Shelley that Jane Williams had probably received her copy (McAleer, *The Sensitive Plant*, pp. 180, 182–84).

14. Euthanasia, the heroine of Mary Shelley's *Valperga,* was Shelleyan in character and drowned at sea (vol. 3, chap. 12).

*To Mrs. Thomas — Albaro Wednesday [?15 January 1823][1]

A contrary fate, my dear Mrs Thomas, has attended my promised call upon you. First it was so hot—then it rained—then a wind arose scattering all the blossoms of Albaro & I hate wind—then my boy got a violent cold & cough, so that I could not leave him—& now, he being better, has transferred it to me & I keep house for a few days—I hope only a very few days—So this is a full, true & particular account of my being tied by the leg on our dreary hill.

Will you take pity on me & send me a book to amuse me, while my head is too confused & aching for anything except a a novel. Any one will do though never so old—So it be neither Smolletts or Fieldings or Scotts for those I have near at hand. Miss Burney—Mrs Ratcliffe—or the last of Scott—that would indeed be a treat.

I send the second no. of the Liberal—You know my crime therein—On Monarchy & the Scotch Character is by Hazlitt—on Longus by a Mr Hogg—(not the Aitrick Shepherd—but an extremely clever man & a friend of mine)—the rest are by Hunt.[2]

Have you any Examiners?—Might I ask you (it is very impertinent) not to keep the girl who brings this as she is not my servant

Compts to Mr Thomas

Most truly Yours
MaryShelley

Any news of a nurse for Mrs Hunt.

ADDRESS: A Madame / Madme Thomas. UNPUBLISHED. TEXT: MS., Pforzheimer Library.

1. The second number of the *Liberal* was published on 1 January 1823. The earliest it could have reached Mary Shelley was 13 January.

2. See 7 January [1823] to Trelawny.

When you get this letter, my dear Trelawny, your voyage will be at an end. I am however anxious to hear of its conclusion. We have had & continue to have frightful weather, and if it be not better with you, your arrival at Rome will be much retarded. I write with the suspicion that you will not receive my letter—So I shall be shorter than would otherwise be the case.

You will hear at Rome that it is all compleated & how it has been done. You will see Mr Freeborn (whom pray thank in my name) & Hunt in a letter he writes to Mr Severn will mention your arrival & that you will probably have the goodness to call upon him. Mr Severn was the friend of Keats; he seems to have been mainly instrumental in bringing the present ceremony to a termination—Pray call on him—And tell me also if Sir Charles Styles[1] was not one of the persons who made one at the funeral. Mr Severn has written Hunt an account of it—and that dreary weight of doubt is now off my mind.

Indeed I do believe, my dear Trelawny, that you are the best friend I have—& most truly would I rather apply to you in any difficulty than to any one else[2]—for I know your heart, & rely on it at present I am very well off, having still a considerable residue of the money I brought with me from Pisa & besides I have received £33 from the Liberal.[3] Part of this I have been obliged to send to Claire. You will be sorry to hear that the last account she has sent of herself is that she is seriously ill. The cold of Vienna has doubtless contributed to this—as it is even a dangerous aggravation of her old complaint. I wait anxiouly to hear from her. She is still at Madme Henneickstein's. I sent her 15 Napoleons—& shall send more if necessary & if I can. LB. continues kind—he has made frequent offers of money—I do not want it—as you see.

I wrote to you addressed to Dunn at Leghorn—if he forwards that letter to you at Rome you will see from it that Sir T. Shelley refused to give any answer to Hanson's application—Lord Byron has written to Sir T.S. himself & the answer <u>can</u> arrive in about 10 days.

Perhaps when you are at Rome you will not dislike calling on a Mr Brunelli who was at one time the English Vice Consul there. Miss Curran left 2 pictures of me & of Claire in his possession to give to us if we wished[4] —He has not that of Shelley I fear, but you might enquire about it.—

I still turn towards Florence away from this hateful place Marianne's situation will probably keep us here until June [ ] At any ra[te] I rely on seeing you again next summer—You [ ] not stay [ ] than a month or two at Rome—& Roberts [ ] not venture to Naples in the heat I am sure.

Adieu. As soon as I hear from you I will write again; but as I said, I suspect this letter may never reach you—as usual with us the wind howls & the rain descends & as usual with me—I am as melancholy as the dreary night itself—All is over for me—I endeavour to be resigned; but I cannot but repine when I think of last winter—then I had nothing to desire—now I have nothing to fear—& in a short, short time I trust I may repose in that divine City beside my set Sun.

Affectionately Yours
Mary Shelley.

[*P. 3, top*] Severn's Address—
No. 18—Via di San Indoro
Secondo Piano.
[*P. 4*] Claire wrote to you directed to Leghorn

ADDRESS: Edward Trelawny Esq. / Ferma in Posta / Roma. POSTMARKS: (1) GENOVA; (2) 6 FEBB[RAIO]. PUBLISHED: Jones, #167. TEXT: MS., Bodleian Library (MS., Shelley, Adds., c. 6, ff. 3–4).

1. Joseph Severn's letter of 21 January 1823 to Brown says "Sir C. Sykes" attended the funeral. The Reverend Richard Burgess, who read the burial service, left a memoir that lists "Sir Charles Slyte?" as attending (Angeli, *Shelley and His Friends in Italy*, p. 318). I have been unable to find information about a "Sir Charles Sykes"; Sir Thomas Charles Style (1797–1879), however, is listed in *Burke's Peerage.*

2. Trelawny had written on 11 January that he would consider it "a breach of friendship should you employ anyone else in services that I can execute" (*S&M*, IV, 911).

3. John Hunt's unpublished letter to Leigh Hunt says that Mary Shelley was paid £36. William H. Marshall conjectures that she may have received the additional £3 later or that the discrepancy was due to a mistake or accident (*The Liberal*, p. 148).

4. See 26 July 1822. On 11 April Trelawny wrote to Claire Clairmont: "Dearest, I have got possession of a portrait of you—by Miss Curran—it is an excellent likeness" (Trelawny, *Letters*, pp. 46–47). Trelawny obtained both Claire Clairmont's and Mary Shelley's portraits, as Mary Shelley had requested, but he kept them. Mary Shelley tried unsuccessfully throughout her life to retrieve her portrait from Trelawny (St. Clair, *Trelawny*, p. 189).

TO [?MRS. SAUNDERS]

A[l]baro Friday
[?February–March 1823][1]

My dear Madam

I return the Examiner and should be much pleased to have another, which I will send back sooner than I have done this, but you said that you were in no hurry for it. Lord Byron says that he returned the last one that he had to Dr Alexander.[2] You mentioned that you could lend me the Edinburgh and Quarterly Reviews, Mr Hunt would be very glad to see them.

This weather confines us in our windy and solitary prison;—I cannot ask you to come, but if you receive any news concerning Trelawny will you let me know where he is & what he is doing. My Compliments to Mr. Saunders.

Sincerely Yours—Mary Shelley.

PUBLISHED: Jones, #170. TEXT: MS., Pierpont Morgan Library.

1. Trelawny's letter of 11 January 1823 to Mary Shelley indicated that the

rapidity and uncertainty of his movements would cause a break in their correspondence until he reached Rome in February (*S&M*, IV, 909–10). Mary Shelley's request for information about Trelawny suggests that this letter was written sometime in February or March, before she had any word directly from him.

2. Dr. James Alexander, an English physician at Genoa, who attended Byron. Dr. Francesco Bruno, the physician who went with Byron on the Greek expedition in July 1823, was recommended by Dr. Alexander (Marchand, *Byron*, III, 1052, 1078).

To Lord Byron [Albaro] Sunday [?2 February 1823][1]

The more I read this Poem that I send, the more I admire it. I pray that Your Lordship will finish it.—It must be your own inclination that will govern you in that, but from what you have said, I have some hopes that you will. You never wrote any thing more beautiful than one lyric in it—& the whole, I am tempted to say, surpasses "Your former glorious style"—at least it fully equals the very best parts of your best productions.

Truly Yours—MWS

ADDRESS: To the Rt. Honble / Lord Byron. PUBLISHED: Jones, #165. TEXT: MS., John Murray.

1. On 25 January 1823 Byron sent Mary Shelley "a few more scenes of the drama before begun [*The Deformed Transformed*]" (Byron, *Works*, VI, 165).

*To Jane Williams Albaro. Feb 19th Feb 20th [1823]

You do not write, my best Jane—and anxious as I am to hear of your welfare I am half angry when post after post I hear nothing from you. Indeed I hear from nobody—the Gisbornes never write—my father's business letters come once every six weeks & that is all. I live in entire solitude, & never communicating with any one or hearing from any one I feel as if I belonged to another world. It is true I am in the same house with the Hunts, but I find myself too irritable & too little adapted to other society than my solitary thoughts to mingle with them. My child is my only companion—I read—write & walk, alone in all things. My thoughts never rest, & bitterly agonizing as they are, yet they are dear to me as uniting me to my lost one. The weather is now become mild and spring like—though we have a continuance of scirocco & rain very unlike dear Pisa—In all my solitary walk & musings when the past does not wholly occupy me I think most of you—your sufferings—and what you may now be doing. When may I hope to see you? I hope we shall meet in Italy & that my wayward fate will not necessitate me to return to a country I hate more & more (if that be possible) so that the idea that Sir T.S. [*Timothy Shelley*] should require my return makes me tremble.—As yet of course you cannot have heard from Ned's brother—but the rest of your affairs may be in a state of forwardness—Is Mr Alexander alive and does he assist you?—how is your Mother & what of Sarah? Remember, dear girl that your & Edward's recounts & conversations have made me so familiar with all your friends that you can mention none who are strangers to me. Do you find any relief in the society of the Miss Temples?—Have you seen Cox?[1]—

I dare say that you have built airy hopes for poor C— [*Claire*] upon the information that I sent you in my last. But nothing but evil has followed. LB. told me that he had acceded to Mrs M.'s [*Mason's*] proposition—but these were mere words, & nothing was done when I received a letter from her saying that C— was dangerously ill—that Lord Mountcashell's death[2] had straitened them so much that she had no money to send & urging me to press LB. to come to a conclusion, as her funds were of course low. I went to LB. & told him that he or I must send some money. The choice was too inviting—I had, as he knew, just received a few pounds from the Liberal—& he thought that if in depriving myself, I was necessitated to apply to him it would then be time to unloose his purse strings—so I sent 15 Napoleons. Mrs M. was shocked at this & wrote him a letter which ought to have moved him, but which has I believe produced no effect.—I have not heard since from C— nor has Mrs M. but I am of course very anxious to hear—poor girl! her dispiacere[3] joined to the cold of Vienna has caused her glandular complaint to make a serious attack—If she gets better her only hope is in sea bathing—she must quit Vienna & her prospects there—but if LB. continues thus hardhearted & Sir T.S. does nothing for me what can I do? He salves it over to his own conscience I believe (& for the sake of human nature, I trust) with the idea of repaying me when I want it—& of that he has made frequent offers—but it will be a peculiar & most temporary necessity indeed that would make me borrow from him—For there after all is the sting—it is a loan to me, a gift to C— I trust all these details to your discretion, my dear Jane, & entreat that you will not mention them to a living soul. I wrote last wishing to communicate a piece of good news—& now to shew you the fallacy of my hopes.

I dare say that you know more or as much of Ty [*Trelawny*] as I do—I have only had one letter from him from Piombino. I have heard however from Rome. All is at rest there (would I were too!) He sleeps beneath the tomb of Cestius

> The grey walls moulder round, on which dull Time
> Feeds,[4]—Do you not know that verse of Adonais—All

that passage which joined to many other motives kept me firm in my choice, when all opposed it—All my thoughts now tend & all my actions will be bent towards a journey to that beloved city, whose blue sky is the tomb of those I best love. Solitary as I am, I feed & live on imagination only—feelings are my events—sorrow, deep, deep & eternal my companion—Indeed I am so much alone that I should soon forget how to converse with any but the dead & absent, were it not for my child. This is not right perhaps, but the discontent & restless wretchedness I feel in society is to be exchanged for all the ⟨solitary⟩ bitterness of companionless hours. Yesterday as I was reading I thought I heard him call me—⟨I thought⟩ not his spirit—but he my companion & not lost Shelley—the revulsion of thought agonized every nerve—& gave too too much reality to the knowledge that I was deceived

As I said I see little now of my companions—Poor Marianne advances in her pregnancy & as yet we can conclude nothing—It is not surprizing that she suffers, for such a situation makes even the healthy suffer, how much more one whose frame is so shattered & weak. But I hope it will go well with her. She is much teazed by servants & 6 children are no small burthen to her spirits, especially under her circumstances—but if she gets through the present crisis well & removes to Florence, as is proposed, in the Autumn, I hope life will afford her some of the pleasures that she is capable of enjoying as long as Hunt continues well & kind. You may guess to whom I allude in that last word—Her[5] arrival would be a death blow to poor Marianne—but if it be delayed, yet some time or other I fear it will occur. Thornton, who is an excellent boy, w^{d} be a great comfort to her, did not the neglect of his education here at th[is] desart & barbarian Albaro make her uneasy in the reflexion of the time he is losing—Their youngest child is the best little fellow in the world—affectionate, docile, lively & clever he is her great comfort. Hunt suffers from the scirocco—he writes for the Liberal & is in better spirits on the prospect of its success.—The G.—[*Guiccioli*] has just lost her sister Carolina, the flower of the family, by a consumption—she appears much grieved—I saw her yesterday—she had heard the news 4 days before & she told me she was so unhappy that she had not seen LB. once during that time—Strange between lovers—for that which is the flower of love is the consolation one receives in misfortune.—I have not a good opinion of her or I s^{hd} pity her—but her unamiable jealousies & falsehoods have destroyed what remained of affection in his heart, though he clings to her as two birds of opposite breed in one cage—there they are—& what is there better to do?

Again I return from these who are nothing, to you, my dearest Jane—How are your children? Percy still remembers Duli & Za-zane & says that they must come back to Toscana. Kiss my little God-daughter many times & tell me if she continues to resemble dearest Edward. My lost Clara was so like Shelley—methinks I should be better consoled if she had been spared for me—but destiny has fated me to hopelessness & sorrow—& I have endured miseries that make the air a pall—the breeze a dirge—the earth a grave—& heaven a vault—far beyond all that, I place my only hopes.

If you have any means of instigating Peacock to send those papers I so earnestly desire pray use them. Hogg has not written at all & Mrs Gisborne has entirely forgotten me—the arrival of these papers will be the only pleasure I can conceive of receiving and they should not grudge it to me.

I leave this space to mention if tomorrow I hear from C— for you will probably be as anxious as I, to hear what turn her malady takes.

Feb 20th) I close my letter but will write again if I receive any intelligence from Vienna—Let me hear from you as soon as you can & as often as you can

Ever & ever affectionately Yours
MaryW. Shelley

ADDRESS: Mrs. Williams / Mrs. Cleveland / 24 Alsop's Buildings—New Road / London / Londres / Inghilterra. POSTMARKS: (1) GENOVA; (2) FPO / MR. 6 / [18] 23; (3) 12 NOON 12 / MR. 6 / 1823. UNPUBLISHED. TEXT: MS., Abinger MS., Bodleian Library.

1. [?George] Cox was an old friend of Edward Williams's and godfather to Rosalind, "Dina" (Williams, *Journals and Letters*, p. 101; *SC*, VI, 817, 830–31).

2. Mrs. Mason's annuity had stopped when Lord Mount Cashell, her legal husband, died on 27 October 1822 (McAleer, *The Sensitive Plant*, p. 177).

3. "Misfortune."

4. *Adonais* 50. 1.

5. Bessy Kent (see 2 March 1817 to Marianne Hunt, n. 2; 10 April [1823]; 9–11 September [1823]).

To Lord Byron

Albaro Teusday— [25 February 1823][1]

My dear Lord Byron

I am indeed at a loss to conceive of what is at present to be done; there is no law to help me, & certainly no feeling that can be of service to me with a man who could make that insolent & hardhearted proposition about my poor boy.—That did a little overcome my philosophy. If the persecuted Liberal[2] still continues that may in some degree prevent my burthening any one in my present evil fortune—if not some other means may be thought of. Perhaps if I were in England he might be shamed into doing something, but the difficulty of getting there, & the dearness of living when arrived, would I think destroy all good that could accrue from such a journey; though doubtless my being in Italy does my cause no good.

I sent a copy of the letter last night to my father that I might as soon as possible have his opinion & advice upon it. Your Lordship's also would of course be gratifying to me—but I fancy that you feel as I do, that the affair is hopeless.

I have been expecting Don Juan but I fear your Lordship's illness has been the cause of its delay[3]—perhaps this fine weather will cure you—

Very truly Yours
Mary Shelley

ADDRESS: To the Rt Honble / Lord Byron. PUBLISHED: Jones, #171. TEXT: MS., John Murray.

1. On 24 February Byron sent Mary Shelley Sir Timothy Shelley's letter stating his refusal to aid her and his willingness to maintain Percy only if she gave up custody of him (unpublished Byron MS., Pierpont Morgan Library). That day, she wrote in her Journal: "But today melancholy would invade me—& I thought the peace I enjoyed (such a word indeed does not befit)me) was transient—and that fate which has so relent[l]essly brought me to this lowest pitch of fortune, would not permit me to establish myself in my airy height, but make me feel my mortality

in every trembling nerve. Then that letter came to place its seal on on my prognostications—Yet it was not the refusal or the insult heaped on me that stung me to tears—it was their bitter words about our boy—Why I live only to keep him from their hands—How dared they dream that I held him not—far more precious than all save the hope of again seeing you—my lost one—but for his smiles—where should I now be?—"

On 14–18 February Godwin wrote Mary Shelley that he had received a copy of Sir Timothy Shelley's response to Byron (Abinger MS.). Godwin's letter is Italian postmarked "3 Marzo." Mary Shelley's mention in this letter of sending her father "a copy of the letter last night" is in reference to a letter that would have been written on the Tuesday before she received Godwin's letter.

2. John Hunt, as publisher of the *Liberal*, had been indicted in December 1822 for printing Byron's *The Vision of Judgment*, which the Constitutional Association claimed to be a villification of the memory of George III. News of the indictment reached Genoa on 23 December, and Byron arranged for legal counsel to defend Hunt and also offered to return to England himself if that would help. John Hunt was brought to trial and found guilty on 15 January. On 19 June 1824 he was sentenced to pay a fine of £100, considered by the *Examiner* as a kind of victory, in that it did "not bear any proportion to the pretended flagrancy of the offence" (Marshall, *The Liberal*, pp. 126–31, 205–9).

3. Byron's letter of 24 February refers to his being ill for three days. Truman Guy Steffan infers that Mary Shelley had by this time copied Canto 13, written by Byron between 12 and 19 February (*Byron's Don Juan*, I, 308).

To Lord Byron

[Albaro] Teusday ½ past 2 P.M.
[?25 February 1823][1]

My dear Lord Byron

I cannot call on the C.G. [*Countess Guiccioli*] today or I should be glad to do so, that I might have an opportunity to converse with your Lordship.

It appears to me that the mode in which Sir T.S. [*Timothy Shelley*] expresses himself about my child plainly shew by what mean principles he would be actuated—he does not offer him an assylum in his own house, but a beggarly provision under the care of a stranger.

Setting aside that I would not part with him. Something is due to me—⟨Every⟩ I should not live ten days seperated from him—If it were necessary for me to die for his benefit the sacrifice would be easy—but his delicate ⟨health⟩ frame requires all a Mothers solicitude—nor shall he be deprived of my anxious love & assiduous attention to his happiness while I have it in my power to bestow it on him. Not to mention that his future respect for his excellent father & his moral well being greatly depend upon his being away from the immediate influence of his relations—

This perhaps you will think nonsense & it is inconceivably painful to me to discuss a point which appears to me as clear as noon day—besides I loose all—all honourable station & name when I admit that I am not a fitting person to take care of my infant—The insult is keen—the pretence for heaping it upon me too gross—the advantage to them if the will came to be contested would be too immense—

As a matter of feeling I would never consent to it—I am said to have a cold heart—there are feelings however so strongly implanted in my nature that to root them out life will go with it—

I am delighted to hear that you are well—Don Juan will not annoy me—I am obliged to occupy myself closely to curb in some degree the agitation that in spite of all my efforts possesses me.

Most truly yours
Mary Shelley

I will come down to Casa Saluzzi tomorrow

PUBLISHED: Jones, #168. TEXT: MS., John Murray.

1. The text of this letter and the specification of the hour written suggest that it was sent the afternoon of 25 February, after Mary Shelley had received a response (unlocated) from Lord Byron to her letter written earlier that same day (see Teusday—[25 February 1823]).

TO THOMAS JEFFERSON HOGG

Albaro—Near Genoa
Febry 28th [1823]

My dear Friend

I am truly obliged to you for the Message that you sent me through Mrs Williams "You have not the heart to write to me!"[1]—No wonder! Miserable wreck as I am—left from the destruction of the noblest fabric of humanity, to tell of it—to mourn over it—& mark its ruin—who can visit me even in thought without a shudder—who can communicate with me without being shadowed by the misery which penetrates me. Our divine Shelley has left me, my dear Jefferson, your fellow collegiate, one who always loved you—the best—but to you I need not praise him.

I do not write to you merely to pour forth the bitterness of my spirit. Although our connexion was marked by storms; & circumstances led me often into erroneous conduct with regard to you, yet now bereft of all, I willingly turn to my Shelley's earliest friend, & to one whom I am persuaded, notwithstanding all ⟨looks⟩ thinks kindly of me. I write to ask your advice. I believe you know my character sufficiently to be aware how deeply it is tinged with irresolution & an incapacity of action. Hitherto I have had little to do with forming any mode of action, even in the common occurences of life—If I have interfered in the legislative—I have had nothing to do with {the} executive part of our little government—I am aghast when I have any thing to do—but a crisis must come, & I must determine on something. You have some knowledge of my lost Shelley's family; you will neither be actuated by prejudice or the contrary, I wish therefore to discuss my affairs with you. Will you not lend me your best intelligence to aid me—for indeed I am a poor hand in these matters.

When Jane returned to England I had at first determined to accompany her, thinking it necessary for my interests to be on the spot—& that when in London any application to Sir T.S. [*Timothy Shelley*] would be more effectual than while I was abroad. Lord Byron dissuaded me from this—his arguments were shortly these: that I spent all my money in a journey; that I had none or a very miserable home to receive me—& that all arrangements with my father-in-law could be managed as well in my absence from England. Attached from a thousand reasons to this divine country, dismayed at the prospect of wretchedness that awaited me in London I readily acquiesced. LordB. was executor—he promised to take the most active part in fulfilling the duties of an office he accepted. He had every right to advise me. So I came to Genoa & have resided under the roof of the Hunts, husbanding my means, & awaiting the result of the negociations made for me.

First (at My father's request) LordB. wrote to his Solicitor Hanson to communicate with Whitton concerning me. The result might be guessed—Sir T. S. would give no reply. Lord B. then wrote to Sir T.S. himself, a letter which had my ⟨?entire⟩ approbation. An answer arrived the other day. After reprobating my conduct, saying that he suspects me of having estranged his son's mind from the respect due to Lady S. & himself (you know the parties & are aware What canting nonsense this is) he refuses to interfere in any of my concerns. As for my boy, if I bring him to England, and will place him under the care of such a person as he will approve, he will afford him a suitable, tho' limited maintainance

Now this is my situation, & what shall I do? This letter found me leading a most solitary life, immersed in study, occupied by no external circumstance except the care of my darling boy—and having found in this mode of life the only balm I can conceive for the miseries I have endured. At present living with the Hunts, I spend little. I have still some money remaining from the sum I possessed on my arrival in Genoa, I have received some money from the Liberal, & if that publication continues, shall continue regularly to receive more. Such are the benefits attendant on the continuance of my present situation. Peace & solitude. But again LB. now offers to provide means for my return to England—We may be scattered—LB. will probably leave this part of the world—the Liberal may die—I cannot burthen the Hunts—I am without resource—and this future, I own, terrifies me.

Shall I then come to England?—You may guess that I do not make it a question whether I will part with my boy. He is my all. My other children I have lost, & the pangs I endured when those events happened were so terrible, that even now, inured as I am to mental pain—I look back with affright to those periods of agony—I have lost my support, my friend, my chosen & only one—my tree of life is felled & I live only in the little sprout that shadows greenly its fearful ruin. I could not live a day without my boy. Let them persuade me that my existence is detrimental to his future prospects and I will not burthen the earth any longer— but go to Rome & die. But I live persuaded that his delicate frame requires maternal solicitude —& that in my affection & attentions he will pass a childhood of happiness, whatever evils may afterwards befal him. That LB. should have counselled my acquiescence does not surprize me. But the very idea of such a doubt threw me for several days into a state of agitation I cannot describe. If I go to England will they not try to force him from me? It would require force indeed & I would die in the struggle—but one cannot look forward to such contests with equanimity. But other ideas suggest themselves. LordB. will (as you suggested) write to Lord Holland to interest himself for me.—If on my arrival in England Sir T.S. finds me protected by people whose rank he respects he may consider me a fitting person to have the charge of my infant. I wish his childhood to be prosperous. Italian skies of themselves shed prosperity—but looking towards England we cannot find that except in the mansions of the rich—& one wishes that he should be properly recognized & protected by his father's family. They will of course be much more prejudiced against me than they are, if I, unprotected, young & tireless, reside abroad—out of their English pale—the sanctuary of virtue & propriety—They will look on me indeed as a black-black sheep if I do not hasten to place myself beneath all the benefits of their clouded atmosphere & foggy virtue—I shall be da paragonare with the Queen alone.[2]

I love Italy—it sky canopies the tombs of my lost treasures—its sun—its vegetation—the solitude I can here enjoy—the easy life one can lead—my habits now of five years growth—all & everything endears Italy to me beyond expression. The thought of leaving it fills me with painful tumults—tears come into my eyes—I prognosticate all evils. Yet if I stay how very desolate I may become—The Hunts are very kind—but they are poor. Hunt in his generous nature is delighted to be of use to me—& I am not too proud to accept an obligation; gratitude is to me a pleasing feeling—but I shrink from linking my fate too closely—& then I would not for worlds burthen them. If I should be left alone—without the means of proceeding to England. I thought that I ought to follow LordB's advice in staying, ought I not to follow it in going? though his idea that I ought to part with mine own Shelley's babe invalidates his advice—Could I ever cease to find my sole comfort in having him perpetually with me—watching the dawings[3] of his mind, inspiring him with due respect for his unequalled father, & spreading joy over his infant years? What! shall I proclaim myself unworthy to have the care of my boy?—Never—Even if I could live & do it I would not—& if I were persuaded that I ought, then I should die.

If you are at all acquainted with the Entail of my Shelley's property you best know what confidence I may put in the validity of his will. If that will stands I shall be rich one day, & the present moment alone is to be provided for. If that stands my boy's fortune will depend on me & I become in every way his fitting guardian.

Again—I arrive in England poor to nothingness—I reside (even if that can be) in my father's house—poverty & misery around me—anxious care—but that must be mine wherever I am.

Yet my present life is a peaceful one. I see little even of those with whom I live—that is not their fault, but mine. I study—I write—I think even to madness & torture of the past—I look forward to the grave with hope—but in exerting my intellect—in forcing myself to real study—I find an opiate which at least adds nothing to the pain of regret that must necessarily be mine for ever.

Thus, my dear Jefferson, I send you a true picture of my situation You can shew it to M[rs] Williams—And she may help you to understand it. Again I appeal to you for your counsel—what shall I do? Consider that my child's interest is the question to be solved—I would do all, sacrifice all for him. What is best for him, is best for me. Let that consideration guide you{.} all sacrifice will be light to me made for his benefit—Study, tranquillity—Italy & all its gentle airs may go to the winds, if that they should, be best for him—care—poverty—& the ills of England will be welcome to me if they conduce to his benefit. I will do all but part with him—though if that should be necessary (but it is not) I would die—but what child could be benefited by the death of a mother whose life hangs upon his.

Pardon me that I have thus troubled you. Pardon me that I recall to your memory & force your attention to a hapless being—who since she last saw you has been tamed by every misery under the sun; and Who hopeless & wishless of any good in this life, prays daily for death when her life is no longer useful to the only tie that remains for her. Sorrow came upon me in my youth—& now still young—I have lost all even to wishing for. My only relief is in the exercise of my mind, the improvement {of} my understanding & the acquirement of knowledge. I fear & fly society—my child is my sole companion—I wish only for this grave like tranquility, if it be consistent with his prospects—& if indeed it can in any way continue under the present circumstances.

If I return to England I shall see you & in talking to you of your lost friend I ⟨expect⟩ shall find one of the very few consolations that I can expect to find in that country. I do not think that you will find me what I was. but tamed to submission to my har[s]h fate, grateful for kindness & as full of affection as one devoted to the past, & future beyond life—& looking on the present as a dark passage that must be gone through—tolerant—fearful—easily agitated but still reserved & diffident—what more? I have talked long enough of myself—if you see me again you will judge for yourself—if not, still think with kindness of the selected & chosen one of your friend, his constant companion & truest, perpetual Mourner—As one whom I believe to have been most sincerely attached to him—as the spectator of the ⟨earliest⟩ first years I spent with him, I must ever turn to you as a true friend

Most sincerely Yours
Mary Shelley

ADDRESS: T. Jefferson Hogg Esq / 1 Garden Court / Temple / Inghilterra / London. POSTMARKS: (1) GENOVA; (2) FPO / MR. 13 / 1823. PUBLISHED: Scott, *New Shelley Letters*, pp. 138–44. TEXT: MS., Pforzheimer Library.

1. In Jane Williams's letter of 12 February she wrote: "Hogg desires me to tell

you he would write to you himself but he cannot find it in his heart" (Abinger MS.).

2. "Compared with" Caroline of Brunswick (see 19 July 1820, n. 7).

3. Mary Shelley may have meant to write *dawnings*, or perhaps she was using the Scottish *dawings*, which means the same thing.

TO LORD BYRON Wednesday—Casa Negroto [5 March 1823][1]

I have received a letter from my father today, & should be glad to see your Lordship, if possible before the Post goes out to England. If it be not inconvenient to you would you come up this evening at your usual hour? or will you mention a convenient time when I can see you at your own house?

Pardon this annoyance, your own kindness has caused it—& I hope that that kindness is sufficient to render you not very impatient under the trouble it has drawn on you.

Salute Mad[me] Guiccioli for me

Truly Yours,
Mary Shelley

ADDRESS: To the Right Honble / Lord Byron / &c &c &c. PUBLISHED: Jones, #174. TEXT: MS., John Murray.

1. Godwin's letter of 14–18 February is Italian postmarked "3 Marzo." In Godwin's Journal, he also records writing to Mary Shelley on 18 March, 6 May, and 30 May 1823 (dates of receipt: c. 31 March, c. 19 May, and c. 12 June).

*TO JANE WILLIAMS Albaro. March 7th [1823]

You will probably have heard from my father, my best Jane, the result of LB's letter to Sir T.S. [*Timothy Shelley*]—It threw me into such a state of agitation for some days, that I hardly knew what to think or do; nor was this diminished by LB's saying that the proposal about my child ought to be accepted. I believe you know how much the "moods of my mind"[1] are at the mercy of the people about me. I can, I do, live in solitude; I can act independantly of the opinion of others; but the expression of that opinion if it be in opposition to mine shakes my nature to its foundations. I differed from LB. entirely; in the worldly as well as the moral view of this question; but I literally writhed under the idea that one so near me should advise me to a mode of conduct which appeared little short of madness & nothing short of death Then he said I ought to go to England; and I thought so too. But afterwards I doubted & fell into a fit of Pirrhonism[2] (which is still on me) and in an access of it I wrote a letter to Hogg, which you may possibly have seen. Methinks I ought to return to see what can be done, and entrench myself within the English pale. And again I think that this {is} a futile idea; that there I should be involved in {a} train of circumstances and solicitations, to which I am by no means equal; the course of which would make me supremely wretched, and in which after all I should not succeed: I think that I can maintain myself, and there is something inspiriting in the idea. Yet wishing to do the best for my boy, I am full of doubts. I shall stay with Marianne until her confinement, & in the mean time I wait for my father's advice, and Hogg's—and your's, dear friend, if you will send it me: for being on the spot you can judge better than I of the necessity or uselessness of my journey. LB. will write to Lord Holland,[3] but if I am not in the country, I do not see that it will be of any great use—after Sir. T.S.'s letter I can do nothing with him (if I can do any thing in any case) if I am not in England. I see very little of LB. he does not come here; & you may guess that my visits to Casa Saluzzi are, like those of Angels—"short, & far between."[4]

I indeed see no one. The spring is coming up slowly, and though so different from the last that we, happy flower girls, spent together; yet to me it is better than winter, for I am more free. I can walk—I take my solitary walks. I am no longer confined to one room, to hear the wind howl, and the rain patter. Even the hated sea wears a milder appearance. As I look on it sparkling beneath the sun, bounded by majestic promontories, and overlooked by the tower-crowned Appenines, I cannot help thinking that He—a disembodied spirit must still love those scenes in which he took so great a delight when with me, & that he may now hover over his ancient haunts. I saw the other day a white sail at a distance, and with a kind of madness of deception, I thought—there they are! I will take a boat & go out to them. But I must not weary you with the fantastic reveries of one given up to solitary & strange thought

I have heard from Charles Clairmont at Vienna. Claire is better and expects to engage herself soon to a Russian lady, & to go to that country.[5] This is a dangerous experiment for her, as her complaint is far from being cured, and the cold may have the worst effect on her. I know that Mrs Mason will say that she will not survive a Russian winter—& has dissuaded her in strong terms. But what can be done? Something may happen next winter; but I am too much accustomed to the dread of, and to the arrival of evil to build any thing upon lucky accidents. And what accident can be lucky for me? I am internally persuaded that however I may be annoyed by poverty, yet that when I am richer, some sinister event will spoil all, and make any acquisition of fortune weigh light in the scale of my cares.

I hear nothing at all of Ty [*Trelawny*]—which rather annoys me as his is a sea voyage—& if I were given to nervous fears, I might fancy a thousand things. But sufficient for the day—you know the rest[6]—& surely in our cases, my poor girl—we have a sufficiency of evil. Gabrielle is <u>disperata</u>. She goes out no where except to Mass & then escapes to Mrs Thomas, who is not very well pleased at being lugged into so disagreable an affair. I fortunately am too far off—but the other day I was surprised by a dirty epistle brought by a blacksmith, probably thrown to him out of window, from her, asking for intelligence—fortunately (as I then thought) I had none—& sent a very cold answer. Suppose her letters (which she dispatches in this heroine-like style) should fall into W's [*Wright's*] hands—they are couched in such terms that a duel must ensue—so figurativo her real care for Ty's life.

It seems to me, dearest Jane, that for us "the worlds great age begins anew" and "the years" (not the golden ones) "return."[7] You are gone back to your Mother's house—to Maria's[8] temper—to all the circumstances that marked your early youth. And I am threatened with a renewal of my girlish troubles. If I go back to my father's house—I know the person I have to deal with; all at first will be velvet—then thorns will come up—in fact it could not last long. This makes me more than ever inclined to my Italian poverty and my literary exertions. By the bye you do not mention the "Liberal" or my tale in it.[9] It is not an author's vanity that makes me say this—but I am a young beginner and want a little encouragement or criticism. You will have seen my novel by this time. I have requested my father to send you a copy[10]—and you must make my apologies to Hogg that I cannot send [him] one—& to Mrs Gisborne also—if it be worth while; but she has so entirely forg[ot]ten me, that it may not be necessary. My father says that he has curtailed i[t] greatly. Would that I could gain enough this way to make me completely indepe[n]dant. Staying with the Hunts (though they are kind, especially Marianne, whose disposition is free from any particle of meaness) yet in many ways does not suit me—but these are evils which do not disturb me greatly—I study—I have my child with me—and although not one moment—oh! not one—even the smallest division of time! is free from acute mental pain—I bear all with tolerable patience.

Your prospects, dear Jane, depend greatly on our beloved Edward's brother; I am anxious to hear of his arrival.[11] He may make your situation far less embarassing How vexatious that your sister, should spoil the slight tranquillity you might have enjoyed under your Mother's roof—and your children are yet too young to be a consolation to you. I am delighted to hear they are well—in this month is little Rosalinds birthday—I wish I could send her an Italian gift—but you must buy her some little thing to give her from her "Godmother." If it is settled that I remain here I have requested my father to get the £8—I mentioned & to give it to you. I do not think that my order would have any effect—Peacock as executor is the right person—but he will not take the trouble to send me the papers that I have almost prayed for (as Taaffe says) on my mental knees. Do you know—that when very poor, we divided our greatest acquisitions of money (got actually by pawning) with him. And that until he got his present situation he received regularly from our income (a third less than his present one) above £100 a year.[12] After this can you be surprized at Harvey[13]—perhaps he has grown rich—if so there is no hope of justice from him Holcroft wrote a ballad with this moral

The poor man alone,
When he hears the poor moan
Of his morsel, a morsel will give.[14]

And this is true as truth. Why even my stingy neighbour has only grown incorrigible since he came into his fortune last year.[15] He never took to saving before—saving, the characteristic fault of the Papalangi's[16] Do you remember [?king Finow]. Adieu—write as often as you can—

Most affectionately & for ever your own—Mary Shelley.

[*Cross-written*] You can always send me anything by sending it to my address to Mr John Hunt at the Examiner Office—with a polite note requesting him to forward it in the next box to his brother. Don't cross your letters—write smaller & on larger paper—but crossing is a thing very annoying as it destroys legibility—pardon this assurance—but I do not read your letters over half so many times as I should, if they were not crossed—

ADDRESS: Mrs. Williams / Mrs. Cleveland / 24 Alsop's Buildings / New Road / London Inghilterra / Londres. POSTMARKS: (1) GENOVA; (2) FPO / MR. 22 / 1823; (3) 12 NOON 12 / MR. 22. 1823. UNPUBLISHED. TEXT: MS., Abinger MS., Bodleian Library.

1. *Alastor*, lines 161–63.

2. Pyrrhonism, i.e., skepticism.

3. In her letter of 12 February Jane Williams had mentioned Hogg's suggestion that Byron contact Lord Holland and ask him "to suggest to Sir Timothy the propriety of making a moderate allowance for the maintenance" of Percy, since the child might inherit the title "& to support to honour of the family." Hogg argued that Sir Timothy Shelley was more likely to be favorably influenced by Lord Holland's intercession than by Godwin's (Abinger MS.).

4. Robert Blair, *The Grave*, line 588.

5. Claire Clairmont had agreed to accompany Countess Zotoff, the daughter of Prince Kurakin, a Russian minister, to Petersburg, where she would become the companion to the Countess's teenage daughters. Her salary was about £75 annually. On 22 March Claire Clairmont left Vienna with Countess Zotoff, and for almost a year she wrote to no one (*CC Journals*, p. 297).

6. "Sufficient unto the day is the evil thereof" (Matt. 6:34).

7. *Hellas*, lines 1060–61.

8. Maria Baird, Jane Williams's sister.

9. See 7 January [1823] to Trelawny, n. 5.

10. *Valperga* was published by G. and W. B. Whittaker in February 1823. In a letter of 14–18 February Godwin wrote to Mary Shelley: "Your novel is now fully printed, & ready for publication. I shall send you a copy either by Peacock's parcel or John Hunt's. I have taken great liberties with it, & I fear your amour propre will be proportionably shocked. I need not tell you that all the merit of the book is exclusively your own. The whole of what I have done is nearly confined to the taking away things that must have prevented its success. I scarcely ever saw any thing more unfortunately out of taste, than the long detail of battles & campaigning, after the death of Beatrice, & when the reader is impatient for the conclusion. Beatrice is the jewel of the book; not but that I greatly admire Euthanasia; & I think the characters of Pepi, Bindo, & the Witch, decisive efforts of original genius. I am promised a character of the work in the Morning Chronicle & the Herald, & was in hopes to have sent you the one or the other by this time: I also sent a copy of

the book to the Examiner for the same purpose" (Abinger MS.). Godwin's Journal records 19 February as the publication date.

11. Captain John Williams, a natural or reputed brother of Edward Williams, was an officer in the Eighth Light Dragoons, stationed in India. Jane Williams, who alluded to him as her husband's half brother, expected him to aid her when he returned to England (letter to Mary Shelley, 27 March 1823, Abinger MS.). This explains information Peacock sent to Mary Shelley on 8 August 1822: "Regiments have embarked for Bengal to relieve others. Amongst the latter will be the 8th Light Dragoons. They are expected home about the spring or summer of next year" (Peacock, *Works*, VIII, 230). As late as 27 March 1823 Jane Williams did not know that John Williams had died at sea on 20 January 1823 (Edmund Blunden, "The Family of Edward Williams," *Keats-Shelley Memorial Bulletin* 4 [1952]: 49–50; see 31 May [1823]).

12. See *MWS Journal*, 12 January 1815, and White, *Shelley*, I, 541, concerning the Shelleys' aid to Peacock.

13. Beauchamp Harvey, an old friend of Edward Williams (Williams, *Journals and Letters*, p. 113).

14. Thomas Holcroft, "The Song of Gaffer-Gray," lines 39–41.

15. The death of Lady Judith Noel, Byron's mother-in-law, on 28 January 1822, had brought him an annual income of about £2,500 (Marchand, *Byron*, III, 970–71). Byron's letter of 18 January 1823, in which he writes: "I *loves lucre*," acknowledges his "recent and furious fit of accumulation and retrenchment" (Byron, *Works*, VI, 163).

16. Perhaps Mary Shelley's neologism for Catholic-English and therefore an allusion to Byron's decision to educate Allegra in a convent and his occasionally positive words about Catholicism (Marchand, *Byron*, III, 977–78).

To Lord Byron — Albaro Sunday [30 March 1823][1]

My dear Lord Byron

The 15th Canto was so long coming even after I had heard that it was finished, that I began to suspect that you thought that you were annoying me by sending me employment. Be assured however on the contrary, that besides the pleasure it gives me to be in the slightest manner useful to your Lordship, the task itself is a delightful one to me.

Is Aurora a portrait?[2] ⟨She is⟩ Poor Juan I long to know how he gets out or rather into the net. Are the other Cantos to be published soon?

I have had no letters. I wait with no pleasant expectation for the result of my father's deliberations—it little matters which way he decides for either to go or stay are equally disagreable to me in the situation I now am. But the present state of things cannot & shall not last, though I see but dimly what is to come in lieu of it. I think it will be England after all—that will be best for my boys health & perhaps the least unexceptionable part for me to take.

I hope this fine weather has cured all your incommodi

Truly Yours obliged
Mary Shelley

Will you lend me those verses on Lady B. that Hunt had a few weeks ago[3]

ADDRESS: To the Right Honble / Lord Byron. PUBLISHED: Jones, #173. TEXT: MS., John Murray.

1. Mary Shelley's references to Canto 15 suggest that this letter was written on 30 March. Byron completed Canto 15 on 25 March (Steffan, *Byron's Don Juan,* I, 319).

2. Aurora Raby, *Don Juan* 15. 43.

3. Possibly "The Charity Ball."

TO LORD BYRON Monday Albaro [31 March 1823][1]

My dear Lord Byron

I am afraid I annoy you very much by intruding myself and my affairs on you. I had hopes at one time not to have troubled any one; but fate is innimical to me.

I have received a letter from my father who thinks well of what I mentioned to your Lordship when I last saw you, rather more than a month ago, of a letter to Lord Holland. I cannot go to England until after Mrs Hunt's confinement, & you seemed then to think that in the interim it might be well if my father saw Lord Holland, introduced by a letter from you. Do you still think so—and would you write?

I send you my father's letter that you may judge better—you will smile at the idea of Hunt's wishing to keep me—I am no such Gods-send to any one—& he would find a better consoler—though I have entire hope that it will not be needed & all will go well.

I am sufficiently out of spirits. The idea of maintaining myself in England I own frightens me. I—who nine days out of ten am too agitated & miserable to write at all.—However I hope my fortitude will re-awaken some of these days and in the mean time I have sufficient for the present. That is to say if the 3rd No. of the Liberal Comes out[2]

Again I entreat your Lordship to excuse me—Your own kindness is indeed my only excuse—retract that, & I shall have none—& without one I will not sin.

Yours Obliged
Mary Shelley

I would come down—but I have found that there is small chance of seeing you when I do—

ADDRESS: To the Rt Honble / Lord Byron. PUBLISHED: Jones, #176. TEXT: MS., John Murray.

1. This letter indicates that Mary Shelley first discussed the possibility of Byron's writing to Lord Holland more than a month earlier. Jane Williams's letter mentioning Lord Holland was Italian postmarked 26 February, which suggests that the Monday on which Mary Shelley wrote this letter was 31 March. This date is corroborated by Mary Shelley's reference to a letter received from Godwin, since the letter he wrote on 18 March would have been received about 31 March (see [5 March 1823]; 7 March [1823]).

2. The third number of the Liberal was published on 26 April 1823 and included Mary Shelley's article "Madame D'Houtetot" (Marshall, *The Liberal*, p. 174).

To Lord Byron [Albaro] Wednesday. [2 April 1823][1]

My dear Lord Byron,

I could not well wait for you yesterday, but I do not intend to write to my father until next week.[2] In the interval perhaps you can come up here; or if not, if you will let me know when I can conveniently see you, I will come down to Casa Saluzzi.

I am very grateful to you for Your kind offers yesterday. In part I must avail myself of them to get to England but I know too well how many claims you must have on you and have been myself to long in a situation where more limited in our means yet no one was satisfied with the little we did, not to have pity on the situation of one to whom all look up to as their prop, & be assured that I shall presume as little as possible on your kindness, & your demonstrations of good will, will not cause me to tire those feeling, although I own that the expression of them is highly gratifying to me.

I hear that you have begun Your 16th Canto. I trust that your Lordship will make use of me, in the only way I can be of service to you as long as my residence near you gives you the opportunity

Truly Ys Obliged
MaryS.

PUBLISHED: Jones, #172. TEXT: MS., John Murray.

1. Mary Shelley's reference to Canto 16 indicates that this letter could not have been written until the first Wednesday after 29 March, when Byron began writing Canto 16 (Steffan, *Byron's Don Juan*, I, 309).

2. Godwin's letter of 6 May acknowledged receipt, on 18 April, of a letter (unlocated) from Mary Shelley stating her intention to return to England (for Godwin's letter, see *S&M*, IV, 940–41).

To Edward John Trelawny [Albaro c. 5 April 1823][1]

I am most truly grateful to you, my dear Trelawny, for the additional benefit you have conferred upon me by placing the ashes of my Beloved Shelley apart from others. But, my dear friend, you give too short an account of all this—You write to one whose heart & soul is in every letter penned on the subject, and there are several circumstances connected with what you have done, that appear obscure to me; I therefore write immediately that my letter may reach you before you quit Rome and I entreat you, by all your kindness towards me, to answer me immediately, by return of Post if you can.

Is the place you have selected for my Shelley within the Enclosure of the burying Ground?

Where is this Burying Ground?—Is it not near the Tomb of Cestius on the further side from the Porta S. Paolo—near Monte Testaccio?[2]

In enclosing a spot around the grave you have fulfilled my earnest wish—

Will you tell me what the inscription on the tomb is—how are you planting it—have you placed a cypress—& how will you guard against violation of & provide for the care of what you have done. It occurred to me that for a moderate stipend the monks of a neighbouring convent would be good guardians since they would be permanent ones. We shall one day be both richer & my first hope is to place an enduring mark to denote where his spoils lie & to prove that no earthly creature ever had hearts & friends more entirely & truly devoted to him than my lost Shelley.

My heart is beneath that weed grown wall. Would that I were really there! My first act of freedom will carry me there—but now I am a slave—who so great a one as a poor person—& I shall soon perform a far different & most hateful journey. I return to England. Sir T.S. [*Timothy Shelley*] has refused to provide for me—yet in such a way as leaves a hope that he might be brought to another determination if I were not abroad—for he acknowledges the rights of my boy—if he were in England—I go—with great regret—yet less than I once had—in poverty & dependance Italy loses half its charms, if I live I shall return able to do all here that I desire —If not—still I shall return. I know that I shall suffer a great deal in England—& I own that there is not the prospect of a single feeling unembued with pain. But I submit. But for my boy I should soon be free from all these trammels and it is for his good that I devote myself.

I shall wait here until after Mrs Hunt's con[finement] for I will not leave her until I see what dan[ ][3] detain me until June when you talk of retur[ ] trust that I shall see you before I go—b[ ] A place of peril for you—the most ha[ ] where you are never either well or happy [ ] forgive myself if I were the means of draw[ ] meet in some other town on the road to [ ].

LB. continues kind and attentive [ ] for England.

I will write to you more at length at Florence [ ] I only recur to the subject that has occasioned this letter [ ] Do write to me before you quit Rome answering my questions which may appear trifling—but they are of the utmost importance to me—for as I said, my deepest, realest, & most eternal feelings—& my never resting thoughts are ever beside His Tomb.

Hunt desires to be remembered to you—& begs me to request you to tell Mr Severn that he writes to him tomorrow. I will write to Rose as you desire.[4] When do you think of going to Paris?

Happy Trelawny, you are at Rome—What a [ ] sound that name has ever been to me—how I [ ] loved that City—Now it contains my all.

Trust to the sincere Attachment of

[M]aryShelley

ADDRESS: Edward Trelawny Esq. / Ferma in Posta / Roma. POSTMARKS: (1) GENOVA; (2) [ ] APRILLE. PUBLISHED: Jones, #175. TEXT: MS., Bodleian Library (MS., Shelley, Adds., c. 6, ff. 5–6).

1. On 2 April Trelawny wrote Mary Shelley that displeased with the location of Shelley's grave, he had selected "the only interesting spot. I enclosed it apart from all possibility of sacrilegious intrusion and removed his ashes to it, placed a stone over it, am now planting it, and have ordered a granite to be prepared for myself, which I shall place in this beautiful recess (of which the enclosed is a drawing I took), for when I am dead I have none to do me this service, so shall at least give one instance in my life of proficiency" (*S&M*, IV, 930–31). In this letter, Mary Shelley indicates that she is writing immediately in order to receive a response from Trelawny before his planned departure from Rome around 12 April. This, together with the trace of a single-digit postal date, suggests that the letter was written around 5 April.

2. Trelawny's letter of 27 April answers Mary Shelley's questions (*S&M*, IV, 933–35). Part of Trelawny's answer is included in Mary Shelley's letter to Maria Gisborne of 3–6 May [1823].

3. Manuscript eradicated, affecting several lines.

4. Trelawny had asked Mary Shelley to respond on his behalf to a letter from his "old friend Rose" telling her "everything," expressing his pleasure at hearing from her, and saying he would go to Paris to see her at "the first opportunity" (*S&M*, IV, 931).

*To Jane Williams — Albaro. April 10th [1823]

Your letter, mine own Jane, does but confirm all that I feel and know about England and my residence there—Ma che vuol che la dico?[1] A number of circumstances impel my return, yet not exactly those on which you lay so great a stress. And yet I may be wrong there. I own that with all drawbacks I fancy I could maintain myself better here than there. But then I must depend upon My father for active exertion in gaining employment for me and selling what I produce—he makes no offers and I know how necessary it is to depend on oneself alone. LB. strongly advises my return—he is still very kind to me & makes offers of a generous nature. He will profit by the will & therefore every motive will induce him to keep his word.[2] But he piques himself on giving good advice & I must follow it, or lose my credit with him—which stands greatly I believe on my known admiration of his writings and my docility in attending to him. He will probably leave this part of the country about the time I fix for my return—he will go where for a time communication will be difficult—& he would go with the reflection that I was self willed—whereas if I obey him, he cannot find fault with the result. His idea is that my boy ought to be in England—that he ought to be seen by some of his father's relations. Indeed, you surprize me by saying that wise heads think that my presence might hurt my negociation with my father-in-law. He expressly makes it one of his two conditions for providing for my child that he should be in England—& my only excuse for applying again without fulfilling this, would be, that I had not the means. After LB's letter, which said all that could be said, another would be useless, unless by some alteration in my circumstances, it could wear somewhat a new form. If I can make friends in

England, if I can interest any of the millions of Shelleys uncles & cousins—or people of higher interest such as you mentioned in your former letter, something might be done. Above all, by my lost One's will I come in nearly for the whole property on Sir T.S. [*Timothy Shelley's*] death—it would be well that for that I were somewhat known—that my boy was looked on by someone of the family. Then consider—I cannot continue to live under Hunt's roof. LB will be absent[3] if he goes, T—y [*Trelawny*] will go too—the Liberal looks dismal.[4] I have therefore made up my mind to return after I have seen Marianne safe through her confinement. And now I will no longer annoy you with this ungrateful subject—I have so many other things to say, & having resolved—so be it—at least I shall see you, my poor girl—I may help you to support your weight of discomfort—we will build castles for the future. For instance such a one as I dreamt a few night's ago. First there was Ned & my beloved Shelley, there was a strange bustle—suddenly you and I became such as we are, and we prepared to return to England—I saw the boxes pact & all the preparations for a journey when I thought that you and I turned down a pathway that led through a wood beneath the brow of a rocky hill. Imagination cannot conceive any thing more lovely than this spot; which has haunted me ever since. By its vegetation it must have been Italy—the rich foliage of the trees—the verdure of the grass, the beauty of the flowers, the picturesque & tree grown rock—are all before me—& we were told that we were to remain there until our reunion with our lost ones. If I do not die I trust I shall one day be independant—when I hope that all that nature can do to heal our wounds, she will perform.

I heard from Trelawny the other day—he has enclosed me a drawing of my Shelley tomb—that is to say the old wall of Rome under which the slight tablet rests that marks the place. If the climate of Rome would permit me to take my child there, I would go, & then no motive would be strong enough to take me away—but that must be my grave & not my living residence—nothing can be kinder than Trelawny—and every act proves more the goodness of his heart. He is now at Rome—he removes soon to Florence, & will then come here—I have advised against his return to this place, but since I wrote other circumstances have occurred. I confide them to your discretion, my dear Jane, and entreat you not to mention them to any one, for if they do not come to pass, LB. would be sorry that they should be known. A person from the Greek Committee in London & several Greeks have requested him to go over there—to observe the state of the country & cause—& to be of what use he can. He has replied that he will go if they prove to him that the Provisional Government will be glad of his presence—& they promise to procure an official invitation for him in three months time. I think he will go—because he hates Genoa—because Pierino[5] is half mad with joy at the very idea—because Greece has many charms for him, & his pride also will be gratified—He has requested me to invite Trelawny to go with him (if he goes) & in the mean time you will be glad to hear that he is actually buying arms—causing cannons to be cast—has promised to give the "Bolivar" to the Greeks & seems to be animated by a good spirit in this affair. As to the G— [*Guiccioli*] as she is very artful I cannot pretend to judge of her motives or designs—but she does not oppose herself.

As to the Hunts I hardly know what to think—I am enclined to suspect that they will return in [*to*] England, notwithstanding their declarations to the contrary: the great thing is to see Marianne safe through the approaching crisis. H. has had the humanity to permit her to decide concerning the coming of Miss K.[6] and she has placed her veto on it, so it will not be for the present. H. could not at so terrible a moment have acted against her wishes—& I think it would have killed her if that most selfish of human beings had arrived to disturb by her self will & violence the comparative peace she enjoys. I remain here till that time be passed. I seldom see any of them I am alone reading & studying & suffering. I strive for fortitude & courage—sometimes I get a glimpse of these things—but generally nervous agitation—incapacity of anything except walking up & down the room & dreaming of the past—regret—vain wishes & dispair are my dayly occupations. I look with inconceivable horror on the future—whatever turn affairs take I see no good for me—when I can read & exert my mind I find my only consolation in those exercises—but sometimes I cannot engage myself in any thing.—The doubt I was in for a long time about my return was the cause of excessive agitation—now, though I have chosen for the worser part, I am more calm. I have returned to my books—Spring is dressing all in green, the blossoms are passing away—we have had some heavy rains—& I expect to find vegetation much advanced when I revisit my solitary haunts—it is not the cheerfulness of spring that brings ought [*aught*] of cheerfulness [   ] but the only relief I find is in nourishing a romantic & exalted tone of mind [   ] in thought about that above me—thus all the operations of nature—the c[   ] the air, the springing green feeds the current—allows it not to pause—& thus I create a veil for the dull reality. I get wings for my spirit—& my lonely rambles are not without their inspirations—while among others & enclosed by my four walls—I droop & all is as blank as the reality—I strive to communicate with the beloved spirit of him who was mine—and I feel nearer to him while beauty clothes the earth & bathes the breeze in sweetness. All my hope—my expectation my life is in this kind of madness.

Your account of the occurences at Paris is curious—& how more & more does it assimilate your situation to my Mother's heroine.[7] I am grieved indeed you suffer by the coldness of people from whom better might have been expected—at least Wallace—as a man accustomed to danger & risque, he ought to feel sympathy for the unfortunate—You do not surprize me with what you say of Cox[8]—he is married—you do not fall in the way of his dayly intercourse—& constant sight is almost the only way of exciting the interest of commonminded persons. The paragraph from the Brighton paper[9] is almost wonderful—one would almost think that someone put it in to give a false idea that dearest Ned was not my Shelley's companion—but those who could have done that, could not have known other circumstances mentioned in so singularly exact a manner.

As I do not come to England until June write again, my dear girl. England! what a fearful sound!—best I submit—well—perhaps as you seem to find some relief in the intercourse of persons of liberal sentiments I may enlarge that sphere for you. Pray tell me if Medwin is in Paris—& if he is, where? as I should wish to see him as I pass through—& should even write to him first to get an apartment for me for the few days I may stay there. C—[*Claire*] writes to say she is better. Mrs M. [*Mason*] is very angry with LB.[10] and I do not wonder—but I am grateful to him for his kindness to me and if he [*cross-written*] continues as he promises my gratitude will prevent my being angry with him. I shall see when I depart if his actions are on a parr with his professions, & if they are why, my dear Jane, I shall be very glad—truly obliged—not a little surprised & not less reconnaissante. —Peacock has I hear at last sent my box, but with out giving me notice of it, or telling me the name of the vessel—so it will be delayed & every inconvenience attend my getting it—I own that I agree with you about the title of my book[11]—but all alterations that have been made since I read it to you in my little room at Pisa have been made by my father. As Hogg is on the circuit I suppose that he has not yet received my letter. I wrote to him for advice but I seem to have come to a conclusion without. Can I then leave dear—dear Italy?—I often think that my scene will close before I again pass the Alps, or that some obstacle will arise higher than they to keep me here—Would that it could be so!—Adieu dear Jane God & good spirits & our Spirits guard you—I am growing terribly religious—LB. says—what are you a Christian? no I were not religious—if I were—but I have a firm faith—& I place my hope in those aspirations that lead me to my Lost One

Again adieu, my best Jane—Percy remembers Dulie. he is well

Ever affectionately yrs
MaryShelley

I have some crowns of yours you know—tell me if you would like that I should buy any thing here for you.

ADDRESS: Mrs Williams / Mrs Cleveland / 24 Alsops Buildings / New Road / London / Inghilterra—Londres. POSTMARKS: (1) GENOVA; (2) FPO / AP. 22 / 1823; (3) 12 NOON 12 / AP. 22 / 1823. UNPUBLISHED. TEXT: MS., Abinger MS., Bodleian Library.

1. "But what can I say?"

2. Shelley bequeathed £2,000 to Byron. Byron renounced claims to this legacy when he was confronted with Hunt's argument that Byron owed Mary Shelley £1,000 as a result of losing his bet with Shelley over whether Lady Noel (Byron's mother-in-law) or Sir Timothy Shelley would die first (Marchand, *Byron*, III, 1079–80; see also [c. 2] July [1823]).

3. On 5 April Edward Blaquiere, a member of the London Greek Committee, and Andreas Luriottis, a representative of the Greek government, visited Byron. By the end of their conversations, Byron, who in the summer of 1822 had contemplated such a plan, offered to go to Greece to fight for Greek liberty (Marchand, *Byron*, III, 1027, 1061).

4. The financial failure of the second number of the *Liberal*, Byron's growing disaffection, and the prosecution of the *Liberal* for Byron's *The Vision of Judgment* all contributed to its final demise with its fourth number, published 30 July 1823 (Marshall, *The Liberal*, pp. 162–63, 196–98).

5. Teresa Guiccioli's brother, who accompanied Byron to Greece.

6. Bessy Kent (see 2 March 1817 to Marianne Hunt, n. 2).

7. The heroine of *The Wrongs of Woman; or, Maria* was married to a scoundrel. Medwin had written Jane Williams that her legal husband (whom she referred to as "my evil genius") was involved in a variety of crimes, including forgery of checks and attempted murder, and was sought by the Paris Police (Jane Williams to Mary Shelley, 27 March 1823, Abinger MS.; and Lovell, *Medwin*, pp. 136–37).

8. Jane Williams had depended on Wallace and Cox, friends of Edward Williams, for aid on her return to England. Cox was negotiating on Jane Williams's behalf with Edward Williams's stepmother to obtain a picture of Edward Williams. Disappointed with Cox's handling of the matter, Jane Williams regretted "having selected him for such a mission; he is a fool and cold hearted and a luke-warm friend often does you more mischief than a bitter enemy. Medwin would have been a better person for he is sincere at all events to me" (Jane Williams to Mary Shelley, 27 March 1823, Abinger MS.).

9. An account of an Edward Williams who was missing from his lodgings at Brighton and was found drowned several days afterward, and whose half brother was a captain in the Light Dragoons. The circumstances sound like a garbled version of the Shelley-Williams drowning.

10. See 12 January [1823].

11. Jane Williams had written: "I do not approve of the change in the title The 'life & Adventures' always remind me of Jack the Giants Killer or Mother Hubbard ——'Castruccio Prince of Lucca' was dignified and was more expressive of the nature of the work; but I may be wrong it is only my own suggestion" (27 March 1823, Abinger MS.; see also 7 March [1823]).

To Teresa Guiccioli

[Albaro] domenica [*Sunday* May–June 1823][1]

Mia Cara—Sono desperata—accioche mi trovo senza una penna nel mondo, e⟨d anche⟩ la Hunt non ne ha per prestarmi—E festa e non c'è rimedio se voi non avrete la bonta di mandarmi una mezza dozzina.

Se avete finito col secondo numero del Paris Monthly reveiw,[2] mi farete un grand'piacere mandandomilo.

Che tempo! voleva mostrarvi il mio passeggio ma bisogna aspettar per il ritorno del sole—volete intanto, se non piove venir ascostarvi al mio foco, che non fuma, e mi fa un agradevole compagnia, or a che il cielo è annuvalato. Vorrei che c'erà ballo a Casa Saluzzi per far Byron e voi venir quà su—ma pensate che io parto fra poco e lascioro la mia Italia e voi altri pure, cosi sarebbe una cosa affatto gentile se Egli e voi mi farete questo piacer

Addio Mia Cara—le penne per pietà—

V. Aff[ma] A.
Mary Shelley

[*Translation*]

My Dear—I am desperate—because I find myself without a pen in the world, and ⟨even⟩ Hunt does not have any to lend me—It is holiday and there is no remedy if you will not have the goodness to send me half a dozen.

If you have finished with the second number of the Paris Monthly review,[2] do me the great favor of sending it to me.

What weather! I wanted to show you my walk but need to wait for the return of the sun—do you want, in the meantime, if it does not rain, to come and draw near to my fire, which does not smoke, and pay me an agreeable visit, now that the sky is cloudy. I would like there to be a ball at Casa Saluzzi to make Byron and you come up here—but think that I am departing before long and I will leave my Italy and you others also, therefore it would be a truly kind thing if he and you would do me this favor.

So long my dear—the pens for pity's sake—

Your affectionate friend
Mary Shelley

ADDRESS: a Madame/ Madme la Countesse de Guicc[ioli]. PUBLISHED: Palacio, *Mary Shelley*, p. 603. TEXT: MS., John Murray. TRANSLATION: Ricki B. Herzfeld.

1. Since Mary Shelley mentions her impending departure "fra poco" ("shortly"), this letter may have been written as early as May, when her decision to return to England was made (see 3–6 May [1823]), or as late as the end of June. At the beginning of July Mary Shelley became quite angry with Byron (see [c. 2] July [1823]); the friendly reference to Byron in this letter suggests that it was written prior to the quarrel.

2. *The Paris Monthly Review of British and Continental Literature* published a dozen numbers between 1822 and 1823 (Palacio, *Mary Shelley*, p. 603).

To Maria Gisborne May 3rd (May 6th) Albaro [1823][1]

My dear M[rs] Gisborne

Your letter[2] was very pleasing to me since it shewed me, that it was not want of affection that caused your silence: Utter solitude is delightful to me, but in the midst of the waste, I am much comforted when I hear the quiet voice of friendship telling me that I am still loved by some one, & especially by those who knew my Shelley and have been his companions. You do well to say that it is an almost insurmountable difficulty in expressing your thoughts that causes you to be silent. For though occupation or indolence may often prevent your exerting yourself, yet when you do write, yours are the best letters I receive, especially as far as clearness & information goes.

I had a letter today from Trelawny at Rome concerning the disposition of the earthly dress of my lost one. He is in the Protestant burying ground at that place, which is beside, & not before, the tomb of Cestius. The old wall with an Ancient tower bounds it on one side & beneath this tower, a weed grown & picturesque ruin, the excavation has been made. T—y has sent me a drawing of it—& he thus writes,—"is placed apart, yet in the centre, & the most conspicuous spot in the burying Ground. I have just planted six young cypresses & 4 laurels, in the front of the recess, which you see in the drawing, which is caused by the projecting part of the old ruin. My own stone"—(T—y you know, one of the best & most generous of creatures, is eccentric in his way) "a plain slab, till I can decide upon some fitting inscription, is placed on the left hand—I have likewise dug my grave—so that when I die, there is only to lift up the coverlet, & roll me into it—You may lay on the other side, or I will share my narrow bed with you, if you like. It is a lovely spot. The only inscription on S. stone, besides the cor cordium of Hunt, are three lines I have added, from Shakespeare

—"Nothing of him that doth <u>fade</u>,
But doth suffer a sea-change
Into something <u>rich</u> & <u>strange</u>

"This quotation by its double meaning alludes both to the manner of his d—h & his genius. And I think the element on which his soul took wing, & the subtle essence of his being mingled, may still retain him in some other shape. The water may keep the dead, as the earth may, & fire, & air. His passionate fondness might have arisen from some sweet sympathy in his nature; thence the fascination which so forcibly attracted him, without fear or caution to trust an element, which almost all others hold in superstitious dread, & venture as cautiously on as they would in a lair of Lions"—

This quotation is pleasing to me also, because a year ago, T—y came one afternoon in high spirits with news concerning the building of the boat—saying—oh—we must all embark—all live aboard—"We will all suffer a sea-change," and dearest Shelley was delighted with the quotation—saying that he w[d] have it for the motto of his boat—Try— says in another part of his letter, "I have been digging & planting myself—there are 7 or 8 cypresses & as many laurels, about the tomb or rather I should say tombs, for I have completed one for myself & yesterday laid it down on the left of S. as they both stand on a very steep bank, I thought it necessary to put additional security to prevent their being moved, either by rain or otherwise —every thing is now most satisfactorily arranged."

Captain Roberts (Jane will tell you who he is) is just come from Rome. He confirms all that is said in this letter. Tell Jane I passed yesterday evening with him & talked a great deal of her & dearest Edward. I was pleased by the enthusiasm with which he spoke—He declared that he had never met a man to be compared him– in Nobleness & amiability of Nature—together with a nameless charm that pervaded all his converse. Roberts had bought the hulk of that miserable boat—new rigged her—even with higher Masts than before—he has sailed with her at the rate of 8 knots an hour—& on such occasions tried various experiments, hazardous ones, to discover how the catastrophe that closed the scene for us two poor creatures happened. It is plain to every eye. She was run down from behind. On bringing her up from 15 fathom all was in her—books, telescope ballast, lying on each side of the boat without any appearance of shifting or confusion—the topsails furled—topmasts lowered—the false stern (Jane can explain) broken to pieces & a great hole knocked in the stern timbers. When she was brought to Leghorn every one went to see her—& the same exclamation was uttered by all—She was run down. by that wretched fishing boat which owned that it had seen them.[3]

I have written myself into a state of agitation—if I continued my letter it would only be to pour out the bitterness of my heart. Oh this spring is so beautiful the clear sky shines above the calm murderer—the trees are all in leaf & a soft air is among them—The stars tell of other spheres where I pray to be—for all this beauty while at times it elevates me—yet in stronger words tells me—that he, the best & most beautiful is gone

> Oh follow! follow!—
> And on each herb, from which heavens dew had fallen
> The like was stamped, as with a with a withering fire,
> —And then
> Low, sweet, faint sounds, like the farewel of ghosts
> Were heard: oh, follow, follow, follow me.[4]

I will finish my letter Monday—God bless you: good night. I often see him—both he & dear Edward in dreams—perhaps I shall tonight—at least I shall not be in sleep as I am now—the clinging present is so odious—

(May 6th) I finish my letter. You will soon see me in England. It is not my own desire, or for my own advantage that I go—but for my boy's—So I am fixed—and enjoy these blue skies & the sight of vines & olive groves for the last time. I hope indeed to return—all my hopes are set upon that but that is in case I get richer one day—if not I trust I return for my repose. I am sorry to hear the melancholy account you give of your situation & am truly sorry that Henry does {not} gain the success that his talents deserve. I wait here to see Mrs Hunt safe through her confinement—In her critical situation among strangers & not speaking a word of Italian—without an English servant (the one she brought over has made a scapatura) Hunt speaking badly—& this vile Genoese destroying that little, my presence is necessary at least to keep up her spirits. That passed, the fear of the advancing season will make me begin my journey as quickly as possible. I should in any case have feared an Italian summer for my delicate child—the climate of England will agree with him. LB. is very kind to me, & promises that I shall make my journey at my ease, which on Percy's account, I am glad of. He is much improved poor boy—& cannot speak a word of English —Remember me to M^{r} G [*Gisborne*] & Henry

Did the End of Beatrice[5] surprise you. I am surprised that none of these Literary Gazettes are shocked—I feared that they would stumble over a part of what I read to you & still more over my Anathema.[6] I wish much to see it—as my father has made some curtailments—but the vessel has not yet arrived. Is not the catastrophe strangely prophetic[7] But it seems to me that in what I have hitherto written I have done nothing but prophecy what has arrived to. Matilda[8] fortells even many small circumstances most truly—& the whole of it is a monument of what now is—

Adieu, My dear Friend—Give my very tenderest love to Jane when you see her

Affectionately Yours,
Mary W.Shelley

ADDRESS: Mrs. Gisborne / 33 Kings St. West, / Bryanstone Square / London / Inghilterra / Londres. POSTMARKS: (1) GENOVA; (2) FPO / MY. 20 / 1823; (3) 12 NOON 12 / MY. 20 / 1823. PUBLISHED: Jones, #177. TEXT: MS., Bodleian Library (MS., Shelley, Adds., c. 6, ff. 7–8).

1. Jones, taking his text of this letter from a copy, dated the letter 2 May but noted that it was dated 3 May in all other printed texts. The original letter bears the date "May 3rd Albaro"; further, Trelawny's letter, which Mary Shelley received that day, is postmarked "3 MAGGIO."
2. Dated 17 March 1823 (Gisborne, *Journals and Letters*, pp. 93–98).
3. See 15 August 1822; 17–20 September 1822.
4. *Prometheus Unbound* 2. 1. 153–55, 157–59.
5. *Valperga*, vol. 3, chap. 7.
6. *Valperga*, vol. 3, chap. 3, in which Beatrice curses the "author of her being."
7. See 12 January [1823].
8. See 15 August 1822.

TO DANIEL ROBERTS

Albaro. May 6th Monday [1823][1]

My Dear Roberts

As I wish much to see the views of Rome of which you spoke, perhaps you would send them to Mrs Thomas—where I would come to look them over.

I had a letter Friday from Trelawny, dated Rome April 27—he bids me tell you that he had received your 2 letters & had answered the first—Asks if you join the Broughtons in Switzerland—talks of going thither himself, & requests that you would ask Beeze[2] if he would go with him, & live on shore. But the idea of the Greek Expedition may alter all this & LordByron seems bent upon going. He says that he leaves Rome the following day after that on which he wrote—

This fine weather will assist you in your drawing.[3] And may tempt you to come to Albaro—Adieu

Yours obliged
MaryShelley

PUBLISHED: Jones, #178. TEXT: MS., Pforzheimer Library.

1. The sixth of May, 1823, was a Tuesday.

2. One of the men previously employed on Byron's *Bolivar*.

3. In Roberts's letter of 1 May to Mary Shelley he wrote that he had "procured leave to take a panorama view of Genoa, which leave expires in 15 days" (Abinger MS.).

TO EDWARD JOHN TRELAWNY Albaro. May 10th [1823]

My dear Trelawny,

You appear to have fulfilled my entire wish in all you have done at Rome. Do you remember the day you made that quotation from Shakespear in our dining room at Pisa, mine own Shelley was delighted with it & thus it has for me a pleasing association. Sometime hence I may visit the spot which of all others I desire most to see. At present I visit it in imagination, and living as I almost entirely do in the exercise of that faculty, I can in this instance, aided by your sketch, almost believe myself to be under that divine sky, near that weed grown tower, looking on the pyramid of Cestius —knowing that the spoils of the most noble of earth's creatures is near me & fondly trusting that his spirit is near too.

It is not on my own account, my excellent friend, that I go to England[1]— I believe that my child's interests will be best consulted by my return to that country—In every case I should have dreaded an Italian summer for him; and when the time comes for asserting his rights, it would not be well to pounce down suddenly among them, unknown and unprotected. Desiring solitude and my books only, together with the consciousness that I have one or two friends who although absent, still think of me with affection— England of course holds out no inviting prospect to me. But I am sure to {be} rewarded in doing or suffering for my little darling, so I am resigned to this last act, which seems to snap the sole link which bound the present to the past, and to tear aside the veil which I have endeavoured to draw over the desolateness of my situation. Your kindness I shall treasure up to comfort me in future ill—I shall repeat to myself—I have such a friend; and endeavour to deserve it.

Do you go to Greece?[2] Lord Byron continues in the same mind. The G— [*Guiccioli*] is an obstacle—and certainly her situation is rather a difficult one. But he does not seem disposed to make a mountain of her resistance; and he is far more able to take a decided than a petty step in contradiction to the wishes of those about him. If you do go it may hasten your return hither. I remain until Mrs Hunts confinement is over. Had it not been for that, the fear of a hot journey would have caused me to go in this month— but my desire to be useful to her and my anxiety concerning the event of so momentous a crisis has induced me to stay. You may think with what awe & terror I look forward to the decisive moment—but I hope for the best— She is as well, perhaps better than we could in any way expect.

I had no opportunity to send you a 2nd No of the Liberal—we only received it a short time ago—& then you were on the wing. The third number has come out,[3] and we had a copy by post—It has little in it we expected but it is an amusing number and LB. is better pleased with it than any other

You do not mention your Eliza—perhaps you have heard through the Lowes[4] of her well being—But I trust that I shall see you soon and then I shall hear all your news—I shall see you—but it will be for so short a time—I fear even that you will not go to Switzerland—but these are things I must not dwell upon—partings & seperations—when there is no circumstance to lessen any pang—I must brace my mind—not enervate it—for I know that I shall have much to endure—

I asked Hunt's opinion about your epitaph for Keats[5]—He said that the line from Adonais though beautiful in itself—might be applied to any poet in whatever circumstances or whatever age that died—and that to be in accord with the two stringed lyre you ought to select one that alluded to his youth & immature genius. A line to this effect you might doubtless find in the Adonais

Among the fragments of my lost Shelley I found the following poetical commentary on the words of Keats—not that I recommend it for the epitaph—but it may please you to see it.

"Here lieth one, whose name was writ on water,"
But ere the breath that could erase it, blew,
Death, in remorse for that fell slaughter,
Death, the immortalizing writer, flew
Athwart the stream, and Time's Monthless torrent grew
A scroll of Chrystal, emblazoning the name
Of Adonais—

I have not heard from Jane lately—she was well when s[he] last wrote, but annoyed by various circumstances and impatient of her lengthened stay in England. How earnestly do I hope that Edward's brother will soon arrive & shew himself worthy of his affinity to the noble and unequalled creature she has lost, by protecting one to whom protection is so necessary, & shielding her from some of the ills to which she is exposed.

Adieu, my dear Trelawny.—Continue to think kindly of me and trust in my unalterable friendship

Mary Shelley.

ADDRESS: Edward Trelawny Esq / Ferma in Posta / Firenze / Florence. POSTMARKS: (1) [GE]NOVA; (2) 13 / MAGGIO. PUBLISHED: Jones, #179. TEXT: MS., Bodleian Library (MS., Shelley, Adds., c. 6, ff. 9–10).

1. In his letter of 27 April Trelawny urged Mary Shelley to remain in Italy and share his income rather than "encounter poverty and bitter retrospections" in England (*S&M*, IV, 935).

2. With Byron (see 10 April [1823]).

3. The third number of the *Liberal* was published on 26 April.

4. Eliza Trelawny (1816–29), Trelawny's second daughter by his first wife, Caroline Julia Addison (*SC*, V, 45). Mary Low is identified by Trelawny as his

"Pisa friend." In a letter of 15 May 1823 Trelawny informed Claire Clairmont that he had not heard of Eliza for nearly two years (Trelawny, *Letters*, pp. 40, 59). Trelawny's letter of 10 January to Mary Shelley, in which he says he has not heard a word from Mrs. Johnson for nearly two years, is also a reference to Eliza, since the Johnsons were her "adopted" parents (Trelawny, *Letters*, p. 121).

5. "Here lies the spoils / of a / Young English Poet / 'Whose masters' hand is cold, whose silver lyre unstrung' / —And by whose desire is in[s]cribed / 'That his name was writ in water.'" (Previous printings of this text have printed *master-hand* for *masters' hand*. See Trelawny, *Letters*, p. 54, and Marshall, *Mary Shelley*, II, 74; the text here is taken from the Abinger MS.) Trelawny asked for Hunt's opinion of the epitaph, which was not put on Keats's tombstone (Gay, "The Protestant Burial-Ground in Rome," pp. 48–49).

TO MRS. THOMAS Albaro. Wednesday [?14 May 1823][1]

My dear Mrs Thomas,

I enclose the Bill of lading which I received today. I see it is dated the 30th April so god knows when my case will come. You were so kind as to say that Mr Thomas would look to it when it entered Porto Franco, I send this bill to you.

Is there any hope of getting the books I mentioned from the Library. I should like to add—to that list. Targioni Viaggij[2] in Toscana in (I think) 12 volumes—the miscellaneous works of Ariosto—consisting of nine—satyres & Comedies and the following works of Boccaccio

De montibus-silvis-fontibus-lacubus—

De Casibus Virorum & Foeminarum illustrium.

De Claris Mulieribus

All his letters latin & Italian

Amorosa Visione—Ninfale Fiesolano

But I am most anxious about the books I mentioned first.

When you have done with the Liberal[3] will you send it to Cap^n^ Roberts—

What changeable weather! The invalids suffer by it—I am not among them—but I love cloudless skies too much to be at my ease in a sirocco—I hope you are quite well—

By the bye do not fancy that Mrs Hunt was not extremely happy that Thornton should visit your Richard—She expects the latter saturday, and if you still continue so obliging as to wish it—Thornton will return his visit the sunday after. The reason of his not seeing you last sunday I will explain when I see you—

Compliments to Mr Thomas

Very truly Yours
MaryShelley

Will you give the piece of nankeen to the bearer

Has Mr Saunders got Boswell's life of Johnson in his Library

Have the Indians (cioè the Indian vessel) any scarfs—or small shawls of Chinese crape—worked or unworked—<u>black</u>—and would you tell me the price.

Do you know where Mrs Hunt could get a shawl 7 palms square—of silk, blue, or purple—or almost any colour except red—& which ought not to cost more than 40 livres—I saw some 6½ square but that is too small—

I know you will pardon the impertinence of the commissions but I can hardly pardon myself.

If inconvenient to answer directly—keep the bearer quante vuole.—

PUBLISHED: Jones, #180. TEXT: MS., Pierpont Morgan Library.

1. Peacock's letter of 15 April informed Mary Shelley that about a month earlier he had sent a case containing almost all the papers she had requested on the *Berbice*, Captain Wayth, and that he would send a bill of lading subsequently (Peacock, *Works*, VIII, 232–34). Since Mary Shelley says that the bill of lading is dated 30 April, the earliest Wednesday that this letter could have been written was 14 May. Mary Shelley had requested the contents of the case on 29 September 1822.

2. Giovanni Targioni-Tozzetti, *Relazioni d'alcuni viaggi fatte in diverse parti della Toscana* . . . , 2d ed., 12 vols. (Florence, 1768–69).

3. The third number of the *Liberal* (see 10 May [1823], n. 3).

*To JANE WILLIAMS — Albaro. May 31st [1823]

Dearest Jane

I write to you once again before I settle the date of my departure from dear Italy. This depends upon the period of Marianne's confinement, which we now expect daily, but which may not happen this week or even ten days. If all goes well with her I shall then make short delay. If our worst fears are realized—I suppose Bessy will immediately come out, and I must stay until then—But I have every confidence that nothing of evil will ensue—She is weak & suffers greatly—but care and anxiety & trouble augmenting the natural debility of her shattered frame renders this what we must expect,—She goes her full time & that is much.

Poor girl! Every Evil seems poured upon you—& this is the last blow—I hoped much from Jack, & now instead of hopes we have added to their loss the feeling of compassion for his children.[1] You do not mention whether you have returned to your Mother's house,[2] or what is become of Maria.[3] I hope that my being near you will afford you some pleasure—as to utility—the time for that is past with me, & all I can hope is not to be a burthen. As to the will I trust that it is good, for my little Percy's sake—I do not expect ever to profit by it—You will laugh at this as I am in good health; but many of my presentiments have come true—many years ago I completely foresaw my present situation—You know I am a dreamer—& my amusement in solitude has often been to picture my future life—not drawing the colours from probability or desire—but letting them take their own course—more than four years ago—in this kind of second sight, I saw myself desolate and alone—My William who then lived & on whom I so fondly doted, gone—beloved Shelley vanished.—Again, I had always a strong presentiment that Percy would be my last child—so much so that last summer without at all adverting to the accident that actually came to pass,[4] I never expected that it would all come to its natural conclusion—I wished it—I tried to figure it to myself but in vain—And so now I am perfectly persuaded that I shall never fill, what to my indolent disposition, in all that regards the care of money, appears an annoying situation—that of having the management of a fortune.—If Sir TS. [*Timothy Shelley*] would only permit me to remain here with a moderate income, he would fulfill the height of my wishes as far as regards myself. I give myself 10 or 12 years more of life—& in Claire's style I am almost tempted to prognosticate that 37 will be written on my tomb—long enough in all conscience—if I live longer—until 40—I shall amaze them, & be something more learned & wise than is suspected—but that will not be—such are my presentiments. I in vain attempt in imagination to form an idea beyond the period I have mentioned—all is obscurity & darkness—& so no doubt it will be—

No more of myself—yet I am not enclined to write about those around me—since it would require many written words to explain the state of things and I can relate all in so short a time when I see you. LB. is fixed on Greece—he gets rid of two burthens; the G— [*Guiccioli*] & the Liberal[5] —the first is natural, though I pity her—the second ought not be, & need not be, but so it is. The Hunts go to Florence. They cannot stay here—for the desertion & solitude would overcome H. They had better not return to England, if they can possibly help it—for they live cheaper here—can educate their children more cheaply—& the climate will be beneficial to both—Trelawny is not yet arrived—I believe that he will accompany LB. to Greece since he has been invited. I am glad of this—action will do him good—& it will break off his connection in this place, which is an odious one. I expect him every day—but from his uncertain & dilitory disposition it may be some time yet before he comes. Roberts is here, waiting for him, I see him now and then.

My father in his last letter[6] says that his house would only be a temporary residence for a few days—As I never am well in London, & should be very averse to confine my boy's free motions within the circuit of a town—I shall seek some country residence. I shall be solitary but I am accustomed to this & it pleases me—I am better & happier when alone—my monotonous course interrupted only by a few visits now and then from those I love. I hardly know a creature in England—& do not wish to enlarge this circle—I do not expect to have any <u>relations</u> with the <u>family</u>.—And in seeing you I shall see the only one I greatly love in the land of clouds—My first free act will be my return to Italy—if I ever leave it—for I sometimes wildly think that will never be—But to talk of matter of fact—I do not know what you mean by talking of my return to Pisa—I do not dream of such a journey—thank you for your attentions about that—but I have hopes that I shall be enabled to travel post—

I have had no news from Claire or her brother, but I [ ] that she is on her road to Russia where I hope she wi[ ] & then persuade her Count to bring her to Italy.

We have a divine Spring—there are no walks here—or shady lanes—but one gets up a hill, through alleys of stone walls—& then from the height one sees a complete garden—the excess of cultivation here is wonderful—every inch of ground is planted—Pergolas of grapes have french beans growing beneath their shade—& the fields are all divided into small strips sown with corn or vegetables & shaded by olive fig or pear trees—often in the midst of a podere[7] a fierce torrent rushing down from the hills is chained in between two high stone walls—and every now and then, the struggling power bears away a part of its dungeon and shews to open day its ungovernable & savage nature amidst all the arts & cares of cultivation—the summits of the hills are bare—& it seems as if every vestige of earth would be swept into the sea beneath—if these eternal stone walls did not keep it from descending—the sea too—is so wonderfully beautiful. He must be there, dearest Jane—he loved his mists & airs—it promontories—its clearness—& its beauty—and methinks I feel his spirit wandering will { } the spirit of loveliness about the caves & solitudes of these shores—these thoughts possess me so much, that in a very short time, the sight of the Mediterranean would become a necessary part of my existence—I sit on a rock that overhangs it, until intensity of thought becomes a painful heavy chain—Yet all this thought—this whirl of ideas which is never still is the part of my being I prize & cherish most—I am annoyed by all that recalls me to real life—& never feel so—not happy—but less wretched as when my thoughts are most entirely beyond the hateful present—& this dress of clay which I long to throw aside—Adieu—my best girl—love me ever & confide in the entire affection of—MaryShelley

You will not answer this letter—& I shall write again as soon as dates &c are fixed—You shall have your pelisse & what else you want. Let me not forget to tell you, that in a letter I shall expect from you—at Paris—to mention how you managed at the English Custom house with dear Ned's drawings—

[*P. 1, top*] Just four years ago my boy was dying at Rome—& my misfortunes began—a year ago—I thought to die myself—w[d] that I had & "that the flowers of this departed spring were fading on my grave!"[8]—

ADDRESS: Mrs Williams / Mrs Cleveland / 24 Alsop's Buildings / New Road / Inghilterra / London / Londres. POSTMARKS: (1) GENOVA; (2) FPO / JU. 12 / [1]823; (3) 12 NOON 12 / JU. 12 / 1823; (4) 12 NOON 12 / JU. 21 / 1823; (5) NOON [ ]. J[U] / 182[3]; (6) [crown] To be / delivered / Free. UNPUBLISHED. TEXT: MS., Abinger MS., Bodleian Library.

1. A reference to the death of John Williams, Edward Williams's brother, who left four children (see 7 March [1823], n. 11).

2. Jane Williams had moved to a lodging because of repairs being made on her mother's house (Jane Williams to Mary Shelley, 27 March 1823, Abinger MS.).

3. Jane Williams's letter of 12 February had revealed the impending separation of Jane Williams's sister Maria Baird from her husband (Abinger MS.).

4. The miscarriage Mary Shelley suffered on 16 June 1822.

5. For a discussion of Byron's withdrawal from the *Liberal*, see Marshall, *The Liberal*, pp. 164–69.

6. Godwin had written on 6 May 1823 (*S&M*, IV, 940–41).

7. "Farm"; see 28 August 1819.

8. *The Cenci* I. 3. 138–39.

TO EDWARD JOHN TRELAWNY — Genoa June 9, 1823

Lord Byron says, that as he has not heard from Greece, his going there is uncertain; but if he does go, he is extremely desirous that you should join him, and if you will continue to let him know where you may be found, he will inform you as soon as he comes to any decision.

PUBLISHED: Jones, #182. TEXT: Trelawny, *Recollections*, pp. 162–63.

*TO LORD BYRON — Albaro Saturday [14 June 1823][1]

My dear Lord Byron

I have had a letter from Trelawny today which I must answer by return of post—He expresses the greatest willingness to accompany your Lordship to Greece, and anxiety lest you should change your resolution, which resolution he says has excited great praise and admiration every where—Is your vessel hired—& is your going more certain than when I last saw you?—Trelawny says that he is willing to stake his all in the Grecian cause—

Truly Y^s obliged
Mary Shelley

ADDRESS: [*not written by Mary Shelley*] Rt. Hon. / Lord Byron. UNPUBLISHED: Jones, #181, in summary. TEXT: MS., John Murray.

1. Trelawny's letter, dated 10 June, is postmarked 14 June (Abinger MS.). Trelawny wrote that should Byron remain "in Italy—writing—I shall push my way on to Madrid—and fight as a volunteer with the Spaniards." Two other items in this letter give some details about people referred to in Mary Shelley's letters. Trelawny tells Mary Shelley that he receives letters from Gabrielle Wright but cannot write to her "as the channel by which I sent my letters is stopped—or rather Mrs T—'s [*Thomas's*] patience or friendship run dry." He also writes that Rose was delighted with his "letter by proxy" (see [c. 5 April 1823]).

*TO JANE WILLIAMS — Albaro [c. 2] July [1823]

My very dear Jane

I have delayed writing both to you and my father a long time, hoping that I might mention the date of my departure in my letters. But I wait in vain, and things have taken so strange a turn, and the delay is so much greater than I expected that I find at last I must write while still in a state of uncertainty. I write to you in preference to my father, because you to a great degree understand the person I have to deal with, & in communicating what I say concerning him, you can viva voce add such comments, as will render my relation more intelligible

The day after Mariannes confinement, (the 9th of June)[1] seeing all went so prosperously, I told LB. that I was ready to go, & he promised to provide means. When I talked of going post, it was because he said that I should go so, at the same declaring that he would regulate all himself. I waited in vain for these arrangements—But not to make a long story, since I hope soon to be able to relate the details, he chose to transact our negotiation through Hunt; and gave such an air of unwillingness & sense of the obligation he conferred, as at last provoked H. to say that there was no obligation, since he owed me a £1000[2]—"Glad of a quarrel straight I clap the door!—"[3] still keeping up an appearance of amity with H. he has written notes & letters—so full of contempt against me & my lost Shelley that I could stand it no longer, and have refused to receive his still proffered aid for my journey[4]—This of course delays me I can muster about £30[5] of my own; I do not know whether this is barely sufficient, but as the delicate constitution of my child may oblige me to rest several times on the journey, I cannot persuade myself to commence my journey with what is barely necessary, I have written therefore to Trelawny for the sum requisite, and must wait till I hear from him.

I see you, my poor girl, sigh over these my mischances—but never mind; I do not feel them. My life is a shifting scene, & my business is to play the part alotted for each day well—& not liking to think of tomorrow, I never think of it at all—except in an intellectual way—and as to money difficulties—why having nothing, I can lose nothing. Thus as far as regards what are commonly called worldly concerns, I am perfectly tranquil, & as free or freer from care as if my signature should be able to draw £1,000 from some banker;—⟨I want for⟩ The Extravagance & anger of LB's letters also relieves me from all pain that his deriliction might occasion me. And that his conscience twinges him is too visible from his impatient kicks & unmannerly curvets—You w^d laugh at his last letter to H— where he says concerning his connection with Shelley that "he let himself down to the level of the democrats."

In the mean time Hunt is all kindness, consideration and friendship—all feeling of alienation towards me has disappeared even to its last dreg—He perfectly approves of what I have done. So I am still in Italy—And I doubt not that it is its sun, & vivifying geniality that relieves me from those biting cares which would be mine in England, I fear, if I were destitute there. But I feel above the mark of fortune and my heart, too much wounded to feel these pricks, on all occasions that does not regard its affections "s'arma di se, e d'intero diamante"[6]—thus am I changed—too late alas! for what ought to have been, but not too late, I trust, to enable me, more than before, to be some stay & consolation {to} you, my own dear Jane.

I very much wished not {to} have been in a crow[d] these melancholy days—now that the year is fulfill[ed] every hour & feeling reminds me of what is ever & for ever before me. How quickly this year has past— methinks it was but yesterday we parted—but why should I renew in you thoughts that must eat into your soul, & haunt you through every recess of your mind. I live in that world & in those scenes, & thus the present & its capricious changes appear dreams not worthy my attention.—One only thing afflicts me—to leave Italy—& if I could in any way dispose of my writings without being in England, I w[d] remain here, but that cannot be.

I have not heard from Claire a long time—& have not written to her from the same causes that has prevented my writing to you. Will you let my father know what I have said of my affairs, & explain to him at the same time the primum mobile of LB actions—Meaness—the Greek Expedition will not blind you—thus he walks off triumphantly from these shores with his untouched thousands, and he has already p{r}epared many designs for their safe analyssis from their Greek journey—the Reatreat of his 9,000 will be worthy of the pen of another Zenophon.[7] I have already sent packages by sea.—2 cases with books & one box of clothes—they go by the Jane—Captain Whitney, & are directed to my father's house.

God bless you, my best girl. I shall set out the moment I hear from Trelawny, so somewhat poorer in cash—but rich to overflow in all the many feelings—sorrow—love & futurity that make my world, I shall embrace you & give you all the comfort [*p. 1, top*] that you can receive from

Your affectionate friend
Mary Shelley

I should come by sea if Hunt w[d] let me

ADDRESS: Mrs Williams / Mrs Cleveland / 24 Alsop's Buildings / New Road / London / Londres / Inghilterra. POSTMARKS: (1) GENOVA; (2) FPO/ JY. 15 / 1823; (3) 12 NOON 12 / JY. 15 / 1823. UNPUBLISHED: Jones, #183, in part. TEXT: MS., Abinger MS., Bodleian Library.

1. With the Hunts' seventh child, Vincent Leigh Hunt.

2. Edward Williams recorded in his Journal for 25 December 1821: "It was on this day that Lord B. and S. proposed to give a thousand pounds to the other who first came to their estate" (p. 119). Hunt's claim of the debt owing was the result of the death of Lady Noel on 22 January 1822 (see 10 April [1823], n. 2).

3. Pope, *Episle to Dr. Arbuthnot*, line 67.

4. Marchand (*Byron*, III, 1085–86) and Moore (*The Late Lord Byron*, pp. 404–22) recount details of the quarrel. Moore places the responsibility for the quarrel with Hunt and contends that Hunt secretly appropriated for his own use a provision of £30 made by Byron for Mary Shelley.

5. Trelawny and Mrs. Mason gave Mary Shelley funds (Trelawny, *Letters*, pp. 67–68; McAleer, *The Sensitive Plant*, p. 182). On 1 July Hunt informed Byron that "under certain circumstances" Mary Shelley would ask Trelawny for the money and that she "is not aware of my saying a word to you on this point" (Moore, *The Late Lord Byron*, p. 441).

6. Unidentified.

7. Xenophon (c. 430–after 355 B.C.), Greek historian, whose *Anabasis* records the story of the ten thousand Greek troops who, deserted by their commanders in Persia, made their way safely back to Greece after a five-month march.

To Teresa Guiccioli[1] [Albaro ?2–10 July 1823] (*a*)

Chere Contessina votre billet m'à fait vraiment plaisir[2] . . . le sentiment de l'inimitié est si penible que c'est un g^d soulagement pour moi de trouver que le poison m'est pas arrive jusque a vous. Je vous remercie sans fin pour vos offres—mais si je dois comprendre que vous voulez etre mediatrice entre Ld Byron et moi Je crains qu'il ne vous reussira pas. Je n'eprouvais aucune repugnance a l'idee de recevoir des obbligations et des cortesies d'un ami—et je me figurais ou pour mieux dire je me flattais que LB serait content de me retenir non seulement avec les liens de l'amitie mais aussi de la reconnaissance. Mais maintenant tout est fini—et celui qui me m'estime pas ne peut pas etre mon Bienfaiteur.

Ld Byron ayant dit qui lui serait desagreable de me voir vous voyez que je ne puis avoir le plaisir d'aller vous chercher chez vous mais je serais charmee de vous voir chez moi.

[*Translation*]

Dear Contessina, Your note gave me much pleasure[2] . . . the feeling of hostility is so painful that it is a great consolation to me to find that the poison has not reached you. I thank you truly for your offers—but if I am to understand that you want to mediate between Lord Byron and myself, I fear that you will not succeed. I felt no repugnance to the idea of accepting obligations and kindnesses from a friend—and I imagined, or to put it better, I flattered myself that LB would be glad to bind me with ties not only of friendship but also of gratitude. But now all is over—and he who has no esteem for me cannot be my Benefactor.

Ld Byron having said that it would be disagreeable for him to see me, you realize that I cannot have the pleasure of calling on you, but I would be charmed to see you here.

PUBLISHED: Origo, *The Last Attachment*, pp. 330–31, in English. TEXT: MS., unpublished, of Teresa Guiccioli's "La vie de Lord Byron en Italie." TRANSCRIPTION: Mihai H. Handrea.

1. This and the other two letters dated [?2–10 July 1823] are responses to Teresa Guiccioli's attempt to mediate the differences between Mary Shelley and Byron over the money for Mary Shelley's return to England. Although Mary Shelley certainly wrote these letters in Italian (as she did all her correspondence with Teresa Guiccioli), forty years later, Teresa Guiccioli transcribed them in French in "La vie de Lord Byron," her unpublished biography of Byron. The originals of the letters are unlocated.

2. Teresa Guiccioli here interjected, "lui repondait Mme Shelley" ("Mme Shelley responded to her"). In "La vie de Lord Byron," Teresa Guiccioli refers to herself in the third person.

*To Teresa Guiccioli[1] [Albaro ?2–10 July 1823] (*b*)

Chere A pour vous dire la verite ma position genante ne me pese pas autant sur le coeur que les expressions de LB sur moi et plus encore sur Shelley.

Tout sentiment ennemi me fait grande peine. Vous pouvez donc etre certaine du plaisir que vous me ferez en offrant ma proposition d'amnistie; et si lui l'accepte tout sentiment penible disparaitra de mon ame. D'un Ami j'accepterais tout—et si lui me temoignera la moindre signe d'amitie—et si de nouveau il sera content de me faire du bien je lui aurais encore cette nouvelle obbligation—et je lui serais reconnaissante. Agreez encore que je vous repete tout ce que j'eprouve pour votre Cortesie et conte . . .

[*Translation*]

Dear Friend, to tell you the truth my difficult position weighs less heavily upon my heart than LB's expressions about me and, even more, about Shelley. All ill feeling pains me greatly. You may then be assured of the pleasure that you will give me in presenting to him my proposal of conciliation; and if he accepts it, all ill feelings will disappear from my soul. From a friend I would accept anything—and if he shows me the least sign of friendship—and if he again is happy to help me, I would feel a renewed obligation to him—and would be grateful. Let me express again my gratitude for your Kindness . . .

UNPUBLISHED: Origo, *The Last Attachment*, p. 331, in English (incomplete). TEXT: MS., unpublished, of Teresa Guiccioli's "La vie de Lord Byron en Italie. TRANSCRIPTION: Mihai H. Handrea.

1. See [?2–10 July 1823] (*a*).

To TERESA GUICCIOLI[1] [Albaro ?2–10 July 1823] (*c*)

Cara Contessina—je sens vraiment toute la valeur de vos sentiments amicales dans les circonstances actuelles et je vous en suis reconnaissante . . . Je me semble presque que vous etes plus affligee de cette mauvaises affaires que moi meme. J'ai souffert tant et tant que j'ai perdu la faculte de m'inquieter pour des choses qui regardent uniquement l'argent.

Je suis trop pauvre pour perdre encore les Amis—et si l'Amitie de LB me manque tout le reste ne vaut pas beaucoup—et ne pourrais pas etre accepte per moi. J'offre de tout mon Coeur l'Amnistie entre nous et si Ld Byron veut bien oublier tout ce qui il a eu de penible a souffrie de moi et pour moi, s'il reconnait ce que Shelley merite ce sera avec un vrai plaisir que je lui souhaiterais de vive voix ce que je fair maintenant par ecrit un heureux voyage et tout le success que je me flatte que ses projets auront en Grece . . . Vos offres si pleines de cordialite m'ont fait g^d^ plaisir et je suis avec la plus g^de^ sincerite votre Amie Af.

Mary Shelley

[*Translation*]

I value deeply your friendly feelings in the present circumstances and I am grateful to you . . . It seems to me that you are almost more pained by this bad business than I am myself. I have suffered so much that I have lost the capacity of worrying about matters that relate solely to money.

I am too poor to lose my friends as well—and if I lost the friendship of LB the rest would not be worth much—and I could not accept it. I propose with all my heart a conciliation between us and if Ld Byron is willing to forget anything painful he may have endured from me and on account of me, if he recognizes what Shelley deserves, it will be with real pleasure that I will wish him in person what I express now in writing, a good voyage and all the success I feel certain his plans will have in Greece . . . Your cordial offers gave me great pleasure, and I am very sincerely your affectionate friend.

PUBLISHED: Origo, *The Last Attachment*, pp. 331–32, in English. TEXT: MS., unpublished, of Teresa Guiccioli's "La vie de Lord Byron en Italie." TRANSCRIPTION: Mihai H. Handrea.

1. See [?2–10 July 1823] (*a*).

TO LORD BYRON Albaro July 13 [1823][1]

Dear Lord Byron

I did not wish to spare myself the pain of taking leave. We understood from Conte Pietro to-day that you did not embark till tomorrow evening or mid-day at the earliest.[2] I intended therefore to settle this pecuniary matter[3] first by letter, there being better subjects for discourse in this world; & then to come down & bid you farewel, which I will do accordingly if you please, tomorrow morning.

In the mean time as the message which Mad. Guiccioli has been kind enough to transmit to me, still leaves me an uneasy sense of vagueness in my mind, will you do me the favour to state in whose hands you have left this matter & what is it's precise nature

Yours sincerely

PUBLISHED: Jones, #184. TEXT: MS., Bodleian Library (MS., Shelley, Adds., d. 5, f. 86).

1. This text is taken from an unsigned copy of the letter by Mary Shelley. On 12 July Teresa Guiccioli enclosed messages from Byron to Mary Shelley and Hunt in her letter to Mary Shelley (Abinger MS.; Origo, *The Last Attachment*, pp. 346–47).

2. Byron and Pietro Gamba left on 13 July at 5:00 P.M.; however, the weather prevented them from sailing until 17 July (see 23 July [1823]). Just as Byron left, Mary Shelley arrived at Casa Saluzzo, at Byron's request, to comfort Teresa Guiccioli (Marchand, *Byron*, III, 1087).

3. In her letter of 12 July Teresa Guiccioli mentioned that Hunt knew that Byron had left orders for his financial affairs, probably with "Signor Barry." Byron placed his financial matters at Genoa in the hands of Charles F. Barry, a partner in the banking firm of Messrs. Webb & Co., (Moore, *The Late Lord Byron*, p. 214). Exactly what arrangements Byron made remains unclear; however, it has been suggested that Hunt took for himself funds that Byron provided for Mary Shelley (Moore, *The Late Lord Byron*, p. 420).

To Jane Williams Albaro July 23rd [1823]

Dearest Jane

I have at length fixed with the Vetturino;[1] I depart on the 25th My best girl, I leave Italy—I return to the dreariest reality after having dreamt away a year in this blessed and beloved country.

Lord Byron, Trelawny Pierino Gamba &c sailed for Greece on the 17th Ult. I did not see the former. His unconquerable avarice prevented his supplying me with money, & a remnant of shame caused him to avoid me. But I have a world of things to tell you on that score when I see you. If he were mean T—y [*Trelawny*] more than balanced the moral account. His whole conduct during his last short stay here has impressed us all with an affectionate regard and a perfect faith in the unalterable goodness of his heart. They sailed together: LB with £10,000 Ty with £50—and LB cowering before his eye for reasons you shall hear soon. The Guiccioli is gone to Bologna—e poi cosa fara? Chi lo sa? Cosa vuol che la dico?[2] He talks seriously of returning to her, and may if he finds none of equal rank to be got as cheaply—She cost him nothing & was thus invaluable.

I travel without a servant. I rest first at Lyons. But do you write to me at Paris. Hotel Nelson—it will be a friend to await me—Alas! I have need of consolation—Hunt's kindness is now as active & warm as it was dormant before; but just as I find a companion in him I leave him. I lea[ve] him in all his difficulties, with his head throbbing with overwrought thought, & his frame sometimes sinking under his anxieties. Poor Marianne has found good medecine, facendo un bimbo,[3] & then nursing it, but she with her female providence is more beset by care than Hunt. How much I wished & wish to settle near them at Florence—but I must submit with courage and patience may at last come and give opiate to my irritable feelings.

Both Hunt and Trelawny say that Percy is much improved since Maria[4] left me. He is affectionately attached to Silvan[5] & very fond of il Bimbo nuovo, kisses him by the hour & tells me come il Signor Enrico ha comprato un Baby nuovo a Genova forse ti dara il Baby Vecchio,[6] as he gives away an old toy on the appearance of a new one.

I will not write longer. In conversation, nay almost in thought, I can at this most painful moment, force my excited feelings to laugh at themselve and my spirits raised by emotion to seem as if they were light; but the natural current and real hue overflows me & penetrates me when I write—and it wd be painful to you & overthrow all my hopes of retaining my fortitude if I were to write one word that truly translated the agitation I suffer into language.

I will write again from Lyons where I suppose that I shall be on the 3rd of August—Dear Jane—can I render you happier than you are? The idea of that might console me. At least you will see one who truly loves you & who is for ever Your affectionately attached

MaryShelley

If there is any talk of my accommodations, pray let M^{rs} G [*Godwin*] understand that I cannot sleep on any but a hard bed—I care not how hard so that it be matresses

ADDRESS: Mrs Williams / Mrs Cleveland / 24 Alsop's Buildings / New Road / Inghilterra London / Londres. POSTMARKS: (1) GENOVA; (2) FPO / AU. 7 / 1823; (3) 12 NOON 12 / AU. 7 / 1823. PUBLISHED: Jones, #185. TEXT: MS., Pforzheimer Library.

1. See [c. 3] December 1818, n. 2.

2. "And then what will she do? Who knows? What can I say?"

3. "Having a baby."

4. A servant. Mrs. Mason wrote on 24 June of Maria's arrival at Pisa (Abinger MS.).

5. The Hunts' sixth child, [James] Henry Sylvan, was the same age as Percy Florence.

6. "Since Mr. Henry has brought a new Baby at Genoa, maybe he will give you the Old Baby."

TO LEIGH AND MARIANNE HUNT

Asti [Turin and Susa]
July 26th [–27, 1823][1]

Dearest Friends—Very Patient & Patient Very[2]

How do you do—I am very well—I think so—I think Percy is very well my boy is a good boy—I think so—you will receive this letter from your affectionate Mary Wollstonecraft Shelley I hope—I love you—I think I do—I love Henry Sylvan, & Mary Florimel Leigh Hunt Hunt I hope—& so kiss her, one of you, if she be good—& Thornton also to whom I shall write soon—& Baby Nuovo—and the rest in a lump, scape grace Jhonny—giggling Swinny & Percy the Martyr.

My dear Hunt—I passed through very pretty scenery after leaving you at Borgo the ravine closed in, & the river wound gently under hanging woods—As evening came on however the vale opened—we descended the staircase of hills & came to this wide landing place call{ed} Piedmont—The olives have gone—(not a leaf for Bessy)—the vines are stunts th[ ] wide, unhedged, undiversified—Such is the approach to Alessand{r}ia where I [ ] day—between that town & this we had some undulations, some trees, poplars be[ech] ash—a wide river—greenish grass—cows & altogether a scene not unresembling what I remember of English scenery. Asti being the native town of Alfieri my attention was awakened to observe, the scenes of his childhood & I was pleased with these indications of the picturesque—but before arriving here the hills again disappeared—the town is low built & insignificant—& after trying all I could to believe that an old wall was romantic and at length concluding that it was not, I find the prettiest thing about Asti is its name. Not that it is ugly—but it is plain & so different from my own Tuscany that—[ ] I think nonsense not to be so sorrowful, than an Albaro scirocco, with its blotted sky, wailing sea & howling wind, w^{d} be nothing to it—

Percy is very good & does not in the least annoy me— In the state of mind I am now in the motion & change is delightful to me —my thoughts run with the coach & wind & double & jerk & are up & down & forward & most often backward till the labyrinth of Crete is a joke in comparison to my intricate wanderings—They now lead me to you—Hunt you rose early—wrote—walked—dined whistled sang & punned most outrageously the worst puns in the world—My best Polly, you full of you chicks & your new darling—yet sometimes called "Henry"—to see a beautiful affect of light on the mountains—did you indeed begin to cut a profile—{"}oh Polly"—Well, dear girl I have a great affection for you, believe that, & dont talk or think sorrowfully unless you have the toothach—& then dont think but talk infinite nonsense mixed with infinite sense— & Hunt will listen as I used—Thorny—you have not been cross yet—oh my dear Thorny (dont be angry, Polly, with this nonsense) do not let your impatient nature ever overcome you—or you may suffer as I have done—which God forbid!—be true to yourself—& talk much to your father who will teach you as he has taught me—it is the idea of his lessons of wisdom that makes me feel the affection I do for him—I profit by them—so do you—may you never feel the remorse of having neglected them when his voice & look are gone, & he can no longer talk to you—that remorse is a terrible feeling—& it requires a faith & philosophy immense not to be destroyed by the stinging monster.

⟨Joh Jhonny⟩ Johnny—I ⟨write⟩ thought of two verses on you in the coach today—I send them that your papa may revenge himself for my disdainful laughing ⟨sometimes⟩ at his puns by laughing also disdainfully at this lame nonsense

Well, Johnny how fares it with ve{r}ses & puns—
  Do your couplets or bon mots e'er win you a dinner?
Is Spenser still dearer than tartlets or buns?—
  Still hunting for thoughts, & in that race a winner?—

Now think my dear Johnny, can jag rhyme with bad?
  Or mischeif & merriment tag two good lines?
But, as you now see, bad answers to sad
  And   are very fair rhymes—

(Do you, Hunt, put in two words that rhyme—one meaning goodness the other mirth—I cant think of one for the life of me—laugh as much as you please{)}

Good night—dear children—there is a howling wind—but I hope you are all asleep for it is on the stroke of eleven—again good night—I shall soon be asleep

Sunday—7 o'clock PM.

Safe arrived at Turin—The country between this & Asti is very pretty—meadows of green with cattle feeding, hills covered with low vines or woods of poplar beech & ash streams & all that would remind you of England & for which reason you w^{d} like it—It is pretty & must have many delightful walks. The people about Turin are very ugly & such a costume this is the head costume of the contadine being made of stiff starched muslin—they all wear these caps—the citoyennes wear them also though of another fashion—less strange but not prettier—"Oh! very well Sir"—Hunt, I wont be answered so—"oh very well Sir!" Hunt, I pour out a glass of water—"Indeed Ma'am"—[ ] oh you feel the dash in your face & the water trickling from your hair down your innocent nose—but oh! the new Jacket! What will Marianne say to naughty Grandmamma—Marianne is not in the way but moral Mary observes—"If ever I heard of rich—well, this is one way I must say!"—

"Well I say nothing—but one thing I will say"[3]—blessed the man who first invented baths—after the dusty roads I get into one and refresh myself most delightfully—At Asti there were mineral baths—here they were common warm water.—Plenty of linen, & the damage, Marianne, at Asti 32 soldi—here 33—including a handsome present to the attendants.

Tomorrow, dear absent ones, is the anniversary when 9 years ago I quitted England with Shelley—& now I return—never mind—sufferance is the badge of all our tribe—I will make an order of the badge & so it may feel lighter.

Do not wait for my letter from Lyons to write to me at Paris—but write Saturday August 2nd or if it better please you Monday 4th (Shelleys birthday) at latest—direct to me at Hotel Nelson, Fauxbourg St. Germain

Farewell, My Children—think kindly & often of the

Affectionate Grandmo[ther]
MaryWShelley

What did Marianne say to my having left my watch?—dont send it by any but a safe opportunity—& in the mean time I pray you get it mended, or it will be quite spoilt.—

I hear voices, as you used to hear them at Pisa—they are in harmony & the bass is pleasing—My heart is a park well walled in with many doors Many alas! have been locked too long—but Music is the Master key to all of them—

I sh^{d} have tried to have got you some music here but it is sunday—& I go at day break tomorrow—at Lyons I will buy some—if there is any, & send it you by the Vetturino when he returns—Adieu

I was too late for the post yesterday evening at Turin, & too early this morning, so, as I determined to put this letter in the post myself I bring it with me to Susa, & now open it to tell you how delighted I am with my mornings ride—The scenery is so divine—the high dark Alps first, on this southern side tipt with snow, close in a plain—The meadows are full of clover & flowers and the woods of Ash elm & beech descend & spread and lose themselves in the fields—stately trees in clumps or singly arise on each side, and wherever you look you see some spot where you dream of building a house & living for ever. The exquisite beauty of Nature and the cloudless sky of this summer day soothes me, and makes this 28th so full of recollections as it is, almost pleasurable. Wherever the spirit of beauty dwells he must be—the rustling of the trees is full of him—the waving of the tall grass—the moving shadows of the vast hills—the blue air that penetrates their ravines & rests upon their heights—I feel him near me when I see that which he best loved—Alas! Nine years ago he took to a home in his heart this weak being, whom he has now left for more congenial spirits & happier regions—She lives only in the hope that she may become one day as one of them.

Absolutely, my dear Hunt, I will pass some 3 summer months in this divine spot—you shall all be with me—there are no gentlemen's seats or palazzi—so we will take a cottage which we will paint & refit—just as this country inn is, in which I now write clean & plain—We will have no servants—only we will give out all the needle work—Marianne shall make puddings & pies to make up for the vegetables & meat which I shall boil & spoil. Thorny shall sweep the rooms, Mary make the beds—Johnny clean the kettles & pans & then we will pop him into one of the many streams hereabouts & so clean him Swinny, being so quick, shall be our Mercury—Percy our gardener—Sylvan & Percy Florence our weeders & Vincent our plaything—& then to raise us above the vulgar we will do all our work keeping time to Hunt's symphonies we will ex[ ] our sweepings & dustings to the March in Alceste—We will [ ] meals to the tune of the laughing trio and when we [ ]ad we will lie on our turf sophas while all who [ ] voices shal[l] chorus in "Notte giorno faticar"[4]—You see [my pap]er is quite out so I must say for the last time Adieu, God bless you.—MaryWS—

ADDRESS: Leigh Hunt Esq / Casa Negrotto / Albaro / Genova. POSTMARKS: (1) GENOVA; (2) PI O4 P / SUZE; (3) 1 AGO. PUBLISHED: Jones, #186. TEXT: MS., Bodleian Library (MS., Shelley, Adds., c. 6, ff. 11–12).

1. On 25 July 1823 Mary Shelley and Percy Florence left Albaro for England.
2. Mary Shelley's nicknames for Marianne and Leigh Hunt. This letter also contains her own nickname, "Grandmamma," a reference to her care and concern for the birth of Vincent and the welfare of Marianne Hunt.
3. *Don Juan* I. 52.
4. From Mozart's *Don Giovanni.*

TO JANE WILLIAMS St. Jean de la Maurienne—July 30th [1823]

My best Jane

I wrote to you from Genoa the day before I quitted it, but I afterwards lost the letter; I asked the Hunts {to} look for it & send it if found, but ten to one you will never receive it.[1] It contained nothing however but what I can tell you in five minutes when I see you. It told you of the departure of LB & Trelawny for Greece, the former escaping with all his crowns & the other disbursing until he had hardly £60 left. It went to my heart to borrow the sum from him necessary to make up my journey but he behaved with so much quiet generosity that one was almost glad to put him to that proof and witness the excellence of his heart. In this & in another trial he acquitted so well that he gained all our hearts—while the other—but more when we meet—

I left Genoa Friday 25th Hunt & Thornton accompanied me the first 20 miles—this was much you will say for Hunt—But thank heaven we are now the best friends in the world—he set his heart on my quitting Italy with as comfortable feelings as possible; & he did so much, that notwithstanding all the wrenching & riving such an event, joined to parting with so dear a friend, inflicted upon me, yet I have borne up with better spirits than I could in any way have hoped—It is a delightful thing, dear Jane to be able to expend one's affection upon an old & tried friend like Hunt, & one so passionately attached to my S— as he was & is: it is pleasant also to feel oneself loved by one who loves him—You know somewhat of what I suffered during the winter during his alienation from me; he was displeased with me for many just reasons, but he found me willing to expiate as far as I cd the evil I had done, so his heart was again warmed; & if my dear friend, when I return you find me more amiable & more willing to suffer with patience than I was, it is to him that I owe this benefit—& you may judge if I ought not to be grateful to him. I am even so to LB—who was the cause that I staid at Genoa and thus secured one whom I am sure can never change—

The illness of one of the horses detains me here an afternoon, so I write, & shall put the letter in the post at Chamberi. I have come without a servant or companion—but Percy is perfectly good & no trouble to me at all—We are both well—a little tired or so—Will you tell my father that you have heard from me & that I am so far on my journey—I expect to be at Lyons in 3 days & will write to him from that place. If there be any talk of my accommodations, pray put in a word for a <u>hard</u> bed—for else I am sure I cannot sleep

So I have left Italy—and alone with my child I am travelling towards England—What a dream I have had ⟨& as⟩ is it over?—Oh no for I do nothing but dream—realities seem to have lost all power over me—I mean as it were, tangible realities—for where the affections are concer{n}ed calamity has only awakened greater sensitiveness.

I fear things do not go on well with you, my dearest girl—you are not in your Mother's house and you cannot have settled your affairs in India—mine too.—Why I arrive poor to nothingness & my hopes are small except from my own exertions; & living in England is so dear—my thoughts will all tend towards Italy, but even if STS [*Sir Timothy Shelley*] shd do any thing he will not I am sure permit me to go abroad—At any rate, dear Jane, we shall be together awhile—we will talk of our lost ones, & think of realizing my dream—Who knows?—Adieu—I shall soon see you & you will find how truly I am your affectionate—

MaryShelley

ADDRESS: Mrs Williams / Mrs Cleveland / Alsop's Buildings / New Road / London / Londres. POSTMARKS: (1) P.R.P.P.; (2) P. 37. P / LE PO[ ]T [ ]; (3) FPO / AU. 9 / 1823; (4) 12 NOON 12 / AU. 9 / 1823. PUBLISHED: Jones, #187. TEXT: MS., Abinger MS., Bodleian Library.

1. Mary Shelley's letter of 23 July was found and mailed, and it arrived in England on 7 August 1823.

TO LEIGH AND MARIANNE HUNT

St. Jean de la Maurienne—Savoy
Pont Bon Voisin— July 30th
August 1st [1823]

I am detained here, my dear Children, a whole afternoon by the illness of one of the horses—the quiet solitude of the inn is painful to me so I try to forget myself in writing to you—Pardon me therefore, Very Patient, (if you read my letter through) and you, Patient Very (if you like it when read) that I write often. Consider I am at a dismal inn all alone—my heart is often on the point of sinking within me, but I strive with the foul fiend & take refuge in the idea of those I love; with my pen in my hand I can drive off the evil hour—& then sleep comes, then waking and once in the carriage I can defy the Devil, for motion keeps up my spirits & sets my thoughts gadding at full gallop through all the regions of the has been, is, & to be.

I put my letter to you in the post at Susa[1] & hope you will get it safe, but I think it runs some hazard of miscarrying—I put in one for Mrs Mason at the same office & the post master asked me, where Pisa was? dove è quella Pisa? were his words—Credat Christianus (as Hunt says)—ma è veeero. I was not so much delighted with the passage of Mont Cenis as I expected, but this was because I had formed a wrong idea of it—Covered as it is for 8 months of the year with a heavy covering of snow, of course there can be no trees on its heights—but it is curious to see its crags, recesses & plains covered with luxuriant grass, & flowers; the excessive green & watriness of these rocks, which seem themselves thawed into life, is a pleasant contrast to the snow many feet deep which was on them when we crossed them in the month of March.[2] I am now however in the midst of the most divine scenery you can imagine—or rather I was this morning, & know I shall be tomorrow, just this spot yields in beauty to several others—The immense mountains are covered with pine forests & a deep and rock-vexed river flows through the depth of the ravine through which we wind—the rocks themselves, except where quite perpendicular are covered with underwood & weeping willows & birch hang over the waterfalls which rush down through every fold of the mountain into the noisy & gurgling river. Above the pine covered sides of the mountains high & bare peaks arise, flecked with snow—while in the midst of the forests, meadows and glades of exquisite verdure are contrasted with the dark colour of the trees. I am pleased also with the inhabitants. The roundness & softness of their features is refrshing after the cut and dry aspect of the Italians. The latter, even the best looking among them, often seem as if they had walked out from a picture or down from a pedestal with just as much of soul as the canvas or marble can bestow; there is a sensitive look about the flesh of these people, which seems to have evapourated among the Southerns under the influence of their sun and when pretty they look good natured. They are very quiet too, no brawling no talking loud, so that a village seems a solitude, & in the very midst of one I have not heard the thousandth part of the noise which so annoys Marianne in one single family;—I have heard a dispute or two today under my window—but it was carried on with gentleness and politeness & their most vigorous negative was—vous avez raison, Monsieur, mais ayez la bontè de reflechir:[3]—Neither have they any of the scepticism of the Italians in their manners & tones. If they laugh it is with good humour, & they speak to you with the easy but perfect good breeding so common in France—the beggars even smile amiably if you give them rather more than they expect & say bien obligeè with a really thankful air—while the Madame & Monsieur they use in common to all ranks from a princess to (literally) the beggar is a symbol that they claim kindred with & afford sympathy to all.

Such are my impressions hitherto, & you see that they are not in favour of the Italians. My Vetturino who has only crossed Cenis once before is quite transported with the cordial reception & recognitions he meets with among these mountaineers—What will Marianne say?—will she think that I am turning traitress to dear Italy?—not so—the inhabitants were never favourites with me—I had been habituated to many of their defects until I was hardly aware of them, but the ⟨contrast⟩ absence of them strikes me as agreable Still I love & turn to Italy as the place where all my delights were centred & where ⟨only⟩ I can feel most forcibly that I am still united to those I have lost—besides I like its country & the life & the daily habits one has there better than any others—Besides & besides I love Italy with all my heart & all my soul & all my might & all my strength (you know the catechism, Hunt) and all my hopes are centred in returning there.

I will tell you something I think droll. Near Cenis, & above it, is a high mountain called the Mugone—the snows are yet upon its height, & the approach to the summit is difficult & must be made on foot—it requires a day to go and a day to return; when you arrive at the top you find a peak of naked rock and a little chapel with an image of the Madonna Nera. A great concourse of people flock to this height in the middle of August & fanno festa, people come even from as far as Turin to make holiday here. Now this pleases me—this is something like—one can conceive of animals, dogs & cows, going to pleasant places to enjoy themselves—but it belongs to that queer animal man alone, to toil up steep & perilous crags, to arrive at a bare peak; to sleep ill & fare worse, & then the next day to descend & call this a feast—the feast of the soul it must be—now, dear Patient Very, is not this a trait after your own heart.

I have another thing to say, & even if you dont agree with me, you will pardon poor Grandmamma for her impertinence. I dont think you either of you saw Thornton's letter to Mr Lamb[4]—he begins it by saying that he is going to write to him & will tell him how the Genoese pass the day—he has then copied what, in its place, was cleverly written, a description of how the men women & children of Genoa pass the day—having copied this, he adds that he has nothing more to add but love to Miss Lamb &c.—not a word of his being in Ovid, of any of the things that it w^d^ please Lamb to hear—this is pure laziness, but as he does nothing but abuse the Genoese it might give Lamb a false idea of his character—had he not better write another letter—let him send it to me at Paris & it will be in time—& so now, if I have spoken out of season, forgive me—indeed I am sure you will, or I should not write as I do.

Percy has been writing a letter for Baby—he is now sealing it & then mounts on horseback (on a chair) to carry it—he has been very good & is no trouble to me at all—How are you all? My heart is with you all—and I long to see if when in England I can do any thing to alleviate your cares.—When will the happy day come when we shall meet again?

Pont Bon Voisin—August 1st

After quitting St. Jean I got into a country I knew but too well—and one spot in particular, a wood covered knoll, I had walked on with S— & my lost William. It was a rainy day too—but however to diversify the scene at mid-day I picked up two walking tourists [F]rench gentlemen, who came on with me to Chamberi, glad to escape in my machine from the pouring rain—they were no great things but excessively good natured—and when I had resisted a piece of Percy's self-will successfully, the elder one, the father of 6 children, observed "Madame—vous avez du caractere.{"}

All the scenery of Savoy is beautiful & I know it well—This mornings ride was perfectly delightful—after passing la Montagne des Eschelles, whose dark high precipieces towering above, gave S— the idea of his Prometheus,[5] we wound along a ravine, whose sides & rocks covered with trees & underwood are more picturesque even than the vale of the Alps & the river where not perfectly white with foam was of that green hue one often sees in Italian pictures—This scene, however, though bosky wanted the excessive richness of foliage of La Maurienne, and besides it wanted the higher mountains with their pine forests and naked peaks.

I am now just entered this town, one half of which belongs to Savoy and the other to France—it is divided by a river & a bridge on each side on which the friendly centinels keep looking at each other & examining the effects of those who pass: the town has a good name for a frontier one—Pont bon Voisin—I am now on the French side and have just had my effects not examined by the custom house officers—they were very polite & only just lifted up the lid of one box—It was droll enough however when the superior officer uttered a witticism & the man below him in office laughed, the superior rebuked him—saying ne riez pas—you ought not to laugh while employed on this business—"Il vaut mieux rire que pleurer pourtant{"}[6]—replied the man—non pas pleurer—replied the other but you ought to be serious during your occupations.

[The q]uiet of these people still strikes me as very agreable—I do not know how the English will seem—but the absence of loud voices violent gesticulation & eternal clack gives even to the lower orders an air {of} gentleness & good breeding that even the highest Italians want—I speak of the men particularly, having seen some of the male sex who have their hats properly on their heads and look almost like gentlemen.

Tomorrow I shall be at Lyons—thence to Paris I hope to proceed by a quicker mode of conveyance—I shall have letters from you there, that is one comfort—It seems a day since I left you and yet it was this day week that I saw my poor Polly sleeping or pretending to sleep under net—and that I parted with patient Very, who ⟨fully acquitted himself⟩ entirely fulfilled the beau ideal of the character implied by that name.

Again & again how are you all, dear friends? & when do you go to Florence? And has my Polly walked yet[7] and how go lessons & masters? & by the bye i miei saluti al Signor Agostino Ginocchio—Many kisses to all the children & particularly to Henry & baby nuovo—so no more at present from your affectionate Grandmother

Mary Wolls^ft^ Shelley.

Does Hunt send me a letter for Horace Smith

[*P. 1, top*] For fear that any accident may have happened to my Susa letter write to me at Paris immediately on the reception of this—directed at the Hotêl Nelson Faubourgh St. Germain

ADDRESS: Leigh Hunt Esq / Albaro / Genova / à Gênes—l'Italie. POSTMARKS: (1) GENOVA; (2) 6. AGO. PUBLISHED: Jones, #188. TEXT: MS., Bodleian Library (MS., Shelley, Adds., d. 5, ff. 83–85).

1. Mary Shelley's letter of 26 [–27] July to the Hunts bears a Susa postmark.
2. March 1818 (see *MWS Journal*, 26–30 March 1818; *CC Journals*, 8 April 1818).
3. "You are right, Sir, but have the goodness to reflect."
4. Thornton Hunt was a favorite of Charles Lamb, who expressed his admiration in his poem "To. T.L.H.," written while Hunt and his family were in the Surrey Gaol (February 1813–February 1815) and first printed in the *Examiner* of 1 January 1815 (Blunden, *Leigh Hunt*, pp. 72, 85–86, 88).
5. Jones points out that Mary Shelley omitted this fact in her 1839 note on *Prometheus Unbound* (*MWS Letters*, I, 240, n. 1).
6. "It is better to laugh than cry however."
7. A reference to Marianne Hunt's confinement on 9 June 1823.

To Leigh Hunt

Sunday—Lyons—August 3rd (Tuesday August 5th [1823]

My dear Hunt

I arrived at Lyons yesterday evening and remain here until tuesday evening. This repose will, I trust, entirely restore Percy & will give me time,

I hope to receive your letter, which is not yet arrived. I have taken my place in a public conveyance, not the diligence. I shall travel all tuesday night & the day of Wednesday—& then repose a night & a day at Dijon—then again a night & day of travelling—the same of repose & sunday afternoon I arrive at Paris. This I dare say will appear to you a queer mode of proceeding, but it was the best I c^d manage—I c^d not think of travelling 3 successive days & nights—Veturino travelling is detestable from the slowness of the motion—& posting w^d be too expensive; but in this mode I unite cheapness swiftness & repose—"Indeed Ma'am"—Well are not these two good things in travelling?—"Just so"—

I have sent you a Juvenal by my Veturino who brought me here & now returns to Italy—I sought for English books but could find none so I only send a Paul and Virginia[1] for Thornton. I send you also the Music of the "Clemenza di Tito"[2]—it cost only 17 francs so I was tempted—I went to the Music shop to buy some for you, but my ignorance both of what I ought to buy, & what you have, so puzzled me, that I was glad to settle on safe ground in buying Mozart—Remembering my Polly's preference I tried to get some of Handel, but there was none—You have "Ah! Perdona"—but I do not think that you have "Deh prendi un dolce Amplesso"—and besides there must be many other things in an Opera of Mozart.—By the bye send me a list of what music you w^d like to have—& what you have, that if I see any cheap I may know what I am about: & tell me also the name of that air of Handel's of which you are so fond—I do not mean, "He was despised & rejected of Men"—but the other of which you know only a few notes.

Have you received my two letters one impostata at Susa, the other at Pont Bon Voisin—they will have shewn you how I got on during the first days—I look back with surprize to the tranquillity I was able to preserve at that time—but this is to be attributed to your kindness, my dear friend, for the idea of leaving affectionate hearts behind me consoled me; it still preserves in an outward & visible form the bond that must ever exist between me & Italy.—Now I turn southward and ask: What are you doing?—if you are not a rebel against all your own diaphragmatic theories you are taking a long walk this fine evening—and you, Marianne, have you not been out? How is Thorny's temper, Johnny's verses—Mary's "Deuce takeits"—Swinburne's quiet looks, & serious attention, while the Master is there, Percy's Martyrdom—Henry's "Magnificent eyes"—& little Vincent's gentle smiles?—pray tell all & each that their exiled Grandmother will receive no greater pleasure than the news of their improvement—She sends them all a kiss—Percy wants to send Sylvan a play thing, but that must be reserved for England, he even says that if Baby—Henry[3]—w^d come here he w^d give him his new barroccio.[4]

From the quai here that overlooks the Rhone, we see Mont Blanc—This mountain is associated to me with many delightful hours—We lived under its eye at Geneva—& when at Lyons[5] we looked with joy at its sublime

Dome. It is in itself so magnificent—the utmost heights of Cenis & the Mungone were only flecked with snow—Mont Blanc has still on its huge Mantle, and its aiguilles, purer than the whitest marble, pierce the heaven around it—the sight of this might have given Michael Angelo a still finer idea of a "dome in the air"[6] than the Pantheon itself. I wonder, my best friend, if in other planets & systems there are other sublimer objects & more lovely scenes to entrance Shelley with still greater delight than he felt at seeing these wondrous piles of earth's primæval matter—or does he only feel & see the beauties we contemplate with greater intensity—I fear that if he c^d send us any of his Poetry from where he now is, the world w^d find it more unintelligible & elementary than that which we have. He loved Nature so enthusiastically that one is irrisistibly led to imagine his painless spirit among its divinest combinations—In society, even of those he loved, I do not feel his presence so vividly as I do when I hear the wind among the trees;—when I see the shadows on the mountains—the sunshine in the ravines, or behold heaven and earth meet, when she arises towards it or the clouds descend to her. During the winter how horrible was the sound & look of the sea, but I began to love it & fancy him near it when it sparkled beneath the sun; yet after all, dear Hunt, I was surprised to find that I felt his presence move vividly during my journey through the ravines of the Alps, near the roar of the waterfalls & the "inland murmur"[7] of the precipitous rivers. How I sh^d delight to make a tour with you among these scenes—feeling him & all about him as you do—still you w^d know him better, if you visited these spots which he loved better than any others in the world.

(Tuesday August 5th

I have your letter & your excuses & all.—I thank you most sincerely for it, at the same time I do entreat you to take care of yourself with regard to writing—Although your letters are worth infinite pleasure to me—yet that pleasure cannot be worth pain to you—& remember, if you must write, the good hacnied maxim of multum in parvo and when your temples throb distill the essence of 3 pages into three lines & my "fictitious Adventure" will enable me to spin them out & fill up intervals not but what the 3 pages are best—but "you understand me"—And now let me tell you that I fear you do not rise early since you doubt my ore matutine, be it known to you then, that on the journey I always rose before 3 o'clock that I never once made the Veturino wait—& moreover that there was no discontent in our jogging on, on either side—so that I half expect to be a Santa with him—He indeed got a little out of his element when he got into France—his good humor did not leave him but his self possess he c^d not speak french & he walked about as if treading on eggs.

When at Paris I will tell you more what I think of the French—They still seem miracles of quietness in comparison with Marianne's noisy friends; and the women's dresses afford the drollest contrast with those in fashion when I first set foot in Paris in 1814—then their waists were between their shoulders & as Hogg observed they wore rather curtains than gowns. Their hair too, dragged to the top of the head & then lifted to its height appeared as if each female wished to be a tower of Babel in herself—now their waists { } long (not so long however as the Genoese) & their hair { } flat at the top with quantities of curls on the temples—I remember in 1814 a frenchman's pathetic horror at Claire's & my appearance in the streets of Paris in Oldenburgh (as they were called) hats—now they all wear machines of that shape & a high bonnet w^d of course be as far out of the right road as if the earth were to take a flying leap to another system.

After you receive this letter you must direct to me to my fathers—(pray put WG Esq. since the want of that etiquette annoys him—I remember Shelley's unspeakable astonishment when the Author of Political Justice asked him half reproachfully why he addressed him "M^r" G.) 195 Strand—and since the 21st is the day[8] I suppose I ought to write to Florence however when in Paris I will calculate the time & direct accordingly. Remember Via Val Fonda[9]—I will send you the number of the House from Paris—I think it was called Palazzo Morano or Morandi—but the number will settle that.

Well, my dear Hunt, I must not clack any more or Marianne will think me as bad as Marin—except that you can silence me by not reading me—I hope you have taken measures that Mrs Mason sh^d have Valperga—Do you write a criticism of it?[10]—if ever I write another novel it will be better worth your criticism & more pleasing to you than this—After all Valperga is merely a book of promise, another landing place in the staircase I am climbing—I often think of Alfred & of Triamond[11]—you must send me the list of books I must consult for it—

I hope Marianne thinks of me with kindness—& that the children remember me—Percy was playing at playing with Henry all day yesterday & generously gave the shadow all his play things—How are Polly's nerves & the bell & the empty house & how goes on the Jacket—the Jacket with the definite article—has Henry yet profaned it with fruit soiled hands?—God bless you all—& bless you, dear Hunt, for all the good you have done me—do me & are about to do—

faithfully yours MaryWShelley

The Veturino will take my packet to Mrs Heslops,[12] will Marianne tell her to give him a livre or two for his trouble—I saw a letter to Lord C. Murray[13] in the Post Office here today—can he have returned or not gone—Percy has just informed me with a lau[gh] {"}Mary dice mio mano— Mary non dice mia mano"[14]—while chattering to himself in the coach he tells long stories of "Una Mor[ ]da va su un albore [*albero*] per cercar un gatto{"}[15]—

ADDRESS: Leigh Hunt Esq / Albaro / Genova / Gênes—L'Italie. POSTMARKS: (1) P. 68. P / LYON; (2) GENOVA / 13 AGO. PUBLISHED: Jones, #189. TEXT: MS., Bodleian Library (MS., Shelley, Adds., c. 6, ff. 13–14).

1. J. H. B. de Saint Pierre, *Paul et Virginie* (Paris, 1789). Mary Shelley may have sent the translation by Helen Maria Williams (London, 1795). Williams (1762–1827), British author and supporter of the ideals of the French Revolution, had known both Godwin and Wollstonecraft. Aware of their acquaintanceship, Shelley called on her in Paris in 1814, but she was out of town (Dowden, *Shelley*, I, 352).

2. A Mozart opera.

3. [James] Henry Sylvan, the Hunts' sixth child.

4. "Wagon."

5. May–August 1816 at Geneva; 21–25 March 1818 at Lyons.

6. Shelley, "The Cloud," line 80.

7. Wordsworth, "Lines Composed a Few Miles above Tintern Abbey," line 4.

8. The Hunts left Genoa for Florence on 22 August. They remained briefly at Florence and then settled at Maiano, a suburb of Florence (Blunden, *Leigh Hunt*, p. 208).

9. Palazza Marini, 4395 Via Valfonda, the Shelleys' residence from 2 October 1819 to 26 January 1820.

10. Hunt did not review *Valperga*. The *Examiner* noticed *Valperga* only in a brief, favorable review on 2 March 1823 (p. 154).

11. By the beginning of October, Mary Shelley decided against writing a historical novel about Alfred the Great (see 2–5 October [1823]). Triamond is the Knight of Friendship in Spenser's *Faerie Queene*.

12. Edward Williams noted that a "Mr. Heslop and two English seamen" brought the *Don Juan* from Genoa to Shelley on 12 May 1822 (Williams, *Journals and Letters*, p. 148).

13. Lord Charles Murray (1799–1824) had gone to Greece to fight for Greek liberty (see 10 October [1824], n. 5).

14. "Mary says my [*masculine form*] hand—Mary does not say my [*feminine*] hand."

15. "A [?] goes up a tree to look for a cat."

To Leigh Hunt — Dijon—August 7th [1823]

Well, my dear Hunt, how do you do? I am Mary Shelley I hope—though like the little woman in the story book—I begin to doubt "if I be I"—I am & I was so-so tired—Well I have bidden adieu to night travelling & public conveyances in France—Such a machine—figure to yourself a thing worse far worse than the worst, worst English heavy coaches—so dirty—Well, I got into it—The man had deceived me & shewed me better so I was not prepared—I got in & the first thing I did was to dash away a foolish tear & the second to philosophize—Have I not promised Hunt to be patient, & will he not be pleased if I am?—Then I thought—when in a garden or a wood or a palace one can fancy the plants, the trees or the encrusted walls a part of us, but in such a place as this one must confine ones identity to the small sphere of one's own person—here am I and my boy—entire, well—with a little atmospher around us, that nothing may touch—then I thought how I might be worse off, and recollected what I had seen that morning—a poor young woman arrive in the diligence with child on her knee which she was evidently nursing, looking so tired with a pink hectic flush on her check—so suffering & yet so patient—Thinking of this I began to {be} ashamed of wanting philosophy—I thought that I might if I chose be the Sultaness you wished me to be—I would make myself a downy couch of pleasant thoughts—my wishes sh^{d} be my coursers & my attendants a thousand memories & gentle feelings—So I got over my disgust—but all w^{d} not do to conquer real inconveniences—the uneasy position—my child asleep on my knees, put me into such pain & exhausted me so greatly that I was more dead than alive in the morning—& most philosophically determined not to endure such another night. By the evening, we arrived here—where I have slept & although bruised & battered, non c'è male—so I have engaged a veturino & shall jog on in my old style—the carriage is a good one however, & I shall be alone—& solitude is company—for I never feel so perfectly lonely as when, among a crowd, I feel the want of that protection to which I have been used. How I felt this at Lyons—in the coach they were jog trot people & perfectly civil—but a wretch—such a wretch at Lyons had the impudence to say something to me—I did not say a word, which I dare say you will think was saying my worst—but there are certain situations that one never foresees as possible, and so one is perfectly unprepared—I startled my gentleman however, who muttered something about my not understanding French & left me—to be a goose—& weep—Well that is over too—

The Inn at Lyons was a very nice one & very cheap & the people civil though my solitary mode of proceeding somewhat surprises them—and a servant would in that way have been a convenience to me—though as far as trouble & Percy goes she w^{d} not have been of the least use—I now go Veturino again & shall be in Paris in five days, I hope.—I have engaged my carriage however only for Auxerre, where I arrive Saturday evening—& I may find it as cheap to post thence to Paris.—Although I would not risk another night & day's journey like the last, yet it is pleasant to look back & find that I have done a five days work in 24 hours—but it {is} no joke to be taken really ill at 2 in the morning on a desart road, with rain & muddy roads—and other people in the machine & all kinds of discomfort around one—

I have not written today however, my dear friend, to give you an account of my disasters—now over—but to correct a mistake in my Lyons' letter—I told you in that to direct in future to the Strand—which was a dreary oversight on my part—as soon as you know that I am arrived my letters there will be safe—for I shall get them early the moment they come but in my absence, unless you write for M^{rs} G's [*Godwin's*] most certain and attentive perusal, do not send any letters there. The best place w^{d} be perhaps at your brother John's—as I shall have probably an account with him & he is a man of business—& also this will only be for a short time—until I am settled—direct therefore to London in future, as I shall to Florence unless I hear from you to the contrary—

And so my dear Polly is overwhelmed with packing, meddling chicks &

disobedient, clacking servants—Heaven get you safe through it, my best Polly—safe to Florence, where you may set up the ark of your rest & be at peace for one while. Passing through the plain of Lucca & the Val di Nievole you will see much of the scenery of Valperga—If you stay to rinfrescare there, my dear friend—go to the top of the tower of the palace of Guinigi an old tower as ancient as those times—look towards the opening of the hills, on the road to the Baths of Lucca, & on the banks of the Serchio & you will see the site of Valperga and towards the west you will see a dark wood where they will tell you there are the ruins of a castle which Castruccio built—& that wood is the scene of the incantations where Castruccio & Tripalda appear—If you have time you can go to the Church of San Franceno—then fuore now dentro delle Mura & half way up the aisle on the right hand side you will see on the wall a slab to the memory of Castruccio & underneath this newer one the little old one which contains the inscription I have quoted.[1]

Have you heard any news—I heard some very displeasing to me—the Basilica of San Paolo fuore delle Mura at Rome was burned down—because the geese must needs roof it with the cedar of Lebanon—& of the 24 stupendous marble columns taken from the tomb of Adrian, which in height perfection, & the exquisitely beautiful lilac tinge of the Marble, were unequalled in the world, are all calcined & destroyed, one only excepted—thus time & his servitor destruction are still at work to efface the [ ] of the men of ancient times & our children will see less than we have seen—unless Herculaneum is dug out—Do-e-by-g-d-

The other news is that the F. [*French*] want to make peace in S. [*Spain*][2] That the "Gallant General" is holding out at Casogne & has been wounded & in a letter published of his to another town in Spain shews himself indeed the "Gallant General"—And how goes on our "Gallant Bard" & his crowns & his helmets & his Bolivar canon—& he, worth all & a thousand times more, his companion[3]—you say there is a letter for me from him[4]—I am glad of this—& tell me too what you have done with his letter to Mrs W. [*Wright*] that I left with you. If you have read it—(& you may) you will see that it ought to be delivered—perhaps Mrs Thomas might—or if Mrs Heslop wd give it into her own hands it will do—

You see, when I get a pen, and have plenty of time on my hands how I run on & fill my paper—are these "Gigantic paragraphs"[5]—you see I have a memory—I have indeed, my very dear friend—or my dear friend, very, I will remember all you have told me, all you have taught me, & besides I will bear in mind to love you & yours to the last day of my life—

So now with a Grandmother's blessing to your children, and a Great grandmother's fondest blessing to you and Marianne, I bid you be good children, & to take care of your respective healths—Hunt ought to take a little quassia every morning—& Marianne a little egg flip every night—This is in the right style is it not—however really and truly follow my advice & you may be the better for it. Shelley found quassia very good—it strengthens the digestion—put a tea spoonful of the shavings into a glass of cold water when you go to bed & the next morning before you dress drain the water & drink it—just try this—or put half a pound in a bottle of madeira wine & take a wine glassful half an hour before dinner—now laugh as I do at my own—not nonsense but sense for it may do you a great deal of good—adieu—I depart at 1 o'clock P.M.—it is now 11 A.M.—

Your respectable aieule[6]

Mary W S.

[*P. 2, top, upside-down*] If you write any letters on the journey pray follow my example & put them in the post yourself—People of inns never put them in any place place—but the fire—& the money in their pockets—what think you of this for a witticism—rather stale—but it will do for a beginner—

[*P. 1, top*] Only think of a hand organ, & a miserable french tune—oh! Italy!

ADDRESS: Leigh Hunt, Esq. / Albaro / Genoa, / Gênes—l'Italie. POSTMARKS: (1) DIJON / CHAMBERY / C.F.3.R; (2) 18. AGOSTO. PUBLISHED: Jones, #190. TEXT: MS., Bodleian Library (MS., Shelley, Adds., d. 5, ff. 67–68).

1. At the conclusion of Valperga, III, 269: "EN VIVO VIVAMQUE / FAMA RERUM GESTARUM / ITALICÆ MILITIÆ SPLENDOR; LUCENSIUM DECUS ETRURIÆ ORNAMENTUM CASTRUCCIUS GERRIS ANTELMINELLORUM STIRPE / VIXI PECCAVI DOLUI / CESSI NATURÆ INDIGENTI ANIMÆ PIÆ BENEVOLI / SUCCURRITE BREVI MEMORES / VOS MORITUROS" ("Behold I live and will live, the fame of Italian history, the splendor of war, the glory of Lucca, the ornament of Etruria, Castruccio from the line of Gerius and Antelminelli. I have lived, I have sinned, I have grieved. I have yielded to demanding nature. You who wish well, come to the aid of a pious soul. You who are about to die, for a brief moment remember me").

2. On 7 April 1823 a French army, led by Louis Antoine de Bourbon, Duke of Angouleme, invaded Spain for the purpose of quelling the revolution begun in 1820 and restoring full power to Ferdinand VII.

3. Byron and Trelawny. Byron had three elaborate helmets made—for himself, Pietro Gamba, and Trelawny. The most elaborate one, for himself, bore the motto "Crede Byron." Hunt claimed that Trelawny declined to wear his helmet (Hunt, *Lord Byron and Some of His Contemporaries*, I, 119–20). For details concerning the history of the helmets, see Marchand, *Byron*, III, 1078. Byron kept the two one-pounder cannon from the *Bolivar* when he sold the vessel to Lord Blessington (Byron, *Works*, VI, 223). According to Pietro Gamba, Byron took with him "ten thousand Spanish dollars, in ready money, and bills of exchange for forty thousand more. There were, likewise, some chests of medicine for a thousand men for a year" (Marchand, *Byron*, III, 1087).

4. From Leghorn, dated 23 July 1823 (*S&M*, IV, 950–51). His letter refers to a Mary Shelley letter not located.

5. See 28 August 1819.

6. "Grandmother."

To Jane Williams Paris. August 13 [1823]—Hotel Nelson

Dearest Jane

Your letter advising me to remain in Italy, reached me here[1] at first it made me very melancholy thinking that I might have remained where my heart still is—but reflection has led me to the same decision as that which leads me to London, and your arguments are so many more in favour of my journey. I have indeed no hopes from Sir TS [*Timothy Shelley*]—and of course {I} should not seek to see him—In his letter to LB—he said that he w[d] provide for my boy, if in England & with any one of whom he should approve, I dare say he will stick fast to the last condition & so make the other null. You say, dear girl, that <u>my friends</u> might dispose of my writings for me, but will you tell me which?—You are coming away—My father has never made the slightest offer of the kind, & on the contrary has evidently <u>shirked</u> the office. The Gisbornes are the only people in England who have offered their services, & a thousand reasons make them little fit. It is far less easy to do things by letter than you imagine. As to a periodical publication with Hunt, his situation is extremely precarious just now & he feels it so: so much so, that although I <u>know</u> that my remaining would have pleased him, yet he never urged more than my speedy return. It is for that I shall strain every nerve—to return if possible with you in the spring—what say you, my friend—If I can get any thing, I <u>will</u> get a sufficiency for the journey—I shall leave my father in law without excuse—I shall arrange for the publication of my S.—'s Mss.—I shall establish a correspondance with a bookseller.—And perhaps (though this is last & with a most hypothetical <u>perhaps</u> before it) I may, as I doubt not that the will is valid, raise at a great loss some little sum—say £50 a year or even less which will just help me on, and render the task of self maintanance more easy. Your argument is that my friends c[d] do all this—my dear child, I have waited a whole year for these friends but they are not even yet in embryo; so I am like the farmer in the fable of the lark & her young ones, now going to take the harvest into my own hands, & if in any way I only reap tares, why now I do not even get straw. I have 3 good friends in the world, and I ought to be content since they are proof—I have you, dear girl,—you I trust love me. I have Hunt, whom with his characteristic enthusiasm has me now as much at heart as I was out of it a little while ago. And I have Trelawny, by whose aid I made up the money sufficient to come to England—and when I tell you all of him that I can, in addition to what you know already, you will have admiration for "the rough outside with the gentle heart."

I hope also when in England to be of use to Hunt & arrange his affairs for him—thus I consider this a visit only & all my hope & trust will be to return with you. In the mean time I will not repine—fortune is adverse to me but nothing that has to { } ⟨my⟩ with money shall draw ⟨my⟩ a tear from my eye[2]—⟨if I have⟩ not having been all I sh[d] have been, I will at least bear my penance well & not making my S.— so happy as he deserved to be I will at least make him happy where he is now, if he can be conscious of my constancy & patience

You talk of Hunt's means being mine in disposing {of} his works—why he has none except through his brother—& he depends much on my personal interference even in that quarter; it is so impossible to do any thing in absence, except through the help of a zealous friend.—thus all has combined to lead me to England, may all equally combine in a few months time to send me out of it. I shall not send this letter till I have settled the period of my leaving Paris. I am much knocked up by my journey & during the last 2 day was really ill with fever which has gone after a nights repose, but left me very weak—so I must collect a little strength. I shall try also to see H. Smith[3]—and then for England, with prospects as cloudy as its sky, & with the expectation of but one pleasant sensation—that of seeing you—tell me, my best girl—shall we not return to Italy together?

Your commission is not fulfilled as it ought to have been from the reason you guess—I had however bought Mrs G. [*Godwin*] a gown of the common twilled black silk & that you shall have.—Adieu Bless you, dearest, & your babes—Percy asks if "Dulie" è in Inghilterra—

Thinking again—I will put my letter in the post today that you may know & inform my father that I arrived in Paris last Night—I shall write to him when I have fixed the date of my departure.—Adieu—my heart is heavy after all. My great consolation is, that my boy is well—Will you tell the Gisbornes how soon I hope to see them

Ever Affectionately Yours
Mary W. Shelley

I like this Hotel—the people are uncommonly civil—

ADDRESS: Mrs Williams / Mrs Cleveland / 24 Alsops Buildings / New Road / London / Londres. POSTMARKS: (1) P PAYE PARIS; (2) FPO / AU. 16 / 1823; (3) 12 NOON 12 / AU. 16 / 1823. PUBLISHED: Jones, #191. TEXT: MS., Pforzheimer Library.

1. Jane Williams's letter of 17 July has a French postmark of 8 August 1823 (Abinger MS.). Jane Williams and Hogg discussed the question of Mary Shelley's return to England. He strongly believed she should remain in Italy (see Norman, *After Shelley*, pp. 10, 16, 17–18).

2. The words from this point through ". . . at least" have been omitted in previous publications of this letter.

3. Horace Smith had intended to settle near the Shelleys at Florence in the fall of 1821. His wife's illness altered their plans, and they remained in France, living at Versailles until their return to England in 1825 (*PBS Letters*, #662).

To Leigh and Marianne Hunt

Paris—August 13th
Thursday 14th [1823]

My dear Friends

I arrived here last night quite knocked down (as a Genevese Dr used to say, meaning knocked up—he understood a little English, & wished to speak it idiomatically)—I could hardly get on during the last two days, exhaustion having brought on fever—& all caused by that odious diligence and those delightful warm baths. A night's good rest has much restored me, & I am about to sally forth, to seek for other letters from Italy, & send mine to H.S. [*Horace Smith*]—

The letter from Jane was full of advice to me to remain in Italy—she says that she hopes that she shall arrange her affairs in November & will return in the Spring—I shall work hard to return with her—and once more there, with the security of obtaining the little I want, the rest may go to the winds, and Sir T. S. [*Timothy Shelley*] live to the age of Methusalem if he will—in the mean time "Rabshaka" (how do you spell his name pray tell me the book Chap. & v. "sat on a wall."[1] What say you, shall I not by next summer hear Ah Perdona sung by one who sings it better than all the Opera singers in the world, my favourite David included (Marianne will allow this piece of praise, I know, without calling it flattery—I have heard her say as much—& other people have their ears about them.) It warms my heart to think of this; for England is not an ice house to receive or give sunbeams, but one to freeze all pleasure and emotion. Poor Jane says, alluding to your, Hunt, affectionate zeal for me with the D. in M. stores.[2] "I glory in Hunt's manly and spirited conduct, he was indeed worthy to be the chosen friend of our S. & this is (& I know he will think so) the ne plus ultra of all praise"—There is more flattery, Polly—but it is not mine, you know. I confine my praise to smaller matters—Hesperian curls—the front of———Mont Blanc—The Apollo's throat (that's Thornton) the hands of king Solomon & the (last but not least) Left Leg—all other perfections are Marianne's; witness the Jacket.—Well Jane's letter made me melancholy thinking that some one thought I might have been spared this Journey—yet I could not—but I trust & hope to accompany her on her return.

My amiable Teacher, do not fear to annoy me by your didactics, & above all be assured that they will be religiously attended to. Marianne pays a compliment to my understanding on account of my attention to your admonitions—I am afraid affection & (strange to say) pride, had as much to do with it as understanding. My affection led me to wish to please you; pride made me glory in feeling that I had a friend who would tell me the whole truth, & in so earnest & kind a manner too—& understanding came in at the fag end to tell me that all you said was just and that I could only become worthy of him by following your lessons. So you see you may take courage, since affection & pride are your allies & reason your mate.

I wish you had opened Trelawny's letter[3]—(I am less scrupulous about T's letters because he shew all his & I never write a word to him that I do not expect to be read by those near him{)}[4] it would only have shewn you trusting—not "curious"—but sure that I had no secrets or reserve I w[d] send it to you, but there is not enough in it to render that worth while. It is full of kindness—& discontent that he cannot aid me more than he has.

He mentions that he wishes that you wd insert in the Examiner the dates of their departure with his name, as he wishes his friends to know where he is, tho' he does not write to them. He adds "Say all that is kind to Hunt* & Marianne from me—they have no friend so anxious about them as I am—or would do so much to serve them, let them put me to the proof when they like—for 'tis unpleasant talking of these things."—he says that LB. disembarked at Leghorn only for a few hours adding: "his attention & professed kindness to me is boundless, he leaves every thing to my direction—if I had confidence in him this wd be well—but I now only see the black side of it—it will eventually possibly rob me of my free agency—so weaving me in with his fortunes that I may have difficulty in seperating myself from them"—His letter is desponding—but I hope he will get up his spirits when he enters into action

I made acquaintance on the road with the English family I mentioned in my letter to Marianne;[5] I recommended them to this Hotel & they are now under the same roof with me: they are very polite & pleasant. I like her particularly—she has that attractive mark of un' anima gentile a gentle sweet voice which is a heavenly grace both in the frail & immaculate sect. She has delighted me just now by telling me that she is passionately fond of gardening—they have 6 children—all boys, Polly—one Henry—who is the prettiest, but Percy is faithful to the Albaro Henry & says—"Voglio Henry—non Henry co' calzoni, ma Henry senza calzone Henry Baby"[6]—She looks so young & fresh that it seems to me impossible that she can be the Mother of all—she cannot be more than seven & twenty—yet she nurses them herself—she is rather pretty & quite unaffected—he is goodnatured but nullo & none of the 6 except Henry, who takes after her, are attractive. Why do I tell you all this about strangers—why because I talk to you of the Alps—the fields & the woods—because I talk to you of all I see & hear, & thus keep up my intercourse which methinks would be spoilt if I did not chat about every thing. And besides Hunt will like to hear of her since, hearing that I went on my lonely way, she was impelled by her good nature to offer her services to one who seemed forlorn.

Thursday 14th—4 oclk. PM.

I have just had a visit from HS [*Horace Smith*]—who was very polite & kind—He says that there is a great outcry against the new Cantos, of DJ.[7] & they have a limited sale—He does not know much English News, except that they brought out Frankenstein at the Lyceum[8] and vivified the Monster in such a manner as caused the ladies to faint away & a hubbub to ensue—however they diminished the horrors in the sequel, & it is having a run—he enquired kindly about you all, and asked me to come to stay at Versailles during the time I waited before going to England—excusing Mrs S—'s not calling that she was not well—he pressed so much that I promised to dine with him tomorrow.—I have spent the morning seeing sights with the

English family I mentioned—the only thing worth seeing was the Pantheon which is pretty—I saw some modern french pictures which are perfectly odious—& to Italian eyes painful.—I have bought Mrs Hunter[9] a Mother of pea{r}l toothpick, very pretty—value 3 franks—How I longed for as many napoleons to throw away in nick knacks, all elegant, & yet which w^{d} have all be{en} useful to you—but I did not dare begin making purchases—Percy runs by my side in all these promenâdes like a little dog, & does not seem to tire I asked him whether you should send him his whip (the loss of which no other replaced to his mind) or whether he would give it to Henry—he says—che mi lo manda—compra Henry un altra—ma non si trova belle fruste tante in questo paese[10]—his journey has made him understand what a paese is, & he logically described it saying—Mamma—quando ci sono molte case, molte, molte, questo è un paese[11]—

Well, Thorny, I have not had you P.S. yet—how are you all my dears—Arrived in Florence safe & well?—How do you like the Venus, how the Niobe how the St. John in the desart—how all you have seen? Welcome—welcome to Fiorenza mia—welcome out of stone walls, solitude & the Union of voices welcome to C. Brown & Carlino—to Severn—to the Cascini. I have received your letter of the 4th of August, dear Hunt, and thank you a thousand times for it—you know how to pour balms into the wounds, I was going to say you make, but that is not just—the wounds were there deep & incurable till you medecined them—Can one's own heart ever deceive one? but I will not enter on so melancholy a subject—thank you—& be happy in the thought of the good you have done—Many happy returns to me? And what to you, dear ones? What happiness for this coming year? Marianne with restored health?—walks by the Arno—along the Cascini—where We often walked & were enchanted by all we saw. The Gallery—the Pitti palace—the opera—studious mornings, out of door afternoons—social evenings—if it were not for these odious cares?—Yet do not think so much of futurity—"sufficient for the day &c{"}—What dreams & prospects I formed—& all now dust—but as evil destroys good, so may good be at times the victor, & who knows the unborn events of a winter that lowers on me with most ungentle aspect—but all changes, & if "in the mean time "Rabshacha sits on a wall" why he might sit lower & the broken masonry might bruise the flesh & the shaken limbs be unable to rise—true—true—much of this is—but a torso of the Ancients is better than a gallery of sound limbed dainty unharmed modern blocks—some of the fragments of an image of unspeakable beauty (our re-union at Pugnano) some glorious relics survive, let us treasure, preserve, glue, join—as an old maid her china, & we will get cups for our water if our wine be indeed all spilt.

I go on talking—Alone in the evening can I do better that [*than*] collect you[12] around me. Besides I am still this side (there is but one <u>this</u> side) of the Channel—Postage is still tolerably cheap, and I may run a little riot with my paper as well as my words.—In England I must think how to save twopence postage by putting two thoughts instead of one into a sentence, and weep, like Milton's devils, from "Gigantic paragraphs"—into such full, overflowing, pressing down of the measure, that each word will be a three volumed novel. For instance in my very direction when I write Florence.F will stand for friend & friend will mean affection & wishes & hopes—l—may be left leg—for Leigh—for length O—O!!! will be an exclamation that will do {to} express wonder at no letters—wonder at many letters—wonder of all sorts—I will not talk more nonsense (if I can help it) finish, Johnny, the many meaning F.l.o.r.e.n.c.e. may imply—or Hunt—do you in the French style write 8 verses each beginning with these letters in succession, & let us see what you can make of it—

This letter will go tomorrow before I go to Versailles—so you will have another letter from me at Paris—and then I enter the Enchanted Island or rather the Isle where all enchantments cease—where there is no sun[ ] & if by chance for a few hours the heaven be free from clouds the dun sky [ ] washed—at least so it is here—Where instead of originals pictures [ ] copies—brick houses for stone palaces, for marble statues, plaster casts—Now dont be tiresome, Marianne & say you w^d like the exchange—my heart echoes back in every beat, a passage of poor Jane's letter—"a cottage in Italy with bread & fruit is better than a dukedom in this dismal country"[13]—I like contrasts—I dont like snow in the winter & rain in the summer—but ice when the sun shines—and serene January's, Nature reposing from her Autumnal fertility, not dying as with us—covering herself with her pall of virgin white & shaking her hairless tresses (there is a bull—but what are foliageless trees) under a tyrant wind.—I do talk on in spite of myself & am angry with myself—if Very patient & Patient Very do not both patronize my clack I never will clack more, I wont—& revenge myself by making myself unhappy—Good night I tell you—It is late, naughty children Why will you keep you poor great grandmother up so long—you will have a headache, Hunt;—as for you Polly, you may sit up with greater impunity—and so I will spend a few minutes more with you now modest Hunt has crept under the zanzaliera[14]—How are you, dear girl?—& how is he? Is he ever cross & silent? if he is just throw a glass of water at him only take care of the Jacket—the same recipe may not be amiss for Thorny if he can't write the PS. For Mary & Johnny a ducking alone will do—How are Henrys [?lamps]—& Vincent, whom I declare is as much mine as yours—& if he turns out all his gentle smiles promise I will prove this—Why I might have taken him away who c^d have hindered me just then?—& what does Swiny say to all the "treasures of his art." And how go the crowns—& the chaste caresses—& the bragings—& veal & ham pies—oh Polly—I hope you have deposited all your nervous feeling in that empty house—& the bell will ring a joyful farewell for you as you go away—Good night now, my Polly—& be not, I conjure you, offended at any of my nonsense—absence seems to give one a right to be wilful, & I am not Very patient or Patient Very—but, alas! very impatient

& impatient very & this may make me say at times ⟨more than after⟩ other than I mean—if I say any thing that can give you pain—

Affectionately your Exiled Grandmother, & very true friend

Mary WS.

You did quite right, H. to enumerate your letters—this is my 6th I[ ] 1 from you at Lyons & 2 at Paris & J—'s [*Jane's*] & T—'s [*Trelawny's*]— I think HS. [*Horace Smith*] looks younger than when I saw him last—

* I have been interrupted just here by some Italians coming into the Court Yd of the inn & playing & singing Italian airs—they sang a buona notte set to an air Jane used to sing.—"And I also lived in Italy!"

ADDRESS: Leigh Hunt Esq / Ferma in Posta / Firenze—Toscanna / Florence—Italie. POSTMARKS: (1) [ ] PARIS; (2) 28 / AGOST[O]. PUBLISHED: Jones, #192. TEXT: MS., Huntington Library (HM 11631); and British Library (Add. MSS. 38,523, f. 75).

1. Rabshakeh (see 2 Kings 18:26–27).
2. Unidentified.
3. Hunt must have forwarded Trelawny's letter of 23 July, French-postmarked 8 August.
4. This explanation is written in a very small hand and squeezed between the preceding paragraph and this paragraph.
5. Letter unlocated.
6. "I want Henry—not Henry with trousers but Henry without trousers Baby Henry."
7. Cantos 6–8, published by John Hunt on 15 July 1823 (Steffan, *Byron's Don Juan*, I, 209).
8. Godwin's letter of 22 July informed Mary Shelley that *Presumption, or the Fate of Frankenstein* would be produced the following Monday (Godwin to Mary Shelley, Huntington Library [HM 11634]). Richard Brinsley Peake (1792–1847) was the dramatist. *Presumption* opened on 28 July and was a success. On 18 August another adaptation of *Frankenstein*, entitled *Frankenstein; or, The Demon of Switzerland*, by H. M. Milner, was produced at the Royal Coburg Theatre, London. A burlesque of Frankenstein by R. B. Brough and William Brough was produced in 1849 at the Adelphi (Nicoll, *English Drama*, IV, 271, 356, 369).
9. In 1803 Ann Kent, Marianne Hunt's widowed mother, married Rowland Hunter, a publisher and bookseller who was nephew and successor to Joseph Johnson, the publisher of Wollstonecraft, Godwin, and many other important literary figures of the age (*SC*, II, 772).
10. "It should be sent to me—buy another for Henry—but you don't find many good whips in this country."
11. "When there are many houses, very very many, this is a country."
12. The manuscript to this point is at the Huntington Library; the remainder is at the British Library.
13. Jane Williams's letter of 17 July (Abinger MS.).
14. *Zanzariera* ("mosquito net").

TO LEIGH HUNT August 18th (August 19th) [1823] Paris

My dear Hunt

I have just returned from spending three days at Versailles.[1] I went to dine & sleep one night, and the Kenny's[2] being there, & my dining at their house, made me remain a day longer than I intended. HS [*Horace Smith*] was very polite as was also Mrs S. [*Smith*] who in truth is in very delicate health; besides Eliza & Horace they have only one child a little girl 2½ years old,[3] all life and spirits & chattering. Eliza is at home, she seems a nice girl enough, and HS— seems happy in his domestic circle, pleased with France which Mrs S. is not, so they will return to England—God knows when! I was pleased to see the Kenny's, especially Kenny, since he is much, dear Hunt, in your circle and I asked him accordingly a number of questions. They have an immense family, and a little house quite full—and in the midst of a horde of uninteresting beings, one graceful & amiable creature, Louisa Holcroft—the Eldest of Holcroft's girls by Mrs Kenny—she is now I suppose about two & twenty, she attends to the whole family and her gentleness & sweetness seems the spirit to set all right—I like to see her & Kenny together, they appear so affectionately attached—You w^d^ like to see them too; very pretty with bright eyes & animated but unaffected & simple manners, her blushes cover her cheeks whenever she speaks, or whenever Mamma is going to tell an unlucky story, which she has vainly endeavoured to interrupt with—"Oh, Mamma, not <u>that</u>."—Kenny has just brought out an extremely successful opera at the Haymarket[4]—It was to have been played at Drury Lane but "Constantia gone! Amazement!" (I made them laugh by telling them this) refused to act if he did not have Elliston's part, which c^d^ not be conceded to him. Poor Kenny is in spirits at the success of his peice, and is not half so nervous as he was, neither apparently or really, as Louisa tells me. I have a sort of instinctive liking for these <u>Authors</u>, & besides was glad to talk of something with a person of observation after having exhausted my Nothings with Mrs S.—so Louisa, Kenny and I drew together in a corner & talked first of the Godwins & then of the Lambs: I will reverse this order in ⟨talking⟩ writing of them to you.

Two years Ago the Lambs made an excursion to France—when at Amiens poor Miss L. was taken ill in her usual way,[5] and Lamb was in despair, he met however with some acquaintances, who got Miss L. into proper hands & L. came on to Versailles and staid with the Kenny's, going on very well, if the French wine had not been too good for him, so I found him no favorite with the S.—s [*Smith's*]. Poor Miss L. is again ill just now. They have been moving, renouncing town & country house to take one which was neither or either—at Islington, I think they said. Kenny was loud in her praise, saying that he thought her a faultless creature—possessing every virtue under heaven. He was annoyed to find L. more reserved & shut up than usual—avoiding his old friends & not so cordial or amiable as his wont—I asked him about Hazlitt—This love-sick youth, jilted by Infelice has taken to falling in love.[6] He told Kenny that whereas formerly he thought women silly, unamusing toys, & people with whose society he delighted to dispense—he was now only happy where they were & given up to the admiration of their interesting foibles & amiable weaknesses. He is the humble servant of all marriageable young ladies. Oh! Polly! Wordsworth was in town not long ago, publishing & looking old—Coleridge is well, having been ill—Procter[7] is ill—& fond of money, as they say—poetical fact! I heard little else—except that the reign of Cant in England is growing wider & stronger each day—John Bull (the Newsp.)[8] attacked the licencer of the theatres for allowing a piece to pass with improper expressions, so the next farce was sent back to the theatre with a note from the Licencer to say that in the farce there were 9 damns—& two equivocal words which considering what John Bull said, he could not permit to pass. —John Bull is conducted by Hooke, a man I know nothing of but whom HS. & Kenny joined in abusing as the publisher & speaker of greater blasphemies, indecencies &c than any person in the world. My utter surprize is, why they have not pounced upon Valperga.—

Well!—they all seemed in a fright at the idea of my being under the same roof as Mrs G. [*Godwin*] they made me promise (readily enough) not to stay more than a few days—"a few days in the Strand, & a few weeks only in England," Mrs K. said, "you will be miserable there." My father, it seems, is in excellent health, & generally in good spirits—but she—well—pazienza!—Kenny did not give a favourable account of William[9] either—vedremo. The Kenny's are to pay me a visit tomorrow when I may hear more.

I was pleased to see HS. looking happy & amiable (synonimes, Hunt?) I do not know what to make of her—the only thing that pleased me was a certain activity of spirit she seemed to have, one likes motion & life. Do you know that S. gets 200 per ann. from Colburn[10] clear, regularly, for writing "al suo aggio—" some times yes, at time no—for the New Monthly —Would not such be a comfortable addition? if it were not too great an addition to Head work—they want amusing & light writing so much, that they are ready to pay anything ⟨to buy it⟩ for it Speak the word & I will try to manage it for you. It w^d^ be better than writing notes for the Italian selection—or that might be done in a more lucrative way.—Shall I offer Colburn by the bye, that selection.[11] Going to the fountain head of the knowledge I found that it was not true that the ladies were frightened at the first appearance of Frankenstein—K. says that the first appearance of the Monster from F.'s labratory down a dark staircase had a fine effect—but the piece fell off afterwards—though it is having a run.—

I have just made my bargain for Calais & go Wednesday noon—(this is monday) I shall arrive next sunday & hope to sail the day after—I am under a little anxiety about my finances—but trust that I have just enough to conclude my journey. I am obliged to travel rather more expensively than I otherwise should—because my health will not permit me to travel at night—I am so very weak, that the slightest exertion almost upsets me, & an emotion throws me into a fever—there was m[usic] at Kenny's—and all at once I heard chords on the harp—the co[mmence]ment of the Indian air you have often heard me mention that [ ] Jane used to sing together[12]—One is so afraid of appearing affected, but I wa[s] obliged to entreat them to cease—& then smothered my tears & pain, for it darted like a spasm through me—in my corner.—It was the only air except one other of E's [*Edward's*]—in the world, I think, that I c^{d} not have heard through without exposing myself—but how could I hear the mimickry of that voice—the witch to recal such scenes.—Let me forget it—the very remembrance makes me melancholy. Well then, quatrini;[13]—I trust that I have sufficient—& enough is as good as a feast, they say—so I shall be economical, without being anxious, for there is no use in that. I will write my last un-English letter to you from Calais.

My dearest Hunt, your letters are a great consolation to me. I feel remorse at the idea of your making your temples beat & your head ache to please me—but how can I forego your kindness? And when I get to England what else but those and the hope of returning to Italy, can keep up my spirits?—and when I see Italy receeding & hope fail, what but your letters, my best friend,—have I left in the world?—You are the tie of the past, the assurance of the future—my Pardoner & teacher—Well I will not be too sentimental—though affection may excuse my feeling, & bodily weakness & solitude the expression.—Goodnight I will finish my letter tomorrow. (August 19th)

The Kenny's have been with me again today and I cannot refrain from telling you what they told me of Hazlitt. Just before the S. [*Scottish*] D. Divorce he met M$^{rs.}$ H [*Hazlitt*] in the St. "Ah you here—& how do you do?"—"Oh very well W^{m} & how are you?"—"Very well thank you. I was just looking about for my dinner"—"Well mine is just ready a nice boiled leg of pork—if you like W^{m} to have a slice"—so he went & had a slice—Miss Lamb—in vain endeavoured to make her look on her journey to Scotnd in any other light than a jaunt. K. [*Kenney*] met H [*Hazlitt*] in the Ham^{std} fields—well sir—he said—I was just going to M^{r}——— theres a young lady there—I don't know—But said K. there was another a young lady of colour you [*cross-written*] were about to marry—has she jilted you like Infelice"—"No, sir, but you see Sir, she had relations—kind of people who ask after character, & as mine smacks, sir, why it was broken off."—K. says that when he met you it was at Lambs after a damnation of his own—when all his wish was that people w^{d} not be sympathizing—& that you seemed to understand this feeling so well, & ate your supper with such appetite, & forced the conversation into the most opposite channels that he was quite delighted "Yes" said Mrs K. "I loved Mr Hunt from that moment"—They both desire to know more of you, & as they talk of Italy next year, who knows? K. is passionately fond of music—Mozart, & Louisa plays uncommonly well. I am more pleased with her the more I see of her. She & K will probably come to Paris tomorrow to take leave of me & perhaps accompany me a few miles out of town—I worked myself into good spirits this evening & it w^{d} have been pleasant but for 2 young ladies whom M^{rs} K has under their care[14]—They are romantic (ugly & crayon)[15] & talk about happiness ridicule the narrow prejudices of K. & L. who say that it consists in cheerfully fulfilling your duties and making those happy around you—"No," they say "there will be no happiness in the world till every thing is capable of demonstration"—Do you understand this? they seek their demonstration in balls theatres finery their notions of romance, & treating ill a poor indulgent father, who is looked upon as the most prejudiced of beings—Miss L. it seems has attacks of a much lighter nature than formerly—she is never violent, & is never removed from home—she has a person to attend her there—she was ill for 3 months when in France in M^rs^ K's house.—

One more letter from Calais & then "to England if you will"[16]—Dear children when shall your exiled Grandmother see you again—they say that my father is anxious to see me—I dread that tie—all the rest is air Adieu dearest Polly; my good chicks, I hope you are all good T. J. M. S. P. HS. & V. a blessing on you all—My dear Hunt adieu believe me

faithfully yours
MaryWShelley

M^rs^ K says that I am grown very like my Mother, especially in Manners—in my way of addressing people—this is the most flattering thing any one c^d^ say to me I have tried to please them, & I have some hopes that I have succeeded.—

HS. tells me that S.T.S. [*Sir Timothy Shelley*] is laid on the shelf and Whitton & Lady S. manage everything—LB. wanted me to write to her—I did not for one hates to beg—should I—or not?[17] t[e]ll me you, good one.

ADDRESS: Leigh Hunt Esq / Ferma in Posta / Firenze / Toscana / Florence—l'Italie. POSTMARK: 2 / SETTEMBRE. PUBLISHED: Jones, #193. TEXT: MS., Huntington Library (HM 2752).

1. Visiting the Horace Smiths.

2. James Kenney (1780–1849) was a prolific playwright. Among his friends were numbered many of the most notable literary figures of the day, including Godwin, Charles Lamb, Washington Irving, and Samuel Rogers. His wife, Louisa Mercier, was the widow of Godwin's close friend Thomas Holcroft.

3. Eliza and Horace were Horace Smith's children from his first marriage. Rosalind, born to his second wife (whom he married in 1818), was named for Shelley's *Rosalind and Helen* (Beavan, *James and Horace Smith*, pp. 123, 157).

4. *Sweethearts and Wives* opened at the Haymarket on 7 July 1823 (Nicoll, *English Drama*, IV, 337).

5. The Lambs visited France in June 1822. When Mary Lamb recovered from this attack of her recurrent mental illness, she was escorted about Paris by Henry Crabb Robinson (1775–1867), diarist, and John Howard Payne, actor and playwright (see 1 June [1824]; Lucas, *Charles Lamb*, II, 89–90).

6. William Hazlitt married Sarah Stoddart on 1 May 1808. In 1819 they separated, and on 17 July 1822 they divorced in Scotland. On the day of the divorce, Hazlitt related to his wife a detailed account of his passionate love for Sarah Walker, who jilted him. Hazlitt had written of his relationship with Sarah Walker, whom he called Infelice, in "Table-Talk, No. 2: On Great and Little Things," *New Monthly Magazine*, February 1822. His *Liber Amoris; or, the New Pygmalion* (London, 1823) gave a full account of this unhappy affair (Wardle, *Hazlitt*, pp. 111, 248, 300–305, 362–65).

7. Bryan Waller Procter (1787–1874) wrote under the name of Barry Cornwall.

On 9 March 1819 Hunt had written Mary Shelley that he had met Procter, an admirer of Shelley's, and had included some of his verses in the *Literary Pocket-Book* (*S&M*, II, 368). (Shelley was highly critical of Procter's writing [*PBS Letters*, #589, #605, #614, #625].) Procter's enthusiasm for Shelley's work led him to support Mary Shelley's edition of the *Posthumous Poems* (see 18 September [1823]).

8. The vigorously Tory *John Bull*, published between 1820 and 1892, was directed at the time by Theodore Hook. For its attacks on Shelley, see White, *Unextinguished Hearth*, p. 385.

9. William Godwin, Jr.

10. Henry Colburn (d. 1855), publisher of the *New Monthly Magazine* and of many novelists of the day, including Horace Smith, Theodore Hook, Lady Morgan, and Mary Shelley (see 15 November [1825]).

11. On 1 September 1824 Hunt wrote Bessy Kent of a fourth offer he had received from Henry Colburn to write for the *New Monthly Magazine* (Hunt, *Correspondence*, I, 232). In 1825 the *New Monthly Magazine* began publishing Hunt's work (Brewer, *The Holograph Letters*, pp. 137–38, 144).

12. Possibly the inspiration of Shelley's "The Indian Girl's Song."

13. "Money."

14. "Two Miss Bryants," who boarded with the Kenneys (Irving, *Journals and Notebooks*, III, 210).

15. Perhaps a reference to their use of lipstick, *crayon de rouge à levres.*

16. *King John* 3. 4. 68.

17. Mary Shelley did write to Shelley's parents (see 9–11 September [1823]).

To Leigh Hunt

[14 Speldhurst Street Brunswick Square]
September 9th (Sep. 11th) [1823]

My dear Hunt

Bessy promised me to relieve you from any inquietude you might suffer from not hearing from me, so I indulged myself with not writing to you until I was quietly settled in lodgings of my own. Want of time is not my excuse, I had plenty—but until I saw all quiet around me I had not the spirit to write a line—I thought of you all—how much! and often longed to write, yet would not till I called myself free. To turn Southward; to imagine you all, to put myself in the midst of you would have destroyed all my philosophy. But now I do so. I am in little neat lodgeings—my boy in bed, I quiet—and I will now talk to you; tell you what I have seen and heard, and with as little repining as I can try, by making the best of what I have, the certainty of your friendship & kindness, to rest half content tho' I am not in the "Paradise of Exiles."[1]—Well—first I will tell you journal wise the history of my 16 days in London. I arrived monday the 25th of August—My father & William came for me to the Wharf. I had an excellent passage of 11½ hours—a glassy sea & a contrary wind—the smoke of our fire was wafted right aft & streamed out behind us—but wind was of little consequence—the tide was with us—& though the Engine gave a "short uneasy motion"[2] to the vessel, the water was so smooth that no one on board was sick & Persino played about the deck in high glee. I had a very kind reception in the Strand[3] and all was done that could be done to make me comfortable—I exerted myself to keep up my spirits—the house though rather dismal, is infinitely better than the Skinner St. one—I resolved not to think of certain things, to take all as a matter of course and thus contrived to keep myself out of the gulph of melancholy, on the edge of which I was & am continually peeping.—

But lo & behold! I found myself famous!—Frankenstein had prodigious success as a drama & was about to be repeated for the 23rd night at the English opera house.[4] The play bill amused me extremely, for in the list of dramatis personæ came, ———by Mr T. Cooke:[5] this nameless mode of naming the un{n}ameable is rather good. On Friday Aug. 29th Jane My father William & I went to the theatre to see it. Wallack[6] looked very well as F [*Frankenstein*]—he is at the beginning full of hope & expectation—at the end of the 1st Act. the stage represents a room with a staircase leading to F workshop—he goes to it and you see his light at a small window, through which a frightened servant peeps, who runs off in terror when F. exclaims "It lives!"—Presently F himself rushes in horror & trepidation from the room and while still expressing his agony & terror ——— throws down the door of the labratory, leaps the staircase & presents his unearthly & monstrous person on the stage. The story is not well managed —but Cooke played ———'s part extremely well—his seeking as it were for support—his trying to grasp at the sounds he heard—all indeed he does was well imagined & executed. I was much amused, & it appeared to excite a breathelss eagerness in the audience—it was a third piece a scanty pit filled at half price—& all stayed till it was over. They continue to play it even now.

On Saturday Aug. 30th I went with Jane to the Gisbornes. I know not why, but seeing them seemed more than anything else to remind me of Italy. Evening came on drearily, the rain splashed on the pavement, nor star, nor moon deigned to appear—I looked upward to seek an image of Italy but the blotted sky told me only of my change. I tried to collect my thoughts, and then again dared not think—for I am a ruin where owls & bats live only and I lost my last singing bird when I left Albaro. It was my birthday and it pleased me to tell the people so—to recollect & feel that time flies & what is to arrive is nearer, & my home not so far off as it was a year ago. This same evening on my return to the Strand I saw Lamb who was very entertaining & amiable though a little deaf. One of the first questions he asked me was whether they made puns in Italy—I said—{"}Yes, now Hunt is there"—He said that Burney made a pun in Otaheite,[7] the first that was ever made in that country: At first the natives could not make out what he meant, but all at once they discovered the pun & danced round him in transports of joy. L. [*Lamb*] said one thing which I am sure will give you pleasure. He corrected for Hazlitt a new collection of Elegant Extracts, in which the Living Poets are included.[8] He said he was much pleased with many of your things, with a little of Montgomery[9] & a little of Crabbe—Scott he found tiresome—Byron had many fine things but was tiresome but yours appeared to him the freshest & best of all. These Extracts have never been published—they have been offered to Mr Hunter & seeing the book at his house I had the curiosity to look at what the extracts were that pleased L. There was the Canto of the Fatal Passion from Rimini several things from Foliage & from the Amyntas. L. mentioned also your conversation with Coleridge & was much pleased with it. He was very gracious to me, and invited me to see him when Miss L. should be well.

One the strength of the drama my father had published for my benefit a new edition of F.[10] & this seemed all I had to look to, for he despaired utterly of my doing anything with S.T.S. [*Sir Timothy Shelley*]—I wrote to him however to tell him I had arrived & on the following Wednesday had a note from Whitton where he invited me, if I wished for an explanation of S.T.S.'s intentions concerning my boy to call on him.[11] I went with my father. W. [*Whitton*] was very polite though long winded—his great wish seemed to be to prevent my applying again to STS, whom he represented as old, infirm & irritable—however he advanced me £100 for my immediate expences, told me that he c^d^ not speak positively until he had seen STS. but that he doubted not but that I should receive the same annually for my child, & with a little time & patience, I should get an allowance for myself.[12] This, you see relieved me from a load of anxieties—I hesitated no longer to quit the Strand and having secured neat cheap lodgings—removed hither last night. Such, dear Hunt is the outline of your poor Exile's history. After two days of rain the weather has been uncommonly fine cioè without rain, & cloudless I believe, though I trust to other eyes for that fact, since the whitewashed sky is any thing but blue to any but the perceptions of the Natives themselves. It is so cold however that the fire I am now sitting by is not the first that has been lighted, for my father had one two days ago. The wind is East and piercing—but I comfort myself with the hope that softer gales are now fanning your not throbbing temples, that the climate of Florence will prove kindly to you, & that your health & spirits will return to you.—Why am I not there? This is quite a foreign country to me; the names of the places sound strangely—the voices of the people are new & grating—the Vulgar English they speak particularly displeasing—but for my father, I should be with you next spring—but his heart & soul are set on my stay, and in this world it always seems one's duty to sacrifice one's own desires, & that claim ever appears the strongest which claims such a sacrifice.

On Tuesday (Sep. 2nd) I dined with Mr Hunter and Bessy & she afterwards drank tea with me at the Strand—She is certainly much improved in countenance. Her mouth which used always to express violence & anger now seems habitually to wear a good tempered smile—Mrs Godwin herself observed the change—this is certainly to Bessy's credit since she is far from happy as you may guess. It would be useless for me to repeat Bessy's news since doubtless she has told you all herself & you already know that the Novello's have from motives of economy, retired to the country.[13]—One thing at Mr Hunter's amused me very much—Your piping Fau[n] & kneeling Venus are on the piano, but, from a feeling {of} delicacy, they are turned with their backs [ ] company. I think of going down to Richmond on Friday & take a last peep at green fields & [ ] leaves before I return to my winter cage. You must know that Jane is a great favourite w[ith] Mrs H. [*Hunter*]—Poor thing she is much persecuted by Edward's Mother in Law[14] Who to save her own credit spreads false reports about her as much as she can. She even called on Mrs Godwin to warn her that I ought not to know her—at the same time that she tells other people that she can never forgive her, for knowing me. England is no place for Jane—how I wish we could leave it together next spring. Hogg & Peacock are both out of town.

I have now renewed my acquaintance with the friend of my girlish days[15]—she has been ill a long time, even disturbed in her reason, and the remains of this still hang over her. She is delighted to see me, although she is just now on the point of going to Scotland for a few weeks. The great affection she displays for me endears her to me & the memory of early days—Else all is so changed for me that I should hardly feel pleasure in cultivating her society. We never do what we wish when we wish it, and when we desire a thing earnestly, & it does arrive, that or we are changed so that we slide from the summit of our wishes & find ourselves where we were. Two years ago I looked forward with eagerness to your arrival, & pictured to myself all that I should enjoy with you & dear Marianne to make a part of our pleasures—You came, 12 dreary months past, I just began to regain your affection & to delight in your society & I am here, to pine for it again. This is life!—And what more have I { } to you with its painful bitterness—sour sweets & sweet sours?—What will happen when I see you again?[16]

Your brother has been out of town all this time. I heard that he was to return yesterday & expect him to call on me today. Of course I did not talk to Henry of all that I have to say to his father. Henry is not handsome. He is stiff in his manners though polite to me. They seem to be going on well and he says that the literary Examiner is succeeding. The truth however is, dear Hunt, that there is nothing in it Except the Indicator which is worth reading—but you will see them and judge. They have offered that I should contribute to fill up the few pages that follow the Criticism on books (which is written by a Mr Gordon, I think is his name) & when I can I will—but I have not that talent which enlivens a half page.—Do you know that your friend Rd Mr Collyer (who so shamefully attacked dearest S.) has been accused of the Bishop's crime[17] & has absconded.—This will become quite a clerical amusement, it unnaturalness befits their habitual hypocrisy & cant—When a man belies his conscience to the world—he will soon bely it to himself and what comes next, may easily be as bad as poor Joslin Adieu dear friend I will finish the rest when I have seen your brother.

(Sep. 11th) I saw your brother yesterday. Being the first time that I saw him you may guess that I looked curiously at him. In features he is very like Henry, but softened from his immoveability of feature by time and suffering. He does not look so old as he is, & LB. w^d envy his unchanged looks, but I do not think him at all like your picture. He was all politeness & even kindness to me—I soon found that I had two feelings to remove in his mind[18]—one your not having managed well with the D in M Stores—the other poor dear M⟨a⟩r.'s [*Marianne's*] extravagance—I believe that I succeeded in both these points at least he said that I did. He spoke with great affection of you & when he went away said, that he was reserved & had the character perhaps of being more so than he was but that he did not wish to be so with you or with me—In fact though obstinacy is written on his brow, & reserve in all his solemn address yet he encouraged me so far that I look forward with less apprehension to the final result of my next conversation with him. I feel that I must not be reserved, nor shall I be so—I told him as it was that he ought to write oftenor, spoke of regular remittances—& urged him to send an immediate one; he said that he would write by the same post as that by which this letter will go, and that I trust will contain a permission for you to draw. I expect to see him soon again. Direct to me 14 Speldhurst St.—Brunswick Square. I will write again speedily—& wait anxiously to hear from you—Keep well—be all well, dear, dearest friends, be as happy as you can, &, while it be of value to you, & even after, depend upon the unremitting affection of your Exiled

MaryWS.

ADDRESS: Leigh Hunt Esq / Ferma in Posta / Firenze / Florence—Italy. POSTMARKS: (1) F-23 / 113; (2) CHAMBERY; (3) ANGLE[TERRE]; (4) 27 / SETTEMBRE. PUBLISHED: Jones, #194. TEXT: MS., Bodleian Library (MS., Shelley, Adds., c. 6, ff. 15–16).

1. Shelley, *Julian and Maddalo*, line 57.
2. Coleridge, *The Ancient Mariner*, 5. 386.
3. At the Godwins'.
4. See 13–14 August [1823].
5. Thomas Potter Cooke (1786–1864). In 1825 Cooke presented *Le Monstre* (that is, *Frankenstein*) in Paris on eighty successive nights (see 11 June 1826, n. 14).
6. James William Wallack (?1791–1864), actor and stage manager.
7. Tahiti. Lamb was referring to his friend Captain James Burney (1750–1821), rear admiral and man of letters, the son of Charles Burney.
8. *Select British Poets, or New Elegant Extracts from Chaucer to the Present Time, with Critical Remarks, by Wm. Hazlitt* (London: William C. Hall, 1824). Hazlitt stated in his preface that the anthology was meant to be an improvement on the Reverend Vicesimus Knox's *Elegant Extracts in Verse*, "at least a third" of which "was devoted to articles either entirely worthless, or recommended only by considerations foreign to the reader of poetry" (Wardle, *Hazlitt*, p. 387). Included in the collection were poems by Lamb, Keats, Shelley, and Hunt. The volume was with-

drawn from circulation almost immediately after publication because the selections from contemporary poets had been reprinted without permissions. The volume was republished the following year, but the contemporary poets were omitted (Wardle, *Hazlitt*, p. 388).

9. James Montgomery (1771–1854), poet and newspaper editor.

10. MWS, *Frankenstein*.

11. In response to Mary Shelley's letters to Sir Timothy Shelley and Lady Shelley, Whitton wrote on 3 September inviting her to call on him that day or the next but making clear that Shelley's parents refused to see her (*S&M*, IV, 973–74).

12. Mary Shelley misunderstood Whitton, who recommended to Sir Timothy Shelley that he make an allowance of £100 per annum for Percy Florence but made no recommendation on Mary Shelley's behalf. By the end of November, however, Sir Timothy Shelley agreed to make an annual allowance of £100 for Mary Shelley as well. All funds provided by Sir Timothy Shelley were to be deducted from the estate Mary Shelley would inherit upon Sir Timothy Shelley's death (Ingpen, *Shelley in England*, pp. 574–75).

13. The Novellos had moved to Shacklewell Green. Vincent Novello (1781–1861) was a famous composer and performer of music. With his son Joseph Alfred he founded, in December 1828, the publishing firm of Novello & Co., which is still in existence today. In 1808 Novello married Mary Sabilla Hehl (?1787–1854), who wrote a number of stories and novels and was respected as a woman who possessed both intellect and charm. The Novellos had eleven children, four of whom died in infancy or childhood (see 27 June [1825] for a list of ten of the children; the child missing is Julia Harriet [?1820], who died in infancy). The Novellos held frequent musical evenings in their home and were the friends of many noted figures in the world of literature and music, among them Hunt and Lamb. The Shelleys first met the Novellos on 8 March 1818 (*MWS Journal*). Upon her return to England, Mary Shelley was reintroduced into the Novello circle by a letter from Hunt, and she (along with Jane Williams, who had been introduced upon her return by a letter from Hunt) quickly became an intimate friend of the Novellos and members of their circle. The Novellos' eldest daughter was Mary Victoria (1809–98), who married Charles Cowden Clarke (1787–1877) on 5 July 1825. Clarke, an author and publisher, had numerous literary associations. He was a friend of the Lambs, the Hunts, and the Novellos and is credited with introducing the young Keats to poetry at his (Clarke's) father's school at Enfield. Individually and jointly, the Clarkes wrote many stories, essays, and books, several of which give details of the lives of the Novellos and their circle, including Mary Cowden Clarke and Charles Cowden Clarke, *Recollections of Writers* (London, 1878); and Mary Cowden Clarke, *My Long Life: An Autobiographic Sketch* (London, 1896) (see Altick, *The Cowden Clarkes*, pp. 1–8, 42–47, 68.)

14. *Mother-in-law* then referred to the mother of one's spouse or a stepmother. Since Jane Williams refers to Edward Williams's mother-in-law as "Mrs. Williams" (see, for example, Jane Williams's letter to Mary Shelley, 27 March 1823, Abinger MS.), we may conclude that Mary Shelley was writing about Williams's stepmother, Mary Ann Williams, rather than, as Jones speculated, a former mother-in-law of Williams's, implying a former marriage by Williams (*MWS Letters*, I, 315, n. 1).

15. Isabella Baxter Booth. Godwin recorded in his Journal that "Mrs. Booth & fille" dined with him and Mary Shelley on 3 September (Abinger MS.).

16. This sentence is omitted in Jones's text.

17. Reverend William Bengo Collyer (1782–1854), "Licentious Productions in High Life," *The Investigator, or Quarterly Magazine* 5 (October 1822): 315–73. Hunt denounced Collyer's vicious personal attack on Shelley in "Canting Slander, to the Reverend William Bengo Collyer," *Examiner*, 22 September 1822 (Reiman, *The Romantics Reviewed*, Part B, III, 1170–99). In the *Morning Chronicle* of 25

August 1823 Reverend Collyer publicly refuted accusations of homosexual activity, stating that the two instances cited were of a medical nature.

18. John and Leigh Hunt were divided over Leigh Hunt's claims to proprietary rights in the *Examiner*. On 3 October 1823 Leigh Hunt wrote to John Hunt: "I have so little time to write, and so great a desire to render the footing on which I am to stand in future, plain and simple, that I will say at once, that I will resume my station in *The Examiner*, to write for it all that I can write both political and literary; in return for which, all matters considered, I will also continue my old share of the profits. You will observe, that whatever I have written, in *The Examiner* or out of it, I have always considered it as my duty to you to take care that you should be the better for it, as far as lay in my power. When you set up the *Literary Examiner*, my notion was, that it was only a part of *The Examiner* in another shape, and that not being able to do more for us both with the *Liberal*, I returned to my *Examiner* tasks. I never dreamed of its being a "secession" from *The Examiner*, or most assuredly I should have paused before I struggled to get up a new paper in conjunction with new hands" (Brewer, *The Holograph Letters*, p. 158). On 14 October Leigh Hunt wrote to John Hunt: "I have received a letter from Mrs. Shelley, in which she exhorts me to draw upon you, being certain, she says, that you expect me to do so, and have been surprised at my not doing it. Not hearing from you on this point, and having had no friends near me to endorse a bill, if I had drawn it, I confess I never thought of such a thing: But I now do it, having no other alternative" (Brewer, *The Holograph Letters*, p. 158). The dispute resulted, however—despite the intervention over a number of years of Mary Shelley, Vincent Novello, William Hazlitt, Charles Armitage Brown, and others—in an estrangement of the brothers that was not resolved until 1837 (see Brown, *Letters*, for extensive details of the controversy).

To Leigh Hunt

September 18th [1823] 14 Speldhurst St.
Brunswick Sq.

My dear Hunt

There is a tone of melancholy about your letter which I received last night, dated Florence, which makes me melancholy also. God knows I do not wonder at it, care and ill health press upon you, and the sorrows of this strange life have collected themselves into a mighty host to oppress you. But I have not the same despair about you now that you have left the <u>non Cristiano</u> Albaro, and have established yourselves in Florence. You will see I doubt not some old friends there, for somehow or other people pop up in that city whom you imagined hundreds of miles off—you will make news ones too; you will find objects on all sides to amuse and distract you, and that is what you most especially want, for else the very sociability of your disposition preys upon you, and you become at times the most unsocial of men to those near you, because the quicker impulses of your nature stagnate—as they say warm water freezes quicker than cold. You must do your very best to rouse yourself, and I have no doubt you will do your <u>very</u> best—for being Patient and Very, both these qualities will assist you {to} bear and in time to be cheerful.

I hope by this time also you have heard from your brother, and that he has relieved you from some anxieties.[1] I have not seen him since I last wrote; I have been expecting him to call on me every day but he has not—so I shall call on him and learn what I can from him. I own the easiest way of managing the affair seems to me, that, economizing as much as you can, you ought to draw on him when necessary and write to inform him of your bill. This would save you and Marianne much anxiety and in fact be the same thing to him; for you must live, and you would not draw for more than is perfectly necessary. It would simplify the affair, and in the end he would have nothing to complain of, and would feel that.

I spoke to your brother when I saw him concerning the publication of such MSS as I had of our S— and he agreed to it. Since that Procter called on my father to say that two gentlemen great admirers of S— were willing to undertake the risk of such a publication if I would agree to it.[2] The risk I hope is none—I agreed mentioning that I had spoken to JH. Procter saw the latter immediately and then called upon me, shewing a zeal in the affair, which considering that he is an author & a poet pleased me mightily. I am now therefore fully occupied in preparing the MSS. Procter asked me if I would write a biographical notice.—This, just at this moment would I think better come from you.[3] I know you have prepared an article. This you might alter and enlarge, and without making a regular biography—write what we (you & I) would wish to be written. I should afterwards publish a complete edition of S's work—but the present volume would consist of unpublished pieces. (This latter circumstance is not yet settled—perhaps they will all be printed together{)} You have I think my copies of the Essay on Devils—Translation of Cyprian—Witch of Atlas and the Cyclops of Euripides—The Cyprian I could easily transcribe again. The Witch of Atlas I have a copy of corrected by S.—and those vacancies filled up which are in my copy. But I wish that you w^d send me immediately the Essay on Devils and the Cyclops—particularly the latter—for these were a few lines filled up—besides I should wish to see your correction of it & compare it with the orriginal.

Procter pleased me by his errand and also by his manners and appearance. He is evidently vain, yet not pretending, and his ill health is for me an interesting circumstance; since I have been so accustomed to Poets whose frame has been shattered by the mind, that a stout healthy person would rather seem to me a waggoner than a versifier. Yet after all, except the Dramatic Scenes I do not like Procter's style—and, worst of all, have not read much that he has written—so that when he alluded to some part of one of his poems, I am afraid I looked the ignorance I felt—I trust however this unhappy passage was in the Flood of Thessaly,[4] which considering Absence & travelling & arrivals I may be pardoned for not having <u>yet</u> read—I shall set about the task immediately, for he deserves that at least for the attention he has shewn in this affair—and though one need not praise an Author to his face—one must have read him. He said one or two things of LB which made me smile, knowing what is behind the curtain as well as I do—He said that he hoped he would not <u>fight</u> for the Greeks—

I told him that he might be at ease on that point, Helmets so fine were never made to hack—the existence of these helmets by the bye is well known here, as there was a paragraph in the Chronicle describing them[5]—Most people think it a calumny. LB may be happy in the certainty that he cannot be calumniated. There is a small knife for you, dear Polly—so—don't be severe, Marianne. Every one talks of the large sums he is to give—I wonder what Mavrocordato will say to them a few months hence.

I am going tomorrow to Richmond to see Tom[6] perform and to have a sight of the green leaves before their faded forms strew the ground. I am comfortable here as far as I can be in England—and worse than that—in London. My lodgings are neat & quiet—my servant good—my boy in delightful health & very happy & amiable. My time occupied & my thoughts also with how many thoughts of the past. But the future—My father intends to make my returning to Italy an affair of life and death with him, and makes my society appear so necessary to him, that I hardly know what to think or say—pazienza! At present I will not look beyond the present hour—I am here—so I am—where I shall be—Shall will know—and my motto being Alla Giornata—I shut my eyes & will not care.

There is one question I must not forget to ask you—if you write the biographical notice would it be in keeping to dedicate the book to you—& if not, do you think Trelawny would be pleased by a compliment he so richly deserves.[7]

I have just seen your brother, and I find to my great disappointment that he has not yet written to you, having waited to hear from you. There is only one good thing that I have heard, which is that so far from appreciating your delicacy in waiting for his permission to draw, he was perfectly unaware of this circumstance—I therefore reiterate what I said before that you had better draw when you must draw, only informing him that you have done so.—With regard to settled remittances his statement of facts is such, that at present it hardly appears possible to settle any thing—since all is at present on a kind of shifting ground one cannot well understand. I mentioned to him the papers concerning the property of the Examiner—He said that for 2 years you [had] done nothing for it, & he had been constantly employed giving his time and incurr[ing] danger—But he declined being a judge in his own cause & said that he wished that you should put it into the hands of two of your friends who should decide upon what writings ought to be drawn up and he would abide by their decision. He mentioned M[r] Novello & M[r] Procter as friends of yours who understood business. Your brother must be aware that your talents established the Examiner, and that its great falling off is in consequence of your desertion of it. But he says that it is getting up again now. I find that you have not mentioned to him that you want to draw—but I am sure that you will by the time that you receive this letter, so pray do—though drawing in this way it were best perhaps to draw for smaller sums at a time. Your brother repeats that you shall not be in difficulties from the moment that he can have any power to relieve you from them, and declares that he has nothing so much at heart as to relieve your mnid from pecuniary anxieties. He says that for a long time upon lowering the price of the Examiner, they received nothing from it & were even obliged to delay the usual instalments—but it is now rising—The Literary Examiner hardly as yet pays its way. I wish they got better writers for it—else I am convinced the Indicator is the sole cause of its sale.

What do I not wish concerning you, my dear, dear friends—but I do not see clearly what it is best to do—If your health permitted it, how excellent it would be to get some thing from another quarter besides your brother In the mean time I would have you seriously think of this proposition of drawing up writings concerning the Examiner, for it is slipping through your hands—& if help from you is the thing to keep up your share in it, I would not barter that for any share in the Literary Examiner.

You talk of heat—I am over a fire—but heat ought not to hurt you, or Italy must loose half its good for you. It never hurt either of us, and your West Indian blood[8] ought to protect you in some degree. Take care of yourself, dear Hunt—for this bad world cannot spare such as you—Why do cares so press upon you—alas alas why is all that is—& what was the power that snapt our chain last year?—

10 o'clock P.M.) I now conclude my letter, dear Hunt, and I wish I knew what words with which to conclude that might bring a smile to your lips or a happy thought to your mind. How truly you deserve to pass your days in ease, yet day after day goes on & no ease visits you. Yet try to be happy, try to bear life lightly—and I hope you will find some in Florence to render this task more easy—I am far away—my letters written in one mood may find you in another. All might go well if your health were good —in the first place therefore take care of that—dear Very Patient and dear Patient Very my heart enters into all the feelings of yours & sinks with them—but if you both get well a better sun may shine. Adieu, my best friends, confide in the affectionate attachment of your exiled Grandmother

MaryWS.

ADDRESS: Leigh Hunt Esq / Ferma in Posta / Firenze / Florence—L'Italie. POSTMARKS: (1) F23 / 198; (2) ANGLET[ERRE]; (3) CHAMBERY; (4) 4/ OTTO[B]RE. PUBLISHED: Jones, #195. TEXT: MS., Bodleian Library (MS., Shelley, Adds., c. 6, ff. 17–18).

1. See 9–11 September [1823].

2. Nicholas Waller Procter, Thomas Lovell Beddoes, and Thomas Forbes Kelsall guaranteed the costs of publishing 250 copies of Shelley's *Posthumous Poems*. It was long thought that Bryan Waller Procter was a guarantor, but Charles H. Taylor, Jr., has argued that the evidence suggests that Procter's brother was financially involved and that Procter served as intermediary between Mary Shelley and the guarantors (Taylor, *Early Collected Editions*). John Hunt published 500 copies (250 at his own risk) shortly after 1 June 1824. In less than two months 309 copies of the *Posthumous Poems* were in circulation. The remainder were removed from sale at the insistence of Sir Timothy Shelley, whose opposition to Shelley's being brought to public attention threatened the arrangements for an annual settlement for Mary

Shelley and Percy Florence, then being negotiated. To comply with Sir Timothy Shelley's wishes, Mary Shelley was also obliged to place with Peacock the manuscripts she had intended for a volume of Shelley's prose. (For details of the publication and suppression of the *Posthumous Poems*, see Ingpen, *Shelley in England*, pp. 576–86, 618; Beddoes, *Letters*, pp. 1–3, 22–23; and 22 August [1824].)

3. Hunt agreed to supply a biographical notice but later changed his mind (see 13–18 June [1824], n. 6; 8 April [1825]).

4. *Dramatic Scenes, and Other Poems* (London: C. and J. Ollier, 1819); *The Flood of Thessaly* (London: Henry Colburn, 1823). Shelley seems to have admired *Dramatic Scenes* more than Procter's other works (see Procter, "*Dramatic Scenes" and "Marcian Colonna"*, ed. Donald H. Reiman [New York: Garland Publishing, 1978], p. vii).

5. See 7 August [1823].

6. Tom Kent, Marianne Hunt's brother, then an actor (see 13–18 June [1824]).

7. *Posthumous Poems* has no dedication.

8. Hunt's father and grandfather had lived in Barbados (Blunden, *Leigh Hunt*, pp. 2–5).

To Louisa Holcroft — Oct. 2nd [1823] — 14 Speldhurst St.
Brunswick Sq.

My dear Louise

I have not written to you but I have not forgotten you or Versailles, or the Caffè Françoise or your young ladies who get happiness through demonstration & Q.E.D. How are you all? How is Mrs Kenny with her kind heart? How is Mr Kenny whom we walked until he had a sprained ancle. I have been here a month—seeing few people & wishing alack! that I were in Italy, & yet finding myself tied by the leg. If I talk of cloudless skies, my father becomes cloudy, & seems to have my stay so much at heart, that it seems selfish in one so useless as I am, to be worse than useless and give pain. And yet I get very impatient with rainy days, Hackney coaches, spoiled pelisses, "Round & sound, twopence a pound"—cold firesides, dull newspapers & the rest of the daily round. What I enjoy is my quiet which I could get better in Italy, & the best friend I have here would go with me if I went. And I could go for I fancy that my father-in law will make me an allowance, which though poor enough here would be riches in dear Italy—He has already given me a present supply[1]—so that much good at least has been accomplished by my journey though I am sorry to say that I do not think that I look any taller than I did at Versailles, nor hold my head higher, which perhaps Mr Kenny meant—I only do that in Italy where I should be a great lady on £200 per ann. and ramble about mountains & ches{t}nut woods until I should tire you all out. I am well here as so is my boy, whom (though he does not speak a word of English) I can leave for a few hours without his tormenting his keeper as he did poor kind Ellen.[2]

I dare say you will wonder what change I find in London—and I must, say of it, as I did of you, that it is very much grown—& grown out of my knowledge too which was never very extensive: but now I think I could find my way better on foot to the Coliseum at Rome than hence to Grosvenor Square—ought I not to go by Fenchurch St—through Park Lane and so to Fetter Lane which is not far off from Grosvenor Sq. any one will tell me if I ask—But then they speak bad English with so vulgar an accent that I am in despair. I walked up Holborn Hill the other day, repeating to myself Oh when shall I be in Italy again! Why did I ever leave my dolce Nido![3]—

I saw your sister Fanny[4] for a few minutes about 3 weeks ago she seemed very well—I saw Lamb who did not say that I was grown or even altered. M^rs G[5] tells me I look 16—but unluckily strangers unwittingly tell me I look 30. A French Gentleman (in France) who wanted to be very polite, on my mentioning my having seen the Louvre asked me if it was during the peace of Amiens[6] which was, I think in —97 the year I w[as] born. And an English Gentleman in an English stage, hea[rd I] had been at Naples asked me if I was there [ ][7] Lady Hamilton made common cause agains[t] which event took place I think some [ ] Lamb has been ill hitherto but I expect [ ] house on saturday & shall be delighted to see [ ] your message.

Adieu my dear Louise—My love to your Mother, whom for more reasons than one I should be very glad to see again, i.e. at Versailles—I have but one reason to wish to see her here My best remembrances to Mr Kenney —Has Elen forgiven [ ]rgotten) the trouble I gave her—And James and [ ]s & Therese & the young Hercules whose name [ ] they all.

Most faithfully Yours
Mary WShelley

ADDRESS: Miss Holcroft / Dieu vous benisse / Versailles, &c &c &c. PUBLISHED: Jones, #197. TEXT: MS., Pforzheimer Library.

1. £100 per annum (see 9–11 September [1823]).

2. Ellen Holcroft, Louisa Holcroft's sister (see 29 November [1825]).

3. "Sweet nest."

4. Louisa Holcroft's sister Fanny Holcroft, who had written a novel entitled *Fortitude and Frailty*. The Gisbornes had seen her in May 1822 and had found her a "firm loyalist" (Gisborne, *Journals and Letters*, p. 86).

5. Since Maria Gisborne knew the Holcroft family, this could refer to her or to Mrs. Godwin.

6. The Treaty of Amiens was signed on 27 March 1802, bringing peace between Britain and France until war was resumed on 16 May 1803.

7. From this point on the right-hand quarter of the manuscript is missing.

TO LEIGH HUNT

[14 Speldhurst Street Brunswick Square]
October 2nd (Sunday Oct 5th) [1823]

My dear Hunt

I spent a few days about a fortnight ago, at Richmond, in the midst of the Hunters. I wished if possible to see Tom in some character by which I might send M. [*Marianne*] my notion of her brother's performance. But that was impossible. The Manager and his lady of the R. theatre (a gentle couple both nearly 60 years of age—and as fat & wrinkled as need be) are so fond of playing the characters of young lovers in high comedy that poor Tom gets quite in despair. Mrs H. [*Hunter*] is not only reconciled to the stage but buys & makes all his dresses herself, and except now and then a quarrel about the fashion of a jacket Tom's word is law in the house. I was excessively amused by the conversation at dinner the first day I was there, Nancy[1] present. We spoke of Henry H. [*Hunt*][2] & Mrs H. [*Hunter*] said that she did not like him that he was so conceited & pragmatical and that nothing w^d^ do him so much good as getting into some exceeding scrape. "Yes—" said Tom, "His father ought to treat him as Dowton treated his son—finding his pretentions to morality very inconvenient he went to the best looking ladies at the saloon at the ⟨Opera⟩ theatre entreating them to seduce his son, & promising them any reward if they should succeed."— "Excellent!" cried Mrs H. "I only wish these same ladies would get hold of Henry, they w^d^ do him a world of good"—What think you of this Polly?

Last thursday I dined at Mr Novellos with—ah! Hunt!—the Emerald Pin and her Cara Sposo.[3]—She made me a speech on seeing me, which for the life of me I could not answer, for her voice was so exactly like your mimickry of it, that I was quite aghast. They all joined chorus in lamenting your absence and the E.P. became quite eloquent on the topic. They seemed to be going on as of old. Mr A.G. had dared Novello to make his wife have a boiled goose for dinner. At the dinner hour both Novello & the goose were absent—M^r^ G was triumphant and E.P. loud in her applause of M^rs^ N's resistance to the matrimonial yoke. Presently Mr N. came in & his lady ordered his dinner to be brought in—the covered dish, uncovered, discovered the boiled goose in all its non glory—Anastatia seemed a little confounded—M^r^ G— put on his spectacles, at first declared it only pale roasted, but then convinced both he & Mr N. ate heartily of the boiled goose to the scandal of Mr C. C. Clarke[4] and Mr Holmes[5] who ⟨declared⟩ as batchelors w^d^ by no means patronize the spoiling of the goose. We had music in the evening—Beethoven Hayden. Mozart—The March in Alceste & the March in the Zauberflaut—but no singing—on saturday (the day after tomorrow) Jane & I are to go and Mrs B. Hunt[6] is to be there. But a word of Shacklewell and their new House—both odious—the G's are in despair at the removal for they are in King St. again. The house is a huddled nest of 16 rooms—low & small—they have a dismal garden & a damp arbour where they made us moralize—for they are themselves as yet perfectly content—Dio faccia che seguitono cosi[7]—. Do not mention my disapprobation, for one must not put them out of conceit of a place they have taken for 12 years—& on which for economy's sake they have laid out a great deal of money.

You must know that Southey has attacked Elia's religion in the Quarterly & whined over the fate of T.L.H. [*Thornton Leigh Hunt*] (my favourite child) for not having better religious principles instilled into him. This roused Lamb & on the spur of the moment he has written a reply which has appeared in the London Magazine.[8] With regard to religion he turns the tables on Southey, and tells him that no one can tell what religion he is of—tells him that any spirit of joking that he (Lamb) may have on that subject he imbibed from Southey himself—telling him that he had all his life made a jest of the devil—saying: "you have made wonderfully free with, and been mightily pleasant upon, the popular idea & attributes of him. A noble Lord, your brother Visionary, has scarcely taken greater liberties with the material keys and mere Catholic notion of St. Peter. You have flattered him in prose, you have chanted him in goodly odes. You have been his Jester; Volunteer Laureat, & self-elected Court Poet of Beelzebub." —What after this will become of the Satanic school?—Southey has spoken ill of L's friends—he calls them over, mentioning their various good qualities briefly & then more fully enters upon your character & his intimacy with Hazlitt. He says: "Accident introduced me to the acquaintance of Mr L.H.—& the experience of his many friendly qualities confirmed a friendship between us. You, who have been misrepresented yourself, I should hope, have not lent an idle ear to the calumnies which have been spread abroad concerning this gentleman. I was admitted to his household for several years, & do most solemnly aver, that I believe him to be in his domestic relations as correct as any man."—He then alludes to Rimini, disapproving of the subject, but saying that "it has nothing in common with the black horrors sung by Ford and Massinger."[9]—& says that he looks upon the author of Rimini "As a man of taste and a poet." {"}He is better than so, he is one of the most cordial-minded men I ever knew, a matchless fire-side companion. I mean not to affront or wound your feelings when I say that, in his more genial moods, he has often reminded me of you. There is the same air of mild dogmatism—the same condescending to boyish sportiveness—in both your conversations. His hand writing is so much the same with your own, that I have opened more than one letter of his, hoping, nay, not doubting, but that it was from you, & have been disappointed (he will bear with me for saying so) at the discovery of my error."—He alludes to your opinions concerning marriage, which he says are opposite to his own—but he says neither for these opinions "nor for his political asperities & petulancies, which are wearing out with the heats & vanities of youth, did I select him for a friend; but for qualities which fitted him for that relation. I do not know whether I flatter myself with being the occasion, but certain it is, that, touched with some misgivings for sundry harsh things which he had written aforetime against our friend C.—[*Coleridge*], before he left this country he sought a reconciliation with that gentleman (himself being his own introducer), & found it.—L.H. is now in Italy; on his departure to w^{h} land, with much regret, I took my leave of him and his little family—7 of them, Sir, with their Mother—as kind a set of little people (T.H. & all) as affectionate children, as ever blessed a parent. Had you seen them, Sir, I think you w^d^ not have looked upon them as so many little Jonases—but rather as pledges of the Vessel's safety, that was to bear such a freight of love.—I wish you w^d^ read M^r^ H's— lines to that same T.H. "6 years old during a sickness". "Sleep breathes at last from out thee, my little patient boy—(they are to be found in the 47th page of Foliage) & ask yourself how far they are out of the spirit of Christianity. I have a letter from Italy, received but the other day into wh. L.H. has put as much heart, & as many friendly yearnings after old associates, & native country, as, I think, paper can well hold. It w^d^ do you no hurt to give that the perusal also."—

He then turns to Hazlitt—but it is too long to quote—he regrets his instability—but speaks of him with infinite kindness—

I copy all this, dear Hunt, because I am sure it will give you pleasure to find how your friends in England remember you. And you are comfortless I fear there where I w^d^ fain be, in dear Florence. I do dislike this place—yet here I am with little hope of being quickly elsewhere. I was glad to find that you had found an old acquaintance at Florence[10] & shall be happy to see her (could you entrust her with my watch—but do not write to me by her—or by any one, except the post—I have a particular dislike to letters by a private hand—if they have any thing in them worth reading)—What a divine place Italy is! It seems to nurture all gentle feelings & to warm with peculiar sensibility an affectionate heart; its winds whisper a thousand expressions of kindness—clouds vanish from the mind as from the sky—Here!—methinks a cold rain falls on the feelings & quenches the living spark that was lighted there—it is a dreary, rainy cold infeelicissimo paese. When oh when when shall I escape?—I walked the other day with William to the fields about Kentish Town, old friends I doubt not of yours. The day was fine—those fields are particularly beautiful shaded by majestic elms & looking towards the woody uplands of Highgate. Next summer I shall get out to some place like this, & enjoy the best part of England its fields & trees—Yet I love the mountains of Tuscany, its olive copses & chestnut wood, its dancing streams & vine shaded allies & its transcendant sky better than the green grass here.—So you were disappointed with the Venus di Medici—so was I. She is an artful little thing—so unpretending that you almost think her insignificant, but she creeps upon you—she & all her excellencies until you are quite taken with her grace & softness. You go to the gallery that is well—you see some society—that also is well. You did not see the scenery of Valperga—but all Tuscany bears the character of that scenery, though the country around Florence perhaps less than any—it is too much inhabited, too little solitary (N.B. no further notice has been taken of Valperga in the E—r [*Examiner*]—another N.B. did you send the copy of that book to Mrs Mason—if you did not or have one to spare, will you send it across the Apennines to the Guiccioli at Bologna, as I promised her one, & she writes to remind me of the promise—(I have asked her also to get a book or two for me, which she will send you—you will pay her—& forward me the books by the first opportunity—Do you know that the duty on my foreign books comes to £14—the whole packages will cost me £20—so beware of purchases to bring home with you).—

Adieu—dear Hunt, my own Polly—& do you, Polly, write; for I learn more of the real state of things in 3 lines from you than 3 pages from H. God bless you all—dear Grandchildren—you see I have a large sheet of paper & will fill it soon—& again declare myself what I now do enattendant Your affectionate Exile.—

(Sunday Oct 5th) I passed a very pleasant evening at the Novello's yesterday—At dinner there was only Jane & the Lambs—the Gliddons did not come. This was the first time Miss Lamb had come out—they (she in particular) seemed very glad to see me and I go to spend the day at her house on Thursday.[11]—In the evening Mr and Mrs B. [*Blaine*] Hunt came & Mr F [*Francesco*] Novello[12]—we had a great deal of music beginning (to please me) with sacred music—introducing Mariannes favorite hymn from the Flaut[ ]—Afterwards we had several duets &c from Figaro. Looking at Mr F.N—'s [*Francesco Novello's*] Italian phisiognomy & gestu[res I] almost have fancied myself in Italy—I was somewhat disappointed in Mrs B.H—'s singing—but [ ] not in voice. The singers went away early & then we had several pieces from Himmel,[13] as you [ ] desired—they were excessively beautiful, & I dare say I shall think them more so when I hear them again my ears were filled then with Handel & Mozart (by the bye, do send me the name of that air of Handels of which you know only a few bars) and yet I was greatly pleased. Nothing can be more amiable than Mr Novello's manners to me, and I tell you this, because since it chiefly (wholly I may say) arises from your mode of writing to him concerning me you may see with what an active spirit of friendship he is animated towards you.—You know there resides with them C. C. Clarke, who puts one out of all patience with his "charming!" & "beautiful!" as an accompaniment, a little discordant or so, si guasta un po la musica, e si guasta un po le parole, ma pero[14]—with Handel & Mozart—however he is the image of good humor & there is Mr Holmes—Werter the II—passionately fond of music & playing well—& almost in appearance overpowered with the notes his fingers strike Mrs Novello is there ever smiling —& all the children Victoria—che poi e piutosto bruttina[15]—Alfred who is a nice looking boy—the rest I forget except Mary, two years & a half old—the flower of the flock, the only pretty one among them—like I guess Sidney, from Marianne's description of him; & Novello shaking his sides—enjoying his own & your pleasure as he plays—& looking smiling despair when the tingle of a tea spoon clashes with his melody.

Messrs. N. & C. walked part of the way home with us—& I laid hold of the former that I might talk of your affairs to him. I mentioned to him your brother's proposition of referring the question of the E— [*Examiner*] to him & Procter. Novello objected to being a party on the sole score of not understanding the business & feeling himself incapable in consequence of doing justice to either—he mentioned Mr Colson[16] as a fitter person—saying that he had opportunities of proving him & was certain that you had not a more zealous friend in the world. He spoke very highly of your brother, as a man of high honour & generosity (I repeat his words) but allowed that Henry in every way was not a person to whom all the interests of your family ought to be confided. He thought no time ought to be lost (not a moment) in ⟨sell⟩ arranging the terms of this affair—& mentioned that perhaps it w^d^ be best for each brother to name a friend—though Colson as the friend of both w^d^ equally represent both interests & Procter be in—because it is right to have two in such a case. Such, dear friends was the result of my conversation with Novello—than whom none c^d^ appear more warm hearted zealous & friendly towards you—He had not had a hint on the subject before—I took him unawares and thus all he said sprung solely from himself.

Have you thought of your notice for Shelley's works—they will all be printed mingled with what has not before been published—I want very much the Cyclops & Essay on devils. I am now busy writing an Article for the London[17]—after which I shall begin a Novel—not Alfred[18]—more wild & imaginative & I think more in my way. Novello will help it greatly—as I listen to music (especially instrumental) new ideas rise & develope themselves, with greater energy & truth that [*than*] at any other time—thus I am becoming very fond of instrumental music of which before I was more careless—singing confines ones thoughts to the words—in mere playing they form a song for themselves which if it be not more in harmony with the notes at least is more so with ones tone of mind.

Well here is an end of my paper—but not of a tenth part of what I have to say—I intended to have said ten million of things which now I leave to your imagination—I was going to say why I think that you thought too hardly of me heretofore—I am after all the same as then—the same weak fluctuating creature—but not all you say—yet I dont like myself I promise you—either then or now. You can hardly point me out a person whose frame of mind I do not prefer to my own. But this, expressed in these few words will be almost unintelligible to you. And as my paper grows less & less I can only say, my dear Hunt, and dear, dear Polly that I am your

Affectionate friend
MWS

ADDRESS: Leigh Hunt Esq / Ferma in Posta / Firenze / Florence—Italy. POSTMARKS: (1) Catherine St. / Strand; (2) F23 / 205; (3) ANGLETERR[E]; (4) CHAMBERY; (5) CORRISP[ZA ESTERA DA] GENOVA; (6) 23 / OTTOBRE. PUBLISHED: Jones, #196. TEXT: MS., Bodleian Library (MS., Shelley, Adds., d. 5, ff. 71–72).

1. Nancy Hunter, Marianne Hunt's stepsister (see 13–18 June [1824]).

2. John Hunt's son.

3. The Hunts had met their close friends Arthur and Alistasia Gliddon (nicknamed "the Emerald Pin") through the Novellos in 1819. Hunt referred with kind

feelings to Gliddon's snuff and tobacco shop in King Street in his essay "Coffee Houses and Smoking." Arthur Gliddon was also the publisher of Hunt's *Indicator*. Arthur Gliddon's nephew John Gliddon married Mary Florimel Hunt, and Katherine Gliddon, Arthur Gliddon's niece, married Thornton Hunt (Tatchell, *Leigh Hunt*, pp. 58, 61, 62; Hunt, *Correspondence*, I, 192–94, 210–13; *SC*, VI, 796).

4. See 9–11 September [1823], n. 13.

5. Edward Holmes (1797–1859) was a musician and musical commentator. Holmes was a schoolmate and close friend of Keats's at the Enfield School, where he also met his lifelong friend Charles Cowden Clarke. He studied music with Novello and lived with the Novellos for a number of years.

6. Perhaps Mrs. Blaine Hunt, who gave Cecilia Novello singing lessons (Altick, *The Cowden Clarkes*, p. 72).

7. "May God will that they continue like this."

8. Southey's article in the January *Quarterly*, "The Progress of Infidelity," referred to the Elia essays only incidentally, quoting from "Witches and Other Night Fears," which mentions "Dear little T.H." Lamb's response in the October *London Magazine* particularly praised Hunt and Hazlitt. On 19 November 1823 Southey wrote Lamb a conciliatory letter, which Lamb promptly answered, ending their quarrel (Lucas, *Charles Lamb*, II, 108–13).

9. John Ford (fl. 1639) and Philip Massinger (1583–1640), British playwrights.

10. A Mrs. Payne (see 20 October–3 November [1823]).

11. Mary Shelley was also invited to the Lambs' on 15 November, when the Novellos were also invited (Lamb, *Letters* [Lucas], II, 407).

12. Vincenzo Novello's brother.

13. Johann Nepomuk Hummel (1778–1837), Austrian composer, pianist, and conductor.

14. "He spoils the music a little, and spoils the words a little, but however."

15. "Who, then, is rather homely."

16. Walter Coulson (?1794–1860), lawyer, author, editor. At one times amanuensis to Jeremy Bentham, he became a parliamentary reporter for the *Morning Chronicle* and went on to become editor of the *Traveller*, which in 1823 was united with the *Globe* under Coulson's editorship. Among his friends he numbered Hazlitt, Lamb, Clarke, and Hunt.

17. Charles Lamb had recommended Mary Shelley to John Taylor and James Augustus Hessey, proprietors of the *London Magazine*, in September 1823 (MS., Pforzheimer Library). In April 1824 Thomas Lovell Beddoes wrote to Thomas Forbes Kelsall: "Mrs. Shelley has written lately in the London—a paper on ghosts in the March No & 'The Bride of Modern Italy' in the present" (Beddoes, *Letters*, p. 23). F. L. Jones points out that almost half of "On Ghosts" (*London Magazine* 9 [March 1824]: 253–56) was written into Mary Shelley's Journal while she was in Italy. Jones notes that "The Bride of Modern Italy" (*London Magazine* 9 [April 1824]: 351–63) contains Mary Shelley's first literary depiction of Emilia Viviani, who appears as Clorinda. Shelley is depicted in the figure of a seventeen-year-old English artist (*MWS Letters*, I, 272–73. See also 3 December 1820 to Leigh Hunt, n. 5; 7 March 1822, n. 13).

18. See 3–5 August [1823], n. 11.

To Thomas Jefferson Hogg 14 Speldhurst St. Brunswick Square.
Oct. 18 [1823]

My dear Jefferson

In this sunless country the exercise of the affections can alone awaken one from lethargy—I never cling to my friends (cioè to 1 or 2 human beings) as much as now. All is so desolate—Streets, mud—cockneyism—ballad singers—cries—hackney coaches—lodgeings—cheerless solitude—what a compound! let me turn from it.

Am I, Jefferson, the same that you once knew? I seem to myself a dream—Italy was reality—a strange phastasmagoria is painted on this clouded sky. You know how very few friends we ever had in England—Yourself & Peacock were the extent of the Catalogue. Peacock has not yet been to see me; Your letter was a great pleasure to me thro' some accident I never received your answer to my last winters letter consequently I half feared to find you cold & careless—Your letter relieved me from this dread & was a great delight.

I shall expect to see you when you arrive—I have seen the Gibsornes a few times (they are immoveable—& rain & dirt are no great aiders of friendly intercourse) I often see my dear best Jane, she has so affectionate an heart that it is impossible not to love her tenderly for her own sake; and bound up with the reality of my lost life she is as dear to me as any creature that exists.—You will be glad to see my little Italian, he is a fine boy.—Adieu—I am always at home of a morning generally of an evening—

Yours
Mary W. Shelley

ADDRESS: Jefferson Hogg. PUBLISHED: Scott, *New Shelley Letters*, pp. 144–45. TEXT: MS., Pforzheimer Library.

To Leigh Hunt [14 Speldhurst Street Brunswick Square]
October 20th (Nov. 3rd) [1823]

You will be gratified to hear, dear Hunt, that I celebrated your birthday yesterday at the Novellos.[1] He is such a worshipper of yours that it seems to make him ten years younger to do anything to your honour, and this animated his playing, while he sighed over it—That Hunt were here! We had there Frank Novello whom I delight to see; he transports me into Italy by his very best kind of Italian face, manners & speech; his voice too is very delightful, and was the only very good voice there; how we missed you in the duets—There was a Mr Evans treble, & Charles Robertson tenor.[2] He sang with spirit but he wants power sadly—He is looking much older than when I saw him at Hamstead, & he is almost the only person in whom I perceive much change—he made one good pun—They were laughing at him for the pretty figure he cut as Susannah when he bowed to F.N. saying "now I think Susanna has a very pretty Figaro (figure o)"

There was the E.P. [*Emerald Pin*] and Caro Sposo. She was remarkably quiet thinking of old times I suppose. there was my dear Jenny [*Jane Williams*] to whom Ah Perdona! gave a great headach—There was Mr G. Gliddon just returned from patria mia, loving it almost as much as I, and looking the picture of content & good humour—There was of course Mr Clarke with a face like a bird's skull and Werter II i.e. Mr Holmes—You know how delightfully Novello selects and arranges music for such a party —we had first Church music—among it Mi lasci O Madre Amata—Deh prendi un dolce simplessa the Priests song in the Zauberflaüt, & your March in Alceste arranged for sacramental psalms—then we had Ah perdona—sung by ⟨H⟩ C.R. [*Henry Charles Robertson*] and F.N. [*Francesco Novello*]—but not sung as you have sung it—the passion and expression of your voice in certain parts of that—& in the breathless conclusion could not be equalled by these (there, Polly!). After this, airs from Figaro—Cosi fan tutte and D.G. [*Don Giovanni*] had their turn until the singers were quite exhausted. There sat Novello, giving the keys an expression no other creature ever gave, every now and then at a favourite passage, a smile stealing over his features, and giving a little side glance to see who sympathized with him. In short, dear Hunt, if you and my best Marianne had been there the evening would have been perfect. Nor would Mar. have sat like a stone; everybody was occupied by music and when at supper the spirits rose to drink "Leigh Hunt's health" there was nothing to shock her —for neither Jenny or I were anything but pleased—I gave way a little to the "giddy school girl"—After a glee or two the coach came along side & a long after walk from Shacklewell—William[3] makes himself my squire, and he finds the Novellos an immense acquisition for he is passionately fond of music—I was housed by two and now the next morning write to make you enter into some of the pleasure that [was ani]mated by your spirit, which seemed looking over us as your Mercury from its pedestal actually did.

Since beginning to write this letter I have seen your brother. It is useless mentioning business until I have had your answers to my letters on those subjects, for which I am very anxious. With regard to what you say of the L.E. [*Literary Examiner*] you know I perfectly concur—but it is established —to change would have a bad effect—That & the dropping of the L. [*Liberal*] would so affect any new periodical work you undertook that I am convinced that you w^d^ have to wait many numbers without reaping any profit—until the public were satisfied that it would continue—you cd not afford that. The Indicator has an excellent name—the worst of it, is, that in its present form it cannot be bound up with the old Indicator which is a great drawback.[4] As to a Quarterly or Monthly Magazine—besides what I have already said—you being abroad—it must have a competent Editor—a literary one—Neither your brother or Nephew are fit for the task.—I am anxious too to hear what you do about a Notice for S.—I am yet undecided whether to print a Vol. of unpublished ones {or} of the whole together—

I encline to the former—as it w[d] be a specimen of how he could write without shocking any one—and afterwards an edition of the whole might be got up inserting any thing too shocking for this Vol. but I sh[d] be very glad of your opinion. Your brother tells me that you are going into the country. I am very sorry for this. You will have no evening society, nor ever be drawn out to the Opera &c—You will not find so many conveniences for a winter residence in any Italian country house, as in the town, Albaro was one of the best I ever saw, and si figuri the cold there. In short you might as well be in the Great De{s}art as in Italy if you are in the Country in the Winter—Not that it w[d] be so with every one—but I know you, my friend; With all your likings & talents for society you must be sought & drawn out—that cannot happen—& for heaven's sake take care you do not get outside a gate that shuts alle venti quattro—if my opinion and wishes have any weight do not go into the country in the winter. And my dear Polly! she is ill again; how truly sorrowful this is—she must take care of herself—she ought to be relieved from her weight of domestic cares—but how? Except for this ill news your last letter was very gratifying to me. I saw that I was not misunderstood—& I feared that I should be so—Moreover I saw that you sympathized with me—and that was quite right.—I have a world of things to say to you on that & many subjects—but they must be said & when will that be? I detest England more & more—its fogs rains & wind are bolts bars and high walls in the way of enjoyment, even if one had money, and with so little as I have they are unsurmountable. In short, I sigh ardently for Italy, and would give ten worlds to have celebrated y[r] birthday with you at Florence, delighted as I was by the Paradise of Sweet Sounds at the Novellos—I often think you may return except that it appears impossible. Marianne's health, your own—want of money—& yet you w[d] enjoy yourself more here, & once set a going here, if you c[d] keep y[r] health, w[d] earn doubly what you get there—But there are so many ifs—that prophecy veils her eyes, and hope hardly dares raise hers as the Chariots of the Hours pass, bringing with them the Unknown To Come. Adieu, my dear friends, Very Patient and Patient Very—I do not know when I shall finish this letter—but with so large a paper before me—it appears to me best to write this journal wise—& bring you as nearly as possible in contact with scenes that want you both only to be perfectly delightful—Your Exile—MWS—

(Oct. 26th) I went to sup the other night at the Lambs—They have a house at Islington looking over the New River I cannot say much for the beauty or rurality of the spot but they are pleased—They were both in good humour. Lamb told us[5] William was with me that he once made a fable for a Peacock and Hog—Said the Hog—Why go you flaunting about—spreading you tail and waving your neck do you not know that beauty is only skin deep?—Replied the Peacock—O good M[r] Hog how can you say so? I am sure if your beauty was but half as deep as your skin—how handsome you would be. M[rs] Payne is I hear returned[6]—I have not seen her. She has not of course got my watch—do not think I am impatient & so send it by any but the safest of safe hands—but I do want it.—Last night Jane and I were at the Gliddons with the Novello's. We passed a pleasant evening. The E.P. [*Emerald Pin*] is cheerful enough but more quiet than I expected tho' Mr N. says that she is the same as she always was—Mr Novello is my prediletto I like him better & better each time I see him—his excessive good nature, enthusiastic friendship for you—his kindness towards me & his playing have quite won my heart. William & I took a long walk today in the way of Shacklewell—I tried to like it—especially as next summer I must go into the country—(ahime Italia!) & sh^d^ like to go near them. But it is all so ugly—Lamb says, speaking of its neighbourhood—"I like drab coloured fields"—I can endure them if they be sun parched & richly shaded by the fresh grapes but fire dried & embellished by brick kilns—oh questo—no! We dined at the Novello's—She only was at home—Vincenzo came in just as we were going away—but it was a pleasure to see him tho' but for a minute. This walk has tired me, somewhat in body—more in spirits—the dense clouds—& dull scenery made me think of other changes besides sun & mountains & streams. Alas, that I should have been in familiar intercourse with my lost one, wise, imaginative & feeling—what conversations we have had during our walks—now—I must get into the midst of books & study to recollect myself—raise myself from the vile every day life that clings to one—Good hearts (superlatively good—par excellence) have a poetry of their own—and it is sufficiently elevating to mingle with them—but where goodness is negative—the want of refinement and cultivation is annoying and depressing. If I do stay in this odious country any time I must accommodate my mode of life to my mode of thought—and abstract myself entirely where sympathy does not imperiously call me out. Oh what a change, dark &—heavy has come over my scene of life—I struggle like an animal in a net—I can only at times, when I banish thought—endure it—To have lived in Italy w^d^ have been still to have kept a part of my Shelley—here—shades—well never mind—good night—tomorrow—Greek shall lay this evil spirit in the company of Homer I am with one of his best friends—and in reading the books he best loved I collect his acquaintances about me. Adieu dear Hunt—forgive me if I grumble a little—do you know I am a very good girl after all—ask Mr Novello if I am not.—

(Oct. 29th) I have just written to Bessy to ask whether she has heard from you, for your silence both public & private makes me anxious. I saw your brother today—he is in despair at the non appearance of Indicators. Something [ ] must have happened to cause this long[7] suspension—yet no ill I trust Dear Polly, when Hunt does not write why do you not put pen to paper, just to say how you all are, what doing or suffering. One line indeed from you tells me more of the real picturesque state of you all than much from Hunt—but you neither of you write, and guessing on so momentous a subject is a most painful employment.

Hogg is come to town—He came to me immediately—And appears to me (con una cosa di meno)[8] the same as ever. He looks uncommonly well in health—I passed yesterday evening with him and Jane at the Ghisbornes—this little set—Jane, gentle and elegant, Hogg witty, kind & queer, Mr G— inquisitive humble, affectionate & clever & I—they call me an Avalanche non so troppo il perche—forse da qualch [?onni] somigliante al bichiere d'ac[qua[9]][10] together, find out places, & the evening passes delightfully—Henry [ ] quiet—knowing everything & always with some news about [ ] plan—which—God knows—may help change the appearance of the [ ] love her more and more—She is so affectionate, good & kind [ ] know—both being in love with the same person—Ah Polly—[ ] everybody—my oldest & newest friends—& they all assure me that [ ] as may have made me appear so—but I am sure that I am [ ]tachment—Who shd it be but your best friend—dear, kind, open [ ] Jane likes Mrs N— and so perhaps may I—but she is not [ ] words that he is—& so as yet I prefer him.

I kept up my spirits but seeing Hogg was, as you may guess [ ] dreadfully so—but afterwards during the evening—his voice ma[nner] & words unaltered from what they used to be, associated as they are—came often like poignards through me & made me aghast & sad at the miserable change[11]—When in company I fly from these thoughts & take refuge in far greater gaiety than is otherwise natural to me. And once excited if some painful revulsion come not I easily forget myself—& at first carried away soon get beyond & carry with me the spirit of the company.—This will be a strange letter before it is completed: tell me that you are pleased (& not perfectly tired out with this journal kind of writing & I will continue thus—It will at least let you see how I pass a part of my time{)} The rest is spent in solitude—reading—writing—studying—Adieu—[I] hope to hear from you before I close this many wandering rigmarole—

(Nov. 3rd) Having just heard from Bessy that she has not heard from you I send my letter, a swift footed courier, to entreat you to relieve us all from our painful suspense—I would fain persuade myself that it is only il solito modo—and that no sinister event occasioned this painful silence—Yet all things considered—I fear, and know not what to think My S'—s poems are ready—I publish now the unpublished only—I long to know whether you write & what you write as that must determine me—I want the Cyclops particularly—you need not mind the Cyprian, I shall copy that again— I want that part of my own "Choice"[12] I mentioned to you send these two things immediately You had better address them to your brother—But at least dear Hunt, or you dear Polly, write and tell us how you all are.

I had several things to tell you but have no heart now. I saw Procter the other day, he says that he shall write to you. He has much pleased me by the way in which he speaks of our Shelley—How unlike LB. and yet S. eclipses him more than the other. He is not well & that interests me also—as I told you before I have always a sneaking kindness for these delicately healthed Poets.—Poor Keats I often think of him now.

I saw the Novellos at my lodgings sunday. N. [*Novello*] enquired tenderly after you and is very anxious. Write then, good creatures, and relieve us—Your affec[tionate] Grandmother blesses you.

MaryWS

ADDRESS: Leigh Hunt Esq / Ferma in Posta / Firenze / Florence—Italie. POSTMARKS: (1) ANGLETE[RRE]; (2) CHAMBERY; (3) CORRESP[ZA ESTERA DA] GENOVA; (4) [ ] / NOVEMB[RE]. PUBLISHED: Jones, #199. TEXT: MS., Bodleian Library (MS., Shelley, Adds., c. 6, ff. 19–20).

1. Mary Sabilla Novello sent Hunt a letter describing the party she gave in his honor (Hunt, *Correspondence*, I, 208–10).

2. Charles Smart Evans (1778–1849), composer, chorister, organist; and Henry Charles Robertson, who was described by Thornton Hunt as "the agreeable singer who is too nervous to be more than a chorus singer on his native stage" (Blunden, *Leigh Hunt*, p. 361).

3. William Godwin, Jr.

4. Hunt's *Indicator* ran from 13 October 1819 through 21 March 1821 (see 29 December 1820–1 January 1821, n. 2).

5. The following four words were inserted above the line, marked by a caret between *us* and *that*.

6. See 2–5 October [1823].

7. The phrase "happened to cause this long" is given in Sir John Shelley-Rolls's copy of this letter (Bodleian Library). The manuscript of this letter is extremely faded.

8. "Except for one thing."

9. "I don't really know why—maybe from some [?] resembling a glass of [water]."

10. This and the following eleven lines have blanks of two and one-half inches where the ink has faded away.

11. Mary Shelley's *Journal* entry of 19 October 1823 reveals that Hogg's voice unexpectedly affected her in the same way that Byron's had, that is, as one in a conversation in which Shelley's voice should also have been heard.

12. Mary Shelley's poem—written in Italy—commemorating Shelley's death (printed in Grylls, *Mary Shelley*, pp. 297–301).

TO CHARLES OLLIER — Speldhurst St. Oct—28th [1823]

My dear Sir

Will you have the kindness to deliver into Mr John Hunt's hands such copies of Mr Shelley's works as you still retain.[1]—I should be very glad of a single copy of the Alastor if by any chance there should be one remaining.

I hope that Mrs Ollier[2] and yourself are in good health

Your obedient servant
MaryW. Shelley

ADDRESS: Mr Chas Ollier / &c &c &c. PUBLISHED: Jones, #200. TEXT: MS., Pforzheimer Library.

1. Charles Ollier, Shelley's publisher, went out of business in the summer of 1823. On 17 November he responded. Noting that "the sale, in every instance, of Mr Shelley's works has been very confined," he indicated that he had forwarded the following list of works to John Hunt:

160	Epipsychidion	(stitched)	4	Hellas	(sewed)
12	Hellas	(quires)	15	Revolt of Islam	(Bds)
12	Rosalind	D°	41	Adonais	(quires)
12	Prometheus	D°	92	Six Weeks' Tour	D°
12	Cenci	D°	18	Proposal for Reform	(stitched)
3	D°	Bds 1st Edit.			

Ollier, seeking a copy of *Alastor* to complete his own collection of Shelley, had recently been offered the purchase of one, which he was willing to allow Mary Shelley to purchase instead (Abinger MS.; printed in *S&M*, IV, 990–91).

2. Maria Gattie Ollier, whose brothers were friends of Leigh Hunt and Charles Cowden Clarke (*SC*, V, 125).

*To Sir Richard Phillips[1]

[14 Speldhurst Street Brunswick Square]
Friday November 14th [1823]

Dear Sir

On my removal from the Strand[2] this book was mislaid, and this must account though it can hardly apologize for my having detained it so long. I am not well read enough in such questions to comment on your theory; I own I have great respect for that faculty we carry about us called Mind —and I fear that no Frankenstein can so arrange the gases as to be able to make any combination of them produce thought or even life—However happy conjectures must always instruct even if they fail from entirely attaining their object—

With many thanks for your politeness I am, dear Sir

Your obedient servant
MaryW. Shelley

Address: Sir Richard Philipps / &c &c &c. Unpublished. Text: MS., Pforzheimer Library.

1. Sir Richard Phillips (1767–1840), author, bookseller, publisher. Henry Colburn's *New Monthly Magazine* was established to compete with Phillips's *Monthly Magazine.* A political radical, Phillips had been sentenced to eighteen months' imprisonment in 1793 for selling Paine's *Rights of Man.* Phillips also wrote scientific works based on his own speculations rather than on experience or experiment. The work Mary Shelley commented on may be Phillips's *The Proximate Causes of Material Phenomena*, published in 1821 and 1824.

2. That is, when Mary Shelley moved from the Godwins' residence in the Strand to Speldhurst Street on 8 September 1823.

To Charles Ollier

14 Speldhurst St— Saturday.
Nov. 15th [1823]

Dear Sir

In the Literary Pocket Book for 1821 there appeared two extracts, entitled "Sun set" and "Grief"[1]—taken from a longer poem of Mr Shelley's.

You would extremely oblige me if you could inform me where it is probable that I should obtain a copy of this poem.

Excuse this trouble. I hope Mrs Ollier & your family are well—

Your obedient Servant
MaryShelley

ADDRESS: Mr Chas Ollier / &c &c &c. PUBLISHED: Palacio, *Mary Shelley*, p. 605. TEXT: MS., Pforzheimer Library.

1. "Sun set" and "Grief" were excerpts from Shelley's "The Sunset"—lines 9–20 and 27–42, respectively—signed Δ in the *Literary Pocket-Book* (see 29 December 1820–1 January 1821, n. 6) for 1821 (pp. 120–21). Mary Shelley published "The Sunset" in *Posthumous Poems*, pp. 183–84.

*TO CHARLES OLLIER [14 Speldhurst Street Brunswick Square 19 November 1823]

My dear Sir

I am obliged to you for your consideration in keeping for me the copies of the poems—Might I request you to let me know which of these publications was printed at your expence. I am thankful to you also for your offer of Alastor[1] but have I believe obtained one myself—It will be reprinted in the Volume about to be published.

Your Mss (which I have received) were very welcome to me; I am grateful to you for your offers, & would avail myself of them but at present I do not think that there is any thing which ⟨needs⟩ requires my troubling you—

Have the kindness to present my compliment to Mrs Ollier—Dear Sir

Your obedient servant
MaryWShelley

ADDRESS: Mr Chas Ollier / Maida Hill / Paddington. POSTMARKS: (1) T.P / LambsCond St; (2) 7 NIGHT 7 / 19. NO / 1823. UNPUBLISHED. TEXT: MS., Pforzheimer Library.

1. See 28 October [1823].

TO MARIANNE HUNT Novr 27th [1823] London

My dearest Polly,

Are you not a naughty girl? How could you copy a letter to that "agreable unaffected woman, Mrs Shelley" without saying a word from yourself to your loving Grandmother? My dear Polly, to own the truth, a line from you forms a better picture for me of what you are all about than—alas! I was going to say three pages, but I check myself,—than the rare one page of Hunt. Do not think that I forget you; even Percy does not, and he often tells me to bid the Signor Enrico & you, to get in a carriage and then into a boat & to come to questo paese with Baby Nuovo, Henry, Swinburne e tutti—But that will not be; nor shall I see you at Mariano; this is a dreary exile for me. During a long month of cloud & fog how often have I sighed for my beloved Italy—And more than ever this day, when I have come to a conclusion with S.T.S. [*Sir Timothy Shelley*] as to my affairs, and I find the miserable pittance that I am to have. Nearly sufficient [in] Italy—here it will not go half way—it is £100 P^r^ An. Nor is this all; for I foresee [a] thousand troubles. Yet in truth as far as regards mere money matters & worldly prospects I keep up my philosophy with excellent success—Others wonder at this, but I do not, nor is there any philosophy in it. After having witnessed the mortal agonies of my two darling children, after that journey from & to Lerici, I feel all these as pictures & trifles as long as I am kept out of contact with the unholy. I was upset today by being obliged to see Whitton, & the prospect of seeing others of his tribe—I can earn a sufficiency I doubt not—in Italy I should be content, here I will not bemoan—Indeed I never do, & Mrs Godwin makes large eyes & [*at*] the quiet way in which I take it all.—It is England alone that annoys me; yet sometimes I get among friends & almost forget it's fogs. I go to Shacklewell rarely & sometimes see the Novellos elsewhere. He is my especial favourite, & his music always transports me to the seventh Heaven. I have seen Mrs Blaine Hunt there. B.H. [*Blaine Hunt*] is the brother of that Monster Hunt[1] who is concerned in a horrible murder, of which of course you have read, if you ever see Galignani. This is sufficiently distressing to her & she is so gentle & unaffected yet half timid that she inspires one with a wish to pay her distinguished attention. She was much gratified at hearing that you spoke of & begged her kindest Compliments.—I see the Lambs rather often—she is ever amiable & Lamb witty & delightful. I must tell you one thing & make H. laugh. Lamb's new house at Islington is close to the New River, and George Dyer,[2] after having paid them a visit, on going away, at 12 at noon day—walked deliberately in to the water, takeing it for the high road, But as he said afterwards to Procter, "I soon found that I was in the water, Sir;"—So Miss L. & the servant had to fish him out. I must tell you also another thing, which will hardly make you laugh—& yet it will too—Your poor, dear favourite Mr A——r[3]—had married you know beneath him & has at last produced his wife in Society—On being asked by a lady in company—Do you know a Mrs Mitchel—Mrs A——r replied—"I can't say I does, Ma'am, but the same Docter as lays me, lays her."[4]—A——r is very fond of her they say, or as the lady expresses it—"Oh, A——r and me, we lives like doves."—She is said to be beautiful.—I must tell Hunt also a good saying of Lambs—talking of someone, he said —"Now some men who are very veracious are called matter of fact men—but Such-a-one-I should call: a Matter-of-lie man.{"}

I have seen also Procter with his "beautifully formed head" (it is beautifully formed) several times and I like him. He is an enthusiastic admirer of Shelley, & most zealous in the bringing out the Volume of his Poems;

this alone w^d please me, & he is moreover gentle & gentlemanly & apparently endued with a true poetic feeling—Besides he is an invalid—& some time ago I told you in a letter that I have always a sneaking (for sneaking, read open) kindness for men of literary & particularly poetic habits who have delicate health; I cannot help revering the mind, delicately attuned, that shatters the material frame, & whose thoughts ⟨flow⟩ are strong enough to throw down & dilapidate the walls of sense & dikes of flesh that the unimaginative contrive to keep in such good repair. I have seen Peacock two or three times. he looks quite prosperous and I was pleased to hear him speak with feeling of his children.—What wonder? you will say—truly, my dear, I have seen him so seldom go out of himself, that this most instinctive selfish-unselfishness sets him off to advantage. Mrs P. [*Peacock*] is in the country—he goes down to her every saturday He says that Hogg is grown thinner & I suppose he is, since he is not, as you described him, fat; but is the same in person & in every thing (una cosa di meno)[5] as ever, as far as I see, & his colour, which often changes, shews I think that his sensibility remains. I see him sometimes of an evening either here or at the Ghisbornes—and every Sunday he takes a long walk with Mill[6] & Colson. By the bye I must {not} forget to do away any false impression you may have received from Mrs. G—'s [*Gisborne's*] letter about him & Mrs W. [*Williams*] which was I think all a mistake.[7] I see nothing in his manner beyond that interest which every one must take in her, nor in her any consciousness of anything beyond. She is totally free from every particle of coquetry, & the beautiful simplicity of her character which S. & I always admired, now displays itself in all its charms, & the affection I ever had for her is now much strengthened—it is my & I think her greatest delight when we spend hours together talking of one subject only & living over & over again in memory our happy months.

After all I spend a great deal of my time in solitude. I have been hitherto fully occupied in preparing Shelley's MSS—it is now complete, & the poetry alone will make a large Volume. Will you tell Hunt that he need not send any of the MSS that he has (except the Essay on Devils & some lines addressed to himself on his arrival in Italy, if he should choose them to be inserted) as I have re-copied all the rest. We should be very glad however of his Notice as quickly as possible, as we wish the book to be out in a month at furthest & that will not be possible unless he send it immediately; it would break my heart if the book should appear without it.—When he does send a packet over (let it be directed to his brother) will he also be so good as to send me a copy of my "Choice" beginning after the line, "Entrenched sad lines, or blotted with its might;"—Perhaps, dear Marianne, you would have the kindness to copy them for me, & send them soon—I have another favour to ask of you. Miss Curran has a portrait of Shelley in many things very like; & she has so much talent that I entertain great hopes that she will be able to make a good one: for this purpose I wish her to have all the aids possible & among the rest a profile from you.[8] If you c[d] not cut another, perhaps you [could] send her one already cut, & if you sent it with a note requesting her to re[turn it to me after] she had done with it, I will engage that it will be most fait[hfully] returned. At present I am not quite sure where she is, but I [ ] she should be there & you can find her & send her this, I need not [tell] you how you would oblige me—you w[d] oblige "Henry"—if he thus got a good portrait.

I heard from Bessy that Hunt is writing something for the Examiner for me; I conjecture that this may be concerning Valperga—I shall be glad indeed when that comes, or in lieu of it, anything else—John Hunt begins to despair, since he says that without the Indicators the L.E. [*Literary Examiner*] must fail. That the E. is so constituted now, on account of the admission of Advertisements, that any thing not immediately of the day c[d] not be printed in it—& that he despairs of the possibility of setting up anything new.

And now, dear Polly, I think I have done with gossip & business—with words of affection & kindness I should never have done. I am inexpressibly anxious about you all; Percy has had a similar though shorter attack to that one at Albaro, but he is now recovered—I have a cold in my head Occasioned I suppose by the weather—Ah Polly—if the beauties of England were to have only the mirror that Richard III desires, a very short time w[d] be spent at the Looking Glass[9]—What of Florence & the Gallery—I saw the Elgin Marbles today—tomorrow I am to go to the Museum & look over the prints—that will be a great treat. The Theseus is a divinity—but how very few statues they have. Kiss the children—Ask Thornton for his promised & forgotten P.S. Give my love to Hunt & believe me, my dear Marianne, the exiled but ever

Most affectionately Yours, MaryWS.—

Trelawny write to me that he wishes Hunt to send his letter to him to me.

When Hunt writes to M[r] Brown or Severn w[d] you ask him to make enquiries about a Sculptor of the name of Gott—how he is & how {h}is family is—I ask on account of a friend of his M[r] Smith of the British Museum—who is anxious to know

ADDRESS: Mrs. Leigh Hunt / Ferma in Posta / Firenze / Italie / Florence—Italy felice. POSTMARKS: (1) F23 / 190; (2) ANGLETERRE; (3) CHAMBERY; (4) [ ] / 1823; (5) [CORRISPZA DA] GENOVA; (6) 18 DE[CEM]BRE. PUBLISHED: Jones, #201. TEXT: MS., Bodleian Library (MS., Shelley, Adds., c. 6, ff. 21–22).

1. Joseph Hunt and John Thurtell were accused of the spade murder of a Mr. Weare (*Times* [London], 24 November 1823).

2. George Dyer (1755–1841), author, was a friend of the Lambs and Hazlitt. Lamb relates this same anecdote in his essay "Amicus Redivivus." For an account of Dyer, see Lucas, *Charles Lamb*, pp. 144–67.

3. Thomas Massa Alsager (1779–1846), a friend of Hunt, Godwin, Henry Crabb Robinson, Lamb, Hazlitt, and Wordsworth, was financial editor for the *Times*. He also wrote articles about music (*SC*, V, 264–65).

4. That is, assists in a lying-in.

5. "Excepting one thing."

6. James Mill (1773–1836), utilitarian philosopher, who had been appointed to a clerkship in the Examiner's Office of the East India Company in May 1819, along with Peacock (see 29 June 1819, n. 2).

7. In her letter of 17 March to Mary Shelley, Maria Gisborne had described Hogg's considerable attentions to Jane Williams in terms of a courtship which there proved to be (Gisborne, *Journals and Letters*, pp. 94–95; Norman, *After Shelley*, pp. 5–72).

8. See 26 July 1822. Marianne Hunt was adept at cutting silhouettes (see Blunden, *Leigh Hunt*, facing pp. 152 and 328, for her silhouettes of Keats and Hunt). Mary Shelley wanted to include the portrait in *Posthumous Poems*. In June 1824 Beddoes, in Milan, wrote to Procter about bringing the Curran portrait to England, but Beddoes did not bring it (Norman, *Flight of the Skylark*, p. 51).

9. *Richard III* I. 2. 255.

*TO VINCENT NOVELLO [14 Speldhurst Street Brunswick Square]
Teusday Dec[r] 9th [1823]

My dear Friend

I have just seen John Hunt and what he has said requires so much time to re-say in writing that I should be very glad if I could see you, & would come down to Shacklewell on purpose if necessary—I will just mention now these heads 1st—that J.H. [*John Hunt*] proposed to put to arbitration the whole question of Leigh's property in the Examiner;[1] Leigh refuses to suffer that to be ultimately decided by arbiters, & JH says that it would be useless to refer minor questions to them, since he is sure that his own conduct in them w[d] fully satisfy his brother, without the need of troubling others. With regard to the question of property he is willing cheerfully to accede to the decision of the arbiters however partial it might appear to him to be—but that unless his brother consents to the arbitration now or at any other time in future he shall decide for himself on the subject & let his brother then follow what course he thinks fit. Under these circumstances would it not be far better that Leigh should consent to J.H.'s proposal? When I write to him I should certainly say that I think he had better; but I do not believe myself a good enough judge in these matters, nor ⟨believed⟩ am I looked upon by Leigh to be so, nor in any manner am I, to put myself forward as an adviser—but if after thinking on this & perhaps seeing me, when I could explain to you more fully J.H.'s view of the question, would you not write to Leigh on the subject?

With regard to the Arbiters M[r] J.H asked me to say to you that he was sorry that you declined—that he should be perfectly satisfied if you were the only one, & whatever you decided, to that he would submit without a murmur—he is content with Leigh's choice—but thinks that if four were named, naming yourself, M[r] A. Gliddon, C. Lamb & M[r] Coulson, it would be more agreable to all parties

Under these circumstances, until Leigh's concurrence should come for the arbitration I shall not mention the affair to Lamb—I send you the letters—first that you may re-read & shew them to M[rs] Novello, if she wishes to see them, & also to Mr A. Gliddon, who knows from J.H. that Leigh has chosen him, & consequently had better see them—that is to say if you think fit—for mind, Caro Vincenzo—that as I never decide for myself, so do I never state any opinion, more particularly in practical affairs, that I am not willing to give up to that of a wiser judge, which I am sure that you are.

On Sunday, for the honour of the Gentle Cavalier, there can be no talk of business—can you call on me before—or how shall it be settled?—

I expect Clara[2] on thursday—give my love to Mrs Novello & she may give it, if she likes, to my defaulting Cavalier & my defaulting Werter,[3] both of whom I cordially forgive, & please myself with the idea that I shall see in perfect health on Sunday

Affectionately Evr MaryWS.

[*P. 1, top*] if you call just send a line to say when—unless it be before 2 in the afternoon when I am always at home

ADDRESS: Vincent Novello. UNPUBLISHED. TEXT: MS., Brotherton Collection, University of Leeds Library.

1. See 9–11 September [1823].
2. Possibly Clara Novello.
3. Playful names for Vincent Novello, possibly adopted from his wife's use of the term (Hunt, *Correspondence*, I, 210), and for Edward Holmes.

To Leigh Hunt — London. Decr 11th [1823]

My dear Hunt

I am much annoyed at all the vexation that you must have received from your brother's letter; more particularly as much of it, is gratuitous and if you had been in this country and could have seen him the disagreable tone that exists, need never have been adopted. I have seen him several times & both Novello and I are certain that he intends to act in a strictly honourable manner. He is no inditer; he wishes to be consciencious clear in his communications & cannot mix this up in writing with the real feeling that appears in his discourse. I know that in saying this I shall please you, and I will now tell you the substance of what he said.

I saw him on Teusday Dec 9th when he appeared a good deal hurt by your letter & had, I am afraid replied to it in a no{t} very conciliating manner; in fact feeling (I dare say chiefly on Henry's account) the necessity of making a definitive ajustment he was annoyed at your preventing it;—for as he had left to you the choice of arbiters and expressed his determination of abiding by their decision, however unjust it might appear to him to be, he thought you unreasonable in not acceeding. I saw him again yesterday, and after deliberation, he had thought of two ways of settling the matter an account of which I believe he intends sending to you by tomorrow's post. But as he has the knack of giving an ungracious air to his written communications I will tell you what these are as he explained them to me. The first is: that such persons named should look into the accounts of the Examiner, & decide what sum for past labours you should receive, & this should be charged as a perpetual annuity on the paper, & be payable to you & your heirs for ever—& it may be added that if the sale of the paper should ever rise above a certain number this annuity should be encreased—& besides that you should have the right of supplying the Examiner with articles, for which you shall be paid, as your brother says, at such a rate as shall fully content you.—His second proposition does not please him so well, perhaps it may please you more than the first—that these persons should decide what he (J.H. [*John Hunt*]) ought to receive for the labour of editing, & after that is paid that the remaining profits on the paper should be divided between you; you also having the right of writing for the paper & being paid for your articles.—Such are your brothers proposals. I saw Novello this morning & he is to see J.H. on saturday after which he will write to you his feeling and opinion on the subject; I write therefore only to ease your mind & you had better not reply until you have received Vincenzo's letter. This affair must come to some certain conclusion; minor points & past events had better be forgotten; and if these proposals do not please you, I think, my dear friend, that you & Marianne had better talk the matter over & make one yourselves, that is to regard the future only. Vincenzo entreats me to tell you that he hopes that you do not doubt for a moment his wish to give you any pleasure or undertake any labour for you & that if you insist that he will accept the office of arbiter; but he is so little conversant in such matters that he is afraid that he might injure you even when he most wishes to serve you. He thinks that it w^{d} be better to name 3 than 2 persons for this task; & that perhaps your brother had better have the naming of the third; but if you name him, he thinks Coulson the best person as one fully competent in such a question. I think that if you had your brother only to deal with, all this would be needless; but you naturally look forward to the possibility of its being a question between Cousins instead of brothers—& for every reason the affair had better be ascertained & established immediately for if in future you had Henry to deal with instead of his father the exchange would be by no means pleasing. So much for business.

You make one indeed guilty of one of the seven deadly sins (invidia) when you talk of summer weather: cloud, rain, fogs, dirt such are the alternations of our genial sky—it is, this blessed paese a prison & the worst of prisons—God only knows when I shall revisit my dolce nido, but I sigh bitterly for it—this winter at Rome instead of here—I may not dream of such bliss.—My great consolation here is music; the music with which Vincenzo & his friends provide me: I go to the chapel;[1] I have been with Mrs W. [*Williams*] to a concert that they have established & I hear it at his house. He has made me a convert to Haydn—Do you know the piece, "A new healed World"—in his Creation; what a wonderful stream of sound it is; it puts me in mind of those beautiful lines of Milton "Untwisting all the chains that tie The hidden soul of harmony"[2]—by the bye

I have asked you, but you never reply to one's letters to mention to me what that piece of Hande[l] is of which you only know a few bars. I hope Marianne has received {my} letter & will answer it & all in it—& do a part of what I a[sk] her especially about the profile which I very much wish to be one [   ] Miss Curran's hands & I am sure that you will be repaid for [   ] temporary concession by the nearest likeness to our Shelley that can now be had.—

I shall see Bessy today; & as this letter does not go untill tomorrow so I may add a word or two more. You did not seal with my seal al solito[3]—I have asked Mrs Mason if she knows of a safe ha{n}d by which the watch may come to me to send it & this will spare you further trouble about it—It is a very great inconvenience to me not to have it;—being an English one there is no trouble in getting it into this country, so if you have a very safe hand send it without waiting for Mrs M.—Do you remember your promise of asking Severn for a copy of one {of} his portraits of Trelawny—if I were rich I would claim, in a different manner from what I now can do, his promise to Shelley of a likeness of Keats.—Adieu my dear friends, my love to Marianne & your chicks—Percy remembers them all, & in particular Thornton, Baby nuovo & Henry.—He talks bad English now—& has a cough & a cold—ma cose vuole—inquesto inferno gia si sa[4]—I am not always in spirits but if my friends say that I am "good," contrive to fancy that I am so & so continue to love yours most truly

Mary Shelley

Do you think that as the notice that you have written for our S. is now to be prefixed to a volume of his works that it will require much alteration—& his lordship's note be at least left out—he need only be alluded to—yet not disagreably either—I w^d^ not that the notice on such a subject sh^d^ excite inimical feelings in any persons mind—

As your brother must give up he says the L.E. [*Literary Examiner*] this adjustment would free you from the necessity of writing for him; and if at present you did not begin any new work I doubt not that you articles w^d^ receive very high pay from any periodical publication.—

With regard to the arbitrators I have seen Miss Lamb & she assured me that her brother w^d^ feel himself wholly incompetent to the task—I did not (by Novello's advice) shew him the letters.—but Miss L. said that she felt sure he w^d^ refuse—

ADDRESS: Leigh Hunt Esq / Ferma in Posta / Firenze / Florence—Italie / Italy—Florence. POSTMARKS: (1) F23 / 158; (2) ANGLETERRE; (3) CHAMBERY; (4) 1 GEN[NAIO]; (5) CORRISPZA ESTTERA [DA GENOVA]. PUBLISHED: Jones, #202. TEXT: MS., Bodleian Library (MS., Shelley, Adds., c. 6, ff. 23–24).

1. The Portuguese Embassy Chapel, where Vincent Novello was organist and choir master.

2. *L'Allegro*, lines 143–44.

3. "As usual."

4. "But what do you want—in this inferno one knows only too well."

*To [?   ]   [London] Monday [?1824–29][1]

My dear Sir—I am very {sorry} that I was out when you called—The truth is I did not the least imagine that you would call when I remembered that it was Saturday—⟨knowing⟩ fancying that you were always peculiarly engaged on that day, and I was asked quite unxepectedly to go to a morning concert—

You send me the mere beginning of a chapter for a motto—it is difficult so to adapt one I send a few lines from a Manuscript of Mr Shelley—will they suit—I copy them again here

> Amid the desolation of a city
> Which was the cradle and is now the grave
> Of an extinguished people—so that pity
> Weeps o'er the shipwrecks of oblivion's wave

You will find me I think I may promise at home any morning before two during this week—do call as early during it as you can

Yours truly
MWS

[*P. 4*]

> Amid the desolation of a city
> Which was the cradle and is now the grave
> Of an extinguished people, so that pity
> Weeps o'er the shipwrecks of oblivion's wave

> The tigers leap up
> a loud, long, hoarse cry
> Bursts at once from their vitals tremendously[2]
> Shelley

UNPUBLISHED. TEXT: MS., Pforzheimer Library.

1. The date of this letter is most uncertain. The fact that Mary Shelley quoted lines 1–4 of "The Tower of Famine" from manuscript suggests that the letter was written prior to the poem's publication in the *Keepsake*, in 1829.
2. "A Vision of the Sea," lines 92–95.

To Vincent Novello   [London] Monday.
[c. 19 January–9 February 1824][1]

My dear Vincenzo

I was somewhat rash when I promised to send you Hunts next letter—for it has so happened that my letter just received contains such allusions to the affairs of a friend of his & mine that I cannot send it—He writes also to you (I judge so at least from an expression of his letter) & thus there is less need. However as you may not have received yours I will tell you what he says—first he writes in very good spirits infinitely pleased at the settlement made concerning the Examiner, although I am yet to learn, what the arrangement is that he agrees to, & he refers me to his letters to his brother which when I get, I will dispatch to you. His health is better he says—& he entreats me if his brother refuses to publish his Bacchus in Italy[2] to get it from him & sell it for him at the best price I can—As if I were a good person to do such a deed—however I must perform my best—He says "New years day was indeed a new years day—I received all your letters on it, & read them with a change of feeling inexpressible"—this is indeed good news—& he adds "I shall be getting up articles for the Examiner. the old word inspires me. Why cannot you take a run over with the Novello expedition & see our vineyards—{"}

I write "con furia" as I have not a momen[t] to spare and yet wish to save a post—I have received a letter also from Trelawny in Greece[3] Which I have not yet had time to read When shall I see you all—you promised to call—this Week—Give my best love to Mrs Novello.

Affectionately ys
MaryShelley

Poor Jane suffered for her freak—the damp gave her spasms in her chest & she suffered dismally for 24 hours—she is now quite free from pain but weak—kindest messages to your Cavalieri.

PUBLISHED: Jones, #203. TEXT: MS., British Library (Add. MSS. 11,730, f. 180).

1. Since Hunt's letter to Mary Shelley was written after 1 January, the earliest Monday it could have been received is 19 January. On 9 February, Mary Shelley responded to Hunt's letter. Her letter to Vincent Novello was written between these dates, perhaps even on 9 February, which was a Monday.

2. *Bacchus in Tuscany* was published by John Hunt on 1 January 1825 (Blunden, *Leigh Hunt*, p. 207).

3. Trelawny's letter of 24 October 1823 described the status of the Greek uprising and gave accounts of Byron, Gamba, and Mavrocordato (*S&M*, IV, 981–89).

To Leigh Hunt

Feb. 9th London [1824]

My dear Hunt

I intend to write you but a short letter—& should even have deferred writing at all but that we have begun to print and I am anxious to receive your MS. As in the latter part of your letter you say that you will send it immediately upon my asking for it I need hardly answer what you say about putting off the publication for a year—Alas, my dear friend, "there is a tide in the affairs of men"[1]—Shelley has celebrity even popularity now—a winter ago greater interest would perhaps have been excited than now by this volume—but who knows what may happen before the next—Indeed I have given my word to several people—it has been advertised—& moreover, do you, my best friend—assist me in making it complete—send me what you prepare; for it is not yet too late—but if you wait to exchange more letters it will be.

I am very glad to hear that my good Polly has written and that I am to have the letter—se dio vuole—some time or other—and I wish that in return I could send you a budget of good news—but what is there good in the world & above all [   ] miserable country. The Novellos are at Shacklewell—they have just [   ] remained of their furniture from Percy St. & Mrs N. has been so engaged in arrang[   ] that I have not seen much of them for nearly a month—I saw the Lambs last night & they were quite well—⟨We knew one old ?deb⟩ Mrs Williams is well—but as impatient as I of England & the rest of it—she bears herself up very well—but it is very—very hard to fall from the enjoyment of life to a living death.—You have of course heard of the event of your brother's trial[2]—All the world cries out about it—& the Court itself seems displeased with the officiousness of the prosecutors—yet 12 men were found who could give a verdict of guilty—The judgement is not yet passed, & probably will not be yet awhile—for the Judges say that they have too much to do—casting an eye perhaps on a paper which your brother holds when he attends their Lordships' leisure—& not knowing how long they may be kept—Do not frown at this scherzo—upon the whole I am much prepossessed in your brother's favour—he called on me the day before he expected to be sent to prison—expressed his great pleasure in your having agreed to his arrangements—& evinced a sensibility in his manner of which I did not judge him capable—poor fellow! he is hardly used in this world—but cosi va il mondo[3]—

Do you know I have drawn on him for his theatrical ticket for D.L. [*Drury Lane*] till I am half ashamed—& yet go on—the truth is, I have been highly delighted with Kean[4]—he excites me & makes me happy for the time—& in addition the idea of writing a tragedy[5] "that last infirmity of noble minds"[6] has come over me—and though as yet I have thrown all my halting verses into the fire—yet I still dream of the buskined muse & see Kean partly as a study—I wish to do anything to get rid of my enemies—the blue devils—I try hard—every now an{d} then I cut off a head of the hydra—but two pop up instead of one ed eccomi li[7]—

I spoke to your brother about the Bacchus—he said that he had offered it to Colburn who declined—& meant to offer it to others—I will see him soon about it & try what can be done—Ultra Crepidarius[8] does not sell—Gifford is out of fashion—quite forgotten—and even your lines will not stir the waters of oblivion in which he has sunk.—Write your Articles, write your Indicators—your wishing cap[9]—it is thus you will make money—the grand desideratum with us groveling mortals—as for me bien mauvais gré I write bad articles[10] which help to make me miserable—but I am going to plunge into a novel, and hope that its clear water will wash off the ⟨dirt⟩ mud of the magazines—

Oh that you wd answer a letter! Perhaps Marianne will—what of Miss Curran what of the promised profile of my Shelley—what of his verses to you. You ask me what authority I have for asking for Trelawny's letters.—

I only asked for one & it was because he referred me to it in one to me & said that he hoped you w[d] send it

This is a shabby letter—I write at this moment only to entreat you to send the Notice for our volume (send it directed to your brother) as soon as possible—Adieu good friends—be well, happy & good so prays y[r] exiled Grandmother— Mary Shelley.

ADDRESS: Leigh Hunt / Ferma in Posta / Firenze / Florence—Italie / Italy. POSTMARKS: (1) F.P. PAID / FE. 13 / 1824 / 7 NIGHT 7 / ; (2) P24 / 73; (3) ANGLETERRE; (4) CHAMBERY; (5) 28 / FEBB[R]IO. PUBLISHED: Jones, #205. TEXT: MS., Huntington Library (HM 2749).

1. *Julius Caesar* 4. 3. 218.

2. John Hunt had been tried on 15 January for publishing Byron's *The Vision of Judgment* and found guilty (see Tuesday— [25 February 1823], n. 2). Byron had intended to pay John Hunt's fine, and John Hunt hoped Byron's executors might fulfill his intentions, but they did not (Blunden, *Leigh Hunt*, p. 205; Marshall, *The Liberal*, pp. 205–6, 209).

3. "So it goes."

4. Edmund Kean.

5. Mary Shelley wrote some scenes of a tragedy and sent them to Godwin and Bryan Waller Procter (Barry Cornwall) for their judgments. Godwin responded that Mary Shelley had literary talent but not the talent of a dramatist: ". . . you afford an example, to be added to Barry Cornwall, how much easier it is to write a detached dramatic scene than to write a tragedy" (Marshall, *Mary Shelley*, II, 107). Procter responded: "I shall regret very much, if anything which I have said, should induce you to discontinue your play. On the contrary, I have no doubt of your success & beg to offer my services (if they will be at all useful) in introducing it to the theatre. If my play succeeded no one need despair" (Abinger MS.). Procter's tragedy *Mirandola* had been produced at Covent Garden on 1 January 1821 (Nicoll, *English Drama*, IV, 283).

6. Milton, *Lycidas*, line 71.

7. "And here I am."

8. Hunt's *Ultra-Crepidarius: A Satire on William Gifford* (see 29 May 1817, n. 8) was published by John Hunt in 1823.

9. Hunt's "The Wishing-Cap Papers" were published in the Examiner in 1824 and 1825 (Blunden, *"Examiner" Examined*, pp. 117–21).

10. Charles E. Robinson has brought to my attention correspondence between Godwin and the publisher Henry Colburn in which Godwin recommended Mary Shelley as a potential author for Colburn's *New Monthly Magazine*, mentioning that Horace Smith, who regularly published with Colburn (see 18–19 August [1823]), was Mary Shelley's friend (13 December 1823, MS., Victoria and Albert Museum). On 13 January 1824 Godwin sent Colburn Mary Shelley's article "intended for the next number" (MS., Victoria and Albert Museum). Robinson conjectures that this was "Rome in the First and Nineteenth Centuries," which appeared in the March 1824 issue.

*To Charles Ollier

Nov. 11th [error for 11 February 1824][1]
14 Speldhurst St. Brunswick Sq.

My dear Sir

I am obliged to you for the loan of the Literary Pocket Book, which I will return as soon as I can. It will give me great pleasure if you are able to supply me with any of Mr Shelley's MSS.—And I am the more anxious —as they may consist of pieces of which I have imperfect copies, which would thus be rendered complete.

I was pleased to hear from Mr Lamb that he was much interested by your Inesilla—I promise myself the pleasure of reading it within a few days—

dear Sir
Your obedient Servant
MaryShelley

ADDRESS: Mr Charles Ollier / 5 Maida Hill West / Paddington. POSTMARKS: (1) 2. A.NOON. 2 / 11. FE / 1824; (2) 4. EVEN. 4 / 11. FE / 1824. UNPUBLISHED. TEXT: MS., The Robert H. Taylor Collection, Princeton.

1. This letter and Mary Shelley's letter to Hogg dated 11 November are postmarked 11 February 1824. The publication date of Ollier's *Inesilla; or The Tempter, A Romance; with Other Tales* (London, 1824) suggests that the postmark date is correct. Further, Lamb wrote to Ollier on 27 January 1824 to thank him for a copy of *Inesilla* (Lamb, *Letters* [Lucas], II, 417), a letter that would have been written upon receipt of the book and prior to Lamb's expressed interest in it, to which Mary Shelley refers.

TO THOMAS JEFFERSON HOGG [London] Nov. 11th [error for 11 February 1824][1]

My dear Jefferson

I trust that you hold yourself engaged to accompany Jane & I to the theatre on Friday[2]—Be with me by six—I saw Jane today—Dina is convalescent—

How can you empty the mighty vessels of your fearful wrath on so frail a plant as woman?—Do—thats a good child, fall in love & you will become more tender hearted when instead of a weeder of those bending flowers you are turned into a prop—nicely painted green & tied to one by a piece of matting—

Yours in all friendship
MaryShelley

ADDRESS: T. Jefferson Hogg Esq / &c &c &c / 1 Garden Court / Temple. POSTMARKS: (1) T.P / Mar[ ]; (2) 2. A.NOON. 2 / 11. FE / 1824. PUBLISHED: Scott, *New Shelley Letters*, pp. 145–46. TEXT: MS., Pforzheimer Library.

1. See [11 February 1824] to Ollier, n. 1.

2. Perhaps to see Philip Massinger's *A New Way to Pay Old Debts*, which played at Drury Lane on Friday, 13 February 1824. Mary Shelley informed Trelawny that she had recently seen the play in her letter of [?–] 22 March [1824].

TO EDWARD JOHN TRELAWNY[1] London—(March [?–] 22nd) [1824]

My dear Trelawny

I wish I could see you in your Ulyssean dress—your red and gold vest and sheep-skin capote—To you who are in Greece and see her foul as well as her fair side, she may appear barbarous & perhaps odious—but here, where all the every day annoyances of civilization press on one who has passed her best years out of its pale—that sunlit country and its energetic inhabitants seem so much more capable of bestowing pleasure on me that [*than*] the crowded houses of London; and minus the shooting Turks and Woodcocks[2] I do most deeply envy your situation; the opportunities of seeing human Nature, and the interest you must feel in the strange aspect of humanity among these Greeks and Trojans—One is always ready to throw the blame on the mere accidents of life—I might perhaps be as unhappy any where as here; and the delights of Italy might {be} torture to me—I cannot tell; I only know that as I am, I am miserable. The eight years that I passed with our lost Shelley does not appear a dream, for my present existence is more like that—surely his state is not more changed than mine. When I first came to England, change of scene, the seeing old friends and the excitement with which the uncertainty of my situation inspired me, made me, though not happy, yet pass the day unrepining. But now each hour seems to add a load of intolerable melancholy. While alone I can hardly support the weight—when with others, it is almost worse. I think of my converse with Shelley, his incomparable superiority, and besides that he was mine and loved me; I think of Edward; of his virtues and pure friendship, till my heart sinks—The greatest pleasure I have is in company with Jane—When we talk over old times for hours—My other friends are good and kind, but they are so perfectly unlike all that I have been accustomed to, that I enter into a new world when I see them—It is to Jane only that I ever mention Shelley—Do you remember, dear friend, our talks over the fire-side at Genoa?—God knows how wretched I was there; and yet it seems a happy time in comparison to the present—Am I indeed Mary Shelley? the Mary Shelley who gave you almond billêt doux during our Pisan regales? and who ⟨almost forgot⟩ erred into wildness, untamed as she was by any sorrow?—Mary Shelley now is but a ghost of that—but I will not vex you with my repinings—It is a pleasure to me at least to write to you—to recall images of the past, which you also will remember with pleasure—to think that I shall see you once more, & to know that in the mean time your kind, generous heart feels compassion & affection for me

But instead of these useless repinings I had better fill my paper with what news may interest you—and though that is not much, yet it is always agreable to learn something from the land of the living while in exile (though in pleasant exile) from it. First Jane has settled her affairs in India[3]—she will have no great things—not sufficient to live upon in this country—but she has something secure. Her guardian is dead, & her guardian's heir is very kind to her; he is rich and generous, & although of course she would not avail herself of the qualities—yet it is pleasant to know that there is a post to lean on during the accidents of life.—No one has heard from Claire since last July—this is very cruel of her, since she must be aware that we must all be very anxious about her. I strive to think that her silence is occasioned only by her love of mystery or some other caprice —but I am made very uncomfortable about it. There has been no change in my situation,—except that some circumstances induce me to believe that my father-in-law intends to be more generous towards me than he professed—but I cannot tell until next June, when my quarter is due. As it is—living with the greatest economy, I do not want for money—I lead the same life writing & reading & seeing a few people—dull and monotonous enough, since every hour I detest London and its—infernal (one must use expressive words on some occasions) climate more & more. I saw Miss Whitehead[4] the other day. She is at Islington, but talks of going into the country soon—She said that your Cousin was well.—By the bye I wrote to Mrs Mason about the remainder of the will which you say Mr H. Browne had from the people from whom we rented a house at the Baths of Pisa[5]—in her reply she says: "The result of my inquiries is that no papers whatever were found after your departure, consequently no person can be in possession of the Document you mention by that means: Mrs Turbati (the woman of the house) added that had there been any papers, she must have found them, as she always examines every part of her house herself, the moment strangers leave it."—There is probably some mistake in the place—you described the papers so accurately that I cannot doubt of their being those I sought—I wish I could have them as soon as possible & know exactly the place where M^r^ H Browne got them.

(March 22nd) Mr Hamilton Browne called on me today which was a great pleasure to me, since he is the only person I have seen who has been in your company since we parted on the hill of Albaro. He tells me that a vessel sails for Greece next thursday, so I finish this letter & will send it by this opportunity with a few books—I enquired for works upon Greece but could hear of none. Opinions vary very much with regard to these last Cantos of Don Juan;[6] they are usually considered as a falling off—& so they are in many respects, they want the deep & passionate feeling of the first—but they are unequalled in their strictures upon life & flashes of wit. —These are almost our only novelties; Lady Morgan's life of Salvator Rosa[7] is pronounced dull—St. Ronan's well[8]—one of the worst of the Great Unknown—The reviews I never read;—What more? I have been to the theatre several times to see Kean. I never was more powerfully affected by any representation than by his Sir Giles Overreach[9]—The best scene is worked up to a pitch of passion that I could not have imagined—His tones & looks often remind me of you—& [ ][10] but that is not your stage—You Greek dress—pistols—Suliotes & Woodcock shooting are more in your way. Covent Garden was nearly deserted till they brought out a comedy by that ranter Croly[11]—by which it would seem that the proverb is a true one, that says, that extremes meet—for this comedy is, they say, as broad, vulgar & farcical, as his tragic vein is high flown & bombastic—it succeeds prodigiously.—Parliament is met here and Canning[12] is making a figure—he does not seem at all to like the part he was forced to play with regard to Spain, & said in the House that he would not tacitly acquiesce in such another invasion as that of the French at the risk of any war. They are introducing some ammelioration in the state of the slaves in some parts of the West Indies—during the debate on that subject Canning paid a compliment to Frankenstein in a manner sufficiently pleasing to me. The town however is not full as yet, & the Winter is not begun—And although the Opera House is crowded I have not seen there any of the first Grandees. Medwin is still in Paris—nor have either Jane or I heard from him since Christmas—a pretty fellow! Roberts is shooting in the Maremma with Cap^{n} Hay—The Hunts are still at Florence—longing for England.—How I wish I could change places with them! They would get on well if Hunt would write—but he does not—John Hunt has acted very well towards his brother in the main & I think him perfectly honourable though rough in manner. My volume of our Shelley's Poems is printing—it will be a good sized one.

After all this odious place agrees with me & I am very well. Indeed we have had a mild though rainy winter—& last week we had two really fine days—Percy is grown quite out of your knowledge—Poor Jane is by no means well just now & has during this winter grown fearfully thin—We shall go somewhere into the country in the summer, when I hope she will regain her health.—She has been a great deal annoyed by her sister Mrs Baird,—and I think that her illness has been to a great degree occasioned by this.

I heard the other day from the Guiccioli—She says LB's behaviour to the Greeks has been generous in the extreme! H.B. [*Hamilton Browne*] says that his £4000 has already been repaid to him he is lucky in this—but how will he bear the news that Lord Blessington's bills in payment for the yacht[13] have been protested—I hope you are somewhat richer than you were last autumn but you will never be rich—have as much money as you will—Tell me—by the bye if a Miss Anne Matthews ever resided with you & Mrs T. [*Trelawny*] in Wales—Is there any idea that Captain Shenley will join {   } in Greece—or the slightest hope that I shall see you soon again—Could you [*p. 1, top*] Direct to me at the Examiner Office—38 Tavistock St. Covent Garden Or: through Hunt in Italy.—

PUBLISHED: Jones, #206. TEXT: MS., Bodleian Library (MS., Shelley, Adds., c. 6, ff. 25–26).

1. This letter was written in response to Trelawny's 24 October 1823 letter from the Isle of Hydra, Greece (*S&M*, IV, 981–89).

2. Trelawny had written of "excellent sport between Turk and woodcock shooting."

3. On 12 February 1823 Jane Williams wrote to Mary Shelley: "It will take another year to settle my affairs and it would be folly to leave England till this is done" (Abinger MS.; for Jane Williams and India, see [14–15] January 1821).

4. Trelawny had written in a postscript: "If Miss Whitehead calls on you let her read this letter." In his letter of 26 August 1824 Trelawny gives her full name as Ellen Whitehead.

5. On 6 September 1823 Trelawny wrote Mary Shelley that James Hamilton Browne, who was en route to Greece with him (see Marchand, *Byron*, III, 1093), had lived in lodgings that the Shelleys had occupied at the Baths of Pisa and had discovered "some loose sheets of paper"—a will or deed of Shelley's, each page signed and witnessed. Margaret Mason's response was written on 31 January 1824 and arrived in England on 19 February (Abinger MS.).

6. Cantos 12, 13, and 14 were published by John Hunt on 17 December 1823; Cantos 15 and 16 were published on 26 March 1824.

7. Lady Morgan (née Sydney Owenson), *The Life and Times of Salvator Rosa* (Paris, 1824). Lady Morgan (1776–1859) wrote a number of romances and travel books. Her travel books about France and Italy caused some controversy because of her liberal views. Mary Shelley and Lady Morgan became friends in the 1830s.

8. Sir Walter Scott, *St. Ronan's Well* (Edinburgh, 1824 [for 1823]).

9. A character in *A New Way to Pay Old Debts* (1633), by Philip Massinger.

10. A line and a quarter deleted by Mary Shelley.

11. George Croly (1780–1860). His comedy with songs, *Pride Shall Have a Fall*, opened at Covent Garden on 11 March (Nicoll, *English Drama*, IV, 285). A rector, Croly wrote romances, plays, book reviews (some containing attacks on Byron and Shelley), and poems (two of the latter imitations of Byron). Byron satirized Croly as the "Revd. Rowley Powley" in *Don Juan* 11. 57.

12. George Canning (1770–1827), a British statesman who was credited for his liberal policies while he served as Foreign Secretary, from 1822 to 1827. The Congress of Verona (October 1822) of the Quadruple Alliance gave France a mandate to suppress the Spanish Revolution begun in 1820 (see [26 March 1820], n. 2). On 31 August 1823 the revolutionaries were defeated, and Ferdinand VII was restored to the Spanish throne. Canning, however, had refused to cooperate with the other members of the Alliance in this action, and this led to the dissolution of the Alliance. Canning alluded to *Frankenstein* on 16 March 1824 (Great Britain, *Hansard's Parliamentary Debates*, 2d ser., 10 [1824], col. 1103).

13. Byron wrote to his banker, Charles Barry: "I regret L[d] Blessington's behaviour about the bill: you know that he insisted on buying the Schooner, and had the bargain at his own price. If his bill is not paid, I must make it public, and bring the business, moreover, to a personal discussion; he shan't treat me like a tradesman—that I promise him" (Byron, *Works*, VI, 290).

TO BRYAN WALLER PROCTER — Speldhurst St. 9 May [1824]

My dear Sir

I send the dramas.[1] I do this with less compunction as I know that M[r] Kelsall is possessed of exemplary patience in the way of reading—he read Ahasverus![2]—these are short at least.

This Italian weather puts me in spirits, & seems to restore my faculties—dead during the winter—What a divine night, last night was—calm clear and genial—if such weather continued I should write again—& shall at all events the moment the bustle of my approaching removal is over. I hope you are well

Yours ever obliged
Mary W S.

ADDRESS: B. W. Procter, Esq. / &c &c &c. PUBLISHED: Donner, *The Browning Box*, pp. lxi–lxii. TEXT: Donner, *The Browning Box*.

1. Mary Shelley's blank-verse dramas, *Proserpine* and *Midas*, written in 1820. *Prosperpine* was published in *The Winter's Wreath*, 1832 [1831], pp. 1–20; *Midas* was first published in *Proserpine & Midas: Two Unpublished Mythological Dramas by Mary Shelley*, ed. Andre Henri Koszul (London: Humphrey Milford, 1922), pp. 45–89.

2. Probably Thomas Medwin's *Ahasuerus, The Wanderer: A Dramatic Legend, in Six Parts* (London, 1823).

*TO TERESA GUICCIOLI 16mo—Maggio [May 1824][1]—Londra

Carissima Amica

Come scrivervi? Come esprimere l'alto dolore che mi punge il core? Povera Teresa! siamo ormai sorelle nella infelicità! Temo che una mia lettera sara un raddoppiamento della vostra tristezza, e pur troppo sento che non vi rechera alcuna consolazione. Non posso addoperare i luoghi communi della consolazione, giacche so io che sono falsi. Come dirvi che la pace vi atten dera quando il tempo abbia guarito le piaghe del dolore, e provo che queste piaghe sono immediabile dal tempo? Ogni giorno si sente più al di dentro quanto poco vale il mondo quando l'oggetto amato ci manca. Non ha detto il caro Byron se stesso (egli che conobbe al fondo il cor femenile) che tutta l'esistenza d'una donna dipende dall'amore, ed allorchè perdiamo un amante non ci sia altro rifugio che

To love again and be again undone[2]

Ma noi, cara Guiccioli, siamo private di questo rufugio. Il destino diede ad ambedue i primi spiriti del secolo, perduti loro, non v'è un secondo amare; ed i cori nostri sempremai vedovati, non sono altri che monumenti per dimostrare la felicità ivi sepolta.

E l'ho veduto per l'ultima volta! Non vedro mai più il più bello di tutti gli uomini, quella gloriosa creatura che fu il vanto del mondo; mai piu sentiro la sua voce o leggero la nuova poesia figlia del suo imparagibile genio. Non devo forse sfogarmi in questo modo, e destare le vostre lagrimi ora che i miei occhi sono offuscati della dolorose acque. Ma quando persi la cara metà di me stessa niente mi recò tanta consolazione quanto i di lui lodi—mi pasceva di quei, e mi figuro che voi anche amarete sentire nell'-espressione dell'afflizione d'una amica di Byron, l'eco dei tuoi pianti. Vorrei che fossi presso a te, cara Contessina; parleremmo insieme del diletto Byron, ci rementeremmo del tempo che abbiamo passato insieme—dei nostri passeggi, quando egli veniva devante di noi in tutta la gloria della sua beltà: sarebbero le nostre converzazioni interminabili. Ma non vi manca sicuramente la simpatia degli amici; mi è grata l'idea che siete fra dei cari, e godiate tutto il conforto che la tenera amicizia può dare.

Quanta paura aveste di questo viaggio! ogni giorno sono più sicura che

Dio ci ha dottato col potere di prevedere i nostri mali. Ma siamo tutte quante delle Cassandre; e cosi cieche siamo che non diamo orreccho alla voce silenziale che si fa sentire nell'anima. Si conosce poi la verità allorchè sono le profezie addempite. Quante e quante cose dessero sicura notizia alla Williams ed a me della nostra disgrazia, e voi mille volte poi mi avete detto—Quanto temo questa spedizione.—Temo di annoiarvi ma vorrei sapere tutte le circonstanze di questo disgraziatissimo avvenimento. È la medesima malatia che ebbe a Lerici, non è vero? Esso seppe il suo pericolo? Mi figuro che Pierino vi abbia spedita la narrazione di tutto, e spero di non mostrarmi importuna pregandovi di mandarmi una copia di ciò. Quando vi ha scritto il caro Byron ultimamente? era ammalato allora. State sicura che ogni cosa che mi mandate, ogni copia delle sue lettere, sara sacra per me; nel chiedere questi monumenti dei suoi ultimi momenti sono mossa della vere affezione che sento per lui

La Williams vi prega di gradire l'espressione della sua simpatia. Poverina! Sta assai male lei: è dimagrita al punto di far orrore, e la salute pare affatto rovinato. Per noi altri settentrionalioti non v'è primavera per far risalire i corpi soffranti; il freddo, la pioggia e gli spessi cambiamenti dell'atmosfera indeboliscono e guastono le costituzioni i più robusti; il s[ole] è sempre oscur[ato]. Ma perche parlare di sifatte bagatelle. Questa disgrazia fare[bbe o]scurare il bel cielo d'Italia ed i di lei fiori saranno [per] voi solamente tanti ornamenti per il sepolcro di votro amore. Coraggio intanto, che pare che ci sia nuova legge della natura, e moriremo tutti giovani—Coraggio! sicchè per noi l'ignota via della morta è calcata dai nostri più cari; se quando facciamo questo medesimo viaggio, giungeremo ad un paese sconosciuto, quei che amiamo sono già costà e si affrettarono di farci le benvenute. Morire per noi non sara una seperazione dai bene della vità, ma un raggiungnimento ai tesori nostri rapiti ora dalla Morte.

Beh! Carissima mia, scivetemi col prossimo Corriere. Aspettero con somma impazienza la vostra lettera.—Se vi sia alcuna cosa che volete che faccio—alcuna ambasciata alle genti qui, commandatemi schiettamente, che mi ripeto pur sempe, Cara Guiccioli

Vostra Aff[ma] Amica—Mary Shelley.

[*Translation*]

Dearest Friend
How shall I write to you. How can I express the deep pain that pierces my heart? Poor Teresa! we are now sisters in misfortune! I fear that my letter will make your sorrow more intense, and unfortunately I feel that it will not bring you any comfort. I cannot use the commonplaces of consolation, since I know that they are false. How can I tell you that peace awaits you when time has healed the wounds of pain, when I know that these wounds are incurable by time? Every day one feels more within how little the world is worth when the beloved object is gone. Didn't dear Byron himself say (he who knew so thoroughly the female heart) that the whole of a

woman's existence depends on love, and therefore losing a love there is no other refuge than

To love again and be again undone[2]

But we, dear Guiccioli, are deprived of this refuge. Destiny gave to both of us the first spirits of the age, losing them, there is no second love; and our hearts forever widowed, can only be monuments to demonstrate the happiness buried there.

And I saw him for the last time! I will never again see the most beautiful of all men, that glorious creature who was the pride of all the world; never again will I hear his voice or read his new poetry, the daughter of his incomparable genius. Maybe I should not give vent to my feelings in this way, and arouse your weeping now that my eyes are blurred by these sorrowful tears. But when I lost the dear half of myself, nothing brought me as much consolation as hearing his praises—I fed on those, and I suppose that you also will want to hear the echo of your own lamentations in the expression of the suffering of a friend of Byron. I wish that I were close to you, dear Contessina; we would talk together of beloved Byron, we would recall the time that we have passed together—of our walks, when he would come before us in all the glory of his beauty: these would be our interminable conversations. But surely you do not lack the sympathy of your friends; I am pleased by the idea that you are surrounded by those who are dear to you, and you will enjoy all the comfort that affectionate friendship can give you.

How much you feared this voyage! every day I am more certain that God has endowed us with the power to foresee our misfortunes. But we are all Cassandras; and we are so blind that we do not give heed to the silent voice that makes itself heard within our soul. We then know the truth when the prophecies are fulfilled. How many things gave certain notice to Signora Williams and myself of our misfortune, and you also told me a thousand times—How much I fear this expedition.—I am afraid of annoying you but I would like to know all the circumstances of this most unfortunate happening. It was the same malady that he suffered from at Lerici, isn't that right? Did he know of his danger? I imagine that Pierino has sent you an account of all, and I hope not to appear importunate asking you to send me a copy of it. When was the last time that dear Byron wrote to you? Was he ill at that time? Be assured that anything that you send me, any copy of his letters, will be sacred to me; in asking for these monuments of his final moments I am moved by the true affection that I feel for him.

Signora Williams asks you to accept the expression of her sympathy. Poor thing! She is very ill: she has grown so thin as to cause horror, and her health seems to be truly ruined. For we northerners there is no spring to restore our suffering bodies; the cold, the rain and the frequent changes in the atmosphere weaken and ruin the constitutions of the most robust;

the sun is always clouded. But why talk of such trifles. Your misfortune would becloud the beautiful Italian sky and for you her flowers will be only so many ornaments for the sepulchre of your love. Courage meanwhile, for there seems to be a new law of nature, and we all will die young—Courage! since for us the unknown path of death has been tread by those dearest to us; if when we make this same journey, we arrive at an unknown country, those whom we love are already there and will hurry to make us welcome. For us death will not be a separation from the blessings of life, but a reunion with our dear ones carried off by Death.

Well! My dearest, write to me by the next Courier. I will be awaiting your letter with the utmost impatience.—If there is anything that you might want me to do—any message to people here, ask me frankly, as I again declare myself always, Dear Guiccioli

Your most affectionate friend—Mary Shelley.

ADDRESS: Alla Sua Eccellenza / La Signora Contessa Teresa Guiccioli / A Bologna / nei Stati Pontefici / Bologna—Italy. POSTMARKS: (1) F24 / 30; (2) ANGLETERRE; (3) CORRISPZA EST[ERA DA GENOVA]; (4) [ ]INSTR GENER[ ]LE POST PONT / S.E.O.F. / BOLOGNA; (5) BOLOGNA / 6. GIU. UNPUBLISHED. TEXT: MS., Pforzheimer Library. TRANSLATION: Ricki B. Herzfeld.

1. The news of Byron's death at Missolonghi on 19 April 1824 reached Byron's closest friends on 14 May and the public, on 15 May. Byron's body was shipped to England on the *Florida*, arriving there on 29 June. Pietro Gamba, Byron's companion in Greece, traveled to England at the same time, but on a different vessel so as to avoid attention being called to his sister's relationship with Byron. On 12 July Byron's funeral procession went from London toward Nottingham (passing Mary Shelley's residence as it climbed up Highgate Hill), and on 16 July Byron was interred in the Byron family vault at Hucknall Torkard (Marchand, *Byron*, III, 1229, 1242–43, 1260–63).

2. *Don Juan* 1. 194.

TO JAMES AUGUSTUS HESSEY[1]

14 Speldhurst St. Burton Crescent.
[?24–31] May [1824][2]

My dear Sir

It would give me pleasure if you found a place for the enclosed article in your Magazine, although I fear it comes rather late. If it be not inserted will you have the goodness to return it to me. You will favour me by not mentioning me as the Author of it.

I ⟨am afraid⟩ conjecture that you have already received tributes due to the memory of our lost Poet, but as his friend I was impelled to contribute my mite, and to alleviate my sorrow for his loss by expressing the sincere admiration I had for his genius

I am Your obedient servt.
MaryShelley

ADDRESS: JA Hessey Esq. PUBLISHED: Jones, #207. TEXT: MS., Pforzheimer Library.

1. James Augustus Hessey (c. 1785–1870) was a member of the publishing firm of Taylor and Hessey, publishers of the *London Magazine*.

2. Since Mary Shelley notes that she sends her tribute "rather late, and since news of Byron's death did not reach England until mid-May, we may assume that this letter was written around the end of May. Her tribute was not published. In August the *London Magazine* published Allan Cunningham's article "Robert Burns and Lord Byron," which praised both poets (vol. 10, pp. 117–22).

*To JOHN HOWARD PAYNE[1] 14 Speldhurst Street June 1st [1824][2]

My dear Sir

I was unable to avail myself of the Tickets that you kindly sent last Thursday,—I do not know what day next week Charles II[3] will be performed—but as soon as I possibly can I shall with great pleasure pass an evening I am sure of infinite amusement at C.G [*Covent Garden*]—& shall apply to you for admissions In the mean time, if you can spare 4 Orders for this evening, for any part of the house (I should prefer the boxes) you will very much oblige me

I am, dear Sir
Your obedient Servant
MaryShelley

[*Added by William Godwin, Jr.*] Turn over

Dear H—

This note was ready written when I arrived—but M[rs] Shelley has just discovered that she wants a double order for the boxes for Friday

Ever yous
W.G. Junior

ADDRESS: J. Howard Payne Esq. UNPUBLISHED. TEXT: MS., Pforzheimer Library.

1. John Howard Payne (1791–1852) was an American actor and playwright who collaborated with his friend Washington Irving in writing several plays; from 1842 to 1845 and again in 1851 and 1852 he was American Consul at Tunis. Payne fell in love with Mary Shelley in 1825 (see [28 June 1825], n. 2), but finding that she did not reciprocate his feelings but expressed some interest in Washington Irving, Payne tried to encourage Irving's attentions by giving him Mary Shelley's letters to read. Irving, however, was impervious to his friend's matchmaking efforts. Payne continued to be Mary Shelley's friend until his return to America in 1832. His association with the theater gave him access to free admissions, which he generously provided for Mary Shelley throughout their friendship (*MWS Letters*, II, 347–53; *The Romance* first brought the relationship of the three to light and prints part of Mary Shelley and Payne's correspondence. Sylva Norman suggests that Mary Shelley and Payne met in Paris in 1823 through the Kenneys [*Flight of the Skylark*, p. 64]. For a full-length study of Payne, see Overmyer, *America's First Hamlet*. Overmyer gives a more objective account of the relationship of Mary Shelley and Payne than Sanborn or Jones, who depict Mary Shelley as rather opportunistic in her treatment of Payne. Overmyer also points out that Mary Shelley may have met Payne at the Lambs' or through her half brother, William Godwin, Jr., who was Payne's friend [p. 240]).

2. Only in 1824 did Mary Shelley live at 14 Speldhurst Street on 1 June.

3. Payne's comedy *Charles the Second; or, The Merry Monarch* opened at Covent Garden on Thursday, 27 May 1824 (Nicoll, *English Drama*, IV, 369). *Charles the Second*; *Cozening*; and *Clari* were advertised to be performed on 1 June. (*Clari; or, The Maid of Milan*, by Payne, opened at Covent Garden on 8 May 1823 and contained Payne's famous song "Home, Sweet Home.")

*TO [BRYAN WALLER PROCTER][1]

[14 Speldhurst Street
Brunswick Square] Saturday
[? 12 June 1824]

My dear Sir

You will I hope have received copies of the Poems by this time.—As I do not know the address of Mr Kelsall & Mr Beddoes, will you have the goodness to forward copies to them. I have made out the en{c}losed list of errata[2] which ought to be printed immediately—but I wished to ask you first, if in looking over the volume you found any additional errors

I am, dear Sir
Yours sincerly & obliged
MaryWShelley

Errata

P. 77 1. 5—for
The shapes which drew in thick lightnings
read
The shapes which drew it, in thick lightenings.

P. 139—1 5 for seem, read, seems.
1 6—for shrine read shine

P. 164—Insert a comma at the end of line 4
and then insert this line
The breath of the moist earth is light

---

p. 186 last line—for 1817—read 1819.

P. 221—1 11—for wait, read wail.

UNPUBLISHED. Jones, #208, in part. TEXT: MS., Pforzheimer Library.

1. *Posthumous Poems of Percy Bysshe Shelley* was published during the second week of June (Taylor, *Early Collected Editions*, p. 7). The evidence that this letter was addressed to Procter is found in his letter to Mary Shelley dated "Tuesday Morning," in which he writes: "I have sent to Kelsall about the errata—which he will attend to—I have been in a state of such nervousness as not to be able to read enough for the purpose." He also says, "I desired Kelsall to thank you for the beautiful volume of Poems—I hope he did so" (Abinger MS.).

2. The errata leaf, which was tipped into some copies of the *Posthumous Poems*, contained twenty-four corrections (Taylor, *Early Collected Editions*, p. 17).

To Marianne Hunt London June 13th (June 18th) [1824]

My best Polly

You perhaps will wonder that you have not heard from me, while I have been lost in conjecture as to {the} occasion of Hunt's silence. All I can say in my excuse is this. I have now a letter open before me addressed to you, dated May 9th beginning with these words—"I have delayed writing in expectation of an answer from Hunt; the delay on his part gives me hopes that he will treat me at last with kindness and confidence and send me his MS.—in the mean time I will fill two sides of my paper and the leave the third blank for some days more, in hopes that I may then fill it with acknowledgements for his envoy."—This luckless third page was filled up on June 1st I then sealed my letter, and annoying circumstances have prevented my sending it;—till now, I begin to think that I had better write another, at which task behold me occupied.—It is fifty ages since I heard any news of you, and I long excessively for a letter—how much more do I long that I were with you! truly my mode of life in England is little agreable to me; my only comfort is in my child's growth and health and in the society of Mrs Williams. She had been seriously indisposed the whole winter and it is only on her recent removal from the smoke of London to Kentish Town (12 Mortimer Terrace!)[1] that she has begun to recover —she is so thin—and then she in no way gives herself up, but struggles against debility and ill health to the very last, and is as cheerful as she can be in this cloudy land. The Natives call is summer, while they, as well as I, shiver [ ] fire—the fields may well be green—being well watered—and when it [ ] rain, Nature kindly preserves their complexion by suspending over them a sunproof parasol of clouds—Yet, dear Hunt (if so, not being angry with me, you allow me to call you) the fields on the two!!! fine days we have had were superbly beautiful—I walked to Hamstead Heath on one of them, & on another through the meadows whch divide Hamstead from the Regent's Park & so home by Kentish Town. The smell of hay perfumed the air, the soft tall green grass starred by "buttercups, that will be seen, whether you will see or no"[2]—the elms and grassy lanes all brought old times to my mind.—I long to get out to K.T. [*Kentish Town*] when I shall be near my Janey, but circumstances obliged me to delay my removal until the beginning of June, and now I cannot get lodgings there.—In the mean time I enjoy (when it does not rain) all I can of the country, by help of prodigious walks—Ye Gods—how I walk! and starve—because in spite of all I am too much en bon point—Cosa vuole? quel che dio vuole, sara, e ci vuol pazienza.[3] My walks some times turn towards Shacklewell—that dreary flat,—scented by brick kilns and adorned by carcases of houses—The good kind hearts that inhabit it compensate for it, when once arrived, but it prevents frequent visits—and Mrs Novello's circumstance[4] (as Pamela calls it) now almost entirely prevents her from coming to town. You will not see them in Italy this summer I can bear witness that {it} is not M^rs^ N's, but Vincenzo's fault—he says that if he could bring you all back with him he would not hesitate—but his time would be so short—the way so long—and his pain at leaving you so great—that he puts the ounce of sweet meeting in an opposite scale to the pound of bitter parting, and lo! the smiles kick the beam and the sighs enchain him here.—The Gliddons are evidently a good deal cut up by the removal of their friends; they go there in the rain & return home weary—& the N's say that they will come—& then they do not—in fact the great pleasure of friendship, constant intercourse, is inevitably destroyed—Statia[5] (the "Yes. Mr Hunt.") is grown into a fine tall girl, and though she may not be brilliant is far from silly.—

I cannot I own conjecture why Hunt refused to join his name to mine in my publication[6]—I have been too little accustomed to be treated with suspicion, and am far too secure that I do not deserve it, to know how to conduct myself when treated thus unjustly—that is to say, if suspicion has been the cause of his refusal—I hope that you will soon receive a copy; and I hope that the preface will at least not displease him;—and yet it may—although I have done my best that it should not. During the dreary winter I passed at Genoa, in the midst of coldness & aversion I preserved my affection for Hunt, suspicion is deadly poison to friendship, but I will give mine patience as an antidote, and my naughty Very (Patient no longer) is & must [ever b]e dear to me:—even though he disdains me—as he does.—

Have you heard from Trelawny? I am very anxious to have a letter, since none has been received by him since that which you forwarded. I wish that he had been at Missalunghi, since I doubt not that want of proper attendance caused the melancholy catastrophe of LB's voyage, and his activity & kindness might have prevented it. We have heard from Claire since I wrote—poor girl; She is dismally tossed about, so much so that perhaps she may return to England—To exchange Italy for England is dreary work—but it must be pleasanter than Moscow after all—I think this is all the news that I can tell you—it is very, very long since I have seen Procter—he is much annoyed by his affairs & also by ill health—C. Lamb has suspended his Elia's[7]—My father's 1st vol. of the Hist. of the Commonwea{l}th[8] has come out & sells well I believe—I hope by next spring to publish myself—& shall work hard the moment I get into country lodgings—& before, if my removal continues to be delayed—

And what do you all do with yourselves—out of Florence, you must lead very recluse lives—and I fear all your spirits suffer from want of society—I see few—but those few often;—now Kean plays no more, my only public amusement is the Opera, which is inexpressibly delightful to me.—The Good People of England have shewn taste in it—Notwithstanding Rossini being the fashion & his going to Carlton House[9] & giving concerts under the patronage of the ladies of Almacks[10]—the Singers have each chosen Mozart for their Benefit.—That nice creature la Caradori began it by selecting Don Giovanni for hers, & played Zerlina as well (& that is saying every thing) as la Fodor. Garcia was the Don—in one or two parts he surpassed Ambrogetti, but in others (in la ci darem particularly) he puts me in mind of the Union of Voices, he was so full of graces—& then he pronounces Italian vilely: il Begnis made an enchanting Leperello he is full of comic talent—& truly Italian—La Catalani took Le Nozze di Figaro for her benefit—we had an odious page but the rest was good—the pretty la Begnis made a sweet countess[11]—and Begnis singing of Le vuol balare, was incomparable—sul'aria was encored of course—there are one or two excellent airs in this piece which are spoiled because they devolve on inferior singers—la Vendetta for instance, which Francesco Novello fills full {of} animation & beauty is lost in the stupid Bartolo of the Opera.—The town is extremely full—there are exhibitions of all kinds—two of the ruined city of Pompeii—which the painter has spoiled by covering the glowing earth with an English sky—There are several of fine old paintings which are to me drops of water in the desart—The Claude's bring all Italy before me [*my*] eyes—& thus transport me to Paradise.—

(June 15th) After writing the above I went to St. P. Ch. Y^d {*St. Paul's Church Yard*} to see Bessy concerning this debut of your brother,[12] & it is settled that I go with them on Thursday—so I shall not close this letter until this is decided. Your Mother was infinitely nervous—she spoke with great delight of a letter that she had received from you. Bessy is so changed that you w^d hardly know her again; she is grown plump & contented-looking—this is the more wonderful as she continues to take opium, & could not leave it off without extreme suffering—but it seems to have no other effect on her than to keep her in good health—Nancy[13] was remarkably blooming—her costume is somewhat altered & civilized—I have once or twice seen the nankeens—but white frocks—sashes—& pretty silk kerchiefs are permitted as well as curls—great innovations these.—I heard yesterday from John Hunt that my volume promises to sell well—if I do get & when I get money from it I will send you the things you desire—but I have only £100 p.a. from STS. [*Sir Timothy Shelley*] enough in Italy—but only half enough for England. I shall see Virtue[14] (i.e. Laura—are these synonimous since Petrarch's time?) on Thursday—Mrs Williams is to go also, who is an extreme favourite of your Mother. Adieu for the present.—

(June 18th) I own when I had finished so far—I began to tremble as to what this little space might contain—nor was I altogether comfortable at the idea of going with your mother & sister to witness Tom's defeat—but on the contrary my dear we beheld his most unequivocal triumph the play was Richard III—I do not pretend to say that I like him as I do Kean—but of course he could not act his best on the first night—The first good point of his was—"Was ever woman in such humour won"—and the best thing he said during the whole night was "Richard is himself again"—After he died, not a word was to be heard—nor could Richmond in any way contrive to give out the play for the next night—in fact one could not hear oneself speak the hubbub was so tremendous. C. Kemble[15] at length made Tom go on to meet their repeated calls for him—There was some [*half-line deleted*] opposition but it came principally from the gallery. Poor Tom as you may guess is infinitely delighted to find himself as he says transformed from a poor to a rich man at once—he had refused an offer of £18 p. week—& Kemble is now quite cap in hand to him—When I see him again I shall judge better of his real merits—which one cannot do when he himself was agitated—& one's attention was of course as much directed towards the audience as to towards him—besides we were (in a private box) a great way from the stage—His voice is the best on the stage—& that is the greatest thing in his favour.—However his acting—(as I said) cannot be judged of by last night—Your Mother behaved very well—she took your grandmother with us—The old lady sat as quiet & pleased as possible—Nancy was all anxiety & Virtue sat pale and silent as Marble—or her namesake Your Mother told me to tell you that she w^{d} write as soon as she found her wits—He is to play R. III. again on monday—I had intended not to go—but if they of St. P.—'s insist upon it, I will—Though I had rather see him next in a new character—

Write soon my Polly if Hunt is inexorable & will not write again give my love to him to Occhi turchini[16] & the rest—

Yours affly
MaryWS.

[*P. 1, top*] Direct to me at John Hunts—as I am about to change my lodgings[17]

ADDRESS: Mrs Leigh Hunt / Ferma in Posta / Firenze / Florence—Italy / La Toscane. POSTMARKS: (1) PAID / 18 JU 18 / 1824; (2) ANGLETERRE; (3) CHAMBERY; (4) CORRISPZA EST[ERA DA GENOVA]; (5) 3 / LUGLIO. PUBLISHED: Jones, #209. TEXT: MS., Huntington Library (HM 2753).

1. The Hunts had lived at 13 Mortimer Terrace, Kentish Town, in 1820.

2. Wordsworth, "To the Small Celandine," lines 51–52.

3. "In good condition—What do you want? That which God wills, will be, and one needs patience."

4. In 1824 Mary Sabilla Novello gave birth to her eleventh and last child, Charles, who died in May 1825 (Altick, *The Cowden Clarkes*, p. 47).

5. Clara Anastasia Novello (see 9 December [1823]).

6. Hunt had failed to send Mary Shelley his biographical essay on Shelley for the *Posthumous Poems*; he subsequently published it (see 8 April [1825]).

7. Lamb published nothing between December 1823 and September 1824, when he resumed his "Elia Essays" in the *London Magazine* (Lucas, *Charles Lamb*, pp. 120, 130).

8. *History of the Commonwealth of England from its Commencement to the Restoration of Charles the Second*, 4 vols. (London: Henry Colburn, 1824–28).

9. Home of George IV.

10. A committee of fashionable women who made lists of people to be admitted to balls held at Willis's Rooms (originally Almack's Rooms), 26 King's Street, St. James, from c. 1770 to 1863 (*Leigh's New Picture of London* [London: Samuel Leigh, 1820], p. 446).

11. Maria Caterina Rosalbina Caradori-Allen (1800–1865); Manuel del Pópolo Vincente García (1775–1832); Giuseppe Ambrogetti (1780–?); Giuseppe de Begnis (1793–1843); Angelica Catalani (1780–1848); and Ronzi de Begnis (?1800–1853), wife of Giuseppe de Begnis.

12. Tom Kent's first leading part in a London production was in the title role of *Richard III* at Covent Garden Theatre on 17 June 1824 (*MWS Letters*, #209, n. 6).

13. Nancy Hunter, Marianne Hunt's stepsister.

14. Virtue Kent, a cousin of Marianne Hunt (Hunt, *Autobiography*, II, 19).

15. Charles Kemble (1775–1854), actor and manager of Covent Garden Theatre from 1823 to 1833.

16. "Blue eyes," that is, the baby Vincent.

17. Mary Shelley moved to 5 Bartholomew Place, Kentish Town, on 21 June 1824.

*To Arthur Brooke[1]

June 20th [1824] London

My dear Sir

It is with difficulty that I can find terms to thank you for your kind letter of the 11th inst.—It would be ridiculous to accept as merited the expressions with which your admiration for those to whom I belong has betrayed you, at the same time that believing you to be sincere, I feel at once flattered and confounded by such undue compliments.—You cannot doubt but that I must have felt pleasure in seeing Shelley's devoted admirer, and it is natural therefore that I should feel gratified in finding that your visit has not destroyed the interest you entertained.

From your poems as well as your letter, it is apparent that you have suffered a great deal during life. Nor can I wonder at it—since the same sensitiveness that has distinguished your intercourse with me, must in the system of social intercourse under which we live, have been productive of a thousand disappointments to you. There is nothing more certain in philosophy than that we are born to endure pain, &, as I trust, to be made fitter for the enjoyment at least of wisdom, thro' this inexplicable process. But the young with difficulty bend to this necessity and when in the course of years they are conquered, their energies and excellences are also destroyed in the combat. The secret of life appears to me, to be the power of conquering pain & evil.—It is this feeling that guides me; that animated me in the midst of heart-piercing sorrow, and during the annoying cares of daily existence.—If years do not conquer me, and I trust that I shall die young, I entertain the hope, that I shall overcome misfortune, & continue true to myself & to him with whom my happy years were spent.

Your letter has elicited these remarks although I believe that they are almost impertinent in this place. You are now shaking off the clogging load of despair,[2] and I would fain encourage you in the task. You must not permit sorrow to destroy you, and you will surely find consolation in the exertion of the talents you possess—Being extremely occupied at present

I have only found time to look over your interesting volumes;[3] I promise myself a more attentive perusal hereafter, since what I have already seen leads me to expect much pleasure from them. I doubt not that you have been pleased with the Posthumous poems[4] ⟨I sent⟩ they are of more popular nature for the most part that [*than*] his former productions—I wish that the preface had (in the absence of Hunt's notice) been longer and better, but

Trovaimi all' opra via piu lento a frale
D'un picciol ramo cui gran fascio piega
Adunque
Beati gli occhi che lo vider vivo[5]

It will give me great pleasure to see you whenever you visit this great town, and I hope that time will not be very long delayed. I am about to remove to Kentish Town, will you therefore have the goodness, when you write, to address your letters to—Mr John Hunt.—You will be pleased to find that this gentlem[an] has got off without imprisonment,[6] and this long ⟨threat⟩ pending prosecution is at last ended.—

I must again renew my thanks for your kindness, and I hope soon to hear that you are well in health & more cheerful in mind. My boy is quite well

I am most sincerely Yours
MaryW. Shelley

ADDRESS: Arthur Brooke Esq / Canterbury. POSTMARK: D / JU / 21 / 1824. UNPUBLISHED. TEXT: MS., Pforzheimer Library.

1. Arthur Brooke was a pseudonym of John Chalk Claris (?1796–1866), editor of the *Kent Herald*, Canterbury, and poet, whose works included *An Elegy on the Death of Shelley*. Pleased by his great admiration of Shelley, on 7 June 1824 Mary Shelley gave Brooke the fair-copy holograph manuscript of the first part of Shelley's "Prince Athanase" (which she published in *Posthumous Poems*), and a lock of Shelley's hair (*SC*, II, 896; White, *Shelley*, II, 302, 356, 392–93; Norman, *Flight of the Skylark*, p. 54).

2. His wife had died (Norman, *Flight of the Skylark*, p. 50).

3. Brooke's more recent works included *Thoughts and Feelings* (London: Longman, 1820) and *Retrospection* (London: John Warren, 1822), in addition to his *Elegy on the Death of Shelley* (London: C. and J. Ollier, 1822).

4. Brooke purchased six copies of *Posthumous Poems* (Norman, *Flight of the Skylark*, p. 50).

5. From Petrarch, *Canzoniere*. The first two lines are from poem 307, lines 5–6: "I found myself much more slow and frail in my work / Than a little branch bent by a great burden"; the last two lines are from poem 309, lines 13–14: "Then / Blessed are the eyes that saw him alive."

6. See 9 February [1824].

*To Thomas Jefferson Hogg

[14 Speldhurst Street
Brunswick Square] Monday
June 21st [1824]

My dear Hogg

That you may not trudge in vain to Speldhurst Street and find, poi, the bird flown, I have thought proper to cause you to incur the expence of twopence, to tell you that you will find me at 5 Bartholomew Place—Kentish Town, whither I remove today. It is quite at this end of the village on the right hand side—I hope to see you soon there

Yours Ever
MaryShelley

Address: T. Jefferson Hogg Esq / 1 Garden Court / Temple. Postmarks: (1) 10. F.NOON. 10 / 21. JU / 1824; (2) 12. NOON. 12 / 21. JU / 1824. Unpublished. Text: MS., Pforzheimer Library.

*To [?Charles Ollier][1]

Kentish Town—Friday
[?June 1824–August 1825][2]

Dear Sir

I am in great want of a book which describes minutely the Environs of Constantinople—Whether it be in French or English is no consequence; I do not know any such book—but if you cast your eye over Colburns Catalogue you will perhaps meet with one—& you would oblige me if you would send it without delay.—On second thoughts, as I am quite at a stand, I send a special Messenger Can you give him the Volumes

I am extremely obliged to you for your polite offer of services & as you see take the liberty of availing myself of them—

I am your Obt Sert
MaryShelley

Unpublished. Text: MS., Pforzheimer Library.

1. After the publishing firm of Charles and James Ollier foundered in 1823, Charles Ollier became a literary adviser for Henry Colburn (*SC*, V, 127). Charles Ollier served as intermediary between Mary Shelley and Henry Colburn, and in many instances she called on Ollier to aid her in obtaining books for research.

2. Mary Shelley moved to Kentish Town on 21 June 1824. Constantinople is the setting of the opening of the second volume of *The Last Man.* Since Mary Shelley began *The Last Man* in February 1824 and completed it by November 1825, this letter may have been written as late as summer 1825.

*To [?Charles Ollier] Friday Kentish Town [?June 1824–27]

My Dear Sir

Would you have the goodness to get my two Articles that did not pass from Mr Reading,[1] and forward them to me immediately—It is of consequence that I should have them without delay—

I am, dear Sir

Your ob^t^ Servant
MaryShelley

Unpublished. Text: MS., Pforzheimer Library.

1. Perhaps Cyrus Redding (1785–1850), journalist, who was working editor of the *New Monthly Magazine* (under the nominal editorship of Thomas Campbell) from 1821 to 1830. One of the articles may have been "Roger Dodsworth: The Reanimated Englishman," which would place this letter in 1826 (see Charles E. Robinson, "Mary Shelley and the Roger Dodsworth Hoax," *Keats-Shelley Journal* 24 [1975]: 20–28; MWS, *Collected Tales*, pp. 43–50).

To Thomas Forbes Kelsall Kentish Town, 3 July [1824]

My dear Sir,

I hope in a few days to obtain Miss Curran's present address, when I will write to her on the subject of giving the portrait to Mr. Beddoe's care. If I should be unable to get it, will you (as soon as you can) let me have Mr. Beddoes's address, as I will write to her through him. It is quite necessary that I should write to her myself.[1]

I am, Yours truly & obliged
Mary W. Shelley

Corpses are cold in the tomb—
Stones on the pavement are dumb—
Abortions are dead in the womb
And their mothers look pale, like the white shore
Of Albion, free no more!

Her sons are as stones in the way—
They are masses of senseless clay—
They are trodden and move not away;
The abortion with which she travailleth
Is Liberty smitten to death.

Then trample and dance, thou Opressor,
For thy victim is no redressor,
Thou art sole Lord and Possessor
Of her corpses and clods and abortions—they pave
Thy path to the grave.

Hearest thou the festival din
Of Death and Destruction and Sin—

And Wealth crying, Havock! within—
'Tis the Bacchanal triumph which make[s] truth dumb,
Thine Epithalamium.

Aye, marry thy ghastly wife!
Let Fear and Disquiet and strife
Spread thy couch in the chamber of life—
Marry Ruin, thou Tyrant! and God be thy guide
To the bed of thy bride.[2]

ADDRESS: Thomas Kelsall Esq / 67 Great Portland Street. PUBLISHED: Donner, *The Browning Box*; Jones, #211 (Shelley's poem is omitted). TEXT: Donner, *The Browning Box*.

1. On 8 June 1824 Beddoes wrote Bryan Waller Procter from Milan: "If you see Mrs. Shelley, ask her to remember me, and tell her that I am as anxious to change countries with her as she can be. If I could be of any use in bringing the portrait, etc., it would be a proud task, but most likely I only flash over Florence; entering on the flood of the stars, and departing with their ebb" (Beddoes, *Letters*, p. 32). Beddoes did not get the portrait (see 26 July 1822).

2. Shelley's "Lines Written During the Castlereagh Administration." Donner points out that it was Kelsall and not—as was long believed—Medwin who supplied the text of the poem (taken from Mary Shelley's transcription) to the *Athenæum*, where it was published on 8 December 1832 (*The Browning Box*, pp. 21, 144).

*To John Hanson

July 7th [1824] 5 Bartholomew Place
Kentish Town

Sir

I hear that the remains of our lost and lamented friend are arrived;[1] I suppose that they are in quarantine. I hear that Count Pietro Gamba has accompanied them and I should be very much obliged to you if you would forward the enclosed note to him. For many years he was LordByron's constant companion;—By what vessel did they come, and where is the quarantine passed?—

I do not know how far it would be possible, but I very much wish to see the remains of LByron:—I hope that you will excuse my applying to you, but, as executor, it appeared to me that I could make this request to no other person so suitably as to you. Where will he be buried?—Will it be possible for any person to be present except those who attend on the ceremony?—perhaps you will have the goodness to inform me of the time and place and afford me facilities for being there.

Mr Hobhouse,[2] who knew Mr Shelley personally, although I was never happy enough to see him, will not, I am sure, object to what I ask. It is melancholy indeed when all the attention we can bestow on a friend reduces itself to barren honour to their lifeless remains;—but when nothing else is left, we cling to this little with double earnestness.—

Will you tell Mr Hobhouse that I have received a letter from Trelawny with an account of the last moments of LB[3]—but he will hear every thing of this kind as well from Count Gamba and Fletcher. Trelawny was at Solona when the news of his friend's illness reached him, and he set out immediately for Missalonghi, but all was over when he arrived.

I am, Sir—
Your obed[t] Servant
MaryShelley

ADDRESS: John Hanson Esq. UNPUBLISHED. TEXT: MS., John Murray.

1. See [?24–31] May [1824].

2. John Cam Hobhouse, later Baron Broughton (1786–1869), English statesman, had met Byron at Trinity College, Cambridge, and had been Byron's lifelong friend and confidant.

3. Trelawny had written Mary Shelley on 30 April enclosing a letter detailing Byron's death: "This letter I had intended for Hobhouse—but shall not send it. It is a narrative of facts of Lord Byron's death—Hunt may pick something at it—if he please." According to the account, Trelawny had accompanied Byron everywhere for a period of four years and had been his daily companion, which obviously was untrue. Further, Byron is described as fearful of his own cowardliness in contrast to Trelawny's courageousness (*S&M*, IV, 1006–9). John Hunt took some information from Trelawny's accounts for *Examiner* articles.

TO [JOHN HANSON] Kentish Town Friday July 9th [1824]

Sir

I am exceedingly obliged to you for your ⟨kind⟩ polite attention to my request, and shall avail myself, with many thanks, of the opportunity you afford me for gratifying my wish. I shall be in Great George Street[1] precisely at two o'clock today—

I am Sir
Your Obt—Ser[t]
MaryShelley

PUBLISHED: Jones, #213. TEXT: MS., John Murray.

1. Byron was refused burial at Westminster Abbey. Before being carried to his family vault, his remains were at the house of Sir Edward Knatchbull, 20 Great George Street, London (Marchand, *Byron*, III, 1255).

*TO [?CHARLES OLLIER][1] July 11 [?1824–27] Kentish Town—

My dear Sir

My brother[2] has sent to M[r] Colburn a Manuscript which he is desirous he should purchase—& as I understand that you are in the habit of having the Manuscripts thus sent submitted {to} your judgement, I take the liberty of reccommending it particularly to your notice.

Having it before you I need not describe its nature. My brother has for several weeks read at the Museum—& sought the best means of making a good selection—and his talents are such that I have no doubt that he has been able to execute well the plan he had in view—it will be a good book of the kind—& the particular kind is I believe without any rival in the literary world—I hope sincerely that it will meet with yours and Mr Colburns approbation

I am dear Sir
Your Obedient Servant
MaryShelley

I have not forgot that I still have a book of yours; it shall be speedily returned—I hope that your family is good health

UNPUBLISHED. TEXT: MS., Pforzheimer Library.

1. The contents of this letter and its postscript suggest Ollier as the addressee.

2. William Godwin, Jr., had turned from architecture to a career as a writer. He founded a literary society called the Mulberries and in 1823 had two essays published in the *Literary Examiner*. He was a parliamentary reporter for the *Morning Chronicle* and wrote *Transfusion*, a novel published posthumously by William Godwin, Sr., in 1835 (Brown, *Godwin*, p. 358). William Godwin, Jr.'s book was not published by Colburn; nor have I been able to find any other record of this work.

*TO ARTHUR BROOKE[1] July 13th [1824] Kentish Town

My dear Sir

It is with pleasure that, at your request, I renew my invitation for you to come and see me when you visit London. I am now removed to Kentish Town, and am endeavouring notwithstanding our continual rains, to make the best of an English summer and their vaunted green fields. The scenery about here is really pretty; the lawny uplands are here and there shaded by fine trees, and black patches of distant woods, mark the vicinity of grander objects. What a country Italy would become in the hands of the English, since they contrive thus to adorn this ungenial spot.

I have visited the part of the country where you at present are, but it is many years since I made any stay there. My recollection of it is as of a sufficiently dreary spot, cultivated but without any picturesque charm. A great white cliff can hardly be called grand or an extent of sand interesting; —it is only in narrow bays, and in spots where vegetations decks its shores that the sea side is ⟨interesting⟩ pleasing to me; and in any case inland scenery, with a river or a lake is far preferable. These were always my feelings—now, my bitterest enemy could hardly desire for me a greater punishment than a visit to the sea-side. At any rate I do not dream of removing from the neighbourhood of London, since if I could ⟨bust⟩ break the fetters that keep me here, I should escape altogether and return to Italy. It is there only that I can enjoy even the ⟨sad⟩ shadow of the pleasures which were once mine. For the present I am tied here, but this will not last for ever.

I am happy to hear of the health of your son. My Percy is enjoying with keen delight the freedom of a country residence. He is for ever in the fields and his fairness is at present lost. I am seeking tranquillity in study, in attempts at composition, and in the society of a beloved friend who lives near me, who was Shelley's companion as well as mine, and who shared the grief of my miserable loss;—⟨since in losing by the same fate⟩—Among the consolations which are still left to me, my boy's health & her friendship are the principal.—

I hope that you will be well when I have the pleasure of seeing you again. You will find me at 5 Bartholomew Place Kentish Town

I am, dear Sir, Very truly Y^rs^ MaryShelley

ADDRESS: Arthur Brooke Esq / Mr. S. Chalks—Surgeon / Dover. POSTMARK: J / JY / 13 / 1824. UNPUBLISHED. TEXT: MS., Pforzheimer Library.

1. Pseudonym of John Chalk Claris (see 20 June [1824], n. 1).

*To Arthur Brooke[1] [Kentish Town] Wednesday Evening [?21 July 1824][2]

My dear Sir

I am truly obliged to you for your attention; I am afraid that I cannot walk in the morning of either tomorrow or Friday being very peculiarly engaged just now. I shall see you however, I trust, on Friday Evening when we can talk of it, if it be not too late, & if you prefer a ramble that way to our Kentish Town Uplands.

I am, my dear Sir
Yours Ever Obliged
MaryShelley

ADDRESS: Arthur Brooke Esq / &c &c &c. UNPUBLISHED. TEXT: MS., Pforzheimer Library.

1. Pseudonym of John Chalk Claris (see 20 June [1824], n. 1).

2. The last line of this letter suggests that Mary Shelley had already moved to Kentish Town; the address of the letter suggests that Brooke was again in London. On Friday, 23 July 1824, Brooke called on Godwin, and Godwin also noted "Peacock and MWS au soir" (Godwin, Journal). I have therefore tentatively dated this letter 21 July, the Wednesday prior to Mary Shelley and Brooke's call on Godwin.

To Edward John Trelawny July 28th [1824] Kentish Town.

So, dear Trelawny, you remember still poor MaryShelley—thank you for your remembrance and a thousand thanks for your kind letter.[1] It is delightful to feel that absence does not diminish your affection, excellent, warm-hearted friend, remnant of our happy days, of my vagabond life in beloved Italy, our companion in prosperity our comforter in sorrow! You will not wonder that the late loss of LB, makes me cling with greater zeal {to} those dear friends who remain to me—He could be hardly called a friend—but connected with him in a thousand ways, admiring his talents & with all his faults feeling affection for him, it went to my heart when the other day the herse that contained his lifeless form, a form of beauty which in life I often delighted to behold, passed my window going up Highgate Hill on his last journey to the last seat of his ancestors. Your account of his last moments was infinitely interesting to me. Going about a fortnight ago to the house where his remains lay, I found there Fletcher & Lega[2] Lega looking a most preposterous rogue—Fletcher I expect to call on me when he returns from Nottingham—From a few words he imprudently let fall, it w[d] seem that his Lord spoke of C— [*Claire*][3] in his last moments, and of his wish to do something for her at a time when his mind, vaccillating between consciousness & delirium, would not permit him to do anything. Did F. mention this to you. It seems that this doughty Leporello[4] speaks of his lord to strangers with the highest respect—more than he did a year ago—the best, the most generous, the most wronged of peers—the notion of his leading an irregular life quite a false one. Lady B. [*Byron*] sent for F. he found her in a fit of passionate grief, but perfectly implacable, and as much resolved never to have united herself again to him as she was when she first signed their seperation. M[rs] Claremont (the Governess) is living with her.

His death as you may guess made a great sensation here, which was not diminished by the destruction {of} his memoirs, which he wrote & gave to Moore, & which were burned by M[rs] Leigh & Hobhouse.[5] There was not much in them I know, for I read them some years ago at Venice, but the world fancied that it was to have a confession of the hidden feelings of one, concerning whom they were always passionately curious. Moore was by no means pleased he is now writing a life of him himself, but it is conjectured that notwithstanding he had the MS. so long in his possession, that he never found time to read it. I breakfasted with him about a week ago, & he is anxious to get materials for his work. I shewed him your letter on the subject of LB.'s death and he wishes very much to obtain from you any anecdote or account that you w[d] like to send. If you know any thing that ought to be known, or feel inclined to detail anything that you may remember worthy of record concerning him perhaps you will communicate with Moore.[6] You have often said that you wished to keep up our friend's name in the world, & if you still entertain the same feeling, no way is more obvious than to assist Moore—who asked me to make you this request—You can write to him through me, or addressed to Longmans.[7]

But to quit this ⟨eternal⟩ subject, and to come nearer home—& to return to your welcome letter. In {a} happy hour, it seems, you went to Greece, since you find your element there, & have exchanged inertness for activity—You ask Jane & I to come to you—Would that we could—but Greece is not, at present at least, the place for children, & I fear that our little things will forbid such a delightful meeting. Will you not come & see us in our prison here? I sometimes think that you will run over during the coming winter, assure yourself of the existence of your child, remind your Aunts of their affection for you, & embrace the two poor lost girls, who pine for another climate, for lost & absent friends & for the sun of "azure Italy." Nothing distracts our thoughts & talk from the past. We live near eath [*each*] other now & seeing each other almost daily, for ever dwell on one subject. The time of year (fatal July) if possible recalls it more vividly to us. Fatal July I call it—a fated month both for Jane & I—for good and evil fortune. In this month Jane left England with Edward[8]—On this very day ten years ago, I went to France with my Shelley—how young heedless & happy & poor we were then—& now my sleeping boy is all that is left to me of that time—my boy—& a thousand recollections which never sleep.

Here then we are, Jane & I in Kentish Town—After a long duration of cold & rain we have at last fine warm weather—hot, the natives call it—falsely—but, if it w^d^ last, it is better than <u>hot</u> weather for the temperature is quite delightful. The country about here is really pretty; lawny uplands; —wooded parks, green lanes & gentle hills form agreable & varying combinations. If we had orange sunsets—cloudless noons, fire-flies, large halls &c &c I should not find the scenery amiss—and yet I can attach myself to nothing here—neither among the people—tho' some are good & clever—nor to the places—though they be pretty. Jane is my chosen companion & only friend. I am under a cloud, & cannot form new acquaintances among that class whose manners & modes of life are agreable to me—& I think myself fortunate in having one or two pleasing acquaintances among literary people—whose society I enjoy without dreaming of friendship. My child too is in excellent health—a fine tall handsome boy—

And then for money & the rest of those necessary annoyances—the means of getting at the necessaries of life. Jane's affairs are yet unsettled—She has found a kind friend in the heir of her disceased guardian—he advises her to remove her money from India. This step requires time—& she cannot leave England till all is settled. My prospects are somewhat brighter than they were. I have little doubt but that in the course of a few months I shall have an independant income of £300 or 400£ per ann. during Sir Tim's life[9] and that with small sacrifice on my part. After his death Shelley's will secures me an income more than sufficient for my simple habits

One of my first wishes in obtaining the independance I mention will be to assist in freeing Claire from her present painful mode of life. She is now at Moscow sufficiently uncomfortable poor girl—Unless some change has taken place, I think it probable that she will soon return to England. Her spirits will have been improved by the information I sent her that his family consider S's will valid, & that she may rely upon receiving her legacy.[10] We have had a letter from her, but it details no particulars about her situation, while she complains of its extreme discomfort and the bad effect a Russian winter had on her.

It is very long since I heard from Hunt. Others however have had letters —I fear that he is far from happy—Marianne's health is still bad & they live out of Florence, without any society. I have not, for some time had any

Italian letters—but I have seen your brother-in-law Young Lavers, from Genoa—Alithea is as beautiful as ever—Mrs W. [*Wright*] is still with W. who has never heard of your exploits. Mrs Thomas[11] is in London—but I have not seen her lately. I heard from Medwin the other day[12]—He is at [*letter incomplete*]

[*P. 1, top*] I entreat you to write often—& when you communicate with Mr Bowring[13] to ask him to inform me of your having written & yr welfare. As Mr B. has called on me & offered his services, there is no indecorum in this

PUBLISHED: Jones, #214. TEXT: Keats-Shelley Memorial House, Rome.

1. Trelawny's letter of 30 April enclosing an account of Byron's death (see 7 July [1824]).

2. William Fletcher, Byron's valet (see [12 April 1822] to Byron, n. 3), and Lega Zambelli, Byron's Italian secretary and household steward (Moore, *Accounts Rendered*, pp. 244–49).

3. Claire Clairmont. Marchand suggests that Fletcher's report may well be suspect (*Byron*, III, 1258).

4. The servant in Mozart's *Don Giovanni.*

5. For details of the burning of Byron's memoirs, which took place on 17 May 1824 at John Murray's, in the presence of Hobhouse, Moore, and representatives of Augusta Leigh and Lady Byron, see Marchand, *Byron*, III, 1245–51; Moore, *The Late Lord Byron*, pp. 12–45.

6. This is likely the first of the many instances in which Mary Shelley assisted Moore in his *The Letters and Journals of Lord Byron: with Notices of His Life* (London: John Murray, 1830).

7. Longman published many of Moore's works.

8. This resolves the question raised in *SC* as to when in 1819 Edward and Jane Williams eloped and confirms the first of Donald H. Reiman's two hypotheses (see *SC*, VI, 831).

9. At Whitton's suggestion of 14 June, Whitton and Peacock (representing Mary Shelley) were negotiating with the Rock Insurance Company for an annuity that would provide Mary Shelley with £300 per annum for a charge against Shelley's estate in the event of Sir Timothy Shelley's death in the lifetime of either Charles B. Shelley or Percy Florence Shelley (*S&M*, IV, 1011–13). The negotiations proved fruitless (Ingpen, *Shelley in England*, pp. 585–86).

10. £12,000.

11. See 7 January [1823] to Trelawny.

12. Medwin's letter of 10 July informed Mary Shelley that he was writing the "Memoirs of Lord Byron" based on his copious notes of conversations he and Byron had had at Pisa. He added: "Shelley I have made a very prominent feature in the work," believing Mary Shelley would be pleased. He also assured her that the book would not be published until she had seen it. By 17 July Medwin had probably received £500 from Henry Colburn, who published *Conversations* on 23 October 1824. On 13 August 1824 Medwin again wrote Mary Shelley, this time responding to objections she must have sent him (in an unlocated letter). The *Conversations* appeared in fifteen editions between 1824 and 1842 and caused great controversy, angering particularly Hobhouse and Murray, whose friendships with Byron were shadowed in Medwin's telling (Lovell, *Medwin*, pp. 160–70).

13. Sir John Bowring (1792–1872), author, linguist, member of Parliament, diplomat (knighted in 1854), and first editor of the *Westminster Review* (established in 1824). Bowring, a man of considerable learning and a prolific author,

became a close friend of Mary Shelley's. In his capacity as Honorary Secretary to the Greek Committee, which had supported Byron's Greek undertaking, Bowring had information about Trelawny and events in Greece (Byron, *Works*, VI, 205–11).

To Leigh Hunt — 5 Bartholomew Place—Kentish Town—
July 29th [1824]

I hope, my dear Hunt, that you will soon receive the volume of Shelley's poems, which I have sent you through Mrs Mason. It is I believe selling tolerably well.—Since writing to Marianne I have removed to this part of the world—but this I may say, is the only change that has taken place in my situation—except indeed that alteration in spirit which is occasioned by a miraculous duration of fine weather:—We (i.e. the English—I used to say they ahime! talking of the natives) have not had such a summer, they say, for these five years—manca a shower or two we have not had a mizzle this fortnight—They call is hot—it is not—but it is pleasant weather—a little cloudy or so but so convenient in heat that I echo an Italian image-seller who said to me—sarei contento se durasse.[1]

I had a letter the other day from Trelawny—it was dated Missalonghi, to which place he had come hoping to save or attend on the last moments of LB. but he came too late. The funeral[2] last week passed my house—What should I have said to a Cassandra who 3 years ago should have prophecied that Jane and I—Edward and Shelley gone, should watch the funeral procession of LB. up Highgate hill—All changes of romance or drama lag far behind this. Trelawny is sanguine about the cause and his own personal advancement. He has formed a friendship also for a young man (I suppose a Greek) whom he compares to S. in enthusiasm and talent—He invites Jane & I to Greece and we repeat each other's vorrei as we lament over our stupid English life—but it is impossible—quite impossible to go to Greece, I fear ever, and for the present to Italy. Yet I will not be exiled for ever from that dear, dear country—my good compatrioti may rest assured of that.

What news have I? La Novello, dismal beyond measure in her luckless circumstance, is also not pleased that Vincenzo looks upon Italy {as} impossible for this year. Not but I think that she herself is unequal to the journey. We spent the evening at Shacklewell last Monday Mrs B. [*Blaine*] Hunt sang divinely dove sono—& the air from Nina pazza—La Gliddon was there looking very pretty. Bessy was expected but did not come—I fancy there is some embroglio in St. P.s. Ch. Yd concerning Tom's cara sposa. I never saw Bessy look better than when I saw her last, about a fortnight ago—she appeared cheerful & well—

It is about a month since I saw your brother. He talked of bringing out the Bacchus in Tuscany—but I have seen no proofs or advertisements. He has some hopes that LB's executors will pay his fine & expences, since LB wrote to D. [*Douglas*] Kinnaird ordering that this should be done, but

D.K. [*Douglas Kinnaird*] is not executor, nor is it certain how far they are justified in so doing, & I hardly think that M[rs] Leigh will.

I lead a very different life now from that which I did during the winter something that approaches to my Italian one—Jane & I live near each other, & see each other almost every day—we dwell on the past and dream of future Italy. She, poor girl, has been very ill; but tranquillity & the air here have in a great measure restored her, added to her resolution not to be ill, without which I almost think that she would have been lost. I make hardly any visits except to my father, & endeavour to be as recluse as I can, without giving up the friendship of the very few who are dear to me—Operas and theatres are over for me now in summer time—but while I am near Jane I cannot feel lonely. I hope that my affairs have taken a more prosperous turn, but I am as yet quite in the dark although I indulge a hope that I shall encrease my income this winter—in fact I cannot live in this country for what I have—House rent of itself swallows it nearly up.

I long to hear from you—I fear that you are not well or happy & this long silence on your part seems to arise from that. I wish we could change places—I should not wish for better than the chestnut covered hills & olive groves of Maiano—glowing sunsets, fire flies—the cry of the aziolo[3] the language of the [ ] Tuscans—things associated to me with my happiest days—you would be pleased with a quiet abode in Kentish Town—a stroll through its green meadows & rambles up its gentle hills—very pretty things no doubt, & I make the best of them, delighted to have escaped dreary London, & resolved to enjoy the summer.

Mr. Beddoes (a very great admirer of our S.) is now in Italy. He is to get the portrait[4] from Miss Curran who I fancy is in Rome. Could not Marianne send one of the profiles already cut to Miss Curran (who I know w[d] return it with care) & who by this means would ⟨perhaps⟩ make a better likeness than any that exists at present. I own that my heart is set upon Marianne's doing this for what w[d] I not give for a portrait which while he was with me I so often resolved to obtain & was obliged perpetually to disappoint myself. M. wished for scissars which I had no opportunity of sending—but she has some cut—give my love to her & tell her I throw myself at her feet and implore her to comply with my request. How is she, poor thing? And how is Thorny & dear Henry, whom Percy has not forgotten Percy is a fine tall boy—he goes to school & learns to read & write although as yet—school being quite a new thing—he has made little progress—the chief good is that he is employed & likes his employment—& takes pleasure in going thither.

It will give me great pleasure if either you or Marianne would write—I love you both tenderly & am ever

Yours affectionate
Mary W. Shelley

Hazlitt is married—a nice kind of woman they say.[5] The first M[rs] H paid the new-married couple a wedding visit & was much taken with her successor; this is fact. G. Dyer too is married—a very clean woman, he says—she keps him clean at least & that is much.[6]

ADDRESS: Leigh Hunt Esq / Ferma in Posta / Firenze / Florence—Italy. POSTMARKS: (1) F24 / 67; (2) CHAMBERY; (3) CORRISPZA ESTERA DA GENOVA; (4) 14 / AGOSTO. PUBLISHED: Jones, #215. TEXT: MS., Bodleian Library (MS., Shelley, Adds., c. 6, ff. 27–28).

1. "I would be content if it might last."

2. See [?24–31] May [1824].

3. A small, downy owl whose cry is described in Shelley's poem "The Aziola."

4. See 3 July [1824].

5. Hazlitt married Isabella Bridgwater, widow of Lieutenant Colonel Henry B. Bridgwater, in April 1824 in Scotland, since his divorce was not recognized in England. In 1827 Hazlitt and his second wife separated (Wardle, *Hazlitt*, pp. 380–81, 438–39).

6. George Dyer married a Mrs. Mather, three times a widow.

*TO TERESA GUICCIOLI Kentish Town—11mo Agosto [August 1824]

Cara Amica

Profito della occasione che mi è offerta da il Signore Hamilton Browne per scrivervi, ed esprimere come mi è penosa l'idea del vostro soffrire. O Cara Guiccioli, ben si puo dire che sulla strada della vita crescono pochi fiori, e che le espine ci riscon trono ad ogni passo. Come va? E poi che questione? Siete pur infelice e non trovo consolazione atta per voi. I vostri parenti i vostri amici che vi circondono possono dir più che me, ad influire colla lor presenza, meglio di me, la Vra anima.

Non viddi il sempre caro Byron, oime come fosse possibile di vedere già cambiato dalla morte quel bel sembiante—Andai pero alla casa ove fùrono collocati i preziosi resti, e toccai la cassa che lo contenne. Viddi ivi Fletcher e Lega che stettero come persi senza il lor Padrone.—Sento che Pierono è arrivato ma non l'ho veduto fin'ora-quando lo vedo avra la Va ambasciata—deve esso dolersi molto di questo miserabile fine al suo viaggio.

Pare almeno che il Caro Byron soffri poco dolore—temeva la pena della morte non lo morte stessa, ed aspette l'arriva della medesima con sommo corraggio—i nemici suoi non possono far altro che ammirare l'ultima pena della vita sua—e costoro che lo vogliono bene troveranno consolazione nella lor irreperabile perdita, nella gloria bontà e fortitudine che gli furono compagni fin'all'ultimo momento.

Scriverei più lungamente tutta la storia dell'arrivo qui e le ceremonie funerali ma il Sigre H.B. che Vi vedro puo meglio di me contare tutto ciò. Scrivetemi spesso vi prego e credete sempre nella mia amicizia—Commandatemi se vi sia alcuna cosa che volete che sia fatto qui e fidatevi nel mio zelo. Abbiate cura della vostra salute—se si vive la salute è pur sempre un bene prezioso—senza quella si è una noia ad altri—con quella non soffre ⟨altri che se stessa se no⟩ se stessa.

Salutate per me il Sigre Ruggieri il buono pappà, che soffre coi suoi figli e cosi buono e benevolente, è pur persegui tato dalla fortuna—La Williams vi saluta caramente—poverina, anche essa ha perduta quel che fece la vita sua un Eliso—Percy gode ottima salute—non parla più l'Italiana cosa che m'incresce—per me mi pasco dell'idea di tornare a questo bel paese e di trovare l'imagine della felicità che mi è fuggita in questo dolce clima.

Addio, cara Contessina—Crediato sempre nella mia perfetta amicizia e che pur sempre saro di voi

A^ca^ Aff^ma^ e serva
Mary Shelley

Il mio indrizzo è a me
to the care of Mr John Hunt
38 Tavistock Street
Covent Garden
London

[*Translation*]

Dear Friend

I am taking advantage of the opportunity offered to me by Signor Hamilton Browne to write to you and express how distressing the thought of your suffering is to me. Oh Dear Guiccioli, one may certainly say that on the road of life few flowers grow and that their thorns meet us at every step. How does it go? And then, what a question? You are indeed unhappy, and I can't find a suitable consolation for you. Your relatives and friends who surround you can say more than I and can influence your spirit with their presence better than I can.

I did not see the ever beloved Byron; alas how was it possible to see that beautiful countenance already altered by death—However, I went to the house where his precious remains were placed, and I touched the casket that contained them. I saw Fletcher and Lega there, who seemed lost souls without their Master.—I hear that Pierino has arrived, but until now I have not seen him—when I do, he will receive your message—he must greatly lament this miserable ending to his journey.

At least it seems that Dear Byron suffered little pain—he feared the pain of death, not death itself, and awaited its arrival with extreme courage—his enemies cannot but admire the ultimate suffering of his life—and those who love him will find consolation for their irreparable loss in the glory, goodness, and fortitude that were his companions until the final moment.

I would write more at length about the whole story of the arrival here and the funeral ceremonies but Signor H.B., whom you will see, can recount all of it better than I. Write to me often I pray you and believe in my friendship always—Ask me if there is anything that you might want done and trust in my zeal. Take care of your health—if one lives, health is always a precious blessing—without it one is a nuisance to others—with it ⟨only oneself suffers⟩ one does not suffer.

Greet Signor Ruggiero, your good father, for me, who suffers with his children, he is so good and benevolent and still persecuted by destiny—Signora Williams greets you warmly—poor thing, she also has lost he who made her life an Elysium—Percy enjoys the best of health—he no longer speaks Italian, a thing that I regret—for myself I feed on the idea of returning to this beautiful country and finding the image of the happiness that escaped from me in this gentle climate.

Farewell, dear Countess—Believe always in my true friendship and that I will indeed always be your

Most affectionate friend and servant
Mary Shelley

My address is to me
to the care of Mr John Hunt
38 Tavistock Street
Covent Garden
London

UNPUBLISHED. TEXT: MS., Pforzheimer Library. TRANSLATION: Ricki B. Herzfeld.

TO LEIGH HUNT Kentish Town—August 22nd [1824]

My dear Hunt

Although I know that you wish yourself in England, yet it seems to me as if I wrote to Paradise from Purgatory—Our summer is over and rain and perpetual cloud veil this dreary land. I wish you were here since you wish it, yet from all I hear the period does not seem near. Poor dear Marianne! She goes on suffering, and God knows what would become of her in this ungenial climate. Jane and I dream and talk only of our return, and I begin to think that next Autumn this may be possible. A Negociation is begun between Sir T. S. [*Timothy Shelley*] & myself by which, on sacrificing a small part of my future expectations on the will, I shall ensure myself a sufficiency, for the present, & not only that, but be able, I hope, to releive Claire from her disagreable situation at Moscow. I have been obliged however as an indispensable preliminary, to suppress the Post. Poems[1]—More than 300 copies had been sold so this is the less provoking, and I have been obliged to promise not to bring dear S's name before the public again during Sir. T—'s life. There is no great harm in this, since he is above 70, & from choice I should not think of writing memoirs now and the materials for a volume of more works are so scant that I doubted before whether I could publish it.—Such is the folly of the world—& so do things seem different from what they are, since from Whitton's account Sir T. writhes under the fame of his incomparable son as if it were a most grievous injury done to him.—& so perhaps after all it will prove.—All this was pending when I wrote last, but until I was certain I did not think it worth while to mention it. The affair is arranged by Peacock, who though

I seldom see him, seems anxious to do me all these kind of services, in the best manner that he can.

It is long since I saw your brother nor had he then any news for me—I lead a most quiet life & see hardly any one. Mrs Novello, Vincent C.C.C. [*Charles Cowden Clarke*] & Werter went to Boulogne the other day, whence V. escaped & returned to England, & the other three posted on to Paris, earning pleasure hardly I should think, especially as Mrs N. [*Novello*] appears in a continual fever—The Gliddons are gone to Hastings for a few weeks.—Hogg is on the circuit—now that he is rich he is so very poor—so unamiable & so strange that I look forward to his return without any desire of shortening the term of absence.—Poor Pierino is now in London—Non fosse male questo paese, he says, se vedesse mai il Sole[2]—He is full of Greece to which he is going to return, and gave us an account of our good friend T— [*Trelawny*] which shew [th]at he is not at all changed. T.— had made a hero of the Greek Chief Ulysses—& declares that there is a great cavern in Attica which he & Ulysses have provisioned for 7 years & to which if the Cause fails he & this Chieftain are to retire[3]—but if the Cause is triumphant he is to build a city in the Negropont, colonize it & Jane & I are to go out to be Queens & Chieftanesses of the Island. When T.— first came to Athens—he took to a Turkish life bought 12 or fifteen women—brutte mostre—Pierino says—one a Moor, of all things—& there he lay on his sopha, smoking, these gentle creatures about him—till he got heartily sick of idleness shut them up in his haram & joined & combated with Ulysses. He has quarrelled very violently with Mavrocordato, but I easily divine how all this is—poor Mavrocordato, beset by covetous Suliotes, disliked by the chieftains of the Morea—caballed against by the strangers—poor, while every other chief is getting rich, is drinking deep of the bitter cup of calumny & disappointment.

But to quit Greece & return to England. The Opera House is closed—before it shut I heard Pasta[4] & never was more affected by any scenic representation than by her acting of Romeo—She joins intellectual beauty, grace, perfect tragic action to a fine voice & a sentiment in singing I never saw equalled. When she sees Giulletta in the tomb—when she takes poison, when Giulletta awakes & her joy at meeting is changed to the throes of death, the whole theatre was in one transport of emotion.—The novelty now is the Der Freishutz of Weiber—performing at the Lyceum & the music is wild but often beautiful—when the magic bullets are cast they fill the stage with all sorts of horrors—owls flapping the[ir] wings—toads [hopp]ing about—fierly[5] serpents darting & the [ ] ghostly hunters in the clouds, while every now & then in the [ ] of a stream of wild harmony comes a crashing discord—all forms I assure you a very fine scene, while every part of the house except the stage is invelloped in darkness.

One of my principal reasons for writing just now is that I have just heard Miss Curran's address (64, Via Sistina, Roma) & I am anxious that Marianne should (if she will be so very good) send one of the profiles already cut, to her, of Shelley, since I think that by the help of that Miss C— will be able to correct her portrait of S— and make for us, what we so much desire, a good likeness—I am convinced that Miss C— will return the profile immediately that she has done with it—so that you will not sacrifice it, though you may be the means of our obtaining a good likeness.

I will write soon to Marianne—in the mean time I wish she would write to me since I long to hear from her, & should be very glad whenever you will be kind enough to assure me of the continuance of your friendship although I fear it is gone to the tomb of the Capulets—but I do not deserve this catastrophe—Give my love to your children—Occhi Turchini among the rest—& believe me ever, my dear Hunt

Your faithful friend MaryW. Shelley

[*P. 1, top*] Direct to me thro' y^r brother

ADDRESS: Leigh Hunt Esq / Ferma in Posta / Firenze / Italie / Florence—Italy. POSTMARKS: (1) F24 / 103; (2) ANGLET[ERR]E; (3) CHA[MBE]RY; (4) CORRISPZA ESTERA [DA GENOVA]. PUBLISHED: Jones, #216. TEXT: MS., Bodleian Library (MS., Shelley, Adds., c. 6, ff. 29–30).

1. See 18 September [1823].
2. "This country might not be bad . . . if one could see the sun sometime."
3. Odysseus Androutsos (d. 17 June 1825), a Greek chieftain who controlled most of Eastern Greece from Parnassus to Athens. Odysseus betrayed the Greek cause by making a truce with the Turks, but was captured and killed by Mavrocordato (St. Clair, *Trelawny*, 102, 115–16; *SC*, V, 54–56). Trelawny married Odysseus's sister (see 22–27 February [1825], n. 2). In September 1824 Trelawny sent Mary Shelley "a Description of the Cavern Fortress of Mt Parnassus belonging to General Ulysses commanded by Cap^n E. Trelawny," with the request that she "make an article" of it and have John Hunt publish it in the *Examiner* (Abinger MS.; *S&M*, IV, 1027–31).
4. Giuditta Pasta (c. 1798–1865).
5. A miswriting of *fiery*.

To Thomas Jefferson Hogg Kentish Town. August 30th [1824]

My dear Jefferson

I am happy to say at last that <u>you</u> have some reason to complain of heat, while {the} atmosphere is to my feelings genial and delightful. Court cannot be the best place to enjoy it—and you describe the pains of circuit[1] so vividly that I own while I had wherewithal to buy bread & cheese I would never submit to them—as to the argument, <u>one must do something</u>, I own I should think myself very silly, if I could not find occupation more profitable to mind & body than Bell versus Jenkins. But being a female & not being cut out by nature to make one of your black-stoled & be-wigged company, my word will hardly appear to you law.—& besides Fetter Lane[2] is not my terrestrial Paradise.—

I thank you for your congratulations on the good turn fortune seems about to do me.[3] In such matters I am patience itself. I live quietly, write

—read a little Greek; & having finished the Furioso have begun la Divina Comedia which interests me beyond measure I am reading besides North's trans. of Plutarch's Lives & the Æneid. Virgil is a great favourite of mine—his harmonious style his grace and majesty make interesting an otherwise dull account of war & diplomatics, but where his subject is worthy his style, he may claim rivalship with the greatest Poets—So my mornings pass & my evening are for the most part spent with Jane. You ask me news of her—there she dwells in her flower adorned bower, sometimes gay, sometimes sorrowful always gentle, always dear. Your last letter appeared to annoy her; I do not wish to touch on this subject, especially as I did not see your letter, but I am sure that she, the most open hearted of human beings, can never have deceived you by appearing what she was not, & I think with your great understanding you might contrive to please instead of to annoy "the fair one"—& to make her smile instead of frown—But I fear that se manca una cosa,[4] you are indifferent to her smiles or frowns & if so you will expect what was happened. However I do not wish to turn preçheuse. I would give worlds to see dear Janey happy—if you can make her happy—so—if not—so—but do not, I entreat you add to her annoyances.

It is a slippery & turbulent eminence to which you every now and then exalt some one of us womankind—we inhabit a stormy region, & as a king with golden chains, we cannot at will throw off our Hogg-bestowed sovereignty—Before I came I had an idea of my fall, & that contributed to render the ⟨idea⟩ thought of England less painful—for I am glad, very glad to see you as a friend—and you as far as you understand its duties or are willing to fulfill them will I doubt not be such to me. But to please you I must talk of J. & not myself—Yet what can I say of J. that will please you? If you were disinterested I would tell you that she is in better health, alquanto più contentina forse[5]—but without an interest in life, without being animated by the god of her existence, Love, J. can only live half a life. You did not know her when she possessed all her heart desired, nor beheld the lovely spectacle of her devotion to Edward & her happiness while thus devoted to him—She was not then monitress or precheuse—she did not scold or find fault—she was all benevolence, all cheerfulness.

The G's [*Guiccioli's*] brother, Count Gamba, is now in town and I have seen him several times. Knowing LB. as well as I did, I was very anxious to obtain an account of his last moments—they were peaceful—attended neither by pain or fear. His end was like the closing of a flower at sunset—e cosa era da lui.[6] Medwin is going to publish his account of him & many confidential conversations that LB (when tipsey) had with him. I have done all I can to prevent our circle from being named & he has promised not to mention me—Dear S. will be there however & that is sufficiently annoying. All the world will be there—& M. will make many enemies & do no one any good, least himself—unless the yellow coin he receive for it is to {be} considered a good—If he thinks to gain honour by "I and LordB" he is mistaken—the world soon divines the secret of such intimacies.

I have heard from poor Claire who is still at Moscow. I hope that she will return to Vienna for there she has friends—but Russia & its inhabitants do not seem habitation or companionship for any thing superior to a bear—The climate hurts her health, & the brutality of her associates her spirits. P. [*Peacock*] is in the country—when he returns in Sept. & W. [*Whitton*] shall have seen Sir T. [*Timothy*] my affairs will I suppose commence their snail's progress—at present they are as quiet as stones [ ] From Hunt I have not heard—of him I hear that M. [*Marianne*] is still il[l]—What would each give he & I to change countries at this momen[t] pazienza! I hope to see the sun of Italy next year.

Percy & Jane's children also are quite well,[7] and I more attached than ever to the Green fields & blue fields of Kentish Town—The green fields of Earth which are entombed by houses—the blue fields of sky which are veiled by smoke in London. I hope you return as well in health, wiser & gentler than you went out—& more accommodating to me; for tho' I thank you sincerely for the letters you have lent me, I entreat you not to deny me a loan of the former ones.[8] Have I so many pleasures that you who can bestow a great one on me & who call yourself my friend, should deny it me?

Adieu, my dear Jefferson,
I am Yours Ever
MaryShelley

(The Gisbornes I have seen twice—She is a{s} usual—very amiable & nice.—

ADDRESS: T. Jefferson Hogg Esq / Norton—near Stockton on Tees / Durham. POSTMARK: I / SE / 1 / 1824. PUBLISHED: Scott, *New Shelley Letters*, pp. 146–49. TEXT: MS., Pforzheimer Library.

1. This letter responds to a letter from Hogg of 22 August (*S&M*, IV, 1022–25).

2. One end of Fetter Lane opens into Fleet Street, where students study law at the Inns of Court. Hogg had studied at Middle Temple, one of the Inns of Court, and was called to the bar in 1817 (Norman, *After Shelley*, p. xi).

3. Hogg had written: "It gave me great pleasure to hear that Sir Timothy has proposed to purchase Field Place of you." Since Field Place was Sir Timothy Shelley's home, Hogg must be referring to a proposal that Mary Shelley give up future rights to Field Place. This arrangement was not concluded.

4. "*If something is missing.*"

5. "Somewhat more contented perhaps."

6. "And this was from him."

7. On 26 September Hogg responded to this letter: "It gave me great pleasure to hear such a good account of yourself, of Jane & the children; I have no doubt that the young gentlemen will be much improved by going to school: Kentish Town is much better calculated for them no doubt than London, & they will grow apace, like ill weeds. . . . & Dina seems to be so well instructed by Bonne in the rudiments of modesty, that, when she is old enough to make an interesting catastrophe, she will

no doubt shew the same aversion, wch I applaud & you condemn, to strip herself before sailors" (*S&M*, IV, 1034).

8. Mary Shelley is almost certainly referring to Shelley's letters to Hogg. Hogg's response to this letter makes no mention of her request (*S&M*, IV, 1034–36).

TO THOMAS JEFFERSON HOGG Kentish Town. Oct. 3rd [1824]

You were very good, my dear Jefferson, to thank me for my last letter, as I confess that I wrote it under the influence of that ill temper which you say is peculiar to women, and not to your species, putting yourself forward as the ecce signum[1] of your theory. I was cross, first because you annoyed Jane—the account which you give of the cause of her annoyance differs materially from hers, & I own it amused me; it put me in mind of the beginning of Gay's fable of the "Goat without a beard."[2]—And then more over you insulted my Greek. Do you think that I would exchange the gentle courtesies of life for a smattering of a language of which I shall never be mistress. My defect of verbal memory will prevent my ever attaining proficiency in it—and my character makes me too sensitive (in every sense of the word <u>too</u>) of the demænour of others, and causes me to cling with childish pleasure to the spirit of politeness. It is not for amusement but for the final improvement of my mind that I grub at Greek roots—if I have any intercourse with others it is necessary to the getting any relief from my usual & too-well-caused despondency to be treated with forbearance & attention—if after losing those who gave me their affections, I cannot obtain the courtesy of your species I will cut their acquaintance for ever.

Jane & I lead our usual monotonous life and the approach of winter, rain & mud render us more eager each day for a return to our beloved adopted counrty—We do not here enjoy the pleasures to which we were accustomed under the benign sky of Italy & our situation prevents us from enjoying your English pleasures. Poor & protectorless what have we to do here?—We meet almost every evening & make visits sometimes to our common friends—We have been several times to the Gisbornes—She is my delight. her gentleness toleration & understanding, & not the least of her attractions, her affection for me, render her dear to me. If during the last twenty years she had cultivated her mind while living with a person superior to herself what would she not have become?—petty cares & deference to the judgement of one so entirely her inferior, have narrowed many of her views, still she is a charming personage & her humility sheds infinite grace over all her proceedings. I have been very little out elsewhere since I saw you except my visits to the Strand. I must except a few evenings at the Opera where I enjoyed an unexpected pleasure in Mad^me^ Pasta. I saw her in Romeo. Joined to a graceful form, intellectual beauty of countenance, eyes of deep meaning and irristible sweetness, she possesses a fine voice & a talent for tragic acting which affected me as much as the Sir G.O.[3] of

Kean. She is not perhaps so great, I cannot entirely judge as I saw her only once, but though you may think this strange, her singing added to the pathos of her representation. She produced an electrical effect in the house & haunted my thoughts—even my dreams for several days—then Jane & I went two or three times to der Freischutz—We liked the music & the incantation scene would have made Shelley scream with delight flapping owls—ravens, hopping toads, queer reptiles—fiery serpents skeleton huntsmen—burning bushes and a chorus made up of strange concords & discords produced a fine effect in the, but for the stage, entirely darkened house.

So much for pleasure. For business—I am so patient that I do not complain though nothing is done—Whitton has been to the North[4]—he is now I believe at Field Place, where he promises to aeange [*arrange*] all satisfactorily—he may waste time, but not eternity; since before the end of that Sir Tim or I will be in kingdom Come, where the acres of of the S. estate will probably be of little value—& I am tolerable proof against delay—while I have bread & potatoes what is the rest? the happiness I enjoyed and the sufferings I endured in Italy make present pleasures & annoyances appear like the changes of a mask—I can sometimes for a while enter into the spirit of the game, but my affections are in the past & my imagination is not much exalted by a representation mean & puerile when compared to the real delight of my intercourse [with] my exalted Shelley, the frank hearted and affectionate Edwa[rd] and others then of less note, but remembered now with fon[dness] as having made a part of the Elect.—

I suppose that we shall see you in the course of this month You will find us still at Kentish Town where we intend to spend the last winter, I trust, that we shall remain in England—Sometimes in spite of mud, rain and cold you will stray from your beau-ideal, Fetter Lane, to this ill paved Village—we shall be almost intirely confined here—for Jane will not risk her health nor I my comfort by long peregrinations to your dreary town. Even in winter the country is most delightful, & during its fine days—its uplands naked woods open sky & green meadows transcend the dirt & gloom of streets—

Percy is well—Adieu, my dear Jefferson

I am Yours Ever
MaryShelley

ADDRESS: T. Jefferson Hogg Esq / Norton / Stockton-upon-Tees / Durham. POSTMARKS: (1) S.O. Kentish [Tn]; (2) 7. NIGHT. 7 / OC. 4 / 1824; (3) OQO / 4 / 1824. PUBLISHED: Scott, *New Shelley Letters*, pp. 149–52. TEXT: MS., Pforzheimer Library.

1. "Behold the proof."

2. " 'Tis certain that the modish passions / Descend among the crowd like fashions" (John Gay, "The Goat Without a Beard," *Fables* [London, 1736], p. 66, lines 1–2). In Hogg's letter of 26 September 1824 to Mary Shelley he explained that Jane Williams had been angry at him because he said "all my friends are going to marry" and he "should probably follow them." To Mary Shelley's allusion to Gay's fable, Hogg responded on 16 October 1824 that since the "Goat in the Fable

was a He-goat, it will not apply to the person, for whom you intend it" (copies of Hogg's letters, John Gisborne Notebook No. 8, Abinger Ms.).

3. Sir Giles Overreach (see [?] 22 March [1824], no. 9).

4. Whitton informed Peacock of his return to London on 23 September. Concerning the *Posthumous Poems*, Whitton wrote that contrary to his expectations, based on Peacock's judgment that the copies sold would balance the expense of publication, he had received "a demand" from John Hunt of nearly a hundred pounds, which he refused to pay, "let what will happen" (*S&M*, IV, 1033–34).

To Marianne Hunt — Kentish Town—Oct. 10th [1824]

My dearest Marianne

My interest in you and your dear circle has been excited in the most lively and painful way by the news I have had of you through Bessy. One's first thought is can one not in any way aid these beloved exiles? and then I shrink into myself in despair at my nothingness. If it were not for your's & Hunt's health, I am convinced that Novello's active friendship wou{l}d dissipate other difficulties and restore you to the England you love. In the mean{time} are there not resources by which you might be rendered more comfortable where you are—J.H. [*John Hunt*] says that Colbourn wishes H. [*Hunt*] to contribute to the N. [*New*] Monthly, if this be true he would pay liberally and H. need not feel delicasy towards his brother since the latter has no violent wish that the W.C.'s [*Wishing Caps*] sh^{d} be continued.[1] From what J.H. said perhaps there is a negociation with Colb^{rn} already on foot—if not if I can thro' H. [*Horace*] Smith (who is now in E. [*England*] & expected dayly in London)[2] or in my own person contribute to such an arrangement I pray you employ me. I am anxious beyond measure to hear from you—from you, my Polly, in particular—since you will send me the most vivid picture of what is passing near. Write if you love me.—

I write to you on the most dismal of all days a rainy sunday, when dreary church-going faces look still more drearily from under dripping umbrellas, and the poor plebeian dame looks reproachfully at her splashed white stockings—not her gown, that has warily been held high up and the to-be-concealed petticoat has borne all the ill usage of the mud. Dismal though it is, dismal tho' I am, I do not wish to write a discontented letter but in a few words to describe things as they are with me—a weekly visit to the Strand a monthly visit to Shacklewell (when we are sure to be caught in the rain) forms my catalogue of visits—I have no visitors—if it were not for Jane I should be quite alone—The eternal rain imprisons one in one's little room & one's spirits flag without one exhiliarating circumstance. In some things however I am better off than last year for I do not doubt but that in the course of a few months I shall have an independance, and I no longer balance as I did last winter, between Italy an{d} England. My father wished me to stay, & old as he is, and wishing as one does to be of some use somewhere I thought that I would make the trial and stay if

I could. But the joke is become too serious; I look forward to the coming winter with horror, but it shall be the last. I have not yet made up my mind to the where in Italy, I shall if possible immediately on arriving push on to Rome. Then we shall see. I read, study & write; sometimes that takes me out of myself—but to live for no one, to be necessary to none; to know that—"where is now my hope? for my hope, who shall see it? They shall go down to the bars of the pit, when our rest together is in the dust."[3]—But change of scene & the sun of Italy will restore my energy, the very thought of it smooths my brow. Perhaps never content with the climate, I shall seek the heats of Naples, if they do not hurt my darling Percy.—

And now what news? Mrs N. [*Novello*] is all horrors of the Month expectant—hardly knowing whether she will not leave her home & comforts to spend it in town on account of the Doctor. Poor Statia, feels each day more the falling off & separation that Shacklewell has caused—to poor people it is no joke to pay a visit with the fear of spending 10 shillings before they can get back—& then Shacklewell is so dreary—the road to it so hateful & there you sit watching the clouds & clock—fearful of rain fearful of being too late.—We had a fright the other day fearing that Miss L. [*Lamb*] was going to be taken ill—but she is now quite well, so she will escape this year. I was to have dined there today had it not been for the rain—She always asks most affectionately after you. Procter is married he married A. Skepper last Thursday[4]—of course I shall never see him again. When you spoke of him & H. [*Hunt*] offered me an introduction to him I declined it knowing that since he was connected with M^rs M [*Montagu*], all would happen—as it has happened; since introducing himself to me I have seen him i.e. that his gentleness, poetical taste & conversation would interest & please me, & then that he w^d disappear from my horizon leaving regret behind. He called on me several times last winter and sat several hours, I was very much pleased with him—& I shall never see him again, which pains me. The same paper that announced his marriage gave out the death of Ld C. Murray[5]—I liked his letter to H. I liked the feeling and the conduct of the man & he is gone. Pierino Gamba is in town—I have seen him often & talk over old times.—Hogg is going the circuit, being more queer, stingy and supercilious than ever. Peacock transacts my business with Sir T.S.'s [*Timothy Shelley's*] Solicitor else I never see him. Colson went to France last Spring and has not yet recovered from the enthusiasm inspird by the French women & Notre Dame. Hazlitt is abroad—he will be in Italy in the winter. He wrote an article in the E.R. on the Vol of Poems w^hch I published[6]—I do not know whether he meant it to be favourable or not—I did not like it at all—but when I saw him I could not be angry—I never was so shocked in my life, gau[nt] & thin, his hair scattered, his cheek bones projecting—but for his voice & smile I sh^d not have known him—his smile brought tears into my eyes, it was like a sun-beam illuminating the most melancholy of ruins—lightning that assured you in a dark night of the identity of a friend's ruined &

deserted abode.—Well what more gossip can I send?—There is a naughty story that Eros (Eros, Polly!) was discovered by his most sacred M—y [*Majesty*] with Lady C—ngh—m,[7] that the k. fainted and Eros was obliged to turn from love making to the art of medecine—Of course it is not true —of course—but I say nothing—but this I will say[8]—oh love! it is!—Pray how is Anteros.—

Have you, my Polly, sent a profile to Miss C. [*Curran*] in Rome—now pray do—& pray write—do, my dear girl—Next year by this time I shall perhaps be on my road to you—it will go hard but that I contrive to spend a week (that is if you wish it) at F. [*Florence*] on my way to the Eternal City. God send that this prove not an airy Castle—but I own that I put faith in my having money before that—& I know that I could not if I would endure the torture of my English life longer than is absolutely necessary. By the bye I hear that you are keeping your promise to Trelawny —and that in due time he will be blessed with a name-sake[9]—How is Occhi Turchini—Thornton the Reformed—⟨Jhonny⟩ Johnny—the—what Johnny?—the good boy—Tray?—Mary the merry, Swiny the Sober, Percy the Martyr & dear Sylvan the good?

Percy is quite well, tell his friend—he goes to school & lea{r}ns to read & write—being very handy with his hands—perhaps having a pure anticipated cognition[10] of the art of painting in his tiny fingers. Mrs W—'s [*Williams's*] little girl, who call's herself Dina, is his wife. Poor C— [*Claire*] is at Moscow—at least she will be independant one day—& if I am so soon her situation will quickly be ammeliorated.—Do you know among other chances—I shall probably visit Dublin next summer—

Have you heard of Medwin's book—notes on conversations that he had at Pisa with L.B. (when tipsy) Every one is to be in it & every one will be angry [*cross-written*] he wanted me to have {a} hand in it but I declined —Years ago "When a man died the worms ate him.{"}[11]—Now a new set of worms feed on the carcase of the scandal that he leaves behind him & grow fat upon the world's love of tittle tattle—I will not be numbered among them

Have you received the Vol. of Poems. Give my love to Very—& so dear Very Patient
Adieu

Yours affly
Mary Shelley

ADDRESS: Mrs. Leigh Hunt / Ferma in Posta / Florence—Firenze / Italy. POSTMARKS: (1) PAID / [ ] / 1824; (2) F24 / 59; (3) ANGLETERRE; (4) CHAMBERY; (5) CORRISPZA DA GENOVA; (6) 26 / OTTOBRE. PUBLISHED: Jones, #219. TEXT: MS., Bodleian Library (MS., Shelley, Adds., c. 6, ff. 31–32).

1. On 4 November 1824 Leigh Hunt wrote to Bessy Kent: "I continue to write Wishing-Caps for every other week, and Colburn after repeatedly invited [inviting] me to write in his Magazine, has agreed with me that I shall do so for a year certain and for £150 the first year, at the rate of 16 guineas a sheet; which he says is the largest pay given" (Brewer, *The Holograph Letters*, p. 135).

2. Horace Smith's close association with Henry Colburn was used as entrée for Mary Shelley's own work (see 9 February [1824], n. 10, 7 November [1825]). Mary Shelley's comment here confirms Hyder E. Rollins's conjecture that Smith returned to England in 1824 and not, as A. H. Beavan states, in 1825 ("Letters of Horace Smith to His Publisher Colburn," *Harvard Library Bulletin* 3 [1949]: 363).

3. Job 17:15–16.

4. On 7 October Procter had married Anne Skepper, stepdaughter of Basil Montagu.

5. On 5 October the *Morning Chronicle* announced that Lord Charles Murray had died at Gastouni on 11 August; on 13 October it reported that Murray was being mourned in Greece for his endeavors on behalf of Greek liberty.

6. "Art. X. Posthumous Poems of Percy Bysshe Shelley," *Edinburgh Review* 40, no. 80 (July 1824): 494–514.

7. Eros is probably Sir William Knighton (1776–1836), who had been the Hunts' physician in their "bridal days" (Hunt, *Correspondence*, I, 165). In 1810 Knighton became physician and adviser to the Prince Regent, who as George IV appointed him Keeper of the Privy Purse (*SC*, V, 486–87). Elizabeth Lady Conyngham (d. 1861), wife of Henry Conyngham, first Marquis Conyngham (1766–1832), was the favorite of George IV throughout his reign as King. She exercised strong influence on the King, considerably increasing her wealth through her connection with him.

8. Don Juan I.52.

9. The Hunts' eighth child was named Julia Trelawny Leigh Hunt (1825–60); however, evidence in Marianne Hunt's diary suggests that she was born c. December 1825 (Edmund Blunden, " Marianne Hunt: A Letter and Fragment of a Diary," *Keats-Shelley Memorial Bulletin* 10 [1959]: 31).

10. From Shelley's note to line 534 of *Peter Bell the Third.*

11. *As You Like It* 4. 1. 110: "Men have died from time to time, and worms have eaten them."

To Thomas Jefferson Hogg

[?Kentish Town
?c. November 1824][1]

Dear Jeff. Have you the works of Cicero? I am getting ashamed of my neglect of latin & wish to rub it up—I want to read the orations letters &c of Cicero—if you could lend them {to} me—or tell me how & where I could get a loan of them you w[d] oblige me infinitely

Y[s] truly MS.

ADDRESS: T. J. Hogg Esq. PUBLISHED: Scott, *New Shelley Letters*, p. 146. TEXT: MS., Pforzheimer Library.

1. Mary Shelley's Journal for 3 December 1824 records that she tried to gain both fortitude and calm through studying "philosophic thoughts" and particularly refers to "Cicero's description of that power of virtue in the human mind w[h] renders man's frail being superior to fortune."

To John Cam Hobhouse

5 Bartholomew Place Kentish Town
Nov. 10. [1824]

My dear Sir

I have read over your sheets[1]—& have made the following remarks only. If I had had M[r] Medwin's book by me I might have enlarged them.

P.1.—While the dayly occurences of my life were at all interesting to me I kept a kind of journal—more for the sake of dates than for any thing else. In this I find, on Tuesday, August 27—1816 "Shelley dines at Diodati with Mr H. [*Hobhouse*] and S. [*Scrope*] Davis—& remains there all the evening—they go out for a short time in the boat.[2]—The circumstance is immaterial—but this is a war of facts, & Medwin may appeal to me. There was certainly no storm—but if my memory do not fail me, a hat was wrecked during the expedition. (By the bye Medwin is Captain by courtesy only—is it courtesy to pint[3] a lieutenant a Captain? I am not aware of the etiquette on this point

p.2.—Is not the Cardinal's name Consalvi?[4]—

p.4 Methinks I have heard LordByron complain of the presence of the lady's maid in the carriage—but if you were there, you must know best.—

p.7. LB. was ⟨certainly⟩ incapable of praising his own verses—& was certainly satisfied with the opinion all present had of his talents—Shelley was a warm admirer of his poetry.—

p.10 Mazi was a Sergeant not a Major.[5]

Not being able to refer to the book, I can only mention a mistake or two that I remember to have struck me. The conversation said to have been held at Diodati is fictitious, since I never saw Lewis in my life—and the stories alluded to (with the exception of that of Lewis) were never related. As I have an invincible objection to the seeing my name in print, this were as well passed over—unless you chose to observe that the Preface to Frankenstein proves that that story was conceived before Lord Byron's and Shelley's tour round the lake, and that Lewis did not arrive at Geneva until some time after.[6]

Medwin could also have mentioned that as soon as Dr Nott heard that he was accused of the impropriety of preaching against Shelley, he paid us a visit to exculpate himself from the charge.

How completely he spoils your story of the Definite Article;[7] I have it as recorded by one of abler memory where it cuts a much better figure

You justly remark that LordByron could not have made an inaccurate quotation—his memory was admirable—

Medwin requested me to correct his MS. I declined even seeing it—He afterwards sent me his Memoir of Shelley[8]—I found it one mass of mistakes—I returned it uncorrected—earnestly entreating him not to publish it—as it would be highly injurious to my interests to recall in this garbled manner past facts at a time that I was endeavouring to bring Sir T.S. [*Timothy Shelley*] to reason. When I have the book I will point out a few of these mistatements—The book has been a source of great pain to me, & will be of more—I argued against the propriety & morality of hurting the living by such gossip—& deprecated the mention of any of my connections—to what purpose, you see.

Hence has arrisen a "Narrative of a Voyage &c{"}[9]—When in fact Shelley was never at sea with LordByron—In times past when a man died the worms eat him,[10] now in addition viler insects feed on his more precious memory, wounding the survivors by their remorseless calumnies

Count Gamba has promised that I shall have the book tomorrow when I will again write. He tells me also that he has mentioned to you my wish to have certain letters—but as he gives me hopes that I shall have the pleasure of seeing you, I will defer speaking of these until we meet. Perhaps you will do me the favour to accompany him some morning to Kentish Town.

I have written in great haste—I am, dear Sir

Your Obedient Servant
MaryShelley

ADDRESS: J. C. Hobhouse Esq / &c &c &c. ENDORSED: Mrs Shelley—1824 / November 11. PUBLISHED: Lovell, *Medwin*, pp. 200–201 (almost complete). TEXT: MS., John Murray.

1. Hobhouse's pamphlet "Exposure of the Mis-statements Contained in Captain Medwin's Pretended 'Conversations of Lord Byron'" was intended to prove that Medwin's *Conversations*, published on 23 October 1824, was fraudulent. On 5 November Pietro Gamba assisted Hobhouse by going through Medwin's book and pointing out inaccuracies. On 9 November Hobhouse gave the pamphlet to John Murray. Medwin's description of Byron's quarrel and disassociation with Murray, with no reference to their reconciliation, had considerably upset the publisher, and he was delighted to have Hobhouse's refutation. On 10 November the proofs of the pamphlet were ready, and on that same day they were sent to Mary Shelley so that she could point out any further inaccuracies by Medwin. Hobhouse finally decided not to publish the pamphlet; instead he submitted it as a review to John Murray's *Quarterly*. Murray declined to publish it, however, and it appeared anonymously in the January 1825 issue of the *Westminster Review* (Moore, *The Late Lord Byron*, pp. 94–124; Lovell, *Medwin*, pp. 173–203).

2. Mary Shelley combined two entries: Hobhouse and Scrope Davies arrived on 26 August 1816; they went boating on 27 August (*MWS Journal*).

3. Although Lovell gives this word as *print*," the manuscript clearly reads "pint," which Mary Shelley may have been using according to its slang definition, namely, "praise" or "recommendation" (Partridge, *A Dictionary of Slang*).

4. Cardinal Ercole Consalvi, Secretary of State to Pius VII, was kept informed of Byron's involvement with the Carbonari through spies and police (Marchand, *Byron*, II, 878–79, 887; Byron, *Works*, IV, 460–64).

5. Masi was a sergeant major.

6. Shelley and Byron toured the lake from 22 to 30 June 1816; Matthew Lewis (1775–1818), author of *The Monk*, arrived on 14 August.

7. A fellow collegian of Byron's resented being called "a Mr. Tuke" by Hobhouse, to which Scrope Davies replied that "he supposed Mr. Tuke wanted to be called the Mr. so and so. He ever after went by the name of the 'Definite Article'" (Medwin, *Conversations*, pp. 132–33. The same anecdote is recorded in Williams's *Journal* [28 December 1821]; and Byron, *Works*, V, 427).

8. Medwin appended a memoir of Shelley to his *Conversations*.

9. *Narrative of Lord Byron's Voyage to Corsica and Sardinia during the Year 1821*, anonymously published and fictitious (Lovell, *Medwin*, p. 201).

10. See 10 October [1824], n. 10.

To Mary Sabilla Novello Kentish Town. Dec. 27. [1824]

According to your kind intimation, Carissima mia—fair Jane & myself have been expecting the Cavalieri—the devil a one (if I may be permitted the expression) has yet appeared—In the name of the 7 planets & all Mr Clarke's stars what can they be about?—I trust in the ruler of the same that it is not occasioned by any indisposition of Vincenzo's—As for a visit to Shacklewell while this blessed climate affords only the varieties of rain & wind (snow & ice are to come) an impassable Jordan seperates us—

Dear MarySabilla—if the O.G.[1] is very good & the Lambs forbid us not Jane & I intend to be at Colebrook Cottage[2] on Sunday—Shall we meet there—

In the meantime I beg to say that you receders are very naughty & that Shacklewell was certainly in Shakespeare's head when he talked of the bourne from which no travellers return[3]—there have been more ghosts to give us news of the land he is commonly supposed to mean than visitors from your green—

How is Charles Arthur & all the little folks & womanly Victoria whom I do not & must not include in the list—Percy & M^rs W's [*Williams's*] babes are well—

Twenty kisses such as woman may give to woman on your dear cheek—as for the Cavalieri they may think themselves happy if they obtain our little fingers for the purpose of saluting them

Thine
MaryWS.

Is Werter making love to Miss Foote?[4]
Is Charles [*Cowden Clarke*] married—consequent no more to be heard of?
Is Vincenzo the most faithless of men?—
—(N.B. V. is not the last but the climax!)

ADDRESS: Mrs. Vincent Novello / Shacklewell Green. POSTMARKS: (1) SO Ken [tish T]n; (2) 12. NOON. 12 / DE. 28 / 1824; (3) [ ] EVEN. 4 / DE. 28 / 1824. PUBLISHED: Jones, #221. TEXT: MS., British Library (Add. MSS. 11,730, f. 180).

1. Perhaps "Old Gentleman," slang for "the devil" (Partridge, *A Dictionary of Slang*).

2. The Lambs had moved to Colebrook Cottage, Islington, in September 1823.

3. *Hamlet.* III. i. 79–80.

4. Werter was Edward Holmes. Jones suggests that Miss Foote is Maria Foote (?1797–1867), a well-known actress of the day, but he gives no source (*MWS Letters*, I, 309, n. 1).

*To Teresa Guiccioli [Kentish Town] 30 Decembre.
[December 1824]

Cara Contessina

Quasi non azardo scrivevi dopo la mia passata trascuranza. Ma la mia vita è cosi monotona, che i giorni divengono settimani e mesi avante che me ne accorgo. La vostra cara lettera del 7mo del corrente mi ha fatto vergognare—Non dubito che in quella divina Roma troviate l'ombra della felicità Sotto quel vago cielo contornata dei più sublimi oggetti, si perde nella contemplazione—ditemi, Cara mia, ove dimorete in Roma—voglio figurarmi la V^{a} casa i vostri passeggi—andate tal volta ai giardini Borghese? Se mai vi troviate sotto quel tempietto di Esculapio, pensate che io pure sono stata ivi, e che la godai una rara ed ohime passata felicità—quante volte abbiamo caminati l'adorato Shelley ed io in quel bellisimo posto—andate mai alla Trinità de' Monti—in quella casa la di cui ringhera s'avanza sulla strada il mio prediletto figlio morì—Il Coliseo fu la scena di mille passeggii deliziosi, ed assisi sopra le deserte e solitarie rovine dei Bagni di Caracalla godemmo la vista della primavera, che [?amiro] questo caduto edifizio con bellissimi fiori—Nei pallazzi ove i quadri ci allettarono, in San Pietro—Nel Vaticano, nei Giadini della Villa Doria, ove le vaghe anemoni fioriscono in Sta Maria della Rotonda, su Monte Cavallo, nel Campidoglio nel tristo Campo Vaccino, sono pure i tracci della perduta gioia della mia vita—parlate me dunque, Carissima Teresina, di tutti questi posti—fate il mio spirito accompagnarvi in questo albergo santo—ove un giorno anch'io alberghero.

Iddio solo sa quando! Parlo sempre di questo viaggio e faro il mio possibile di farlo nel autunno dell'anno vegnente—I miei affari son ormai meno ritrosi—ma mille circonstanze possono farmi tratennere—o almeno io, cosi vaga di vi andare, temo gli ostacoli—Quei della Williams son gia appianati—Chi sa dunque cosa verrà—Ma nel momento ch'io credeva di tutto combinare con mio suocero tutta è arrestata perche egli sta male—Morto lui sono ricca e libera; ma mi dispiace sommamente di veder la che la mia tranquillita dipende sopra la vita d'un vecchio—che, se Dio vuole puo vivere una ventaiia di anni—e pure non vorrei aspettar con piacere la morte di nessuna—che mi dia egli i mezzi per tornare e stare in Italia e che vivesse Mill'anni.

Il vostro fratello non ho veduto per qualche tempo; giacche egli è molto impegnato in questo opuscolo.[1] Mi scrise ieri e dice che ne è stanchissimo poi aggiunge—ed anche "di Londra e del fumo, e del rost Beef—e birra sazio fino alla gola—fra diece o 13 giorni al piu son fermo di partire per Grecia attraverso Parigi e Marsiglia"—Spero di vederlo fra poco quando vi riscrivero

Taffe! o mio Dio! Sa egli tutto quanto Medwin ha contato sopra di lui nelle sue "Converzazioni"—Per Dio è infame di cosi assassinare la gente—Salutatelo per me e per la Williams—Vien egli spesso a voi—forse ora che la Regny l'ha' piantato vuol mettere in avanti i di lui servizii, e trovarsi cavaliere servente di V^{ra} Eccelenza—O mia Cara se conoscesti gli uomini che osono aspirare a essere successori di Shelley e Williams—Dio mio—siamo ridotte a questo—Per quante ragioni vorrei fuggire questa cosi detta patria mia—Ma non è non l'amo—e i miei stessi compatrioti li trovo più amabile in Italia che quà—Prego ogni giorno per il di quando non lo vedro piu e quando gia gli Alpi trascorsi mi ritrovero nella dolce vostra patria

God of the best, the brightest,
The dearest spot of Earth,
Where thou hast loved to scatter
Thy gifts of joy and mirth
See how in gloom I wander,
How mournfully I rove:
Alas! alas! this England,
I can no longer love.[2]

Bisogna finire, e scrivo con fretta—Ma quando verra la lettera che mi promettete vi riscrivero a lungo.—O mia cara, siamo sorelle nelle disgrazie—ormai potete concepire la noia che mi reca ogni cosa—se il cielo fosse chiaro—se la terra non fosse umidissima—se il clima fosse alquanto più piacevole non sentirei tanto il peso della vita—Ma questi delizie trovero in Italia—Dio vuole che vi saro in quest'altro inverno—

Addio—amatemi pur sempre e crediate mi per sempre

Vostra Aff^{ma} Amica
Mary Shelley

La Williams vi saluta caramente—sta bene ora. Percy non lo conoscerete più è cosi grande; poverino—è amabile e spiritoso, ed oso sperare qualche conforto da lui

Siete mai stato alle Tomba di Cestio—e qua dove giace le spoglie terrene del Shelley—diteme se mai andate se i cipressi ed altri alberi fioriscono.—ivi anche sara l'ultima dimora mia—

[*Translation*]

Dear Contessina

I almost do not dare to write to you after my past neglect. But my life is so monotonous that the days become weeks and months before I am aware of it. Your dear letter of the 7th of this month has made me ashamed—I do not doubt that in that sublime city of Rome you may find the shadow of happiness. Beneath that lovely sky surrounded by the most sublime objects, one is lost in contemplation—tell me, my Dear, where you are staying in Rome—I want to imagine your house, your walks—do you sometimes go to the Borghese gardens? If ever you find yourself under that little temple of Aesculapius, think that I too was there and that I enjoyed a rare and alas faded happiness—how many times have we walked, the adored Shelley and I, in that beautiful spot—do you ever go to Trinita de' Monti—in that house whose balcony hangs over the street my dearest son died—The Colosseum was the scene of thousands of delightful walks, and seated upon the deserted and solitary ruins of the Baths of Caracalla, we enjoyed the spectacle of spring, that [?   ] this fallen structure with beautiful flowers—In the palaces where the paintings delight, in St. Peter's

—In the Vatican, in the Gardens of the Villa Doria, where the charming anemones bloom—in Santa Maria della Rotonda, on Mount Cavallo, in the Capitol, in the wretched Campo Vaccino, are also the traces of the lost joy of my life—speak to me then, Dearest Teresina, of all these places—let my spirit accompany you in this sacred abode—where one day I too will lodge.

God only knows when! I always speak of this trip and will do all that I can to make it in the autumn of the coming year—My affairs are now less adverse—but thousands of circumstances can hold me back—or at least I, so desirous of going, am afraid of these obstacles—The affairs of Signora Williams are already settled—Who knows then what is to come—But at the moment that I thought to settle everything with my father-in-law, everything was detained because he was ill—If he dies, I am rich and free; but I am extremely sorry to see that my tranquillity depends upon the life of an old man—who, if God pleases, may live another twenty years—and then too, I do not wish to await with pleasure the death of any man—if only he would provide me with the means to return and stay in Italy, then may he live a thousand years.

I have not seen your brother for some time, inasmuch as he is very much engaged with the pamphlet.[1] He wrote to me yesterday and says that he is extremely tired and then adds—and also "of London and of smoke, and of roast Beef—and sated with beer up to the throat—between ten or 13 days at the most I am certain to leave for Greece by way of Paris and Marseilles"—I hope to see him soon, at which time I will write to you again.

Taffe! oh my God! Does he know all that Medwin has narrated about him in his "Conversations"—By God it is scandalous to ruin people in this way—Send regards to him for me and for Signora Williams—Does he come to see you often—perhaps now that Madame Regny has quit him he wants to proffer his services to you and find himself Your Excellency's cavaliere servante—Oh my Dear if you knew the men that dare to aspire to be the successors of Shelley and Williams—My God—we are reduced to this—There are many reasons why I would like to flee this so-called homeland of mine—But not because I do not love it—and these same fellow countrymen are more amiable to me in Italy than here—I pray daily for the day when I will no longer see this country—and when I may once again cross the Alps and find myself in your sweet homeland

God of the best, the brightest,
The dearest spot of Earth,
Where thou hast loved to scatter
Thy gifts of joy and mirth
See how in gloom I wander,
How mournfully I rove:
Alas! alas! this England,
I can no longer love.[2]

It is necessary to close, and I am writing in haste—But when the letter you have promised me arrives I will write again at length.—Oh my dear, we are sisters in misfortune now you can conceive of the tedium that everything causes me—if only the sky were clear—if the earth were not so damp—if the climate were somewhat more agreeable I would not feel the burden of life so much—But I will find these delights in Italy—May God grant that I may be there next winter—

Farewell—love me always and always believe me

Your most affectionate friend
Mary Shelley

Signora Williams greets you warmly—she is well now. You would no longer know Percy he is so big; poor little one—he is amiable and vivacious, and I dare to hope for some comfort from him

Have you ever been to the Tomb of Cestius—it is there where the earthly remains of Shelley lie—if you ever go, tell me if the cypresses and other trees bloom.—my final home will also be there—

ADDRESS: Alla Sua Eccelenza / La Signora Contessa Guiccioli / Nata Gamba / a Roma / Italy / Italie. POSTMARKS: (1) PAID / 31 DE 31 / 1824; (2) F24 / S 14; (3) ANGLETERRE; (4) CHAMBERY; (5) [CORRIS]PZA DA GENOVA. UNPUBLISHED. TEXT: MS., Pforzheimer Library. TRANSLATION: Ricki B. Herzfeld.

1. Pietro Gamba's narrative of Byron's journey to Greece (see 19 February [1825], n. 7).

2. I have been unable to identify the author of this stanza, which Mary Shelley also quotes in her letter to Louisa Holcroft of 6 January [1825]. It is possible that Mary Shelley herself composed these lines.

TO AMELIA CURRAN 5 Bartholomew Place Kentish Town.
Jan[ry] 2[d] [1825]

My dear Miss Curran

A thousand thanks for all the kindness expressed in your letter of Oct[ber] 15—You are now probably settled in Rome. Pisa is a terrible residence for the summer—but without going as far as the Baths of Lucca—or encountering the English, who are particularly odious in such a confined spot—you would have found {a} cool retreat beneath the Pisan Hills—whither we used to far villeggiatura in summer time—& where I passed the happiest years of my life. I envy your Roman abode—every sacrifice would appear to me small to see again that adored Place—I have now better prospects than I had—or rather a better reality—for my prospects are sufficiently misty. I receive now £200 a year from my father-in-law—but this in so strange & embarrassed a manner that as yet I hardly know what to make of it. I do not believe however that he would object to my going abroad—as I dare say he considers that the first step towards Kingdom Come, whither doubtless he prays than [*that*] an interloper like I may be speedily removed. —I talk therefore of going Next Autumn—and shall be grateful to any power divine or human that assists me to leave this desart country—Mine I cannot call it—it is too unkind to me.

What you say of my Shelley's picture is beyond words interesting to me. How good you are! Send it I pray you—for perhaps I cannot come & at least it would be a blessing to receive it a few months earlier—I am afraid you can do nothing about the Cameo—As you say—it were worth nothing unless like—but I fancied that it might be accomplished under your directions—Would it be asking you too much to lend me the copy you took of my darling William's portrait[1]—since mine is somewhat injured but from both together I could get a nice copy made.

You may imagine that I see few people so far from the centre of bustling London—but in truth I found that even in town; poor un-dinner-giving as I was, I could not dream of society—it was a great confinement for Percy—and I could not write in the midst of smoke—noise & streets—I live here very quietly going once a week to the Strand. My chief dependance for society is in Mrs Williams, who lives at no great distance—As to theatres &c how can a "lone woman" think of such things—No—the pleasures & luxuries of life await me in divine Italy—but here privation solitude & desertion are my portion. What a change for me—but I must not think of that—I contrive to live on as I am—but to recur to the past & compare it with the present is to deluge me in grief & tears.

My boy is well—a fine tall fellow & as good as I can possibly expect—he is improved in looks since he was here. C— [*Claire*] is in Moscow still—not very pleasantly situated—but she is in a situation & being now well in health waits with more patience for better times The G—'s [*Godwins*] go on as usual—My father tho' harassed, is in good health, & is employed on the 2nd Vol. of the Commonwealth.

The weather here is astonishingly mild but the rain continual half England is Underwater and the damage done at Sea Ports from storms incalculable—In Rome doubtless it has been different—Rome, dear name; I cannot tell why but to me there is something Enchanting in that spot. I have another friend there; the Countess Guiccioli—now unhappy & mournful from the death of LordB. poor girl—I sincerely pity her, for she truly loved him—& I cannot think that she can endure an Italian after him. You have there also a Mr Taaffe—a countryman of yours, who translates Dante & rides fine horses who perpetually throw him. He knew us all very well.

The English have had many a dose of scandal—first poor dear LB [ ] whom, now, gone, many a poor devil of an author sup[s] fearless [of pu]nishment—then Mr Fauntleroy[2]—then Miss F[oote][3] these ar[e] dying away—the fame of Mr F. indeed has not survived [ ] that of LB bursts forth every now & then afresh—while Miss [ ] smokes most dismally still—then we have had our quantum of fires & misery—& the poor exiled Italians & Spaniards have added famine to the list of evils; a subscription highly honourable to the poor & middling classes, who subscribed their mite, has relieved them.—

Will you write soon—How much delight I anticipate this spring on the arrival of the picture—In all thankfulness

faithfully yours,
MaryShelley

If you see much of Severn, & if you do not think the request indiscreet—would you ask him to give me (or sell me) a copy of a portrait he made of my friend Trelawny.[4]

You will not paint again! How I mourn over this sacrifice of you talents; yet I do not wonder, with your health & nerves occupation must be tedious to you.

I direct to you as before—for that letter reached you—you have sent me no other address—& I do not think that you are in the habit of sending to the Post Office

Is there any truth in the horrible story of the murder of a Mr & Mrs Hunt at Paestum?[5]—

ADDRESS: Miss Curran / All Arco Della Regina / Via Sistina / Roma / Rome—Italie. POSTMARKS: (1) [PA]ID [ ]; (2) F25 / 34; (3) ANGLETERRE; (4) CHAMBERY; (5) CORRISPZA ESTERA DA GENOVA; (6) Imposta il 7 Gennaio; (7) 24 GENNA[IO]. PUBLISHED: Jones, #222. TEXT: MS., Bodleian Library (Shelley, MS., Adds., c. 6, ff. 33–34).

1. See 26 July 1822.

2. Henry Fauntleroy (1785–1824), a banker who was tried on 30 October 1824 and executed on 30 November 1824 for forging documents and fraudulently disposing of stocks.

3. The *Times* (London) of 18 October and 16 November 1824 reported details of Maria Foote's breach-of-promise suit against Joseph Hayne.

4. On 19 April 1825 Amelia Curran responded that she had seen Severn and that he was sending the portrait Mary Shelley had requested (*S&M*, IV, 1062).

5. In a letter of 22 December 1825 to Jane Williams from Rome Thomas Jefferson Hogg wrote that he had seen the place, about a mile from Paestum, where the robbery and murder of the Hunts had taken place. Hogg also mentioned that he had stayed overnight at the inn at Eboli, whose keeper was rumored to have plotted the crime (Norman, *After Shelley*, p. 56).

To Louisa Holcroft

5 Bartholomew Place—Kentish Town
Janry 6th [1825]

My dear Louisa

Do not be angry that I have not written to you during all this time;—or do be angry if that is a sign that you have not forgotten me—but suffer your indignation to be mollified by this letter. To tell you the truth I like letter writing when I am happy but when I am out of spirits it becomes a task—A pen in hand my thoughts flow fast, but then they come from the overflowing of my heart & if that be sad, why make sad a friend by useless complaints—true I cannot forget past happiness—or become reconciled to my present situation—but why talk to you, dear girl, of these things, who young as you are have, I fear cares of your own?

Behold me even as you left me,[1] only more deserted & solitary—behold me in my little room beside my fire—with no change or hope—Well did your Mother prophecy that I should find England intolerable yet she would hardly believe how totally I am exiled here from every thing that can add a charm to life—And the moment of my departure is yet cruelly uncertain—Shall I ever again leave these clouds?—shall I in very truth feel the sun of Italy—view its beloved hills—wander in its Vineyards—again visit those spots sacred to me by every happy tie?—

God of the best the brightest
 The dearest spot on earth,
Where thou hast loved to scatter
 Thy gifts of joy & mirth
See how in gloom I wander,
 How mournfully I rove:
Alas! Alas! this England
 I can no longer love—[2]

You of course see the papers & news therefore would be de trop—I run over the list of our common friends—but all is as usual—The Lambs are well & dear Miss L. has escaped this year without one of her painful visitations. Poole—you have { } of his adventure. Elliston[3] refused him a Free Admission to D.L. Poole wrote & Elliston did not reply. So Poole went to the theatre & sent in his card—E. was in the Green Room surrounded by the Actors—Whoever he cried, wishes to see a man kicked follow me! the scene that ensued You may easily imagine—& Poole brought Elliston before a Magistrate where the "King of his people" sat in infinite Majesty silent & dignified—The Complaint made the Magistrate asked him what he had to say—Nothing—Your bail Sir?—Without a word he pointed to two men attending him & departed with the same ineffable speechlessness.

I have been very sorry to hear from your brother Tom that Elle[n] has been ill. As she has been & I fancy still remains at her Aunt M[rs] Dowling's I have been unable to see her, since I am not acquainted with M[rs] Dowling—but I wish you would request her to do me the favour to call on me—I am but a dull person but she would see her old friend Percy—& the change might amuse her.

Do you ever see W. Irvin?[4]—he talked of visiting England this Autumn—but he has not unfortunately fulfilled his purpose—Remember me to him & tell him I claim his promised Visit when he does come—Moore[5] has been in town—I have not seen him & he has postponed I believe his life of poor dear LB. for the present—Newton the painter passed five weeks at Sir W.S.'s [*Walter Scott's*] Country Seat Abbotsford & a painting as my father tells me, a very clever picture of an hypocondriacal Dandy.

It will give me great pleasure to hear from you, my dear Louisa—& I trust that you will write before long. I hope your Mother is well—How is M[r] Kenney—pray present by [*my*] best regards to them both—& tell me how all your dear Children are. Percy is well—grown tall & taller & thrives in this odious swamp as well as if he were a native of it. I write & seal my letter without communicating with M[rs] Godwin, or I am sure she would send you a thousand kind messages—she often talks of you with affectionate interest—She is not quite so well now as when you saw her—M[ ] same & is very busy writing. [ ] what has become of M[rs] Morris's pink silk go[wn] chains? That best tempered & best dressed of women [e]ntreat you to remember with some pleasure our walks [ ] operatic excursions—the divine Pasta—the loaches that Tom brought us—Miss Labbitt—& the dinner I made you order for M[r] Kenney —What was it?—Mutton broth & {a} great piece of boiled bacon I think—perhaps his Memory will serve better than mine—& then the piece of cold-warm veal brought in as a subsidiary—but then the strawberries & milk made us forget all our cares—Do you think that M[r] Nathan's[6] pantaloons are still in existence?—

Your friend in truest truth
Mary Shelley

What of my pictures?—my little boys & LB. I should like sent as soon as you can find an opportunity.—

I direct as Tom told me he did—I hope that you will get the letter & that it will not by some mischance fall into the hands of any "Beautiful Maid at the Foot of the Hill"—belonging to this Particular Society—or what will she say to Mr Nathan's Pantaloons?—

ADDRESS: Mlle Louise Holcroft / Ala Societè Particuliere / à Versailles / near Paris. POSTMARKS: (1) PAID / 7 JA 7 / 1825; (2) 34[ ] / 25. PUBLISHED: Jones, #223. TEXT: MS., Pierpont Morgan Library.

1. According to Washington Irving's *Journal*, Louisa Holcroft was in London by 17 July 1824 and remained at least through 10 August 1824. Irving's *Journal* also establishes that James Kenney, Louisa Holcroft's stepfather, was in London at the same time. Godwin's Journal indicates that Kenney arrived in London by 13 June and remained at least until 21 September 1824, and it is possible that Louisa Holcroft also visited for this length of time (Irving, *Journals and Notebooks*, III, 366, 378; Godwin, Journal).

2. See 30 December [1824], n. 2.

3. John Poole (?1786–1872), dramatist and miscellaneous writer (see [6 May 1826]); Robert William Elliston (1774–1831), actor and manager of Drury Lane Theatre from 1819 to 1826.

4. Washington Irving was in England from 28 May to 13 August 1824. His *Journal* records his meeting Mary Shelley on two occasions: first on 17 July 1824, when he sat for his artist friend Gilbert Stuart Newton (1794–1835) for a portrait; then on 10 August 1824, when attending a production of James Kenney and Isaac Nathan's *The Alcaid; or The Secrets of Office*, a comic opera presented at the Haymarket Theatre (Irving, *Journals and Notebooks*, III, 366, 378).

5. Thomas Moore.

6. Isaac Nathan (?1791–1864), musical composer and author, wrote the music for Byron's *Hebrew Melodies*. He wrote music for a number of plays, collaborating with James Kenney on *Sweethearts and Wives*, a comedy with music successfully produced at the Haymarket Theatre on 7 July 1823, and on *The Alcaid*. In 1827 Nathan wrote the music for Kenney's *The Illustrious Stranger; or, Married and Buried* (Nicoll, *English Drama*, IV, 337, 592).

*To [John Cam Hobhouse] Kentish Town. Feb. 19 [1825]

My dear Sir

I am going I am afraid to tresspass most unwarrantably on your politeness—I can only say in excuse—that the object to me is important, & since my difficulty arises from restrictions placed by you the virtual majority upon us the weaker portion, I feel as if I had some (the shadow of a shade)[1] claim upon your gallantry.

I have often wished to be present at a debate in the House of Commons —Two circumstances spur this wish at the present time. First I am engaged in a tale[2] which will certainly be more defective than it would otherwise be, if I am not permitted to be present at a debate—And besides the animated discussions now going on, the splendid eloquence displayed, are beyond words objects of attraction to me. I consider it a great misfortune not {to} have heard the debate of last tuesday.[3]

I hear that there is a place, over the roof of St. Stephens[4] where you senators permit us to hear, not seen. Could you introduce me to this enviable post?—would you?—I make the request frankly—deny me in the same manner if I be too intrusive.

Your's was a most powerful article in the W.R.[5]—Dallas[6] must feel rather uncomfortable & I know that Medwin does.—I think Gamba's book decidedly one of the most interesting upon LordByron[7]—it is simple, affecting & praises without praising—

I am, dear Sir

Yr. Obedient Servant
MaryShelley

Unpublished. Text: MS., John Murray.

1. Aeschylus *Agamemnon* 1. 839.

2. Mary Shelley's request to Hobhouse, a member of Parliament, that he arrange her admission was in order to gather details for the political debates in her novel *The Last Man*, published by Henry Colburn in February 1826.

3. On 15 February Canning and Brougham had debated on a petition granting Catholic rights.

4. The meeting hall of the House of Commons.

5. The *Westminster Review* (see 10 November [1824], n. 1).

6. Robert Charles Dallas (1754–1824), a distant relation to Byron by marriage, had aided Byron's early career. In gratitude, Byron had given Dallas the copyright of *Childe Harold* and *The Corsair* as well as letters Byron had written to his mother from abroad. In June 1824 Dallas proposed to publish the latter in *Private Correspondence of Lord Byron including his letters to his Mother . . . connected by Memorandums and Observations, forming a Memoir of his Life, from the year 1808 to 1814*. Hobhouse's efforts to suppress this book failed, and it was published, first in French, then in English, by Galignani in Paris. Byron's one highly critical remark about Hobhouse, cited by Dallas, was used by Hobhouse's enemies to his mortification. One of the objects of Hobhouse's review article in the *Westminster Review* was to prove the deep friendship that actually existed between himself and Byron (Moore, *The Late Lord Byron*, pp. 68–73, 85–91).

7. Pietro Gamba, *A Narrative of Lord Byron's Last Journey to Greece* (London:

John Murray, 1825). Hobhouse arranged for the translation of Gamba's book into English, overseeing and doing some of the translating himself (Moore, *The Late Lord Byron*, p. 115).

To Prince Alexander Mavrocordato [Kentish Town]
22 Feb. 1825

Mon Cher Ami,

Je me profite de la complaisance de M. de Gamba à vous faire parvenir une lettre.[1] Il vous dira de mes nouvelles, si vous en ayez de la curiosite.

Vous dire avec quel interêt je m'occupe des affaires de la Grece. Comme je me rejouis de chacque victoire que remporte votre patrie, et de chaque honneur rendu a vous—sera de vous raconter une tres longue et tres ancienne histoire—longue autant que la liste de vos faits renommés, ancienne autant que notre amitié.

Aussi j'espere que notre gouvernement plus eclairé et plus liberal qu'autrefois, sera pour l'avenir l'ami vrai de la meilleure et plus noble cause qu'existe; et que le nom d'Angleterre sera à jamais cher aux Grecs. En vous sacrifiant Lord Byron, vous nous devez quelque chose. Vous connaissiez ce grand'homme.—La morte fit une tres grand sensation ici, et l'on porte un respect plus entousiastique à sa memoire et ses cendres, qu'à lui vivant.—

Je sçais trop vos occupations nombreux et importants, et je n'attends de vos lettres. Mais si vous trouvassiez l'occasion de me faire parvenir de vos nouvelles, je vous en sçaurois bon gré.—Eh! Mon cher Prince, est-ce-que vous oubliez Pise? vous oubliez votre incomparable ami, mon bien-aimé Shelley?—Vous oubliez les consolations mutuelles, la simpatie reçue de nous, notre aimable coterie, les leçons?—Vous oubliez tout ça?—je no le crois pas, je ne veux pas la croire.

Madame Williams vous salue.—Veuilliez agreer mon cher Mavrocordato, l'expression d'estime et vif interêt avec lequel je me souscris.

Votre Amie tres sincere
MS.

[*Translation*]

My Dear Friend,

I take advantage of the courtesy of M. de Gamba, who will transmit a letter to you.[1] He will give you news of me, if you wish to hear it.

To tell you with what interest I am occupied with the affairs of Greece. —How I rejoice with each victory your country wins, and with each honor that comes to you—will be to tell you a very long and very old story—as long as the list of your renowned feats, as old as our friendship.

So I hope that our government, more enlightened and more liberal than in the past, will be in the future the true friend of the best and noblest cause that exists; and that the name of England will forever be dear to the Greeks. In sacrificing Lord Byron to you, you owe us something. You knew this great man.—The death caused a very great sensation here, and they pay more enthusiastic respect to his memory and his ashes, than to him when alive.

I know too well your numerous and important endeavors, and I don't expect letters from you. But should you find the opportunity to send me news of you I would be grateful. Well! My dear Prince, have you forgotten Pisa? have you forgotten your incomparable friend, my beloved Shelley?—Have you forgotten the mutual consolations, the understanding we gave you, our friendly circle, the lessons? Have you forgotten all that?—I don't believe it, I don't want to believe it.

Madame Williams sends her greetings.—Please accept my dear Mavrocordato, the expression of esteem and deep interest with which I sign myself

Your very sincere Friend
MS.

PUBLISHED: Huscher, "Alexander Mavrocordato." TEXT: MS. (photocopy), Alexandros Maurocordatos Archives, Athens, Greece.

1. Pietro Gamba left London by 6 March (see [6 March 1825]). By 12 March he was at Portsmouth en route to Greece (Teresa Guiccioli letter to Mary Shelley, 25 June 1825, Abinger MS.).

TO EDWARD JOHN TRELAWNY

5 Bartholomew Place. Kentish Town
Feb. 22. Feb 27th [1825]

My dear Trelawny

I hear at last that Mr Hodges[1] has letters for me, and that prevents a thousand things I was about to say concerning the pain your very long silence has occasioned me. Consider, dear Friend, that your last was in date April, so that nearly a year has gone by, & not only I did not hear <u>from</u> you, but until the arrival of Mr Hodges, many months had elapsed since I had heard <u>of</u> you. Sometimes I flattered myself that the foundations of my little habitation would have have shaken by a "Ship Shelley ahoy"—that even Jane, distant a mile, would have heard. That dear hope lost, I feared a thousand things—Hamilton's Brown's illness—the death of many English, the return of every other from Greece filled me with gloomy apprehensions.

But you live,—what kind of life—your letters will I trust inform me—What possible kind of life in a cavern surrounded by precipices, inaccessible! All this will satisfy your craving imagination; the friendship you have for Odysseus does that satisfy your warm heart?—Your Seraglio left behind at Athens—I gather from your last letter & other intelligence, that you think of marrying the sister of your favourite Chief[2]—& thus will renounce England—& worse the English for ever. And yet—no! You love some of us, I am sure too much to forget us—even if you neglect us for a while—but truly I long for your letters which will tell me all. And remember, dear Friend, it is about yourself that I am anxious—Of Greece I read in the papers—I see many informants—but I can learn your actions, hopes, & above all valuable to me, the continuance of your affection for me, from your letters only.

I have nothing new to tell you. I live in the same place, vegetate in the same way—My boy grows taller, I grow older—so that in my melancholy prognostications—I often fancy, so fast does the year change its cypher, that I shall be "a toothless old hag" before we meet again. My affairs are still in close keeping of Sir Timothy's Solicitor, who just affords me wherewithal to live—with promises of better things soon. When the first use to which I shall put my encrease of cash will be to leave this England, where I find neither comfort for past misfortunes or hope of happier days.

I have not heard from Claire since I dispatched her letter to you. Perhaps your packet may contain one to her. I quite forget whether I told you the latest news of Jane—that Ned's Mother-in-law[3] now makes her an allowance—& makes it without restriction or pretention. This dear girl's health is much better than it was last year—We are much together talking of the past—or future (for the present is nought) & we mingle your name in our dreams of both.

The name of LB. which stood its ground for a very long time in this country is now dying away. Medwin's book made a great sensation. He is lately married to a Swedish lady of rank—a baroness by right of birth—a countess by the rank of her late husband—with a good fortune, he says, pretty, & thirty years of age.[4] However the two latter circumstances may be aprocryphal—it is certain that she has some money & consequently that he has made a good thing of it. Moreover I received a letter from him the other day whose seal bears arms topped by a coronet & supported by Griffins with the motto (it might do for Gabè)[5] Nous <u>ne changeons jamais</u>—happy Medwin! he says that he & his bride think of settling at Florence (they are now at Vevai) & that the last two months have been the happiest of his life. His letter is principally taken up with excuses for having (against my earnest desire) published a very blundering & disagreable memoir of our Shelley in his Conversations—& last not least he reports having sold the boat for 20 napoleons—deducts 5 for expences & sends £12 as being the whole of the residue to Jane[6]—Magnificent

Feb. 27th

I now close my letter; I have not yet received yours.—

Last night Jane & I went with Gamba & my father to see Kean in Othello. This play, as you may guess, reminded us of you[7]—Do you remember when delivering the killing scen[e] you awoke Jane as Othello awakens Desdemona, from h[er] sleep on the sopha? Kean, abominably supported, acted divinely—put as he is upon his mettle by the recent events[8] & a full house & applause—which he deserved—his farewell is the most pathetic piece of acting to be imagined. Yet my dear Friend I wish we had seen it represented, as was talked of at Pisa—Iago wd never have found a better representative that [*than*] that strange & wondrous creature, whom one regrets dayly more—for who here can equal him?

Adieu, dear Trelawny—take care of yourself & come & visit us as soon as you can escape from the sorceries of Ulysses

In all truth Y^s Affectionately MWS—

ADDRESS: Edward Trelawny Esq. / &c &c &c / Honoured by Count Gamba. PUBLISHED: Jones, #224. TEXT: MS., Keats-Shelley Memorial House, Rome.

1. An agent of Colonel Leicester Stanhope (1784–1862), a member of the Greek Committee, who had been in Greece (Marchand, *Byron*, III, 1197).

2. Trelawny married Tersitza, the thirteen-year-old half sister of Odysseus, in 1825. A daughter, Zella, was born to them in 1826. In 1828 they were divorced (*SC*, V, 55–58).

3. See 9–11 September [1823], n. 14.

4. On 2 November 1824 Medwin had married Anna, Baroness Hamilton of Sweden, Countess of Starnford (1788–1868) (Lovell, *Medwin*, pp. 205–6).

5. Gabrielle Wright, Trelawny's former lover at Genoa, signed her letters to Mary Shelley "Gaby" (four letters, 4 March through 8 May 1823, Abinger MS.).

6. Medwin had sold that boat that Williams left at Lake Geneva (Lovell, *Medwin*, p. 165).

7. Trelawny later wrote in the left-hand margin of Mary Shelley's letter: "At Pisa 1822 Lord Byron talked vehemently of our getting up a play in his Great Hall at the Lanfranchi it was to be Othelo he cast the Characters thus. Byron Iago—Tre. Othello. Williams Cassio. Medwin Roderigo Mrs Shelley Desdemona Mrs Williams Emilia Who is to be our Audience I asked—all Pisa he rejoined—he recited a great Portion of his part with great Gusto it exactly suited him—he looked it to."

8. Edmund Kean's liaison with a Mrs. Cox led to a lawsuit brought by her husband. Kean was found guilty and fined £800. On 24 January, in the midst of the scandal resulting from the lawsuit, Kean appeared as Richard at Drury Lane and was given an unruly reception by the audience.

*TO JOHN CAM HOBHOUSE

5 Bartholomew Place Kentish Town
Saturday [?26 February 1825][1]

My dear Sir

I write to acknowledge your polite & kind note, as I hear from Gamba that you feared from its being misdirected, that it might not have reached me. I feel truly obliged to you for your promise to facilitate my wish.

Allow me merely to add that if it be impossible for me to attain to hear an interesting & great debate, I shall be glad to peep into St. Stephens, at any time when you shall be assembled, that I may form a correct idea of the geography & modes of going on in your Chamber

I have the honour to be, dear Sir

Y^s obliged & faithfully MaryShelley

UNPUBLISHED. TEXT: MS., Avon County Library (Bath Reference Library).

1. In a letter of 19 February, Mary Shelley had requested Hobhouse's aid in arranging for her to visit the House of Commons. It is likely that this letter was written on the Saturday following.

*To Teresa Guiccioli 5 Bartholomew Place, Kentish Town; London 6mo Febbraio. [February (error for 6 March 1825)][1]

Mia Cara Guiccioli

Alfine il V[ro] fratello è partito; mi dice d'avervi fatto di cio consapevole; ma per Bacco, è molto trascurante egli; che ultimamente mi confessò di non avervi mandati dei nuovi suoi per dei mesi. Per ciò vi scrivo in questo memento, sicchè vi assicura della sua salute e le buone speranze colle quale se ne andata via. Và colla prima parte d'una nuova imprestita fatta da un certo Ricardo ai Greci; ed è caricato dal medesimo di osservare e rapportare la situazione vera della Grecia—del governo e della speranza del di lei trionfo in questa contesa. Questo carico gli è vieppiù piacevole giacche lo fa sperare di tornare in questo nebbioso paese—dal quale dio volesse ch'io mi potessi liberare presto, come ha fatto egli.

Ma Egli pure n'è incantato; il comercio, le manufatture, la campagna cosi ben coltivata, i giardini—i parc, la beltà delle donne, la richezze—tutto era per lui uno spetacolo quasi da teatro dal quale non poteva levare gli occhi. Poi l'apertatura del parlamento; il parlare di Canning e Brougham lo ritenne, e la buona compagnia dei primi della partita dell'opozizione al Ministero. Fù accogliato con somma garbatezza la Hobhouse, Brougham, Kinnaird &c e combinato con questo ci fù un certo amore che gli prese per una biondina Inglese (non saprei che fosse mai) che metteva colmo all'incantesimo. Cosi non fa specia che il poverino persa la ragione, perso tempo, se medessimo quasi perso, non adempì bene i doveri di figlio e fratello.

La Leigh gli rese mille gentilezze—gli dè un anello da lutto ed un ritratto del suo fratello—gli mostrò la Medora e gli chiese se non lo pareva che somigliasse lei a Bÿron. Vorrei (e come!) che partendo da qui Pierino fosse ritornato presso da voi. Vi avrebbe racontato tante cose della Williams e di me; pero la voglia mia è sciocca, che non avrebbe nulla di piacevole a dirvi senonche viviamo colla speranza di visitar Italia avante il il prossimo inverno. Felicità per me qui non si trova; neppur un oblio dei mali; mi figuro che a Roma, nella diletta vità dell'anima mia, lontana dei guai, ritroverei l'ombra del piacere—Chi lo sa! forse lo spietato destino non mai mi levera d'adosso il carico pesante, porzione mia in Inghilterra.

Spero che Pietro vi abbia mandato il suo libro. The last journey of Lord Byron. Mi piace assaissimo—è scritto senza pretenzione ma vi si trova dei fatti interessante ed uno squarcio di Byron vero piacevolissimo; descrive pateticamente gl'ultimi suoi momenti; ci mena seco lui nelle aventure, ed a me che lo conobbi pare di sentirlo e vederlo dire e fare le cose racontate. Ben si vede che è finita con lui la gloria del mondo—destino maraviglioso, inesplicabile, deplorabile in eterno! che nel fior della nostra gioventù ha rapito da noi tre, voi, la Williams ed io costoro che amavamo, costoro che fecero la terra per noi un paradiso e loro spariti la trasforma in un cerchio dell'inferno.

Ma non vorrei attristarvi colla mia tristezza. Piùtosto permettele che vi racconto della novità—non tocando à me, che per me non v'è nulla di nuova—L'ultima storia assai stravagante è della Carolina Lamb[2] che pare esser divenuta pazza. L'altro giorno fece una scena nelle strade di Londra, richiamando la protezione del popolo—gridando che volevano i suoi nemici rinchiuderla—che ebbe veduto il figlio ed il prediletto marito per l'ultima volta, che dovrebbe il popolo salvare lei d'essere strascinata cosi indegnamente, come anni fà salvarono la Regina—e mille cose simili, ma tanto da pazza, che la buona gente d'intorno la lasciò nelle mani di suoi servitori—Questo è ben curiosa, non è vero, Cara Guiccioli?, cosa ne avrebbe detto Byron?—

Tita[3] sta con Hobhouse—trova la donne qui troppo belle, consciosiacosa che non se ne pero innamorare. Gli pare conventi le case dei Signori: si va a mangiare chiamato dalla campanella, e si sono (sommamente la casa del padre di Hobhouse) così serie, così ben regolate che fa disperare uno scherzevole Italiano. Quando torno in Italia cerchero di menar Tita meco. Lega ha l'idea di stabilirsi qui come negoziante di pasta; questo roba non è mangiato qui che dai Signori e si vende caro; Fletcher gli fara compagno nella mercanzia.[4]

Pierino lasciò tra le mie mani parecchi fagotti di fogli, lettere V^{re} al diletto Bÿron—e dei gioiellini dati da voi, al medesimo—cio è una catena fabricata dai V^{ri} capelli—un'anello dei medesimo, [un] cristallo legato di oro e poi il ritratto datogli dalla Leigh, non degno gia del v^{ro} [ ] amante—cosa farei con questi—se trovo una buona occasione potrei mandare i gioielli—ma le lettere terro fin che verrò io—o che trovo uno che va dritto a Roma, che vi le consegnarebbe senza ritardo. In tanto aspeterro i vostri ordini. Queste lettere colle risposte di Byron, che sicuramente teneti, contengono forse la storia del V^{ro} amore, e devono essere interesantissime. Un giorno, non è vero, Contessina cara, scriverete in detaglio questa romanza vera, più romanzesca che niuna romanza falsa—e come tocca ad un uomo celebre come Byron, ed una amante fedelissima come voi, sarebbe impregibile

Percÿ sta benissimo non lo conoscereste più—si ramenta della Contessina di Milord—delle oche della capra—e mi chiede, p[er]che non vai in Italia, Mamma, deh! partiamo domani—Dio buono! faccia che presto ritorno giacche vivere qui è peggio che morire mille mille volte!

Scrivete mi vi prego, cara Amica—Consolatevi il meglio che potete—la W. vi saluta—Credetimi V^{r} Aff^{ma} A^{ca} Mary Shelley.

—Salutatemi il Taaffe.

[*Translation*]

My Dear Guiccioli

Your brother has finally departed; he tells me that he made you aware of this; but indeed he is very negligent; lately he confessed to me that he had not sent you any news of himself for some months. For this reason I am writing to you now, in order to assure you about his health and the high hopes with which he left here. He goes with the first part of a new loan made to the Greeks by a certain Ricardo; and he is charged by the same to observe and report on the real situation in Greece—on the government and the hope of her triumph in this contest. This duty is much more agreeable in that it makes him look forward to returning to this cloudy country—from which God grant that I may be liberated soon, as he has been.

But he is truly enchanted; the commerce, the manufacturing, the well-cultivated countryside, the gardens—the parks, the beauty of the women, the wealth—everything was for him almost a theatrical entertainment from which he could not take his eyes off of. Then the opening of Parliament; the speeches of Canning and Brougham detained him, and the fine company of the first men of the party in opposition to the Ministry. He was received with the utmost geniality by Hobhouse, Brougham, Kinnaird, etc., and combined with this he fell in love with a certain blonde Englishwoman (I would not know who she might be), which put the crown on the enchantment. So it is not surprising that the poor thing has lost his reason, lost time, and almost losing himself, he did not properly fill his duties as a son and a brother.

Madame Leigh paid him a thousand kindnesses—she gave him a mourning ring and a portrait of her brother—she showed him Medora and asked him if it didn't seem to him that she resembled Byron. I would like it (how much!) if, departing from here, Pierino might return and be near to you. He would have told you many things about Signora Williams and me; however my wish is foolish, and he would not have anything agreeable to tell you except that we live in the hope of visiting Italy before next winter. Happiness for me is not to be found here; nor forgetfulness of troubles; I believe that in Rome, in the delightful life of my soul, far from the woes, I would find again the shadow of pleasure—Who knows! maybe cruel fate will never lift the heavy burden from me—my share in England.

I hope that Pietro has sent you his book—The last journey of Lord Byron. I like it very much—it is written without pretension, but one finds interesting facts in it and a really very agreeable excerpt of Byron; it touchingly describes his last moments; it takes us along with him on his adventures, and to me who knew him, I seem to hear him and see him saying and doing the things that are described. One sees clearly that the glory of the world has ended with him—wondrous destiny, inexplicable, forever to be deplored! which in the flower of our youth has stolen from we three—you, Signora Williams, and I, those whom we loved, those who made the earth a paradise for us, and they having vanished, it is transformed into a circle of hell.

But I don't wish to sadden you with my unhappiness. Instead allow me to tell you some news—not relating to me, since for me there is nothing new—This latest very odd story is about Caroline Lamb,[2] who seems to have become crazy. The other day she caused a scene in the streets of London, calling for the protection of the people—screaming that her enemies want to lock her up—that she had seen her son and her darling husband for the last time, that the people must save her from being dragged so unworthily, as years ago they had saved the Queen—and a thousand similar things, but so crazy, that the good people around, left her in the hands of her servants—This is very strange, isn't it, Dear Guiccioli? what would Byron have said?—

Tita[3] stays with Hobhouse—he finds the women here too beautiful, although he does not fall in love. The houses of the Gentlemen seem like convents to him: one goes to eat when called by a bell, and they are (especially in Hobhouse's father's house) so serious, so well ordered, that they make a playful Italian despair. When I return to Italy I will try to bring Tita with me. Lega has the idea of establishing himself here as a pasta merchant; this stuff is eaten here only by Gentlemen and is very expensive; Fletcher will be his partner in the merchandise.[4]

Pierino left in my hands several bundles of papers, your letters to the beloved Byron—and some jewelry given by you to the same—that is, a chain made of your hair—a ring of the same, a crystal bound with gold and then a portrait given to him by Signora Leigh, not at all worthy of your [ ] lover—what can I do with these things—If I find a good opportunity I could send the jewelry—but the letters I will keep until I shall come—or until I find someone who is going directly to Rome, who would bring them to you without delay. Meanwhile I will await your instructions. These letters with Byron's replys, which surely you have, probably contain the story of your love and must be extremely interesting. One day, isn't it true, dear Contessina, you will write in detail this true romance, more romantic than any fictional romance—and since it relates to a man as celebrated as Byron and to a lover as faithful as you, it would be very valuable.

Percy is extremely well, you would not longer recognize him—he recalls the Contessina of Mylord—of the eyes like a goat—and he asks me, why don't you go to Italy, Mamma, ah! let's leave tomorrow—Good God! let me return soon because living here is a thousand, thousand times worse than death!

Write to me I beg you, dear Friend—Console yourself as best as possible—Signora Williams sends you her regards—Believe me Your Affectionate Friend Mary Shelley.

—Send my regards to Taaffe.

ADDRESS: Alla Sua Eccelenza / La Signora Contessa Teresa Guiccioli / A Roma / Rome Italia / l'Italie. POSTMARKS: (1) PAID / 14 MA / 1825; (2) F[ ] / 266; (3) ANGLETERRE; (4) CHAMBERY; (5) 31 MARZO. UNPUBLISHED. TEXT: MS., Pforzheimer Library. TRANSLATION: Ricki B. Herzfeld.

1. Mary Shelley's date almost certainly should be 6 March 1825. She mentions that Gamba attended Parliament and delayed his departure to hear Brougham's and

Canning's speeches. Parliament opened on 3 February 1825, and the speeches referred to took place on 15 February (see 19 February [1825]; and Lord Broughton [John Cam Hobhouse], *Recollections of a Long Life*, ed. Lady Dorchester, 6 vols. [London: John Murray, 1911], III, 85–90). In his Journal Godwin noted that he, Mary Shelley, Jane Williams, and Pietro Gamba attended a performance of *Othello* on 26 February 1825. Furthermore, Teresa Guiccioli indicated in a letter to Mary Shelley that she had last heard from her brother in a letter written from Portsmouth on 12 March (*S&M*, IV, 1064). The postmark dates also support a date of 6 March.

2. Lady Caroline Lamb (1785–1828), novelist and wife of William Lamb (afterwards Lord Melbourne). She and Byron had a love affair from March until September 1812, when Byron broke off the relationship. Caroline Lamb, however, unwilling to part with Byron, found numerous ways to interject herself into his life, including the publication of her novel *Glenarvon* (1816), in which she caricatured him. In 1825 she and her husband were separated.

3. Giovanni Battista "Tita" Falcieri, Byron's servant (see 6–10 April 1822).

4. The pasta-manufacturing company established by Lega and Fletcher failed (see Moore, *Accounts Rendered*, pp. 428–32).

To Leigh Hunt

5 Bartholomew Place—Kentish Town
April 8th [1825]

My dear Hunt

I have just finished reading your Article upon Shelley.[1] It is with great diffidence that I write to thank you for it—because perceiving plainly that you think that I have forfeited all claim on your affection, you may deem my thanks an impertinent intrusion. But from my heart I thank you—You may imagine that it has moved me deeply.—Of course this very article shews how entirely you have cast me out from any corner in your affections—and from various causes, none dishonourable to me, being excluded from society, now more entirely than I ever was—I cannot help wishing that I could have secured you{r} good will & kindness which I prize & have ever prized—But you have a feeling, I had almost said a prejudice, against me—which makes you construe foreign matter into detraction against me (I allude to the, to me, deeply afflicting idea you got upon some vague expression communicated to you by your brother) and insensible to any circumstances that might be pleaded for me. But I will not dwell on this—the sun shines and I am striving so hard for a continuation of the gleams of pleasure that visit my intolerable state of regret for the loss of beloved companionship, during cloudless days that I will dash away the springing tears—and make one or two necessary observations on your Article.—

I have often heard our Shelley relate the story of stabbing an Upper Boy with a fork—but never as you relate it—He always described it in my hearing as being an almost involuntary act, done on the spur of anguish, and that he made the stab as the boy was going out of the room.—Shelley did not allow Harriet half his income—she received £200 a year. Mr Westbrook had always made his daughter an allowance even while she lived with Shelley—which of course was continued to her after their seperation.

I think if I were near you I could readily persuade you to omit all allusion to Claire. After the death of LB. in the thick of Memoirs, scandal, & turning up old stories she has never even been alluded to, at least in any work I have seen. You mention (having been obliged to return your MSS. to Mr Bowring, I quote from memory) an Article in Blackwood—but I hardly think that this is of {a} date subsequent to our miserable loss.—In fact poor Claire has been buried in entire oblivion & to bring her from this even for the sake of defending her would I ⟨think⟩ am sure pain her greatly and do her mischief. Would you permit this part to be erased?—I have without waiting to ask your leave, requested Mr Bowring to leave out your mention that the remains of dearest Edward were brought to England. Jane still possesses this treasure—& has once or twice been asked by his Mother-in-law about it—Once an herse was sent—Consequently she is very anxious that her secret should be kept & has allowed it to be believed that the ashes were deposited with Shelley's at Rome.

Such, my dear Hunt, are all the alterations that I have to suggest and I lose no time in communicating them to you—they are too trivial for me to apologize for the liberty—and I hope that you will agree with me in what I say about Claire—Allegra no more—she at present absent & forgotten—on Sir Tim's death she will come in for a legacy which may enable her to enter into soc[iety] perhaps to marry, if she wishes it—if the past be [ ]

[ ]ther such things are recorded by Galignani—or if recorded how far it is likely [ ] you would have noticed it—My father's complicated annoyances, brought to their height by the failure of a very promising speculation, & the loss of an impossible-to-be-lost lawsuit, have ended in a bankrupcy—the various acts of which drama are now in progress. That over, nothing will be left him but his pen & me—He is so full of his Commonwealth that in the midst of every anxiety he writes every day now & in a month or two will have completed the second volume—And I am employed in raising money necessary for my maintainance & of which he must participate—This will drain me pretty dry for the present— but (as the old women say) if I live, I shall have more than enough for him & me & recur at least to some part of my ancient style of life, & feel of some value to others—Do not however mistake my phraseology—I shall not live with my father, but return to Italy—& economize the moment God & Mr Whitton will permit—My Percy is quite well—& has exchanged his constant Winter occupation of drawing for playing in the fields (which are now useful as well as ornamental) flying kite—gardening &c—I bask in the sun on the grass reading Virgil, that is, my beloved Georgics & Ld Shaftesbury's Characteristics.[2] I begin to live again, & as the Maids of Greece sang joyous hymns on the revival of Adonis, does my Spirit lift itself in delightful thanksgiving on the awakening of Nature to geniality & the feeling of delight in my careful mind.—

Lamb is super-annuated[3]—Do you understand—as Mne [*Marianne*] says·

he has left the India House on $2 \cdot 3^{ds}$ of his income & become a gentleman at large—a delightful consummation—What a strange taste is his That confines him to a view of the New River, with Houses opposite, in Islington —I saw the Novello's the other day—Mary & her new babe are well—he Vincent all over·fat & flourishing moreover—& she dolorous that it should be her fate to add more than her share to the population of the world. How are all yours?—Henry and the rest—Percy still remembers him tho' occupied by new friendships and the feelings incident to his state of—Matrimony —having taken for better & worse to wife Mrs William's little girl—
I wrote to you & to Marianne by a parcel sent to you by Bessy—I suppose you will receive with these letters Bessy's new book[4] which she has done very well indeed & forms with the other a delightful prize for plant & flower worshippers—those favourites of God—which enjoy beauty unequaled & the tranquil pleasures of growth & life—bestowing incalculable pleasure & never giving or receiving pain.—Have you seen Hazlitt?—Notes of his travels appear in the Chronicle[5]—he is going over the same road that I have traversed twice. He surprised me by calling the Road from Susa to Turin dull—There where the Alps sink into low mountains & romantic hills—topped by ruined castles—watered by brawling streams—clothed by magnificent walnut trees—there where I wrote to you in a fit of enchantment excited by the splendid scene—but I remembered—first that he travelled in winter when snow covers all—& besides he went from what I approached & looked at the plain of Lombardy with the back of the Diligence between him & the loveliest scene in nature—So much can relation alter circumstance

Claire is still I believe at Moscow [ ] return to Italy, I shall endeavour to enable he[r] thither also.—I shall not come without my [Jane] who is now necessary to my existence almost.—Thro[ugh] own resources she has recourse to the cultivat[ ] mind—& amiable & dear as she ever was she [ ] every way improved & become more valuable [ ]
[*P. 3, top, upside-down*] Trelawny is {in} the Cave with Ulysses—Not in Polypheme's cave—but in a vast cavern of Parnassus inaccessible & healthy & safe—but cut off from the rest of the World—Trelawny has attached himself to the party of Ulysses a savage Chieftan without any plan but personal independance & opposition to the Government—T— calls him an hero—. Ulysses speaks a word or two of French. T. no Greek.—che ornatissime conversazioni che sengono.[6] Pierino has returned to Greece.
[*P. 2, top, upside-down*] Horace Smith has returned with his diminished family (little Horace is dead)—He already finds London too expensive & they are about to migrate to Tunbridge Wells. He is very kind to me.

I long to hear from you—& am more tenderly attached to you & yours than you imagine—love me a little & make Marianne love me—as truly I think she does—Am I mistaken, Polly?—

Yours affectionately & obliged. MaryWShelley

ADDRESS: Leigh Hunt Esq / Ferma in Posta / Firenze / Florence / La Toscane / L'Italie. POSTMARKS: (1) F25 / 67; (2) ANGLETERRE; (3) CHAMBERY; (4) CORRISPZA ESTERA DA GENOVA; (5) 23 / APRILE. PUBLISHED: Jones, #225. TEXT: MS., Bodleian Library (MS., Shelley, Adds., c. 6, ff. 35–36).

1. Hunt's article on Shelley was offered to the *Westminster Review* as a review of Shelley's *Posthumous Poems.* On 26 December 1825 Rowland Hunter wrote to Hunt informing him that John Bowring would not print the article as it was because "he had shown it to some of Mr. Shelley's most intimate friends," who told him "the facts were not correct" (Brewer, *The Holograph Letters*, pp. 148–49). According to Mary Shelley, Peacock interfered with the publication of the essay because of the agreement he had made with Sir Timothy Shelley that Mary Shelley would not bring to public notice the Shelley name. Hunt published his essay in *Lord Byron and Some of His Contemporaries* in 1828, but he did not change his contention, to which Peacock strenuously objected, that Shelley and Harriet Shelley had separated by mutual consent. Hunt omitted reference to Claire Clairmont but retained the information that Edward Williams's ashes had been brought to England (see 28 December 1825).

2. Anthony Ashley Cooper, third Earl of Shaftsbury (1671–1713), whose chief works are collected in the *Characteristics of Men, Manners, Opinions, and Times* (1711).

3. On 29 March Lamb was retired with a pension of £450, having worked at the East India Company for thirty-three years (Lucas, *Charles Lamb*, II, 140).

4. *Sylvan Sketches*, dedicated to Marianne Hunt (see 2 March 1817 to Marianne Hunt, n. 2). Leigh Hunt helped Bessy Kent in her selections from the poets, which included quotations from Shelley, Keats, Hunt, and Mary Shelley (p. 207 contains a quotation from *Valperga*, III, 2) (see Hunt, *Correspondence*, I, 204–6).

5. From 1 September 1824 through September 1825 the Hazlitts traveled in France and Italy, and Hazlitt wrote essays about the trip for the *Morning Chronicle.* In February 1825, the Hazlitts went to Florence, where they visited with the Hunts (Blunden, *Leigh Hunt*, p. 218). In 1826 the essays were published as *Notes of a Journey through France and Italy* . . . (London: Hunt and Clarke).

6. "What very elegant conversations that ensue." This phrase has been omitted in previous publications.

To John Howard Payne[1]

5 Bartholomew Place Kentish Town
Thursday Eve^{g} [14 April 1825]

My dear Sir

You failed in bringing me Mrs Kenney[2]—Why doubly fail in not calling [here][3] yourself?—It was not until today [that I] heard that our friend was gone to Brighton and I should have despaired of the possibility of inducing you to make this [Nor]th Passage had not the kind God's sent me a substitute in her place—Mrs Harwood[4] called on me today & expressing a great desire to find some opportunity of conversing with you concerning your American friend,[5] I thought that I might venture to say that I [would] ask you to meet her here—& fixed with her [Sunday] Evening (i.e. at 6 P.M.) Will you come & over a cup of hyson ⟨forget⟩ drink to the better delivering of Embassies & that all [messengers] do not set amicable powers by the ears[6]—

When do you expect Mrs Kenney to return?—

I am, dear Sir
Your faithful Servant
MaryShelley

ADDRESS: J. Hayward Esq. / 22 Lancaster Street / Burton Crescent. POSTMARKS: (1) SO [Kentish Tn]; (2) 12. NOON. 12 / AP. 15 / 1825. PUBLISHED: Jones, #226. TEXT: MS., Huntington Library (HM 6797).

1. During this period Payne kept lodgings at two places: at 22 Lancaster Street, Burton Crescent, and at 29 Arundel Street, Strand. Mary Shelley addressed letters to "J. Hayward" at 22 Lancaster Street but used Payne's real name on letters addressed to Arundel Street. From December 1820 through 1 March 1821 Payne was in jail for debts incurred as lessee of Sadler's Wells Theatre. The success of his play *Thérèse, the Orphan of Geneva*, produced on 2 February 1821 at Drury Lane, gained Payne's release from prison. In order to escape duns, Payne went to Paris (where he saw his friends the Lambs in August 1822). Payne left Paris to return to London on 24 October 1823. His two names and addresses in 1825 were in response to financial difficulties connected with his earlier arrest (Overmyer, *America's First Hamlet*, pp. 190–200; Irving, *Journals and Notebooks*, III, 234; Payne, *Letterbook*, January–March 1825). In his letter to Washington Irving of 10 June 1825 Payne relates the difficult time he has had during "the last three or four months," which included rejections of four operas; "moreover, I have been arrested twice, upon an execution and upon a debt, both of which extraordinary good luck enabled me to settle in twelve hours, whereby other creditors have been encouraged to the same experiment, and my habitation is in a state of seige" (Payne, *Letterbook*, 25 June–26 February 1825).

2. Godwin's Journal records visits by Louisa Kenney on 15 and 28 March 1825.

3. Payne cut seven words out of Mary Shelley's letter and sent them back to her to demonstrate that her handwriting was the cause of his visiting her on Monday instead of Sunday (Payne to Mary Shelley, 18 April, MS., Huntington Library ([HM 6772]). Payne's copy of the letter (MS., Huntington Library), however, contains the missing words, which are supplied in this text in brackets.

4. Mrs. Harwood, a friend of Louisa Kenney's, had been bequeathed four thousand acres in Pennsylvania by the widow of Colonel Harwood. Louisa Kenney asked Payne to seek advice from his friend Colonel Thomas Aspinwall (1786–1876), the American Consul in London from 1815 to 1853, about handling the bequest. On 26 April Godwin's Journal indicates that a Mr. A. Harwood called on him.

5. Washington Irving.

6. This reference is explained in Payne's letter of 16 August 1825 to Irving: ". . . some blunder made by Thomas Holcroft in a message, which for a long time stopped all correspondence with Mrs. S., who some months before had written to me frequently for orders" (*The Romance*, p. 20). Thomas Holcroft was the son of Louisa Kenney.

TO JOHN HOWARD PAYNE — 5 Bartholomew Place Kentish Town.
Wednesday Evening. [20 April 1825]

My dear Sir

If I had been at home on Monday Evening we would have mocked the unkind God who introduced such confusion into my ill-formed pothooks— It was ill done indeed after causing me to form a thousand conjectures concerning your absence on Sunday, to lead you to the empty nest the day after—Will you tempt fortune again?—At least I can assure you that you will not find me from home in the morning—though I am just now so implicated as not to be able to fix any evening—but of so distant a date that I hope that your kindness and my good genius will permit us to meet in the interim—Will you walk over. Saturday or Sunday or any other that may be most convenient to you When it will give me to [*the*] sincere pleasure to find that neither the mistakes of spoken or written embassies can make good long their evil influence

I am, My dear Sir
Yours faithfully
MaryShelley

You talk of a walk from the Strand—and mention being here for a few days—but as this here is not geographically described—I venture still you [*to*] address you as before.[1]

PUBLISHED: Jones, #227. TEXT: MS., Huntington Library (HM 6800).

1. See [14 April 1825], n. 1.

TO JOHN HOWARD PAYNE [Kentish Town] Friday Morn^g [22 April 1825]

My dear Sir

I was excessively annoyed to find that you had called fruitlessly yesterday —I had calculated that you would not receive my note in time for a visit & so did not include Thursday "in the bond."—

Will you drink tea with me tomorrow—as a cold of Percy's will detain me at home from my expected engagement—If you are in the Strand you will find stages in James St. Covent Garden every hour—if in Lancaster Street attain the turnpike of Battle Bridge at 10 minutes exactly after any hour being struck, & soon one of our vehicles will pass—which on being directed will set you down at my door—

You see how diligently I try to repair an inconsequence which must not make you think me unpunctual which I am not &

beleive me dear Sir

Very truly Yours
MShelley

ADDRESS: J. Hayward Esq / 22 Lancaster Street / Burton Crescent. POSTMARKS: (1) S[O] Ke[ntish Tn]; (2) 12. NOON. 12 / AP. 22 / 1825. PUBLISHED: Jones, #228. TEXT: MS., Huntington Library (HM 6798).

TO JOHN HOWARD PAYNE Kentish Town Saturday Morning [?30 April 1825][1]

My dear Sir

Thank you for your kind attention in sending me the books—though as far as I have yet gone they grievously disappoint me. It is a melancholy consideration that the Creator of Lanton, Leather-Stockings & my beloved Long Tom should consent to put Lionel Lincoln[2] forth to the world—

You are very good to say all that you do in your letter; you put too high a price upon what was the result of the instinct as it were of self-preservation which led me to cultivate the only society which could alleviate almost unendurable sorrow[3]—But while you disclaim vanity, you must not make me vain—or perhaps worse egoistical—That is the worst part of a peculiar situation, which by making you the subject of over attention to others creates an undue estimation of self in one's own mind—But I am resolved not to allow myself to be in my own way—but to talk and think of something less near at hand—Will you not allow me to preserve this laudable determination?

I was unable to go to the theatre Yesterday evening—But if Virginius[4] should be acted & the thing practicable I should like to see it—If I do not see you before I will write concerning the arrangements for the opera—By the bye—a box would be preferable wherever it might be, if it can be obtained.—

Do not talk of frowns—You are good & kind—& deserve therefore nothing but kindness—But we must step lightly on the mosaic of circumstance for if we press too hard the beauty & charm is defaced—The world is a hard taskmaster & talk as we will of independance we are slaves

Adieu

I am truly Yours
MaryShelley

PUBLISHED: Jones, #229. TEXT: MS., Huntington Library (HM 6799).

1. This date is suggested by Mary Shelley's letter of [?4 May 1825] (see n. 1).

2. James Fenimore Cooper's *Lionel Lincoln; or, the Leaguer of Boston* (New York, 1825). On [24 April] Payne had sent Mary Shelley the "remaining volumes of Cooper's last novel," indicating that the early part pleased him because it reminded him of boyhood memories: "You can scarcely share my interest even in that part, and the rest may strike you as rather common place" (*The Romance*, p. 29). Godwin's Journal indicates that he read *Lionel Lincoln* from 5 May through 14 May, which suggests that Mary Shelley lent Godwin these volumes.

3. Payne, alluding to their conversation of the day before, called Mary Shelley "a heroine in love & friendship & duty to a parent." He referred to a conversation in which Mary Shelley said "she found herself excluded from the world by her devotedness to Mrs. Williams, whose history she explained," and "she also explained herself about her father" (*The Romance*, pp. 28, 30).

4. *Virginius*, by James Sheridan Knowles, was first produced in 1820, in Glasgow and then at Covent Garden on 17 May 1820 (Nicoll, *English Drama*, IV, 339).

TO JOHN HOWARD PAYNE

Wednesday Kentish Town
[?4 May 1825]

My dear Payne

There seems to be an ambiguity about Friday,[1] which makes it better that we should have nothing to do with it. I have seen Virginius & it was on

M[rs] Williams's account that I wished to go—but her health is delicate & she is afraid of going out two evenings together.

The engagement of Saturday I consider fixed as fate—if you will permit it so to be; for we depend upon you as our escort. Will you find yourself between 5 & 6 on Saturday Afternoon at M[rs] Cleveland's (M[rs] Williams's Mother) 24, Alsop's Buildings, New Road, Opposite to Baker Street—Where you will find us, a coach & every thing prepared. Come early because we are musical enough to wish to hear the Overture—& moreover to have our choice of places in the pit.—

Your octavo pages admonish me not to trespass upon your time[2]—Yet will you send me a line to say that you have received this—or I may fancy it pursueing you to Dover, until I hear that it is safely housed with yourself in Arundel St.—

Although You deprecate the subject I must thank you for all "favours received"—& I include kind thoughts as well as kind actions—Although I truly know how entirely Your imagination creates the admired as well as the admiration—But do not I entreat you frighten me by any more interpretations—Although be sure I am & always shall be

Your sincere friend
MaryShelley

PUBLISHED: Jones, #230. TEXT: MS., Huntington Library (HM 6801).

1. *Virginius* was announced for Friday, 6 May, but Payne informed Mary Shelley that it would probably not be performed (*The Romance*, p. 33).

2. Payne had written: ". . . perhaps we may not meet in the week. I am bound to the oar, as you will infer when I mention a contract to manufacture five hundred octavo pages between this and the twenty-fifth. Besides, I am reluctant to wear out my welcome, and would not cast myself between you and 'the taskmaster.' You are therefore safe from my persecution, excepting when you so far oblige me as to require my services, and then nothing shall stand in the way of your slightest wish; and you cannot do me a greater kindness than by giving me opportunities of showing you how much I am in earnest when I say so. Will you deny me that kindness? I am very fortunate in one respect. I can have your company without oppressing you with mine. You are perpetually in my presence, and if I close my eyes you are still there, and if I cross my arms over them and try to wave you away, still you will not be gone. This madness of my own imagination flatters itself with the forlorn hope of a delightful vagueness in part of your note . . ." (*The Romance*, pp. 34–35).

To John Howard Payne

[Kentish Town] Saturday
[14 May 1825]

My dear Payne

The very little pretention I have to a character for consistency is so deservedly lost with you that I hardly dare vindicate it on the present occasion. —But indeed I said that I would go to any thing but Otello[1]—which I saw at Venice & do not care about hearing again—Accordingly when I saw Otello advertised today, I so engaged myself that it will be impossible for me to avail myself of Elliston's ticket—Is this sufficient defence?— What can I say? Without a little encouragement I hardly venture to add that Next Saturday if Tancredi or Romèo—or Nina or any thing but Otello is sang by Mad[me] Pasta it would give me great pleasure to go—or to Cosi Fan Tutte.—Are you, by the bye, tired of playing the escudero to us—It was hard work last time—But as we shall not again stay for the ballêt I hope we shall be able to manage it more conveniently to all parties—But do not disarrange yourself on our account.—

Nor can I unfortunately go to D.L. [*Drury Lane*] on Monday, since I expect a visitor from the Country—I fear to offend by sending back the orders—& so shall use them,[2] unless you wish for them in which case I entreat you to send for them without any scruple.

You refer to a past note of mine—which is dismal—for I forget all I ever said in any note I ever wrote—& the sight of a letter which has been written & sent coming back on me again, I fear more than a ghost—I could not accuse you of any thing bordering on fatuitè.—

I looked out for you at D.L.—but could not find you—I was greatly interested & amused—The Author & Actor are made for each other; the forte of both being tenderness & passion in domestic feelings—

Your note looks as if you remembered all the nonsense I talked rurally with Jane & you & the silent man in Lambs garden[3]—but do you know I am rather given to talk nonsense—& then only half of it was nonsense—a veil—a make-believe which means every thing & nothing, if this is intelligible

I would ask you to call early next week to arrange but I fear octavo pages perhaps you will write—

I am Yours Ever MWShelley

ADDRESS: John Howard Payne Esq. / 29 Arundel Street / Strand. POSTMARKS: (1) SO Kentish Tn; (2) 12. NOON. 12 / MY. 14 / 1825. PUBLISHED: Jones, #234. TEXT: MS., Huntington Library (HM 6802).

1. *Otello*, by Rossini, was announced for 14 May at the King's Theatre. In this letter Mary Shelley also refers to *Romeo e Guilietta*, by Zingarelli; *Tancredi*, by Rossini; *Nina*, by Paesiello; and *Cosi fan Tutte*, by Mozart.

2. On Monday, 16 May, Godwin attended *Faustus* at Drury Lane (Godwin, Journal). Perhaps Mary Shelley supplied him the ticket.

3. Godwin's Journal for 9 May records: " . . . sup at Lamb's, w. MWS Mrs Williams, Mrs Novello, H Payne, Moxon, Talfourd & Price." To Mary Shelley's remarks about the conversation in the garden, Payne responded: "I have no recollection of any particular conversation in Lamb's garden, but be certain of this,—I am determined never to remember anything about you which may not be remembered with pleasure. I know this is making a virtue of necessity, but there are few in the world worthy even of such a resolution, and I am persuaded *you* are one of the few. Whatever you may mean, I shall always be confident you mean as kindly towards me as you can, and more, too, than I have any right to claim" (*The Romance*, p. 43).

TO JOHN HOWARD PAYNE [Kentish Town] Wednesday [18 May 1825]

My dear Payne

There is no Opera on Saturday[1]—I shall like to go to D.L. [*Drury Lane*] & shall engage Mrs Godwin to go with me if she is well enough—perhaps you will meet us at the theatre—But I will write again when all is arranged—

Remember for the Opera I do not want to see Pasta in Otello or Simiramide[2] but in Romèo or Tancredi or Nina &c—any night that they are represented—You are very good to annoy yourself for me in this way

Will you obtain for me 2 or four admissions to C.G. [*Covent Garden*] some night of Miss Foote's[3] performance, as I wish to accommodate Mrs Williams's Mother—Thank you for W. I. [*Washington Irving*][4]—

I write in haste
& am Yours Ever
MaryShelley

Do not trouble your servant, which goes against my conscience—but write by the post.—

PUBLISHED: Jones, #235. TEXT: MS., Huntington Library (HM 6810).

1. On 21 May 1825 "A Grand and Popular Selection of Music: Handel, Haydn, Mozart, Rossini, Von Weber, etc." was to be performed at Drury Lane (*Morning Chronicle*, 21 May 1825).

2. By Rossini. See also [14 May 1825].

3. Payne oblingingly sent orders and places for Covent Garden for Tuesday, 24 May, when Maria Foote was scheduled to appear. (*The Romance*, p. 45). The plays that night were *The Belle's Stratagem* and *Aladdin; or, The Wonderful Lamp.*

4. Payne had a library of American authors, and Mary Shelley often borrowed books from him.

TO JOHN HOWARD PAYNE Thursday Kentish Town. [19 May 1825]

My dear Payne

Pasta advertizes her benefit for next Thursday[1]—And I and some friends have agreed to go. Of course the tickets for such an expedition must be purchased. Will you have the goodness to buy 4 for me—But I should think that no time must be lost. I believe that if 4 box tickets are bought, all of the same box—One is admitted earlier & has the chance of a better seat.—Will you make enquiries about all this for me. I hope to see you at D.L. [*Drury Lane*] on Saturday when you can communicate "progress" I need not say that if you can make it out, how pleased we shall be at your joining us.—You see I take you at your word & will not make any apology, only thanking you very sincerely—

Yours very truly
MaryShelley

ADDRESS: J. Howard Payne Esq / 29 Arundel Street / Strand. POSTMARKS: (1) T.P / La[ ]nd St: (2) 7. NIGHT. 7 / 19 MY / 1825. PUBLISHED: Jones, #236. TEXT: MS., Huntington Library (HM 6808).

1. Pasta's benefit night at the King's Theatre, at which she sang from *Nina* and *Tancredi*, was 26 May.

To John Howard Payne

[Kentish Town] Friday—Noon
[20 May 1825]

My dear Payne

When I wrote yesterday I had not seen Mrs Godwin—nor arranged for tomorrow—so excuse this supernumerary note—I have depended, as you kindly assured me I should have them, on 4 Orders & Places—if I have overstepped the mark let me know without delay; if not it will be sufficient that you send them to Mrs G. [*Godwin*] 195 Strand in the course of tomorrow. I trust that you will do us the pleasure of joining us at the theatre—for I want to see you to thank you in pe{r}son for your kindness—& more{o}ver I have something else to say about the production of a friend of mine[1]

I am yours truly & obliged
MaryShelley

A note from my friends makes me add if you have not already bought the tickets for Thursday not to take any steps about them till I see you—if you have—never mind—Some of us will go at any rate—Adieu

PUBLISHED: Jones, #237. TEXT: MS., Huntington Library (HM 6809).

1. On the basis of Mary Shelley's letter to Payne of 28 June, Jones concluded that Jane Williams was the author of the drama that Mary Shelley asked Payne to read and evaluate (*MWS Letters*, I, 327, n. 1). The correspondence between Payne and Mary Shelley, together with Edward Williams's *Journal*, makes clear that the parties were discussing *The Promise, or a Year, a Month, and a Day*, a play written by Edward Williams in 1821. Payne wrote: ". . . your friend's play" will "not succeed if acted . . . whatever merit it has is literary." He praised some of its lyrical passages but criticized others, calling "the whole affair of the Jew" an excrescence. Finally, Payne referred to the playwright with a masculine pronoun (*The Romance*, pp. 63–67). Williams's *Journal* contains numerous references to *The Promise* that coincide with the information in Payne's letter. On 24 October 1821 Williams wrote: "Employed revising the Jew Scene"; on 9 January 1822 Williams had news that the proprietors of Covent Garden had rejected the play, that "as a literary composition they consider {it} to abound with great poetical beauties, but as {a} drama they are of opinion it would f[ail] in representation" (see also 15 October 1822; 12 January [1823]).

To John Howard Payne

[Kentish Town] Saturday
[21 May 1825]

My dear Payne

I shall be most happy to see you at the theatre this evening[1] though I hope to make such arrangements as to preclude your thinking it necessary to escort me but I am not quite sure—I am extremely obliged to you for the trouble you take for me

Ever Yours MWS

ADDRESS: J. Howard Payne Esq / &c &c &c. PUBLISHED: Jones, #238. TEXT: MS., Huntington Library (HM 6807).

1. See [18 May 1825], n. 1.

TO JOHN HOWARD PAYNE [Kentish Town] Friday Morn[g] [27 May 1825]

Amabilissimo Cavaliere

Will you not think me impertinent if I request you to find for me & to let me know at your earliest convenience the number of Lady Morgan's abode in Berner's Street.[1]—

Will you be so kind as to tell me what you paid for our tickets—that I may relieve my burthened conscience of a part of my debt to you—though the part I feel most, your more than polite kindness, your goodness in annoying yourself so much for me must still remain unpayable.

I have looked but not seen a handsome Spaniard looking out in Kentish Town for two donzellas whose adventures last night were certainly very ridiculous[2]—My head aches this morning from the result though neither ice nor softer flame occasions it—& as yet I am still faithful to W.I.!!!

Yours, My dear Payne
Most truly & obliged
MaryShelley

I hardly dare ask you to come & call considering your occupations—With regard to future Opera's "the streets are so broad & the lanes are narrow"—the impediments so innumerous—that notwithstan{d}ing my adoration of Pasta & admiration of Begnis I fear I must resolve to confine our visits there to one only—to see Romèo.[3]

[*P. 4, upside-down*] By the bye one day (o this vile pen!) next Week I ⟨may⟩ shall go to the Lambs—how far shall you feel inclined to accompany me hither or meet me there—remember this is for my "pleasure" not my "advantage" so do not inconvenience yourself.[4]

PUBLISHED: Jones, #239. TEXT: MS., Huntington Library (HM 6803).

1. Payne responded: "I have sent to a friend for Lady Morgan's address and will let you know the moment I obtain it" (*The Romance*, p. 50).

2. Payne explained the "handsome Spaniard" to Washington Irving: "The allusion in the following note is—to some laughing at the Opera on this occasion about a Spaniard who caught the attention of the ladies in so marked a manner as to attract his—He followed them out—A remark of mine on the Subject induced Mrs S— to ask 'Is that in Grandpapa? It is worthy of him.' Grandpapa had then just been damned—Hence my use of the Signature—" (MS., Huntington Library; *The Romance*, p. 49).

3. Payne responded that de Begnis would perform in *Romeo* on Thursday and Saturday and Mary Shelley had her choice of attendance (*The Romance*, p. 50).

4. To this request, Payne wrote: "Believe me, I shall always be more than 'inclined to accompany' you as 'far' as you may be 'inclined' to let me. So do not talk of inconvenience" (*The Romance*, p. 51).

To John Howard Payne Kentish Town May 30th [1825]

My dear Payne

We prefer Saturday to Thursday,[1]—if we are sure of Romèo for the latter day.

I confess that the greater part of your note is inexplicable to me. Pity what you call my inexperience, and write more intelligibly; it would seem that you fancy that you began to know me better, when in fact you know me less than ever. It is foolish however to guess at an explanation painful to me, in what I own that I cannot understand.[2]

You forget to answer a part of my note—the expence of the admissions. You promised on this occasion to be "an honest man & true"—and I claim your promise with the greater eagerness—since it will save me the trouble of enquiring the prices of Eber.[3]

I am yours ever & obliged
MaryShelley

ADDRESS: John Howard Payne Esq / 29 Arundel Street / Strand. POSTMARKS: (1) SO K[entish] Tn; (2) 12. NOON. 12 / MY. 30 / 1825. PUBLISHED: Jones, #240. TEXT: MS. (envelope sheet), Pforzheimer Library; MS. (letter), Huntington Library (HM 6804).

1. See [27 May 1825].

2. Payne's double entendre was based on Mary Shelley's return to reading Washington Irving: "I am glad you return to Irving, for it is tantalizing to have one's heart in a state of miscellany. What I myself might have thought on Saturday, could I have presumed so far as to feel a personal interest in your fidelity—! Is *ice* a non-conductor? But if it is, how do you convey impressions? With the tenderest paternal solicitude for your inexperience, believe me, Your most affectionate—'GRANDPAPA' " (*The Romance*, p. 51).

Payne's response to Mary Shelley's request that he "write more intelligibly" was: "All I remember of what I wrote is, that some little *badinage* of yours was answered *by badinage*; and that there was some ridiculous play upon words, which, I apprehend, you have taken in a light I never dreamed of. At least, that is the only way in which I can account for your reproof" (*The Romance*, p. 52).

3. John Ebers (?1785–?1830), opera manager, held the lease on the King's Theatre from 1820 to 1827. Payne informed Mary Shelley that the tickets cost a half-guinea each (*The Romance*, p. 52).

To John Howard Payne Kentish Town. May 31. [1825]

A bad conscience you know, my Dear Payne, is proverbially susceptible—And the feeling that what passed last Saturday was not quite en règle made me captious. I accused myself & so did not like to be accused (as I thought:) by another. This explanation must be my apology for looking seriously upon badinage.[1] I was annoyed at finding a picture turn into a Man—

You say nothing of Romèo—unless I hear from you to the contrary, Mrs Williams and I will call in Arundel Street at ½ past six Saturday—though if there is to be a crush that will be too late, unless, as before, you get a ticket for a Gallery box & we can enter the pit from above stairs. The Opera you know begins at seven on Saturday, So we shall not again steal your Lawyer's sugar,[2] but you can join us in our coach.

A part of your present note is very Wrong—very wrong indeed—I can only say that I hold myself altogether the obliged person & that I am your sincere friend

MWShelley

PUBLISHED: Jones, #242. TEXT: MS., Huntington Library (HM 6805).

1. See 30 May [1825], n. 2.

2. Perhaps Mary Shelley was using *sugar* in its slang sense as "money" (Partridge, *A Dictionary of Slang*), in an allusion to Payne's debts.

TO JOHN HOWARD PAYNE

[Kentish Town] Monday [?6 June 1825][1]

My dear Payne

After due consideration, Mrs Williams & I have concluded—

To call in Arundel St. in a coach at half past 6—Without alighting, we will leave bonnets &c which your man Friday will bring to the Opera at the right time—and we shall not stay for the ballêt—If the hour I have mentioned be too early let me know. This is far the best mode of proceeding & will not take us at all out of our way.—

Adieu—Au revoir!

Yours Ever MWS.

PUBLISHED: Jones, #241. TEXT: MS., Huntington Library (HM 6806).

1. The contents of this letter suggest that it was written on the Monday before Mary Shelley's letter of [12 June 1825].

TO JOHN HOWARD PAYNE

[Kentish Town] Sunday [12 June 1825]

My dear Payne

We were altogether unlucky last night—since our Opera was changed and we did not see you—and moreover beheld Clari[1] cruelly murdered—Nothing ever was managed so ill—& parts—quite different from yours in the worst possible taste—We quitted it on an incipient hiss which threatened damnation—

What divine weather[2] I live now—Kentish Town is odorous with hay—Shall you be here today?—I hope not since I go out—but I leave this in case of a call—We were unable to charm the eyes of your Man Friday last night being obliged to enter town in another way

Lamb I hear is not well at all[3]—I hope soon to see you in some manner & I am

Yours ever truly
MaryShelley

PUBLISHED: Jones, #231. TEXT: MS., Huntington Library (HM 6816).

1. *Clari*, a ballet based on Payne's operetta, and *Il Barbiere di Siviglia* were announced for the King's Theatre for 11 June 1825.

2. The weather in that area of England was particularly warm from 6 through 17 June (Godwin, Journal).

3. On 6 June, Henry Crabb Robinson wrote to Dorothy Wordsworth of Lamb's illness, a nervous disorder that began on 27 May, after Lamb attended the funeral of his late brother's widow (Lucas, *Charles Lamb*, II, 149).

To John Howard Payne

[Kentish Town] Wednesday
[15 June 1825][1]

My dear Payne—I write in a desperate hurry with the vilest of pens which I have not time to mend—The enclosed was waiting for you on Sunday as I expected a call—but by mischance it was not given you—

I am afraid that we shall hardly have courage to make another visit to that desperate Coquette the Opera—Unless it were for something very stupendous & very certain—We wish to see Cosi fan tutte but do not wish to be disappointed—but before I decide I must consult my gentle Oracle[2]

Kean!—Yes truly—fire & water for him—On the stage.—the characters? —what will he play? Sir G.O. [*Giles Overreach*]—Othello—Hamlet—of these I am sure perhaps RIII—I do not wish to go Monday but by that day will write & tell you, my very kind & obliging friend—When I will go—

This note—I am ashamed of—& it is ashamed of me—i.e. the white paper is angry at being so streaked

But I am in a hurry

So with many thanks

Yrs truly
Mary Shelley

PUBLISHED: Jones, #232. TEXT: MS., Huntington Library (HM 6811).

1. This date is established by the letter of Wednesday Eveg [15 June 1825].

2. Jane Williams.

To John Howard Payne

[Kentish Town] Wednesday Eveg
[15 June 1825][1]

My dear Payne

I wrote to you today in so great an hurry that I hardly know what I said—And I forgot to add that I should be glad if you could without trouble get me 4 Box Admissions for D.L. [*Drury Lane*] on Friday—for W. [*William*] Tell.—

I found the inhabitants of Gower Place today suffering under a visitation of painters—nor can I extract them from that scent to my hay-odorous Kentish Town until Sunday—Even for that day Mrs G. [*Godwin*] had a scruple of conscience having asked you to call on them ⟨that day⟩—But I told her that if you were disengaged—I did not doubt that you would not excessively repine at the prolongation of your walk—and dared undertake for you (if, as before said, that you were not otherwise engaged) that you you would dine with them here that day.[2] Will you come?—We shall all be happy to see you—It is, I think, 20 years since we met—

We dine at four

Yours every truly & obliged
MaryShelley

ADDRESS: John Howard Payne Esq / 29 Arundel Street / Strand. POSTMARKS: (1) 12. NOON. 12 / JU. 16 / 1825; (2) S.O K[entish Tn] nt. PUBLISHED: Jones, #233. TEXT: MS. (envelope sheet), Pforzheimer Library; MS. (letter), Huntington Library (HM 6812).

1. Godwin's Journal notes that the Godwins moved to 44 Gower Place on 30 May 1825, not in early 1826, as suggested by Brown (*Godwin*, p. 366). The Journal also records that painters were at Gower Place on Wednesday, 15 June.

2. Payne did dine with the Godwins at Mary Shelley's home on Sunday, 19 June (Godwin, Journal).

TO JOHN HOWARD PAYNE [Kentish Town ?c. 20–22 June 1825]

Dear Payne—In haste with a vile pen. I'll dispatch your note to William without delay he is very abominable—He quarelled { } me really before I let him have [?L-S].[1]—& now—but do not fear I will send your note—I am to see you Thursday at Gower Place[2] I believe if you are good enough to go there—Y^{s} truly MWS.

ADDRESS: J. Howard Payne Esq. PUBLISHED: Jones, #252. TEXT: MS., Huntington Library (HM 6821).

1. Although Jones suggests that Mary Shelley was referring here to *Lionel Lincoln*, the initials are not the same, and they are hyphenated, suggesting *Leather-Stocking*, which was Mary Shelley's name for *The Pioneers* (see [?30 April 1825]).

2. The only Thursday in 1825 that Mary Shelley and Payne dined with the Godwins at Gower Place was 23 June. On that day William Godwin, Jr., was also present.

TO LEIGH HUNT Kentish Town. June 27. [1825]

My dear Hunt

You can hardly be ⟨less⟩ more delighted at the idea of returning To Tottenham C^{t} Road and the Hampstead Coachmen, than are your friends that you should return,[1] & return with pleasure, to these things. If you were here just now you would find England in all its glory, and the people complaining of the Italian heat of the weather, though like me, I think you would find qualche differenza But the English expose themselves to the sunny sides of the way at noon & then are angry to find it too warm—

Of course all questions of the future are rife are among us—Where will they live?—I told the N's [*Novellos*] that I thought that you would take Shacklewell on your shoulders & bear it Westward—You could not live there—you who come for the sake of green fields would not be content with drab-coloured meadows & brick kilns—I saw Novello on Sunday and had a long talk with him about you. He desired me to send the kindest messages; and his renovated spirits & health shew with what eagerness he looks forward to the enjoyment of your society. But he told me to entreat you not to set out until you should hear from him again; as he is very anxious to arrange your debts before your arrival—He is a true, ardent & faithful friend to you. I think that your arrival will do them a great deal of good—for poor Mary by going to that place has shut herself out from society & pines—and Vincent has headachs in solitude—You ask about their children;—you know I cannot tell of the advancement of your knowledge on the subject—so for fear of being puzzling I will "tell the tale"—Victoria—now at Boulogne & not to return—Alfred in Yorkshire—Cecilia—Edward about to go to Hazlewood—Emma—Clara—Mary—and Florence—The little boy, Charles Arthur, brought into the world last autumn died a month ago in consequence of a fall—he was a thriving child and this misfortune cut them up a good deal, until revived by the hopes of your return—such is a full true and particular account—

This does not intend to be a long letter or an answer to your last—When we meet, if the Gods permit, I will tell you one or two things which will I think surprize and perhaps move you—move you at least to excuse a little what you do not approve—I continue to live in quietness—the hope & consolation of my life is the society of Mrs W. [*Williams*] To her, for better or worse I am wedded—while she will have me & I continue in the love-lorn state that I have since I returned to this native country of yours—I go or stay as she or rather our joint circumstances decide—which now with ponderous chain and heavy log enroot us in Kentish Town. I think of Italy as of a vision of Delight afar off—and go to the Opera sometimes merely for the sake of seeing my dear Italians & listening to that glorious language in its perfection

Where will you live My dear Hunt & my Polly? And what will you do?—Command me, I entreat you—if it appears that I can be of the slightest use to you. I am pleased to think that Persino (who does not understand a word of Italian) will renew his friendship with your sweet Henry—I long to see Occhi Turchini—and to congratulate Thornton, when he shall be fairly established in an arm chair with his Bingley[2]—Where will you live? Near Hampstead—not in Hampstead perhaps, it is so dear, & so far—but on the road to it, I think you might be accommodated—

There are some empty Houses on Mortimer Terrace—but I believe my good Polly does not like that. My Polly, I traverse the gap fearless at ten at night and Jane & I in some of our disastrous jou{r}nies to see our friends, have passed it much later—Ma faccian loro[3]—We'll talk Tuscan, Hunt, and I shall get more sick than ever for Valle che de'miei lamenti son pieni[4]—So you are about to bid adieu to fireflies—azioli[5] the Tuscan peasantry & Tuscan vines!—but no more of that—our feelings are so different and we have each such excellent reasons for the difference of our feelings on this subject—that we may differ & agree—the same is not the same, you know—Had you seen Italy as I saw it—had I seen it as you we should each be delighted with our present residence, nor for the world's treasure change—Adieu, dear Hunt, & love Y^s^ faithfully—MaryShelley

ADDRESS: Leigh Hunt Esq / Ferma in Posta / Firenze / Florence—Italy / L'Italie. POSTMARKS: (1) F25 / 5; (2) ANGLETERRE; (3) CH[AMB]ERY; (4) [CORRISPZA] ESTERA [DA GENOVA]; (5) [ ] / LUGLIO. PUBLISHED: Jones, #243. TEXT: MS., Huntington Library (HM 2754).

1. An advance from Henry Colburn for work to be written by Hunt enabled the Hunts to leave Italy on 10 September 1825. They arrived in London on 14 October. The Novellos arranged for them to live in Bloomsbury, but in 1826 the Hunts moved to Highgate Hill (Blunden, *Leigh Hunt*, pp. 220–21; Hunt, *Autobiography*, II, 180, 192).

2. William Bingley (1774–1823) wrote and compiled works on a number of subjects. Two of his most popular works were *Animal Biography* (1802), which reached its sixth edition by 1824, and *Useful Knowledge, an account of the various productions of nature, mineral, vegetable and animal* (1816), which reached its seventh edition by 1852.

3. "But they do it."

4. "Vales that are filled with my laments."

5. See 28 July [1824], n. 3.

TO JOHN HOWARD PAYNE

Tuesday November 25th
[humorously for 28 June 1825]
Kentish Town

My dear Payne

Mrs Williams begs me to thank you for her for the attention you have paid to The Drama—She has no idea of making the <u>radical</u> alterations that you suggest[1]—

I am very sorry to have seen you in such ill spirits lately. Methinks I could give you a world of good advice—but I am so little didactic that I do not know how to set about it—And then I hope that it would no{t} come too late—& that by this time you are gay & hopeful—I trust that you will see me before you leave town—if you do leave it, which I hope you will not though this hope is I fear purely selfish on my part—You are good & kind to all except yourself—If you took to being bounteously, as is you wont, courteous towards yourself I think you would arrive at being, as all other objects of your kindness are, quite in good humour, with & grateful for, your own society.—

You made me expect that another letter[2] would have accompanied the book on Sunday—is it indelicate in me to ask for this?—I should not of course unless you had first said that you would be good enough to shew it me—I hope to see you soon & am always your sincere friend

MaryShelley

With regard to Kean; the weather has been so bad that I have not been able to go to town to see the bills—but as I suppose he will play twice this week & no more—I should like to go both times provided it be to Sir Giles Brutus[3]—Hamlet—or in fact to any thing except Richard III—Shylock & Othello—I shall be at My fathers tomorrow evening, perhaps you can call there, or if not, you will I dare say be good enough to write to tell me by the earliest post—What he acts on Thursday & whether you can obtain places & orders for me for that night. If it be inconvenient to you to get 4; 2 will suffice

PUBLISHED: Jones, #244. TEXT: MS., Huntington Library (HM 6814).

1. Payne had suggested extensive revisions for Edward Williams's play and offered to help revise it (see [20 May 1825]).

2. Payne had sent Mary Shelley one of Irving's letters and had promised more. To this inquiry, Payne responded: "I did not send the letter, because I thought I might find others which would answer your wishes quite as well, and which contained less about my petty affairs, with which you have, in one or two instances, been somewhat disgusted, though you have never said so, and never will. The simple truth is, you have generally seen me under the influence of feelings too deeply possessed to allow me to talk about anything which would give me the trouble of thinking, and I remember all the trash to which I have made you listen with a sort of remorse at having, as it were, thus dragged down a fine mind to the worst of commonplace. But, no doubt, it would happen again, so let it rest. I did not think of these things when I mentioned the letter, which cannot strike you as it does me. I will find others for you, but I send this, lest circumstances should give a false colouring to its being withheld. To understand it, it is necessary you should know that Irving's advice has been of great service to me in all literary points upon which I have had opportunities of consulting him. Since chance threw me among pens, ink and paper, he and his elder brother are the only persons who have ever boldly and unhesitatingly encouraged me with the hopes of ultimate success and prosperity . . ." (*The Romance*, pp. 69–70).

On Saturday, 25 June 1825, Mary Shelley had gone to the Godwins' for tea and had afterwards met Payne (Godwin's Journal makes no mention of Payne on that day), who walked home with her. On this walk Payne declared his love, to which Mary Shelley responded that her feelings for him were not romantic in nature. In the course of their conversation, she told Payne that she was interested in a "friendship" with Irving, whose gentleness and cordiality had impressed her. As a result, Payne decided to try to effect a match between the two. On 16 August he gave Mary Shelley's letters to Irving to read, with a covering letter that read in part: "I do not ask you to fall in love—but I should even feel a little proud of myself if you thought the lady worthy of that distinction, and very possibly you would have fallen in love with her, had you met her casually—but she is too much out of society to enable you to do so—and sentiments stronger than friendship seldom result from this sort of previous earnestness for intimacy when it comes from the wrong side" (*The Romance*, pp. 18–19).

Irving entered in his *Journal* for 16 August 1825: "Read Mrs Shelleys correspondence before going to bed" (Irving, *Journals and Notebooks*, III, 510). There is no evidence to suggest that Mary Shelley was aware that Payne gave her letters to Irving to read. In fact, she asked Payne not to make her "appear ridiculous" by "repeating tales out of school" to Irving (see [29 July 1825]), and she might well have considered Payne's actions a betrayal of her trust.

3. Payne's play *Brutus; or the Fall of Tarquin* was first produced at Drury Lane on 3 December 1818 (Nicoll, *English Drama*, IV, 368). On 7 July 1825 Kean selected *Brutus* for his benefit night at Drury Lane (Genest, *English Stage*, IX, 297).

To John Howard Payne

by the thermometer—
November 29. [1825]—Kentish Town
By the calender—June

My dear Payne

I have read with great pleasure Irvine's letter—with greater because it dwells upon your circumstances—You are wrong in thinking that any details of this kind ever annoyed me[1]—Once, I remember, a conversation about William's visit brought so forcibly to my mind scenes that took place now eleven years ago, that I became melancholy—for when will reflection on the happy, unfortunate past cease to have that effect on me? —But I take a real interest in your affairs; & moreover I am too much of an authoress after all, not {to} listen with avidity to the detail of any of the forms of life and the human mind—were it new it would be the more greedily caught up—but I am familiar with difficulties & what you term petty cares—

Well—to leave my defence; W.I's letter pleases me greatly as I said—I trust that you will attend to his advice & be inspirited by his admonitions —While you retire to "solitude & silence" to seek there "health & peace"— I feel sure that you will be more than ever awake to laudable ambition & exiliarating industry—And moreover a little economical—&, then without crossing the Atlantic in reach of the dead you may patch up a native country out of this queer England—or France.—To the feelings of an English woman who has never dreamt of crossing the Atlantic, America appears cut off from human intercourse:—it cannot be the same to you—& therefore I may be in the wrong in my repugnance to your leaving us for it—

Your letter gives me pain, because you feel it & because it seems to place a barrier to any future meeting[2]—Thus it is ever one's hard fate either to be deserted & neglected—or, which turns out the same thing, to be liked too well, & so avoided—few indeed have your kind generosity to offer, & I am sure sincerely offer, to do ⟨me⟩ services—to one thus circumstanced with you—nor do I think that I do other than please you when I ⟨accept⟩ receive your offers not only with thanks but with "acceptance bounteous."[3]—And will do as you bid me & after these last words be laconic, till you greet me with the welcome news that I may shew you all the kindness and friendship I have for you, without doing you an injury.

I shall be glad to see Irvine's letters—& the handwriting, crabbed after reading your distinct syllables, will become as clear to me as LordByron's letterless scrawl—As to friendship with him—It cannot be—though every thing I hear & know renders it more desirable—How can Irvine surrounded by fashion rank & splendid friendships pilot his pleasure bark from the gay press into this sober, sad, enshadowed nook?—

But our conversations shall not end with W.I. if they began with him,[4] which I do not remember—Why indeed should they end at all but go on & grow sober as our years encrease—Nor if you desire to renew them, let a long interval elapse; for I mean only to live ten years longer & to have 37 engraved upon my tomb—In the mean time the Sortes Virgilianae,[5] which I consulted today on the subject of my return to beloved Italy, promised that a magnificent dwelling should be prepared for me there near the rocks which resound far with the dashing of the sea, beside the torrents black with bituminous whirlpools—which means the neighbourhood of Naples of course—Will you come & see me there?—So I shall not see you saturday—though I had fifty wise counsels to give & sage axioms to deliver—Is it so?—friday, I shall look at the bills & see whether I desire orders for Monday & send you word in measured phrase—yet be not too hard with me on this point—for the truth is though I can rein my spoken words—I find all the woman directs my written ones & the pen in my hand I gallop over fence & ditch without pity for my reader—ecce signum!

But you have taken the affair in hand so sagely & methinks, may I say it without the charge of vanity, so disinterestedly that I resign the rule to you & will endeavour to conform to the laws you have enacted—Which still permit me I hope to adhere to truth & subscribe myself, with deep interest in your Welfare,

your friend—MaryShelley

PUBLISHED: Jones, #245. TEXT: MS., Huntington Library (HM 6815).

1. See [28 June 1825], n. 2.

2. Payne's letter of 29 June 1825 contained a description of his initial intention, upon meeting her, to admire her from a distance for fear he might become romantically attached; his subsequent change of mind; and his present determination to again avoid seeing her until his "fever" passed. He wished, however, to remain her "friend in a corner, and to let me see your handwriting, whenever you can find any commission for me to execute" (*The Romance*, pp. 71–73). From Godwin's Journal we learn that either Payne's fever had passed or his determination not to see her had weakened, for on 11 July Payne, the Lambs, and Godwin visited Mary Shelley.

3. *Othello* 3. 3. 470.

4. Payne closed his letter of 29 June: "To return to the point at which our conversations began and have ended—WI—be assured I will act the hero in this business" (*The Romance*, p. 74).

5. See 18 June 1820, n. 9.

*To John Howard Payne

Kentish Town. Saturday Morng
[?July 1825][1]

My dear Friend

Permit me to return the <u>de</u> <u>trop</u> that you sent me—You are only far too good—

I write in haste, as you may guess—Take care of yourself & believe me

Yours ever truly
MShelley

UNPUBLISHED. TEXT: MS., Pforzheimer Library.

1. I place this letter tentatively in July 1825 because it is written on the same stationery as that of Mary Shelley's letter of [29 July 1825]: cream-colored, wove paper with a floral, embossed border and a Turner watermark; these are the only examples of this paper I have found among Mary Shelley's letters.

To John Howard Payne

[?London ?July 1825–32][1]

I know nothing—it is 6 & no one is here—there is barely time—Yet I Think we probably shall—

ADDRESS: J. H. Payne. PUBLISHED: Jones, #248. TEXT: MS., Huntington Library (HM 10791).

1. The seal on this note, "NOT / WORD[ ] / BUT / DEE[D]," may provide a clue to its date and place, since it almost certainly did not belong to Mary Shelley.

To John Howard Payne

[Kentish Town] Monday Morning
[4 July 1825]

My dear Payne

Kean's nights are limited to 3—& Othello & R III are to make up two of these, neither of which Do I wish to see.—But in recompense, we are to have Brutus[1] on Thursday—and my obedience to Papa's orders is rewarded by my having another opportunity of seeing a play I have long wished to see—Can you Get orders & places for me for Thursday[2]—& will you let me know as soon as you can

I am Yrs Ever & obliged MWS.

ADDRESS: J. Howard Payne Esq / 29 Arundel Street / Strand. POSTMARKS: (1) T.P / Crawford St; (2) 7. NIGH[T]. 7 / 4. JY / [1]82[5]. PUBLISHED: Jones, #246. TEXT: MS., Huntington Library (HM 6813).

1. See [28 June 1825], n. 3.

2. On Tuesday Payne wrote: "I send you three admissions for Kean's Benefit and places for four. I retain the fourth ticket, as perhaps I may look in in the course of the evening" (MS., Huntington Library). For "I retain the fourth ticket," *The Romance* text incorrectly reads: "Retain the fourth ticket" (p. 62).

To John Howard Payne [Kentish Town] Wednesday [?13 July 1825]

My dear Payne—I cannot go tomorrow[1] as I feared—but I will go—I shall see my Janey tomorrow & arrange when—And I will write

Very truly Yours
MWS.

ADDRESS: J. Howard Payne / &c &c &c. PUBLISHED: Jones, #247. TEXT: MS., Huntington Library (HM 6823).

1. Payne's note to Mary Shelley (see *The Romance*, p. 77) said that the play for Thursday was changed to the *Coronation*, first produced on 11 July at Covent Garden (Genest, *English Stage*, IX, 310). The *Coronation*, (which played also on 12–15, 17, and 18 July) was an extravagant representation of the coronation ceremony of Charles X of France, which took place on 29 May (Henry Saxe Wyndham, *The Annals of Covent Garden Theatre from 1732 to 1897*, 2 vols. [London: Chatto & Windus, 1906], II, 35).

To John Howard Payne [Kentish Town] Wednesday— [20 July 1825]

My dear Payne

Will you let me have orders for four for Drury Lane for Friday[1]

How does this divine weather agree with you—I find it infinitely agreable—too luxurious a pleasure I allow to have always—for one can do little else that [*than*] sit in perfect ⟨sympathy⟩ quiescence, the genial atmosphere surrounding one—

How goes the world with you except that this weather exhiliarates me, I should be melancholy for I have been annoyed—Yours ever

MaryShelley

If tickets are going a begging—I should like 6 for friday.

PUBLISHED: Jones, #249. TEXT: MS., Huntington Library (HM 6822).

1. Payne wrote that Drury Lane was to close for the season on Thursday, 21 July, and asked if orders for Haymarket would do (*The Romance*, p. 81). *The Hypocrite*, *Intrigue*, and *'Twould Puzzle a Conjuror* were scheduled for Friday performances at the Haymarket.

To John Howard Payne [Kentish Town] Thursday. [21 July 1825]

I sincerly wish, my dear Payne, that you could physician my annoyances for then I am sure they would come to a speedy conclusion—Unfortunately it is not for myself but others that I am uncomfortable—& I feel that always more difficult to bear—

The Haymarket will do very well only let it be for Saturday instead of Friday.[1]—The glory of the time has departed—how d{r}eary these clouds are, & yet I suppose that I am sola in regretting the dear insufferable heat

The orders I ask for are as you may guess for friends but if we continue cool I expect to be tempted to see Liston[2] some of these days—

Yours Ever
MaryShelley

I am not in the slightest hurry for the life of Brown[3]—a Month hence will do.

PUBLISHED: Jones, #250. TEXT: MS., Huntington Library (HM 6818).

1. *The Rivals*, *Midas*, and *Blue Devils* were to be performed at the Haymarket on Saturday, 23 July 1825.

2. John Liston (?1776–1846), famed comic actor, who performed at the Haymarket during most summer seasons from 1805 through 1830.

3. William Dunlap, *Life of Charles Brockden Brown* (Philadelphia: J. P. Parke, 1815). On 24 July Payne wrote: "I send you Brown's life—I saw it yesterday at Col. Aspinwall's and took unceremonious possession" (*The Romance*, p. 80). "Unceremonious possession" refers to Payne's taking the book without permission, since the Aspinwalls were then at Versailles, living in the cottage Payne had himself previously occupied (Irving, *Journals and Notebooks*, III, 504). Payne met Charles Brockden Brown in 1806, and they became good friends at once (Overmyer, *America's First Hamlet*, pp. 66–67).

TO JOHN HOWARD PAYNE

[Kentish Town] Sunday Evening—
[?24 July 1825]

My dear Friend

As the best mode of explaining your wishes to W. [*William Godwin, Jr.*] I enclosed him your letter[1]—at the Morning Chronicle office—where a missive will always reach him—You say nothing of Yourself & the progress of your affair—I await impatiently news of both—

Can you get me a box for the Opera for Tuesday—if you can let me have it if possible by 3 or 4 o'clock as else it is difficult to get a party togeth{e}r—If not for Tuesday, Thursday—but let me know—

Yours Affly
MS.

ADDRESS: John Howard Payne Esq / &c &c &c. PUBLISHED: Jones, #251. TEXT: MS., Huntington Library (HM 10791).

1. This may refer to Payne's note accompanying the *Life of Charles Brockden Brown*, in which he wrote: "Pray do not lend it to William. He is careless, and books come out of his hands slowly and with darkened countenances. But do not tell him I say so" (MS., Huntington Library; *The Romance*, p. 80).

TO JOHN HOWARD PAYNE

Thursday Kentish Town
[28 July 1825]

My dear Payne

I am afraid that I shall not have the pleasure of seeing you tonight as I expected—for Mrs G— [*Godwin*] is again attacked by her painful complaint which naturally makes her averse to the slightest exertion[1]—

This day is perfect—The most faultless one I think we have had—not too warm I trust for any one—If Don Giovanni or Figaro should be acted on the last night of the Opera Jane & I would like to go but not otherwise—If without any inconvenience you can get me 4 or 6 orders for Saddlers Wells[2] I should like it—but do Not stand, I entreat you on any ceremony but be quite sure that I shall consider your declining an indiscreet request as a mark of kindness—

Poor dear Brown—What a delightful person he seems to have been—As for my favourite I. [*Irving*]—Methinks our acquaintance proceeds at the rate of Antediluvians Who I have somewhere read thought nothing of an interval of a year or two between a visit—Alack I fear that at this rate if ever the Church should make us one it would be announced in the consolotary phrase that the Bride & Bridegrooms joint ages amounted to the discreet number of 145 & 3 months[3]

Am I ever to see you again? Hoping that I shall I am eternally

Your very true friend
MaryWShelley

[*P. 4, upside-down*] If you do send me the S.W. Orders pray let me have them or notice of them a day before their date

ADDRESS: J. Howard Payne Esq / &c &c &c. PUBLISHED: Jones, #253. TEXT: MS., Huntington Library (HM 6817).

1. According to Godwin, Journal, Mary Shelley and William Godwin, Jr., dined at the Godwins' on 28 July 1825.

2. On 29 July Payne responded: "I supped with one of my old Wells' Proprietors last night and got undated orders, which are enclosed" (MS., Huntington Library; *The Romance*, p. 84).

3. In his letter of 29 July Payne promised to "remember your impatience, and if antedeluvian modes are to be revived, I will not be an accessary, but do my best to promote customs more compatible with the term to which you have limited your stay in this only world where wedlock is tolerated" (MS., Huntington Library; *The Romance*, p. 84).

TO JOHN HOWARD PAYNE

[Kentish Town] Friday
[29 July 1825]

Not to keep your Messenger, My dear Friend, I write even before I have read Irvine's letter. I trust that I shall see You, because I do not see why the visit should be so painful as I suppose & truly hope that you will soon return to this country.[1]—

Now, My dear Payne, tho' I am a little fool, do not make me appear so in Rue Richelieu[2] by repeating tales out of school—Nor mention the Antediluvians—But I am not afraid; I am sure you love me well enough not {to} be accessory in making me appear ridiculous to one whom I like & esteem, though I am sure that the time & space between us will never be shortened—perhaps it is that very ⟨idea⟩ certainty that makes me, female

Quixote as I am, pay such homage to the unattainable Dulcinea in the Cueva de Montesinos[3]—i.e. Rieu Richelieu

But again be not a tell tale so God Bless you—Give my love, of course Platonic, to I. [*Irving*]

I am Y^s^ Ever
MaryWShelley

I will send Browns life before Monday. & also I's letter.

PUBLISHED: Jones, #254. TEXT: MS., Huntington Library (HM 6819).

1. At Washington Irving's urging, Payne went to Paris, arriving there on 5 August 1825. Irving wanted Payne to meet with Stephen Price, the American theatrical manager, who was to take Elliston's place as manager of Drury Lane in 1826 and who might arrange "an opening" for Payne that "if well managed, will ensure your future ease and support." Payne reached an agreement with Price that would pay him £150 a year for fifteen pieces; if any piece became a great hit, Price would give Payne some additional sum (Irving, *Journals and Notebooks*, III, 505, 507–8).

2. Payne's Paris apartment was at 89, rue Richelieu. On 3 October 1823 Irving had taken over this apartment. Payne moved back into the apartment on 13 August 1825 and shared it with Irving until the latter's departure from Paris on 20 September 1825 (Irving, *Journals and Notebooks*, III, 227, 509, 522). Three days after Payne moved in with Irving, he gave him Mary Shelley's letters to read (see [28 June 1825], n. 2).

3. *Don Quixote*, vol. 2, chaps. 22–23.

To John Howard Payne — Kentish Town. July 30. [1825]

Now that I have read Irvine's zealous & friendly letter, permit me, my dear Payne, to congratulate you on this new arrangement which appears to me to be very advantageous.[1] It is melancholy to think however that you are going to leave us apparently for a long time—The more so as not withstanding my earnest exertions I am now with less expectation than ever of leaving this country. It would give me the greatest pleasure if Jane & I could make out a visit to Paris, to break in on the monotony of the much-dreaded Northern winter—but I have not at this moment any hope of being able to arrange even this little wandering from my English Prison —Quel che sara—sara—Now during this divine weather I am so much happier than I have been for years that I will not by doleful prognostics dash my unaccustomed cheerfulness—If winter would never come I could, with the aid of my darling Janey's sunshiney countenance, not look at a lamp post with UnChristian Desires—

So again you will dwell in Rue Richlieu—dine at the Caffè François—walk in the Tuilleries—carefully looking away from the spot where the Diligence de Versailles puts up at—Now and then take a walk to Rue de la Paix & standing on the threshold of Hotel Nelson—be transfixed one day with the bright vision of the Swallows of Kentish Town—After all you will probably come over here now & then to drive bargains with the London Theatres; in the mean time pray write to me, & be assured that

I take a lively interest in your affairs, and that the news of your prosperity will be a sunbeam even in the midst of the sleet & ice of the coming winter Write to ⟨?Mr Godwin⟩ me all kind of gossip—for I own my failing—I delight in gossip concerning friends even as much as I am annoyed by it when it regards indifferent persons—Ever Yours—MWS.

[*On address sheet*] As your last act of office as Cavaliere Serviente W[d] you get me 2 Haymarket & 2 Lyceum Admissions for any day after Monday next week—

ADDRESS: John Howard Payne Esq / 29 Arundel Street / Strand. POSTMARK: 12. NOON. 12 / JY. 30 / 1825. PUBLISHED: Jones, #255. TEXT: MS., Huntington Library (HM 6820).

1. See [29 July 1825], n. 1.

TO JOHN HOWARD PAYNE   Kentish Town. September 27th [1825]

My dear Payne

I hear from William who heard from your Man Fridey i.e. Lambert that you are shortly expected in Town. And if this does not come too late, it comes to request you to do me a favour on your return. Louisa Holcroft has two or three portraits in keeping for me—One of L. [*Leigh*] Hunt—one of my little lost William—& one, if it still exist, of Lord Byron. If it will not inconvenience you to much, will you give my love to Louise and ask her to consign these to your care & will you bring them for me to London. I suppose there will be a duty to pay, at least on Hunt's—though I cannot tell as it is a chalk drawing[1] & not a painting. That of my child is damaged & they will therefore hardly require any on that—& that of L.B. is too small—but whatever is necessary I doubt not that you will do. Though if it should inconvenience you, do not scruple to decline the commission, quite sure that I shall not take ill your so doing.

Though I am most happy to hear of your return to my beloved country yet I trust this does not arrive from any disappointment in your views; probably you only come for a short period. You will find M[rs] Williams & myself in Statu quo & having no gentle Cavalier to escort us, we have staid like good housewives at our several homes—only once having been to the Haymarket and that on a moral principle—to see "Quite Corre{c}t"[2]—for how could we answer it to our consciences not to take such an advantageous opportunity of improvement—of course throughout the exhibition we were "Quite Correct"—So very correct were we—however that is nothing to the purpose—but I assure you the Moral lesson was not thrown away. By the bye I went also with M[rs] G. [*Godwin*] to ⟨see⟩ hear Tarrare[3]—a more dull composition never was tolerated—but it was considered good taste to admire the music—some of which was tolerable. I never was more shocked that [*than*] by Miss Paton's or rather Lady William's (for she is really married they say) appearance[4]—I never saw a woman so changed & the faces she makes when singing put one in mind of a cat trying to swallow a bone—her feet are the only prettinesses she has left, so I fixt my eyes on that while she feasted my ears—for her singing is good.

I have also been for 10 days to Windsor[5]—where I rambled to my old haunts. Windsor—Eton &c is the only spot of English ground for which I have an affection. We were delighted each morning too by hearing the King's band practise for an hour & a half—the finest band in the world perhaps consisting of 44 wind instruments, whose effect is so much finer than those scraping strings—In sacred pieces they rose to the majesty of an organ—in lighter airs their delicate execution seemed the work of fayry powers. The grand disappointment was that I could not obtai[n] a sight of my liege Lord his Sacred Majesty—It was too provoking—I prepared my best curls & smiles & curtsey & walked up Each day to the castle with my companion vainly—The servants in waiting began to know us & one old fat footman commiserated our fate mightily when we asked for the last time whether his Majesty was expected & told him that it was our last chance—"I am quite sorry, ladies—I am sure his Majesty would have been glad to see you—he is always glad to see & be seen by ladies."—What a flattering prospect—the while thus we fished the object of our angling was seated calmly in a boat fishing for <u>less</u> fish on Virginia Water.[6]

Enough nonsense, you will say, My dear Payne—I have pity on you & cease especially as my paper warns me to add only that I am Y^s faithfully

MaryWShelley

ADDRESS: A Monsieur / M. Howard Payne / No 89 Rue Richlieu / à Paris. POSTMARKS: (1) F25 / 40; (2) ANGLETERRE; (3) Septembre / 30 / 1825. PUBLISHED: Jones, #256. TEXT: MS., Huntington Library (HM 6824).

1. See 28 August 1819, n. 3.

2. *Quite Correct*, a comedy by Caroline Boaden, first produced at the Haymarket (Theatre Royal) on 30 July 1825 (Nicoll, *English Drama*, IV, 269), is the story of a man who stops his habitual slandering of friends and strangers after he unknowingly slanders his own wife and daughter (Genest, *English Stage*, IX, 315).

3. Salieri's *Tarare* (1787), first produced at the Lyceum on 15 September 1825 (Alfred Loewenberg, *Annals of Opera 1597–1940*, 2 vols. [Geneva: Societas Bibliographica, 1955], I, col. 444).

4. Mary Ann Paton (1802–64) had married Lord William Pitt Lennox on 7 May 1824. She divorced him in 1831 and in the same year married the tenor Joseph Wood.

5. Mary Shelley visited Windsor area—where the Shelleys had lived from August 1815 through April 1816 (see 27 July 1815, n. 3)—to gather details; she used Windsor area as the setting for *The Last Man*.

6. An artificial lake in Windsor Park, which covers about 160 acres.

*TO [JOHN BOWRING][1] Kentish Town. October 31. [1825]

A thousand thanks, my dear Sir, for your intelligence concerning my friend—News more interesting has appeared in the Chronicle today[2]—stating his arrival at Zante—apparently if not in a dangerous at least in a very suffering state—May I ask you what you know of this—and whether there is a probability of his coming to England—Rochefoucault's now trite Maxim[3] will occur to you when I own that my sorrow for his pain will be much diminished if I have a hope that it will be instrumental to the bringing him back to his English friends—I am anxious to know as soon as possible all that is known concerning him—as I wish to write to him without delay. I trust to your usual kindness to excuse my unceremonious call on your very valuable time—

I trust that you & your family are well—This divine summer has had a most beneficial effect on my spirits After an interval of two years I live again. God help me—I hope I shall never get back again to {   } chaos of melancholy in which I lived so long—

I am, my dear Sir
Yours faithfully & obliged
MaryShelley

ENDORSED: Kentish Town Oct / 31st / Mary Shelley / Recd [   ]. UNPUBLISHED. TEXT: MS., Pforzheimer Library.

1. This letter was quite likely written to John Bowring, who as Honorary Secretary to the Greek Committee would have had early news of Trelawny's expected return and would have communicated the news to her (see 28 July [1824]).

2. The *Morning Chronicle* of 31 October 1825, reported under the heading "Portsmouth, Oct. 29," the near-fatal attempt on Trelawny's life: "The Sparrowhawk conveyed to Zante the English Captain Trelawney, who took refuge with his brother-in-law Odysseus, from the revenge of the Greeks, in the fortified cave on the summit of Mount Parnassus. A treacherous attempt had been made by two fellows, employed by the Greeks, to assassinate him, for having betrayed their cause. He was shot in the back; one ball passed out in the front of his shoulder, by which he lost the use of his arm, and another passed through his neck and came out at his mouth." Trelawny had not become a traitor to the Greek cause, but Odysseus, whom he followed, had, and newspapers in Austria, France, and England linked the two together (see St. Clair, *Trelawny*, pp. 120–25).

3. "Nous avons tous assez de force pour supporter les maux d'autrui" ("We all have strength enough to bear the sufferings of others"), from *Réflexions ou sentences et maximes morales* (1665), by François, Duc de La Rochefoucauld (1613–80).

*To [?Charles Ollier] Kentish Town 7 November [1825]

My dear Sir

Will you tell me whether Mr Colburn has heard within this week from Mr Horace Smith on the subject of my Romance[1]—If he has not I will write myself to Mr Colburn on the subject without delay.—I have been hindered by one or two circumstances—among others by my little boy having the measles—but he is doing well—

With many thanks for your attentions I am, dear Sir,

Yours truly
MaryShelley

UNPUBLISHED. TEXT: MS., Pforzheimer Library.

1. *The Last Man.* On 22 August 1825 Horace Smith wrote to Henry Colburn: "I forgot to enquire in Burlington St about Mrs Shelley—I hope you have arranged something with her" (Rollins, "Letters of Horace Smith to His Publisher Colburn," p. 365).

*TO [?CHARLES OLLIER] Kentish Town 15 Nov. [1825]

My dear Sir

The title of my book is to be simply "The Last Man, a Romance, by the Author of Frankenstein."[1]—As soon as Mr Colburn has made the communication of which he speaks it will be ready—that is two volumes are quite ready the third will be prepared long before those are printed—Mr Colburn can therefore send it to the press immediately—

My little Percy is convalescent but not quite well

I am, dear Sir, Y^s^ truly

MaryShelley

UNPUBLISHED. TEXT: MS., Fales Library, New York University.

1. *The Last Man* was published by Henry Colburn in January 1826.

*TO CHARLES OLLIER Kentish Town Sunday [27 November 1825][1]

Dear Sir

Would you have the goodness to send me as speedily as you can the last Edition of Wordsworth's Poems—and the first Publication of Keats containing Sleep & Poetry[2]

I consider Percy as well now, though I am still careful of him—thank God it is so well over!

I am, My Dear Sir
Yours truly
MaryShelley

ADDRESS: Mr. Chas Ollier / 8 New Burlington Street. POSTMARKS: (1) [if]; (2) 12. NOON. 12 / NO. 28 / [ ]. UNPUBLISHED. TEXT: MS., Gordon N. Ray.

1. The only 28 November (the date of the postmark of this letter) that occurred on a Sunday during Mary Shelley's residency at Kentish Town was in 1824. Her reference to Percy's serious illness, however, places this letter in 1825, which suggests that she wrote the letter on 27 November and it was delivered the following day.

2. In *The Last Man* Mary Shelley slightly misquoted line 77 of Wordsworth's "Resolution and Independence" (vol. 2, chap. 8, p. 232) and lines 13–14 of his "The World is too Much with Us" (vol. 2, chap. 9, p. 316); she accurately quoted lines 250–51 of Keat's "Sleep and Poetry" (vol. 2, chap. 8, p. 241).

*To John Howard Payne Kentish Town. 29. Nov. [1825]

My dear Payne

I have been sitting pen in hand for some minutes thinking how to begin my letter—I have fifty things to say, but a beginning is often troublesome—so I will rush into medias res at once and say I am sorry to hear that you are not coming over, glad to hear that you may come over. William tells me that you appear in better spirits than you were here; it is cruel in me then to wish you in drear London, a place I never enter bon grè, and I should in a most Irish manner die in it if I lived there. The dear warm summer restored so much of my youth to me that I have {not} yet stumbled into decrepitude again—tho' I well might for I go no where & see no one. Percy has had the meazles and that confined me to the house for nearly a month—during which time I saw little even of my Janey—for not only it rained all the time, but she never having had the disorder was afraid of them for herself and babes. He is now quite well again & I am beginning to emerge on such days as watry Notus[1] will permit me. I am a good deal engaged to{o} in bringing out my Romance which is gone to the press at last. Would it be of any use to you to send you over an early copy. I do not suppose that my name is sufficiently attractive (mind I do not want a Compliment) to raise much curiosity—but if it were a translation or republication[2] might be a speculation to the speculative—such I am not, and it is therefore an hint quite at your service—only if I can serve you in it I shall be most happy to do so:—a circumstance I trust, my dear friend, you do not doubt. It is called "The Last Man." Colburn gives me £300 for it and is bringing it out as fast as possible.

I have not been to the theatre since I wrote—& cannot guess when I shall again—the impracticability of Cavalieri is an excessive annoyance—Jane & I cogitate dayly concerning how we are to manage the Opera this year—One must go there at least—As for the rest—Kean, the sun of the drama has set[3] and the stars are very cloudy—What think you of Wallack[4] in your Brutus? It is very true—he plays it tonight—I would not behold such sacriligious murder for worlds—the English deserve such drear change for having driven my favorite away—and truly people who prefer Wallack to Kean in Brutus, because his moral character is good—deserve to have him—& that is saying the worst.

I have seen nothing of Newton[5]—in fact my father has not called on him for a long time—some morning when the weather is more amiable I will call there with him—By the bye I did see him once—Breakfasting at Kenney's—he, Louisa, Moore, Tom & I adjourned to Newton's where I first saw W.I. [*Washington Irving*][6] Newton was pretending to paint his portrait but it was not like—Is it true that I. is writing more tales?—they say that he is & that they are worthy of the Sketch Book[7]—You must really come to an end of bantering me on that subject—because after all it is all a mistake—& {I} could tell you a fact or two that would astonish you thereon—but I will not.—My old friend Leigh Hunt has returned from Italy with his family[8]—I see a good deal of them and that is the sole change that has taken place in my narrow horizon—I go on as usual—as usual Janey & I meet in the evening & laugh at or with our friends—or talk sadly of times gone never to return.—

I was concerned to hear of poor Ellen Holcroft's death which I am afraid will afflict her Mother. I have written twice to Louise & she has not written to me—Mrs K. [*Kenney*] said that an answer to my first letter was written only she forgot to bring it with her. As I sent my second by a private hand it may never have arrived—or the neglect of both may have arisen of mere carelessness—& I am not a person to take a pique from that—but I should like to know if there is any deeper cause for Louise's silence—I have a great friendship for her—amounting to an affection—& would write again in spite of silence, were I sure that all was above board.—As to the greek—no wonder she would not have a fool—you see womanlike I defend her, not that I am not aware of her defects, but I have a respect even for the defects which occasion self sacrifice—& you seem to have the same feeling. With regard to my 3 pictures I certainly should like to have them—but if you think of coming over at any certain period I can wait until then—there will of course be a duty to pay.

I am glad to hear of the arrangement of your affairs at Paris. If attention to the A. [*American*] Manager's[9] concerns does not impede your writing for the London stage, it is all so much gain—and the pay can not have the impertinence to expect a very great deal. I like your docility in doing it because your friend told you, you ought—What a pleasure it is to shift the burthern of fate to other shoulders. To console oneself by thinking that if one does fall into a pit at least one has not dug it for oneself.

Our newest books here are Moore's life of Sheridan & Kelly's memoirs cooked by Theodore Hook.[10] I have read the former only & was pleased with parts of it though M. evidently shrinks in fear from coming too near the subject & being included in the list of Modern Scandal Mongers, to which honour however his Twopenny Post Bag gives him a fair claim. We have an alarming dearth of scandal just now. Poor dear LordByron—Kean, Miss Foote & Harriett[e Wilson][11] are forgotten but nothing supplies the place—such a calm bodes no good a [ ]ble storm must succeed. I own I had some hopes of supplying the hunger of Ar[ ] I told you I believe that I went to Windsor—my idea was that of course his most sacred Majesty would be en-netted—I should play a kind of high life Palmela[12] & a coronation was the smallest thing in prospect—Alas—men are as flies to the gods[13]—I did not even see his most sacred Majesty.—Do not you as an American & a republican sneer at such notions—such things have been—only all romance at ⟨age⟩ 64[14] w^d^ be wanting & as I cannot live without romance I am afraid that a crown would not have induced me to such a sad reality—

You see what nonsense I write—& I will never write again unless you assure me that no one eyes this trash—I should not write at all if I could not put down all the idle gabble uppermost—& unluckily you have been so indulgent towards me that I feel less remorse in writing nonsense to you than to any one else.

My father has just finished his 2nd Vol. & is well & in good spirits—Mrs Godwin is not the thing in health—or in spirits but I see no cure that I can administer to either. Miss Lamb has just recovered[15] & I shall soon go to see her—it is so long since I had that pleasure that I am quite impatient for it—

And now if you please—or to please me—throw this letter on your sparkling wood fire the moment that you have read that I am

Yours ever
MaryWShelley—

And my 2 P.S.s besides.

P.S. I like people whose hair begins to thin—in fact the rude state of manliness must be qualified by an interesting state of ill health or some like cause for me to feel any tenderness—then ⟨people⟩ at 20 & 30 if not invalids are too independent—at 40 or 45—they become divine

2nd P.S. You told Mrs W. [*Williams*] that when you wanted to forget any one you began by thinking of their faults—which of mine occupies your contemplation—I entreat you to tell me

ADDRESS: John Howard Payne Esq / No 89 Rue de Richelieu / à Paris. POSTMARKS: (1) F25 / [ ]; (2) Dècembre / 4 / 1825. UNPUBLISHED. TEXT: MS., Pforzheimer Library.

1. "South wind."

2. *The Last Man* was republished (in English) in Paris by Galignani in 1826.

3. Kean, given unruly receptions by British audiences because of scandal (see 22–27 February [1825], n. 8), in 1826 went to America, where he met with similar receptions. When, however, he returned to Drury Lane in 1827, he was enthusiastically received.

4. James William Wallack played the part of Frankenstein in the 28 July 1823 production of Mary Shelley's *Frankenstein* (see 9–11 September [1823], n. 6).

5. Gilbert Stuart Newton (see 6 January [1825], n. 4).

6. Biographers have speculated whether Mary Shelley first met Irving in Paris in 1823. Her statement here that she first saw Irving in 1824 (on 17 July) is confirmed by omission of any mention of an earlier meeting in Irving's diligently recorded *Journals*.

7. *The Sketch Book of Geoffrey Crayon, Gent.* (London: John Murray, 1820).

8. The Hunts returned on 14 October 1825 (see 27 June [1825], n. 1).

9. Stephen Price (see [29 July 1825], n. 1).

10. Thomas Moore, *Memoirs of the Life of the Right Honourable Richard Brinsley Sheridan* (London: Longman, 1825); Theodore Edward Hook, *Reminiscences of Michael Kelly* (London: Henry Colburn, 1826).

11. Harriette Wilson (1789–1846), a courtesan, gave details of her many love affairs in the *Memoirs of Harriette Wilson* (London: J. J. Stockdale, 1825). Prior to publication she offered those named the opportunity to buy themselves out of her *Memoirs*, an opportunity a number of notable figures supposedly took advantage of. Over thirty editions were issued the first year.

12. Samuel Richardson, *Pamela, or Virtue Rewarded* (London: C. Rivington, 1741).

13. *King Lear* 4. 1. 36.

14. George IV (1762–1830) had reached his sixty-third birthday on 12 August 1825.

15. Mary Lamb's attack began around the third week of September (Lucas, *Charles Lamb*, II, 155).

To Leigh Hunt

Kentish Town 28 Dec. 1825

My dear Hunt

You may remember that immediately on reading your Mss concerning our Shelley,[1] I wrote to you thanking you for it and pointing out a few mistakes or omissions to be rectified or made, and I sent it back to Mr Bowring with my approval. I could not therefore have spoken of it in the terms quoted as mine.—I afterwards found that Peacock had it & he mentioned to me a circumstance which I wondered had not struck me before—but which is vital. It regards Shelley & Harriet—where you found your reasoning on a mistake as to fact—they did not part by mutual consent—and Shelley's justification, to me obvious, rests on other grounds; so that you would be obliged to remodel a good part of your writing. Peacock was urgent that such a mistake should not pass, and on account of various arrangements with Sir T.S. [*Timothy Shelley*] was unwilling that it should be printed. I should have wrote concerning this to you, but your speedy arrival was announced—and I delayed mentioning it till I saw you.—I have not seen Mr Bowring or communicated with him on the subject since the note mentioned above. Peacock is in possession of the Mss.

I am, My dear Hunt
Yours affectionately
MaryShelley

PUBLISHED: Jones, #257. TEXT: MS., British Library (Ashley 5021, ff. 5–6).

1. See 8 April [1825].

*To John Howard Payne

Kentish Town.
Janry 28—(Feb. 7) 1826

Your letter, my dear Paine,[1] was a very kind and agreable one. I have defered answering till I could announce the departure of my Sibylline Leaves[2] for Paris—which I shall do I trust before I close this letter. Do not appologize, but permit me to thank you, for the length of your epistle—I have a friend whose chief object in writing to her correspondents is to be concise—& consequently she leaves out all one wishes to know—I am by no means of her school—as my 3 vols. will sadly testify, as well as my letters whose small caractery and well filled pages are provocative I trust of a like return. I think the best part of a letter often consists of what one says—after one has nothing more to say—when excuses—replications & intelligence is exhausted & you fairly chat as you would over the fireside.

I know not how to thank you sufficiently for you kind offer of ceding your abode to my darling Janey & me if we were to visit Paris—our abode there is at Hotêl Nelson, Rue de la Paix—so that if we were permitted to trip along the Parisian Causeways we should not be far from Rue Richelieu, though our consciences would force us to negative the idea of ejecting you from your kingdom & lawful dominion over the subject fair whose services you offer—You entice us with a strong allurement when you disclose to us an antidote to the horrors of crossing the Channel—yet cui bono[3] the prescription if we have not wherewith to concoct it?—Will you send Castor & Pollux or any other twin divinities (you see how moderate my demands are) to pilot us unharmed over our saline way?—seriously I regret to say that our hopes are slight of visiting your gay metropolis, this summer—the same obstacles which prevent our taking flight further south to our dear Italy will hinder this minor trip. I intend for Percy's sake to make out if possible a short visit to the sea—no agreable one certainly for I detest the melancholy roar of the destroyer—but for my little darling's health's sake.

I smiled—but the smile was somewhat a mournful one over your account of how you intend to treat your haggling huckster Manager[4]—there are persons with whom it never succeeds to do other than keep to the letter of the bond—whose inharmonious natures give forth discord when touched even by fairy fingers—whom if you permit to get an idea beyond the hard line of a legal instrument or an exact agreement—think that you can never do enough—Keep to your rights and they sympathize in the sordid feeling; but if you enter into the pale of liberality the ideas of their claims become gigantic to the extreme—but there are amiable persons like yourself who cannot encounter these machines—it is as the clashing of the china & brazen vase in the fable[5]—the more delicate the one & the more rough the other, the more is the injury of the former the more the safety of the latter is insured—Your American Manager, if you doubled your generous intentions & then twice doubled those would at the end declare that he had cause to complain—at least so I fear—but there is always an hope that patience and gentleness will mould all with which they communicate to some affinity to themselves—& a person ought never to put aside their good qualities because one of less fine clay does not possess them.

Your account of poor dear Louise is particularly interesting to me[6]—Kenney called on me the other day and brought me a letter from her which I was very glad to receive. Retired as I am and always have been from the crowd every emotion becomes a sentiment and I cannot put aside even minor affections as I see other people do—I am glad therefore to find that Louise has not forgotten me—though according to the present plan of the Kenneys it is very unlikely that we shall meet—for she will continue absent for the present and as I trust that my imprisonment in this island is not to last for ever I shall probably be on the way when she arrives.

I believe that I have been once to the theatre as a matter of duty (with some acquaintances of Mrs G. [*Godwin*]) since I wrote—It was very stupid and the Diavolo Antonio made me nervous—I have not been to the Opera yet—and am afraid that I shall hardly be able to make it out all this season in the absence of our kind escort—However as yet I have not been tempted—for they say it is very bad, & before Easter it is seldom very alluring—but now they have the ugly old and incompetent of voice in lieu of the charming Begnis and divine Pasta—When she appears I must endeavour to hear her. There has been a frost & there is now a thaw—both inconvenient—for the one freezes me into misery & the other is unkind to our feet—yet sometimes scattered here & there we enjoy those dear winter days—when the sun is like a friend—the wind balmy—the sky blue—& the fine tracery of the leafless trees lies in distinct fretwork against it—During such days in Italy Jane and I used to ramble through the lanes in search of violets and return home, to an home which was not then as now the mockery of that name, laden with our sweet spoil.

London in a few weeks may be alive and then I may be able to write a more amusing letter—At present I go no where—when spring comes I will call with my father at Newton's Studio—and exhibitions & Dioramas—and Mathews[7] at the Lyceum &c &c may give topic for various chat which now I have not—My sole amusements now are the evenings we pass with Hunt when Jane & he get up ⟨a songs⟩ our favourite airs together—& we conclude our evenings musical gaiety with a quadrille—not that Hunt dances by the bye—Mr & Mrs Godwin are now far more settled and comfortable than when you saw them—& my father is printing the 2nd vol of his Commonwealth—In spring I know not why one fancies change must necessarily ensue—& one looks forward to it with a feeling of hope—Of themselves the breezes & fresh life is exhilirating—every one looks more cheerful & smiling—they congregate like swallows—it is {a} matter of wonder sometimes that our aristocrats leave their delightful country residences just at the time when they are most delightful to loose the bright May days in town pleasures—but I do not think that they could find spirits for that kind of thing except at that invigorating season—You manage things other[w]ise at Paris—but I do not think I should like Paris s[o] well as London or exchange my pretty suburb for the neighbourhood of the Tuileries

(Feb. 7) I now hear that William has got my book from Colburn[8]—& I hope to learn today that he has sent it to you. The curiosity ex{c}ited by the title frightens me, because of the disappointment that must of course follow. You can form no idea of the difficulty of the subject—the necessity of making the scene ⟨general⟩ universal to all mankind and of combining this with a particular interest which must constitute the novel—If I had at the commencement fore seen the excessive trouble & then (much worse) the state of imperfection in which partly for want of time I was obliged to leave it—I should never have had the courage to begin. Here and there you will find some things to like, but your critical taste will be hurt by it as an whole. When you have read it, will you have the goodness to lend it to Louise, with my entreaty for her to deign to read it thus as a loan, since I am not able to send her one—As I shall write to her to explain.

Mrs Williams desires to be kindly remembered to you— She is now in far better health than when you were here—this is very pleasing—for it was horrible to see her gentleness in a state of suffering—We both nourish an hope of future delight in the possible visit of our eccentric & very dear friend Trelawny—He was obliged to escape from Greece to get medical attendance to his wounds—as two men—(An English man & a Scotchman) had attempted {to} assassinate him to get possession of his Cave of Parnassus & its treasures—His presence will be a gleam of Italian sunshine to our cloudy sky—A most strange fate at the same time that it destroyed the root of my happiness—scattered every leaf—every flower to which it had given birth—a return of any one of these gives me more delight than any other event however prosperous, yet unconnected with my former state of being could produce.

When do you think to revisit England?—and are you at all come to a decision concerning your return to America?—My own feelings (being European) makes me think that having once realized your prospects there, you would hasten back here—thinking (as I do with regard to human beings,) that a middle aged country—more fertile in memories, associations, & human relics than in natural productions is to be preferred to the savage untutored & selfwilled though beauteous vigor of a land just springing from infancy to youth—Therefore if you go I shall by no means despair of your return—

Adieu my dear Paine—believe me ever Ys—MWS.—

ADDRESS: John Howard Paine Esq. / No 89 Rue Richelieu / à Paris. POSTMARKS: (1) PAID / 9 FE 9 / 1826; (2) F26 / 98; (3) ANGLETERRE; (4) Fevrier / 12 / 1826. UNPUBLISHED. TEXT: MS., Pforzheimer Library.

1. Irving also occasionally used this spelling.

2. *The Last Man.*

3. "For whose good?"

4. Payne had sent eight plays to Price as part of their agreement, but Price was dissatisfied with Payne's work. On 27 December 1825 Payne sent four more plays: *The Wooden Leg*, *Rovido*, the *Neapolitan*, and *The Post Chaise.* In his letter of 27 December 1825 to Price, Payne also alluded to the plays already sent: *Mazeppa, The Man of the Black Forest, The Father's Curse, Lovers & Friends, The Inn of the Mountains, Twas I, Peter Sminck*, and *The Doctor of Altona.* On 4 January Payne wrote of Price to Irving: "He endeavoured to crush me when I was a child. I made my way in spite of him. He wishes to injure me now that I am a man. I will make my way in spite of him" (Payne, *Letterbook*, June 1825–February 1826).

5. Aesop's fable of "The Two Pots," which William Godwin, writing under the pseudonym Edward Baldwin, had included as "The Two Jars" in *Fables, Ancient and Modern, Adapted for the use of Children*, 2 vols. (London, 1805).

6. From this point to the end of the paragraph Mary Shelley's words are written above seven meticulously crossed out lines.

7. Charles Mathews (1776–1835), actor and mimic and a friend of the Lambs and Coleridge. In 1824 Mathews elicited bad feelings in the United States by his

imitations of Americans in his *Trip to America*, a one-man show consisting of songs, recitations, imitations, and ventriloquy. In 1826 and 1827 he again gave one-man presentations (see 21 April 1826, n. 4).

8. Godwin, Journal, records that *The Last Man* was published on 23 January 1826.

To John Bowring — Kentish Town 25. Feb. [1826]

Your note, my dear Friend, is on many accounts gratifying to me—But you must not wonder at my fear of intruding—for I know your time to be so valuable—& being myself a broken branch from the tree of life—a solitary creature—I am tainted by that morbid feeling which I dislike, while I at times yield to it of feeling myself neglected & forgotten—Pardon this last apology—I will never make another to you—trusting to the kind sentiments you express, I be vain enough to believe that you really have a pleasure in now and then hearing from me & being asked to do such kind offices as I have before now solicited from you.

Do not think me capricious if I defer my negociation with Dr Schinas[1]—it is not I but another female, Fortune, who is guilty of caprice on this occasion—I must wait a little before I can take the lessons I desire.

Do not be afraid of losing the impression you have concerning my lost Shelley by conversing with any one who knew him about him—The Mysterious feeling you experience was participated by all his friends, even by me, who was ever with him—or why say <u>even</u>;—I felt it more than any other, because by sharing his fortunes, I was more aware than any other of his wondrous excellencies & the strange fate which attended him on all occasions—Romance is tame in comparison with all that we experienced together & the last fatal scene was accompanied by circumstances so strange so inexplicable so full of terrific interest (words are weak when one speaks of events so near the heart) that you would deem me very superstitious if I were only to narrate simple & incontestible facts to you.—I do not in any degree believe that his being was regulated by the same laws that govern the existence of us common mortals—Nor did any one think so who ever knew him. I have endeavoured, but how inadequately to give some idea of him in my last published book[2]—the sketch has pleased some of those who best loved him—I might have made more of it but there are feelings which one recoils from unveiling to the public eye—I have the greatest pleasure in sending you the writing for which you ask.—

I hope you have not been a sufferer by this commercial turmoil[3]—I am very sorry to hear of the illness of your children—My little boy had the measles in the Autumn but is now quite well—

Did I not mention to you that I had a portrait of Shelley[4]—it would encrease your feeling with regard to him—Some fine spring Morning you will perhaps come and see it when I shall again have the pleasure of seeing you—

I am, My dear Sir,
Most truly Yours
MaryShelley

By the bye I have some prose Mss. of Shelley's which I think will interest you—Shall I send them to you?—I have also some letters—but these would be to be read by you only—

The longer poem I send was never published—It was called "The Mask of Anarchy"[5]—and written in the first strong feelings excited by the cutting down of the people at Manchester in 1819—

ENDORSED: Feby 25 1826 / Mrs Shelley / nd 26. PUBLISHED: Jones, #260. TEXT: MS., British Library (Ashley 1537, ff. 2–5).

1. Tentatively identified by Leslie A. Marchand as Dr. Demetrius G. Schinas, a Greek physician and scholar whom Byron knew in Venice in 1816 (Byron, *Letters and Journals*, V, 152, 182). Mary Shelley probably intended to continue her Greek studies with Dr. Schinas.

2. Adrian, one of the central figures in *The Last Man*, was based on Shelley. On 22 March Hogg wrote to Mary Shelley: "I read your *Last Man* with an intense interest and not without tears. . . . the character of Adrian is most happy and most just" (Marshall, *Mary Shelley*, II, 149). Although Mary Shelley's name was not on the title page of *The Last Man*, her name was cited in reviews of the novel. Sir Timothy Shelley stopped her allowance and reinstated it only after negotiations between Peacock and Whitton (Peacock, *Works*, VIII, 238; Marshall, *Mary Shelley*, II, 149–50).

3. During November and December 1825 six London banks stopped payments. A number of publishing firms in London and Edinburgh were bankrupted, including Constable & Co. and James Ballantyne & Co. (causing the financial ruin of Sir Walter Scott, a secret partner in the firm). Credit became uncertain, and the world of publishing was greatly straitened (Royal A. Gettmann, *A Victorian Publisher*, [Cambridge: Cambridge University Press, 1960], pp. 9–10).

4. Mary Shelley recorded in her journal that Shelley's portrait arrived on 7 September 1826. However, this letter indicates that she already had the portrait at the beginning of 1826. She indicated to W. Galignani on 8 January 1829 that she possessed only one portrait of Shelley, which precludes the possibility that she received a second portrait. Furthermore, Amelia Curran makes clear on 2 January 1825 that she had in fact sent her portrait of Shelley, giving Mary Shelley the address to which it was shipped. It is most unlikely that it took a year and a half for the portrait to arrive, which leads to the almost certain conclusion that Mary Shelley received the portrait on 7 September 1825 but misdated her Journal entry (see 26 July 1822).

5. Mary Shelley presented the manuscript of *The Mask of Anarchy*, now on deposit at the British Library, to John Bowring.

To John Bowring — [Kentish Town] 4 April [1826]

My dear Sir

I hope the tomorrow on which you are to call on me, which your journey to Devonshire put off, will soon arrive.

I want you to recommend to me & even to lend me some Spanish books —My stock consists of Calderon[1]—Don Qu{i}xote—Gil Blas[2] & a few other plays—I like old Romances—if you have the Conquista de Granada[3] I should like it—I hope to hear from you soon—

Yours ever & obliged
MaryShelley

ADDRESS: John Bowring Esq / 5 Jeffrey's Square / City. POSTMARKS: (1) 7. NIGHT. 7 / AP. 4 / 1826; (2) SO Kentish Tn. ENDORSED: Apr 4. 1826 / Mrs Shelley / 5. UNPUBLISHED. TEXT: MS., Fales Library, New York University.

1. Pedro Calderón de la Barca (1600–81), Spanish dramatist whose works Shelley had read in September 1819 and November 1820 (see *MWS Journal*).

2. *The Adventures of Gil Blas of Santillane,* by Alain René Le Sage (1668–1747).

3. Possibly *Guerra de Granada,* by Diego Hurtado de Mendoza (1503–75).

TO JOHN HOWARD PAYNE — Kentish Town 21 April—1826

My dear Payne

Are you alive? I hope you are, or my letter may fall into the hands of your executors, which I should be sorry for—however as to be prepared for the worst is the attribute of prudence, I, as a person of prudence (which you know I am) will write only concerning news, the Duke of Devonshire's mission to Muscovia—and the repairs of Our Ambassador's Hotêl at Paris —such are the topics here—while Greece falls and the defenders of Missalonghi are murdered.[1] I take more than common interest in the affairs of Greece because I have known & even had an affection for Greeks, and the apathy with which their rebellion is regarded would surprize me, did I not know that all human beings & the English in particular require flappers, and pretty smart & oft repeated flaps to awaken them to attention.[2]

I am not going to write a long letter; as I consider my writing at all, considering your long silence, rather an hazardous proceeding—, and half suppose that you will looking at the signature exclaim "I once knew her— but really it is so long ago"—I have not been in either in good health or good spirits lately—nor can I tell why, except that being early inocculated with a love of wandering and adventure, my monotonous present existence grows insupportably tedious There is no hope nor any help, which ought to make me contented they say; yet I cannot be so;—I am told I might be worse off—that reflection redoubles my melancholy—I have been happy— I might have continued as I was, had I not been destined to experience every reverse of unkind fortune. These thoughts will not leave me—I detest England; I am weary of all my occupations—I had almost said of all my friends—one only except—she is my saving Angel.

You will laugh at our plan for this summer, which is no other than to spend a couple of months at Calais.[3] It is necessary for the children's health to change air & go to the sea—nor am I without hopes I may gain benefit from the same circumstances. After canvassing the merits of several English

Sea ports—Jane started the idea of Calais—The place is ugly enough, perhaps dull—but I have a partiality for the people of Calais—then there is ⟨a life in⟩ an ex{c}itement in the entire change of scene, language &c—In fact it is a thing decided upon. We chuse Calais in preference to Boulogne, principally because so many of our country people prefer Boulogne to Calais—and secondly—because at Calais there is no cliff and we both hate a white chalk cliff. We intend to migrate the first week in July.

Pasta is at last come; I hope to see her at least once; though they intend to be very chary of orders. La Begnis is not here this season; nor have I been tempted yet within the walls of the Opera House. The other evening we went to hear & were much entertained by Mathews—I had never heard him before—He has one great moral lesson which I wish some of my friends would learn—The eight little Dilberrys, whose 8 little knives and forks exite the sympathizing glances of those convened to eat of the family dinner; the entrance of the same—their qua[rre]l, & their bows, & last the catastrophe of Phubsy (the dog) having run off with one of their <u>coarse</u> meat balls, was very entertaining and will prove I trust, instructive.[4]

I called with my father on Newton to see his picture before it went to the accadamy—and Kenny entreated me to meet him at his place, to which I consented—I went—but no Newton came—K. tells me he wants me to sit to him, but my aristocrasy will not permit me to have my picture detained in his gallery—and I am too poor to pay for it—so this commencement of an acquaintance does not look auspicious. In fact a thousand circumstance in my amphibious situation renders it very difficult for me to make acquaintance to any purpose with any one—I believe you know my notion concerning <u>acquaintances</u>—in society at large they are pleasant, because if you have not many of them you are at a loss continually for (to use a vulgarism) small change—but to one sequestered like myself from the busy crowd, they are annoyances—taking up one's time, and ending in vanity and vexation—But it is only through long time or some stra[nge] arrangement of circumstances that one can mould an acquaintance into a fr[iend]
I have a hope, which serves in a degree to cheer me of seeing a very dear one this summer—Our valued & excellent Trelawny talks of visiting England—there is one drawback, he has married, and one never knows how much a wife may spoil a husband for his ante (not anti) matrimonial friends. My paper is filled—yet this is not a long letter—I have not room to say at large how truly I shall be pleased to hear good news of yourself [*p. 1, top*] and your projects. Have you received my book—W. [*William*] assures me that he sent it per Diligence.—My father is well—Mrs G. [*Godwin*] returns today from Rochester where she went to visit her lately widowed sister.—Jane desires her amicable salutations—she speaks of you with great kindness—Will you answer this letter?—

I am truly yours MS.

[*Side of p. 4*] This letter is very stupid—but I have no hope that the delay of a post or two w^d^ mend it—because lately writing has been a great annoyance to me—and I can hardly force myself to write at all; so for the sake of the good will the attempt vouches for excuse the lame execution

ADDRESS: John Howard Payne Esq / 87 Rue Richelieu / à Paris. POSTMARKS: (1) So Kentish Tn / 2 py P. Paid; (2) 18. PAID. 26 / AP. 25 / 7. NIGHT. 7; (3) F26 / 73; (4) Avril / 28 / 1826. PUBLISHED: Jones, #261. TEXT: MS., Boston Public Library.

1. In April 1826 Missolonghi, long beseiged, fell to the Turks. Greek forces, sorely pressed by Turkish-Egyptian forces since June 1825, looked to Britain for aid. Canning was instrumental in arranging the Anglo-Russian protocol of 4 April 1826 (the basis for a treaty of 6 July 1827 between France, Britain, and Russia), which established Greece as an autonomous though tributary state under Turkish suzerainty.

2. Swift, *Gulliver's Travels*, bk. 3.

3. Mary Shelley, Jane Williams, and their children went instead to Brighton, from approximately 6 August through 3 September 1826.

4. Jones has noted (*MWS Letters*, I, 343, n. 2) the following description of *Charles Mathews' Entertainment for 1826* by Mrs. Mathews in her *Memoirs of Chas. Mathews, Comedian*, 3 vols. (London: Richard Bentley, 1838–39), III, 567–68: "On Thursday, Mathews is invited to dine with his friend, *Mr. Dilberry*, "in a family way.' He is accompanied by *Mr. John Rally*, an imperturbable quizzer. On their arrival, they have first to encounter a black female servant, with a baby *Dilberry*; and then enters *Mrs. Dilberry* in haste, with her *armorial bearings* (bracelets) in her hand. *Mr. Dilberry* they find in the dining-room, in the act of drawing a cork; and Mathews exhibits his contortions and strainings with great drollery. The guests are soon alarmed by the appearance of eight little knives and forks upon the table. The young *Dilberries* soon follow; and, after delighting their visitors during dinner by their elegant irregularities, one of them, after dinner, sings a song, and another plays a lesson on the pianoforte fifty times over. *Mr. Dilberry*, too, attempts a song to an Irish air. The great difficulty is to observe the key; and in the course of his vocal displays he jumbles all the keys together with a facility which it would puzzle a first-rate singer to equal."

*TO JOHN POOLE[1] [Kentish Town] Saturday [6 May 1826]

My dear Sir

Your prudence is wonderful—your foresight miraculous—excelling both is your complaisance for which I am your obliged debtor—It will be necessary for me to know the number of the box & the name in which the places are taken[2]

Pleasant January weather this—What a fatal mistake it is, that there should be an opinion current that England is an habitable country—This is the cause of all commercial distress—the English are a wonderful people—but it is melancholy to see them expend their energies on the cultivation of a swamp—Pray excuse this apostrophe my inspirer is the dear N.N.E. that freezes me at the present moment—Yours very truly

Mary Shelley

ADDRESS: John Poole Esq / 56 Firth St. / Soho. POSTMARKS: (1) SO [KentishT]n; (2) [7.] NIGHT. 7 / MY. 6 / 1826. UNPUBLISHED. TEXT: MS., Pforzheimer Library.

1. See 6 January [1825], n. 3. Godwin's Journal notes that on 1 April Godwin, Mary Shelley, and Poole were at James Kenney's; on 5 April Poole called on Godwin; on 8 April Godwin called on Poole; and on 13 April Mary Shelley and Poole were at the Godwins'.

2. Poole may have provided Mary Shelley with tickets for his comedy *Paul Pry*, which was given at the Haymarket Theatre from 8 through 12 May 1826 (Nicoll, *English Drama*, IV, 386).

TO THE EDITOR OF THE *Examiner*[1] London, 29th May 1826

Sir,—As the Opera season is now drawing near its close, it may appear rather out of date to enter upon the subject of VELLUTI,[2] which your readers will think has already had its share of notoriety. I am partly led however to this communication from the alteration in your own tone. When VELLUTI first appeared, you came forward in your accustomed character of champion of the oppressed; now that he is established you regard him with a less favourable eye: this change I think unjust.

When this gifted Italian first presented himself to our English audiences, I confess that I abstained from seeing him; he was supported by the principal leaders of taste at the Opera, but I feared that this was rather a mark of their liberality than an opinion expressed *ex cathedra* upon his merits. I wished to like him, and feared a disappointment; it was therefore after a long delay that I heard him, and my unbiased impression now is, that justice has not been done him, even by his friends.

It is an easy but an ungrateful task to allude to VELLUTI'S deficiencies, but his merits are more numerous and far more prominent. In person he is tall and slight; there are defects in his form, but these are more than counterbalanced, they are annulled, by the beauty of his attitudes, the noble ease of his walk, and the graceful action of his arms.* The defects of his voice are so glaring as to be evident to the coarsest ears, and are therefore the less to be insisted on by the judicious and delicate. To refer continually to VELLUTI's bad soprano, and his liability to be out of tune, is to imitate a person of my acquaintance, who, in going through the superb galleries of sculpture at the Vatican, was chiefly struck by the ugly faces and stiff ringlets of the busts of various Roman ladies. VELLUTI has notes in his voice rare and perfect; his upper tones are sweet, clear, and true; some of his lower ones claim the same praise. But his chief merit is in his expression, in his perfect gusto, in his mode of linking note to note in a manner that chains the ear and touches the heart.

These invaluable qualities are overlooked by his cavillers, yet they are unattainable by our English male vocalists. A favourite Comedian, who, secure in his acknowledged powers, ought to have disdained such an exertion of them, can no more succeed in giving, in his tuneless attempts, an idea of the graces of VELLUTI's singing, than he can, in the mask of a face which he puts on, pourtray his variable and amiable countenance.

There is a soft and deprecating expression in VELLUTI's eyes, and a patient sweetness in his smile, that ought to have disarmed both critics and mimics. But my intention is to confine myself to his true merits, omitting to descant on the sentiment attached to his person,—a sentiment that the generous and the gentle must instinctively feel, but which it would be labour in vain to attempt to instil into the coarse and the vulgar.

It is hard for an actor to be judged out of his own country. There is a national mannerism in acting on the stage as well as in the private department. Madame PASTA, in her supreme excellence, surmounts this difficulty; but the next step to perfection wants the "touch of nature" that "makes the whole world kin,"[3] and we come to local and arbitrary modes of expression. The comedy of DE BEGNIS, perfect in its kind, is not duly appreciated in London: in the same way, the grace which is peculiar, and the action, which is to a great degree national, may fail, with small fault on his part, of exacting the admiration of VELLUTI's critical enemies. I was pleased to observe that these were few. We have been told, that we must admire him as we should admire the wonderful daub of a man who painted without hands. This is unjust: VELLUTI may take a higher ground, and such, I will not say the liberal, but the judicious, ought to afford to him. Unsupported (with the exception of CURIONI)[4] by any of his fellow actors in a dull opera, with little beauty in the composition of his airs, he succeeded in making a strong impression in his favour. It is said that he feels great pleasure when, on the stage, he is aware of the sympathy and approbation of his audience. He must have been fully gratified the other night. In spite of prejudice, I heard commendations burst spontaneously from the lips of all around, and to descend from the many to the one, I went with kind feelings towards the man, but hopeless of deriving pleasure from the singer; I came away with every sentiment of personal interest realized and confirmed, with the addition of a deep sense of admiration for his singing and acting.

I am, Sir, your obedient servant,
ANGLO-ITALICUS

* I must observe, that VELLUTI's acting perpetually reminded me of his pupil, Madame PASTA. The school is the same. It is peculiarly remarkable in the similarity of their action, when, in the Cavatina in *Tancredi*, PASTA salutes her country, "Ti saluto e ti baccia;" and when, in the *Crocciato in Egitto*,[5] VELLUTI with passionate remorse exclaims, "Aprite o terra!" It is no ordinary praise for VELLUTI, that this accomplished actress should have derived much of her grace and histrionic powers from him.

PUBLISHED: *Examiner*, 11 June 1826. TEXT: *Examiner*.

1. In 1825 John Hunt retired from publishing and his son Henry Leigh Hunt entered into partnership with Charles Cowden Clarke (Altick, *The Cowden Clarkes*, p. 51).

2. Giovanni-Battista Velluti (1781–1861), castrato, whose voice began to fail when he appeared in London in 1825. He was on the whole successful, however, and

was engaged at £2,300 as singer and director of music at the King's Theatre for 1826. (He had received £600 as a singer in 1825.) The controversy that began in 1825 over his failing abilities came to a head in 1826 when his reputation was further assaulted because of his failure to keep his promise of additional salary to the choir for his benefit night, 22 June. This issue was decided against him in the Sheriff's Court. The season at the King's Theatre came to an abrupt end on 12 August (for more on Mary Shelley's defense of Velluti, see 23 June [1826]).

3. *Troilus and Cressida* 3. 3. 175.

4. Alberico Curioni (1785–1875), Italian tenor.

5. *Il Crociato in Egitto*, by Meyerbeer.

*To John Howard Payne — Kentish Town. 11 June 1826

Summer is come at last, my dear Payne, and with it a renewal of life to the exiles from the sun, Would not a Butterfly have a right to complain if in its Chrysalis it felt its wings bound and darkness & cold press hard upon its tender frame? If I am to live in this make believe of an habitable country let me at least doze away its ten months winter and awake young & fresh in June—What shall I do next winter the very idea strikes me with terror. To add to my discomforts during the preceding one, everything has gone wrong with me[1] and death & disease[2] has invaded my small circle to the destruction of its happiness—Well I have my Jane, my souls sunshine still let that suffice for my possession, and all the rest be paid as a tribute to fortune—

After much impatient expectation we have now been to the Opera—In you alone I confide the fatal secret—remember it is one, and be discreet that—Spirit of Chivalry it is true! we went to the pit of the Opera alone together—After all this is a thing to be done without discomfort so that one keeps one's counsel and no person can prate about or[3] it. We spoke Italian all the time are [*and*] were not the least annoyed to be sure as we quitted the house, one or two parties turned enquiring glances on the ladies without shadows (I hope you have read Peter Schlemil)[4] and we heard. Why they have no shadows—how odd shadowless ladies, but our Italian changed the surprise into, ah! foreign ladies often have no shadows —We were comfortably situated as far as the respectability of nos alentours[5] went—behind us were some good folks from Austin Friars—Who said they were rich ambitious and fond of displays and talked of the chief dandy —oh most exploded word of the parties in Bishops gate street street—One old lady beside me with her glass tried to follow the English of the Italian in her book. I put her right as far as I could in dumb show. But when she obstinately turned over the pages of the 2nd act of the "Crociato" in search of the words of Nina I saw no hope of setting her right except by speaking and that was not in the bond—I could understand a little English but not speak a word. The personage before me offered me his book—Apparement, Madame vous êtes etrangère, voulez vous vous profitez de non livre?[6] in my character of Italian I accepted his civility, as an English person I could not—We saw one act of {"}The Crociato" I was agreeably disappointed in Velluti. I had expected pain but rec'd extreme pleasure, he is handsome graceful & with the exception of one or two peacock notes, his tones are sweet & clear, & his expression infinitely sweet—We also saw my divinity in Nina, she acted & sang better than ever—We saw La Brouciad in Venus,[7] & were disappointed—for she is highly extolled. We joined our carriage in waiting without difficulty—only as we passed, Jane said she saw the Spaniard of former celebrity, he saw not us—& you may be sure that while in the house we looked for none, but were quite correct to a miracle—Our second exhibition was to Pasta's benefit This was an impromptu. A friend sent us two admissions, at three-oclock of the eventful day we were at the house, at the opening of the door and got excellent places. Absorbing interest in the acting & singing of this wonderful woman,—took us out of the world and surrounding people. We saw, heard, thought of nothing but Medea[8]—Have you seen her at Paris yet? Have you heard her passionate tones, & beheld her thrilling countenance? Not given at all to demonstration in the way of sensibility, I was quite overcome, and in the scene with her children only by aid of salts and infinite struggle, could prevent myself from making a scene for the edification of all around. Her eyes—her smiles, her look of unutterable woe! Her harmonious shrieks.—No paradox this—wilder and more terrible than any unmelodized expression of despair, might well cause rocks to weep and beast of prey to pity—We were so overcome, that we could not stay to the ballet. Enough of the opera you will say—yet I have little else to say or think of agreable. Mrs Kenney is in London. I met her once at Gower Place, and was to have dined with her—but it has not yet been more fully arranged. Mrs Godwin has been seriously ill with an inflammatory attack. My father is quite well—in better health and spirits than I have ever seen him—The 2nd Vol. of his Commonwealth has come out—and Colburn has covenanted for two more volumes on the same terms as the preceding ones. So while his health lasts and he can write he is under no pecuniary difficulties. We have so few friends in common, that I can tell you little news—Marshall[9] is well, as also the Lambs—I saw them a week ago. They were as amiable and kind as ever. As to public news you at Paris know as much as a recluse at Kentish Town—Town is emptying for the elections Burdett & Hobhouse are reelected without opposition. The King has attended the Ascott races—Is not all this very interesting—? We still intend to cross to Calais.[10] I do not think that we shall remain entirely stationary there—But I am afraid we shall not make out Paris—which disappoints me as I had hoped so to do. Do you ask if I will speak to you if you come to see us? What a question! or what is—or what is in me that should make you think that I should repay your kindness with impertinence? or that I should not feel friendship for one whom I believe to be truly my friend? However you are a favorite of my Janey—which {"}makes assurance doubly sure"[11]—as to your second dilemma—Whether the pleasure of meeting will be outweighed by the pains of after separation you must consult yr. own philosophy on this point—if you think that I will then remain at Paris, do not see me until I am old and ugly & you will neither come to see me or leave me—It is perhaps wise so to do. Talking of meeting and separation this reminds me, that we expect in the autumn the delight of embracing our past and dear friend Trelawney. He has recovered from his wounds and will return to this country for a time—Though our meeting were to be but for five minutes I could not not see him for a Thousand worlds—He belongs to my past life to days of bliss—of Paradise before the fall—common place as I am become now only to see him will remind me vividly that once Shelley once Edward were my companions—and that I was not always the poor little, rooted rain-drenched plant of pensees[12] I am now. I have to ask you to do me a favor—I know that yr. time is much occupied so that—if from that or any other reason—you find the request de trop—refuse, I shall not take such a refusal ill—I assure you A friend of mine has a young gentleman under the following circumstance—He is a lad of 14—respectably connected—who is to have a situation in a Banking House at Paris—as soon as he is qualified for it—that is when he knows French accounts &c—For this it is necessary to send him to school in France. He is an orphan—& his protectors are by no means rich—They have made enquiries about a school, and have learnt the names of—Ancien Lycee Napoleon—now Louis le Grand—R—Autune and Lycee Rue des Capucines—Fauxbourg le Havre[13]—They wish to learn the terms of these and whether his heatlh—&c &c would be well taken care of—Perhaps without applying to either you may know of a fitting school. It must not be expensive—But as he has no friend in Paris, it were desirable to be particular as to the attention paid to health & cleanliness. If you are able to afford me the information desired let it be as speedily as convenient—adieu, my dear Payne. I hope this letter will find you well and prosperous

Believe me
Yr since{re} friend
Mary Shelley

We go to Velluti's benefit on the 18th. How goes on Frankenstein of Porte St Martini?[14]

UNPUBLISHED. TEXT: Copy, Payne, *Letterbook*, June 1825–February 1826.

1. In order to conform with Sir Timothy Shelley's demands, Mary Shelley signed *The Last Man* "By the Author of Frankenstein." Reviews, however, mentioned the Shelley name, much annoying Sir Timothy and causing him temporarily to withhold funds from Mary Shelley (see Peacock, *Works*, VIII, 238–39).

2. News of the attempt on Trelawny's life reached Mary Shelley on 31 October 1825; in November 1825 Percy Florence had a serious case of the measles; Mrs. Mason's health continued very poor; and Mrs. Godwin was quite ill. On 29 November 1825 Mary Shelley wrote Payne about the death of Ellen Holcroft; in January 1826 Peacock's second daughter, Margaret, died at the age of three; on 21 April 1826 Mary Shelley mentioned the death of Mrs. Godwin's brother-in-law.

3. At this point there is a one-inch blank space in Payne's transcript.

4. Adalbert Von Chamisso, *Peter Schlemilhls wundersame Geschichte* (Nuremberg: Schrag, 1814), is the story of a man who sold his shadow to the devil.

5. "Our surroundings."

6. "Apparently, Madame, you are a foreigner, would you like to make use of my book?"

7. Mlle Brocard performed in the ballet at the King's Theatre in 1826 and 1827; in 1826 she first appeared in *La Naissance de Venus* (Ebers, *The King's Theatre*, pp. 305, 393).

8. Johann Simon Mayr's *Medea.*

9. James Marshall, or Marshal, as Godwin always referred to him, was a contemporary of Godwin's and had been his friend since Godwin was seventeen. Mary Shelley described him as "a translator and index-maker, a literary jobber." It was Marshall who introduced Godwin to the Boinville circle (see 6 April 1819 to Leigh Hunt, n. 7), and Godwin who introduced Shelley (*SC*, I, 436–37; III, 254–55).

10. See 21 April 1826.

11. *Macbeth* 4. 1. 82.

12. I.e., pansies (see 26 July 1822, n. 4).

13. The Lycée Louis le Grand, still in existence, and the Lycée rue des Capucines Fauxbourg le Havre, now called Lycée Condorcet.

14. Jean de Palacio has supplied me with a review of the production of *Frankenstein* at the Theatre de la Porte Saint-Martin from *Le Globe: Journal Litteraire*, 17 June 1826. The review was generally unfavorable, particularly condemning Cooke, saying that his performance could have been equaled by an amateur. Praise was reserved for the set, particualrly for the reality of the sea and storm scenes.

To Charles Cowden Clarke — 23 June [1826] — Kentish Town

Dear C.C.C. Here is defence II of my poor dear Velluti[1]—Do not say that it is too enthusiastic—Wherefore should not the enthusiasm he excites be published as well as the criticisms against him?—He is a gentle graceful angelic being—too much the reverse of coarse natures to be relished by them—If he has not all the boasted energy of that vain creature <u>man</u> he has what is far better, a strength all his own, founded on the tenderness & sympathy he irrisistibly excites. You see how cautious & cold I am in my expressions <u>to be</u> <u>printed</u>, in comparison with the real warmth that is obliged to find unworthy exit in cut & dried phrases—

—I leave the last paragraph to your good judgement—The statements therein I know to be true—but if you think it as well not to attack the people of the Opera House cut it out Velluti himself is thoroughly & reasonably disgusted, & will not again engage himself at the theatre—The omission will shorten the letter which you may think as well—Pray, pray get it in & so deeply oblige

Yours ever & truly
MWS.

Perhaps instead of cutting out all the last paragraph the omission might commence from the words <u>He had wished to have the rehearsals</u> &c since that which goes before is defence & not attack—& the facts ought to be known Pero facciate voi—siete Padrone![2]

[*Enclosure*]

Velluti.
To the Editor of the Examiner

Sir

It can only be considered as a continuation and a summing up of the letter I had before the honour to address to you, if I now add to what I then said on the subject of Velluti, the conclusions drawn from an attendance at his benefit on Thursday night.

Madame de Staël has observed, that there are many things, and those among the most lovely and delightful in the world, which unless we admire with enthusiasm we do not admire at all: we must be, as it were, instinctively attracted and charmed, or the spell is wholly without avail, and there is no medium between fervent admiration and cold distaste. From the extreme contrariety of sentiments expressed concerning the subject of this letter, it would seem that he is thus circumstanced; so that it is merely justice that when his ⟨enemies⟩ censurers are so eager to come forward to express their disapprobation, that his admirers should be permitted to record their approval with that zeal which this accomplished singer has found means to inspire. Having however already expressed my opinion concerning him, an opinion, which founded on sentiments imbibed at the eye and ear, is not to be overthrown by a mere battery of words, it is needless to reiterate assertions, to be opposed by counter:assertions. Leaving therefore the general discussion to the arbitration of each individual who has heard him, I will confine my remarks to the representation of the night of the 22nd

The Opera then selected, Aureliano in Palmira, was, it seems, composed by Rossini expressly for Velluti, and brought out twelve years ago at the theatre of La Scala at Milan, and has never since been sung by him. It bears marks of its design and would be better understood in Italy, where the audience pay no attention except to particular airs, carrying on during the rest of the piece all the small talk of a private converzazione in their respective boxes, and do not labour like the audience of Thursday to attend to the heavy intermediate scenes with which the composition abounds. The house was well filled and Velluti on his appearance was greeted with an enthusiasm which did honour to the audience, and was acknowledged by him with that grace peculiar to him, and with that mixture of gentle timidity and mild consciousness of desert which always animates him. His most pleasing airs occur in the second act. I will freely allow that those who were not delighted with the soft expression and perfect taste displayed in his execution of the air "Soave immagine," can never be converts to his style. The compass of his voice was ⟨to⟩ be particularly to be remarked in it, and the immediate transitions from his clear upper notes to the mellow sweetness of his lower ones was effected with the greatest flexibility and command of voice. It was rapturously received and that as well as the lighter movement of "Sorgete miei cari," and the terzetto, "Vive saran nostr'anime" would have been encored, had not the house reluctantly yielded to manifest tokens of weakness of his part. He is labouring under a severe cough; the result we fear of our ungenial climate. But if he returns for the winter to restore his health in his native country, we trust that his friends here will secure his re:appearance in the spring, and that during next season our opera will not be deprived of its bright ornament. To avoid the usual and annoying ceremony of being called for after the piece, at the close of the finale, before the curtain fell, he came forward to make his acknowledgements to the audience. But that was not allowed to suffice and he was forced to appear again. This fervent desire to express approbation was not confined to a mere knot of partizans. It partly sprang from the general determination to protect and encourage a gifted stranger, who has been oppressed, and who yielded himself to their award: but it chiefly arose from the interest and admiration spread universally around; his critics were invisible, and the whole audience shewed themselves eager to confer upon him the honours of a well earned triumph.

Though I am afraid that I transgress my limits, yet I must add one word more. I would ask why so much carelessness has been shewn in the getting up of the piece; the more remarkable from its contrast with the perfection with which Medèa was first exhibited. Velluti is not to be blamed for this. He has been indefatigable in his exertions; as one token of them he delayed his night[3] a week, when the town was emptying, and each day must have been attended by a pecuniary loss. He also suspended his Academia for the sake of bestowing more time on its preparation; is this to be called over anxiety? If it were so, it must be attributed to the opposition which he has en{c}ountered, and is the reverse of all sordid feeling: He had wished to have the rehearsals carefully attended; but this desire excited the resentment of the gentlemen of the Orchestra; they considered it an encroachment on their freedom; war was declared, and if they came it was only to disappear again, and to leave the most important spartiti to shift for themselves. I believe that of all little worlds, the little world of the Italian Opera House is without exception the most perfect specimen of the evils of anarchy.

I am, Sir,

Your Obedient Servant,
Anglo:Italicus

Londone 23. June. 1826.

ADDRESS: C. C. Clarke Esq. ENDORSED: The initials signify / Mary Wollstonecraft Shelley. / and are in her own handwriting, as is the / whole letter. / Charles Cowden Clarke. PUBLISHED: Jones, #262, and II, 354–56. TEXT: MS., Luther A. Brewer Collection, University of Iowa.

1. See 29 May 1826 for Mary Shelley's first defense; this second defense was not published.

2. "But do as you wish—you are the Boss!"

3. The performance given for his benefit.

*To Charlotte Figge   Kentish Town Saturday—1 July [1826][1]

My dear Charlotte

Long ago you said you would go to the Opera with me—& that your sister in-law, Mrs Figge would also do me the favour to accompany us. I have got 4 orders for tonight—Janey does not go—so if you will with amiable & graceful compliments ask Colonel & Mrs Figge[2] & yourself to accompany me, it will just fill up the number & be very agreable—

If you say yes expect me to dinner at five—I hope you are not engaged— The opera is Aureliano I believe—and I delight in Velluti—so I think will you

Yours—my dear Charlotte

Very truly & ever
MaryShelley

Address: Miss Figge / 5 Church Street / Paddington. Unpublished. Text: MS., Princeton University Library.

1. The only year that Mary Shelley resided at Kentish Town in which 1 July fell on a Saturday was 1826. *Aureliano in Palmira*, by Rossini, to which Mary Shelley refers in this letter, was first produced in London on 22 June 1826 (Loewenberg, *Annals of Opera*, I, col. 636; see also 23 June [1826]).

2. *British Army Lists* for 1830 records a Lieutenant Colonel Edward Figg, Royal Engineers.

To John Howard Payne   [Kentish Town] Friday [28 July 1826][1]

Welcome to England to, my dear Friend—I am in society & can only say these words I will write you by post immediately

Ys Ever truly
MaryShelley

Address: JH Payne Esq. Published: Jones, #263. Text: MS., Boston Public Library.

1. The date of this letter is established by Mary Shelley's letter of 29 July [1826].

To John Howard Payne   Kentish Town 29 July [1826]

When your messenger came I could not write having people with me . . . thank you for the books . . . I intended to ask you to give me the vol. of L[ord] B[yron]'s works, see how our intentions coincide as I perceive that the copy of my foolish book destined for you vous a manque [?]. You must allow me to replace the deficiency by exchanging your Paris Edition for my copy . . . I shall be glad, very glad to see you . . .

[P.S.] I am, they say, grown thinner. I am a year older than when you saw me last. Years until 50 improve a man, after a Miss is out of her teens, they only injure a woman.

Published: Jones, #264. Text: *MWS Letters*, from *Carnagie Book Shop Catalogue*, no. 68 (September 1938), item 454.

*TO MRS. CLINT[1] Kentish Town 5 August [?4 August 1826][2]

My dear Mrs Clint

I believe Jane mentioned to you that we had received orders for the Opera tomorrow which she commissioned me to send you. I hope you will go & be gratified—You will see my pretty Velluti[3]—tho' I am not sure that you & Mr Clint will like him—as a hint I just insinuate that to like him, is a sure means of pleasing me—I leave Mr Clint to conjecture my meaning—only e{n}treating your pardon for my impertinence

If you were not both kind and good I would make a thousand apologies for not having called—in truth I am greatly disappointed at not having seen you again before quitting town—But when I return, I promise myself no infrequent intrusion into the parlour of Gower Street—

With kind Compts to Mr Clint

I am yours truly
MaryShelley

UNPUBLISHED. TEXT: MS., Pforzheimer Library.

1. The wife of the artist George Clint (1770–1854), who painted portraits of Edward and Jane Williams (see pp. 277 and 276), Mary Shelley (unlocated), and a posthumous portrait of Shelley (see White, *Shelley*, II, 519). Clint was famous for his miniatures of actors and actresses, who often visited his studio-home at 83 Gower Street.

2. Mary Shelley dated this letter 5 August, but her references to "orders for the Opera tomorrow" and Velluti suggest that it was written on Friday, 4 August [1826]. A date of 5 August would mean that the opera was scheduled for a Sunday, which was prohibited by British law. Velluti, however, did sing in Rossini's *Aureliano of Palmira* at the Kings Theatre on Saturday, 5 August 1826 (*Morning Chronicle*, 5 August 1826). Since Mary Shelley gave no year on this letter and Velluti sang in London in both 1825 and 1826, she might have written the letter on Friday, 5 August 1825, in reference to Velluti's performance in Meyerbeer's *Il Crociato in Egito* on Saturday, 6 August 1825 (*Morning Chronicle*, 6 August 1825). We know, however, from Mary Shelley's letters of 29 May and 11 June 1826 that she first heard Velluti in 1826. Furthermore, Mary Shelley indicates at the close of this letter that she is about to leave town for a while, and Godwin's Journal makes clear that she was in London throughout August 1825.

3. See 29 May 1826, n. 2.

*TO RUDOLPH ACKERMANN[1] Kentish Town. Saturday Morning.
[5 August 1826]

Mrs Shelley presents her Compliments to Mr Ackerman and as she is leaving town, she will be obliged to him to address his communication to her next week, to the care of Mr Godwin 44·Gower Place·Gower St. She is glad that her story ⟨has⟩ will be inserted in the Forget me Not[2]

ADDRESS: ——— Ackermann Esq / Repository / Strand. POSTMARKS: (1) T.P. / Gt Russel St C.G; (2) [4.] EVEN. 4 / [ ] AU / [ ]; (3) [ ] / 1826.
UNPUBLISHED. TEXT: MS., Pforzheimer Library.

1. Rudolph Ackermann (1764–1834), publisher and bookseller. Ackermann

introduced the illustrated annual, a compilation of literature and art, to English publishing. His *Forget-Me-Not*, under the editorship of Frederic Shoberl (1775–1853), was first brought out in November 1822 and was continued until 1847.

2. Possibly "Lacy de Vere," anonymously published in the 1827 *Forget-Me-Not* (pp. 275–94). Alice G. Fredman has pointed out to me that this story shares with Mary Shelley's other tales for the annuals the themes of sibling devotion and unmotivated, fatal hatred. Furthermore, she was interested in the last-of-the-line figure (as in *The Last Man*), and this story tells of the end of the de Vere family through the deaths of Blanche and Lacy de Vere. The story also includes a cave, used as a haven by the de Veres against their enemies, which may have been drawn from Trelawny and Odysseus's cave in Greece (see 8 April [1825]).

To Leigh Hunt — Brighton. 12 August. 1826

My dearest Hunt

I write to you from an hill almost as high as Albaro—but oh how different! Figure to yourself the edge of a naked promontory, composed of a chalk soil without a tree or shrub—but before I describe further, I pause —supposing that you may have visited this bald & glaring spot—or if not, I am, if my very obtuse muse will permit me—about to write an article on my experiences here[1]—which had I the graceful art some have of tricking out the same, would be amusing—it will comprise an account of an excursion we have made to Castle Goring[2]—thro' a truly English Country—I mean in the best sense of the word—shady lanes—flowery hedges—wooded uplands—rich farms—& rose-bedecked Cottages—one village in particular so took our fancy that we mean at the expiration of another week, to leave the barreness & expence of Brighton & to immure ourselves in a pretty little rural lodging in that same place. I will, if you see no objection, send my article to you, & you will contrive to get it inserted for me—in fact my scant purse makes me seriously intend to indite an article or two—if I can be sure that they will be inserted—but it is dispiriting & annoying to write on purpose not to be printed as our friend H. [*Hogg*] says. I have an idea of another article. I have been reading a book "The English in Italy" (pray tell me if you can, who it is by) very clever amusing & true—Lady Charlotte Bury has also written one on the same topic, & Lady Oxford too—I think of writing a criticism on these with a few anecdotes of my own as sauce piquante—Do you think it will do for the N.M. [*New Monthly*]?[3]—

I have seen no one here, for I have not yet called on the Smiths—I shall however before we retreat to Suniton[4]—Mrs Cleveland (Jane's Mother) leaves us tomorrow & we expect to {   } very tranquil—A little amusement to our taste would be very acceptable—but since we cannot get that, we forge merriment out of dulness itself—You know my Janey's cheerful—gay & contented ⟨mood⟩ temper—I cannot be sorrowful while with her—& though with many thoughts to annoy me—I lose while with her the drear melancholy that for months has devoured me, & am as gay as herself—I cannot express to you the extreme gratitude I feel towards this darling girl, for the power she has over me of influencing me to happiness—Often when I have spent solitary hours in fruitless & unwise tears, one glance at her clear brow & glad smile has dismissed the devils & restored me to pleasurable feeling—She is in truth my all—my sole delight—the dear azure sky from which I—a sea of bitterness beneath—catch alien hues & shine reflecting her lovliness—This excessive feeling towards her has grown slowly, but is now a part of myself—and I live to all good & pleasure only thro' her—

How is Marianne? I fear that all has not gone as well with her as it ought; & I am anxious to hear the result of her indisposition—How are the Gliddons—dear & good creatures—how very hard that they who knew so well how to appreciate their happiness & to turn good fortune to good account should be snatched from some of their chief pleasures. Yet while they still enjoy that best gift of heaven—the true Gliddonic cheerfulness & good humour, they cannot be so much to be pitied, as many better visited by fate—Nor in considering this peculiar & family attribute a special gift of the deity—would I detract from the merit of each & all of them in cultivating this donation—it is so easy to repine—so easy to accuse heaven earth & the laws of nature—so easy to waste in endless tears & dark grief—but to smile at ill luck & bear with unaltered brow hateful employments & care for tomorrow—hic labor hoc opus est[5] (there is a piece of blueism for you—true blue with a false concord I fear—for I cannot remember the gender of labor) God bless them all & help their undertakings—I trust Anne will already have met with an artist who will appreciate her talent & put her in the right way—I am sure that she will succeed in that best & most amiable of all the arts.

I do not think that we shall exceed our time here—I trust that we shall find you on our next walk up the Hill as well as England has made you ever since your return—looking how unlike West's Florentine picture[6]—how unlike when I first saw you in the Vale of Health—better & younger than either—⟨with shirt collar turned back & that [ ] boy. [ ] of appearance⟩ I scratch out because Marianne will laugh & you will think that I am flattering you—which she will not—I cannot pretend to say what were the looks of the black muzzled personage were, who first cried havoc & let slip[7] the darts of little Cubid—but certainly he is ten years younger than he was ten years ago—ten—no nine—is it not—when first, having imaged a kind of fair ruddy light haired radical—I saw in the bust & flower adorned parlour those dark deep eyes looking from under those wise brows—Basta poi—What more—Adieu—the last word of all—Addio—& then à riverderti—dear Italian—how I delight in your [ ] paroletti—Carissimo Amico—Addio—pensi talvolta [ ] con tutta quella bontà solita tua—e l'affezzione dovuto a una che ti ama pur sempre[8]

God bless you, embrace your children for me & give an especial kiss to Mary's pretty eyelids—& the smiling mouth of my Vincenzo—Occhi Turchini Marianne—is more mine than yours—by your own confession—Do you understand Marianne?—God bless you too dear girl—Yours affly my kind friends

MaryShelley

There are in James St. here two neighbouring butchers one is called Venus & the other Myrtle—this is as bad as the consecration of the Jasmine—

I beg your pardon—I meant to have taken special care in writing to you that my ys weres not g's—but I write in haste & console myself with knowing that the worst will be a little laughing & quizzing which I do not dislike from friends & take no credit for my indifference—it may proceed from vanity—partly it proceeds from satisfaction that while you laugh nothing very bad is behind in the way of reprehension

ADDRESS: Leigh Hunt, Esq. / Cutbush's Cottage / Highgate. POSTMARKS: (1) Crawford St; (2) 2. A.NOON. 2 / 14. AU / 1826; (3) 4. EVEN. 4 / AU. 14 / 1826. PUBLISHED: Jones, #265. TEXT: MS., Huntington Library (HM 2755).

1. "A Visit to Brighton," *London Magazine* 16 (December 1826): 460–66, attributed by Charles E. Robinson. Mary Shelley's letter of 24 August 1826 to John Howard Payne seems to repeat part of the article's statements about Brighton.

2. Castle Goring was built by Sir Bysshe Shelley, Shelley's grandfather, but was never completed. It is said to have cost him £80,000. After the death of Sir Timothy Shelley, Percy Florence sold Castle Goring for £12,000 (White, *Shelley*, I, 10).

3. "The English in Italy," published anonymously in the *Westminster Review* (October 1826, pp. 325–41), reviewed three books: Lord Normanby's *The English in Italy*, 3 vols. (London, 1826); *Continental Adventures: A Novel*, 3 vols. (London, 1826); and Anna Brownell Jameson, *Diary of an Ennuyée* (London, 1826). The review is reprinted in *CC Journals*, pp. 441–57.

4. That is, Sumpton (see 24 August 1826).

5. "Hoc opus, hic labor est" (Virgil *Aeneid* 6. 129), meaning "This is really work."

6. In 1824 William Edward West (1788–1857) painted Hunt's portrait, which was for a time mistaken for a portrait of Shelley (see White, *Shelley*, II, 530–38).

7. *Julius Caesar* 3. 1. 273.

8. "Little words—Dear Friend—Goodbye—think sometimes [ ] with all of your customary goodness—and the affection due to one who will always love you."

*To John Howard Payne — Brighton 24 August. 1826

My dear Payne

I had thought to write to you before—but time flies—halt though it do the while—and I hardly know, to tell the truth, whether I have been here three days or three weeks—or even three years—Monotony of occupations confounds every idea of time—day succeeds to day—each sister {to} the other.—Read the papers about Brighton & you will hear that it is the gayest of places—a Royal Duke—A Secretary of state and shoals of fashionables are here—but the hermitesses know nothing of all this—the gates of the world are shut against them, and they live as limpets on a rock, belonging neither to sea or land—

For such as we are, solitary and quiet, Brighton is the worst place in the world—verdure and trees and running streams would be to us like a choice and dear society—but on this barren chalk promontory, it is necessary to forget the negation of all natural beauties in town pleasures—the white sea with it dazzling glare surrounds us on three sides—and the spot of rising ground on which we are perched boasts neither shrub or blade of grass—true from our windows we overlook the whole of the Brighton Park—the word is a burlesque—mauvaise plaisanterie pourtant[1]—as like a park is the little railed incircuit of treeless flowerless chalky downs on which these good people have bestowed the name, ⟨of Park⟩, to a real one, as is a skeleton to a birth night beauty—nay less so—from a well proportioned skeleton you might guess that beauty had there found rough materials whereon to raise it fairest temple—in this place we only perceive the impossibi{li}ty of veiling with in any verdurous veil the naked bones of the earth exhibited at Brighton.—

We have been fortunate in having fine weather—but unluckily M[rs] Williams has been indisposed ever since we have been here—I on the contrary have been better than I had been for a long long time—that is in spirits where my chief disease resides—Secure of seeing a beloved and smiling face during the day, I rise with cheerfulness and give care to the winds—when I return—when winter comes—I fear—most drearily I fear!

I hope you go on prosperously, and that when I return to town I shall find you thriving—I suppose we shall leave this place at the latter end of next week—as Jane's continued indisposition and the extreme ugliness of the place deprives us of any wish to prolong our stay—We had thought when we first came of running away from this barren hill top—and of embowering ourselves in the prettiest little village in the world—the village of Sumpton—whose latticed cottages—orchard grounds—rich farm yards and copse besprinkled hills quite charmed us during a little excursion we made—But this intention depended on one or two circumstances which have gone wrong—so here we remain.

I suppose there is no news in town—the world has grown very dull of late—the English world that is—which [ ] always as dim as its sky unless a storm give it relief—[ ] Ah Italy! did ever poor girl pine for an absent lover or lover for his far distant mistress, as I do for thee!

Adieu, my dear friend, we shall soon meet again—M[rs] Williams desires her kind remembrances

I am yours truly & obliged
MaryShelley

ADDRESS: John Howard Payne Esq / 29 Arundel St. / Strand / London. POSTMARKS: (1) BRIGHT[ON] / AU 25 / 1826; (2) A / 25 AU 25 / 1826. UNPUBLISHED. TEXT: MS., Harvard University Library.

1. "A silly joke however."

*TO JOHN HOWARD PAYNE Kentish Town Monday Morng
[4 September 1826]

I am returned from Brighton, my dear Payne, and shall be glad to see you when you can, as the poets say, wend this way—I hate coming back—I detest this place—I long for a further flight to which with God's blessing there shall be no such sudden return—I hope you have been well

I am yours very truly
MShelley

ADDRESS: John Howard Payne Esq / 27 Arundel St. / Strand. POSTMARKS: (1) T.P / Gt Russel St C.G; (2) 7. NIGHT. 7 / 4. SP / 1826. UNPUBLISHED. TEXT: MS., Wellesley College Library.

TO AN EDITOR[1] [Kentish Town c. October 1826]

It is no doubt very kind in M. Palma (who is, we believe, a Piedmontese Lawyer) to give us information respecting our own countrymen—but the authority on which he heard that T. [*Trelawny*] was maintained by LB. must have been anything but good—The assertion is altogether unfounded. Mr. T. is a gentleman of ancient family (son of the late Col. T.B. [*Trelawny Brereton*]) from whom he inherited property sufficient to preserve him from the temptation of being dependant on any one[2]—even if a remarkably generous & independant spirit wd not make this, under any circumstances the last accident that cd befall him—Parry—who is one of Count Palma's authorities, speaks of "half a dozen adventurers, such as Capt. T. and Mr. Humphreys." P. [*Parry*] must have given to this word "Adventurer" a meaning different from that which Co[u]nt P. [*Palma*], whose knowledge of the E. [*English*] language is not more accurate than his knowledge of E. characters, attributes to it—Adventurer is not always used by Englishmen as by Frenchmen—in the sense of a person without property or principle—seeking a livelihood by dishonest shifts—nor could it be applied to T.—to whomever else it may be applied—But what Parry means or says is of little consequence

PUBLISHED: Jones, #266. TEXT: MS., Bodleian Library (MS., Shelley, c. 1, f. 512).

1. Count Alerino Palma's book *Greece Vindicated* (London: James Ridgeway, 1826) contained critical remarks about others who wrote about Greece, including "Messrs. Bulwer, Emerson, Pecchio, Humphrey, Stanhope, Parry and Blaquiere." William Parry, Bryon's military associate, secretly assisted by Thomas Hodgskin (see William St. Clair, "Postscript to *The Last Days of Lord Byron*," *Keats-Shelley Journal* 19 [1970]: 4–7), had written *The Last Days of Lord Byron* (London: Knight & Lacey, 1825) to vindicate Byron. In the course of discussing Parry's book, Palma stated that Trelawny had been maintained by Byron. In a letter dated 25 August–2 September 1826, Trelawny wrote to Mary Shelley that Palma was "a lying rascal" and asked her to consult Hunt as to what action to take against Palma (Trelawny, *Letters*, pp. 104–6; Oscar José Santucho and Clement Tyson Goode, Jr., *George Gordon, Lord Byron: A Comprehensive Bibliography of Secondary Materials in*

English [Metuchen, N.J.: Scarecrow Press, 1977]). The remainder of this letter and any contemporary publication of it remain unlocated.

2. Charles Trelawny Brereton died in 1819, leaving Trelawny a life income of £300 per annum (St. Clair, *Trelawny*, p. 41).

*TO WILLIAM GODWIN, JR.

Kentish Town Saturday
[?14 October–November 1826][1]

My dear William—I send you the print of LB—the likeness grows on one—I fancy the very tones he used to utter when he wore that fastidious upturned expression of countenance[2]—If you can get a notice of it in other papers thro' your interest in Thwaites Mudford[3] &c—I should consider it a particular favour done to myself & feel truly obliged. Can you not?—pray try—

I wish you w[d] always with an enitial mark in my copy of the O.G. your articles—Which were Payne's last week?

Yours Ever
MaryShelley

This likeness striking at [*as*] it is was cut from memory—merely with scissars—without any drawing at all.

ADDRESS: W. Godwin Esq Jun / &c &c &c. UNPUBLISHED. TEXT: MS., Pforzheimer Library.

1. The date of this letter is based on Mary Shelley's reference to "the O.G.," which was *The Opera Glass for Peeping into the Microcosm of the Fine Arts, and more especially the Drama*, a weekly publication under the editorship of John Howard Payne; it first appeared on 2 October 1826 and ceased publication after twenty-four issues, in March 1827 (Overmyer, *America's First Hamlet*, pp. 267–68).

2. On 5 November 1826 a silhouette of Byron by Marianne Hunt was published in the *Examiner* with a description of the silhouette by Robert Hunt and a description of Byron by Leigh Hunt. Hunt's description mentions Byron's "face turned gently upwards" (Blunden, *"Examiner" Examined*, pp. 242–43).

3. William Mudford (1782–1848), author, journalist, and editor of the evening *Courier*.

TO ALARIC A. WATTS[1]

Kentish Town—30 Oct. [1826]

Sir

The absence of M[r] Lyndsay[2] from this country has occasioned considerable delay in his & my answer to your obliging letter. I now enclose you the packet, he has consigned to my care for you.

I have no small pieces either of my own or of M[r] Shelley's which I can offer you—and I am too much occupied at this moment to attempt the composition of any. The only MS.S. I could offer you—are a prose tale which would about fill 9 pages, I should guess of your work—and 2 short mythological dramas—on the subject of Proserpina & Midas—I would send these now, but I am convinced that your work must be too far advanced to allow the admission of pieces of their length. If you please you can have them that you may judge how far they will be admissible in your next years publication.

I beg to return my thanks for the elegant little volume you have had the politeness to send me. I had of course seen it before—the plates are extremely beautiful, and superior to anything of the kind that I have seen.

I am, Sir,

Your Obedient Servant
MaryShelley

Will you excuse me if I say that in consequence {of} my habit of withdrawing my name from public notice, I should be glad that my signature were not added to your interesting autographs.[3]

ADDRESS: Alaric Watts Esq / &c &c &c. PUBLISHED: Jones, #268. TEXT: MS., Pforzheimer Library.

1. Alaric A. Watts (1797–1864) was editor and proprietor of *The Literary Souvenir*, an annual.

2. Until this edition, David Lyndsay has been accepted as the actual name of the author of *Dramas of the Ancient World*, which in 1822 was read and admired by many, including the Shelleys (see 12 April 1822 to Medwin). Thirty-two letters, dated 1821 through 1829, to William Blackwood, publisher of Lyndsay's *Dramas* and a number of Lyndsay's short stories, reveal that David Lyndsay was a pseudonym and that the author was bound by a promise not to acknowledge his authorship but that sometime in the future his true identity would be made known to Blackwood (Lyndsay's letters to Blackwood are at the National Library of Scotland). The letters also reveal that Lyndsay had the best Scottish blood in his veins; he was several years younger than Byron (whose fame he aspired to equal); he was fluent in many languages; and he was well acquainted with Charles Lamb, "though as Lyndsay he does not know me." In his 16 January 1825 letter Lyndsay informed Blackwood that he was "well-acquainted with Mrs. Shelley." In another letter, c. November–December 1825, he wrote: "with Mrs. Shelley, who is indeed a fine Creature and a million times too good for the party to which she is so unlucky as to belong—I am intimate she is publishing now with Colburn, and from the infinite care with which she has written, I imagine she is anxious to controvert some opinions that have gone abroad as to her cherishing those adopted by her Husband—she had incurr'd an idea that you had been severe in your strictures upon Shelley's writings and character, and I was well pleas'd to be able to prove the contrary, by whole pages of Maga [*Blackwood's Edinburgh Magazine*], in which Shelley is declar'd to be, and treated like, a Scholar and a Gentleman—she was much gratified by your review of Valperga, but declar'd that in her delineation of Castruccio Bonaparte (whom she hates) never enter'd her mind—she has a very powerful mind, and with the most gentle feminine manner and appearance that you can possibly imagine."

These letters, which deal largely with placing his works in *Blackwood's Magazine* or with other publishers, mention the titles of many of his short stories, including his collection, *Tales of the Wild and Wonderful* (London: Hurst and Robinson, 1825).

In January 1822 Blackwood wrote Charles Ollier to learn of the reception of *Dramas* in London and to find out whether Ollier knew the identity of the author. He did not. Eliza Rennie, however, in *Traits of Character*, tells of meeting the author of the *Tales of the Wild and Wonderful*: ". . . certainly Nature, in any of its wildest vagaries, never fashioned anything more grotesque-looking than was this Miss Dods. She was a woman apparently between thirty and forty years of age; with a cropped curly head of short, thick hair, more resembling that of a man than of a woman. She wore no cap, and you almost fancied, on first looking at her, that some one of the masculine gender had indulged in the masquerade freak of feminine habiliments and that 'Miss Dods' was an alias for Mr.—. . . . My astonishment at her appearance was unbounded, and I had some difficulty to keep myself from betraying this, and to conceal the laughter I longed to indulge in; but the charm and fascination of her manner, the extrarordinary talent which her conversation, without pedantry or pretence, displayed, soon reconciled me to all the singularities of her appearance, and checked all inclination to mirth; and I quickly ceased to wonder at 'Doddy,' as she was familiarly termed by Mrs. Shelley and her intimate friends, being so especial a favourite. She was a great linguist, being thoroughly versed in almost every European language, and, taken altogether, a person of very remarkable mental endowments. She was a contributor, she said, to 'Blackwood's Magazine,' and announced herself as the author of a book called 'Tales of the Wild and Wonderful.'

The events of her own 'wild and wonderful' subsequent career I will not enter upon or touch. She resided many years at Paris where 'she died and was buried' " (I, 207–9).

I have examined the handwriting of the letters signed "David Lyndsay" and two Abinger Manuscript letters to Mary Shelley signed "D" and "MD Dods." The identity of the handwriting confirms that "David Lyndsay" was the pseudonym of Mary Shelley's friend M. D. Dods, or "Doddy." From the will of the fifteenth Earl of Morton I have further learned that the author's full name was Mary Diana Dods and that she and her sister Georgiana Dods Carter were the "reputed" daughters of the fifteenth Earl (Scottish Record Office, RD5 / 345, p. 416; for references to the will in these letters, see 28 July 1827, n. 7; 7 August 1827; 15 August 1827 to Jane Hogg).

Mary Diana Dods was a prolific writer and translator of stories, and at one point she tried her hand at a tragedy, which she expected to be presented by Charles Kemble (Lyndsay to Blackwood, 23 March 1823). Although the stories Mary Shelley forwarded to Alaric A. Watts on behalf of her friend were too late for inclusion in the *Literary Souvenir* (the preface of the 1827 edition notes Watts's regret that the articles received from "Mr. David Lindsay" and the author of Frankenstein were too late for inclusion), perhaps it was Mary Shelley who placed "Lyndsay's" "The Three Damsels: A Tale of Halloween" and "The Bridal Ornaments: A Legend of Thuringia" in Ackermann's *Forget-Me-Not* for 1827 (pp. 79–86, 393–416).

By the summer of 1827 Mary Diana Dods and Mary Shelley were assisting Isabel Robinson Douglas (see [19 February 1827], n. 1) to leave England (see 28 July through 31 August 1827). Isabel Robinson Douglas's situation and Mary Diana Dods's relationship to it will be fully treated in volume 2 of these letters.

3. Watts included in his Annual facsimiles of autographs of living authors.

TO HENRY COLBURN Kentish Town Monday [?30 October 1826][1]

Dear Sir

A friend of mine, Mr David Lyndsay,[2] who is now abroad, has written to me, requesting me to propose a work of his to you. You have of course heard of Mr Lyndsay as the Author of "Dramas of the Ancient World"—and latterly of "Tales of the Wild and Wond{er}ful{"} The former work in particular met with considerable success & was highly spoken of in all literary circles—It is indeed a production of genius. His present work is of the same cast— though on even a more poetical plan. The title of some of the Dramas will convey some idea of it "The Revolt of the Wilderness"—"The Festival of the Earth"—"The Wedding of Undine" &c &c The work is not yet complete, but M[r] Lyndsay informs me that it will be ready to send by the time he hears from me. If you should feel disposed to purchase this work he would be most happy to treat with you.

He begs me to add that he is already far advanced in a poetical translation of a German drama held in high estimation in Germany called Der Zauber Liebe—Magic Love. the name of the Author (I think but he has forgotten to mention it) is Alarn. It is of the length of Faust, but M[r] Lynds[ay] intends somewhat to abridge it. He describes it as a poem of the highest imaginative order.

I shall be very glad if you should deem ⟨it⟩ fitting to enter into a negotiation with my friend—

I am, Dear Sir,
Your Ob[t] Servant
Mary Shelley

ADDRESS: Henry Colburn Esq / New Burlington St. PUBLISHED: Jones, #269. TEXT: MS., Huntington Library (HM 20167).

1. Mary Shelley used the stationery on which this letter is written, watermarked "HAGAR & SON / 1826," from c. October 1826 through c. February 1827.

2. See 30 October [1826], to Alaric A. Watts n. 2.

TO LEIGH HUNT

5 Bartholomew Place—Kentish Town
30th October 1826

My dear Hunt

Is it—or is it not right that these few lines should be addressed to you now? Yet if the subject be one, that you may judge better to have been deferred—set my <u>undelay</u> down to the account of overzeal in wishing to relieve you from a part of the care, which I know is just now oppressing you:—too happy I shall be if you permit any act of mine to have that effect.

I told you long ago that our dear Shelley intended on rewriting his will to have left you a legacy; I think the sum mentioned was £2,000. I trust that hereafter you will not refuse to ⟨receive this⟩ consider me your debtor for this sum, merely because I shall be bound to pay it {to} you by the laws of honour, instead of a legal obligation. You would of course been better pleased to have received it immediately from dear Shelley's bequest—but as it is well known that he intended to make such an one it is in fact the same thing, and so I hope by you to be considered.[1] besides your kind heart will receive pleasure from the knowledge that you are bestowing on me the greatest pleasure I am capable of receiving.

This is no resolution of today; but formed from the moment I knew my situation to be such as it is. I did not mention it, because it seemed almost like an empty vaunt, to talk and resolve on things so far off. But futurity approaches[2]—and a feeling haunts me as if this futurity were not far distant. I have spoken vaguely to you on this subject before—but now, you having had a recent disappointment, I have thought it as well to inform you in express terms of the meaning I attached to my expressions. I have as yet made no will; but in the mean time, if I should chance to die, this present writing may serve as a legal document to prove that I give and bequeath to you the sum of two thousand pounds sterling. But I hope we shall both live—I to accomplish Dear Shelley's intentions; you, to honour me so far as to permit me to be their executor.

I have mentioned this subject to no one; and do not intend; an act is not aided by words—especially an act unfulfilled. Nor does this letter, methinks, require any answer—at least not till after the death of Sir Timothy Shelley[3] —when perhaps this explanation would have come with better grace—but I trust to your kindness to put my writing now to a good motive

I am, My dear Hunt
Yours affectionately & obliged
MaryWollstonecraftShelley

To Leigh Hunt Esq.

PUBLISHED: Jones, #267. TEXT: MS., Bodleian Library (MS., Shelley, Adds., c. 6, ff. 37–38); there is a copy in the Humanities Research Center, University of Texas at Austin.

1. The next nine words are inserted between "considered" and the following paragraph.

2. Charles Bysshe Shelley had died of tuberculosis at Field Place and was buried on 16 September, leaving Percy Florence Shelley as his father's heir.

3. By the time Sir Timothy Shelley died in 1844 Mary Shelley had accumulated large debts. She wrote to Hunt on 20 April 1844 referring to this letter written twenty years before and proposed to substitute for her original offer of £2,000 an annual annuity of £120 paid quarterly, to continue to be paid to Marianne Hunt should she survive Leigh Hunt.

TO HENRY COLBURN

Kentish Town Wednesday
[?October 1826–27][1]

M[rs] Shelley would be obliged to M[r] Colburn if he could send the books by the bearer, as she is at an actual stop for want of them

PUBLISHED: Jones, #270. TEXT: MS., Pierpont Morgan Library.

1. The date of this letter is uncertain. I place it here because I have no record of Mary Shelley being in direct contact with Henry Colburn prior to [?30 October 1826].

TO JOHN HOWARD PAYNE

Kentish Town 22. Nov. [1826]

My dear Payne

You have not been tempted by fogs or mist or rain or mud and all the dear English variety of fine weather to come to Kentish Town. I write now to say that M[r] Hogg on coming to town asked me your address, I gave it {to} him, the same as on this letter—but he was told that you were not there—tho' my friend Jefferson has little truly of the appearance of that which William was mistaken for. His address is 1 Garden Court—Temple —so if you wish to renew your Paris acquaintance[1] you can leave a card there.

You are now I suppose in all the agonies of rehearsal[2]—when crowned with triumph, you will I trust come to receive my congratulations

Yours ever truly
MaryShelley

Janey & I promise ourselves admission for the Dame Blanche—

ADDRESS: J. Howard Payne Esq / 29 Arundel St. / Strand. POSTMARKS: (1) S.O Kentish Tn; (2) [7. NIG]HT. 7 / [ ]23 / [ ]. PUBLISHED: Jones, #271. TEXT: MS., Berg Collection, New York Public Library.

1. According to his account of his continental tour, Hogg visited Paris in February 1826 (*Two Hundred and Nine Days*, 2 vols. [London: Hunt and Clarke, 1827], II, 298–309). Mary Shelley's comment that both William Godwin, Jr., and Hogg had been told Payne was not at the Arundel address suggests that Payne still had not cleared the debts that led to his earlier arrests.

2. Payne's opera *The White Maid*, an adaptation of Scribe's *La Dame Blanche* (Paris, 1825), was presented at Covent Garden on 2 January 1827 (Nicoll, *English Drama*, IV, 369).

To John Howard Payne   Sunday. Kentish Town [?1827][1]

My dear Payne

I return the papers—infamous trash![2] they are not worth looking at.

I & Jane think of going to the Lambs on Wednesday. Will you meet us there? If any thing should prevent us, I will let you know

Yours Ever
MS.

ADDRESS: J. H. Payne Esq / &c &c &c. PUBLISHED: Jones, #258. TEXT: MS., Huntington Library (HM 6826).

1. This letter is written on the same kind of stationery as Mary Shelley's letter of 2 September 1827—heavy woven, cream-colored, 8 14/16″ × 7 5/16″, with a watermark comprising elaborate 3-inch feathers and ribbons over the initials TM&M. I therefore tentatively assign it to 1827, the earliest year my records indicate that she used this paper.

2. When John Joseph Stockdale (1770–1847) was prosecuted for publishing the scandalous *Harriette Wilson's Memoirs* (see 29 November [1825]), he defended himself by publishing, from December 1826 through February 1827, *Stockdale's Budget*, which circulated scandal from English upper-class society, to prove that the *Memoirs* were not exaggerated. As Shelley's first publisher, Stockdale had letters from Shelley dated 1810–11. These he inserted in *Stockdale's Budget* to illustrate that he was a Christian gentleman trying to redeem a young atheist (Cameron, *The Young Shelley*, pp. 291–92; for Shelley's letters to Stockdale, see *PBS Letters*). Mary Shelley's comment in this letter was quite possibly in reference to these papers.

To John Howard Payne [Kentish Town 6 January 1827]

My dear Payne

Since ever to see you again is past my hope I write to congratulate you on the success of the White Maid[1]—since tho' the Newspapers shew their want of gallantry towards her—the public are I heare infinitely pleased. I long to see it—but I hear that you are not permitted many orders—and I can more patiently postpone my visit as this weather kills me—I have a very bad cold—& could not venture out till I or the weather change for the better—Nevertheless I hope you will not find it incovenient to facilitate my acquaintance with the piece a week or so hence.

I want to hear if you have further intelligence concerning Murray's proposal concerning Mr Shelley's works[2]—I believe the family obstacles will be obviated—and if Mr Murray still entertains the idea—I should be glad that he should know that it is practicable Can you serve me, as you kindly said you would on this occasion

I really think a walk to Kentish town would do you good—What say you? Will {you} drink tea with me Tuesday Evening?

Yours ever
MaryShelley

ADDRESS: J. Howard Payne Esq / 29 Arundel St. / Strand. POSTMARKS: (1) S.O Kentish Tn; (2) 7. NIGHT. 7 / JA. 6 / 1827. PUBLISHED: Jones, #272. TEXT: MS., Historical Society of Pennsylvania.

1. See 22 November [1826], n. 2.

2. Payne corresponded with John Murray from as early as 8 January 1814, when he offered Murray the English copyright of the *Memoirs of the War in the Southern Department of the United States* (1812) of General Henry Lee ([1756–1818], the father of Robert E. Lee), until at least 29 June 1831, when Payne proposed to translate the best dramatic literature of France for Murray's "Family Library series." On 23 October 1826 *The Opera Glass* announced the death of a friend of Payne's, the great French tragedian François Joseph Talma (Overmyer, *America's First Hamlet*, p. 268); on 25 October 1826 Payne proposed writing a memoir of Talma for Murray. Murray's interest in Shelley's works may have been expressed in the course of correspondence concerning Payne's Talma proposal. It appears that Murray did not accept any of Payne's many projects (MSS. of Payne's letters, John Murray).

*To John Howard Payne Kentish town Thursday [?11 January 1827]

Many thanks, my dear Payne, for your information concerning Murrays offer. The copyrights are all mine. How far in my present situation I can sell them to Murray, I have not yet decided. In the meantime he may be informed that I am the person to whom to apply—Can you guess how far Murray would choose to be purchaser of a romance from me—the subject is a good one—an English Historical one, a little before the Reformation[1]—true it is not begun because I have been so harassed that my thoughts have not been free & besides I want encouragement

You are wrong very wrong to shut yourself up so—Your health will suffer and then what will not suffer when that fails—? I am afraid Miss [*?P*][2]—of C.G. [*Covent Garden*] is annoying you—I do not wonder the theatre quashed amateurs & actors—

W. [*?William Godwin, Jr.*] came too home

Adieu Yours ever
M Shelley

UNPUBLISHED. TEXT: Payne, *Letterbook*, 1815–33.

1. Mary Shelley's fourth novel, *The Fortunes of Perkin Warbeck, A Romance*, published in 3 volumes by Henry Colburn and Richard Bentley in 1830.

2. Mary Ann Paton was originally scheduled to sing the lead in *The White Maid*. When she withdrew, Payne criticized her in *The Opera Glass* (5 December 1826), to which she replied in the *Times* (London) (9 December 1826). The press gave *The White Maid* bad notices, and Overmyer suggests that these may have been partially motivated by Payne's attack on the popular singer (Overmyer, *America's First Hamlet*, p. 270).

To John Murray [Kentish Town] January 13, 1827

I write merely to say that the copyrights[1] are mine, and that if you wish to make such a purchase, I should be happy to enter into a negotiation with you upon it.

PUBLISHED: Jones, #273. TEXT: Smiles, *John Murray*, II, 309.

1. According to Samuel Smiles, John Murray first approached Sir Timothy Shelley about acquiring the copyrights to some of Shelley's works (Smiles, *John Murray*, II, 309).

To [?Charles Ollier] Kentish Town 16 Jan. [?1827][1]

My dear Sir

I wrote to Mr Colburn about ten days ago—offering to undertake the translation of a french work strongly reccomended to me by Mr Peacock—Thierry's History of the Norman Conquest[2]—I have had no answer—Does this mean that he declines my proposal?—

I have a work called L'Osservatore Fiorentino[3]—A work much esteemed in Italy—which contains a history of the principal buildings of Florence—with many curious anecdotes & interesting traditional stories about that City—In the Italian this work consists of 8 thin octavo volumes—For the English reader a judicious abridgement might be made in one volume forming an interesting work. Would you mention it to Mr Colburn—& let me know whether it would suit his views.

I suppose there is no chance now of his purchasing the Copy right of Frankenstein

I am dear Sir
Yours truly
MShelley

PUBLISHED: Jones, #274. TEXT: MS., Chapin Collection, Williams College.

1. This letter is written on stationery watermarked "HAGAR & SON / 1826," which Mary Shelley first used in October–November 1826.

2. *Histoire de la conquête de l'Angleterre par les Normands, de ses causes, et de ses suites jusqu'a nos jours*, 3 vols. (Paris, 1825).

3. See 17 April 1821.

TO JOHN HOWARD PAYNE

Park Cottage[1] Monday
[19 February 1827]

What can I say to all this stupid tracasserie of Dame Fortune—Shall I play again & will you help me to win—Suppose you get tickets for me (4) & places (6)—for Wednesday at the Lyceum—if you can let me have the former & hear of the latter at Papa's tomorrow evening (by 8)—if not then can you send them to me Wednesday Morning—If this does not succeed—the———I leave you to finish the phrase pray do it en{e}rgetically—I say Amen

Yours
MS.

ADDRESS: J. H. Payne / 29 Arundel St / Strand. POSTMARKS: (1) T.P / Mar [ ]; (2) 10. F.NOON. 10 / 19. FE / 1827. PUBLISHED: Jones, #275. TEXT: MS., Huntington Library (HM 10793).

1. The address from which Mary Shelley wrote this letter reveals that her intimate friendship with the family of Joshua Robinson (d. 1841) had begun by February 1827, rather than the following summer, as is often assumed. Little is known about the Robinsons. Mary Shelley was particularly the friend of Isabella (who married Sholto Douglas), Julia, and Rosa (who became the wife of Aubrey William Beauclerc in 1840). Others identified as family members are Louisa (who married Major Lockhard Maclean in 1834), Alfred ([1804–58], a solicitor), George, Julian, and Eliza Agnes (who married Henry James Perry in 1844). (I am indebted to Emily W. Sunstein for supplying me with some of this information.) Mary Shelley made frequent and lengthy visits to their home, Park Cottage, Paddington, and often used the Robinsons' address for mail when she was not permanently domiciled.

*TO [?JOHN HOWARD PAYNE]

Thursday Park Cottage
Paddington. [?February 1827–32][1]

I shall read your tragedy with great pleasure—which is saying much, since I am to be critical a task I love not—& do not think that I understand—Depend however that I will do my best—& be candid—send it to me here—I will return it speedily

Get me the tickets if you can for the Haymarket for next —
Have you better interest at the Lyceum—& have you any at the French Theatre at W. London—Let the admissions be for four & let me have them as long beforehand as you can

Ever Y^s truly
MS.

I left the blank wishing to see the bills—After all I do not much care which Wednesday will do—but if the Rivals were acted Friday or Saturday I had rather—any day will do with the "Green Eyed Monster{"}[2] if you can let me know which a day or two before hand

If I return your M.S. to Lancaster St. (What number?) will that do?

UNPUBLISHED. TEXT: MS., Anthony Collection, New York Public Library.

1. See [19 February 1827], n. 1.
2. *Othello* 3. 3. 166.

TO EDWARD JOHN TRELAWNY — Kentish Town. 4 March 1827

My dear Trelawny—Your long silence had instilled into me the delusive hope that I should hear you sooner than from you. I have been silly enough sometimes to start at a knock,—at length your letter is come.[1] [By] that indeed I entertain more reasonable hopes of seeing you. You will come—Ah, indeed you must; if you are ever the kind-hearted being you were—you must come to be consoled by my sympathy, exhilarated by my encouragements, and made happy by my friendship. You are not happy! Alas! who is that has a noble and generous nature? It is not only, my noble-hearted friend, that your will is bountiful and your means small,—were you richer you would still be tormented by ingratitude, caprice, and change. Yet I say Amen to all your anathema against poverty, it is beyond measure a torment and despair. I am poor, having once been richer; I live among the needy, and see only poverty around. I happen, as has always been my fate, to have formed intimate friendships with those who are great of soul, generous, and incapable of valuing money except for the good it may do—and these very people are all even poorer than myself, is it not hard? But turning to you who are dearest to me, who of all beings are most liberal, it makes me truly unhappy to find that you are hard pressed: do not talk of old age and poverty, both the one and the other are in truth far from you,—for the one it will be a miracle if you live to grow old,—this would appear a strange compliment if addressed to another, but you and I have too much of the pure spirit of fire in our souls to wish to live till the flickering beam waxes dim;—think then of the few present years only. I have no doubt you will do your fortunes great good by coming to this country. A too long absence destroys the interest that friends take, if they are only friends in the common acceptation of the word; and your relations ought to be reminded of you. The great fault to us in this country is its expensiveness, and the dreadful ills attendant here on poverty; elsewhere, though poor, you may live—here you are actually driven from life, and though a few might pity, none would help you were you absolutely starving. You say you shall stay here but a short time and then go to Italy—alas! alas!

It is impossible in a letter to communicate the exact state of one's feelings and affairs here—but there is a change at hand—I cannot guess whether for good or bad as far as regards me. This winter, whose extreme severity has carried off many old people, confined Sir Tim, for ten weeks by the gout—but he is recovered. All that time a settlement for me was delayed, although it was acknowledged that Percy now being the heir,[2] one ought to be made; at length after much parading, they have notified to me that I shall receive a magnificent £250 a year, to be increased next year to £300.[3] But then I am not permitted to leave this cloudy nook. My desire to get away is unchanged, and I used to look forward to your return as a period when I might contrive—but I fear there is no hope for me during Sir T.'s life. He and his family are now at Brighton. John Shelley, dear S.'s brother, is about to marry,[4] and talks of calling upon me. I am often led to reflect in life how people situated in a certain manner with regard to me might make my life less drear than it is—but it is always the case that the people that might—won't, and it is a very great mistake to fancy that they will. Such thoughts make me anxious to draw tighter the cords of sympathy and friendship which are so much more real than those of the world's forming in the way of relationship or connection.

From the ends of the world we were brought together to be friends till death; separated as we are, this tie still subsists. I do not wonder that you are out of heart concerning Greece; the mismanagement here is not less than the misgovernment there, the discord the same, save that here ink is spilt instead of blood. Lord Cochrane[5] alone can assist them—but without vessels or money how can he acquire sufficient power? at any rate except as the Captain of a vessel I do not see what good you can do them. But the mischief is this,—that while some cold, unimpressive natures can go to a new country, reside among a few friends, enter into the interests of an intimate and live as a brother among them for a time, and then depart, leaving small trace, retaining none,—as if they had ascended from a bath, they change their garments and pass on;—while others of subtler nature receive into their very essences a part of those with whom they associate, and after a while they become enchained, either for better or worse, and during a series of years they bear the marks of change and attachment. These natures indeed are the purest and best, and of such are you, dear friend; having you once, I ever have you; losing you once, I have lost you for ever; a riddle this, but true. And so life passes, year is added to year, the word youth is becoming obsolete, while years bring me no change for the better. Yet I said, change is at hand—I know it, though as yet I do not feel it—you will come, in the spring you will come and add fresh delight for me to the happy change from winter to summer. I cannot tell what else material is to change, but I feel sure the year will end differently from its beginning. Jane is quite well, we talk continually of you, and expect you anxiously. Her fortunes have been more shifting than mine,[6] and they are about to conclude,—differently from mine,—but I leave her to say what she thinks best concerning herself, though probably she will defer the explanation until your arrival. She is my joy and consolation. I could never have survived my exile here but for her. Her amiable temper, cheerfulness, and never ceasing sympathy are all so much necessary value for one wounded and lost as I.

Come, dear friend, again I read your melancholy sentences and I say, come! let us try if we can work out good from ill; if I may not be able to throw a ray of sunshine on your path, at least I will lead you as best I may through the gloom. Believe me that all that belongs to you must be dear to me, and that I shall never forget all I owe to you.

Do you remember those pretty lines of Burns?—

> A monarch may forget his crown
> That on his head an hour hath been,
> A bridegroom may forget his bride
> Who was his wedded wife yest'reen,
> A mother may forget her child
> That smiles so sweetly on her knee,
> But I'll remember thee, dear friend,
> And all that thou hast done for me.[7]

Such feelings are not the growth of the moment. They must have lived for years—have flourished in smiles, and retained their freshness watered by tears; to feel them one must have sailed much of life's voyage together—have undergone the same perils, and sympathised in the same fears and griefs; such is our situation; and the heartfelt and deep-rooted sentiments fill my eyes with tears as I think of you, dear friend, we shall meet soon. Adieu,

M. S.

. . . I cannot close this letter without saying a word about dear Hunt—yet that must be melancholy. To feed nine children is no small thing. His health has borne up pretty well hitherto, though his spirits sink. What is it in the soil of this green earth that is so ill adapted to the best of its sons? He speaks often of you with affection.

[*P. 1 top*] Direct {to} me at W. Godwin, Esq., 44 Gower Place, Gower Street, London.

ADDRESS: Edward Trelawny, Esq., / To the care of Samuel Barff, Esq. / Zante, The Ionian Isles. ENDORSED: Received 10th April 1827. PUBLISHED: Jones, #277. TEXT: Marshall, *Mary Shelley*, II, 153–57.

1. See Trelawny, *Letters*, pp. 108–9.

2. See 30 October 1826 to Leigh Hunt, n. 2.

3. Mary Shelley's settlement was increased to £300 with the June 1829 quarter only after she wrote many imploring letters to Whitton (Ingpen, *Shelley in England*, p. 603).

4. On 24 March 1827 John Shelley married Eliza Bowen. Their son Edward, born 1827, became fourth Baronet in 1889, when Sir Percy Florence died without issue (Ingpen, *Shelley in England*, pp. 589–90).

5. Thomas Cochrane, tenth Earl of Dundonald (1775–1860), admiral, had agreed to take command of the Greek Navy. When he arrived in Greece in 1827

his objectives were frustrated by insufficient ships, overexpenditures, and lack of funds. By December 1828 he had resigned his command.

6. Jane Williams and Thomas Jefferson Hogg began to live as husband and wife sometime between April and July 1827.

7. The last stanza of the "Lament for James, Earl of Glencairn," somewhat misquoted.

*TO JOHN HOWARD PAYNE Kentish Town 30. March [1827]

My dear Payne

When you were better you said you would come to K.T. [*Kentish Town*] You do not come yet notwithstanding I hope you are convalescent—Pray let me know—& when I shall see you.

Mrs Godwin begged me when I wrote to say how sorry she was to hear of your illness—

Moreover, how goes the world with you? The smile she put on to me is now exchanged for a frown; but I expect the smile to return ere long

Yours Ever
MS.

ADDRESS: John Howard Payne Esq / 29 Arundel St. / Strand. POSTMARKS: (1) SO [Kentish Tn]; (2) 7. NIGHT. 7 / MR 30 / 1827. UNPUBLISHED: last paragraph in Jones, #277. TEXT: MS., Pforzheimer Library.

MARY SHELLEY AND LEIGH HUNT TO EDWARD JOHN TRELAWNY Kentish Town—Easter Sunday [8 April] 1827

Will this letter find you in your summer isle, my dear Trelawny? Yes—and again & again I fear, my missives will find you there while you defer from spring to autumn & autumn to spring your long promised visit. Your last letter was so truly sad that I long to hear from you again in such a mood as a summer sun may inspire—I never wonder at any melancholy in winter time—during the long drear winter we have endured I could well have streaked sheet after sheet with woe begone reflections—in summer we feel at least that nature is kind to us, and the affection she excites makes us happy in spite of care and sorrow. This is to be an eventful summer to us, and I regard with much anxiety yet with great hope, the changes it will witness. Janey is writing to you & will tell her own tale best. The person to whom she unites herself is one of my oldest friends—the ⟨old⟩ early friend of ⟨my⟩ our S.—It was he who chose to share the honour, as he generously termed it, of S's expulsion from Oxford—And yet he is unlike what you may conceive to be the ideal of the best friend of Shelley. He is a man of talent—of wit—he has sensibility, and even romance in his disposition, but his exterior is composed, and, at a superficial glance, cold. He has loved Jane devotedly and ardently ever since she first arrived in England, almost five years ago—At first she was too faithfully attached to the memory of Edward—nor ⟨afterwards⟩ was he exactly the being to satisfy her imagination—but his sincere & long tried love has at last gained the day. He is by profession a barrister, and thus she will continue to live in England He has a private fortune besides which is now somewhat embarrassed by paying the fortunes of his younger brothers & sisters, on his fathers death—but in time it will be considerable—and I shall have the pleasure of seeing her freed from pecuniary cares and difficulties—able to display her taste & elegance in the way she best likes; creating an ⟨temple of beau⟩ abode replete with every graceful adornment. Nor will I fear for her in the risk she must run when she confides her future happiness to another's constancy & good principles. He is a man of honour—he longs for a home, for domestic life, & he well knows that none could make such so happy as Jane—He is liberal in his opinions, constant in his attachments;—if she is happy with him now, she will be so always—for he appreciates her merits—and, in every body's opinion is much improved, softened & humanized by his intercourse with her. Of course after all that has passed it is our wish that all this shall be as little talked of as possible—the obscurity in which we have lived favours this. We shall remove hence during the summer, for of course we shall still continue near each other—& I—as ever, must derive my only pleasure and solace from her society—I am dead to all other hope—if you returned—yet you would not make one of us—you will leave us quickly again—yet it will be great happiness to have you again with me, tho' for a short time—Will you not come?

Hunt has asked me to leave space for him in this letter, as he wishes to write to you—he has not been well lately but the summer probably will give him health—I have no news for you of friends—it is long since I heard from Miss Whitehead—I wrote to her as you told me. Claire is still in Russia—I had a letter a day or two ago from Medwin—he is doing the great man at Florence—giving parties &c—the English were very shy of him on account of his Conversations—but if he regales them that of course will wear off. Of myself I have no good news to communicate—I believe I wrote to you last while I entertained the hope that my money cares were diminishing—but shabby as the best of these shabby people was—I am not to arrive at that best without due waiting & anxiety—nor do I yet see the end of this worse than tedious uncertainty. Shelley's only brother, a young man about 21—has lately married in Ireland—I am to see him when he comes to London but have small expectation of reaping good from his visit. Adieu, my ever dear Friend; while hearts such as yours beat, I will not wholly despond—my existence depends on the sympathy & affection of those I love—do you then, for my sake love ever

yours MS.

[*From Leigh Hunt*]

Dear Trelawney,

Though you have not heard from him a long while, do not forget that there is one Leigh Hunt, who has never forgotten you, nor ceased to think & talk of you with his friends. If I have not written to you, Mary Shelley will have told you that I have written of you, & perhaps she has told you also that I am now writing of you again. Every body in England is being guilty of Memoirs; so I am dragged in to be as guilty as the rest, & am very shamefully going to tell how many excellent friends I have had, [?&] who they are. You know [w]ho was the dearest & most excellent of them all, & who lov[ed] him as well as myself. Be sure neither of them are omitted, nor some of the most touching & trying moments of their lives. This, however else you may regard it, will at least shew you how you live in the hearts of your friends; let their voices reach you as little as they may. In truth, I deserve to be forgiven, for being an ill correspondent; for my life, since I saw you, has passed in little but hard writing & harder intervals of ill health. I am obliged, now, to indite this letter on a mantle-piece, for fear of stooping my head and bringing the blood up in my cheeks; nor have I written any thing but similar letters for these two months. But I am now getting better again. Then for another set to at writing, and then, I suppose, for another bout of illness. Well; "God help the wicked", as Falstaff says. Here am I with a wife & eight children, desiring nothing but health to work hard with, & willing to make the utmost of this pretty green world, which the godly so abuse, & close to me lives Mrs. Coutts, dying of God knows how many thousands a year & too much beef-steak. I would fain (not to be scandalous) kill her with a more elegant dish; but I am told that she loves the solid goods of this life, and takes them to consist in beef & burliness, & what this age has gracefully termed "heavy wet", which you must know is porter. Do you not long for some in Zante? That is natural enough. I wish you & I had bodily faculties worthy of our thought, & could pitch into another's islands, like Congreve rockets. I would descend suddenly upon you, like a very odd seraph, bringing a pot of Whitbread entire; & you should return me the visit with some Chian wine, which I suppose is about as good as "Etruscan". Marianne begs her very kindest remembrance, & is heartily yours. You know we have a little female Trelawney in our family, but we doubt whether in the course of three or four weeks, we shall not deprive her of her name, & bestow it upon a <u>male</u>. This is "secondo", as the Italians say.[1] Dear Trelawney, write us a word of remembrance, & tell us that our hopes of seeing you in the summer are well founded. I heard from Brown a little while since. He & Kirkup are still living together at Florence, & both well. Severn is ditto at home. Mary & Jane tell you, of course, all sorts of pleasant gossip of themselves; but they do not tell you perhaps what I can; to wit, the l[adies a]re both looking remarkably well. Mary never looked better [ ] so well, if such things were lawful to say of ladies.

[*Mary Shelley adds upside-down between Hunt's pages:*] The writing to which dear Hunt alludes is a ⟨comment on⟩ mention of you in an Article in a Magazine some time ago,—I have not space here to copy it—but in it he says—The writer of this Article had a sudden & short intimacy with Mr Trelawny before he went to Greece— But under such circumstances which cram the feelings of many years into one—& make a brief acquaintance look old. No man could { } a manlier or a nobler part than Mr T did under those circumstances—And when the writer heard of his alledged defection from the cause of liberty he laught it to scorn.—Poor darling Hunt—my heart bleeds for him—and I dare not look forward with regard to him—but I must not make uncertain ill news travel so far—He deserves all possible good—but this {is} an hard world—& he is treated ill on all sides in every way by God & Man.—And alas all I can do is to watch & weep over the progress of the evil. The paper today said that Lord Cochrane had [ar]rived in Greece which [ ] not will save it—the steam Vessel built here has burst [ ] is destroyed—so much for many thousands of Greek debt—The state of public affairs is in the highest degree interesting—Canning by a coup de maitre got himself mamed [*named*] Prime Minister on which the high Tories resigned—& today we have news that Canning and the moderate Whigs have coalesced—This I think is good news for Greece—for they are all liberal—and Brougham I am sure is favourable to their cause—A contradiction appeared today concerning the Greek Steam Packet—they say it sails remarkably well.—Let me hear from you very soon—Your plans—your movements—there is nothing in the world in which I am so much interested as these—Adieu.

[*P. 1. top*] Direct to me in future ⟨to⟩ at my father's 44 Gower Place—Bedford Square

ADDRESS: Edward Trelawny Esq / To the care of M. Sam Barff / Zante—The Ionian Isles. POSTMARKS: (1) F27 / 263; (2) 17. MAG; (3) OFFICIO DELLA POSTA GENERALE / RRE[ ]; (4) CORFU / 26 MAGGIO / 1827. PUBLISHED: Palacio, *Mary Shelley*, pp. 605–7. TEXT: MS., Jean de Palacio. TRANSCRIPTION OF HUNT'S LETTER: Jean de Palacio.

1. This suggests that Marianne Hunt suffered a miscarriage, or that the child born did not long survive, since the next known Hunt child is Jacintha Shelley Leigh Hunt (May 1828–1914).

*To THOMAS JEFFERSON HOGG

[Kentish Town] Thursday [10 May 1827]

My dear Jeff.

Peacock is to see Sir Tim tomorrow—& I believe that you share with me my certainty that after sufficient annoyance this affair will come to a good conclusion.[1] I hope therefore you will not think me indiscreet in asking you to lend me £7—to meet one or two detestable bills that I must pay this week—If you can let me have the money by Saturday Morning

Scusi l'incomodo—drear necessity must be my excuse—& if I am troublesome in asking I shall have the merit at least of punctually repaying

Yours Ever
MShelley

ADDRESS: T. Jefferson Hogg Esq Garden Cour[t] / Temple. POSTMARK: 7. NIGHT. 7 / MY. 10 / 1827. UNPUBLISHED. TEXT: MS., Abinger MS., Bodleian Library.

1. Whitton, on behalf of Sir Timothy Shelley, and Peacock and his solicitors Amory & Coles, on behalf of Mary Shelley, negotiated a settlement whereby Mary Shelley was guaranteed an annual income of £250, to be increased to £300, repayable when Percy came into Shelley's estate (Ingpen, *Shelley in England*, p. 591).

*To [?][1] [Kentish Town c. 14 May 1827]

At the instance of Mr Whitton, Sir T.S's [*Timothy Shelley's*] solicitor, I agreed to sign a bond engaging to repay Sir T.S. the sums of money [*I*][2] had received of him (amounting to nearly £1,0,00 [*£1,000*]) on the event of my coming into possession of the property left to me by Mr S.—which depends on the conti{n}gency of my son surviving Sir T.S.—Mr W. drew up the bond, and sent it for our perusal; in it there is a clause by which I bind myself to pay this £1000 in six months from the date of the bond, giving the trustees of the bond (W. & his partner) the power to sell the whole or any part of my reversionary interest, to make good such payment at the expiration of 6 months.

I was advised to object to this clause. W. is offended by my objection and say[*s*] that [*a*] clause binding the party to pay in six Months is inserted as a matter of course in all bonds of a like nature and [*is*] not intended to be acted upon. And that I shew an insulting distrust of Sir T.S. & his solicitor.[3]

I wish to know whether the clause really is usual and a matter of form only: Or whether it is singular and extorionate.

M

UNPUBLISHED. TEXT: MS., Pforzheimer Library.

1. Mary Shelley was to sign a security for £1,000 for funds already received from Sir Timothy Shelley. On the advice of Amory, Mary Shelley objected to the six-month clause in the security, which angered Sir Timothy Shelley and delayed the completion of the arrangement. Mary Shelley's letter of 29 May to Sir Timothy Shelley assures him or her trust and confidence. This letter, however, shows that Mary Shelley sought a legal opinion other than Amory's. Her explanation in this letter of Whitton's identity and her reference to "my son" rather than "Percy" suggests that she did not address this letter to Hogg, upon whom she occasionally called for legal advice.

2. This letter was corrected by another hand. The corrections are given in brackets.

3. On 17 May Amory and Coles wrote Whitton that they regretted that their letter was "taken in a manner which was not intended." They explained that they had sent one part of Mary Shelley's letter to show that her "consent to your deed was given on the ground you put, that of mutual confidence" and they hoped Mary Shelley would not suffer by their action (Abinger MS.).

To Mrs. Bartlett Kentish Town—19 May—1827

My dear Mrs Bartlett

I am sorry that the present object of my writing is to announce the necessity I am under of quitting Kentish Town. In about a month from the present time I leave town for the country[1]—and the period of my return is uncertain. Besides that family reasons will I believe oblige me when I may return, to take up my residence quite at the other end of London.—

I had intended to defer this communication until I should pay you my debt—but as another week may elapse before the final arrangement of my affairs I am unwilling to give you so short a notice of my intention of leaving you. If any circumstances should make it convenient to you for me to quit you sooner I will endeavour to hasten my departure—otherwise I think in a month ⟨or five weeks at the outside⟩ from this time I shall be obliged to quit town.—

I sincerely thank you for your politeness towards me and your kindness to my little Boy. With the truest wishes for your health & happiness I am

Yours truly
MaryShelley

ADDRESS: Mrs. Bartlett / &c &c &c. PUBLISHED: Jones, #279. TEXT: MS., Bodleian Library (MS., Shelley, Adds., d. 5, ff. 99–100).

1. Mary Shelley left Kentish Town after 24 July 1827. By 28 July she addressed a letter to Jane Williams Hogg from Sompting.

To Sir Timothy Shelley Kentish Town—29. May. 1827

Sir

It is the subject of great anxiety to me that the period of my signing the deed drawn by Mr Whitton is again delayed,—and I am the more mortified since it appears that this delay is occasioned by a communication of mine. When Mr Whitton proposed to me that on the contingency of my inheriting on Bysshe's will, I should repay the sums advanced and to be advanced by you to me and my child, I immediately acceded to this arrangement as being just and proper. Mr Whitton wished that the deed he should draw, should be seen and approved by a Solicitor on my part. Mr Peacock named Mr Amory, and Mr Whitton was satisfied with this nomination. As soon as the affair was put into the hands of a Solicitor, I of course considered myself obliged to act under his directions, and in consequence of Mr Amory's objections all this delay has occurred.

For myself I do not hestiate to say that I put every confidence in you, Sir Timothy, and that I feel perfectly secure that my interests are safe in your hands, and I am ready to confide them to your direction. It is hard therefore that while I am satisfied with the arrangements you make, that the objections of my advisers should subject me to the dreadful embarassments with which I am now struggling. It was in February last that Mr Whitton announced to me your intention of allowing me £250 per ann. since then I have received no supply—I have lived on credit—the bills incurred are now presented for payment, and neither have I funds to defray them, nor any by which I can continue to exist.

I do not understand business; and I do not mean to bring this subject before you as a question of business. The interest you shewed for my son encouraged me in the hope that you also will be desirous of facilitating my earnest wish of bringing him up properly. As by Bysshe's confidence in me I inherit a considerable property I consider it perfectly right that I should repay the sums you advance to me for his support—but the means for his support I can only obtain through you. I am sure that you will not permit a question of forms merely to interfere with the welfare of your Grandson and the respectability of his Mother. It is a great misfortune to me that I am not permitted to see you.[1] It would have been a great happiness to me if, left a widow, I could have been under the protection of Bysshe's father. This good is denied to me; but let me entreat you to enter into my situation, and not to delay in relieving me from the humiliations & distresses to which I am subjected. I believe that Mr Whitton feels assured that confidence may be safely placed in me and will not advise any further postponement in the desired settlement.

Let me entreat you therefore, Sir Timothy, to direct that the deed in question may be immediately prepared for my signature. Every day is of consequence to me; your kind feelings will I do not doubt, cause as few to intervene as possible before I am relieved from my embarassments.

Percy is quite well, and often speaks of you; I hope it will not be long before he has the honour of seeing you again

I am your obliged & obt Servant
MaryShelley

ADDRESS: Sir Tim. Shelley Bart. ENDORSED: 29th May 1827. PUBLISHED: Jones, #280. TEXT: MS., Bodleian Library (MS., Shelley, Adds., c. 6, ff. 41–42).

1. Although Sir Timothy Shelley saw Percy Florence from time to time, he adamantly refused to meet Mary Shelley.

To William Whitton — Kentish Town 29 May 1827

Dear Sir

I enclose you my letter to Sir Tim, and reiterate my request that you will have the goodness to use your influence with my father in-law to bring this painful affair to a conclusion. I feel assured that you are persuaded that confidence may be placed in me—and on my part I am ready to put every confidence in Sir Timothy—

I am Sir—
Yr Obt Servant—MaryShelley

ADDRESS: W. Whitton Esq. ENDORSED: 29th May 1827. PUBLISHED: Jones, #281. TEXT: MS., Bodleian Library (MS., Shelley, Adds., c. 6, ff. 39–40).

To William Whitton Kentish Town—4 June. 1827

Sir

I am sorry that my letter to Sir Timy Shelley is not satisfactory. I beg you will attribute my failure to my utter igorance of business—and my not knowing exactly what it was necessary that I should say. I thought that when I expressed my perfect confidence in Sir Timy, and my readiness to sign the deed in question, that I should efface any disagreable impression made by my letter to Mr Amory.[1] The explanation of that letter is simple. I had, at your wish, confided the conduct of my affairs to Mr Peacock. I ⟨wrote⟩ copied the letter—which certainly when he composed he had no intention it should contain any expressions offensive to Sir T. Shelley—You told me that it conveyed the idea that a foundation was to be laid by it for a suit in Chancery—I am sorry that it should have been so ill worded—I utterly disclaim any such intention or thought on my part. I beg to retract any expressions that could give rise to such an idea, or that detract at all from the perfect confidence I feel in Sir Timothy.

I trust that my present communication fills up any omission in my last. If not, and if you will let me know that such is the case, I will call on you at any hour you will appoint that I may learn by what act or word of mine I can bring this painful negociation to a conclusion.

I am most anxious to make the required concessions and to sign the deed—My situation is one of struggle and embarassment—Besides the debts I have been obliged to incur—I made arrangements (when on the interview of Sir Timy with Mess. Peacock and Amory, I thought the negociation on the eve of terminating) to quit Kentish Town. I cannot delay my departure more than a fortnight or three weeks—and yet without money I cannot discharge my bills here. Permit me to request as a personal favour to myself that you would kindly use your influence with Sir Timy—and as speedily as circumstances will permit, make such communication to him as will bring this distressing delay to a termination.

May I be allowed to ask what the circumstance is to which you allude as having occurred in Sir Timy's family.

I am, Sir—Your Obt. Sert
MaryW. Shelley

Endorsed: 4 June 1827 / Mrs Shelley. Published: Jones, #282. Text: MS., Bodleian Library (MS., Shelley, Adds., c. 6, ff. 43–44).

1. See [c. 14 May 1827].

*To John Howard Payne [Kentish Town] Friday [15 June 1827]

My dear Payne

I am sorry I was not at home on Sunday—I seldom or never engage myself before hand on Sunday—tho' of course I walk when nothing keeps me at home—a line from you would have that desirable effect—May I expect to see you next Sunday? Sunday[1]———I go soon out of town—So pray come if you can

Yours Ever truly
MaryShelley

ADDRESS: J. Howard Payne / 29 Arundel St. / Strand. POSTMARKS: (1) T.P / Holborn [ ]; (2) 4. EVEN. 4 / JU 15 / 1827. UNPUBLISHED. TEXT: MS., Pforzheimer Library.

1. Mary Shelley wrote *Sunday* twice, no doubt recalling that her unclear *Sunday* caused Payne to call on her on Monday, 18 April 1825 (see [14 April 1825]).

*TO TERESA GUICCIOLI 3zo Luglio [July]—1827—Kentish Town

Cara Mia Contessina

Quanto tempo c'è che non siamo scritte! Quasi due anni! Ma non mi sono scordata di voi—parlo continuamente di voi colla Williams—e pensiamo sempre al felice tempo quando fummo tutte vicine l'una a l'altra. Voleva scrivervi quando sentii da Medwin che foste partita da Roma—ed ora mi dice il medesimo che vi siete di ritorno. Mi spiccio a ricomminciare la corispondenza interrotta. Ahime—Amica cara—non siamo scordate dalle disgrazie—il Vostro amato fratello![1] l'abbiamo perduto—che colpo per voi ed il povero Pappa—Questa vita si chiama bene un passo doloroso, quanto abbiamo noi penate—giovane ancora.

Comminciava una lunga lettera per voi—raccontando gli avvenimenti di questi lunghi mesi di silenzio—ma se non siate a Roma—se non vi giunga questo foglio, non vorrei dare tal detaglio a chi che sia che forse leggera questo vergare mio. Vi diro adunque solamente che sto bene, io ed il mio figlio—e subito che tengo la vostra risposta a questa vi riscrivero.

V'è una cosa pero che bisogna aggiungere a queste poche linèe—per che preme il tempo. E vi prego mia cara, di rispondere senza indugio. L'Amico intrinseco di Bÿron—Moore,—scrive ora la vita del vostro Amante.[2] Mi è venuto vedere—Mi parlava di voi—diceva che dopo il libro di Medwin era inutile che voi cercaste l'oscurità, ma che in parlando di voi—voleva sentire primamente da voi il vostro sentimento e se vi fosse cosa alcuna che vorreste dire. Tengo dal Caro Pietro il fagotto delle tue lettere a Bÿron—se mi permetterle potrei da queli far un <u>ebauche</u> della vostra storia per Moore—Ma non vorrei far nulla senza il vostro consentimento Moore e gran'amico del Caro Bÿron—Vi stima—e gli fara caso parlare di voi in un modo degno —E poi mi promette che io legga quel che scrivera di voi—e che non stampera cosa che io non approva—Potete fidarvi adunque, Cara Guiccioli, alla mia amicizia—ed alla sua delicatezza—all'onore suo. Che dite. Forse avete lettere di Byron che vorreste contribuire—Rispondete subito e state sicurra che io staro vigilantissima—e se mi mandate la vostra volonta—quella sara legge per me. Hobhouse dà ogni facilita a Moore—Cosi questo suo libro avra un carattere autentico—Moore vi saluta rispettosamente e vi prega di acconsentire a questo proponimento.

Non potrei dirvi—Mia Cara Amica—quanto piacere reco dalla società di Moore—Non parliamo di altro quasi che di Byron— e non ci ne stanchiamo mai—Ma più di questo—no—fin' che sapro se voi riceverete sicuramente questa lettera.

Addio Mia Cara Contessa—Mi par mill'anni che non vi vedo—che non rivedo la mia Italia Amate me sempre—che mi ripeto sempre

V^{ra} Aff^{ma} A^{ca} Mary Shelley

Vi rammentate di quella letterina Inglese che Egli scrisse al fine della Vostra Corinna[3]? Vi dispiacerebbe di darmi una copia—Indrizzate la Vostra lettera

Mrs Shelley
W. Godwin Esq.
44 Gower Place.—Bedford Sq.
London

[*Translation*]

My Dear Contessina

How long it's been since we have written to each other! Almost two years! But I have not forgotten you—I continually speak about you with Signora Williams—and we always think of the happy time when we were all near to one and other. I wanted to write you when I heard from Medwin that you might have left Rome—and now he tells me that you have returned. I hasten to begin again our interrupted correspondence. Alas—dear Friend—we have not been forgotten by misfortune—Your beloved brother![1] we have lost him—what a blow for you and your poor Father—This life is justly called a sorrowful passage, how much we have suffered—young still.

I started a long letter for you—recounting the events of these long months of silence—but if you are not at Rome—if this letter does not reach you, I do not want to give such detail to whomever might read this letter of mine. I will tell you therefore only that I am well, I and my son—and as soon as I have your reply to this I will write again.

There is one thing however that it is necessary for me to add to these few lines—because time is important. And I beg you my dear, to reply without delay. The intimate friend of Byron—Moore—is now writing the life of your Lover.[2] He came to see me—He spoke to me of you—he said that after Medwin's book it was useless for you to seek obscurity, but that in speaking about you—he wanted to hear chiefly from you your feeling and if there might be anything that you would want to say. I have from Dear Pietro the bundle of your letters to Byron—if you allow me I could make from these a rough outline of your story for Moore—But I do not want to do anything without your consent. Moore is a great friend of Dear Byron—He respects you—and it will please him to speak of you in a deserving way—And then he promises me that I can read that which he will write about you—and that he will not print anything that I do not approve—You may have confidence then, Dear Guiccioli, in my friendship—and in his tact—in his honor. What do you say. Perhaps you have some letters of Byron's that you might want to contribute—Reply immediately and be assured that I will be extremely vigilant—and if you send me your wish—this will be the law for me. Hobhouse gives every accommodation to Moore—Therefore this book will have an authentic character—Moore respectfully sends you his regards and begs you to consent to this purpose.

I cannot tell you—My Dear Friend—how much pleasure I receive from Moore's company—We speak of almost nothing besides Byron—and we never tire of it—But more than this—no—until I know that you will receive this letter for certain.

Farewell My Dear Countess—It seems a thousand years to me since I have seen you—since I have seen my Italy—Love me always—as I again declare myself always

Your most affectionate friend Mary Shelley

Do you recall that little English letter that he wrote at the end of your Corinne[3]? Would you mind giving me a copy—Address your letter

Mrs Shelley
W. Godwin Esq.
44 Gower Place.—Bedford Sq.
London

ADDRESS: Alla Sua Eccellenza / La Contessa Teresa Guiccioli / a Roma / Rome. Italy. POSTMARKS: (1) PAID / 5 JY / 182[7]; (2) F27 / 229; (3) ANGLETERRE; (4) PONT / BEAUVOISIN; (5) 19 LUGLIO. UNPUBLISHED. TEXT: MS., Pforzheimer Library. TRANSLATION: Ricki B. Herzfeld.

1. Upon his return to Greece, Pietro Gamba became a colonel in the Greek Army. He died of typhoid in 1827 (Origo, *The Last Attachment*, p. 387).

2. Mary Shelley wrote in her Journal on 26 June: "I have just made acquaintance with Tom Moore—He reminds me delightfully of the past and I like him much—There is something warm & genuine in his feelings & manner which is very attractive—and redeems him from the sin of worldliness with which he has been charged." On 2 July she wrote in her journal that she had breakfasted with Moore the day before and they had spoken about Shelley and Byron; she also wrote that she felt perfectly at ease with Moore and welcomed his company because "I have been so long exiled from the style of society in which I spent the better part of my life." On 11 July her Journal entry notes that Moore had left town; that his singing "is something new & strange & beautiful!"; and, again, that his visits gave her much pleasure. Moore's purpose in calling on Mary Shelley was to secure her aid in acquiring material for his biography of Byron, a favor she willingly provided (see 28 July [1824], n. 6). Only two fragments of Mary Shelley's letters to Moore have been located, but his many letters to her, spanning the years 1827 through 1841, are evidence of the long friendship that developed between the two writers (see Moore, *Letters*, II; and Betty T. Bennett, "An Unpublished Letter from Thomas Moore to Mary Shelley," *Notes and Queries*, 23, no. 3 [March 1976]: 114).

3. (1807), by Madame de Staël.

TO MARY LAMB Kentish Town 22 July 1827

My dear Miss Lamb

You have been long at Enfield[1]—I hardly know yet whether you are returned—and I quit town so very soon that I have not time to—as I exceedingly wish—call on you before I go—Nevertheless believe (if such familiar expression be not unmeet from me) that I love you with all my heart—gratefully & sincerely—& that when I return I shall seek you with, I hope, not too much zeal—but it will be with great eagerness.

You will be glad to hear that I have every reason to believe that the worst of my pecuniary troubles are over—as I am promised a regular tho' small income from my Father-in-law—I mean to be very industrious <u>on other</u> <u>accounts</u> this summer—so I hope nothing will go very ill with me or mine.

I am afraid Miss Kelly[2] will think me dreadfully rude for not having availed myself of her kind invitation—Will you present my Compliments to her—& say that my embarassments—harassings & distance from town are the guilty causes of my omission—for which with her leave I will apologize in person on my return to London.

All kind & grateful remembrances to Mr Lamb—he must not forget me[3] nor like me one atom less than I delight to flatter myself he does now, when again I come to seize a dinner per force at your Cottage—Percy is quite well—& is reading with great extacy the Arabian Nights—I shall return I suppose some one day in September—God Bless you

Yours Affectionately MaryW. Shelley

PUBLISHED: Jones, #283. TEXT: MS., The Philip H. & A. S. W. Rosenbach Foundation.

1. The Lambs moved to Enfield in September 1827, remaining there until May 1833 (Lucas, *Charles Lamb*, II, 187).

2. Fanny Maria Kelly (1790–1882), actress, was an intimate friend of the Lambs. On 20 July 1819 Lamb proposed marriage to her, and despite her refusal they remained lifelong friends (Lucas, *Charles Lamb*, II, 12–15).

3. Lamb answered this letter on 26 July (Lamb, *Letters* [Lucas], III, 109–11).

TO JOHN HOWARD PAYNE Kentish Town Monday [24 July 1827]

Adieu, dear Payne—for a few weeks—I hope to be in better spirits when I see you again—and that some good fortune will attend us both—Take care of yourself—& preserve for me the friendly kindness you have ever shewn.

Thank you for the books—I will return them when I return

God bless You

Ys Very truly MS.

ADDRESS: J. Howard Payne Esq / 29 Arundel St. / Strand. POSTMARKS: (1) SO Kentish Tn; (2) 12. NOON. 12 / JY. 24 / 1827. PUBLISHED: Jones, #284 (almost complete). TEXT: MS., Washington University Library.

*TO JANE WILLIAMS HOGG[1] Mrs. Burry—Sompting near Shoreham—Sussex. 28 July 1827

Loveliest Janey—to thee tranquillity and health! How are you? You were far from well[2]—I do not fear any new disease, but how is the old one—does the bright lily raise its head lightly & cheerfully?—God send it may never in the slightest degree droop! it is—ma pero I am not sure that male eyes will not trace these lines, so I will endeavour to be as demure as an old maid—I wonder if you will understand the fitting supplement to that unfinished sentence. It is a pleasant thing to turn in one's mind's eye to a friend's sweet home & know that there is tranquillity there—I have now your drawing-room before me, with all its adornments—the kind & happy Giver of Good & the Fairy girl who has created the kindness—the happiness, the gift—the Good—the all. Is my pretty Filleule[3] with you & brave Med?—kiss both the dear children for me.

We are here calm & I trust contented—at least every outward & visible sign betokens peace. I did not tell you that Mary Hunt was to go with us—indeed it was only arranged the day before I saw you for the last time & then my head was full of—Sono veramente grato per questo piacere—incuramente mio procurero questo bene—The cosa fir querta[4]—I was in the Kentish Town Stage with M^arianne & she gave me so dreadful an account of Mary in so careless a tone, that I felt impelled to put in my feeble aid to endeavour to save a child of whose dispositions I have a favourable opinion—Doddy & Isabel[5] did not object—& she is in fact a great resource to us here being old enough to be the gouvernante to Percy & young enough to amuse herself in his game[ ] Monday we begin schooling—Heaven send that indeed we do—we intend it—& hope not to add another stone to the pavement of l'Inferno.

I am happy to find sweet Isabel well—she is anxious about D— [*Doddy*] from whom we had a most melancholy letter this morning—poor pet—she is very dreary & alone—She cannot visit you till she has quatrini & they arrive far slower than the snail of the story—still though circumstances must make her[x] [*p. 3, upside-down*] [x](I am stupid to have left these blanks to be so awkwardly fill up—it was thro' inadvertance) gloomy—good will come soon—Lord M. [*Morton*] is to be buried on Monday—the will will be read—& certainty will come.[6]

I must tell you all our plans hazard à merveille[7]—We arrived tired to death at Worthing at 4 on Tuesday—had tea—& slept—Worthing by the bye is a horror—the best dressed young ladies go about in scanty nankeen pelisses—straw pokes with pea green ribbons—& green crape veils made blue here & there as the sea [*p. 4, upside-down*] spray—on Wednesday morning we Fly it to Sompting with our traps—the lodgings were empty—we took them & established ourselves directly the people are civil & apparently honest—indeed all the villagers & country people are courteous à l'Italienne—we have beautiful walks—& shady embowered places where {we} sit & work & read. In truth so much am I delighted with my life here that I dwell more & more on a plan which I have long cherished—of living wholey in the country about 15 miles from town—Whitton certainly made out that Sir Tim would like this—I should see my family seldomer perhaps but far more comfortably—& even you—bright friend—but this is all <u>en</u> <u>l'air</u> as yet—I fear the future far—far too much to like to dwell on it.

Adieu then—take care of the prettiest, most graceful—blue-eyed Bride this world ever saw—For every body's sake love yourself tenderly—& think with gentle kindness of her <u>who for years</u> has been your devoted

Mary S—

Isabel says that she pictures your fairy home & its presiding Grace & wishes all good to it——

[*P. 4, side*] I have opened my letter to say that Isabel is M[rs] Douglas here—LHunt does not know my friend's name—but Mary's report will be of M[rs] D.— [*Douglas*]

ADDRESS: Mrs Hogg / Mrs Wilson / 8 Maida Place / Edgware Road—London. POSTMARKS: (1) SHOREHAM / PENNY POST; (2) A / 20 JY 30 / 1827; (3) 10. F.NOON. 10 / JY. 30 / 1827. UNPUBLISHED. TEXT: MS., Abinger MS.

1. The name and address on this letter indicate that the union of Jane Williams and Thomas Jefferson Hogg took place before Mary Shelley's departure from London.

2. This letter and Mary Shelley's letters of 7 and 22 August to Jane Williams Hogg make clear that the latter was pregnant. Although biographies of Jane Williams Hogg and Thomas Jefferson Hogg make no mention of a child born of this pregnancy, a daughter was born to the Hoggs c. November 1827 (unpublished Mary Shelley letter to Teresa Guiccioli, 4 December 1827, Pforzheimer Library). The Paddington Parish Registers, The Greater London Record Office, record that the child was baptized Mary Prudentia at St. Mary's Church, Paddington, on 21 January 1829, and was buried at St. Mary's at the age of eighteen months, on 23 May 1829. Hogg's mother and one sister were named Prudentia. (The Hoggs' second daughter, born in 1836, to whom Mary Shelley stood godmother, was named Sarah Prudentia, the first name after another of Hogg's sisters.) It is possible that the Hoggs' first daughter was named in honor of Mary Shelley.

3. "Goddaughter," that is, Dina.

4. "I am truly grateful for this pleasure—without effort I will gain this benefit—The thing was."

5. Mary Diana Dods (see 30 October [1826] to Alaric A. Watts, n. 2) and Isabel Robinson Douglas (see [19 February 1827], n. 1).

6. George Douglas, fifteenth Earl of Morton (b. 1761), died on 17 July 1827 and was buried on 30 July. Since he left no legitimate progeny, he was succeeded by his cousin, George Sholto Douglas, who became the sixteenth Earl of Morton (*The Scots Peerage*, ed. Sir James Balfour Paul [Edinburgh, 1909]). The will of the fifteenth Earl, dated 14 August 1824, provides an annuity of £100 per year for Mary Diana Dods and an equal annuity for her sister Georgiana Dods Carter "for the love favor and affection which I leave and bear to my reputed Daughters" (Scottish Record Office, RD5 / 345, p. 416).

7. "Risking wonder."

*To Jane Williams Hogg Sompting 7 August—1827

Your letter, my poor girl, is sufficiently distressing—How infinitely does the unkind Person of ours love to harrass & torment—Are you better when this reaches you? If not I really think you ought to have advice—& advice from an eminent man—for I am sure that some of your most painful symptoms would admit of cure. That dreadful irritability ending in tears which you describe, puts me in mind of my sufferings at Lerici[1]—but I think mine were greater—& they were accompanied by a depression of spirits, beyond any thing I had ever felt before, the gloomy shadow of the dark hour whose night still invelopes me. Let me hear if you are better,—for such a state of being cannot go on without some result.—

We are as happy here as a beautiful country sunshine & peace can make us. The children are divinely good—& amused by all the farming arrangements to use Isabel's universal word) that they see every where going on—harvest is hardly yet begun—and I never beheld it wear so splendid an appearance—the golden wheat laughs in the sunshine and the straw coloured barley waves its head languidly from its weight of grain—the many fine elms which decorate our village and its near lanes adorn these fields and enable us to stroll among them at all hours. Our nearest sea port is a little town called Lancing and we sit in solitude on its beach far away from Watering Place intruders. In the evening towards Sunset we ascend the upland behind our house & view an immense extent of Coast—While the boundary Sea stretching far round forms a large segment of a circle giving occular demonstration of the form of our globe—the clear blue of our skies stains its waters with a similar dye & the white sails of the numerous craft, play in the sunshine—the earth at our feet is clad with corn & sprinkled with villages & groves of trees—behind us the hills would add perfection to the scene were they covered with wood—but they are bare downs, yet though wild, uncultivated, & unlovely, they are still picturesque. Isabel's health does not permit her to enjoy these beauties to their full extent—she is afflicted with violent headachs & is frequently quite oppressed by fever—D's [*Doddy's*] letters do not medecine her ills, and her extreme anxiety concerning the future makes her restless—yet I flatter myself that she is much better here, than if she remained at Highgate.

What you say of my Country plan has reason in [it]—Winter & lack of friends are dreadful evils—but I do not [ ] how I shall escape these in London. We have long ago deci[ded] that winter is even worse than summer in town. I have no friends there—& neither spirits nor means to seek them; those I had are changed and gone—long ago I said to you—fairest—that though clinging to your affection as my only good—it would no longer be what it was when we defied every peril—& were wet thro' & thoroughly uncomfortable in company—laughing the while as if we were kittens in clover—Happy days those, my Janey—you are too prosperous for them now—& prosperity & I have an adamantine wall between us. I intimately feel that my best hope of the only good I ask, peace—will only visit me in such a scene as this—even though its ugly cover turn its pretty one away, & Prosperine becomes the ⟨six⟩ nine Months bride of Pluto.

I am glad Jeff liked the purse, nor wonder that he was pleased at fancying I gave it him—because we have that dear gift from heaven that we are pleased at receiving kindnesses even from those for whom we feel no very enthusiastic affection. Tell him I pray heartily [*cross-written*] that his happiness & joys may be greater than Jobs after his temptation—& keep to yourself if you will the secret that the a{r}dor of my prayer arises from the indissoluble link now existing between your happiness & his.

I have not heard from the Hunts—so pray send me news about them—Isabel is writing to her Papa beside me—she says—if you wont close your letter till I have finished mine I will say a thousand pretty things to lovely Janey—but now—And she turns her bright eyes, a little clouded the while, again on her paper—poor baby how she hates her task. I am delighted with your account of my pretty Dina—pray console dear Doddy for[2] she is very sorrowful—& has reason to be so—or has had, I trust I may say—for I hope by this time the contents of the will have been communicated to her & are favourable[3]—but we have not heard as we expected this Morning.

Adieu, Most graceful of the daughters of Eve—be also the happiest & think with kindness of your

MS.

ADDRESS: Mrs Jefferson Hogg / Mrs Wilson / Maida Place. Edgeware Road / London. POSTMARKS: (1) SHOREHAM / PENNY POST; (2) A / 8 AU 8 / 1827; (3) 10. F NO[ ] / AU[ ] / 1827. UNPUBLISHED. TEXT: MS., Abinger MS., Bodleian Library.

1. A reference to the miscarriage Mary Shelley suffered at Lerici on 16 June 1822.

2. A blank of one and a half inches is left, perhaps for the seal. Generally, however, Mary Shelley did not take this precaution, which explains why some words were torn from her letters.

3. See 28 July 1827, n. 7.

*TO JANE WILLIAMS HOGG Sompting—15 August—1827

Alas, my sweet girl—how very unkind is our person to us—Your state of ill health weighs heavily on me—I can not endure to think that the Lily of the World droops—and that any thing but happiness should dwell in your blue eyes. Pray, pray take care of yourself—no wet walks to Hampstead—no yielding to the slowness of others, till coaches are lost—&c—remember all depends upon care:

Ah! how could our wrong Person have the heart to take from us the World's Splendour[1]—What a dreadful event for all & every part of habitable earth—I can conceive of no substitution that can compensate in any way for the loss we have sustained.—And foreign nations will feel it even more—for Brougham & others may continue, under the King's present liberal system, the improvements with Canning commenced—but his foreign policy cannot but feel deeply the failure of his tact & knowledge of the subject.—

In the midst of melancholy a letter from D. [*Doddy*] gives us some life —Small indeed is the thing done—[*full line scratched out*] nor do I exactly know what future course of action can be founded on it—but in some way I suppose the plan of going abroad will be put in execution—when or how must be decided when D. & Isabel meet—as yet the mere fact of the continuance of the Annuity and a possibility of something more years hence, is all we know.[2] But certainty succeeding to the worst doubts, is so delightful, that we have hailed this small good with pleasure.

For myself—You say I look forward gloomily & I do. I cannot endure to return to the Kentish Town mode of things & in spite of all, I cling to my country plan—where pleasures that I love—the sights & splendours of earth & sky—will come to my door—instead of my being forced to overcome my laziness to seek them—As yet my schemes are in embryo—but will it not be a pleasant change for you in your three months widowhood[3] to come to me in my cot & enjoy country pleasures?—At any rate I shall remain <u>in</u> London until after the Christmas holidays—when Percy's school must be fixed upon, & I shall remove to its vicinity.

We have had clouds & rain succeeding our brilliant days & divine moonlight nights—but the rain was soft & warm—and walking yesterday night after it had ceased, though the clouds were thick & dark—we found the change delightful—& the south west wind balmy though languid.—The harvest is now getting in—so that we are losing some of our beauties;—by degrees the Bride of the Sun will throw aside her nuptial ornaments—till she assume the dark weeds of her widowhood—and the thing I fear, winter —will enwrap her.——

I have had no letters from any one except th[e] Guiccioli. She writes kindly—& speaks with great sor[row] of the loss of her Brother—which preys on her father's health. The Pope had ordered her to join her husband —which she did, but he was so intolerable in every way, that she obtained from the Santo Padre—another decree of divorce & they are separated for ever. She says she thinks of us both very often & desires tanti saluti alla gentile Mrs W. [*Williams*] ——No letter from Trelawny! What does this mean?—Have you written to Claire? I have so very many foreign letters to write that their number frightens me, & I write none.——

I wish I heard that Dina were with you—though till you gain a little strength I fear even the gentle darling would be too much for you—Give her a kiss from Marraine—& one also to my frank hearted Meddy—— Remember me in the kindest way to poor dear Mammina—Ask her if there is any thing I can get for her from Brighton. Good news of the Shorediches is I fear an hopeless concern—Remember me to the Clints especially Signor Georgio.[4]

I have no news from any one—the G's [*Godwins*] are al solito W. [*William*] is in the country.——I have had one short note from Marianne, Harding has some hopes of Swinburne[5]——Let me hear from you soon—my lovely one—for I am all anxiety on your account—the more that peace being now around me—I wait in fear for a tempest—from which Messer Domine guard me God bless you, my bright beauty—Isabel repeats God bless her—love

Ever Y^s—MS.

ADDRESS: Mrs Jefferson Hogg / 8 Mrs Wilson / Maida Place / Edgeware Road—London. POSTMARKS: (1) [SHO]REHAM / [PE]NNY POST; (2) A / 16 AU 1[6] / 1827; (3) 10. F.NOON. 10 / AU. 16 / 1827. UNPUBLISHED. TEXT: MS., Abinger MS., Bodleian Library.

1. George Canning died on 8 August (see [?–] 22 March [1824]).
2. See 28 July 1827, n. 7.
3. When Hogg would go to the circuit courts in Northumberland and Durham (Norman, *After Shelley*, p. xii).
4. See [5 August 1826] to Mrs. Clint, n. 1.
5. Swinburne Hunt died on 22 September 1827.

TO WILLIAM WHITTON At Mrs Burry's Sompting near Shoreham Sussex 15 August 1827

Sir

I should not write so soon, but that I fear, that if I deferred, my letter would not find you in Town. I am for the present in a country lodging, where of course credit is out of the question, and the most serious consequences would ensue from any delay in my quarterly allowance. According to the arrangement you were so kind to make, on the First of September one will be due to me. Shall I before hand send up a receipt in the form you will dictate—and will you as soon as due either be so good as to enclose a cheque to Mr Peacock or send me a bill on a Brighton Banker. Excuse the anxiety I must naturally feel on the subject, when punctuality in receiving this payment, is my only resource for life.

May I ask how Sir Timothy is—& if his spirits have recovered the late dreadful shock?[1]—When you see or write to him, I should feel extremely obliged to you if you would express from me my grateful thanks for his attentions to my poor boy and his kindness towards myself.

Percy is very well indeed—The fresh country air and sea baths have added to his look of perfect health. This makes me the less regret a short delay in putting him to school. Mr Peacock has meanwhile promised to make enquiries concerning one; My plan is that it should be at a short distance from town and that I should reside close to it—this will be quite necessary at first while he is a day scholar—& afterwards I should not choose to be at any distance from him.—

I am sure your sense of my unprotected situation will lead you readily to excuse my troubling you—and I feel secure that you will add to the obligations I already owe you, that of a speedy & favourable answer

I am, Sir
Your Obedient Servant
MaryShelley

ADDRESS: William Whitton Esq / King's Road / Bedford Row / London. POSTMARKS: (1) SHOREHAM / PENNY POST; (2) A / 16 AU 16 / 18[ ]. ENDORSED: 15th August 1827 / Mrs Shelley. PUBLISHED: Jones, #285. TEXT: MS., Bodleian Library (MS., Shelley, Adds., c. 6, ff. 45–46).

1. Possibly the death of George Canning (see 15 August 1827 to Jane Williams Hogg).

*TO TERESA GUICCIOLI Sompting—Sussex 20 Agosto [August]—1827

Mia Cara Contessina

Con quanto piacere ricevè la carissima vostra lettera! Era pure trista il lungo silenzio fra di noi—nato non so come, ma che non finiva mai. Mi stimo felice che abbiate la bontà d'assicurarmi che dalla parte vostra sia caggionata dalle circonstanze sole—e che mi conservate la preziosa vostra Amicizia. Cara Amica—le vostre disgrazie, mi toccano sul vivo. Povero Pierino mi fù caro come fratello vostro, come compagno ultimo di Byron—le sue proprie qualità poi commandavano la mia stima ed affezione—me trattò sempre con somma gentilezza—Che colpa terribile! che fatal inimicizia del destino! Dite pure il vero, mia Cara—la vita è una pena faticosa—e la dolce pace, per la quale sospiro, non si trova che dopo passando tra la notte della tomba, a trovaremo il quel soggiorno dilettevole ove ora dimorano i nostri Cari. Dovrei consolarvi—e piango vosco—Compatite se la simpitia vera tien luogo della consolazione.

Pure viviamo in questo mondo;—e durando la vita, bisogna che le interessi della vita, almeno quelli degli anni, occupassino la Nostra attenzione. Perciò vi raccontero, Mia Cara, il cambiamento che gli anni ha fatto nella mia situazione—vi rallegrerete che sia piùttosto buono—L'anno scorso morì il figlio maggior di Shelley; in consequenza il mio Percy è divenuto erede del titolo e della maggior parte dei beni del suo Nonno. Il Nonno l'ha veduto questa primavera—fù incantato dalla beltà e gentilezza di mio figlio—[?parese], e disse che lo fece rammentare di quel che fu Shelley nella sua fanciullezza. E contento che stasse [ ] meco, e mi dà da vivere. La sua età avanzata e la debole sua [ ]dere che non molti anni passeranno avante che godessi l'indipendenza—se pero sta sempre buono che viva mill'anni—Voler la sua morte è un peccato della l'anima mia sara innocente. Intanto non vuol permettermi di lasciare Inghilterra—si vanta d'essere "a true Englishman"—vuol che il nipote non errasse da tal virtuosa strada—ed io poi sono prigionera. Subito che fù stabilito questo affare lasciai Kentish Town. Sono qui per i bagni di mare per Percy. Il paese è piccolo assai, ma piacevole i contorni belli—la campagna ricca—abbondante—i contadini cortesi—e la vista del mare dà magnificenza ad un paesaggio che altramente lo manca. Sto qui con una mia Amica che amo ⟨passionamente⟩ teneramente e che sente per me la più vivace amicizia. Dio volesse che potessimo stare sempre insieme, e nella di lei società troverei qualche rimedio ai miei molti mali—Ma fra poche settimane verra il suo marito—partiranno per Parigi—quando io tristissimamente tornero a Londra. Come compagna per il mio Percy menara meco Mary Hunt chi è divenuta molta dolce ed amabile.

Non mi parlate nella vostra lettera dell'Amico Signor Hogg—nè del suo amore per la gentile Williams—pero avete saputo da lui le sue speranze—ormai adempite—Felice! la sorte sua mi pare troppo fortunato per questo sventurato Mondo. Ma come l'ama veramente è degno del dono che Dio gli ha dato. Era lungo tempo avante che essa costante alla memoria del suo Odoardo poteva condursi ad acconsentire ai di lui desideri—si fece la sposa questa Primavera passata. Dimmorano in Londra—sicche egli come Avvocato è necessitato di star ivi quasi sempre. Godo della sua felicità—ma non son punto mossa a eseguire l'esempio suo. Cara Amica, come potesse la moglie di Shelley degnare amore gli u[omin]i d'oggidi. Forse ci sono dei degni, ma non si fanno mirare—e per[ciò] eccomi sempre la Shelley—e sulla tomba mia spero che sara scritto questo nome diletto.

La seconda vostra lettera non mi è venuto alle mani. Moore, uomo impazientessimo, sta inqueto fin'che arriva.[1] Bisogno a perdonare la sua poca pazienza intorno a questo oggetto—dà tanto pregio alla vostra amabile aiutanza, e si stima cosi fortunata che voi lo ne stimate degno. Ricevè una sua lettera ieri—Vi saluta e vi ringrazia di core per la promessa—Forse avete trovate che la storia Vostra si tira un lungo—Sara meglio allora (se non sono spedite quando riceverete questa lettera) di scriverla sopra larghi fogli mandandomi una foglia alla volta— —Scritto di fuore "Single Sheet". Quanto piacere reco dalla Vostra compiacenza. Faccio un bene al Nobile Amico Nostro—e poi a Moore—che come attaccato al nostro Byron—come uomo affatto da bene—come Poeta, dotato di un genio impregibile, mi è caro.—Egli sta quasi sempre in Campagna colla moglie; cosi lo vedo poco. Ma durando la rare sue visite a Londra vien spesso a trovarmi.—

Siete adunque ai bei Bagni di Lucca—Che sito dilettevo[le] Quanto son romanzeche quelle montagne orne da Castagni—irr[igate] da torrente—quel rumor eterno del Serchio—le balze verde—le pietre enorme—i bagni medesimi cosi salutevole—Veramente è un Paradiso proprio. Stetti ivi quando primo venivamo in Italia—ai Bagni di Villa—mi rammento dei terribili tuoni ch'ivi si facevano sentire—tremo per voi, Cara—Ah! i tuoni non ci sono qui—quella voce orrenda—quando raramente la sento, mi parla del Paese lontano—amato—sacro—giacche lo calcò lui che piango sempre—che sara sempremai l'oggetto dei miei dolorosi sospiri

Pensate Mia Cara Amica che le Vostre lettere sono per me un vero bene—Conservatimi la vostra amicizia e forse il cielo pietoso quando meno l'aspetto scioglerera la mia catena e mi permettera di respirare l'aria dolce di Italia—Sono più a malinconica che il solito ora—che la Morte del nostro dotato Canning mi sta sul core—come si fosse stato amico mio—Sapete che ha lodato il Mio Frankenstein nel House of Commons nei termini onorevole[2]—gratissimi a me—A povera Inghilterra—orbo Mondo—che disgrazia irreparabile e per voi la perduta di questo grand'uomo.

Non dubitate, Cara, niente sara fatta colle Vostre lettere che non farete voi stessa—se avete alcuni di Byron—che permetterete d'essere stampate—o altre suoi manuscritti Moore vi sara grato—Addio—La posta va via—

Indrizatte a me come ultimamente—44 Gower Place Gower [ ]

Hai letto Il mio Last Man—Troverai in Lord Raymond ed il Conte Adrian Ritratti deboli ma mi lusingo per voi non dispiacente di B. e S— ma questo è un segreto Addio

Mi ripeto Vostra A^{ca} Aff^{ma} M Shelley

[*Translation*]

My Dear Contessina

With how much pleasure did I receive your dearest letter! The long silence between us was really deplorable—begun I don't know how, but never ending. I consider myself fortunate that you have the goodness to assure me that on your part it was caused only by circumstances—and that you keep your precious friendship for me. Dear Friend—your misfortunes cut me to the quick. Poor Pierino, he was dear to me as your brother, as the last companion of Byron—his own qualities also commanded my esteem and affection—he always treated me with the utmost courtesy—What a terrible blow! what mortal enmity of fate! Indeed tell the truth, by Dear—life is a difficult punishment—and the sweet peace, for which I long, one does not find until after passing beyond the night of death, when we will find that delightful residence where now our Dear ones dwell. You must console yourself—and I cry with you—Pardon if true sympathy takes the place of consolation.

Yet we live in this world;—and as long as life continues it is necessary that the concerns of life, at least those of age, occupy our attention. Therefore I will tell you, My Dear, the change that the years have made in my situation—you will be glad that it is rather good—Last year Shelley's eldest son died; in consequence my Percy became the heir to the title and to the major portion of the property of his Grandfather. His Grandfather saw him this spring—he was enchanted by the beauty and gentleness of my son— [?] and he said that he caused him to remember how Shelley was in his childhood. He is satisfied that he stay [ ] with me, and he gave me living expenses. His advanced age and his weakened [ ] that not many years will pass before I will enjoy my independence—if however he continues to remain fit, so that he lives a thousand years—To wish for his death is a sin from which my soul will be innocent. Meanwhile he did not want to permit me to leave England—He is proud of being "a true Englishman"—wants his grandson not to stray from this virtuous road —and I then am a prisoner. As soon as this affair was settled I left Kentish Town. I am here for the sea bathing for Percy. The town is very small, but pleasant the surroundings are beautiful—the countryside rich—abundant— the country people courteous—and the view of the sea gives a grandeur to a landscape that otherwise would lack it. I am here with a friend of mine who I dearly love and who feels the liveliest affection for me. God grant that we might stay together always, and in her company I might find some remedy for my many sorrows—But within a few weeks her husband is coming—they are leaving for Paris—at which time I will very sorrowfully return to London. As companion for my Percy I am taking Mary Hunt with me who has grown very sweet and charming.

In your letter you don't speak of our friend Signor Hogg—nor of his love for the gentle Williams—but you knew from him of his hopes—now realized—Fortunate! his fate seems to me too lucky for this unhappy World. But as he truly loves her he is worthy of the gift that God has given him. It was a long time before she, faithful to the memory of her Edward, was able to bring herself to assent to his wishes—she became his wife this past Spring. They are residing in London—since he as a Lawyer is required to be there almost always. I rejoice in her happiness—but I am not at all moved to follow her example. Dear Friend, how could the wife of Shelley condescend to love the men of today. Maybe there are some who are worthy, but they don't show themselves—and therefore here I am always Signora Shelley—and I hope that this beloved name will be written on my tomb.

Your second letter has not reached my hands. Moore, a very impatient man, is uneasy until its arrival.[1] You must excuse his lack of patience concerning this subject—he places so much value on your gracious help, and he thinks himself so fortunate that you consider him deserving. He received one of your letters yesterday—He greets you and thanks you from his heart for your promise—Perhaps you have found that your story is very long—It will be better in that case (if you have not sent them when you receive this letter) to write it on large sheets sending me one sheet at a time— —with "Single Sheet" written outside. What pleasure your kindness causes me. I am doing good for Our Illustrious Friend—and then for Moore— who as one fond of our Byron—as quite a good man—as a Poet, endowed with an inestimable talent, is dear to me.—He is almost always in the Country with his wife; therefore I see little of him. But during his infrequent visits to London he often comes to see me.—

Well then you are now at the beautiful Baths of Lucca—What a delightful spot—How romantic those mountains adorned with chestnut trees are —watered by the streams—that eternal noise of the Serchio—the green cliffs—the enormous rocks—the baths themselves so health-giving—Truly it is a real Paradise. I was there when we first arrived in Italy—at the Baths of Villa—I recall the terrible thunderbolts that one hears there—I tremble for you, Dear—Ah! the thunderbolts are not here—that terrifying noise—when rarely I hear it, it speaks to me of that faraway Country—beloved—sacred—since it was tread upon by him for whom I mourn eternally—who will always be the object of my grievous laments.

Consider My Dear Friend that your letters are a true good for me—Keep your friendship for me and perhaps when I least expect it the merciful heaven will unleash my chain and permit me to breathe the sweet air of Italy—I am more melancholy than usual now—since the Death of our learned Canning weighs on my heart—as if he had been a friend of mine—Did you know that he praised my Frankenstein in honorable terms in the House of Commons[2]—extremely pleasing to me—To poor England—bereft World—what an irreparable misfortune the loss of this great man is for you.

Do not fear, Dear, nothing will be done with Your letters except what you will do yourself—if you have some of Byron's—that you will allow to be published—or other manuscripts of his, Moore would be grateful—Addio—the mail is leaving

Address me as the last time—44 Gower Place Gower [ ]

Have you read my Last Man—You will find in Lord Raymond and Count Adrian faint portraits but I hope not displeasing to you of B. and S—but this is a secret Addio

I repeat myself Your Affectionate Friend M Shelley

ADDRESS: Italy / Alla Sua Eccellenza / La Contessa Guiccioli / Ferma in Posta / Ravenna. POSTMARKS: (1) SHOREHAM / PENNY POST; (2) A / PAID / 21 AU 21 / 1827; (3) F27 / 276; (4) No 2; (5) ANGLETERRE; (6) CORRISPZA ESTERA DA GENOVA; (7) S.E.O.F. / BOLOGNA / [ ] DEI LE POST [ ]. UNPUBLISHED. TEXT: MS., Pforzheimer Library. TRANSLATION: Ricki B. Herzfeld.

1. Moore wrote to Mary Shelley on 17 August 1827: "Pray, urge the Guiccioli for me. I have already experienced the good effects of your application to her, for Mr Barry of Genoa writes to me that he thinks she is much inclined to contribute materials to my work" (Moore, *Letters*, II, 574).

2. On 16 March 1824 (see [?–]22 March [1824]).

*TO JANE WILLIAMS HOGG — Sompting. 22. August—1827

That you are better, and that you are content, my lovely Girl, is delightful news to me—I have watched with anxiety the progress of your feelings at this crisis—I hailed with pleasure the satisfaction you felt when the mist, fear had spread before the p{r}ospect, cleared away, & brightness shone forth—the great thing to be desired now is, that your mind should awaken to its full activity, that you should find pleasant occupation & recreation. I almost fear that this will hardly be, till you are in an house of your own, with your children about you;—then, in a very short time, you—most beautiful of Loadstones, will attract round you an atmosphere of elegance, which the few you desire to know will delight to respire—drear November[1] and its fatal event once past, and my chrysalis will expand into a butterfly

—I have no hopes for myself—for you my hopes are high—why then say that I have none for myself—if you are happy, my best hopes revive.—Still, as far as I am personally concerned, I cling to my country plan, & shall at least try it—I look back with disgust to my Kentish Town life—but I think I can arrange a mode of being in the country, which will give me the best chance for peace—the only blessing I ask—If I find myself mistaken, I can but confess my error & reform—all we are told that Messer Domine asks of mortals, though they are seldom so merciful towards each other.

We have indeed lost the best part of the year—it is agreable enough now—the showers intermit sufficiently for us to walk on rainy days—& on fine ones, there is a balminess in the air, & a freshness in the sensations it inspires, that breathes of health—But I deeply regret for myself that we have bid farewell to those heats in which I luxuriate—& feel that every moment is full of Enjoyment—God forgive you, Jeff will say—& indeed for the sake of others, I must own that my pleasure is sinful—Isabel finds great benefit from the change—the warmth makes her bilious & ill—lately too she has suffered from oppressive headachs—I do not understand her maladies & cannot prescribe—what cures her one day seems to create the evil the next—she is now abstaining almost entirely from meat, and as her headachs are better, this may be a good plan. Our lives are the embodyings of quiet—our only peep at the world is when we take the children to bathe at Worthing—this place is filling, and flounces & hats have succeeded to nankeen pelisses & pokes—but there is neither elegance nor fashion—a pretty girl or two there are—their names Robson & Meacock—basta poi—si sa la radice di tal pianta[2]—Not one Man have we seen, except an ugly Guardsman one day, who appeared as dropt from the clouds—& vanished like a meteor. For the rest I read a little Greek, write walk—work—and the days fly.—We have very pretty walks, & extend them each day—making voyages of discovery, and always finding our trouble compensated by what we find.

I am glad to hear Doddy talks of visiting us soon—Isabel [ ] delighted with her promises of going abroad—and I suppose that there [is] small doubt but that they will soon cross to France—I should call your news of the Shorediches very good—were good, good to them—at any rate it puts off the evil hour, & that is much in our philosophy. My affectionate Compliments to Mammia—I sincerely join you in lamenting the impracticability of that unattainable good—Hunt's society—⟨as well love one⟩ I do not hear from them—I wrote praising Mary—the poor child is perfectly uneducated, & giddy to a wonder, but perfectly docile, & has not displayed the slightest movement of ill temper since she has been with us—she is affectionate—& while she thinks of it, eager to please—surely much may be made of such a disposition.—I wait for my September money & then will write to Claire, Trelawny, Tom &c—I wish you would write to the former without delay—pray do—or I must without the smallest drop of milk—No news—no news!—Trelawny in the winter—a back way to the most graceful & inefficient of Conjunctions—the lovely sufferer's hour of trial past such are the hopes you hold out—this last will probably be the only one of the three goods that we shall achieve—but Messer Domine shall receive from me thanksgiving infinite for that one—Every blessing attend you—Jeff is included in that prayer now of course—Isabel says Amen—Take every care of the divine Fairy for the sake of, among many

MS.—

ADDRESS: Mrs Jefferson Hogg / 8 Mrs Wilson / Maida Place—Edgware Road / London. POSTMARKS: (1) SHOREHAM / PENNY POST; (2) A / 2 [ ] AU 2 [ ] / 1827; (3) 10 F.NOON. 10 / AU. 23 / 1827. UNPUBLISHED. TEXT: MS., Abinger MS., Bodleian Library.

1. When Jane Williams Hogg expected to give birth.
2. "Enough then—one knows the root of such a plant."

*TO JOHN HOWARD PAYNE — Sompting Near Shoreham—Sussex—
22. August. [1827]

My dear Payne

When I saw you last I was so overwhelmed by the sense of recent misfortune—so perfectly dispirited by a last dire instance of the enmity of fate,[1] that I in vain endeavoured to shake off the appearance of sorrow—my only resource was to seek from your kindness, a pardon for the silence & dulness, from which I could not extricate myself. The same kind heart will, I know rejoice that I am again at peace. It is true the evil I deplored still exists & must continue, and when I return to town I shall be again subjected to its influence but while I am here, I am at peace—the beauty and seclusion of this spot are paradise to me, and I live from day, happy, if I could always live thus;—the future is my only pain—I put it off, & seek to forget it as much as I can. I have a friend with me here, a lady of beauty & talents, & above all, to my wounded heart, warmly attached to me—I have my boy, and Leigh Hunt's daughter—& we form altogether a loving family, in whose circle I revive from wretchedness.—Having escaped from the selfishness of sorrow, my sympathies expand, and I become eager to know the fortunes of those for whom I have an affection. I hope you believe that I am deeply interested in all that concerns yourself—tell me how you are getting on—Whether you have as yet entered on your projected work from which I augur great success—I am anxious also about your health, which has by no means recovered from its late shock.—I hope you really attend to it—for all of good depends on it.—Perhaps new plans & prospects have opened on you—pray let me hear from you on all these subjects.—Of friends too, do not forget to tell me—Soon after coming here, I had a kind letter from Charles Lamb—he is deep in concocting a farce,[2] from which in despair he thinks of discarding the plot—how curious are these divisions of talents with which we mortals are endowed—one would think the Creator formed us thus, to prove more decisively that we are social animals—& yet we, as Rousseau says, turning his good to our evil, make it the source of perpetual reprehension—& instead of each bringing his mite to help the other, we quarrel all round, because they are not as we are.

How would you like my solitude?—There is no gentry about—our villagers are simple & courteous—and the style of country is as placid & unpretending as themselves—Looking down on it from the Uplands, one would hardly call it beautiful, were it not for the wide embracing sea, into whose bosom our nook of land creeps so that we seem to have got to the very uttermost verge of the world—a few steps more, & one could get out of it—a tempting thought!—since of my own will, I must not yield to it, I only wish fortune would do the deed for me—for though now, life is pleasant enough, the future is so replete with the promise of evil, that to escape from it, I would willingly betake myself to the last best remedy—But that must not be.

I have heard nothing of William since I left town—have you any news of any Friends?—Is Washington Irving's book yet announced?[3]—Do you ever see any thing of Newton?—who says I do not like pictures, because he found me sitting turned from his—I readily forgive the slander from its occasion—when he next sees me at the Exhibition I hope I shall be more luckily employed.

Do you not lament our miserable loss? You Americans lo[o]k disdainfully on our European politics, yet you must regret the Ma[n] who might have regenerated our liberty, and given to the world a gl[ ] that without him, it will never attain.—I love & admire the King for his endeavours to fulfill Canning's wishes[4]—but how can a Work man achieve a work when his matchless instrument is broken?

Adieu—I hope this little surprise will find you prosperous, and that you will welcome it as the gentle Shadow Of One, who will always be delighted to hear of your good fortune

Yours Most Truly
MaryShelley

ADDRESS: J. Howard Payne Esq / 29 Arundel St. Strand / London. POSTMARKS: (1) SHOREHAM / PENNY POST; (2) A / 23 AU 23 / 1827. UNPUBLISHED. TEXT: MS., The Philip H. & A. S. W. Rosenbach Foundation.

1. On 13 July Mary Shelley wrote in her Journal: "My friend has proved false & treacherous! Miserable discovery—for four years I was devoted to her—& I earned only ingratitude. . . ." Mary Shelley had learned that Jane Williams Hogg had spread stories among their mutual friends of the Shelleys' life in Italy that cast Mary Shelley in an unfavorable light. In her letter to Jane Williams Hogg of [?14 February 1828] Mary Shelley expressed her deep disappointment. That letter also gives details of the cause of the estrangement and Mary Shelley's reasons for continuing their friendship. The seven-month interval between Mary Shelley's discovery of Jane Williams Hogg's gossip and the confrontation between the friends was perhaps the result of Mary Shelley's concern for Jane Williams Hogg's extremely poor health during her pregnancy and a lengthy recovery period after the birth of Mary Prudentia.

2. Lamb's letter of 26 July described his "tragi-comic" farce and commented: "I want some Howard Paine to sketch a skeleton of artfully succeeding scenes through a whole play, as the courses are arranged in a cookery book . . ." (Lamb, *Letters* [Lucas], III, 110).

3. Washington Irving sent the first volume of *A. History of the Life and Voyages of Christopher Columbus* (London: John Murray, 1828) to John Murray on 29 July 1827 (Irving, *Journals and Notebooks*, III, xxiii).

4. On 6 July 1827 the Treaty of London—which provided that if the Turks refused an armistice in their war with the Greeks, allied forces would support the Greek cause—was concluded between Britain, France, and Russia. On 16 August the allies demanded an armistice from Turkey. When the Turks refused, the allies instructed their naval forces to prevent supplies from reaching Turkish forces in Greece.

*To Jane Williams Hogg Sompting—26. August [1827]

My pretty Janey—Our unkind M.D. [*Messer Domine*] has taken a freak into his head, that is beyond measure annoying—The people here have let their lodgings over our heads—& having let them superexcellently well—they have paid no attention—neither to our comfort, nor the legality of their proceedings—& yesterday night told us that their new lodgers came in on Wednesday—they are grasping people, & will gain by these latter about four times as much as they do by us—In consequence we must go tomorrow to look for lodgings, & remove without milk—can any thing be so orribile scelerato & all that?——More over this is my situation—I wrote to Whitton to tell him where I was—& where to send my quarter—he has promised that the First of September past, he will send—my quatrini, if I had continued here, would have lasted excellently well—but the additional pound or two of seeking lodgings & moving—& paying up all here, will drain me quite dry—& I shall have nothing to begin with. Will you ask Jefferson to lend me £10 till my quarter is paid. Since before he so readily & kindly complied with my request I confide in his doing so now—Ask him to send it by return of post—that is—you will receive this letter tomorrow, after he has left you—although I should like it, yet it will hardly be possible for you to send it tomorrow—sent on Tuesday, I shall receive it early Wednesday Morning, before the hour of our migration. It is necessary I should have it on that day—because there are no other lodgings in Sompting—& we shall perhaps remove some miles off—& therefore it will be impossible to put off payments here—We resolve to go to a Farm House, & shall take the direction of Arundel in looking for one—the spot in our minds eye is between Arundel & Little Hampton both being ten miles from here—& four miles apart—Si vedra[1]—I am annoyed beyond measure & so is poor Isabel; having given up every other hope but that of peace—is it not hateful that we should be deprived of that? This 1827 has been a complete year of ill luck—to unhouse—to disarrange all ones arrangements—even the extra expence—is all a wordless annoyance, which you will understand & pity.

I hope I shall not inconvenience Jeff—in a week or two he will be repaid certainly—& I trust wholly to his kindness—as che fare se non mi lo manda non saprei[2]

Pity the poor girl, who for the life of her, ca[nnot] get dry land for the sole of her foot—nor quiet for the soul of her body—the diavolo take these money loving Burrys—and tranquillity & movelessness take, I pray, your tempest shaken

MS.

Remember, Beauty—I am wholly dependant on this remittance & am anxious till it arrives che far senza[3] I have no idea—do let there be {no} delay

ADDRESS: Mrs Jefferson Hogg / 8 Mrs Wilson / Maida Vale, Paddington / London. POSTMARKS: (1) SHOREHAM / PENNY POST; (2) A / 27 AU 27 / 1827; (3) 10. F.NOON. 10 / AU 27 / 1827. UNPUBLISHED. TEXT: MS., Abinger MS., Bodleian Library.

1. "I'll see."
2. "I do not know what to do if he does not send it to me."
3. "What to do without it."

*TO JANE WILLIAMS HOGG Sompting—28—August—1827

A thousand thanks for your promptitude, my very kind Janey, which I hasten to acknowledge—& to tell you the course of our movements—We had enjoyed the real country too well, to be able to bear the idea of a frequented or a desolate sea-port—We heard of a pretty & cheap lodging about a mile this side of Arundel—& thither Isabel & I went yesterday—but it was let—We went on to Arundel, & took lodgings—the only ones there, in the town—which is ancient, small, picturesque—our lodgings are much better than these—& cheaper—so I hope to cover the expence of moving. The only inconvenience is, that we cannot go into them till next Monday—non c'era rimedio[1]—so we stay from Wednesday till Monday at the Cabarêt of this village,—you may direct here therefore to me all this week.—I think when the annoyance of moving is over, we may profit by the change—our windows look over the country at Arundel—so we shall hardly feel ourselves in a town—& it is too small a one to cramp our walks. Here we love the country for rusticity's sake—the cornfields, trees, lanes, & hedges—but at Arundel we have something more—the picturesque Castle—the wooded heights—the river—the woods themselves, combine to form scenery of the loveliest description. we shall be four miles from Little Hampton—and the whole country is interspe{r}sed with park land.—Such, at a first view are the pregii[2] of our new abode—add to which a school for Percy, which is a gran' bene—& I expect we shall be very comfortable.

Isabel desires thanks for your prescriptions—If her illness were merely headachs, I think its cure might be found in diet;—but she suffers extremely from Asthma—the purer air of France may relieve this—but I think she ought to have advice—Walking up hill, or against the wind—or walking fast at all, gives her intense pain in her chest—let her rest a little & she is perfectly well—this must be asthmatic—her general health has been better these last days—She enjoyed greatly our excursion to Arundel yesterday—the day indeed was fatto inver per noi[3]—a cool wind, & a brilliant but not burning sun—we walked over to Worthing at 8 in the morning, & took a Fly-ette—(you know the thing I mean) for 12/d for the day—it took us along the road you know, past Castle Goring[4] to Arundel—& then round by Little Hampton, home—nothing could be more beautiful than the country which improves continually to Arundel—& then it seems to converge into a semicircle of not very high but precipitous and wood covered hills—these have in their very bosom, the old romantic Castle & at their foot the straggling town—the Arun flows from the open ravine they form, and meadow or park land is spread along the plain.

I am I confess very glad to hear that dear good Jeff does not leave you—Your weak health & your uncertain arrangements make it very necessary that you should not be alone—I wrote not the word fatal with my Sibylline spirit, but in the Dillonic[5] meaning of fate-full—The power of Destiny I feel every day pressing more & more on me, & I yield myself a slave to it, in all except my moods of mind, which I endeavour to make independant of her, & thus to wreath a chaplet, where all is not cypress, in spite of the Eumenides. I am glad the vision of Kentish Town has past [ ] for though I so deeply & delightedly enjoyed your society there, ye[t] it was on the whole a disturbed and unreal dream—& one's many anxieties pursued one inveterately throughout—I could not return to the like again.—By the way I have written to poor dear Claire—As I wrote, my heart melted within me at the thought of her dreariness, and I was impelled (& do not repent my impulse) to make her, if she could not contrive an Italian journey, a cordial invitation to share my fortunes here—the grand annoyance of Mrs G. [*Godwin*] will be neutralized, if we are in the country—Do you think she will come?—If she pass the winter at St. Petersburgh—it will be easy to sail thence direct for London.—

I shall hear from you in a day or two with the other £5—let me know what news of the Hunts—it is three weeks since I had Marianne's note—but this is only al solito—otherwise I should fear for Swinburne.—I am glad for pretty Isabel's sake that D. [*Doddy*] now seriously thinks of les culottes[6]—I do not expect this person—as Isa names D—for two or three weeks—

[*Cross-written*] Take care of {your} sweet self—be happy—& contrive to nicher yourself speedily when you may take Dina to your arms again & build around you a fairy bower where all the Princes of the earth might come to admire the perfection of grace & beauty—& which too happy Jeff. will call his own. Love to Mammina—the children are delightfully well

God bless the desires of your heart prays Your MS.———

What an horrible affair of poor Miss Paton[7]—married to that wretch by his footman—& the monster[8] will be received after thus deceiving her—& living on her labours; this is prerogative of Manhood! Messer Domine—I am grateful to you for several things, but for nothing so much as my gender—in fact, dear, except the feminine what is amiable except our pretty N—— the word is too wrong I must not write it, but I shall certainly decline only haec & hoc dilecta vel dilectum[9] Jeff. must not see this.——

ADDRESS: Mrs Jefferson Hogg / 8 Mrs Wilson / Maida Vale Place / Paddington—London. POSTMARKS: (1) SHOREHAM / PENNY POST; (2) A / 29 AU 29 / 1827; (3) 10. F.NOON. 10 / AU. 29 / 1827. UNPUBLISHED. TEXT: MS., Abinger MS., Bodleian Library.

1. "There was no solution."
2. "Merits."
3. "*Was made indeed for* us."
4. See 12 August 1826, n. 2.
5. Perhaps a reference to Lord Henry Augustus Dillon (1777–1832), with whom Mary Shelley had become acquainted. (Godwin's Journal records that Lord Dillon visited Mary Shelley on 2 April 1827. On 16 September 1827 Mrs. Mason wrote to Mary Shelley: "I am glad you like Lord Dillon whom I have never seen—Does he ever talk of returning to Italy? I wonder how any one who has lived ten years in Florence can exist in London" [Abinger MS.]). While Lord Dillon was in Italy, he also knew Medwin and Hunt (Lovell, *Medwin*, pp. 221–22). Lord Dillon published two romances, *Rosaline de Vere* (London: Richter, 1824) and the *Life and Opinions of Sir Richard Maltravers* (London: n.p., 1822), the latter critical of Georgian society; *Eccelino da Romano* (1828), a poem in two volumes; and a variety of military and political commentaries, including works advocating Catholic rights.
6. French for "breeches."
7. Perhaps Mary Ann Paton (see 27 September [1825]). The *Times* (London) of 6, 7, and 25 August 1827 indicates that because of indisposition, Miss Paton would not be appearing as scheduled in a new opera at the English Opera House.
8. There is a space of one and a quarter inches in the next three lines to make room for the seal.
9. Mary Shelley declines the participle of *diligo* (the verb meaning "to love above all others, to single out for love") only in the feminine and the neuter genders, suggesting that except in the case of "N——" (unidentified), she has no use for "especially beloved" in the masculine gender.

*TO JOHN HOWARD PAYNE Sompting—30 August [1827]

My dear Payne

Since it is possible that I may have the pleasure of seeing you during my sojourn away from town, I write to tell you of a changement de demuere—I have been obliged to give up my lodgings to other people—& remove next Monday to Arundel—this it is true is ten miles further from Brighton, but a machine will easily bring you to us—Arundel is a most beautiful town—& it & its Castle may figure well in your volumes, so this is an additional inducement, besides the sight of your fair Friend, to make twenty miles seem ten. It is not Mrs Williams who is with me—but take care of your heart when you come—for though my friend is a sweet little girl—

she is married.—⟨Talking of⟩ Apropos of your ⟨distrusting⟩ heart—are you not glad of Louisa's success?[1]—I must write to congratulate—poor darling girl—how pleased she must be—& she has so few pleasures that I am delighted that she should enjoy this one.—Any news you send me is a god send—for our seclusion is perfect—therefore, after all intelligence about yourself, in which I am so truly interested, pray fill your letters with gossip.—

I wish you to do a thing for me—& if you could do it on the day you receive this, & send me the result by return of post, you would greatly enhance the favour.—I have heard that Colonel Lincoln (remember Lincoln) Stanhope[2] is dangerously ill—& for a particular reason (dont try to guess it, for I defy you, I never saw him, even at the Opera, so it is not Amore) I wish to know the truth. Will you send to Harrington House, Stable Yard—St. James—& without mentioning names—ask—Whether Colonel Lincoln Stanhope is there—or where he is—whether he is better & what is his illness—Can you do this without inconvenience—for by so doing, you will convenience me greatly.

I hope to hear, kind Friend, that you are quite well—When is it probable that I shall see you?

Most truly Yours
MS.

Remember I trust to your discretion—my name on no account must be hinted.———I do not go to Arundel till Monday—so direct your answer to me here

ADDRESS: John Howard Payne Esq. / 29 Arundel St. Strand / London. POSTMARKS: (1) SHOREHAM / PENNY POST; (2) A / 31 AU 31 / 1827. UNPUBLISHED. TEXT: MS., Pforzheimer Library.

1. Louisa Holcroft married John Badams (d. 1833), manufacturing chemist and a friend of Carlyle. The Payne, *Letterbook*, copy of this letter substitutes *nuptials* for *success*.

2. Lincoln Edwin Robert Stanhope (1781–1840), son of the third Earl of Harrington.

*TO JANE WILLIAMS HOGG — Somting—31st August 1827.

Pardon this letter—sweet Janey, it is most likely useless—but if not quite useless it is absolutely necessary—You said in your last letter that you would forward the other £5 to our new abode—this would have done very excellently if we had removed hence on Wednesday—but five days at a cabarêt will render it necessary for me to receive it here—the fear of a mistake makes me write—we quit this place on Monday, therefore will you send it by return of post—Next week I hope Whitton will be true to his word—What would I give to have no doubt of receiving my pittance to a day—however as W. [*Whitton*] has promised I ought not to doubt—Il prezzo[1] of small beer has weaned us from our village—& we long for our removal. I hope, pretty One, to hear of your entire convalescence take care of yourself—Isabel has arrived thro' care at a better state of health—She is dictating to me a thousand pettinesses of how her wrecked frame deserves not new rigging from so fair a hand as thine—but I will not write such modest proprieties—What a delight it would be if she were to attain tolerable health—Adieu—I write in a hurry as the thought came on me late that it would be prudent so to do—A thousand thanks for your speedy assistance of the half wrecked

MS.

Oime i venti son omai passato sono gia vecchia![2]

ADDRESS: Mrs Jefferson Hogg / 8 Mrs Wilson / Maida Place—Paddington / London. POSTMARKS: (1) SHOREHAM / PENNY POST; (2) A / 1 SE 1 / 1827; (3) 10. F.NOON. 10 / SP. 1 / 1827. UNPUBLISHED. TEXT: MS., Abinger MS., Bodleian Library.

1. "The price."

2. "Alas the twenties have now passed I am already old." On 30 August Mary Shelley was thirty years old.

Index

Page numbers are cited once within an entry or subentry, even though an entry may occur on a given page several times; likewise, references to notes are listed only once per page. Regardless of the order of their appearance, entries found in the text of letters are cited first, followed by those found in the notes—e.g., *262, 262n.*

THE JOHNS HOPKINS UNIVERSITY PRESS

This book was composed in Linotype Garamond text and hand-set Garamond display type by Maryland Linotype Composition Company from a design by Susan Bishop. It was printed on S. D. Warren's 50-lb. number 66 Offset Cream paper and bound in Joanna Arrestox linen cloth by Universal Lithographers, Inc.

Library of Congress Cataloging in Publication Data

Shelley, Mary Wollstonecraft Godwin, 1797–1851.
The letters of Mary Wollstonecraft Shelley.

Bibliography: v. 1, pp. xxix–xxxvi.
Includes index.
CONTENTS: v. 1. A part of the elect.
1. Shelley, Mary Wollstonecraft Godwin, 1797–1851—Correspondence. 2. Authors, English—19th century—Correspondence. I. Bennett, Betty T. II. Title.

PR5398.A4 1980 823'.7[B] 79–24190
ISBN 0–8018–2275–0 (v. 1)

Pardon this letter sweet Jones, it is most likely useless – but if not quite useless it is absolutely necessary – You said in your last letter that you would forward the other £5 to our new abode – this would have done very excellently if we had removed hence on Wednesday – but five days at a cabaret will render it necessary for me to receive it here – ~~the~~ fear of a mistake makes me write – we quit this place on Monday, therefore will you send it by return of post – Next week I hope Whitton will be true to his word – What would I give to have no doubt of receiving my pittance to a day – however as W. has promised I ought not to doubt – ~~there are~~ A puzzo of small beer has scared [?] us from our village – & we long for our removal. I hope, pretty One, to hear of your entire convalescence take care of yourself – Isabel ~~[illegible]~~ has arrived thro' come [?] at a better state of health – She is dictating to me a thousand prettinesses by how her wrecked frame deserves not new rigging from so